Essentials

Autodesk®

Vault Basic 2022

August 2021

AUTODESK.
Authorized Publisher

Published by
ASCENT Center for Technical Knowledge
630 Peter Jefferson Parkway, Suite 175
Charlottesville, VA 22911

866-527-2368

www.ascented.com

AS-VLT2201-BES1NU-SG // IS-VLT2201-BES1NU-SG

Contents

Preface

The Autodesk® Vault Basic 2022 Essentials learning guide introduces Autodesk® Vault Basic 2022 to end users and CAD administrators. Autodesk® Vault Basic is the foundation module of the data management solution from Autodesk, enabling users to consolidate and organize all product information securely for easy reference, sharing, and re-use purposes.

This learning guide is intended for users and CAD administrators who need to access their design files from Autodesk® Vault Basic. It focuses on capabilities for managing design files and related documentation. Hands-on exercises are included to reinforce how to manage the design workflow process using Autodesk® Vault Basic.

Important:

- *Refer to the Course and Classroom Setup section for installing the practice files and setting up the database.*
- *Refer to the Course Workflow section for understanding the placement of chapters and the dependencies between course exercises.*

Topics Covered

- Introduction to Autodesk Vault features
- Basic Vault Tasks
- Working with Vault and Autodesk® Inventor®
- Working with Vault and AutoCAD®
- Working with Vault and AutoCAD® Electrical
- Working with Vault and AutoCAD® Mechanical
- Working with Vault and Autodesk® Civil 3D®
- Common Vault Tasks
- Organizing and Populating a Vault
- Managing Vault

Prerequisites

- Access to the 2022 version of the software, to ensure compatibility with this guide. Future software updates that are released by Autodesk may include changes that are not reflected in this guide. The practices and files included with this guide are not might not be compatible with prior versions (i.e., 2021).
- This guide is designed to teach new users the essential elements of using Autodesk Vault Basic 2022 for managing files and projects. The primary focus of this guide is on using Autodesk Vault with Autodesk® Inventor®. The guide also includes lessons on working with other software, such as AutoCAD®, AutoCAD® Mechanical, AutoCAD® Electrical, and Autodesk® Civil 3D.
- It is highly recommended that you have a good working knowledge of Autodesk CAD programs and a working knowledge of one or more of the following products:
    - Microsoft® Office
    - Autodesk® Inventor®
    - AutoCAD®
    - AutoCAD® Mechanical
    - AutoCAD® Electrical
    - Autodesk® Civil 3D
    - Microsoft® Windows® 10

Free Autodesk Software for Students and Educators

The Autodesk Education Community is an online resource with more than five million members that enables educators and students to download for free the same software used by professionals worldwide (see website for terms and conditions). You can also access additional tools and materials to help you design, visualize, and simulate ideas. Connect with other learners to stay current with the latest industry trends and get the most out of your designs.

Get started today - register at the Autodesk Education Community and download one of the many Autodesk software applications available.

Visit www.autodesk.com/education/home/

Note: Free products are subject to the terms and conditions of the end-user license and services agreement that accompanies the software. The software is for personal use for education purposes and is not intended for classroom or lab use.

Course and Classroom Setup

Before you start the course, you must install Autodesk Vault Basic and the course data sets. Autodesk Vault Workgroup or Autodesk Vault Professional software can also be installed and used however please note that the course was created using the Autodesk Vault Basic software and therefore the screenshots reflect the Autodesk Vault Basic interface.

Installing the Practice Files

To install the data files for the practices:

Download the Practice Files ZIP file using the link on the Practice Files page in the learning guide. Unzip the zip file to the C: drive.

The path for all the chapter folders should be C:\AOTGVault\.

After you install the data, this folder contains all the files required to complete each exercise in this guide. If Autodesk Vault software has been previously used on the computer, restore default settings for the user interface

Installing Autodesk Vault

You must install and run this courseware from individual computers. You cannot run the courseware from a shared server. Do not install the courseware on a computer that stores your working vault data.

Install both Autodesk Vault Basic Client and Autodesk Vault Basic Server on each computer. See the Autodesk Vault Basic installation media for installation instructions.

Course Setup Information

By default, the data files for each exercise are placed in the C:\AOTGVault folder. Be aware that if you select a different installation location, you might need to manually edit some of the supplied project files to modify their library search paths. These folders contain parts, assemblies, drawing library files, and other files required by the practices.

The practices are designed to be used back-to-back from start to finish. It is recommended that you log in to Autodesk Vault at the beginning of each exercise and when finishing an exercise, you should exit Autodesk Vault. The chapter folders contain subfolders holding documents for the chapter practices.

If you are using any of the following Autodesk® software applications in conjunction with Autodesk Vault, they must also be installed:

- Autodesk Inventor
- AutoCAD
- AutoCAD Mechanical
- AutoCAD Electrical
- Autodesk Civil 3D
- Classroom Environment

The courseware is intended for use in an instructor-led environment. If you plan to use the courseware on your own in a non-classroom environment, you must set up Autodesk Vault correctly. Before you set up your system, you should be aware of the following:

Do not use a production vault for the practices. It is recommended that you set up a separate vault on a separate vault server.

If you plan to repeat an exercise, you must remove any files that were added to the vault when you previously completed the exercise. It is recommended that you delete the entire vault and start again with a new vault.

Do not attempt these practices on a production vault server until you are familiar with the procedures that are covered.

Setting up the Database for the Practices

Before you start any exercise, you need to perform the basic setup for this course. You must:

- Create a vault
- Add a user

Note: You must have Autodesk Vault installed.

Create a Vault

1. Click *Start menu>All Programs>Autodesk>Autodesk Data Management>Autodesk Data Management Server Console 2022*.
2. In the Log In dialog box:
   - For User Name, enter **Administrator**.
   - Leave Password blank.
   - Click OK.

Autodesk Data Management Server Console is displayed.

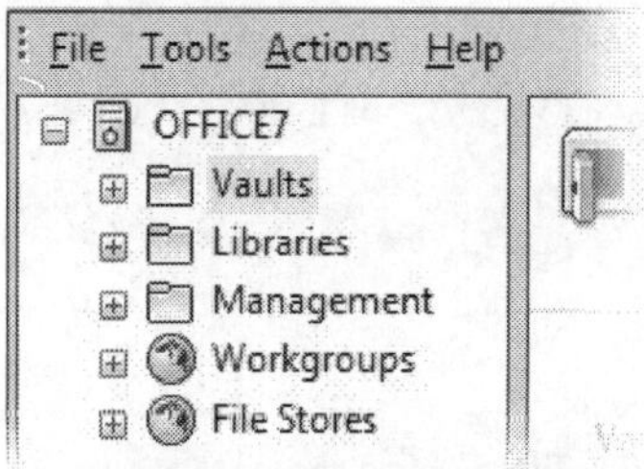

3. Right-click Vaults. Click Create.
4. In the Create Vault dialog box, in New Vault Name, enter **AOTGVault**. Click OK.

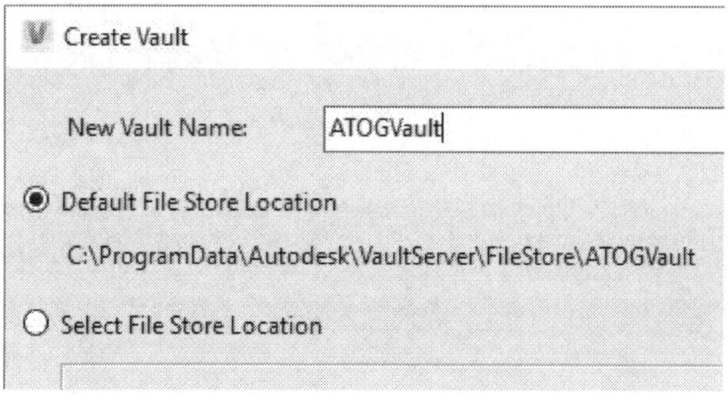

5. Click OK. The vault is added to the list of vaults (you might need to click on the + sign next to Vaults to see the list).

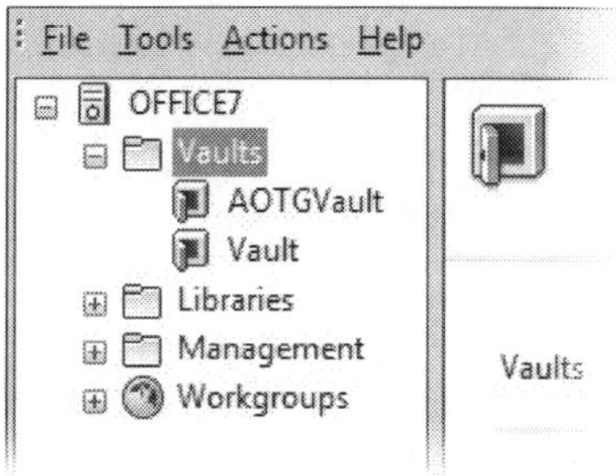

Add a User

1. Click *Tools menu>Administration*.
2. On the *Security* tab, click Manage Access....
3. In the User and Group Management dialog box, click New.
4. In the New User Profile dialog box, enter the following information:
   - In First Name, enter **Vault**.
   - In Last Name, enter **User**.
   - In Display Name, enter **vaultuser**.
5. Click Accounts and select Vault Account. Leave password blank. Click OK.
6. Click Roles.
   - In the Add Roles dialog box, select Document Editor (Level 2).
   - Click OK.
7. Click Vaults.
   - Select AOTGVault and then click OK.
   - Ensure that Enable User is checked.
   - Click OK to close the New User Profile dialog box.
8. Click *File menu>Exit* to close the User and Group Management dialog box.
9. Click Close to close the Global Settings dialog box.
10. Click *File menu>Exit* to close the Autodesk Data Management Server Console.

Course Workflow

The following table outlines dependencies between course practices. The practices in some chapters can be completed without first completing practices in previous chapters.

Chapter	Practices
Introduction	Complete the setup instructions in this chapter. No practices are included in this chapter.
Chapter 1: Introduction to Autodesk Vault	No practices are included in this chapter.
Chapter 2: Basic Vault Tasks	The practices in this chapter are the first course practices. You must complete the practices in the order in which they are presented.
Chapter 3: Working with Vault and Autodesk Inventor	Complete the practices in this chapter after completing the practices in the Basic Vault Tasks chapter. If you complete the practices in this chapter without completing the previous practices, some screen captures will differ from your views of files in the vault.
Chapter 4: Working with Vault and AutoCAD	Complete the practices in this chapter after completing the practices in the Working with Vault and Autodesk Inventor chapter. If you complete the practices in this chapter without completing the previous practices, some screen captures will differ from your views of files in the vault.
Chapter 5: Working with Vault and AutoCAD Electrical	Complete the practices in this chapter after completing the practices in the Working with Vault and Autodesk Inventor chapter. If you complete the practices in this chapter without completing the previous practices, some screen captures will differ from your views of files in the vault.
Chapter 6: Working with Vault and AutoCAD Mechanical	Complete the practices in this chapter after completing the practices in the Working with Vault and Autodesk Inventor chapter. If you complete the practices in this chapter without completing the previous practices, some screen captures will differ from your views of files in the vault.
Chapter 7: Working with Vault and Civil 3D	Complete the practices in this chapter after completing the practices in the Working with Vault and AutoCAD Mechanical chapter. If you complete the practices in this chapter without completing the previous practices, some screen captures will differ from your views of the files in the vault.
Chapter 8: Common Vault Tasks	Complete the practices in the Working with Vault and Autodesk Inventor chapter before completing the practices in this chapter.
Chapter 9: Organizing and Populating a Vault	You can complete the practices in this chapter without completing previous course practices.
Chapter 10: Managing Vault	You can complete the practices in this chapter without completing previous course practices. Some screen captures might differ slightly from your view of files in the vault.

In This Guide

The following highlights the key features of this guide.

Feature	Description
Practice Files	The Practice Files page includes a link to the practice files and instructions on how to download and install them. The practice files are required to complete the practices in this guide.
Chapters	A chapter consists of the following - Learning Objectives, Instructional Content, Practices, Chapter Review Questions, and Command Summary. • **Learning Objectives** define the skills you can acquire by learning the content provided in the chapter. • **Instructional Content**, which begins right after Learning Objectives, refers to the descriptive and procedural information related to various topics. Each main topic introduces a product feature, discusses various aspects of that feature, and provides step-by-step procedures on how to use that feature. Where relevant, examples, figures, helpful hints, and notes are provided. • **Practice** for a topic follows the instructional content. Practices enable you to use the software to perform a hands-on review of a topic. It is required that you download the practice files (using the link found on the Practice Files page) prior to starting the first practice. • **Chapter Review Questions**, located close to the end of a chapter, enable you to test your knowledge of the key concepts discussed in the chapter. • **Command Summary** concludes a chapter. It contains a list of the software commands that are used throughout the chapter and provides information on where the command can be found in the software.
Appendices	Appendices provide additional information to the main course content. It could be in the form of instructional content, practices, tables, projects, or skills assessment.

Practice Files

To download the practice files for this guide, use the following steps:

1. Type the URL ***exactly as shown below*** into the address bar of your Internet browser, to access the Course File Download page.

   Note: If you are using the ebook, you do not have to type the URL. Instead, you can access the page simply by clicking the URL below.

   https://www.ascented.com/getfile/id/corysanthesPF

2. On the Course File Download page, click the **DOWNLOAD NOW** button, as shown below, to download the .ZIP file that contains the practice files.

3. Once the download is complete, unzip the file and extract its contents.

   The recommended practice files folder location is:
   C:

Note: It is recommended that you do not change the location of the practice files folder. Doing so may cause errors when completing the practices.

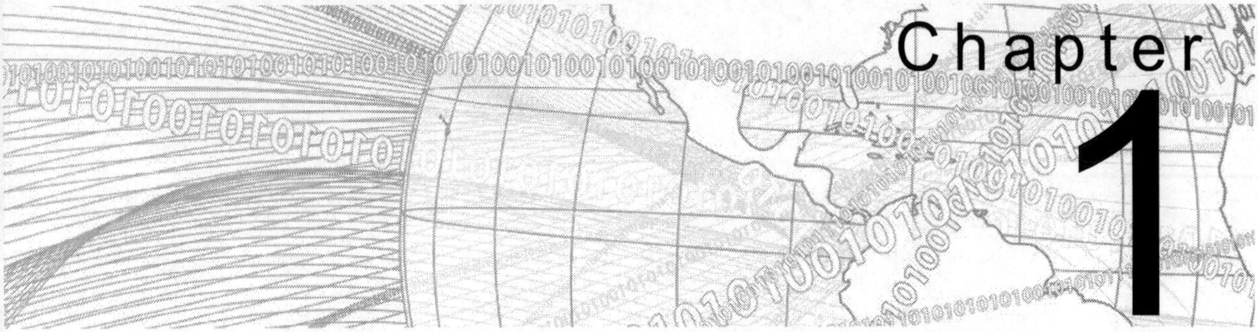

Introduction to Autodesk Vault

This chapter provides an overview of Autodesk® Vault features and functionality. You learn how to use Autodesk Vault to manage engineering design data in a secure, centralized location.

Learning Objective in This Chapter

- Describe the features and functionality of Autodesk Vault.

1.1 Autodesk Vault Overview

Overview

Autodesk Vault is a secure, centralized storage solution for your design data. In this lesson, you learn about the features of Autodesk Vault, the components of a Vault installation, and how you can extend Vault to manage revisions and engineering changes.

In the following image, Autodesk Vault, a stand-alone application, is used to view the history of an Autodesk® Inventor® file that is stored in a vault.

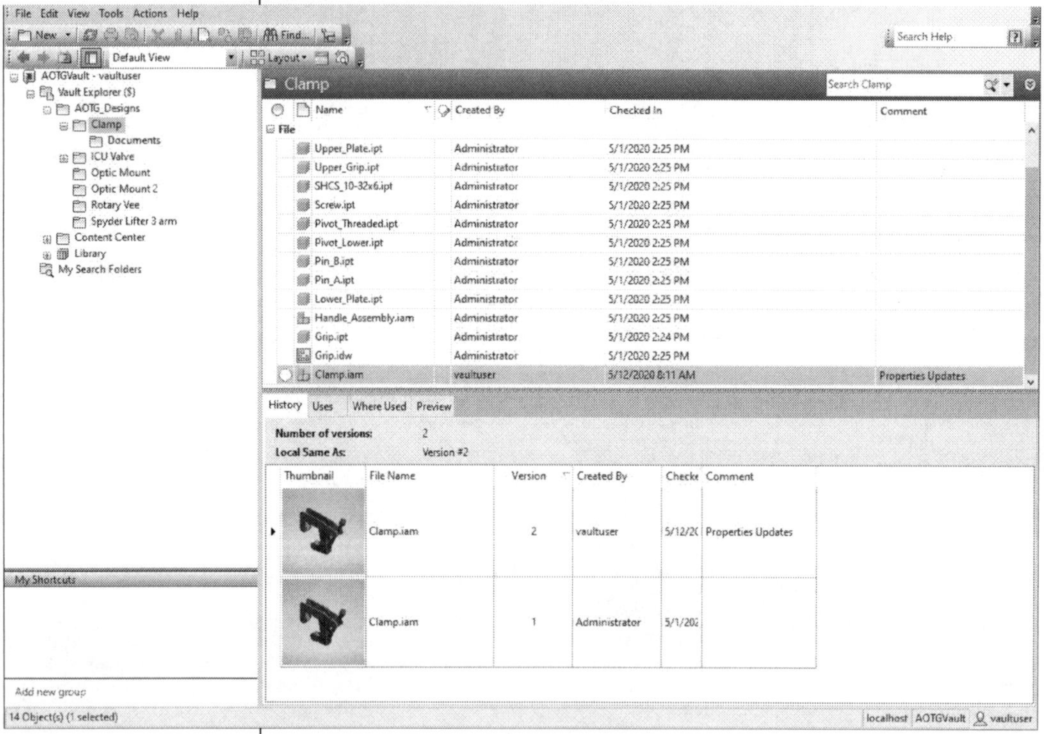

Objective

After completing this lesson, you will be able to:

- Describe the main features of Autodesk Vault.
- Describe the components of a Vault server.
- List the clients you use to access a vault.
- Describe the workflow to edit a file stored in the vault.
- Describe how you can extend the capabilities of Autodesk Vault to include management of revisions, bills of materials, and the change process.

About Vault

Autodesk Vault is a file management and version control system that you use to manage your project files. Vault offers security, version management, multi-user support, and integration with Autodesk applications.

In the following image, the versions of a design are shown in Autodesk Vault, a standalone client that you use to perform common tasks.

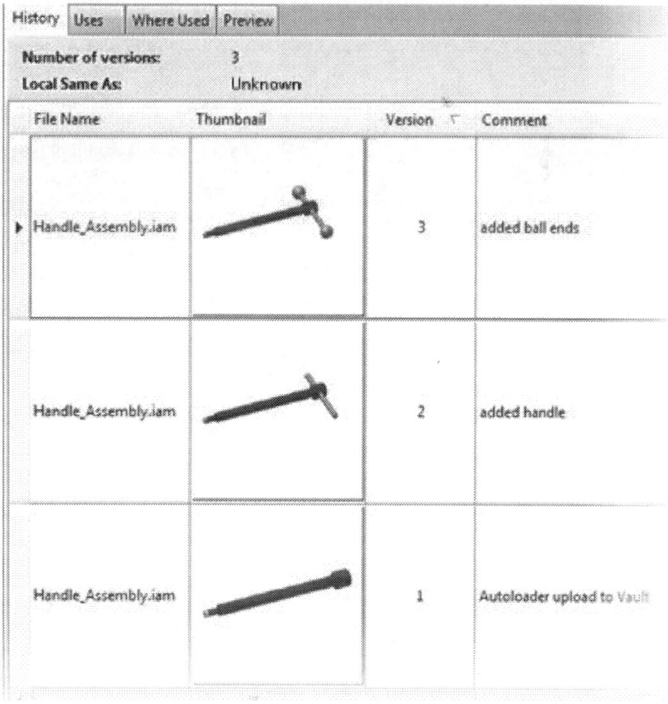

Centralized Storage

You can use Autodesk Vault to manage all your project files regardless of file format. This includes files from Autodesk Inventor, AutoCAD®-based products, Autodesk® 3ds Max®, Autodesk Revit products, AutoCAD Civil3D®, FEA, CAM, Microsoft Office, PDF files, and more. You can organize all your files and keep them in one central location for easy access by all members of the design team.

You organize files in the vault the same way that you organize files outside of the vault. You create folders and then add files to those folders as shown in the following image.

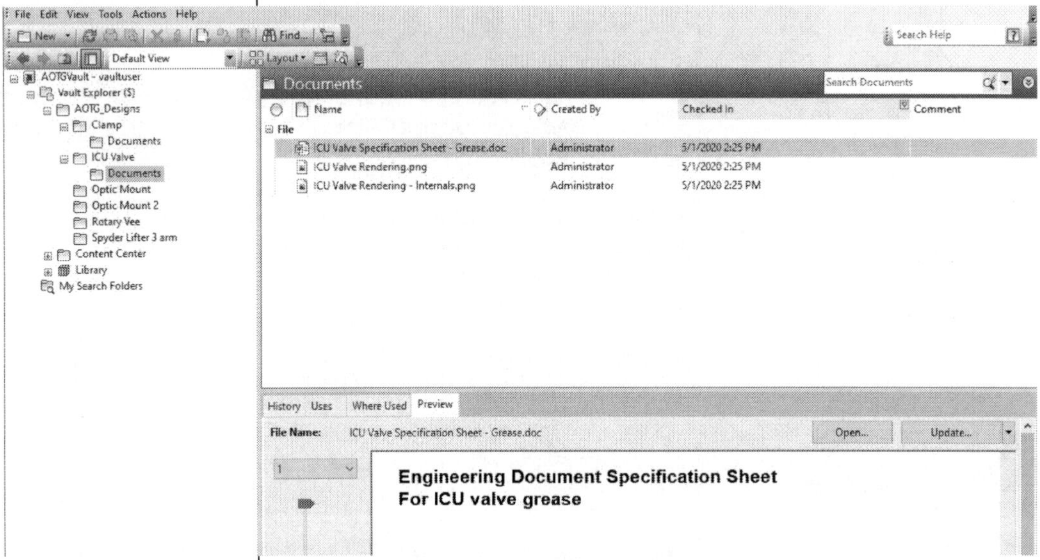

Multi-User Support

Autodesk Vault supports a single user on a single workstation or multiple users with a shared server as shown in the following image.

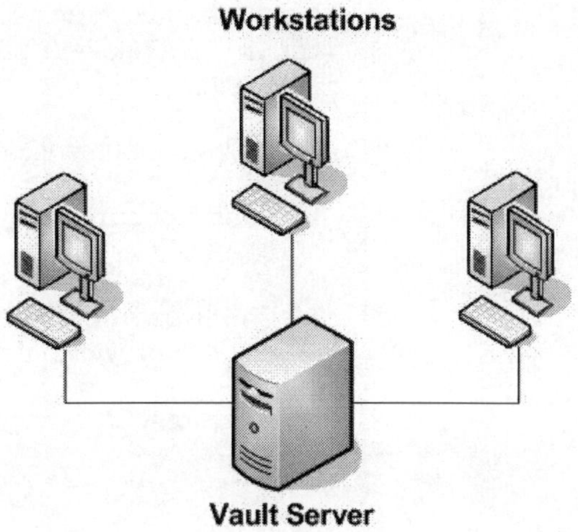

Check out and check in capabilities prevent more than one user from editing a file at one time, and enables all members of the design team to work together. Feedback via status icons and properties keeps all members of the design team informed of the status of files.

Security

Autodesk Vault provides an extra level of security over the standard file system. As shown in the following image, all users must log in to access design data. Autodesk Vault tracks each user's activities so that you can determine who modified a file. Because you cannot easily delete files, and because all file versions are retained, past versions are never misplaced or overwritten.

The following authentication options are available:

- **Vault Account**: Requires a Vault-specific user name with a password.
- **Windows Account**: Uses Windows Active Directory credentials, which are entered for you.
- **Autodesk ID**: Uses Autodesk ID credentials.

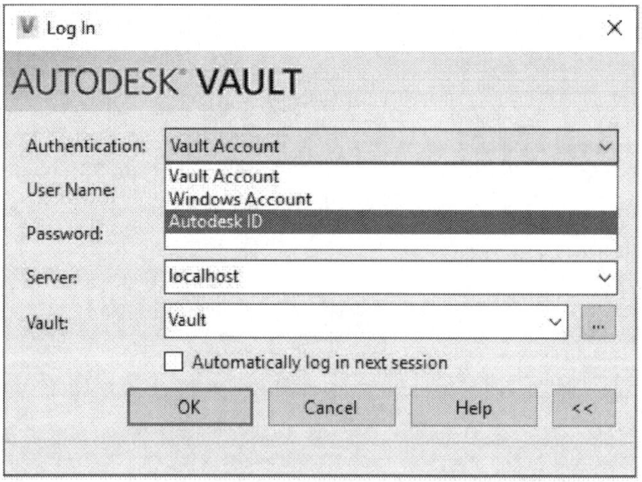

Version Management

Autodesk Vault stores every version of a file and its dependencies. You can view any previous version and its associated files or roll back the design to a previous version. In the following image, the three versions of an Autodesk Inventor assembly are displayed in Autodesk Vault, a stand-alone application that you use to view the contents of a vault.

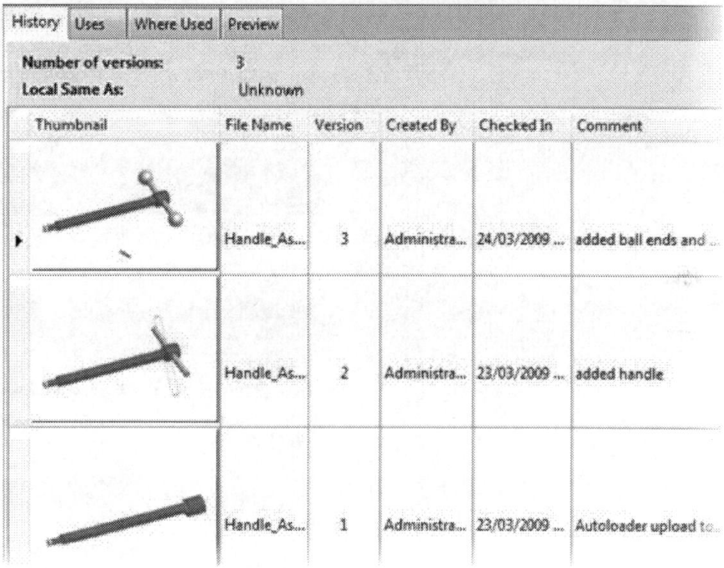

File Relationships

Autodesk Vault understands the relationships between files and maintains those relationships for you. If you rename or move files in the vault, the required parent files are updated so the correct relationship is maintained.

You can view file relationships to determine how a change might impact other designs. For example, before you edit a file, you can determine which designs use the file so that you understand the scope of your changes. In the following image, the Where Used information indicates which designs use an Autodesk Inventor part file.

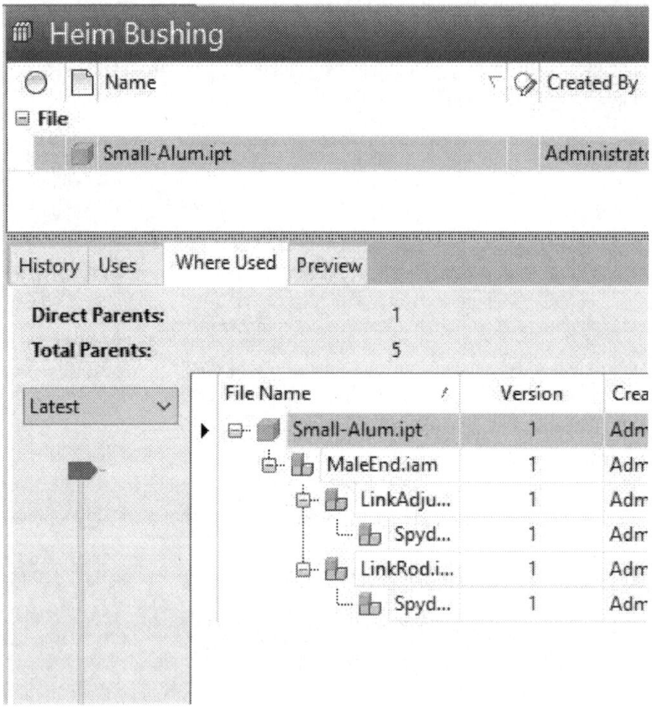

File Properties

When you add a file to Autodesk Vault, the file's properties are extracted and saved in the database. Additional properties are added to the database, including your user name, the version number, the date, and comments. Using Vault, you can view file properties and search for files based on their properties.

The following image displays the Find tool, which you use to find a file based on its properties.

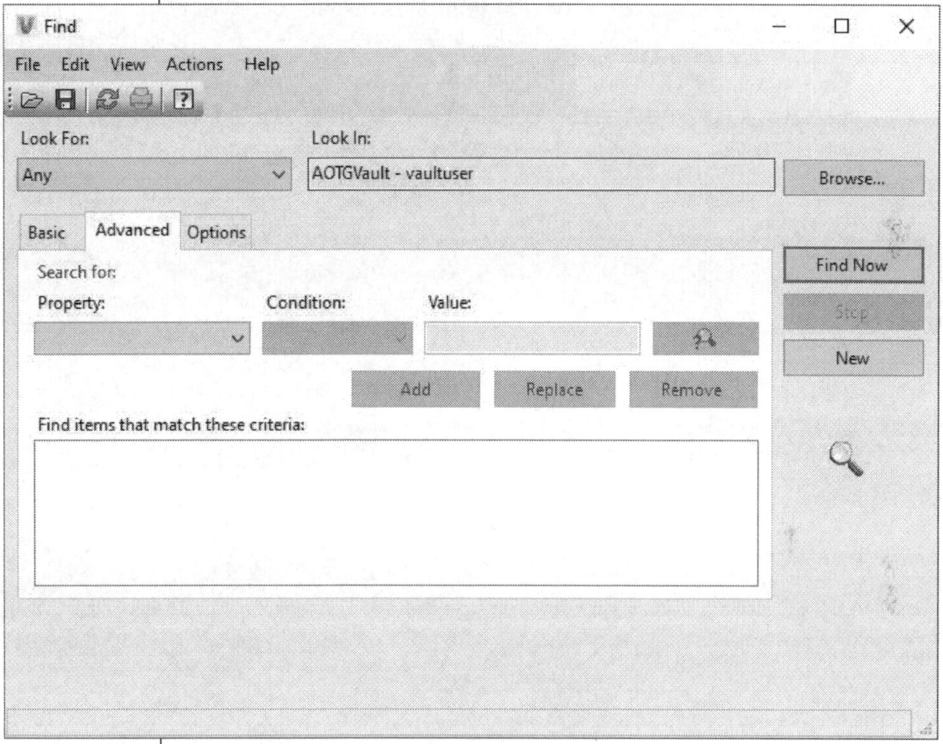

Integration with Applications

Autodesk Vault is integrated into Autodesk® Inventor®, AutoCAD®, AutoCAD® Mechanical, AutoCAD® Electrical, Autodesk® Civil 3D®, Autodesk® 3ds Max®, Microsoft Office and more. The integration provides commands within the application that you can use to perform most Vault tasks without leaving the application.

For example, the Vault client interface for Autodesk Inventor includes a Vault browser. Icons indicate each file's status and shortcut menus give access to common Vault commands as shown in the following image.

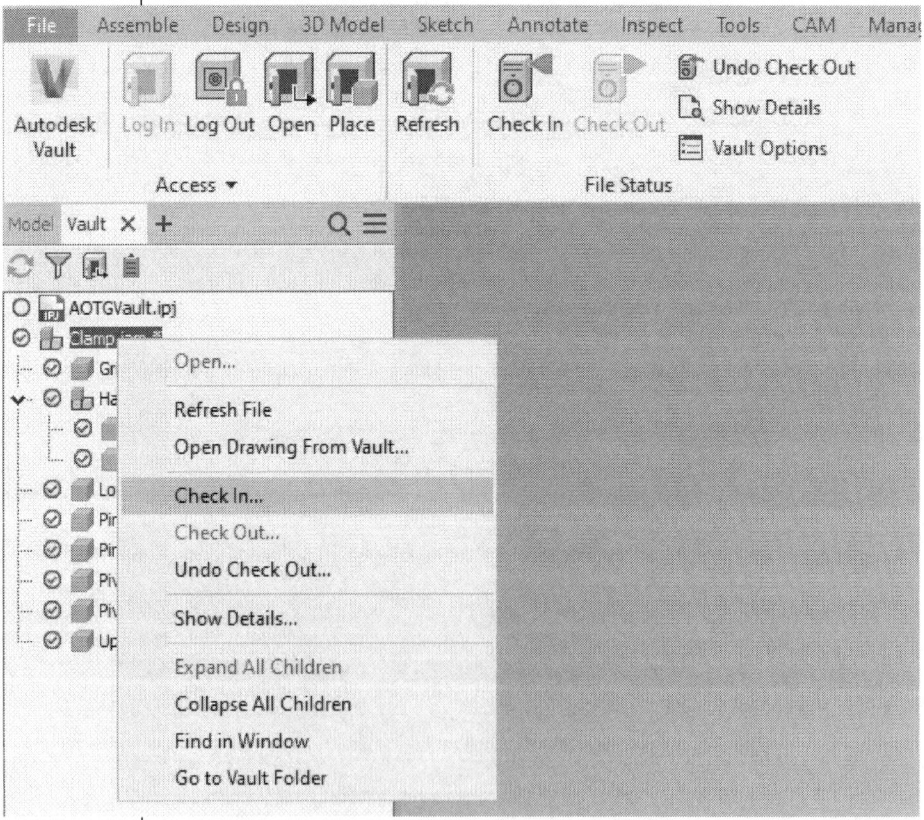

Sharing Project Files with Other Users

Autodesk Vault makes it easy to keep other members of the design team up-to-date by automatically publishing visualization files, such as DWF™ and DWFx, each time a file changes. You can publish to a shared folder outside the vault. Project Sync is available in Vault Professional.

Autodesk Data Management Server

About the Vault Server

The vault server consists of a computer and the software required to manage the vault itself and the transactions between the vault and the vault clients. The server can be located on a single workstation to support a single user or it can be located on a shared workstation or server to support multiple users.

The vault server includes a secure database that stores file properties and file relationships so you can quickly search across all your designs or determine where files are used. The server also includes a secure file store where the versions of your design files are stored. You create, manage, and maintain vaults and content center libraries with the Autodesk Data Management Server (ADMS) software.

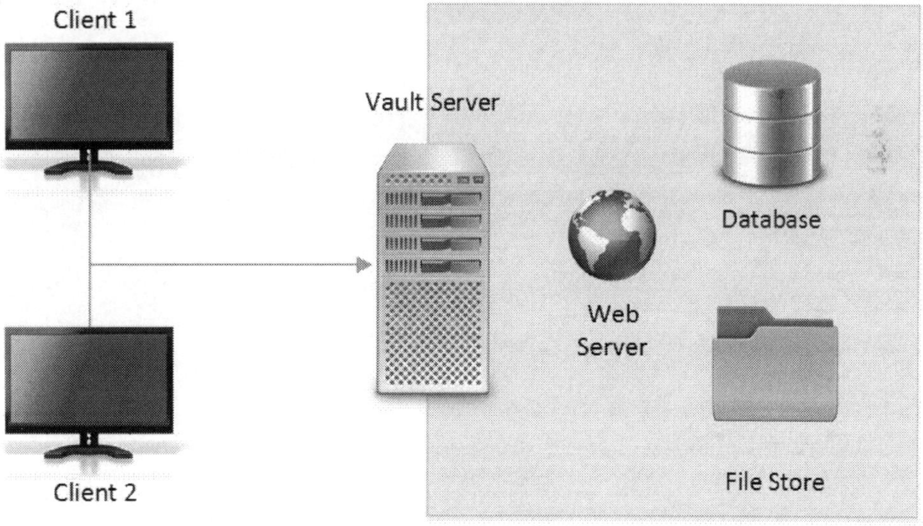

In a typical multi-user installation, the Vault server software is installed on a server that is accessible by all workstations throughout a network. The vault clients, including Vault Explorer and the Vault add-ins for specific applications, are installed on each workstation.

In a single-user, single-workstation environment, the server and clients can be installed on a single workstation as shown in the following image.

About Autodesk Data Management Server Console

Autodesk Data Management Server (ADMS) Console is an application that runs on the vault server. You use ADMS Console to perform maintenance and management tasks on vaults such as:

- Creating and deleting vaults.
- Backing up and restoring vaults.
- Moving vault databases and file stores.
- Purging unneeded versions of files.
- Defragmenting vault databases.

The ADMS application is shown in the following image.

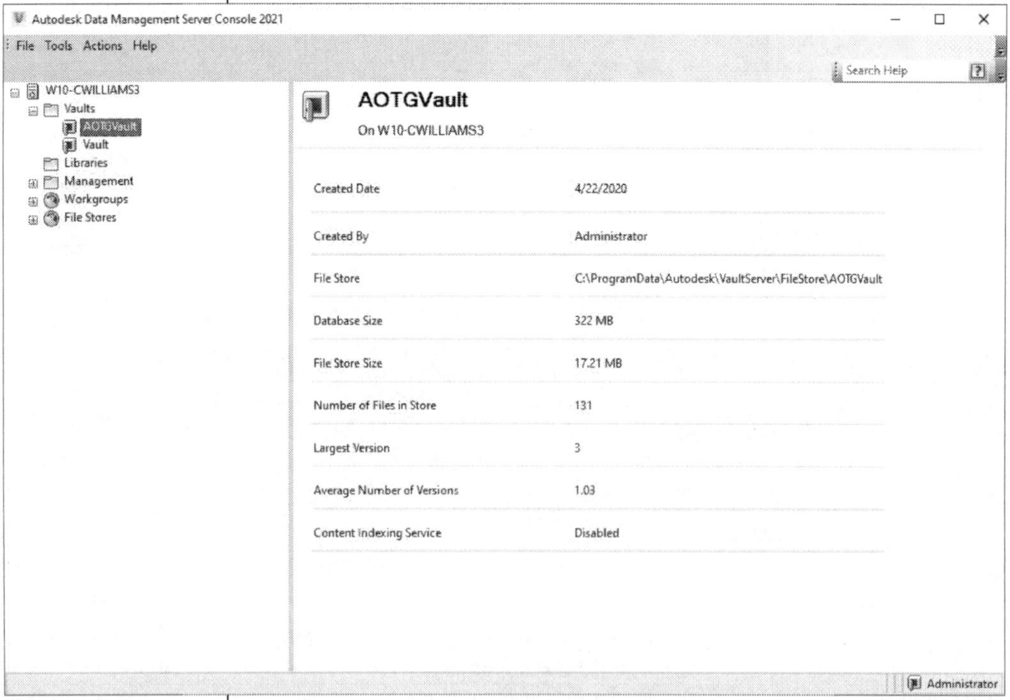

Vault Clients

You access files in the Vault using vault clients that run on your workstation. You use a stand-alone client to perform common tasks on all files and folders in a vault. In each application that you run, you use the built-in client to seamlessly work with the files associated with that application. The following image displays the Vault client.

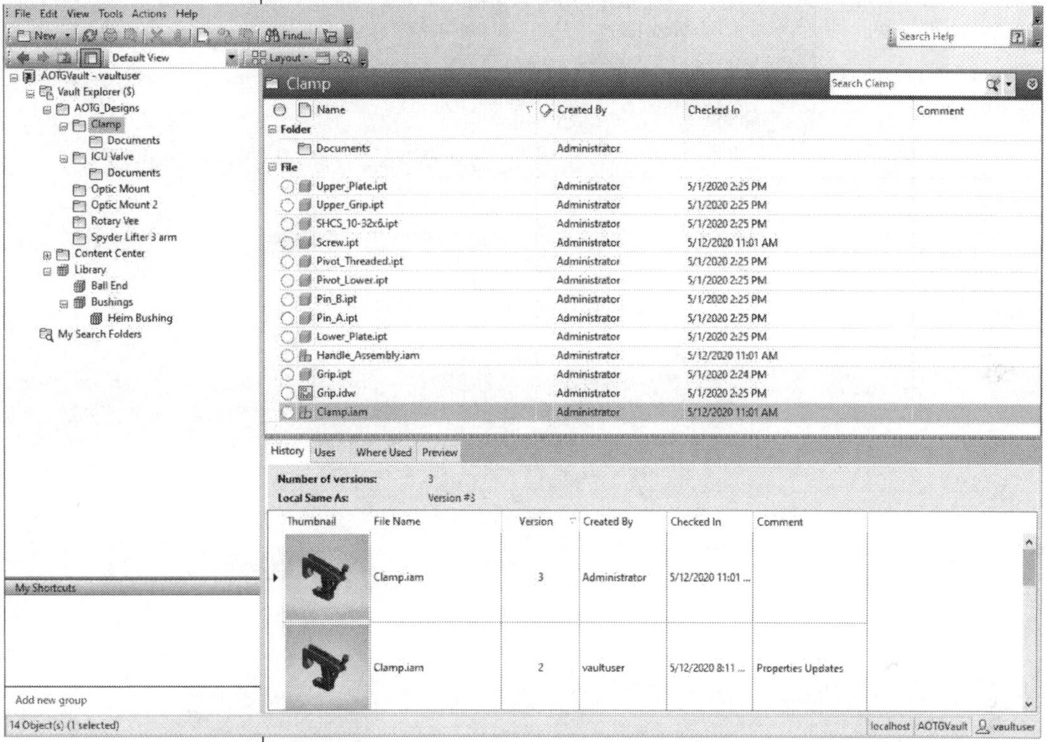

About Autodesk Vault

Autodesk Vault is a stand-alone application that you use to perform vault tasks such as:

- Viewing files and properties.
- Determining the status of a file.
- Finding designs based on file properties.
- Viewing the history of designs.
- Viewing file relationships to determine where a file is used.
- Moving and renaming files.

- Copying an existing design as a start point for a new design.
- Creating folders in a vault.
- Checking out files and opening them (in the corresponding application).

The Autodesk Vault client application is shown in the following image.

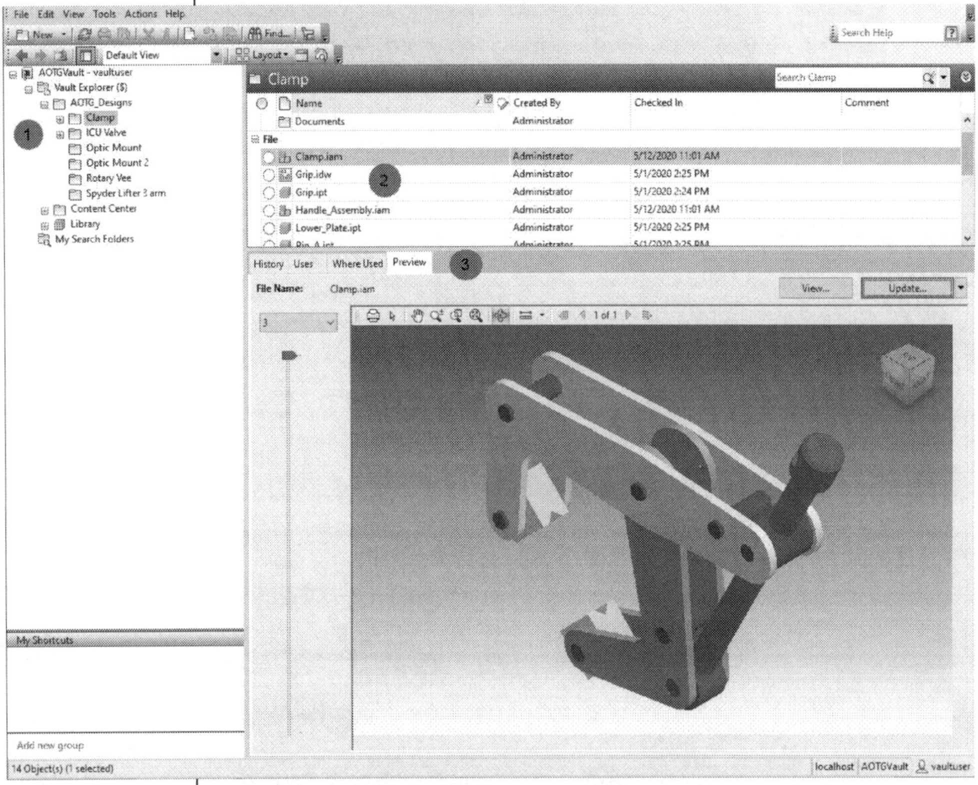

1. The folder structure indicates how files are organized in the vault. You organize files in the vault using the same techniques that you use to organize files on a local drive.

2. The file pane lists the contents of the selected folder. Details for each file are shown such as the current status, the latest version number, who checked out the file, and comments. You can customize the file pane to show any of the properties that are stored in the vault.

3. The tabs provide access to detailed information on the selected file, file history, and relationships to other files. The Preview tab displays the associated visualization file.

Autodesk Vault Add-ins for Applications

The add-ins that you use are integrated into your application. Vault add-ins are available for most Autodesk products and for Microsoft Office applications. Using commands built in to each application, you can perform common editing-related vault tasks such as the following:

- Determining the status of files.
- Adding files to a vault.
- Checking out files and opening them in their associated application.
- Getting files from the vault.
- Checking files in and out of the vault.

For example, in Inventor, you can access common vault commands from either the ribbon or a toolbar as shown in the following image.

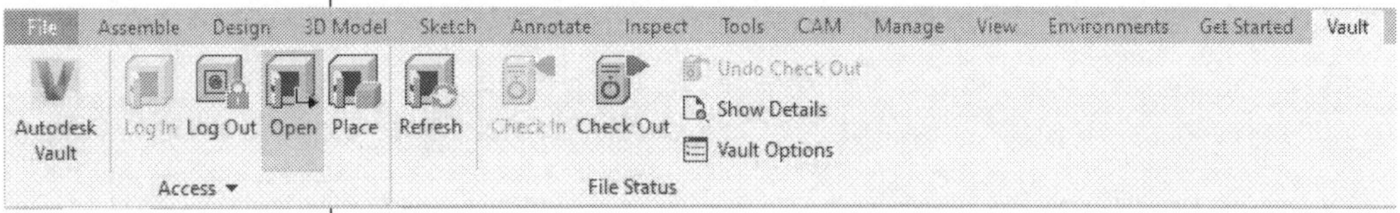

A Typical Workflow

To work on files from the vault, you get a copy of the files onto your local working folder. To edit the files, you check them out. After editing the files, you check them back in to return them to the vault.

Process: A Typical Workflow

The following steps describe a typical workflow for editing a file from the vault. Details on how to use Vault with specific applications are presented in later chapters.

Step	Description
Get a copy of the file from the vault	The first step is to get a copy of the files from the vault onto your local computer. The vault contains the master copy of all the files so that all users have access to the latest versions. When you are editing files, you always work on copies of the files on your local computer. The local copy of the file is copied to the working folder on your workstation as shown in the following image. 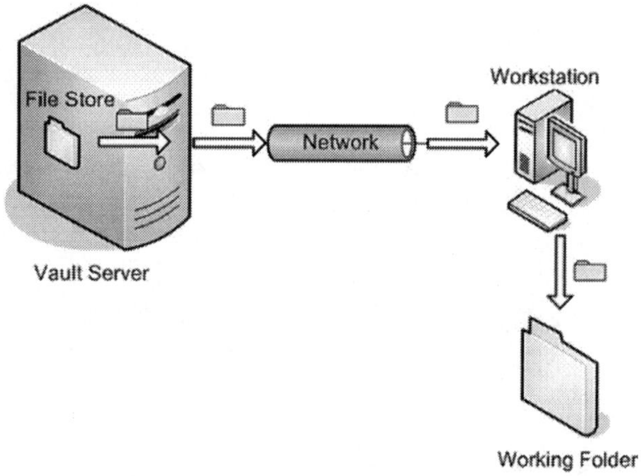
Check out the files to edit	Once the files are on your computer, you work on them as you normally would. Before you edit a file, however, you must check it out of the vault. This informs all other users of the file that you have it reserved for editing and prevents them from editing the same file. Multiple users can have copies of the same files on their computers but a file can be checked out to just one user at a time. Other members of the design team can still get read-only copies of files from the vault for viewing or for reference in their designs or can check out another file in the same model for editing.

Check in the completed files	Once you finish editing a file, you check it back in to the vault. When other users check the status of the files, they will be informed that you have finished editing the file and they can refresh their local copies of the model files to get the latest version from the vault. When you check in a file, the local copy of the file is copied back to the Vault server as shown in the following image. The previous version is not overwritten— the file and its dependencies are saved so you can recall the previous version of the model at any time. 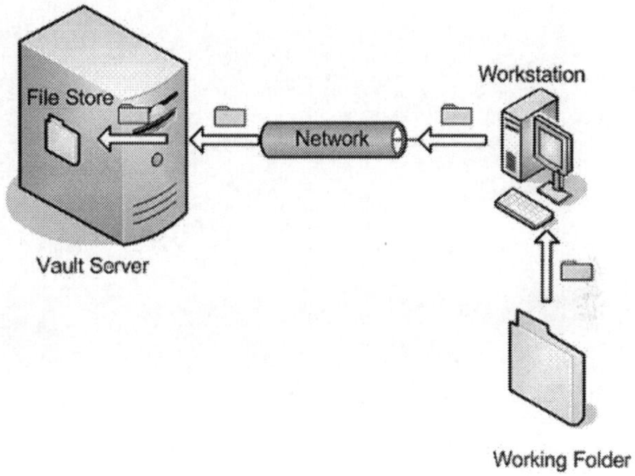

Key Points

- You do not work on files in the vault. You work on files on your local computer that you have copied from the vault.
- You must check a file back in to the vault in order to update the copy in the vault.

Extending Vault Basic

As your needs grow, you can extend Autodesk Vault Basic by purchasing Autodesk Vault Workgroup or Autodesk Vault Professional. Each application builds on Vault by adding capabilities to manage revisions, bills of materials, and the engineering change process. Autodesk Vault Basic forms the basis for all of these applications and continues to provide secure storage, version management, property management, and collaboration capabilities.

1.2 Chapter Summary

In this chapter, you learned about the features of Autodesk Vault and how Autodesk Vault is a secure, centralized storage location for managing engineering design data.

Having completed this chapter, you can:

- Describe the features and functionality of Autodesk Vault.

Chapter 2

Basic Vault Tasks

In this chapter you learn how to log in to Autodesk® Vault, use the Autodesk Vault user interface, and work with non-CAD files.

Learning Objectives in This Chapter

- Log in to Autodesk Vault.
- Describe elements of the Autodesk Vault user interface.
- Set the working folder, create folders in the vault, add non-CAD files, check these files out and edit them, check the files in, and then view the versions of the files.

2.1 Accessing the Vault

Overview

In order to work with and manage files placed in the vault, you first must be able to access them. This lesson covers methods of accessing files in the vault.

One of the important benefits of working with Autodesk Vault is security. Your files are protected and only authorized users can access them.

Objectives

After completing this lesson, you will be able to:

- Use vault clients to access data in a vault.
- Use Autodesk Vault to view and manage files in the vault.
- Use an application's vault add-in to access files in the vault directly from the application software.
- Log in to a vault to access the files in the vault.

About Vault Clients

Autodesk Vault is a client/server application, which means it has a server component and clients that access the data in the server. The server and client can be installed on the same computer, but in most cases the server is installed on a different machine. The default server name is localhost. If the server is installed on a different machine, change localhost to the server name.

Definition of Vault Clients

A client is a front-end interface used to access data on a server. In Autodesk Vault, the data resides in the Autodesk Data Management Server. Clients are installed on the workstations that will access the data in the vault.

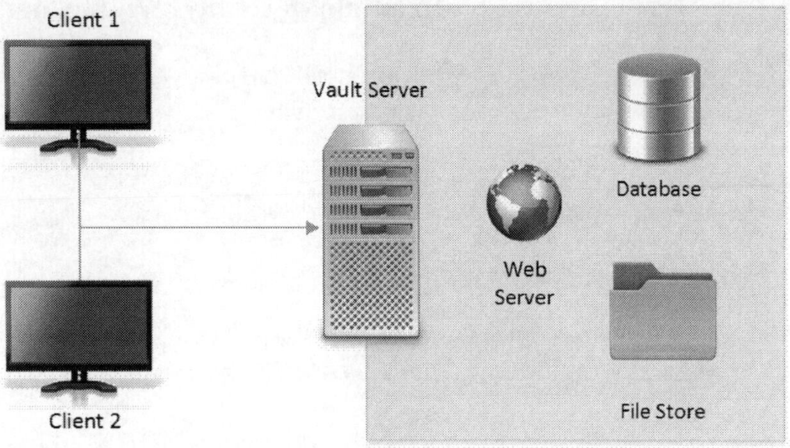

Vault Clients

There are two main types of clients for Autodesk Vault:

Client	Definition
Autodesk Vault	Autodesk Vault is a stand-alone application for viewing files in the vault.
Vault Add-ins	Vault add-ins are modules that integrate Vault functionality into software applications. They enable you to log in and out of the vault, check files in and out of the vault, use shortcuts and saved searches to files in the vault, and manage file versions. There are many add-ins for Autodesk® design software such as Autodesk® Inventor®, AutoCAD®, AutoCAD® Mechanical, AutoCAD® Electrical, Autodesk® Civil 3D®, Autodesk® Alias®, etc. There is also an add-in for Microsoft Office applications.

Vault Clients Are Like Web Browsers

A web browser is an application that displays content (or in other words, accesses files) from web servers on the Internet. As you surf the Internet, the web browser requests the files from the servers and displays them in the browser window.

The concept behind a vault client is similar but more powerful. You open files from the vault (check out files) using the Vault add-ins, and check in the files. You use Vault to view and manage files and folders in the vault. And unlike in a web browser, only authorized users can access the files in the vault.

Example of Using a Vault Client

In Microsoft Word, you access the Autodesk Vault toolbar and log in to a vault.

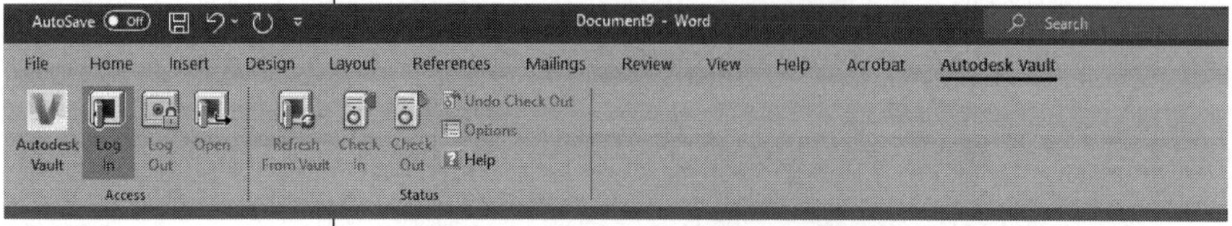

You then open a file from the vault, check the file out, edit it, and check it back in.

About Autodesk Vault

Autodesk Vault is a stand-alone application for viewing and managing the files in the vault. When you open a vault, the Navigation pane on the left side displays the folder hierarchy of the vault.

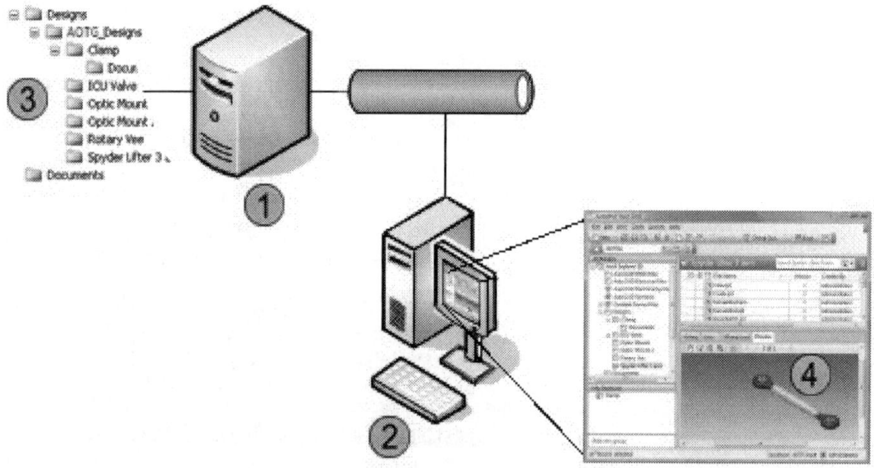

1	Autodesk Data Management Server containing the vault
2	Workstation with Vault
3	Folder hierarchy in the vault
4	Vault showing the folder hierarchy in the vault

The following image displays an example of a vault. The contents of a folder are shown in the Main pane to the right. Below the Main pane is the Preview pane, which displays versions of files selected in the main table. You can also use the Preview pane to determine parent-child relationships and to preview the files.

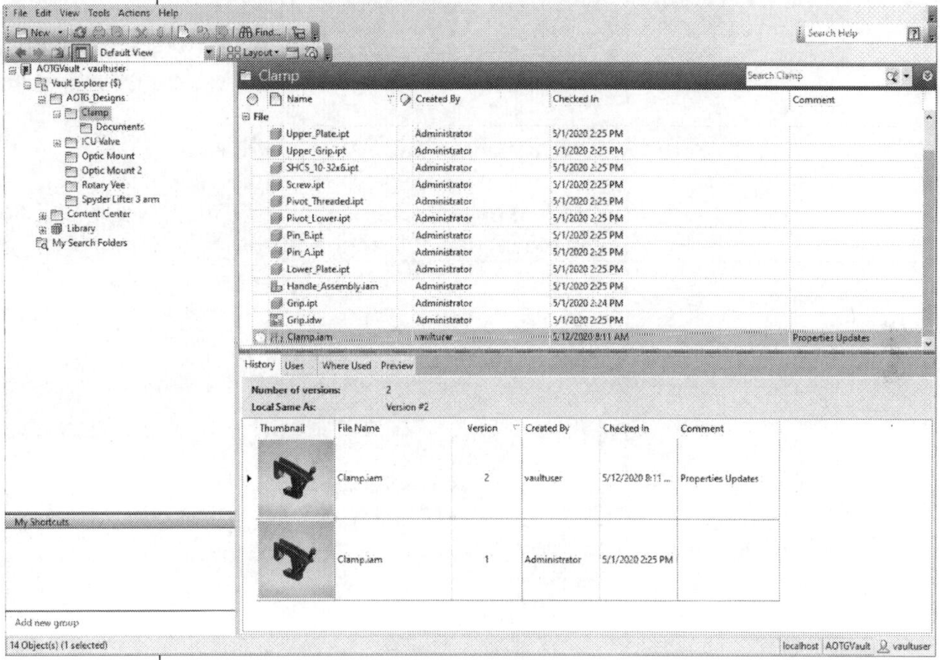

Uses of Autodesk Vault

You use Autodesk Vault to do the following:

- View a vault folder hierarchy and create and remove folders.
- View files in a folder.
- Search for files.
- Preview files, their versions, and their relationships.
- Create and use shortcuts to searches, files, and folders.
- Add non-CAD files to the vault.
- Check files in and out of the vault.
- Copy a design.
- Perform administrative tasks, such as creating new users and assigning roles (administrative access required).

Open CAD Files Using the Correct Add-in

By default, you cannot add design files, such as Inventor or AutoCAD files, directly to Autodesk Vault or drag and drop them into Autodesk Vault. You must use the Vault add-in for the application to open and check files in and out of the vault, thereby maintaining all file relationships.

This option can be disabled in Autodesk Vault, but it is highly recommended that you leave this restriction in place.

Example: Use Autodesk Vault

To find an older version of a file in the vault, use Autodesk Vault to log in, navigate to the folder in the Navigation pane, and then click the file in the Main pane.

The History tab in the Preview pane displays the versions of the file.

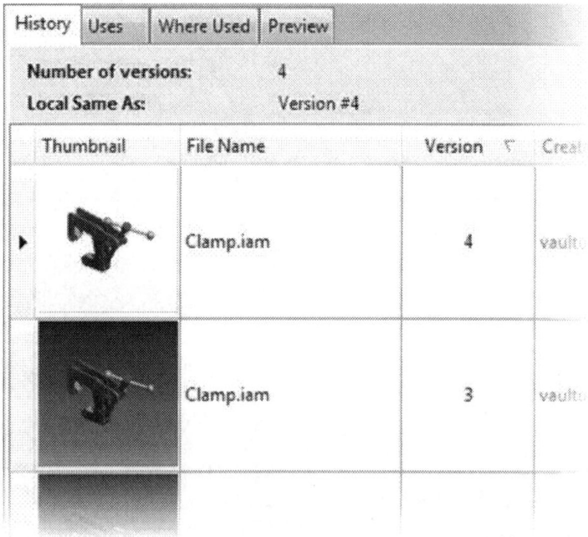

If required, you can get a previous version to open and edit.

Vault Add-ins

A Vault add-in is installed with an application and gives you access to vault files directly in the application.

For CAD applications such as Autodesk Inventor and AutoCAD, the Vault Add-In also helps maintain the relationships between files as they are checked in and out of the vault.

Vault Add-In for Autodesk Inventor

When you are working in Autodesk Inventor, you have direct access to Vault and the files that it contains. To access Vault from the ribbon in Autodesk Inventor, select the Vault tab and click Log In on the Access Panel.

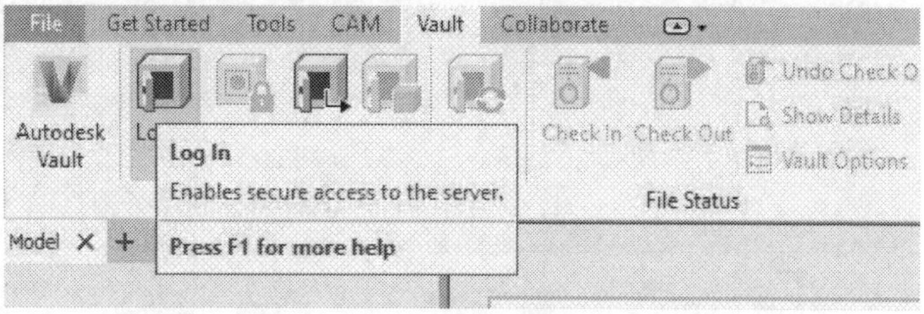

Note: If you do not see the vault browser, select Vault.

Once you are logged in, you access the vault using the Vault browser as shown in the following image.

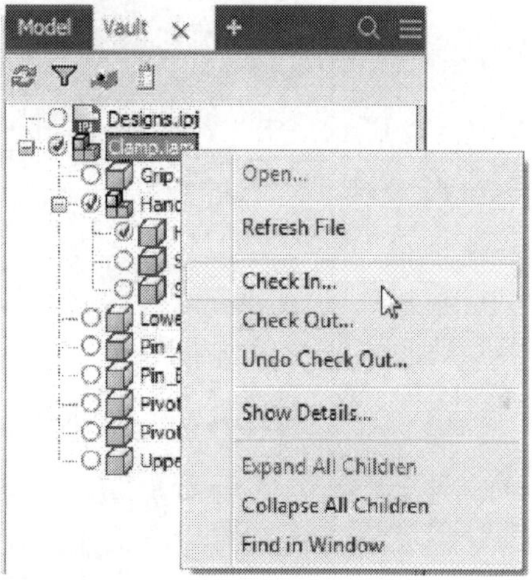

Vault Add-In for AutoCAD

When you are working in AutoCAD, you have direct access to Vault and the files that it contains. To access Vault from AutoCAD, on the ribbon, select the Vault tab and click Log In on the Access Panel.

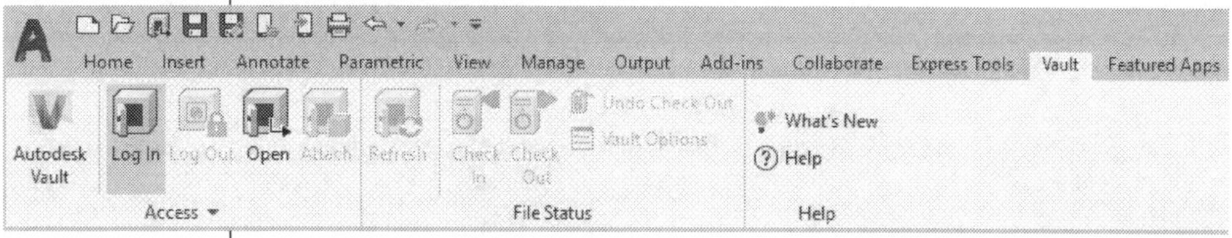

The Vault Add-In for Microsoft Office

You can log in to the vault from the Autodesk Vault toolbar.

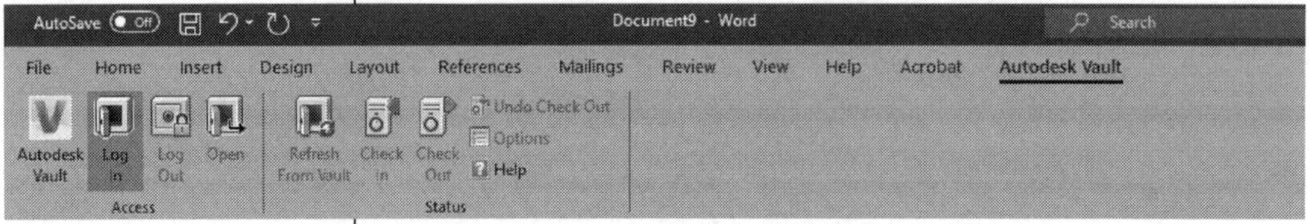

Vault Add-ins for AutoCAD Mechanical, AutoCAD Electrical, Autodesk Civil 3D, and others

When you are working in one of the other add-on software, you have access to Vault and the files that it contains directly from the application. Accessing Vault is similar to accessing it from AutoCAD and Inventor.

Logging in to Autodesk Vault

Autodesk Vault requires users to log in to access the vault data. This is part of the security features of the Autodesk Vault. By creating user accounts and setting up user roles, administrators can control access to the vault.

When you log in to a vault, you are given access based on your assigned role in the vault.

Guidelines for Accessing the Vault

- Use a unique user name and password: If multiple users are to access the same vault, then each user should be assigned their own user name and password. Ask your Vault administrator for your log in information.
- Use one vault: It is recommended you have only one vault for all your designs. You can have additional vaults for training and special purposes, but your production data should reside in one vault.

Accessing the Content Center Libraries

The Autodesk Data Management Server can also manage the content center libraries for Autodesk Inventor. Installing Content Center libraries in ADMS is done to save space on the user workstation and if you have custom content libraries that are shared between users. The Content Center libraries are not installed by default during the server installation. Instead they can be selected as an option to install.

If you only want to access the Content Center libraries in the vault, you can select Content Center Library Read Only User. You do not need to log in to the vault and you obtain read-only access to the Content Center libraries.

If your content libraries were installed as desktop content and not with ADMS, you do not need to log in to the vault to access the content center.

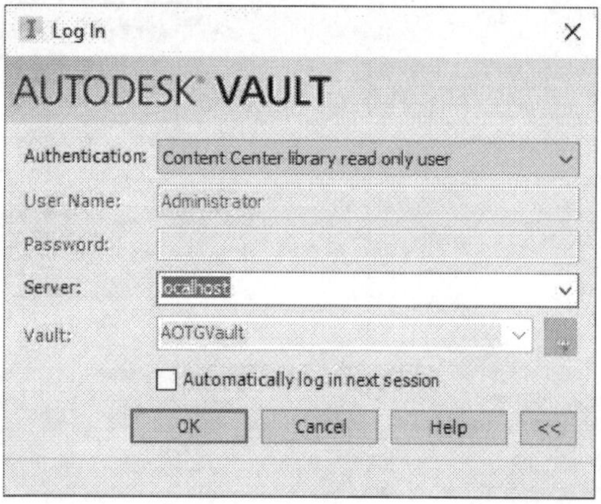

Access Separate Servers for the Content Center and Vault

The Autodesk Data Management Server enables you to use one server for both content and vault data, or you can use separate servers, so your content center data can be installed on your computer while the vault data is accessed from a different computer. You can set this up in Autodesk Inventor in the Connection Options dialog box.

To access the Connection Options dialog box, click the Application Icon>Vault Server>Connection Options.

Procedure: Logging In to Vault

The following steps describe how to log in to a vault.

1. Click Log In.

   Note: The steps to log in can vary from one application to another, but the Log In dialog box and the following steps are the same for all clients.

2. In the Log In dialog box, enter a user name and a password.
3. For Server, enter the server name or leave as the default localhost if the server is installed on the same computer as the client.
4. For Vault, enter the name of the vault you want to access.

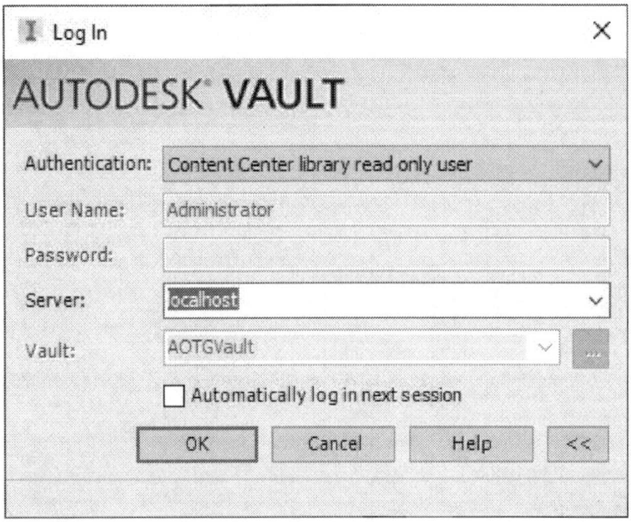

Logging in to the Vault Is the same from Any Client. The steps to log in can vary from one application to another, but the Log In dialog box is the same for all clients.

Note: If you cannot remember the name of the vault, click [...] to the right of the Vault list. The vault (or vaults) available on the server will be listed.

2.2 Autodesk Vault User Interface

Overview

This lesson describes the elements of the Vault user interface.

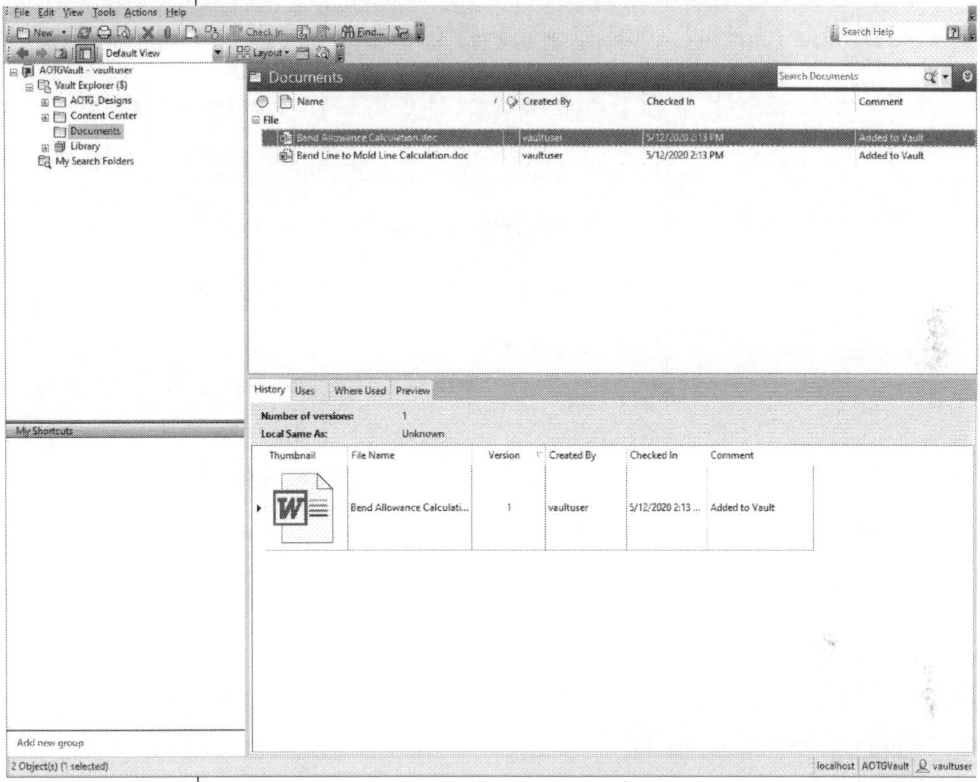

You can use Autodesk Vault for viewing and managing files in the vault, creating and removing folders, managing file history, and more.

Objectives

After completing this lesson, you will be able to:

- Use the Autodesk Vault interface to access files and folders in the vault.
- Use the Navigation pane to navigate in the Vault folder hierarchy and access saved searches.
- Use the Main pane to list files in a selected folder in the vault.

- Use the Preview pane to view a file, view a file's version history, and view the file's parent-child relationships.
- Save your searches and reuse them when required, and navigate to specific folders or files using shortcuts.

Vault Explorer UI

Vault provides a way to access the Vault files and folder structure. The organization of the Vault user interface makes it easy to use.

Elements of the Vault User Interface

The Vault user interface contains the:

- Navigation pane
- Shortcuts pane
- Main pane
- Preview pane

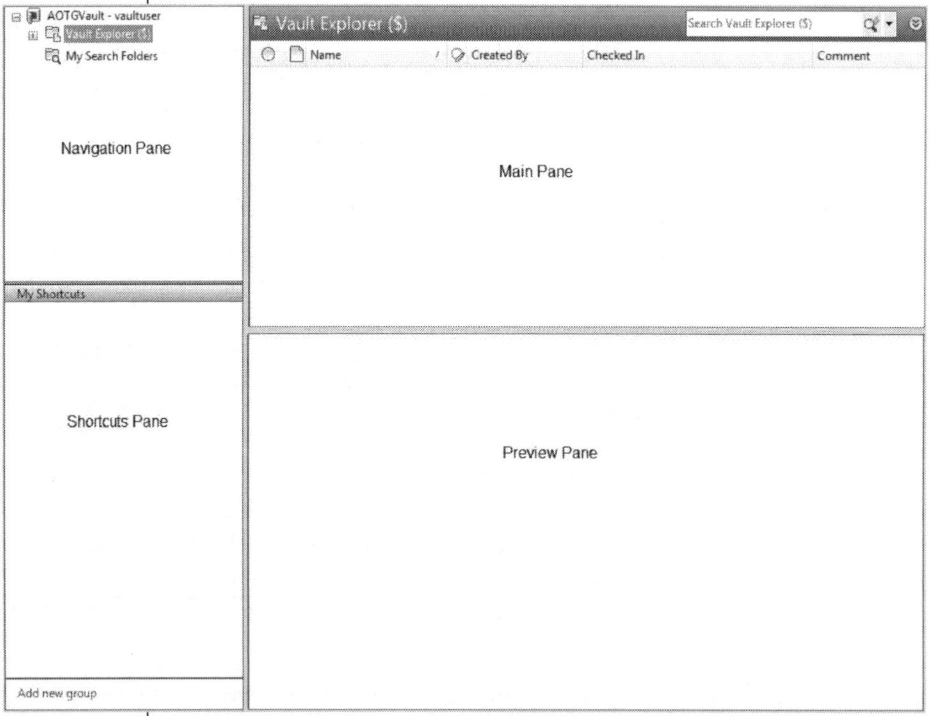

The navigation and shortcuts panes show data in a tree format, while the main and preview panes show data organized in a column format.

In the main and preview panes, each column represents a field. You can resize, rearrange, or group these columns. You can easily sort the contents of any column from ascending to descending order. By customizing the panes to display what you need, you can quickly view important information without extensive searching.

Example User Interface

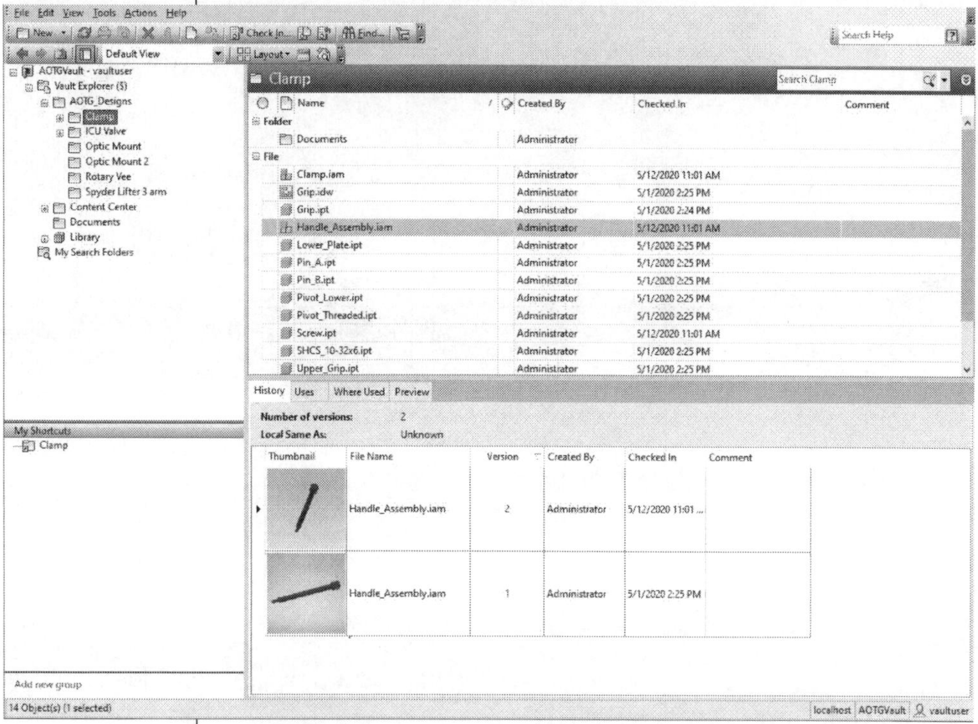

The Navigation pane displays the folder hierarchy of the vault and the saved searches. The saved searches are unique to each user and are saved in the user's profile in Windows, rather than in the vault.

The Shortcuts pane contains shortcuts that you use to quickly navigate to folders and files in the vault. These shortcuts are unique to each user and are saved on each user's workstation, rather than in the vault.

You can toggle off all panes except the Main pane from the View menu.

You can access Vault commands from the menus, toolbars, or shortcut menus.

Navigation Pane

The Navigation pane is a tree structure that displays the Vault folder hierarchy and is used to navigate the folders in the vault.

About the Navigation Pane

The Navigation pane (also called the tree view), located on the left side of the Autodesk Vault window, displays the folders that have been defined in the vault.

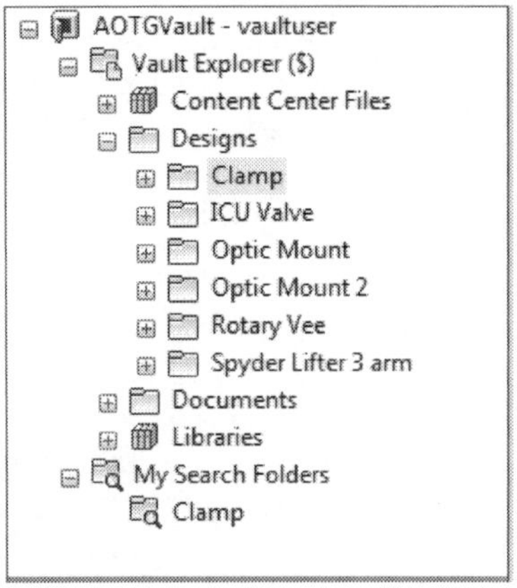

The folders contain the data that has been checked in to that specific folder location.

This folder hierarchy in the vault matches the logical folder structure under the working folder. The Vault folder structure controls the working folder structure to maintain file locations when you use Vault commands such as Check In and Get.

The Navigation pane is also where you find your saved searches.

Functions of the Navigation Pane

The following functions are available in the Navigation pane shortcut menus.

Function	Description
New Folder	Creates a new folder in the vault.
New Library Folder	Creates a new library folder in another library folder.
Add Files	Adds files to the vault from your computer.

Check In	Checks in all files in the selected folder from the same folder under the working folder, if the files exist and are checked out. If the file is changed, the version number in the vault increments. Also unlocks the vault copy so other users can check the file out to make changes.
Get	Copies the selected files to the local workspace. It can also copy related files, and check out the selected files to the user for editing.
Check Out	Checks out all files in the folder. It does not create a local copy of the files in the working folder.
Undo Check Out	Removes the check out for that user. Changes made to the local files remain on the user's workstation, unless the Replace Local Copy is selected.
Create Shortcut	Creates a shortcut to the folder in the Shortcuts pane.
Delete	Deletes the folder or the saved search.
Rename	Renames the folder or the saved search
New Label	Creates a new label at that specific point in time of all the files and their versions in that folder.
Go to Working Folder	Opens the corresponding working folder in Windows Explorer. Note: If the folder does not exist, the vault will create the folder structure required for this local path.
Expand All	Expands all subfolders.
Collapse All	Collapses all subfolders.
Details	Opens the Details dialog box, where you can change the working folder or map the folder to a shared server if it is a library folder.

Example of Using the Navigation Pane

A design has reached a new milestone. To record this milestone, you navigate to the design folder, right-click, and click New Label. You enter a new label and a comment to create the label.

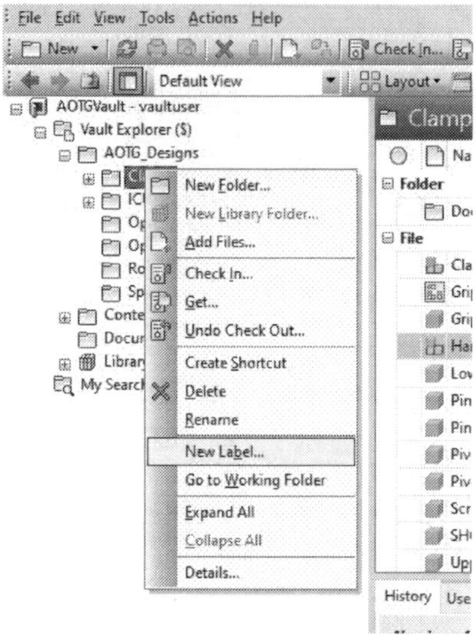

Main Pane

The Main pane lists files in the selected folder or the results of a search.

About the Main Pane

If you check out a file and another user logs in to Autodesk Vault, the status of your checked-out file is displayed to that user.

The Main pane displays the most recent version of the files that are stored in the folder that is selected in the Navigation pane. Vault status for each file is also displayed in the Main pane. You can customize the columns displayed here to display other properties of the files.

You can use the search box to perform basic searches or expand the search box to build a more advanced query of the data.

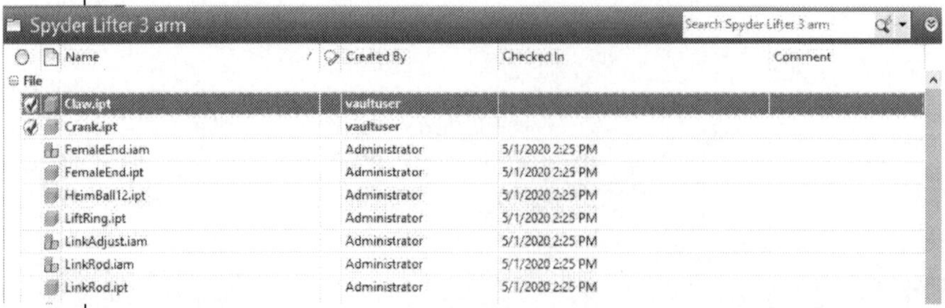

Functions of the Main Pane

The following functions are available in the Main pane shortcut menus by right-clicking the files.

Function	Description
Open	Opens the file using the application associated with the file format and checks out the file for editing.
View in Window	Opens the file in a viewer in a new window if a viewer is associated with the file format.
Check In	Updates the vault with changes you've made to the checked out file so that other users can get the new version from the vault. If the file is changed, the version number in the vault increments. Also unlocks the vault copy so other users can check the file out to make changes.
Get	Copies a specified version of the file(s) from the vault to your working folder. The default is the latest version. This action enables you to specify which, if any, files are designated as checked out to you. This enables you to edit the files and prevents others from editing the same file.
Check Out	Checks out the selected file. It does not create a local copy of the files in the working folder.
Undo Check Out	Abandons changes. Checks the file back in without creating a new version and without copying the file back to the vault. If you select Replace Local Copy, the local version returns to the way it was before you checked it out. You can only use the command on files that you currently have checked out, rather than on files checked out by other users.
Copy Design	Copies a design. You can rename the files and select which files to copy and which files to reference from the original files.
Create Shortcut	Creates a shortcut to the file in the Shortcuts pane.
Delete	Deletes the file. You cannot delete a file if it is checked out or is marked for use in a label.
Purge	Deletes previous versions of a file. Can be used to save space in the vault.
Rename	Renames the file using the Rename wizard.
Go to Working Folder	Opens the corresponding working folder in Windows Explorer.

Go to Folder	Navigates to the folder where the file is stored in the vault.
Details	Opens the Details dialog box to display information such as File Type, File Status, Location, etc.

Example

To see the status of the files in a design, you start Autodesk Vault, navigate to the required folder, and select it.

The list of files in that folder is displayed in the Main pane. In the following image, the Vault status column (to the left of the Checked Out By column) displays the status of the files, and the Version column displays the version number of the latest version of the file in the vault. The Checked Out By column displays who has checked the file out. By default this is not the view of the Main pane; however, it can be customized like this to show all the required information.

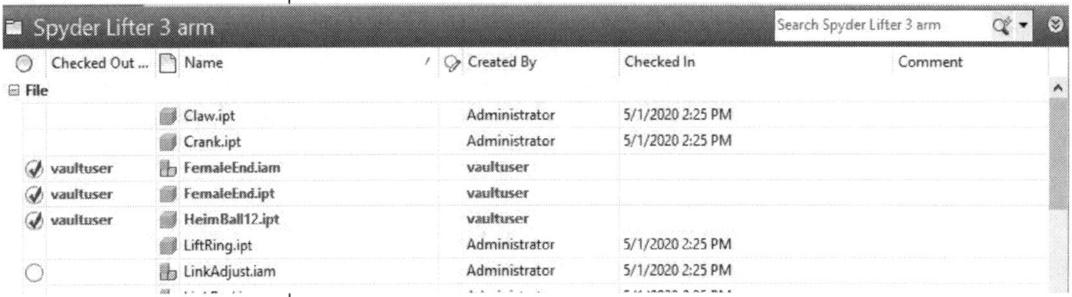

Preview Pane

The Preview pane is used to view a file, view a file's version history, and view the file's parent-child relationships.

About the Preview Pane

The Preview pane is located at the bottom of the main Autodesk Vault interface. This pane displays the history and file relationships for the file that you selected in the Main pane.

History Tab

The History tab displays the available versions of the file.

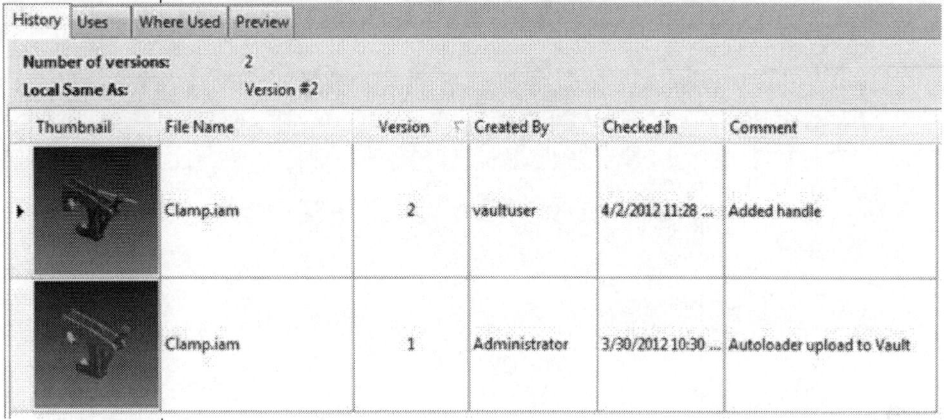

Uses Tab

The Uses tab displays the files that make up the selected file. For example, if you select an assembly and then click the Uses tab, the parts that make up the assembly are displayed.

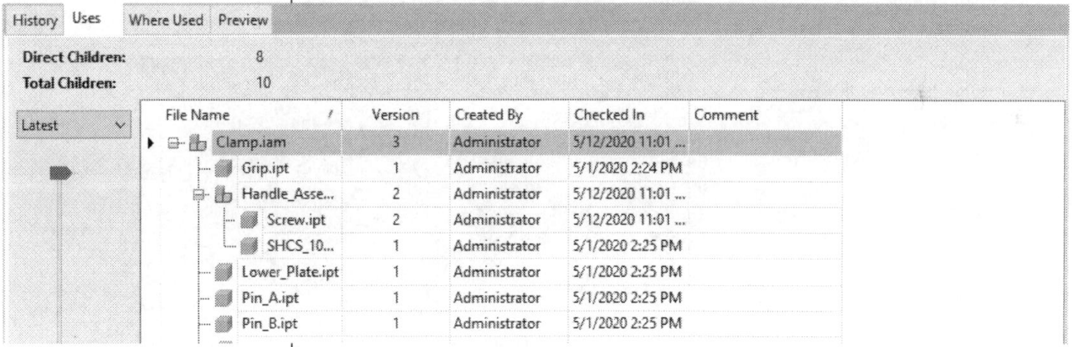

Where Used Tab

The Where Used tab displays where the selected file is used or referenced. If you select an individual part, the assembly and drawing file where the part is used is displayed.

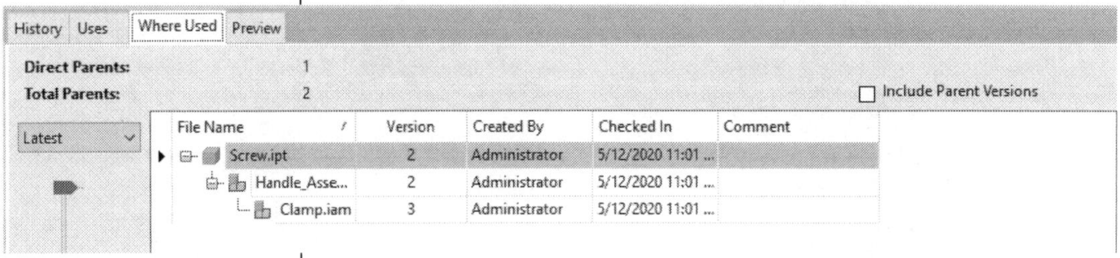

Preview Tab

The Preview tab displays a carousel view of the file. In addition to viewing a thumbnail of the selected file, you can also cycle through historical versions of the file. The file version or revision is displayed at the top of each thumbnail and the last check-in date is displayed at the bottom.

For files, such as Inventor parts, assemblies, and drawings, Vault attaches a visualization file to the selected file. When the thumbnail is selected, the visualization file is loaded, if it exists. Vault can create these visualization files automatically when the file is checked in from Autodesk Inventor or AutoCAD. You can create visualization files by clicking Update.

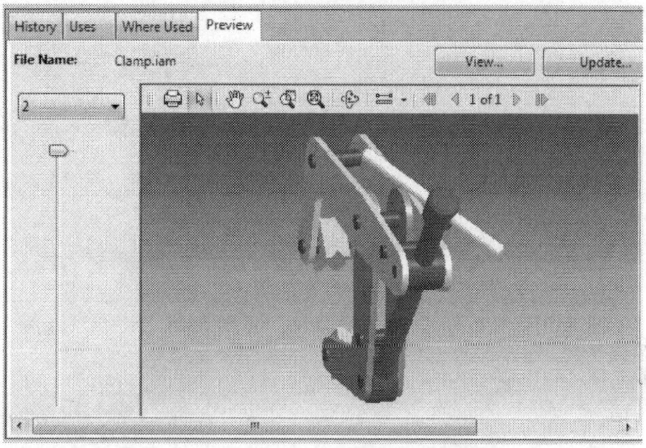

If a file does not have a visualization file attached, you can view the file with an external viewer. Click Open to view the file. The files in the vault are downloaded to a temporary folder on your computer and the viewing software is opened.

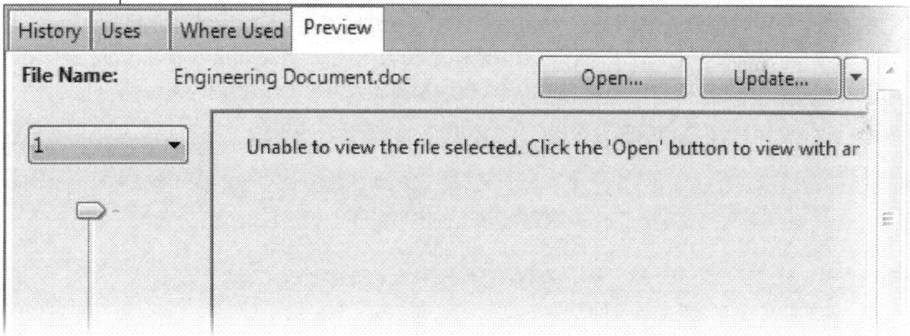

Functions of the Preview Pane

When you right-click a filename in any of the first three tabs of the Preview pane, the same shortcut menu options as those in the Main pane are available.

The Preview tab has functions related to viewing the file and updating the visualization files.

Example

To view different versions of a design, you select the file in the Main pane and then click the History tab in the Preview pane.

You can customize the columns in the Preview pane if you want to display or hide thumbnails of the file versions.

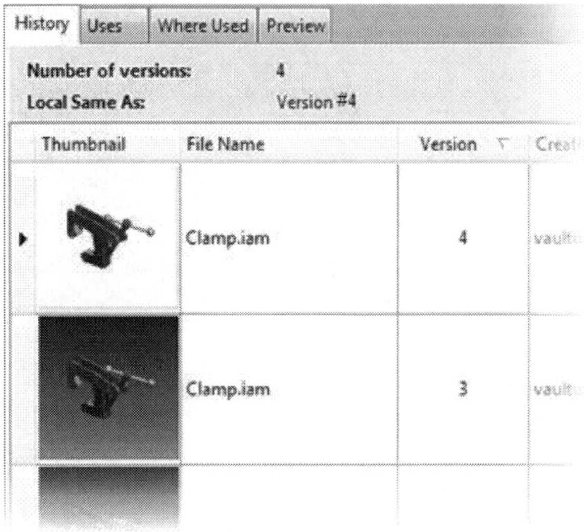

Shortcuts and Saved Searches

Reentering search criteria again and again to find files in a vault is a repetitive and unnecessary task. Searches can be saved and used again when required.

Navigating folders in the Navigation pane and files in the Main pane again and again is also unnecessary. Create shortcuts pointing to folders or files.

About Saved Searches

You can save any search using Find (Basic or Advanced). You can save the search criteria as a search folder that is displayed under My Search Folders in the Navigation pane. To run a search, click on a search folder. Vault runs the search and the results are displayed in the Main pane.

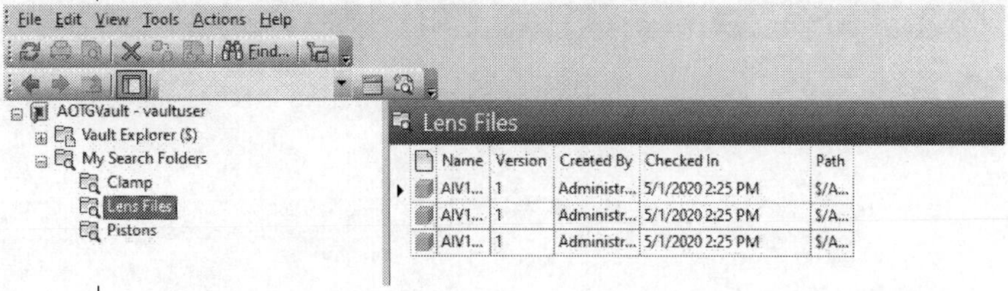

Vault saves searches for each user account so that your saved searches are accessible only to you.

About Shortcuts

Vault displays shortcuts in the Shortcuts pane. To create a shortcut, right-click any file or folder and click Create Shortcut.

You can organize shortcuts into groups. This simplifies how you can navigate to a file or folder.

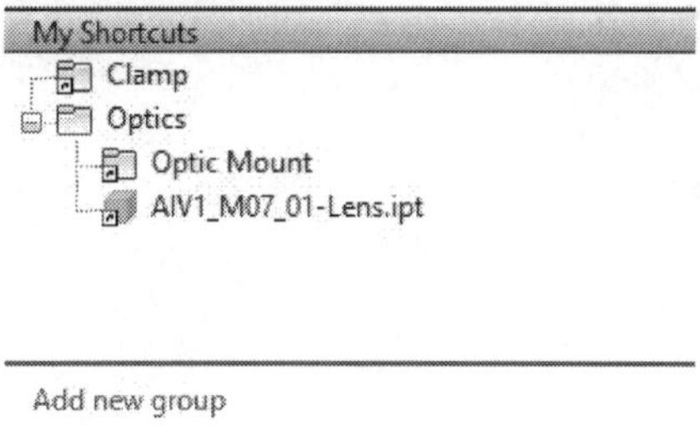

Vault saves shortcuts for each user account so that your saved shortcuts are accessible only to you.

Example

The following image displays a sample of shortcuts in Vault. Note how the shortcuts are organized into groups by design and function.

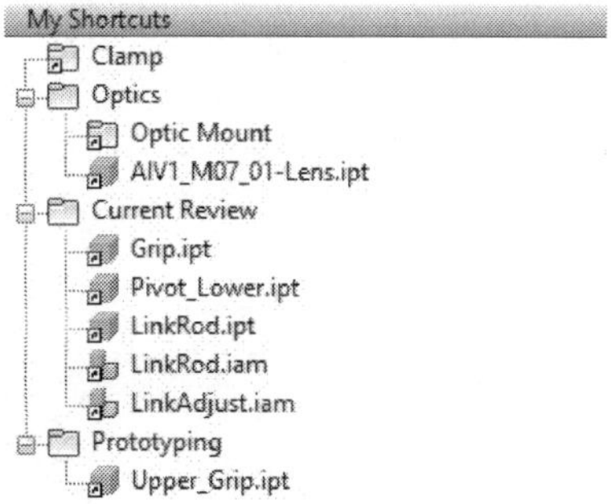

Practice 2a Use the Vault Interface

In this practice, you log in to vault, create a new folder, and add two files.

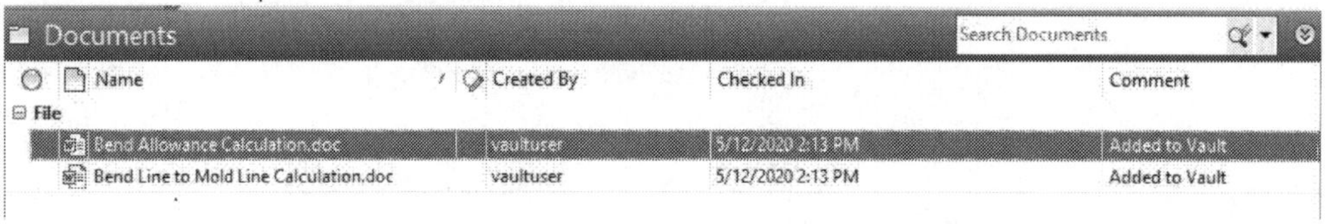

The completed practice

*If you did not create a vault named **AOTGVault** and a user named **vaultuser** during the database set up, refer to the **Preface** and follow the instructions in the sections **Create a Vault** and **Add a User** respectively to create the vault first and then the user.*

1. Start Autodesk Vault. Log in using the following information:
   - For User Name, enter **vaultuser**.
   - For Password, leave the box empty.
   - For Vault, select AOTGVault.
2. Review the vault structure in the Navigation pane. The current vault is empty.

3. In the Navigation pane, right-click the vault root folder ($). Click Details.
4. In the Details for '$' dialog box, click Change. Navigate to *C:\AOTGVault\ VaultWorkingFolder*. Click OK.

5. Click OK to close the Details dialog box.
6. In the Navigation pane, right-click the vault root folder ($). Do the following:
   - Click New Folder.
   - For Folder, enter **Documents**.
   - Click OK.

7. In the Navigation pane, right-click the Documents folder. Do the following:
   - Click Add Files.
   - Navigate to *C:\AOTGVault\Chapter2\Documents*.
   - Select Bend Allowance Calculation.doc and Bend Line to Mold Line Calculation.doc (use the CTRL key to select both files).
   - Click Open.

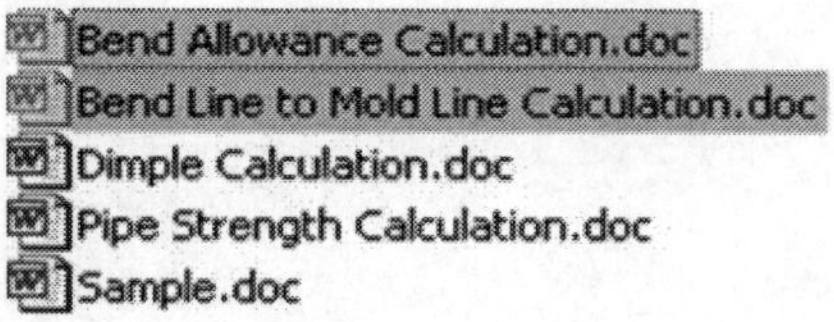

8. In the Add Files - Multiple Files dialog box, under Enter comments to include with this version, enter **Added to Vault**. Click OK.

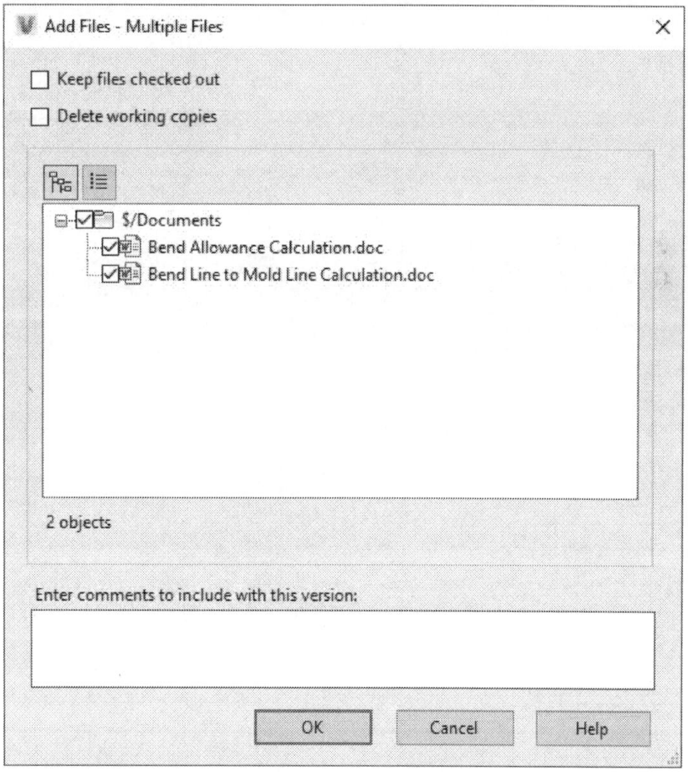

9. In the Navigation pane, double-click Documents. The two Word files are displayed in the Main pane.

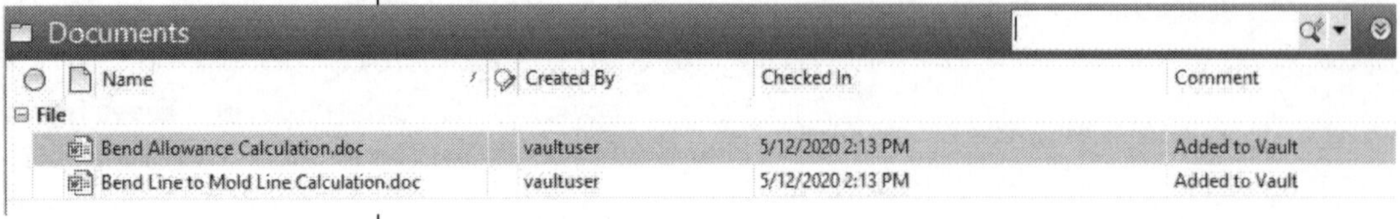

10. In the Main pane, click Bend Allowance Calculation.doc. Note the file details displayed in the Preview pane.

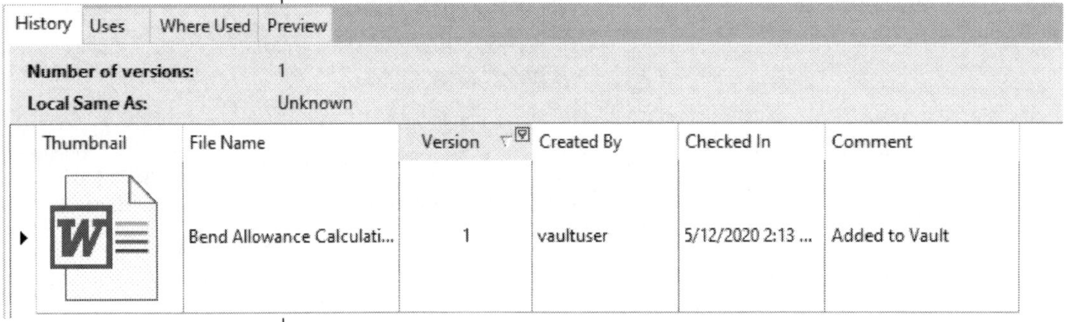

2.3 Working with Files and the Vault

Overview

To use Autodesk Vault, you define folders in the Navigation pane. These folders and their structure match the familiar structure from Windows Explorer. You also specify where files that are checked out go on your local drive.

This lesson displays the basic workflows that you use to add and edit non-CAD files. Supporting engineering documents are frequently created using Microsoft Word, Excel and PowerPoint. These and other non-CAD files can also be added to the vault.

Objectives

After completing this lesson, you will be able to:

- Create new folders and set the working folder to start working with files in the vault.
- Use Add Files in Vault to add non-CAD files to the vault.
- Use Autodesk Vault to check non-CAD files out of and in to the vault so they can be edited.
- Use vault status icons to determine the status of files in the vault.
- Manage file versions to view the history of a file and retrieve older versions.

Folder Structure

In order to accommodate a large number of designs in the vault, a correct folder hierarchy is required. Create folders in the vault to keep your files organized, just like the folders on your hard drive.

In addition, you need to set up a working folder that represents the root of the vault.

Creating Folders in Vault

You use folders to organize your files in the vault in the same way that you organize files on your computer. You create folders using the main menu or the Navigation pane shortcut menu.

When creating folders, in the Navigation pane, click the existing folder that you want to create a new folder under, and then right-click and click New Folder on the shortcut menu.

If you are creating the first folder in the vault, click the Vault Explorer root (defined by $). Folders can be renamed or moved if required.

Library Folders

Files stored in library folders are commonly used in multiple designs and are not changed. Files placed in a library folder should be considered read only; they cannot be edited.

To create a library folder, you click the root ($), and then right-click and click New Library Folder on the shortcut menu. Subfolders of a library folder will also be a library folder.

About the Working Folder

When you get a file from the vault to view or check out a file to edit, the file is copied to the working folder on your local computer. By default, the working folder is set to the folder Vault under My Documents.

Although you can set a working folder for each folder, you usually set one working folder for the root of the vault (indicated by $). When you check out a file, the folder structure used in the vault is created automatically below the root's working folder, thereby replicating the folder hierarchy from the vault on your local computer. Note that the vault does not duplicate all folders in the local workspace. It only duplicates the folders required for the files that you have local copies for.

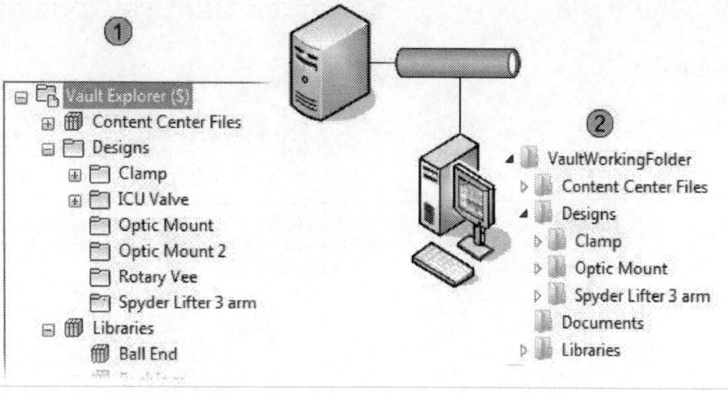

1. File structure in the Vault, with the root ($) mapped to *C:\AOTGVault\VaultWorkingFolder.*

2. File structure in the working folder, duplicating the vault folder hierarchy as files are checked out from the vault

To set the working folder for the vault root folder, right-click the root folder in the Navigation pane and click Details. Click Change, and then select a folder on your local computer. Only perform this on the Vault Explorer root folder ($).

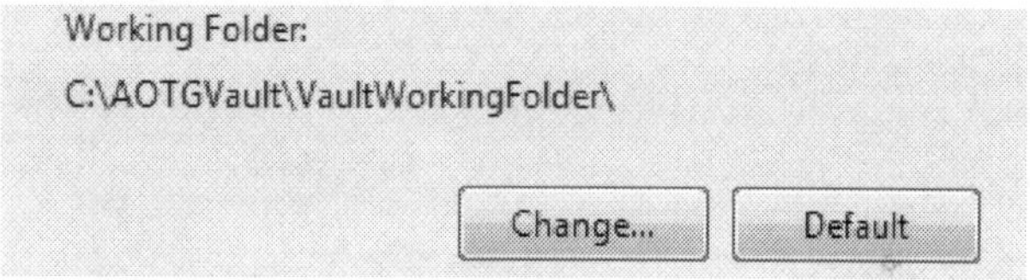

Set the Working Folder Once

It is recommended that you do not change the working folder once you start working with files in the vault. Changing the working folder will create duplicate folder structures on the local computer, and might cause problems resolving files in your CAD application.

Example: Using a Consistent Working Folder

A Vault administrator can set the working folder to a fixed folder that users cannot change. This minimizes confusion and simplifies file maintenance and folder management tasks.

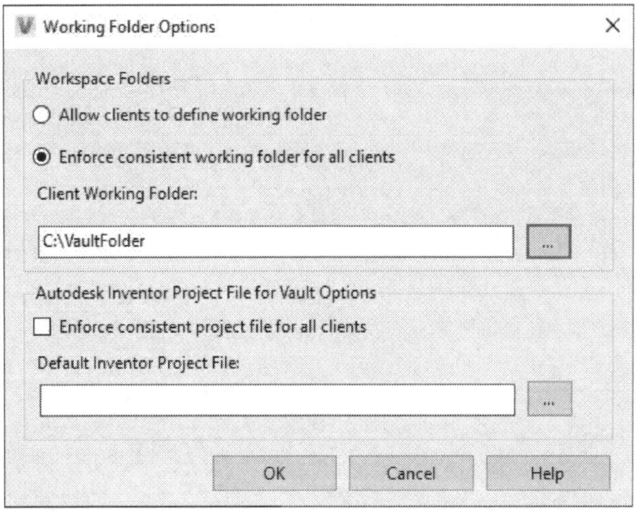

With the defaults set, Vault creates the same working folder, *C:\VaultFolder*, for everyone on their local computer. The folder structure in the vault will be mirrored in this folder on all users' computers as they work with files from the vault.

You will learn more about administrative Vault tasks later in the course.

Adding Files

Autodesk Vault can manage any file format that you add to the vault.

When you add files to the vault, they become available to the rest of the design team in a centralized location. Using Vault, you can also track the version history of the files that are added to the vault so that you can retrieve a previous version of a particular file.

Procedure: Using the Add Files Tool in Vault

The following steps describe how to add files to the vault using the Add Files tool. This method is the simplest but also the most restricted.

Note: Do not add CAD files this way; it is recommended that you use the Vault add-in from the CAD application.

1. In the Navigation pane, right-click the folder to which you want to add files. Click Add Files.

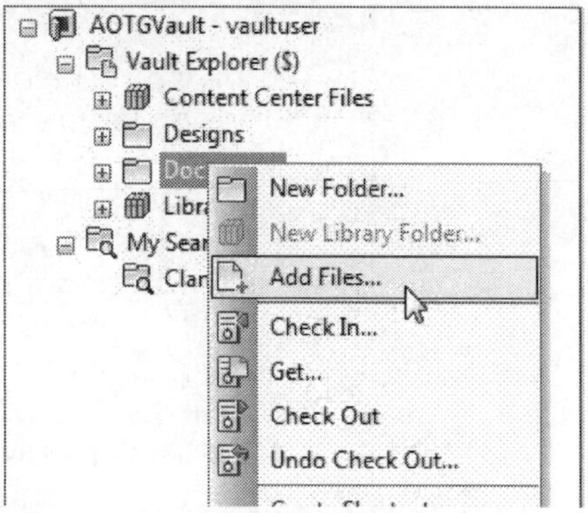

2. Select and open the files from your computer.
3. In the Add Files dialog box, review the files to be added. Then enter a comment.

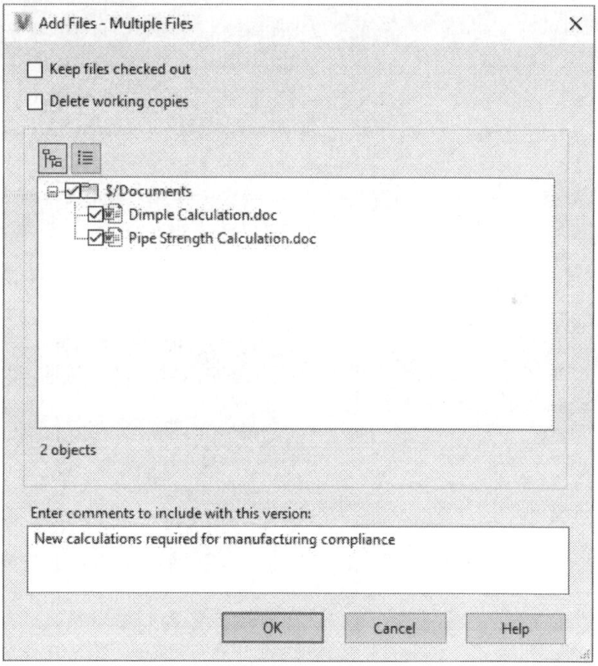

4. Click OK. The files are added to the vault.

Procedure: Adding the Files from the Application Using the Vault Add-in

This method is recommended for design files. To add files to the vault using this method:

1. For Autodesk Inventor files, copy the files to a folder in the Vault working folder. For AutoCAD and other application add-ins you are prompted for the location in which to place the file in the vault if it is opened outside the Vault working folder.
2. Open the files with the application.
3. Check the files into the vault.

Procedure: Using Advanced Tools such as Autoloader

This is a very powerful and very fast method to add existing Autodesk Inventor projects to the vault. Autoloader is a separate application that can be executed.

Guidelines for Adding Files to the Vault

You can use the Add Files tool in Autodesk Vault to add files to the vault, but you should follow these guidelines:

- Adding files using the Add Files tools in Vault is recommended only for non-CAD files. Examples of files that you can load include Microsoft Office documents, Adobe PDF files, and image files.

- Using the Add Files tools on files that have links results in the files being added to the vault, but a Uses or Where Used search reveals no parent or child dependencies. Opening one of these files from the vault might not work because the links might not resolve correctly.

- When you transfer a file to the vault, the copy in the vault becomes the master copy. When you want to edit the file, you check it out of the vault. Ensure that you are working with the latest version on your local computer.

Working on Files

Before you can change a file that is in the vault, you must check it out. After you revise the file, you check it back in to the vault to give the rest of the design team access to the latest version.

You check non-CAD files in and out of the vault using Autodesk Vault. You can also use Open from Vault to check the files out and open the application to edit the files.

Checking Out a File Using Vault

To edit a file, you must copy it locally and check it out of the vault. The Get command copies the file from the vault to the working folder on your computer where you can open it with the associated application. The option also enables you to specify whether the file is checked out at the same time that it is copied locally.

When you check out a file, other users cannot check it out for editing. This prevents more than one person from simultaneously modifying the file. Other users can still view or use a read-only copy of the file.

A separate Check Out command enables you to check out the file; however, does not copy a local version to the working folder for editing.

Undo Check Out

If you check out a file, edit it, and then decide not to save your modifications, you can undo the checkout. When you use this option, a file that you checked out is checked back into the Vault without the modifications. The file does not have a version. You should delete your local copy or get the latest version from the vault to overwrite your local copy with the latest version from the vault.

Check In

After you revise a file, you use the Check In command to copy the file from your computer back into the vault.

When you change a file and check it in, it becomes the latest version of the file in the vault. The previous version is not overwritten; it is marked as a previous version and you can recall it at any time.

When you check a file in to the vault, the file is available for another user to check out. If you are working in a design team, you can inform other users that they should update their local copies to reflect the changes that you made.

Delete Working Copy

When you check a file back in to the vault, if another member of the design team checks out the file and modifies it, your local copy is no longer current. If you delete the local (working) copy after you check the file in, you must get the latest copy from the vault the next time you want to view or edit the file. This prevents you from using old data.

Procedure: Editing a File Using Vault

The following steps show how to check out and edit a file using Vault.

1. Right-click the file to be edited. Click Open.

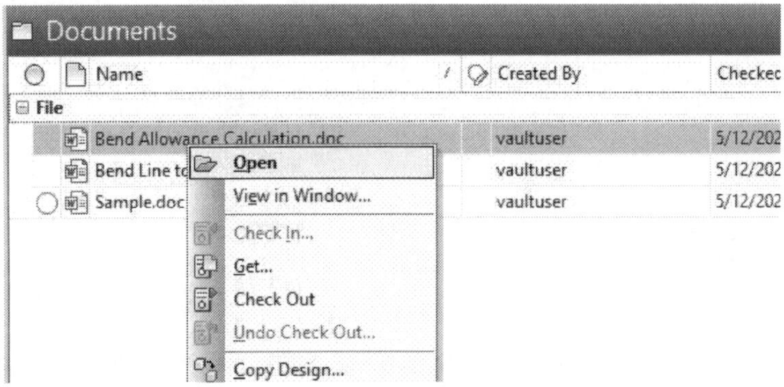

2. Click Yes when you are prompted to check out the file.
3. The file is checked out and opened in the default application for editing.

Procedure: Checking Out a File Using Vault

The following steps show how to check out a file using Vault.

1. Right-click the file to be checked out. Click Get.

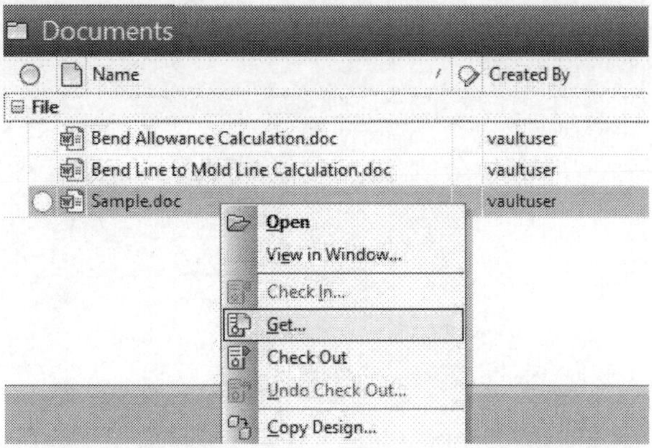

2. The Get dialog box has two settings: collapsed and expanded. In the Get dialog box, select Expand (>>).

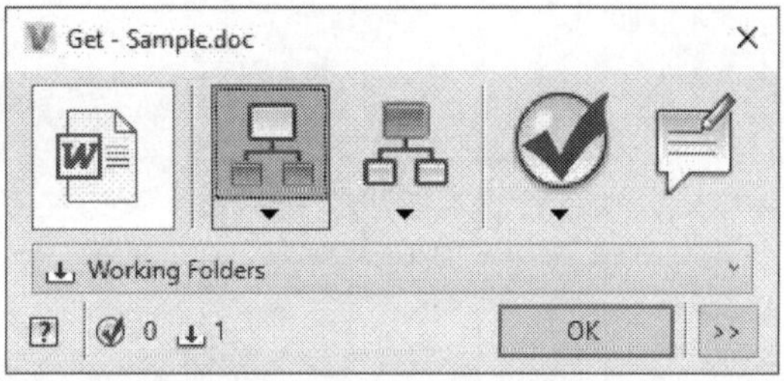

By default, the Get dialog box is collapsed. If you want the dialog to stay uncollapsed every time you open it, click Pin.

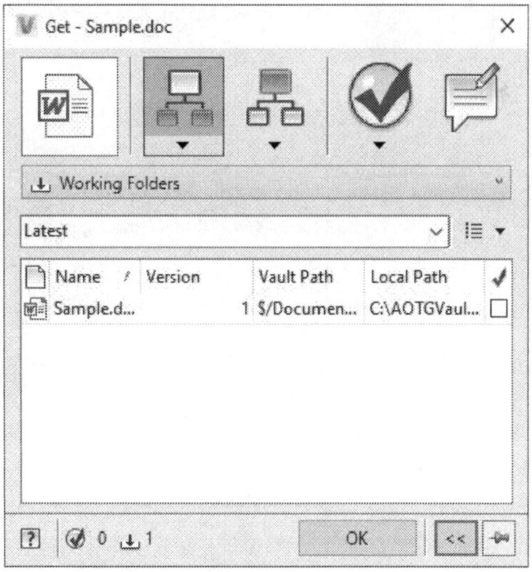

3. To check out the file and not just download a copy to the working folder you must select the Check Out Files option on the compressed view or select the check box adjacent to the filename in the expanded view. Click OK. The file is checked out.

Check Out Options

Option	Description
Include Children 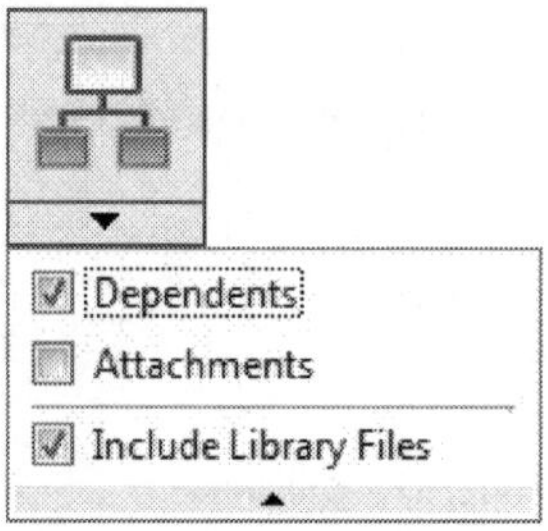 	You can automatically include specified children files for check out whenever you check an object out of the vault. **Tip:** Hover the cursor over Include Children at any time to see the current inclusion settings. Click Include Children to add the specified children file formats to the current list of files. Click the drop-down arrow below Include Children to change the children types to be included when the button is clicked. You can disable the feature by clicking it again. All include settings are ignored until the button is enabled again.
Include Parents 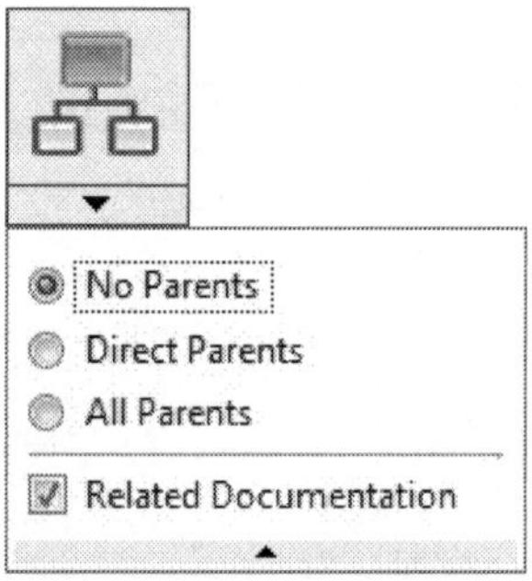 	You can automatically include specified parent files for check out whenever you check an object out of the vault. **Tip:** Hover the cursor over Include Parents at any time to see the current settings. Click Include Parents to add the specified parent file formats related documentation to the current list of files. Click the drop-down arrow below Include Parents to change which parent types, if any, are included when the button is clicked. You can disable the feature by clicking it again. All include settings are ignored until the button is enabled again.

Check Out  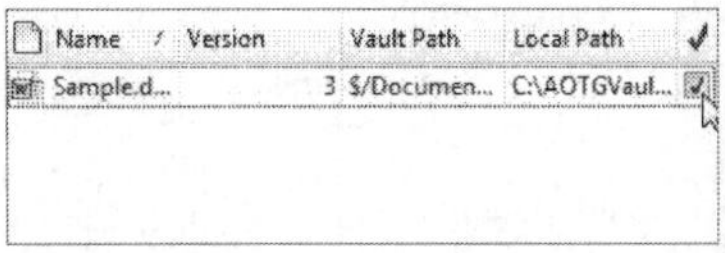	Check Out provides a fast way to select all the objects listed for check out. You can also set it so that whenever the button is clicked, only the objects you initially selected when you launched the Get dialog box are selected. This is a useful feature if you have enabled the Include Children or Include Parents buttons and want a fast way to select everything for check out. **Tip:** Hover the cursor over the button at any time to see the current settings. Click the drop-down arrow below Check Out to change your settings for what happens when the button is clicked. **Selection Settings** Source Selection: Selects only the files that were initially highlighted in the main view when you launched the Get dialog box. All Files: Selects all files listed in the Get dialog box. **Note:** You can also select the files to check out in the expanded Get dialog box.
Working Folders drop-down list 	You can specify whether you want to use the default working folder or select another folder to store the local copies of the objects that you download. You can also select no working folder.
Comments 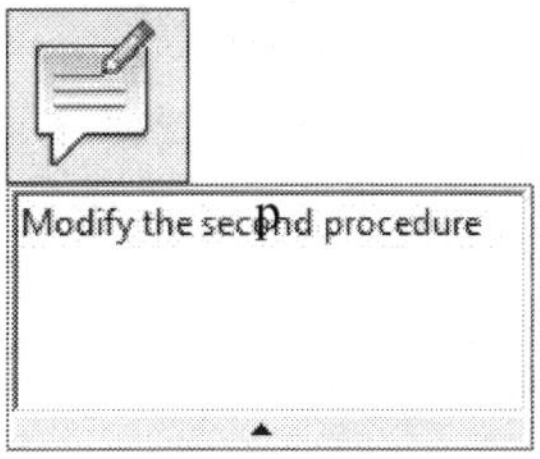	Click Comments to add a description or document the purpose for checking out the selected files. **Tip:** Hover the cursor over Comments to see any comments already recorded. This is displayed to others that might want to access the file while it is checked out to you.
Select Version 	You can get and optionally check out the current (Latest) version or any past versions available in the vault.

Procedure: Checking In a File Using Vault

The following steps show how to check in a file using Vault.

1. Right-click the file to be checked in. Click Check In.

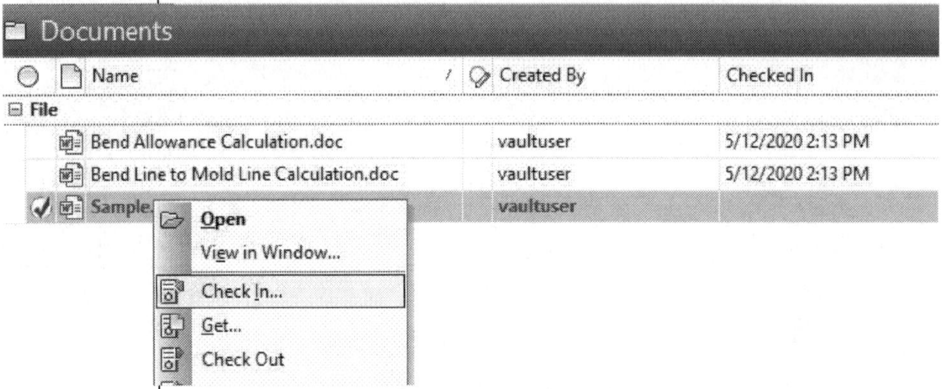

2. Select the options in the Check In dialog box, if required.

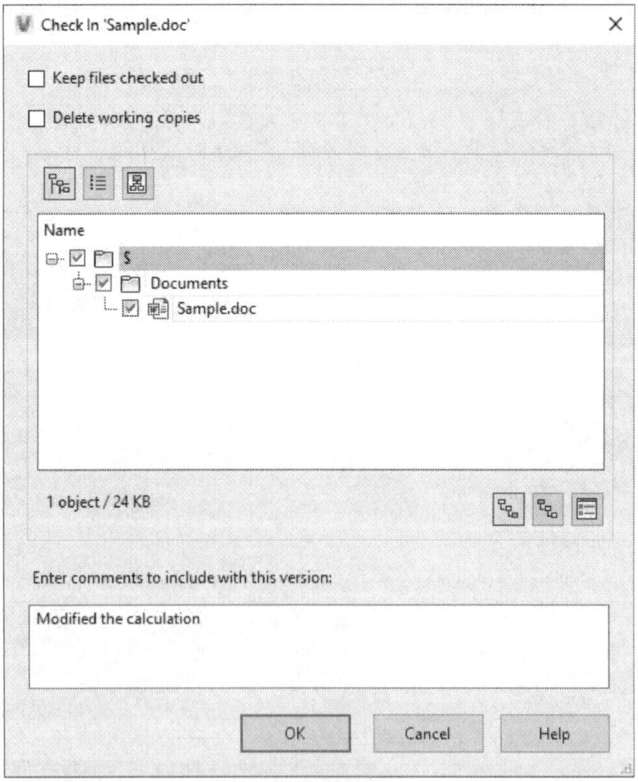

3. Click OK. The file is checked in.

Check In Options

The following options are available in the Check In dialog:

Option	Description
Keep files checked out	Check the file back out immediately after you check it in. You can use this option to secure a filename for a new file and prevent someone else from using the same filename. You can also provide an updated file for other members of your design team but keep the file checked out for further editing.
Delete working copies	Remove the local copy of the file after you check it in. This ensures that you always have the latest version of the file.
Enter comments to include with this version	Enter a comment to let others know why you checked the file in or to include other pertinent information.

File Status

Introduction to Determining File Status

When a design team works with files in the vault the status of files are likely to change often. The ability to see the status of a particular file is crucial in design collaboration.

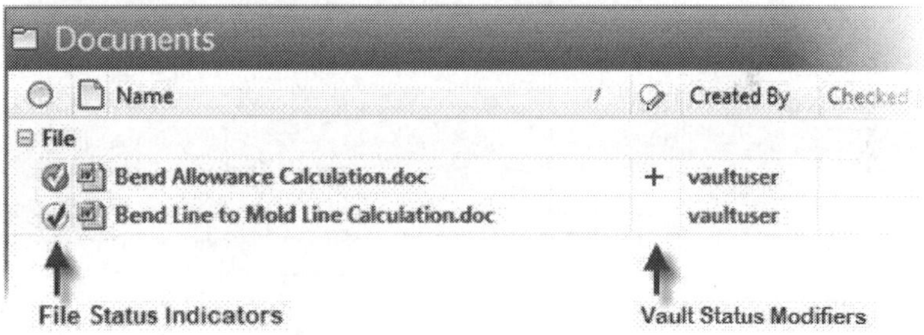

Status Icons (Autodesk Vault Basic)

The status icons are a combination of a background color and foreground symbol. The foreground symbol can be one of the following:

Icon	Description
	If there is no checkmark, x, or lock displayed, the file is in the vault and available to be checked out.
✔	File is checked out to you.
✖	File is checked out to another user.
+ (Vault Status	Local copy has saved edits.

The background symbol can be one of four:

Icon	Description
	If there is no circle, then there is no local copy.
○ (white)	The circle signifies that the local copy exists on your computer. The white background means the local copy is the same as the one in the Vault.
● (green)	The circle signifies that the local copy exists on your computer. The green background means that the local copy is newer than the one in the Vault.
● (red)	The circle signifies that the local copy exists on your computer. The red background means that the local copy is older than the one in the Vault.

The combination of both foreground and background icons gives different states for the files in the Vault:

Option	Description
	If no icon is displayed, the file is in the vault and available to be checked out but there is no local copy.
(white)	File is in the vault and available to be checked out. The version in your working folder is the same as in the vault. This is also referred to as the Latest Version.
(green)	File is in the vault and available to be checked out. Local copy is newer than the vault version. This typically means that your local file was changed without checking it out.
(red)	File is in the vault and available to be checked out. Local copy is older (out of date).
	File is checked out to you. You do not have a local copy. **Note:** This can happen if you check out the file while working on one computer then move to another computer and log in to vault again, or if you change the Working folder location after checking out the file.
(white)	File is checked out to you. The local copy is the same as the vault.
(green)	File is checked out to you. The local copy is newer, which means it was edited but not checked back in yet.
(red)	File is checked out to you. This typically means that you started with a version for the vault that was older than the latest version, and then checked it out to promote it to the latest version.
	File is checked out to another user. You do not have a local copy.
(white)	File is checked out to another user. You have a local copy which is the same as the one in the vault.
(green)	File is checked out to another user. The local copy is newer than the Vault copy.
(red)	File is checked out to another user. Local copy is older (out of date).
	File has attachments. Expand the tree to see what files are attached.
	File is not in Vault. You can add the file using Check In.
	Folder in the vault that is a library. A library folder is a special designation meaning the files in this folder are not intended to be edited when used in context of another assembly.

Versions of Files

In the life of a product, from conception through development to supporting the design, it is important to maintain a history of all the files and any engineering-related documents. Autodesk Vault automatically manages versions as files are revised and checked back in. Vault keeps a history of the files, so that you can retrieve any version of a file at any time.

File Versions Always Increment

When you add a file to the vault, it becomes version 1. When the file is checked out, it is temporarily assigned the next version number; the previous version remains unchanged. The permanent version number is not assigned until the modified file is checked back in. If the file is unchanged when it is checked back in, it does not receive a new version number.

Procedure: Viewing File Versions

The following steps show how to view a file's history in the Preview pane.

1. In the Main pane of the Autodesk Vault window, select the file.
2. The History tab of the Preview pane displays all versions of the selected file.

Procedure: Getting the Latest Version of a File

If you want to view the latest version of a file to see whether the changes affect your design, you can get a read-only copy even if someone else has the file checked out. You can view the file but not edit it, because it is not checked out to you.

The following steps teach you how to see the latest version of a file.

1. In the Main pane of Autodesk Vault, right-click a file. Click Get.

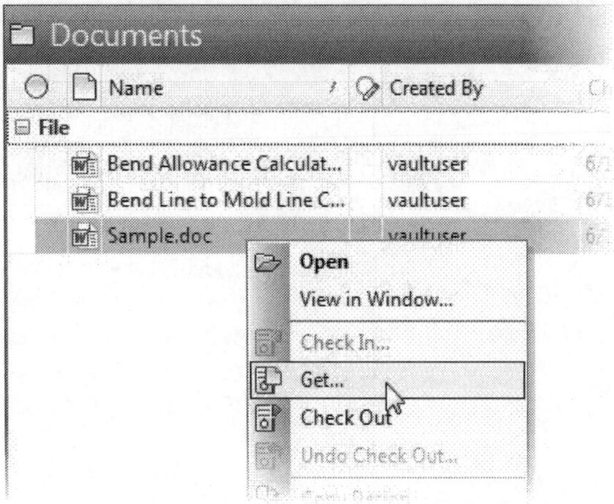

2. In the Get dialog box, select Expand (>>).
3. In the Get dialog box, note that the version defaults to Latest. Also, the checkbox in the last column of the Check Out list is off by default. Select this to display a checkmark in the box. It checks the file out and gets the latest version.

By default, the Get dialog box is collapsed. If you want the dialog box to stay uncollapsed every time you open it, click Pin.

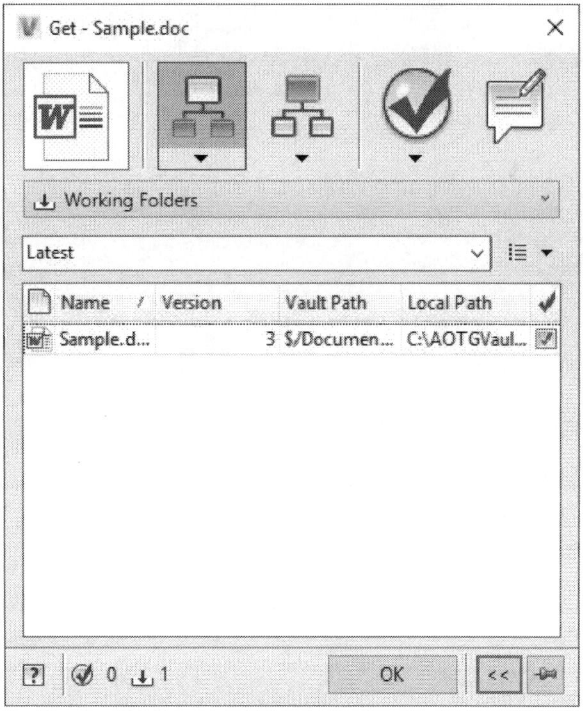

4. Click OK. The file is checked out.

Procedure: Getting the Previous Version of a File

When you retrieve a previous version of a file, Vault does not check the file out. Instead, it places a read-only copy of the file in your working folder. You can either view the copy or use it to roll back to a previous version.

The following steps show you how to get a previous version of a file.

1. In the Main pane of the Autodesk Vault window, right-click a file that has more than one version as shown. Click Get.
2. The Get dialog box opens. Expand the dialog box.
3. In the Select Version drop-down list, you will see multiple entries. The Latest and Version 3 (in this case) are usually (but not always) the same. Since we want to get a previous version, select version 2.

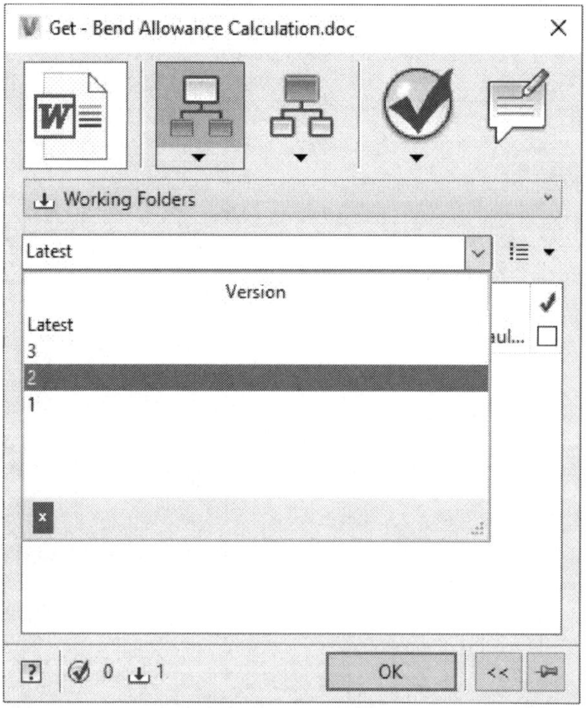

4. Select the Include Children or Include Parents settings to include any children or parent files for that version, as required.
5. Click OK.

Note: Expand is normally closed, so the download location is not displayed by default. It is always good practice to accept the default which is the Working Folder together with the directory selected in the Navigation pane. However, if you just want to send someone a copy of the file(s), you might want to change this so it is downloaded to your desktop for easy retrieval or so that you do not overwrite the current copy in the Working Folder.

Procedure: Rolling Back the File in the Vault to a Previous Version

Once you get a previous version of a file, you can use it to roll back the copy in the vault to a previous version.

The following steps show you how to roll a file in the vault back to a previous version.

1. In Autodesk Vault, Vault reports that the file is checked out.

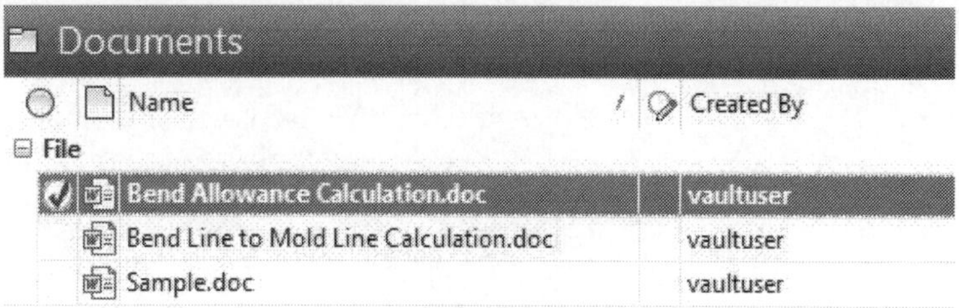

2. Select the file, right-click and select Get.

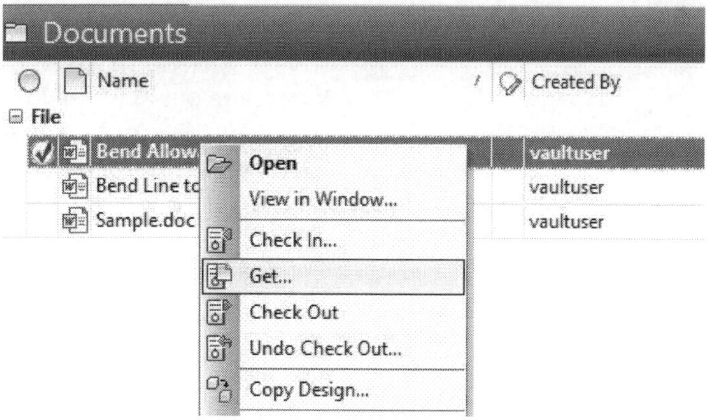

3. The Get dialog box opens. Note that the filename is in blue font and its tooltip warns you that the file is checked out. In the Select Version dialog box, select a previous version.

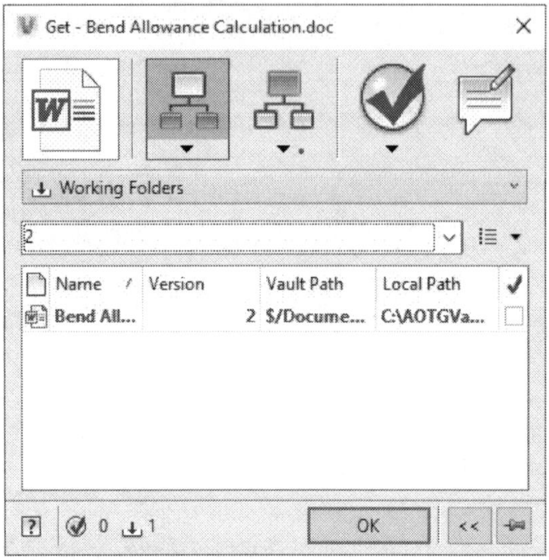

Figure 2–1

4. Click OK. A dialog box opens that warns you that you are going to overwrite the data. Click Yes.

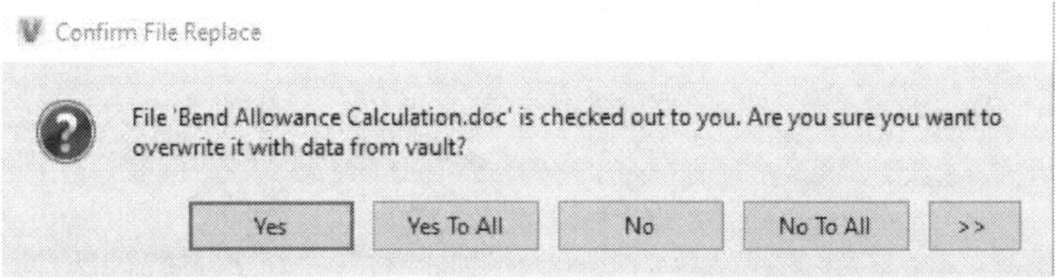

5. The file status in the Main pane is updated to indicate the file is checked out to you but the local copy is older.

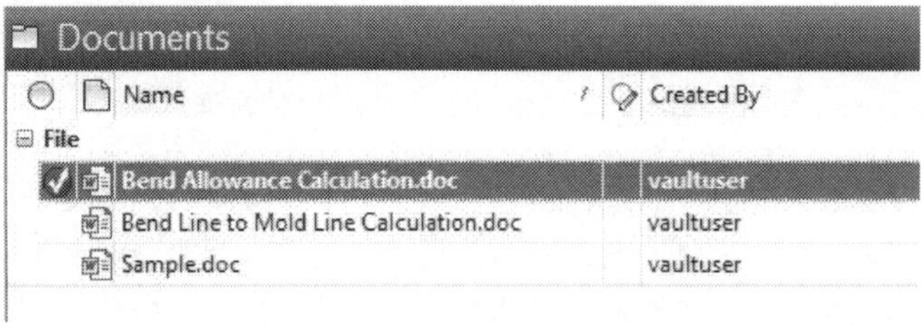

6. Follow the Check In process to check the file back in. It is strongly suggested that you indicate in the comment field that a previous version has been restored as shown.

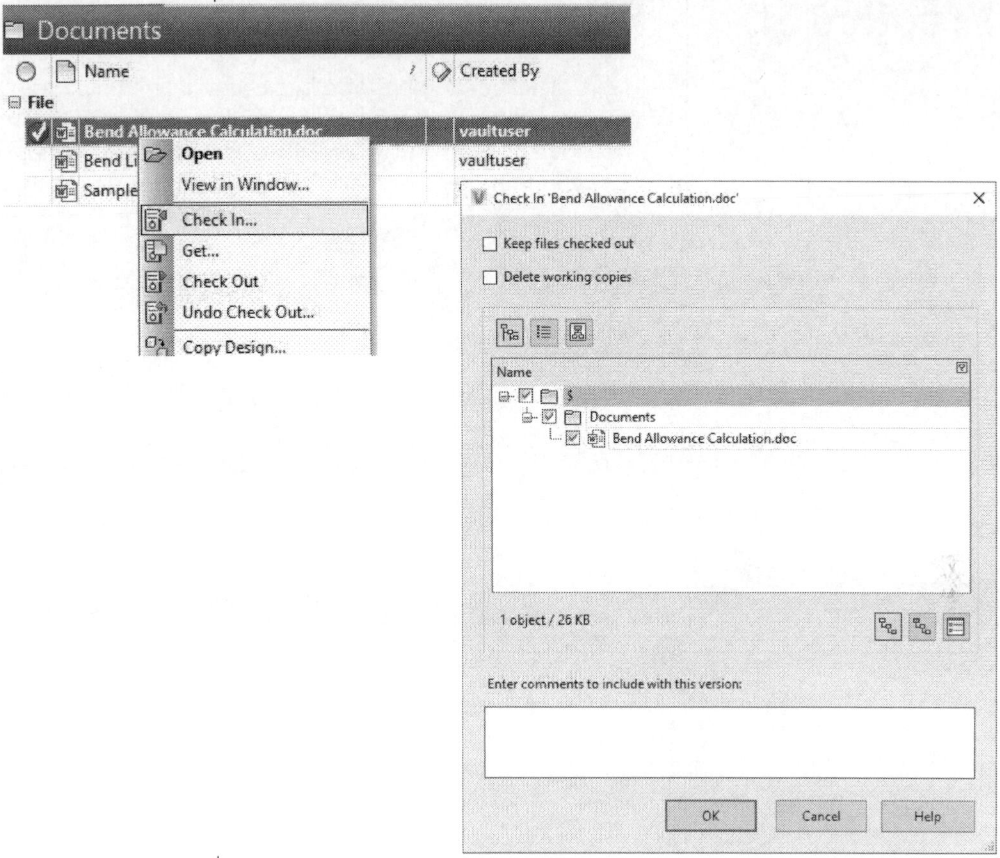

Note the result. The file version has been rolled forward to version 4, which is the same as version 2.

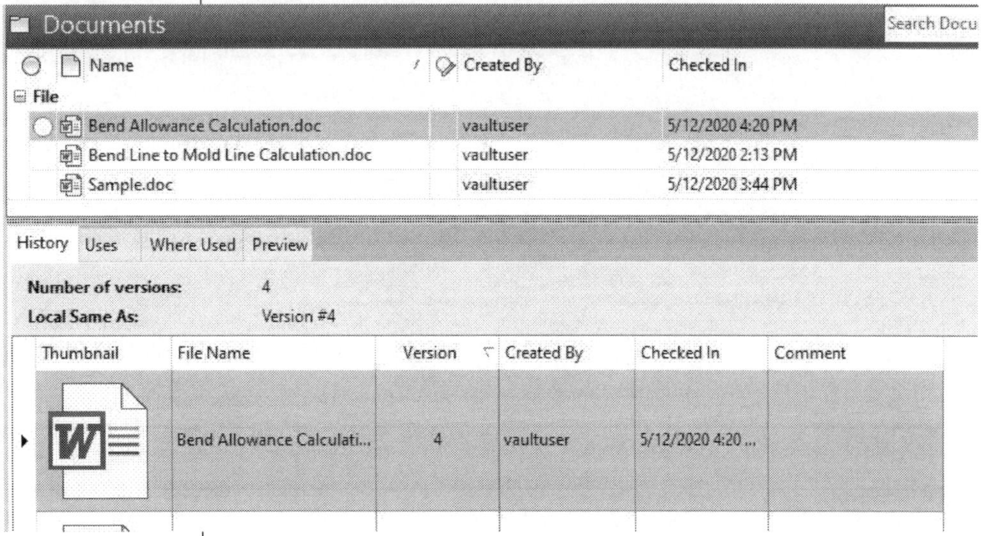

Practice 2b Perform Basic Vault Tasks

In this practice, you perform basic workflows using non-CAD files. You add a document to the vault and edit the document and then check it back in. You will then view the file versions in the vault and then get the previous version, view it, and then get the latest version.

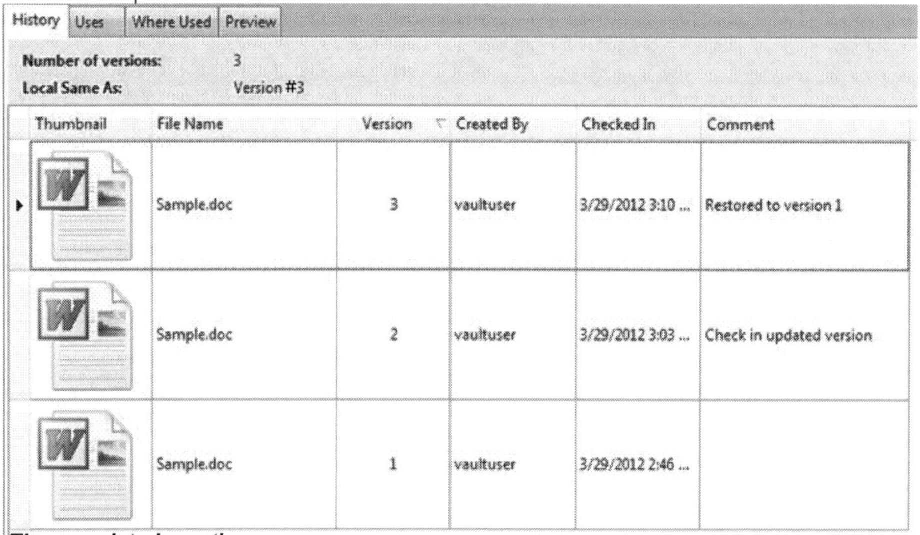

The completed practice

Task 1 - Add a document to the vault.

1. Start Autodesk Vault. Log in using the following information:
    - For User Name, enter **vaultuser**.
    - For Password, leave the box empty.
    - For Vault, select AOTGVault.
2. In the Navigation pane, right-click the vault root folder ($). Click New Folder.

    Note: Steps 2 through 5 are only required if you did not do the previous practice and have not created a Documents folder in the vault.
3. For Folder, enter **Documents**. Click OK.
4. In the Navigation pane, right-click the vault root folder ($). Click Details

5. In the Details for '$' dialog box, verify that the working folder is set to *C:\AOTGVault\VaultWorkingFolder.*

   If it is not set, click Change and set it to *C:\AOTGVault\VaultWorkingFolder*. Click OK.

6. In the Navigation pane, right-click the Documents folder. Click Add Files.
7. Navigate to *C:\AOTGVault\Chapter2\Documents.* Select Sample.doc. Click Open.
8. In the Add Files dialog box, under Enter comments to include with this version, enter **Version 1**. Click OK.

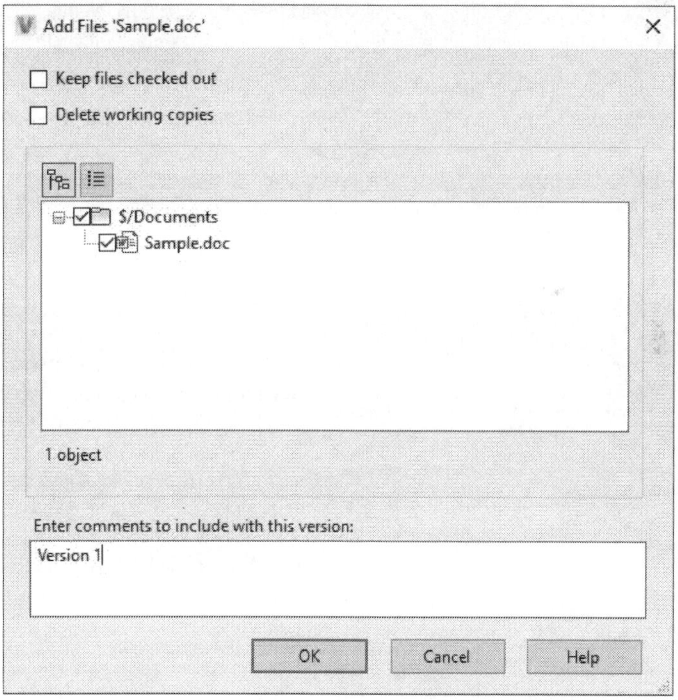

9. In the Main pane, verify that the Sample.doc file is listed and in the Preview pane that the version is 1.

Task 2 - Edit a document and check it back in.

1. In the Main pane, right-click Sample.doc. Click Open.

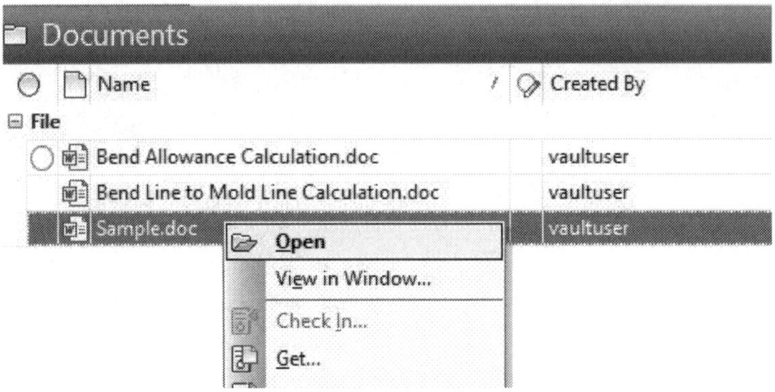

2. In the Open File dialog box, click Yes to check out the file for editing.

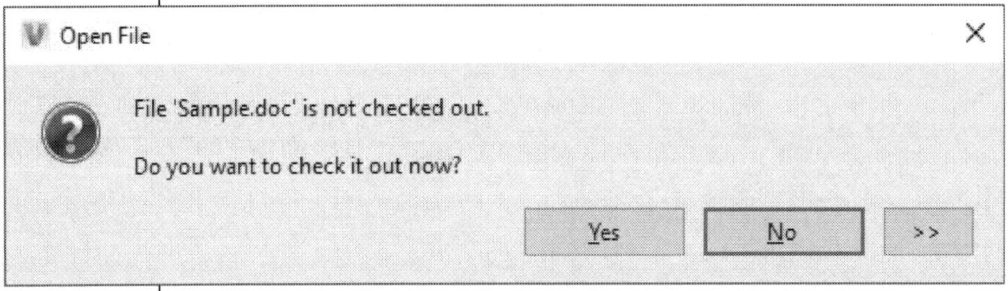

3. The document opens in Microsoft Word. Revise the document by adding a line of text to it and then save it by using the standard save file workflow in Word.

4. Open Windows Explorer and navigate to *C:\AOTGVault\VaultWorkingFolder\Documents.*

   Note that the Sample.doc file has been copied to the folder from the vault.

5. In Microsoft Word, on the ribbon, verify that the Autodesk Vault tab is visible then do the following:

   - Click the Autodesk Vault tab.
   - Click Log In.
   - Enter **vaultuser** to log in to AOTGVault. The password is blank.

6. Click Check In.

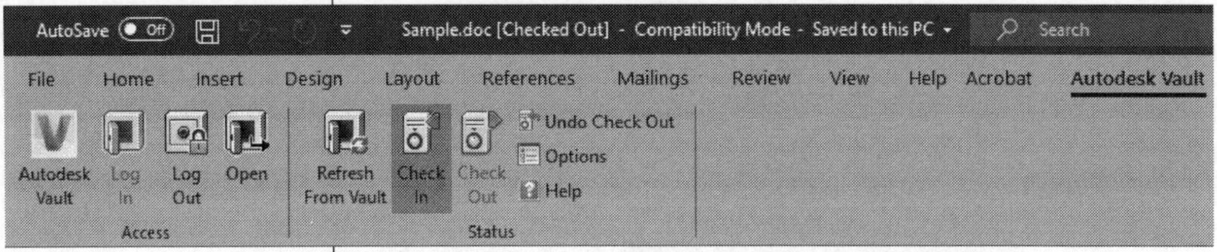

7. In the Check In dialog box, do the following:

   - Select Close file and delete working copy.
   - Under Enter Comments to include with this version, enter **Check in updated version.**
   - Click OK.

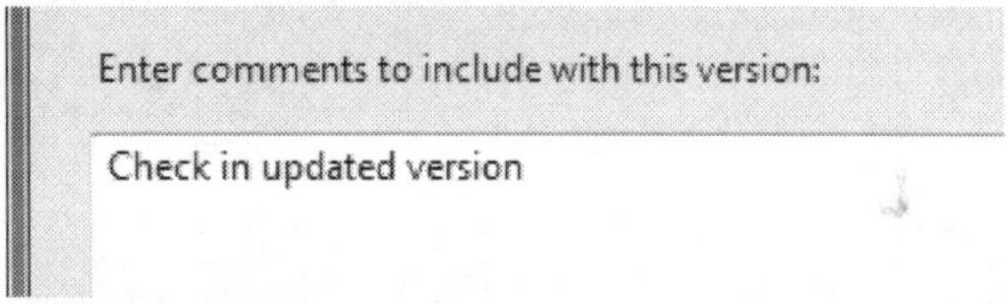

8. Click Yes when asked to confirm the deletion of the Sample.doc file.

   In Windows Explorer, note that the Sample.doc file has been deleted from *C:\AOTGVault\VaultWorkingFolder\Documents.*

Task 3 - View the file version in Vault Explorer.

1. In Vault, click View menu>Refresh or select Refresh on the toolbar.

2. Select Sample.doc in the Main pane and then select History in the Preview pane.

   In the Preview pane, note the two versions and the comments next to each one.

   Note: You might need to select the Show All Versions checkbox on the right side.

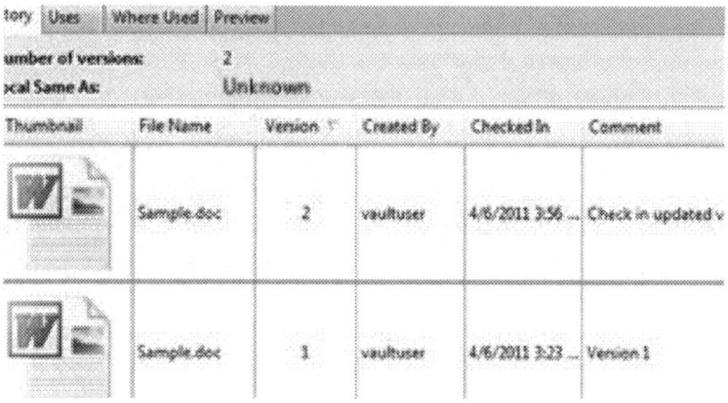

3. In the Main pane, right-click Sample.doc. Click Get.
4. In the Get dialog box, click Expand (>>) and select the checkbox next to the filename to mark it for check out.
5. Click OK to check out the file and download the latest version to the working folder.
6. Repeat step 3 to display the Get dialog box again.
7. Select version 1 in the Select Version drop-down list.

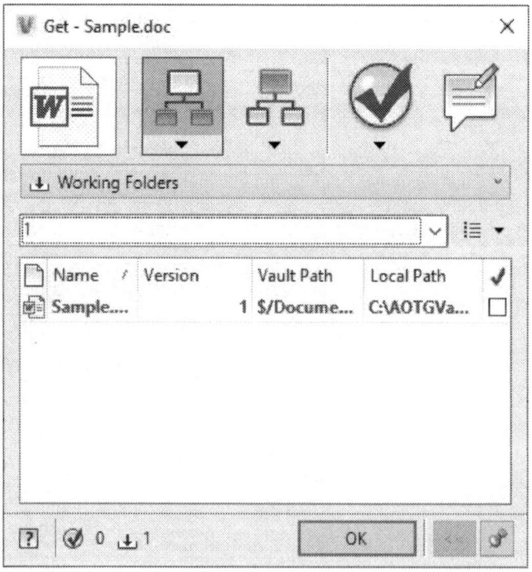

8. Select OK to Check the file out and download version 1 to the working folder.

9. Select Yes when the Confirm File Replace dialog displays warning you that you are going to overwrite the version in the working folder.

10. Note the Main pane and the status of the file.

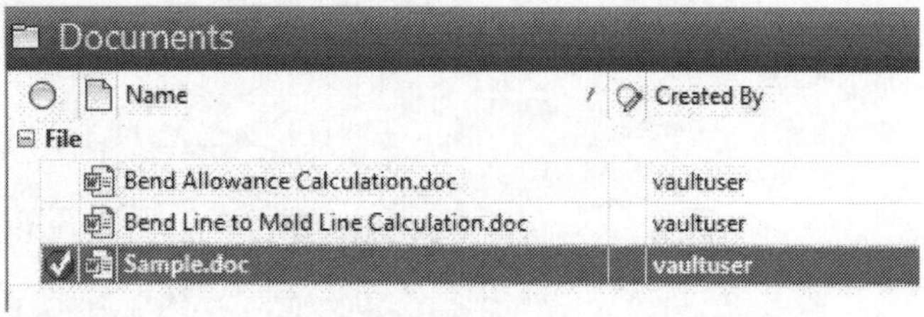

11. Select the file in the Main pane one last time and right click to get the context menu. Click Check In to check the file back in.

12. In the Check In dialog box enter the comment Restored to version 1 in the Enter comments to include with this version field. Click OK.

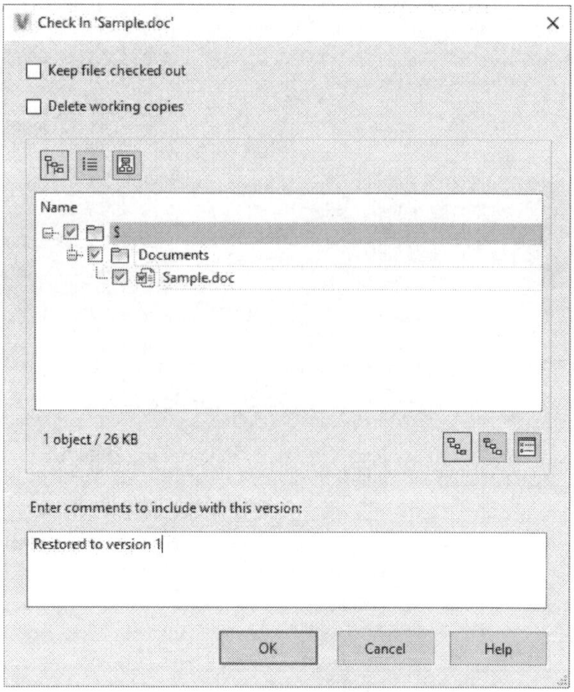

13. In the Main pane, note the change in status for Sample.doc.

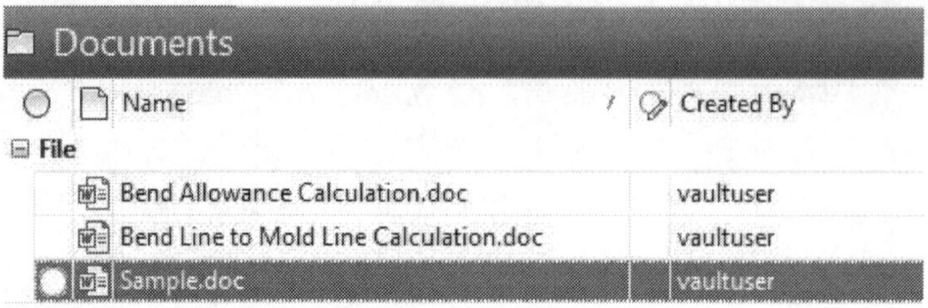

14. Right-click Sample.doc. Click Go to Working Folder.

15. In Windows Explorer, double-click Sample.doc.

    In Microsoft Word, verify that the version of the file is original and does not contain the line of text you added. Close Microsoft Word without saving the file.

16. In Vault, right-click Sample.doc. Click Get. Select Version 2, do not Check Out the file. Click OK and click Yes to overwrite.

    Vault copies Version 2 in the vault to the local working folder and updates the status of Sample.doc in the Main pane.

    The icon indicates that the file is not checked out but the local copy is older than the file in the vault.

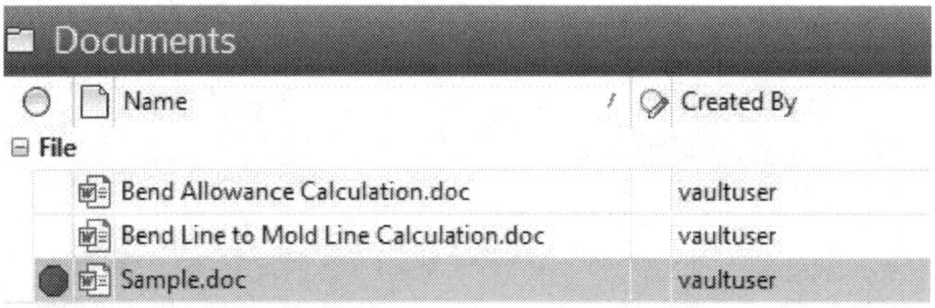

17. Right-click Sample.doc. Click Go to Working Folder.

18. In Windows Explorer, double-click Sample.doc.

    In Microsoft Word, verify that the version of the file is the modified one and contains the line of text you added. Close Microsoft Word without saving the file.

2.4 Chapter Summary

Autodesk Vault is a secure environment in which you can work with your files. In this chapter, you learned how to access the vault and navigate the user interface to add and work with files in the vault.

Having completed this chapter, you can:

- Log in to Autodesk Vault.
- Describe elements of the Autodesk Vault user interface.
- Set the working folder, create folders in the vault, add non-CAD files, check these files out and edit them, check the files in, and then view the versions of the files.

Chapter 3

Working with Vault and Autodesk Inventor

In this chapter, you learn how to use Autodesk Autoloader to add designs and library files to a vault. You learn how to check files out of the vault, edit them in Autodesk® Inventor®, and then check them back in. You also create a new file in Autodesk Inventor, place it in an existing subassembly, and check the modified files back in to the vault.

In order to streamline your vault workflows, you also learn how to specify the default response for common dialog boxes and suppress some of the dialog boxes so they are never displayed.

Learning Objectives in This Chapter

- Use Autodesk Autoloader to add Autodesk Inventor files to a vault.
- Use common vault tasks in Autodesk Inventor.
- Manage Autodesk Inventor designs in a vault.
- Manage Model States.

3.1 Adding Inventor Models to a Vault

Overview

When you start working with Autodesk® Vault, the first step is often to add one or more existing projects to the vault. In this lesson, you learn how to add existing projects using Autodesk Autoloader. You also learn how the vault is organized so that you can add and retrieve files successfully.

Objectives

After completing this lesson, you will be able to:

- Describe how Autodesk Inventor files are organized.
- Organize designs before loading them into the vault and control the creation of visualization files for files loaded to the vault.
- Add existing projects to the vault using Autodesk Autoloader.

How Autodesk Inventor Files Are Organized

Autodesk Inventor models can contain a large number of files. Models can include parts that are unique to the design, and standard parts such as fasteners, bearings, or hydraulic components that are shared by many designs. These files must be organized so they can be added to and retrieved from the vault and shared with other designs.

Before you add files to a vault, you should have a basic understanding of how Autodesk Inventor files are organized in the vault and how Autodesk Inventor uses project files to locate, move, and rename design files.

About Inventor Project Files

In Autodesk Inventor, a project file must be active before you can work with other files. Project files include several settings that Inventor uses to find model files. When Inventor opens an assembly, it looks for the subassemblies and parts that make up the assembly in the locations specified in the project file.

In the example below, the Workspace, Libraries, and Content Center Files folders specify where Inventor searches for files. Note that all of the paths are relative to the location of the project file.

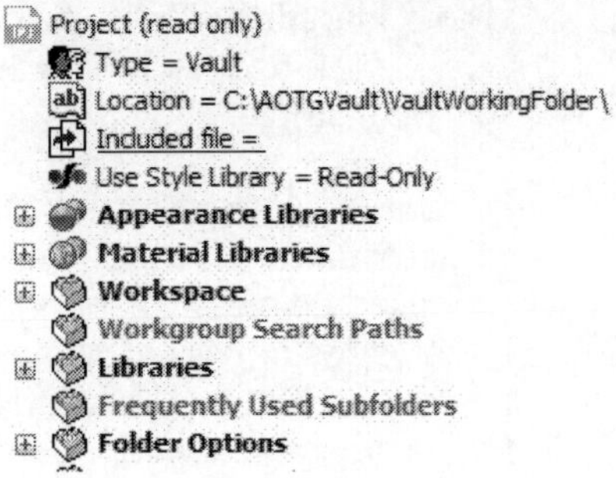

Organize your vault so you use one project file no matter how many designs you have in the vault. The project file is stored in the vault and you must ensure that you have the latest copy in your local working folder. A default Autodesk Inventor project file can be set by your administrator in Vault (Tools>Administration>Vault Settings and click Define for the Working Folder).

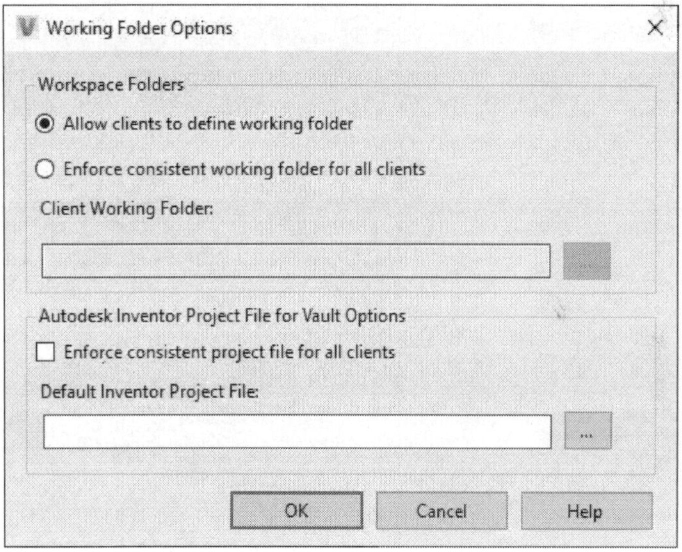

About Library Files

Library files are parts or subassemblies that can be used in more than one design and do not normally change. Library files are treated as read-only files.

Examples of library files include:

- Common purchased components such as fasteners, hydraulic cylinders, or motors. These can be regular parts, iParts, or iAssemblies.

- Manufactured parts or subassemblies that don't change, such as weldments or brackets that are used in several designs.

Library files are organized and treated differently than regular files. Library files are stored in a special type of folder in the Vault called a library folder and are treated as read-only files. In Autodesk Inventor, the project file includes a path to the library files so that the files can be located when the assembly that contains them is opened.

In a typical installation, the library files are copied from the vault to your local computer as they are required. When you place library files in a design, you can place them directly from the vault or from the local storage location.

About Content Center Files

Content center files are standard parts that are placed from the content center. They are similar to library parts because they are treated as read-only components. They have their own search path in the project file and are normally stored in folders that are separate from other library parts.

In the following example, the content center files are stored in their own folder in the vault. The folder icon indicates that the Content Center Files folder is a library folder.

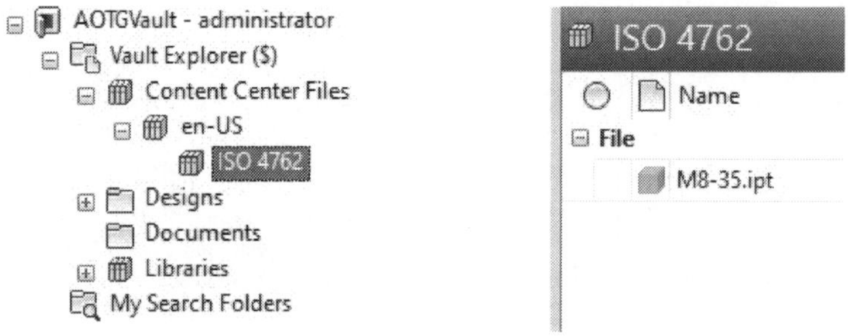

How the Vault Is Organized

There are a number of ways to organize Autodesk Inventor files in the vault. Before you add these files to the vault, you must learn how the files are organized so that you add files to the correct locations.

For best results with Autodesk Vault, a single project file is stored in the root of the vault, one level above the model and library folders. Your designs are stored in subfolders below one of the folders. Vault stores content center parts under one library folder. Another folder contains folders for other library parts as shown in the image.

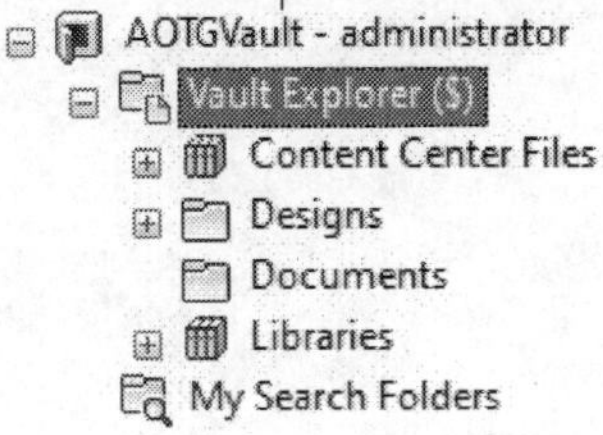

Vault stores each design in a separate folder below the top-level Designs folder. Subfolders help you to organize the model's files as shown in the image. You can organize the folders by product, customer, or other methods that meet your design requirements.

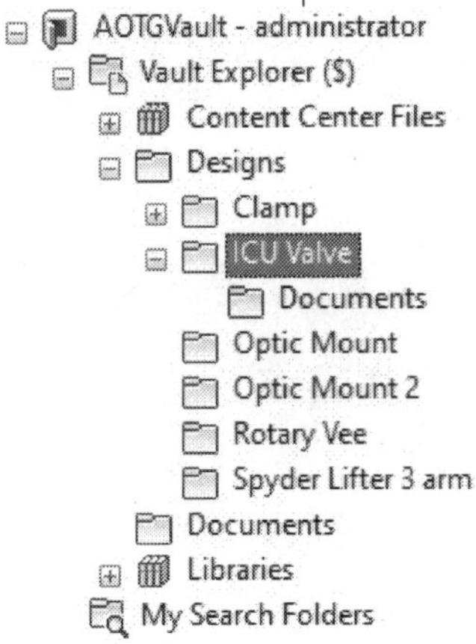

When you work on files, Vault automatically creates local folders to match the structure in the vault. The following image displays the local working folder after you download two designs from the vault. The structure and the relative location of files are identical to the vault.

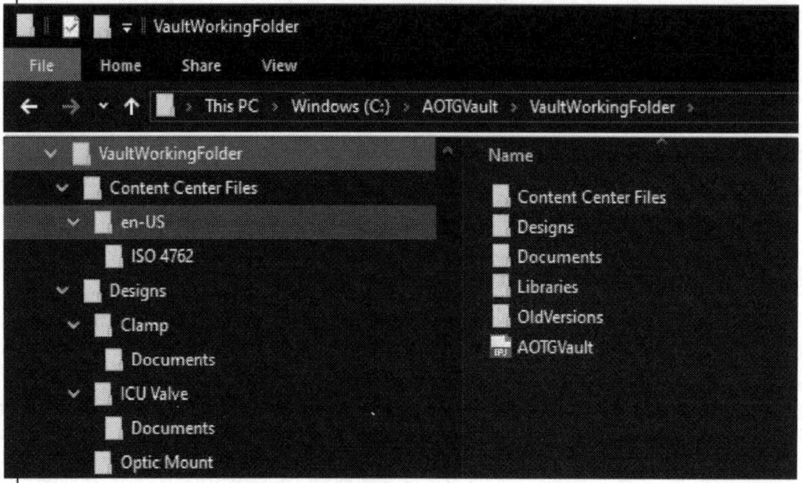

Autodesk Autoloader

Autodesk Inventor files typically contain relationships to other files. For example, an assembly file has references to its parts and subassemblies, and a drawing file has references to the models documented on its sheets.

To maintain the references when you add the files to a vault, you must add Autodesk Inventor files to the vault using one of the following:

- From inside Autodesk Inventor, using the Autodesk Vault for Inventor add-in.
- Using Autodesk Autoloader, a stand-alone application that prepares and uploads existing designs to the vault.

About Autodesk Autoloader

Autodesk Autoloader is a stand-alone application that you use to prepare and upload files from existing Inventor designs to the vault. Autoloader works with all project types including isolated, semi- isolated, shared, single-user, and Vault.

Autoloader helps you to prepare your models for uploading and verifies that files are ready to upload. Autoloader works with one project file at a time and uses the workspace, workgroup, library, and content center files paths from the project file to locate the files to upload. Any files that fail to resolve are reported so you can fix the problem before Autoloader collects all of the files and uploads them to the vault.

If you use Autoloader to upload files to an empty vault, Autoloader creates the required folders for you in the vault. Autoloader also creates a single project file that contains all of the correct paths so you can immediately start to work on your models with Autodesk Inventor.

Autodesk Autoloader also includes non-Inventor files found in the folders in the selected project file. These files are not attached to Autodesk Inventor files, but you can use Vault Explorer to attach them to other files after they are uploaded to the vault.

Hint: Multiple Project Files

Autodesk Autoloader selects the active project file to resolve file references in the selected Autodesk Inventor documents. You can activate the required project file before starting Autoloader, or you can select a different project file in Autoloader after selecting the folder to upload to the vault.

About Visualization Files and Vault

Visualization files display CAD files in Autodesk Vault. Autodesk Autoloader can optionally create the files from all of the Inventor files it loads into the vault. The creation of visualization files for large datasets can take considerable time. You can toggle off the creation of these files as you add the files to the vault and then use the Task Scheduler to create them for all or some of the files in the vault. You can also use Update to create or update the visualization file on demand.

Vault stores the visualization files in the vault and uses them to display the CAD file on the Preview tab, as shown in the following image. A visualization file can be either a DWF™ or DWFx file.

Vault stores a visualization file in the same folder as its associated CAD file, but the visualization file is hidden by default.

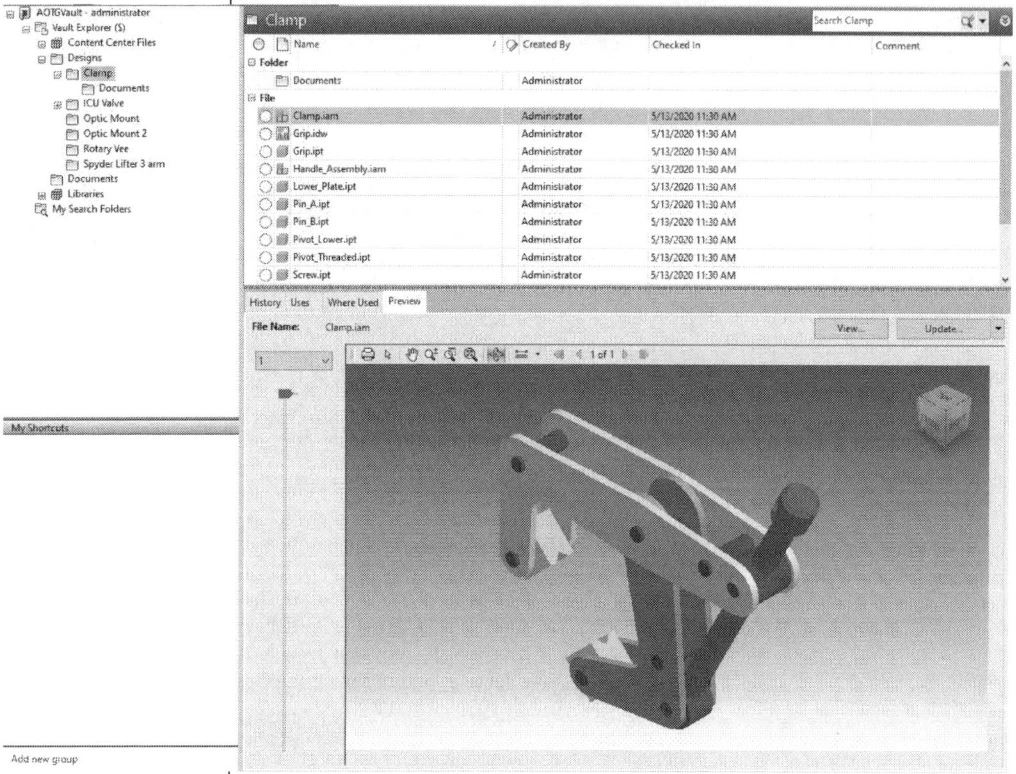

Hint: Visualization File Administration

If your Vault administrator has disabled the visualization attachment options in order to save space in the vault, Vault does not automatically create the visualization files.

Adding Inventor Files to a Vault

Autodesk Autoloader guides you through the process of organizing and uploading files to the vault. It ensures that all related Autodesk Inventor files in the project can be resolved prior to uploading to the vault. You can filter the files that are uploaded, including non-Inventor files in the selected folder and its subfolders.

Autodesk Autoloader helps you resolve any file relationship problems and find duplicate files before uploading the files to the vault. All errors must be resolved before Autodesk Autoloader can upload the files to the vault.

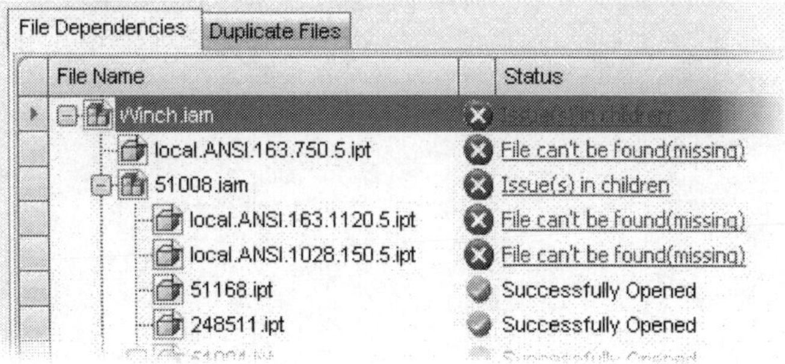

Procedure: Uploading to Vault with Autodesk Autoloader

The following steps describe how to upload existing Autodesk Inventor designs to the vault using Autodesk Autoloader.

1. Note the top-level folder of your existing designs.

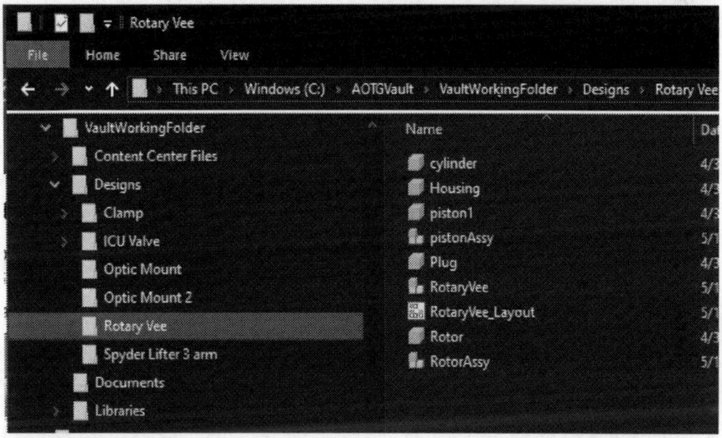

2. Start Autodesk Autoloader. (Start>All Programs>Autodesk> Autodesk Data Management>Tools> Autodesk Autoloader 2021 for Vault)
3. Click Next.
4. Click Select Folder.

5. Select the top-level folder for the designs you want to upload to the vault. Click OK.

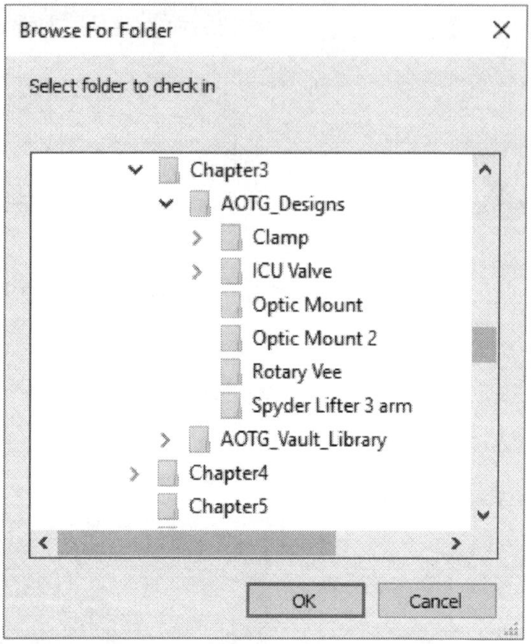

6. Select the existing project file that Autodesk Autoloader uses to determine the files to upload to the vault. Click OK.

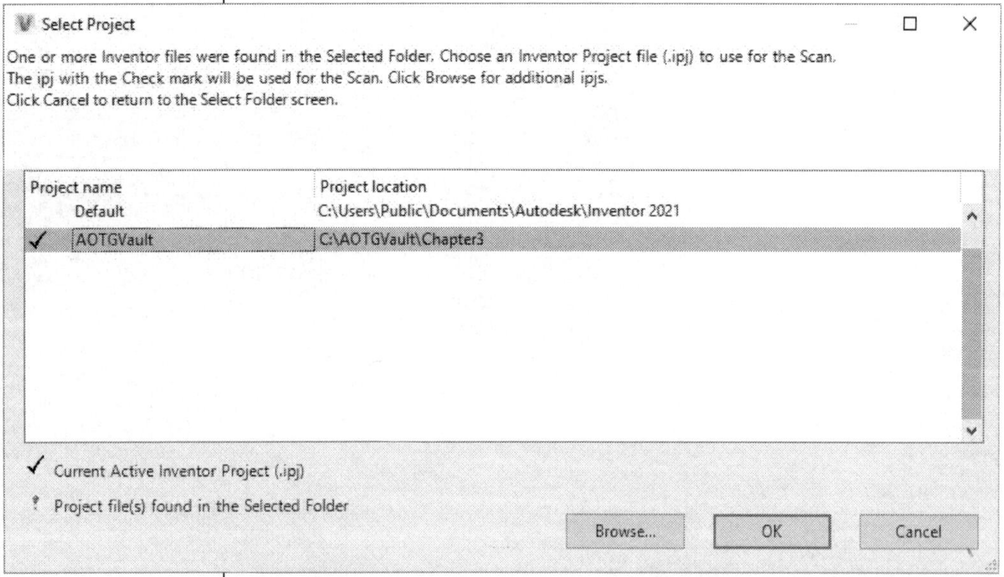

7. Click Next.

8. Click Scan to set Autodesk Autoloader to scan all files in the selected folder and subfolders. File relationships are confirmed during the scan and other referenced files, such as library parts, are added to the list of files to upload. If required, fix any reported problems and then restart Autodesk Autoloader. To resolve issues, you can also open files from within the Autoloader. Rerun the Scan to recheck the files.

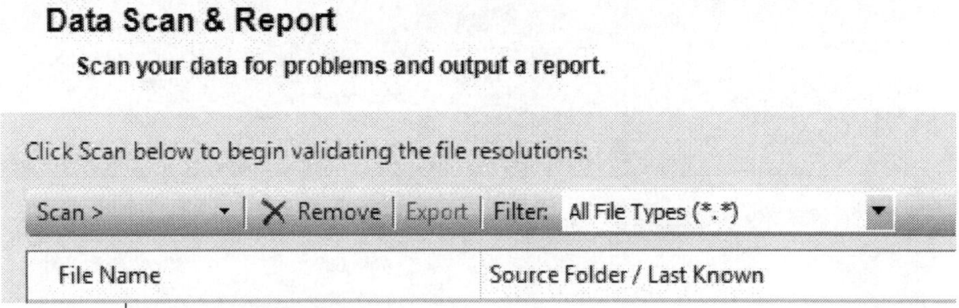

9. Click Next
10. Log in to the vault.
11. Map the generated folders in the vault to the corresponding folders in the existing project folder.

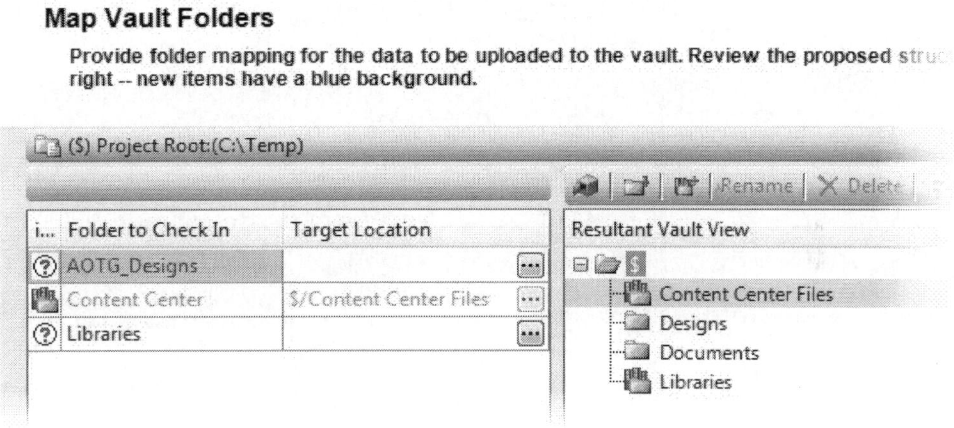

12. Click Next.

13. Optionally, filter the files to be uploaded to the vault. You can include or exclude specific Inventor file formats and non-Inventor files.

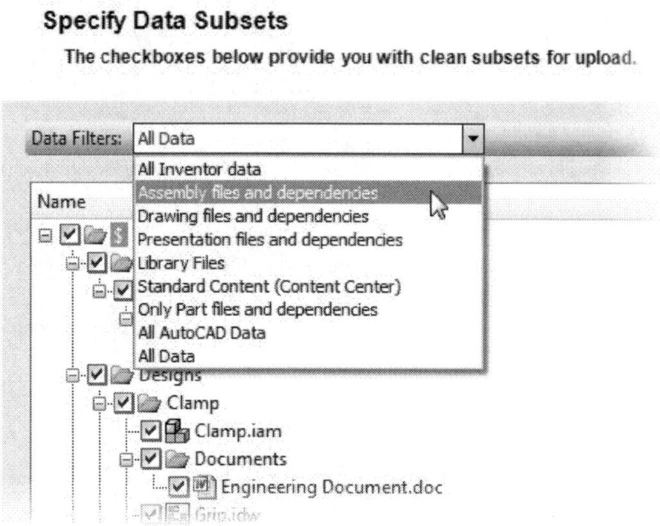

14. Upload the files to the vault. You can optionally generate a visualization file of each Inventor file before it is uploaded to the vault.

Practice 3a Add Existing Projects

In this practice, you use Autodesk Autoloader to add Autodesk Inventor models to a vault. Autodesk Autoloader organizes the existing files for you and creates the recommended folder structure in the vault.

The completed practice

Task 1 - Prepare existing designs.

1. Open Autodesk Inventor. Close any open files.
2. On the ribbon, click the Get Started tab>Launch panel>Projects.
3. If the AOTGVault project is displayed in the Projects dialog box, make it the active project by double-clicking on it and skip to Step 7.
4. If the AOTGVault project is not displayed in the Projects dialog box, click Browse.
5. Browse to *C:\AOTGVault \Chapter3.*

6. Select AOTGVault.ipj.
7. Click Open. Selecting the file will set it to the default.
8. Click Done to close the Projects dialog box.
9. Close Autodesk Inventor.
10. Start Autodesk Autoloader. (Start>All Programs>Autodesk>Autodesk Data Management>Tools>Autodesk Autoloader 2021 for Vault).
11. On the Welcome page, click Next.
12. On the Select Data Source page, click Select Folder.
13. Browse to: *C:\AOTGVault\Chapter3\AOTG_Designs*.
14. Click OK.
15. In the Select Project dialog box, click OK to accept AOTGVault.ipj as the project file.

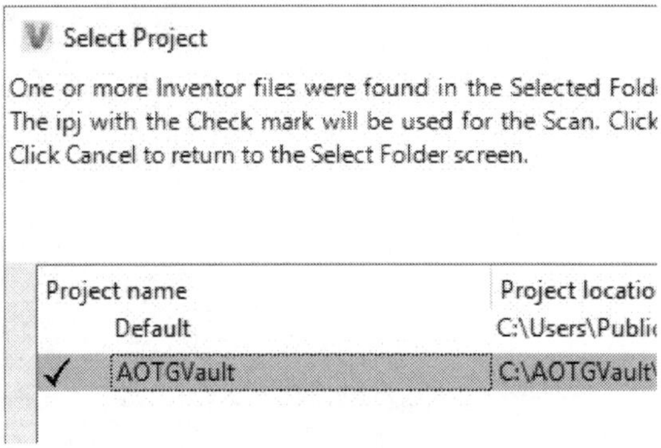

16. On the Select Data Source page, the folders beneath the AOTG_Design folder are displayed.

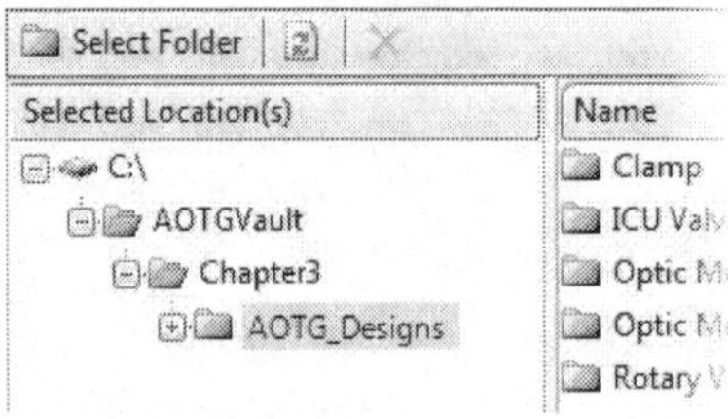

17. Click Next. The files to be scanned are displayed on the Data Scan & Report page.

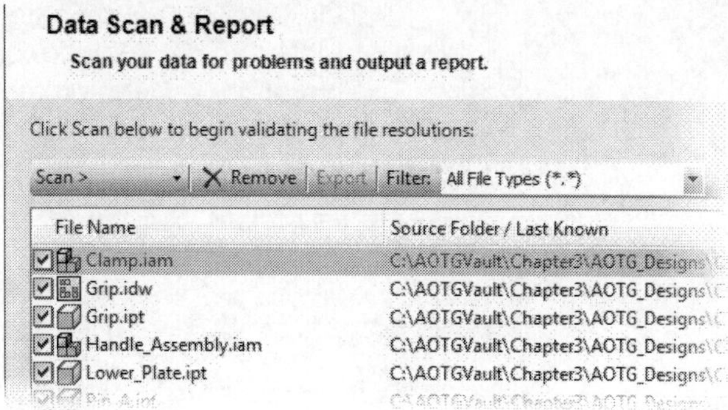

Task 2 - Add designs to the vault.

1. Click Scan.
2. When the scan is complete, click OK. Scroll through the results. All files should have opened and resolved successfully.
3. Click Next.
4. Log in to the vault using the following information:
   - For User Name, enter **Administrator**
   - For Password, leave the box empty.
   - For Vault, select AOTGVault. You might have to select the button next to the Vault field to open the Vaults dialog. Select AOTGVault and then OK to select the database.

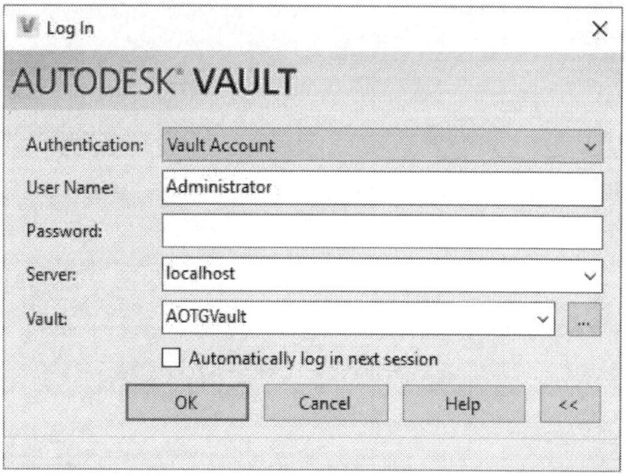

5. On the Map Vault Folders page, mappings from project folders to vault folders are listed on the left. The vault hierarchy is listed on the right.

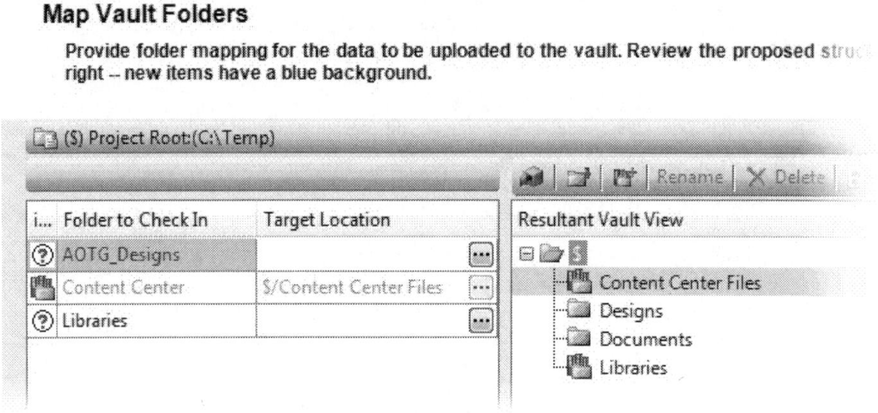

6. In the Folder to Check In list, double-click AOTG_Designs.

7. In the Browse Vault for Folder dialog box:

   - Click Designs.
   - Click the Direct Mapping check box to toggle it on.
   - Click OK.

   The AOTG_Designs folder on the local computer is mapped to the \Designs folder in the vault.

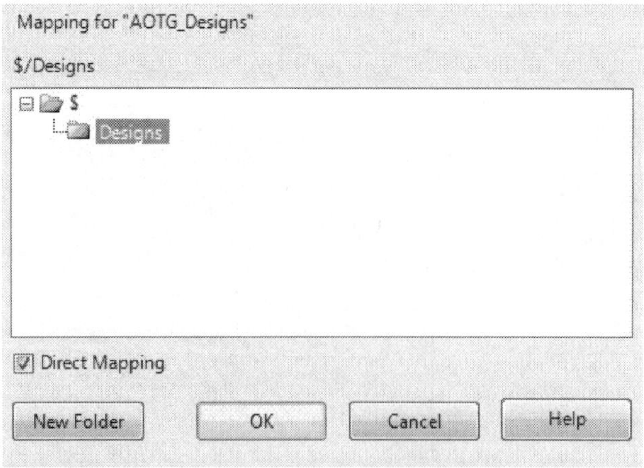

8. In the Folder to Check In list, double-click on Libraries.

9. In the Mapping for Libraries dialog box, select the $ folder and click OK.

10. In the Map Folder list, AOTG_Designs should be mapped to $/Designs, and Libraries should be mapped to $/Libraries.

11. Click Next to start the Copy & File Redirection Progress process.

12. When the process is complete, click Next.

13. On the Specify Data Subsets page, review the list of files selected for upload. Note that non- Inventor files are included in the list.

14. Select the Create Visualization Attachment check box to toggle on the creation of visualization files from the uploaded files. A confirmation dialog will warn that the selection could impact performance. Click Yes to confirm that you want Vault to create visualization files.

15. Click Upload.

16. The files are uploaded to the vault as reported in the Autoload Progress & Report dialog box.

    Note: Vault creates all visualization files before the files are uploaded to the vault. This might take a few minutes to complete.

17. When the process is complete, note the location of the report file on the Autoload Progress and Report page under Status.

18. In Windows Explorer, navigate to the report file (XML format). Open the report in Excel selecting the Open file with the following style sheet applied option to view. Review the report then close the file.

19. In the Autoloader dialog box, click Done.

Task 3 - View the Files in the Vault

1. Start Autodesk Vault. Log in using the following information:

    - For User Name, enter **vaultuser**.
    - For Password, leave the box empty.
    - For Vault, select AOTGVault.

2. In Vault, click Vault Explorer ($). Autoloader creates a single project file named Designs.ipj for all designs in the vault.

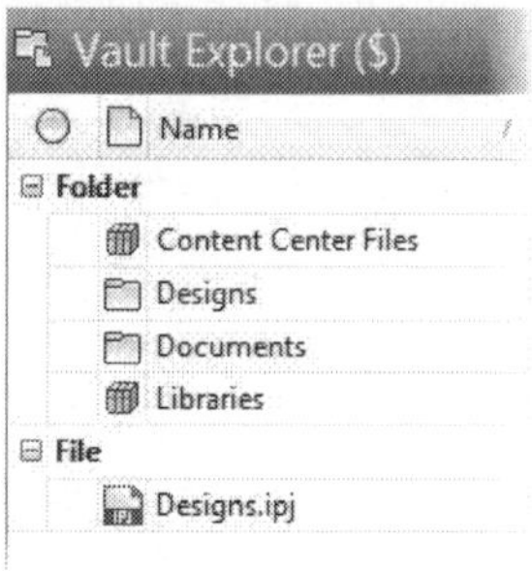

3. Expand the Designs folder. Click the Clamp folder. Files for the clamp design are listed.

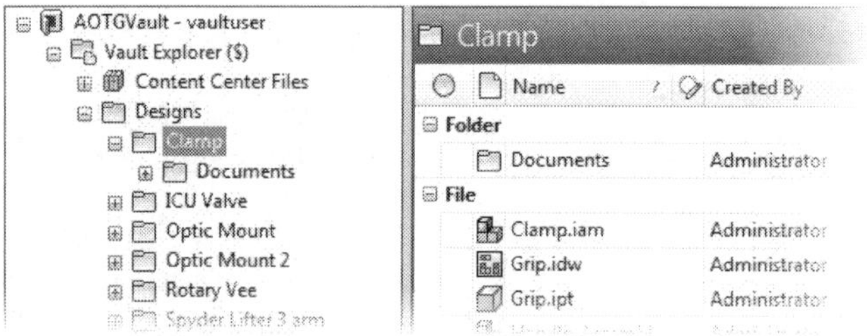

4. In the Clamp folder, select Clamp.iam.
5. Click the Preview tab. Click the Version 1 image.

   The visualization file of the clamp assembly is displayed. View the model using the rotate, zoom, and pan tools.

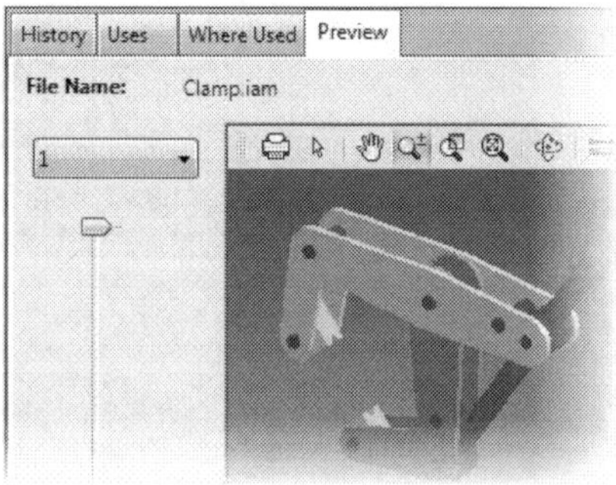

6. Close Vault.

3.2 Common Vault Tasks in Autodesk Inventor

Overview

In this lesson, you learn how to work with Autodesk Inventor files and Autodesk Vault. You perform typical Vault tasks using the Autodesk Vault for Inventor add-in and Autodesk Vault.

Objectives

After completing this lesson, you will be able to:

- Access Vault commands from Autodesk Inventor.
- Describe a typical workflow for editing Vault files in Autodesk Inventor.
- Get files from a vault to your working folder.
- Edit Autodesk Inventor files retrieved from a vault.
- Save Autodesk Inventor files to a vault.

Autodesk Vault for Autodesk Inventor

When you work with Autodesk Inventor files, you use Autodesk Vault and the Autodesk Vault for Inventor add-in to perform common vault tasks including getting files, checking files in and out, and viewing the file history. Because the add-in is tightly integrated into Autodesk Inventor, you can perform most tasks directly from Inventor without having to switch to another application.

Procedure: Logging in to a Vault from Autodesk Inventor

Before you access a vault from Autodesk Inventor, you must log in to a vault from Inventor, even if you are already logged in through Autodesk Vault. The following procedure describes how to log in to a vault from Autodesk Inventor.

1. On the ribbon, click the Vault tab and click Log In on the Access panel.

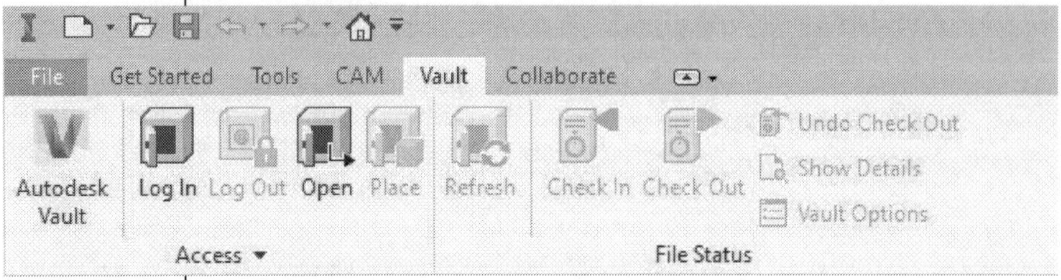

2. Enter your user name and password.

Accessing Vault Commands

The Autodesk Vault for Inventor add-in enables you to perform common vault tasks without leaving the Autodesk Inventor application. You can access all vault tasks on the Vault tab of the ribbon.

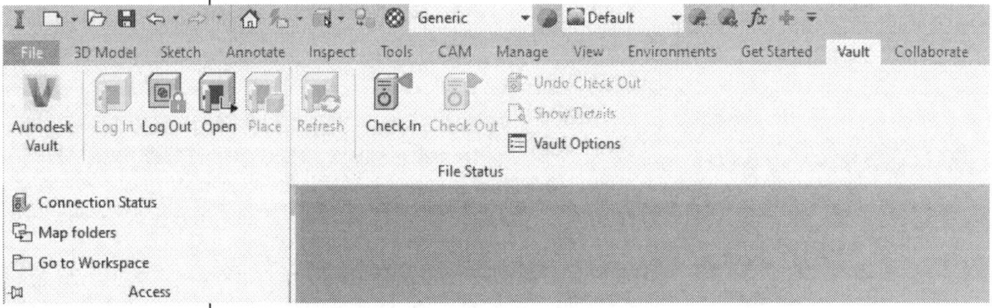

About the Vault Commands

The Vault tab on the ribbon includes the following commands.

Option	Description
Autodesk Vault	Opens the Autodesk Vault application. Equivalent to opening the application from the Start menu or a desktop shortcut.
Log In	Connects to a vault. You must log in to a vault before you can retrieve or check out files.
Log Out	Disconnects from the vault.
Open	Browses the files in the vault and opens a file. The selected file is retrieved to the corresponding local working folder and opened. All referenced files are also copied to the local working folder structure.

Place	Places a file from the vault into the current assembly. When you select a file from the vault, the file is copied to the local working folder and then placed into the current assembly. It is the equivalent of getting the latest version of the file to the local working folder and then using the Place Component command.
Connection Status	Displays the status of the connection to the vault.
Map Folders	Specifies where Inventor files are stored in the vault. Used only when a working folder has not been set from Vault.
Go to Workspace	Opens Windows Explorer in the current project file's workspace.
Refresh	Checks for newer versions of the active file and its referenced files on the vault. Replaces local files if the files in the vault are newer.
Check In	Updates the vault with changes that you have made to the checked-out files. If the local copy of a file is changed, the local file is copied to the vault and the version number in the vault increments. Other users can use Refresh to get the latest version of the file to update their designs. Also, the vault copy is available for other users to check out.
Check Out	Marks the files as checked out to you. Enables you to edit the files and prevents others from editing the same files. Optionally copies the latest version of the files from the vault to your working folder. You cannot use this command to get the initial model files from the vault; the command works for files that are already open in Inventor.
Undo Check Out	Abandons changes. Checks the file back in without creating a new version and without copying the file back to the vault. If you select Replace Local Copy, the local version returns to its state before you checked it out. You can only use the command on files that you currently have checked out, not on files checked out by other users.
Show Details	Displays all versions of the active document stored in the vault.
Vault Options	Displays the Options dialog box where you can set defaults for Vault prompts.

About the Vault Browser

When you work with the Vault in Autodesk Inventor, you access most Vault commands from the Vault browser. This browser can be displayed by selecting Vault as shown in the following image.

You can use the browser icons and tooltips to determine the status of files. When you move the cursor over a filename, a tooltip is displayed that includes additional information about the file as shown in the following image. The icons are similar to those in Autodesk Vault.

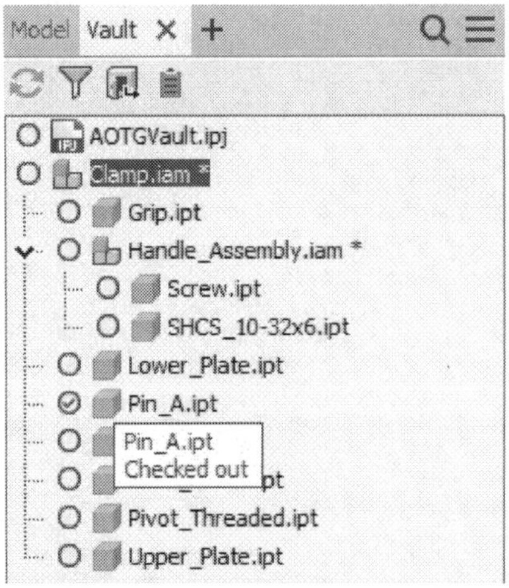

Vault Browser Shortcut Menus

You can use the shortcut menus in the Vault browser to access Vault commands, as shown in the following image. Different commands are displayed depending whether you right-click the browser background or a file.

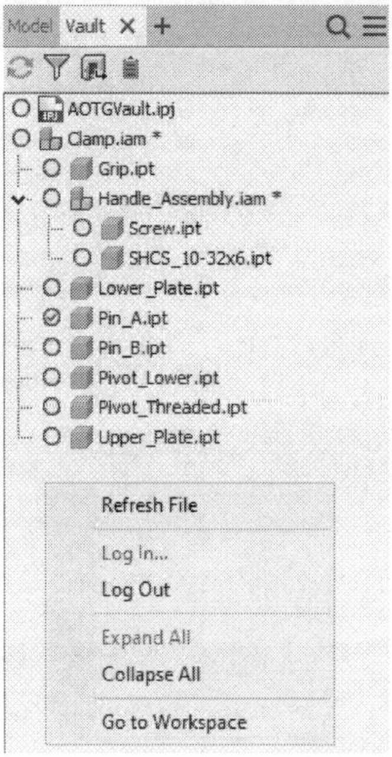

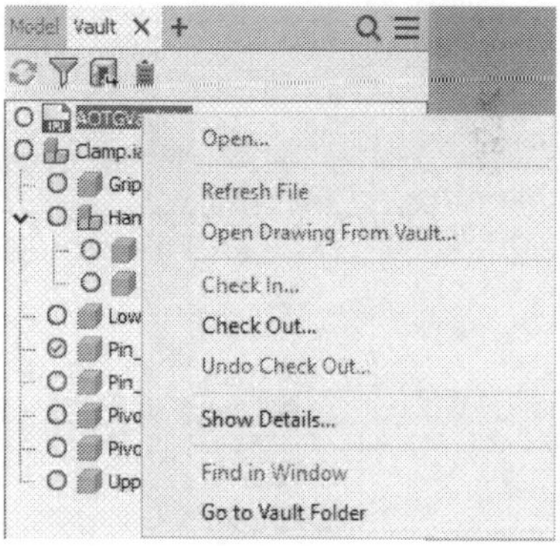

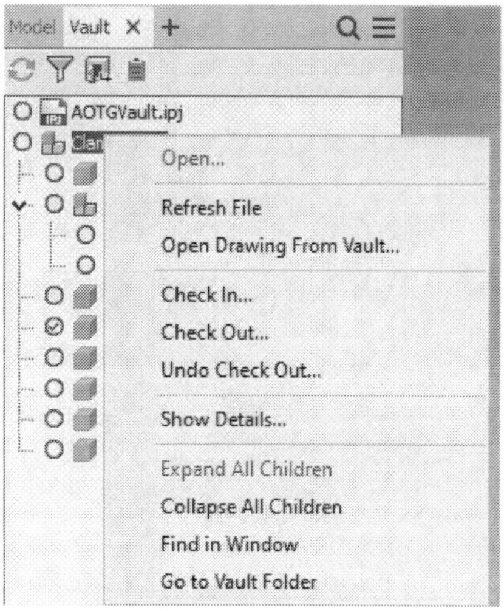

Vault Menu Commands

Some of the commands are the same as those on the Vault tab of the ribbon. The following commands are unique to the browser shortcut menus. Depending on the file, not all will be displayed.

Option	Description
Open	Opens a file in Inventor.
Refresh File	Gets the latest version of the selected files. Useful when someone else on the design team updates a file and you need to get the latest version of the file
Check In	Checks the selected files into the vault.
Check In Out	Checks the selected files out for editing.
Undo Check Out	Abandons changes. Checks the file back in without creating a new version and without copying the file back to the vault.
Show Details	Displays the version history of a file in the vault.
Expand All Children	Expands an assembly to show all children (not available for non-assembly components)
Collapse All Children	Collapses an assembly to hide all children (not available for non-assembly components)
Find in Window	Adjusts the display to show the selected assembly or part. Useful for large assemblies.

Vault Browser Commands

You can find commands to manage the Vault browser display and open the Autodesk Vault application at the top of the Vault browser.

Option	Icon	Description
Refresh Vault Status		Refreshes the status of all files in the Vault browser. You can determine whether another member of the design team checked out, modified, or checked in a file. Does not affect model files.
Filter		Filters the files displayed in the Vault browser.
Go to Vault		Opens the Autodesk Vault application.
Show/Hide Vault Status Modifier		Toggles between showing and hiding the vault status modifier that displays after the filename in the Vault Browser. It is called the Choose Properties icon in the Vault Workgroup and Vault Professional software and enables you to select the properties you want to display after the filename in the Vault Browser.

Typical Edit Workflow

When you work with files from the vault, you never work directly with the files in the vault. You get a copy of the files to your local working folder, check out the files to edit, edit the files, save them locally, and then check the new versions of the files back in to the vault.

Procedure: Editing Files from a Vault

The following steps outline a typical workflow for retrieving Autodesk Inventor files from the vault, editing the files, and then returning the new versions to the vault.

1. In Autodesk Vault, get the latest project file from a vault to your working folder.

   You normally retain this copy of the project file in your local working folder. You do not need to get the project file each time you want to edit a model from the vault.

2. In Autodesk Inventor, activate the project file.
3. From Autodesk Inventor, log in to the vault. Open an existing model directly from the vault using Open from the Vault tab on the ribbon. If required, display the Vault browser and check the status of files to see if they are available for editing.

4. In Inventor, edit the existing files, add new files to the model, or create new documents using your normal workflows. Vault automatically prompts you to check out the associated files, as required.

   In the following image, the browser icons indicate that Clamp.iam, Handle_Assembly.iam, and Handle.ipt are checked out to you and that the local files are newer than the ones in the vault.

5. If required, add existing files to your design from the vault. You can place files directly from the vault using the Place command from the Vault tab on the ribbon. If new components are added from outside of the vault, they will be marked that they have not been uploaded to the vault.

6. Save the new files and the files that were modified to your local working folder structure. Update the modified files and add the new files to the vault by checking in the top-level assembly.

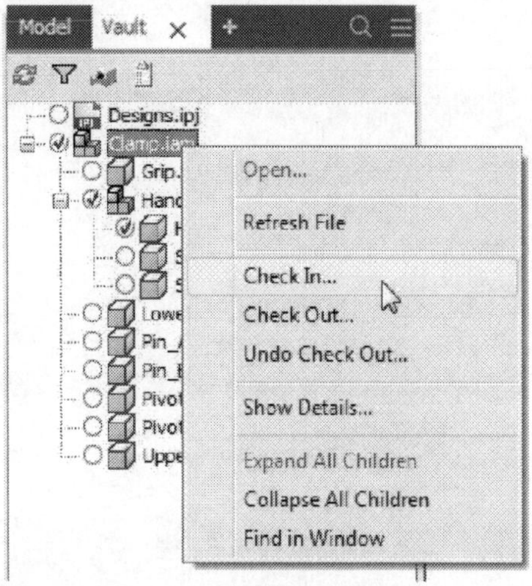

7. Review the versions in Autodesk Vault.

   In the following image, the History tab displays the latest and previous versions of the model.

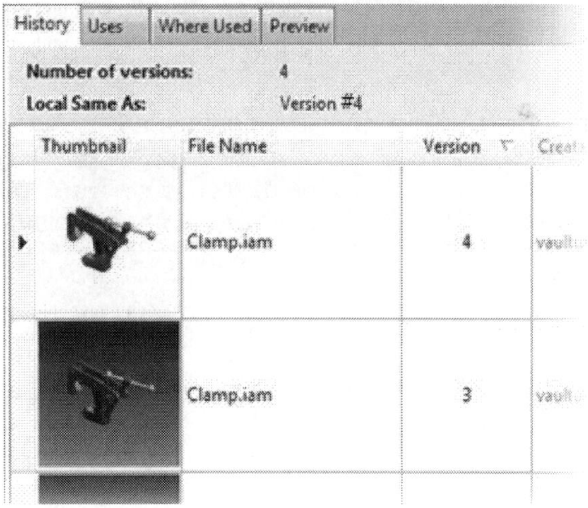

Getting Files from a Vault

When you work with files that are stored in a vault, you get a copy of the files from the vault to your local computer using commands from Autodesk Inventor or Autodesk Vault. Once you have a local copy of the files, you edit them as you normally do.

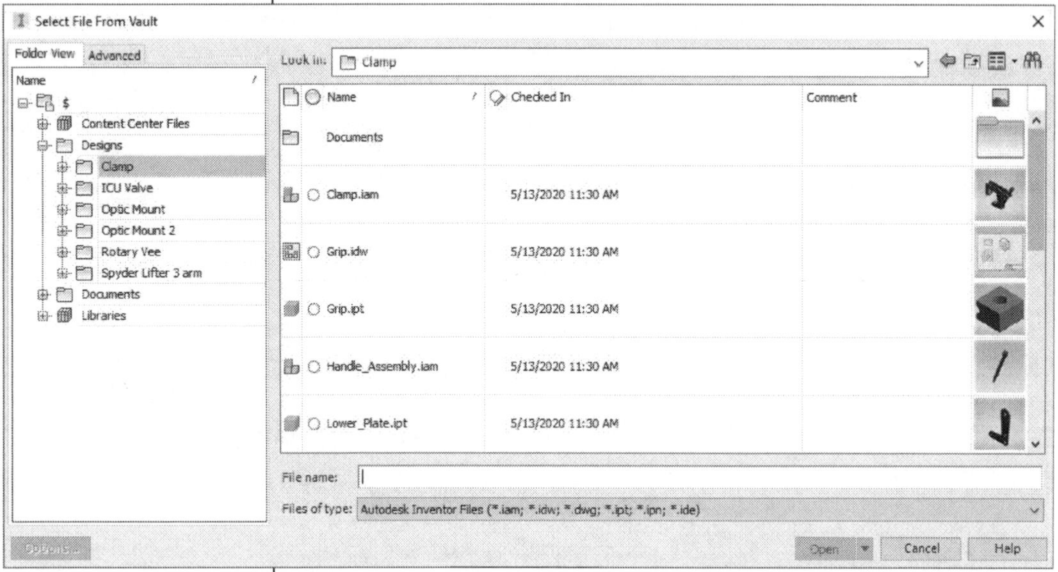

About Getting Autodesk Inventor Files from the Vault

If you are already in Autodesk Inventor, use the Open command from the Vault tab on the ribbon. It gets the latest versions of all of the files to the working folder and then opens the selected file in Inventor. You can also check out one, some or all files using options in the Select File from Vault dialog box.

Open from Vault Options

The Open command in Autodesk Inventor is the recommended method for opening files from the vault. Selecting this command will display the Select File From Vault dialog which has several features, as shown in the following image.

The Select File From Vault dialog box is similar to the standard Open dialog box. It also includes the following unique features.

<table>
<tr><th>Feature Description</th><th>Description</th></tr>
<tr><td>Accesses shortcuts and searches that you created in Autodesk Vault when Advanced tab is selected. Helps you to quickly locate files in the vault. Allows you to easily navigate to a folder when the Folder View tab is selected.</td><td>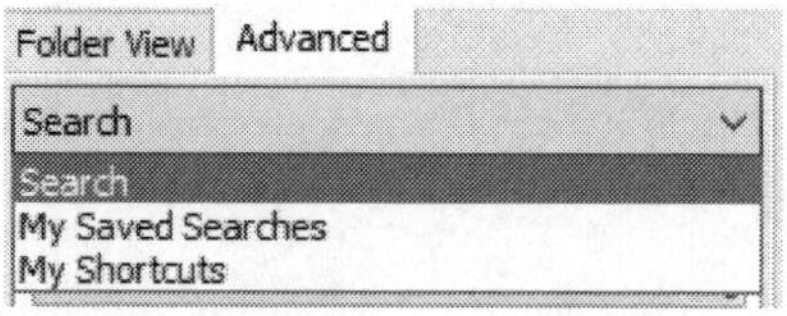
</td></tr>
<tr><td>Opens files as read only or as checked out. The default is to open all files as read only (not checked out).
You can open the selected file only and check it out or display a list of all files and select which files to check out.</td><td>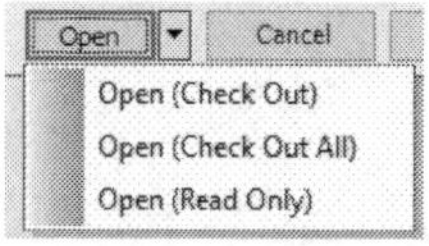
</td></tr>
<tr><td>Finds files in the vault using a keyword search with an option to Search By Property.</td><td>

</td></tr>
<tr><td> Finds files in the vault using the same search tools that you use in Autodesk Vault.</td><td>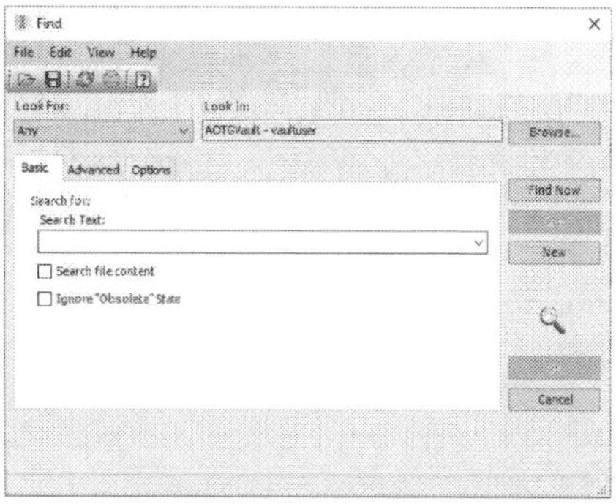
</td></tr>
</table>

Getting Files

You can use the following commands to get Autodesk Inventor files from the vault.

Application - Command	Description
Inventor – Open	Gets a copy of the latest files to the local working folder and then opens the selected file in Inventor. By default, the files are not checked out. Optionally, you can select which files to check out. This is the recommended method for most workflows.
Vault – Open	Opens and optionally checks out the selected file in Inventor.
Vault – Get	Gets a copy of the latest files to the local working folder, overwriting any locally stored versions of the same files. Optionally checks out the file. Does not open the files in Autodesk Inventor.
Vault – Checkout	Checks out the file. Does not open the files in Autodesk Inventor.

Editing Autodesk Inventor Files

Once you have a copy of the files to edit in your working folder, you must check the files out before you can edit them. When you check out a file from the vault, the vault is notified so that others cannot check out the same file and the read-only property of the local file is removed so you can edit your copy of the file.

About Checking Out Files

Before you edit files, the files must be checked out to you. When you check out a file, the file is reserved to you; other members of the design team can get read-only copies of files for viewing but are prevented from checking out the same files for editing.

When you start to edit a file in Inventor, that was not previously checked out, you are prompted as to whether to check out the file.

Procedure: Selecting Which Files to Check Out

1. When you Open files from Inventor, you can use the Check Out commands illustrated below. You can specify to check out the selected file, all the dependent files, or open it as read-only.

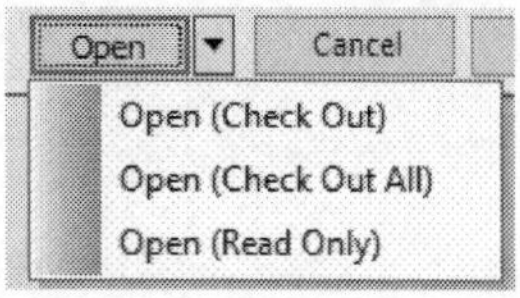

2. In the image below, the user selected Clamp.iam and used the two Check Out options. The dialog on the left results from specifying Open (Check Out) and the dialog on the right from specifying Open (Check Out All).

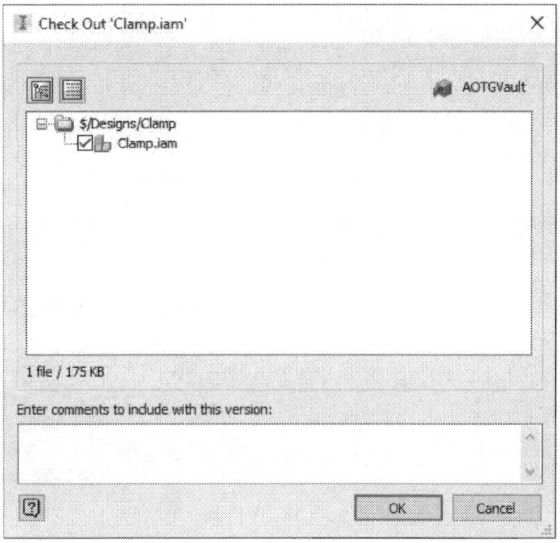

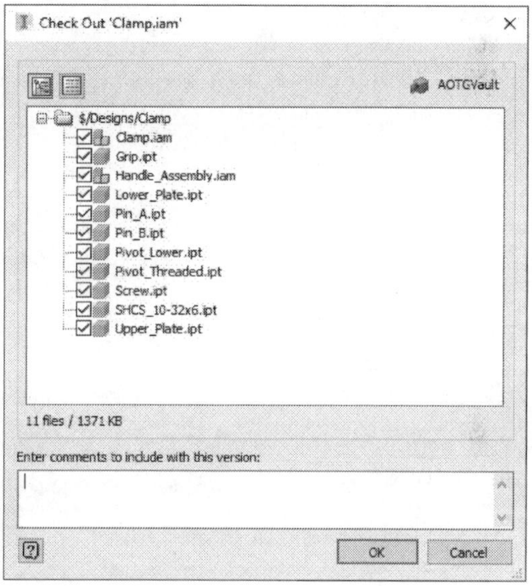

3. When you specify Check Out All, you can then selectively choose which files to check out by de-selecting specific files as illustrated below where all files except SCHS_10-32x6.ipt will be checked out.

4. If you open the file as read-only and later want to check it out, you can use the Check Out command from Inventor. You can control which parents or children are also checked out using the Settings option. In this example, the user selects the Handle Assembly and then selects the Settings option. In the Settings dialog box, you can specify which other files to open.

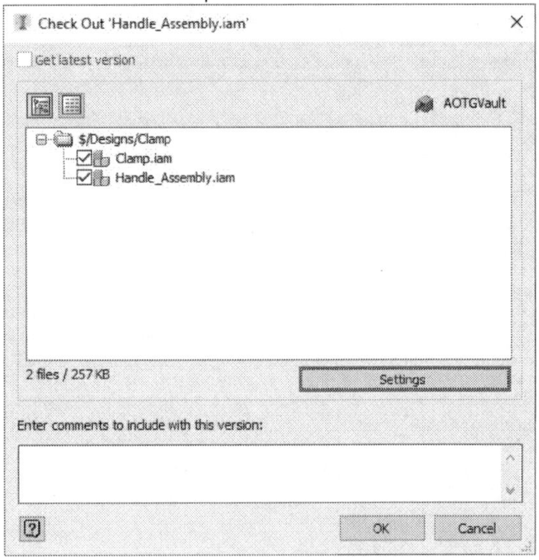

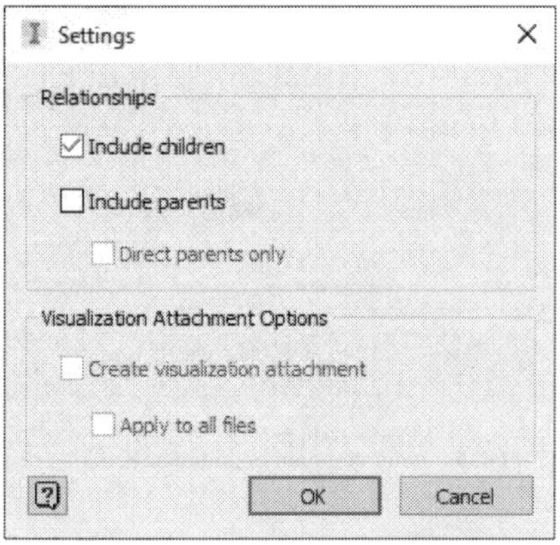

5. Since the user specified Include children, when the Settings dialog box is dismissed the Check Out dialog box now contains the children of the Handle Assembly.

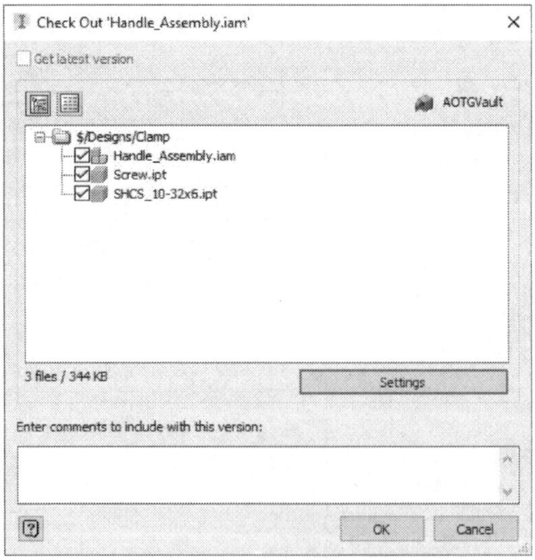

Note: If you use the Get command from Autodesk Vault, you have more control over the parents, children, and other files in the vault to check out to the local working folder.

Hint: Streamlining Your Workflows

To streamline your workflow, you can set default options for all Vault dialog boxes. If you use the same options all of the time, you can suppress the dialog box so the command runs without showing the dialog box.

Guidelines for Checking Out Files

Whether you check files out immediately or as required depends on your working environment:

- If you opt to check out the files when using either the Get command from Autodesk Vault or the Open from Vault command in Autodesk Inventor, the files that you select are checked out to you immediately, thereby reserving them for you to edit. Other members of your team are notified that you have the files reserved and they cannot edit them.
- If you get the latest versions without checking the files out of the vault, Inventor will prompt to check out files when opened, thereby saving you from checking them out manually. Working on a multi-user team does not prevent other users from checking out the file before you do, though it might prevent you from checking out the file when you need to.

Saving Files to a Vault

If you modify local copies of files, you need to check in the updated files from your local working folder to the vault.

Checking Files in to the Vault

When you have finished editing a file, save it locally and then check it back in to the vault. If the local copy of the file is different than the copy in the vault, the local copy of the file is copied to the vault and another version of the file is created. If visualization publishing options are set, a new DWF or DWFx file is also generated and attached to the new file.

You can use the Vault browser to determine which files need to be checked in. For example, the following image displays the Vault browser for a design. The green icon with a checkmark indicates that you have checked out and modified the parts and saved them to your local working folder. The Vault Status Modifier (shown as (+) after the filename), indicates that the local copy has saved edits. You can access the Check In command from the Vault browser shortcut menu.

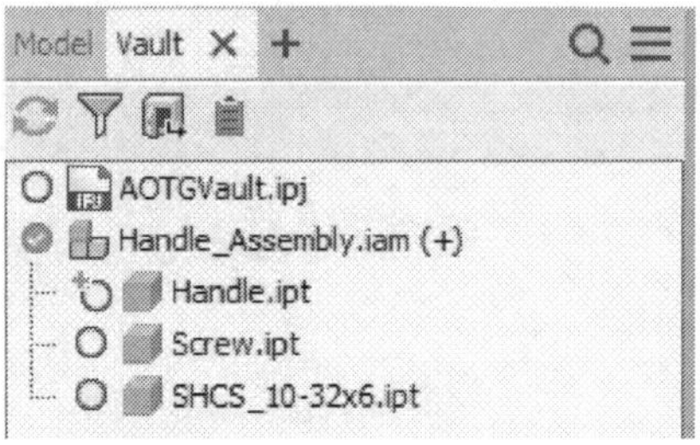

Guidelines for Check In Frequency

The frequency with which you check in files depends on your working environment. Frequent check- ins can result in a large vault database and file store because each time you check in a modified file, another version of the file is added to the vault. However, you can purge versions at any time to reduce the size of the vault. When you check in your designs, consider using a comment or label for versions that you want to keep so that you can easily exclude those versions if you purge the vault.

Check files in to:

- Save the model at a significant point in the design cycle. When you check in the file, a version of the file is saved in the vault.
- Inform other team members of changes that affect their portion of the design. When you check in files, other team members can get the latest versions from the vault to their computers.
- Save a design at a possible rollback point. When you check in a file, another version is created. You can roll back the design to a previous version at any point in the future.
- Save a version to help document design changes.

- Keep a safe copy of your design. Depending on your working environment, your local working folder might not be backed up. If you save a copy to the vault, the vault copy should be backed up on a regular basis.

About Visualization Files

Autodesk Vault uses visualization files to display CAD files. By default, Vault automatically creates visualization files whenever you add or check in files to the vault. Visualization files can be DWF or DWFx files.

If the model file does not have an associated visualization file, you can still view the file in Autodesk Vault. However, viewing takes significantly longer because Vault must transfer the original files from the vault to a temporary folder on your computer before the viewing application opens them.

Vault enables automatic visualization file publishing by default but the Vault administrator can disable it in order to save space in the vault.

Check In Settings

The Check In dialog box is shown in the following image. Several settings and options are applicable to Autodesk Inventor files. The dialog box options vary slightly depending on if you are checking in through Inventor or Vault. The image displays the check in options from Inventor.

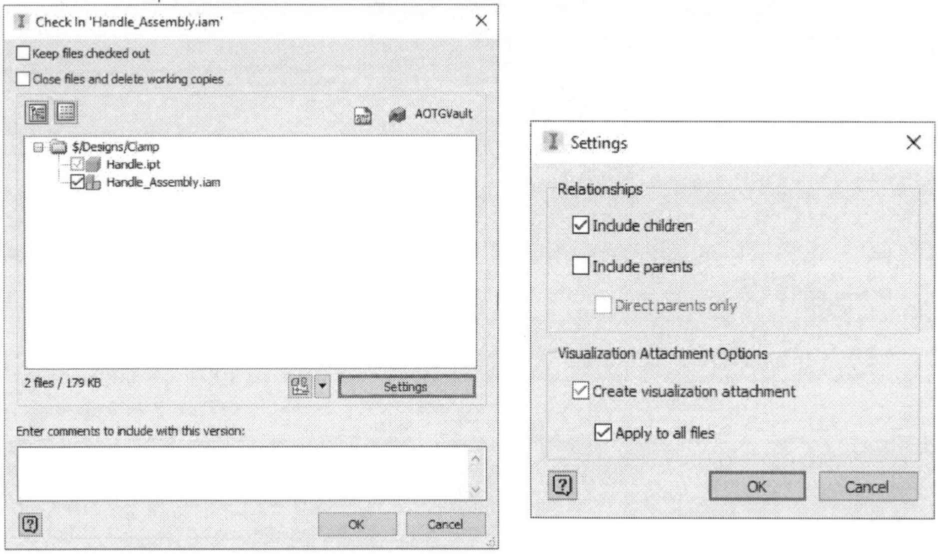

The settings that are applicable to Autodesk Inventor files include:

Setting - Option	Description
Keep files checked out	Checks the file in but keeps the local copy checked out. Updates the vault so other members of the design team can get the latest changes but keeps the files checked out so you can continue to edit them.
Close files and delete working copies	After the files are checked in, they are closed and the local copies are deleted. The next time you work on the files, you must get a copy of the latest files from the vault. This option is only available if all newer local files are checked in to the vault.
Include children / Include parents	The same as check out options.
Create visualization attachment	Creates DWF or DWFx files. Visualization files are created only for files that are different than the files in the vault.
Related files are included/excluded	Includes local drawings and/or presentation files that are not loaded in the current session when you enable the functionality using Include Related Files.

Abandoning Changes

If you decide to abandon changes that you have made to the local copy of a file, you can undo the checkout to remove the checkout flag from the file in the vault. The local copy of the file is replaced with the latest file from the vault, returning the local file to the way it was before you checked it out. The restored local file is automatically reloaded in Inventor. You can undo checkouts on files that you have checked out, not on files checked out by other users.

Practice 3b Edit Autodesk Inventor Files

In this practice, you learn how to work with Autodesk Inventor and Vault. You log in to the vault, get a model, add a new part, and check the files back in to the vault. You then review the model in Vault Explorer.

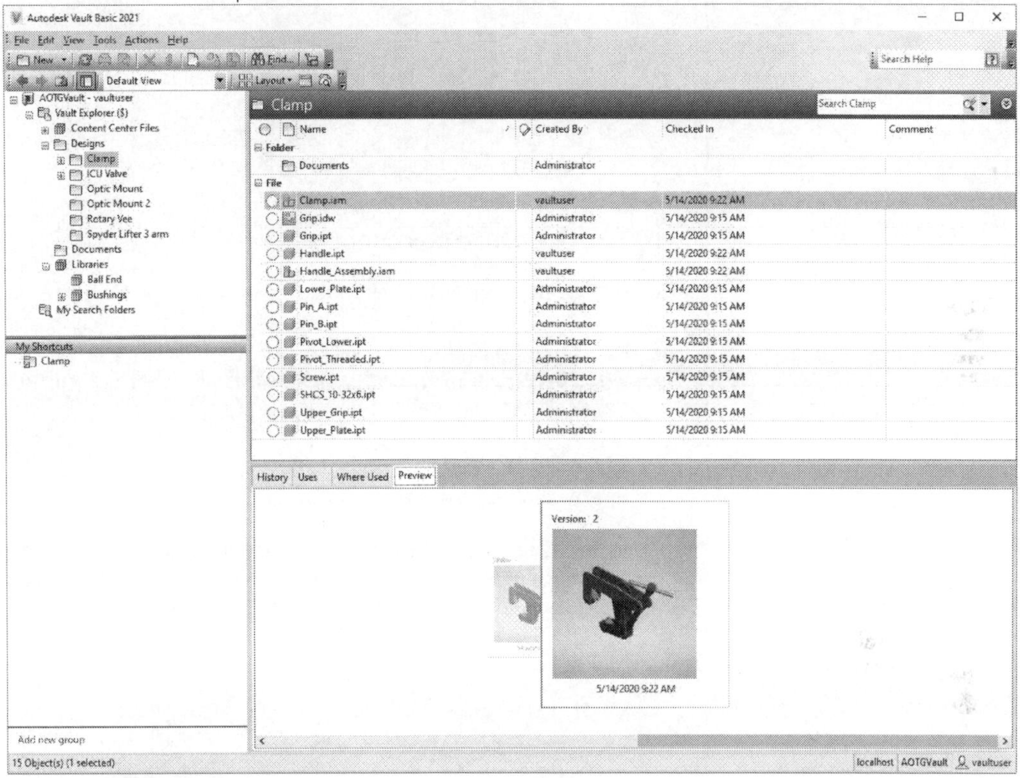

The completed practice

Task 1 - Edit Inventor files.

1. In Inventor, start Autodesk Vault by selecting Vault menu>Autodesk Vault. Use the following information:
   - For User Name, enter **vaultuser**.
   - For Password, leave this box empty.
   - For Vault, select AOTGVault.
2. Click Vault Explorer ($). Click File menu>Set Working Folder. Set the working folder to: *C:\AOTGVault\VaultWorkingFolder.*

Note: If you did the practice in the previous chapter, you might have already set the working folder and do not have to set it again.

3. In the Main Pane right-click Designs.ipj and select Get to copy the file to the working folder.

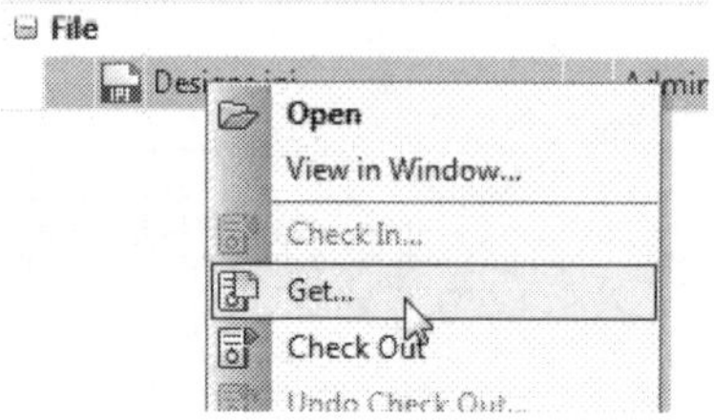

4. The Get dialog box opens.

5. Click OK.

6. Right-click Designs.ipj. Click Go to Working Folder. In Windows Explorer, confirm that the file was downloaded to: *C:\AOTGVault\VaultWorkingFolder.*

7. In Vault, browse to Vault Explorer($)\Designs\Clamp. Right-click Clamp.iam and select Get.

8. In the Get dialog box, ensure that Include Children is selected. The download count should be 11. Click OK.

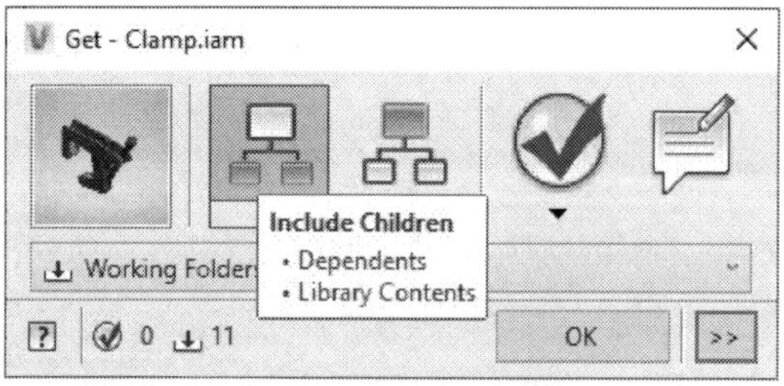

9. Start Autodesk Inventor.

10. On the ribbon, select the Vault tab and click Log In on the Access Panel.

    - For User Name, enter **vaultuser**.
    - For Password, leave this box empty.
    - For Vault, select AOTGVault.

11. On the ribbon, select the Get Started tab and click Projects on the Launch panel. Select Browse.

12. In the Choose project file dialog browser to: *C:\AOTGVault\VaultWorkingFolder* and select Designs. This will select the project file and make this the active project.

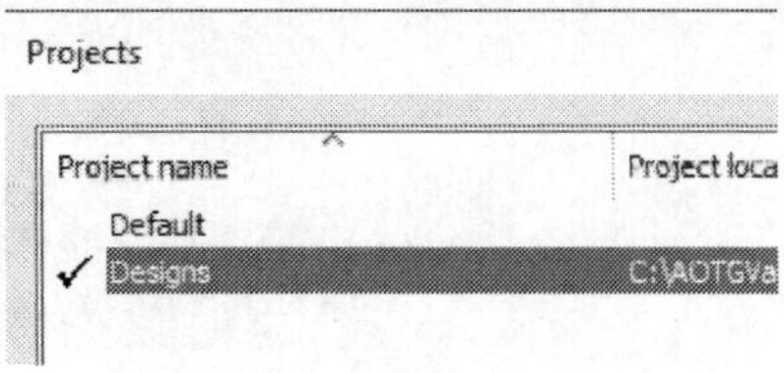

13. Click Done to close the Projects dialog box.

14. Open Workspace\Designs\Clamp\Clamp.iam.

Task 2 - Add a new part.

1. In the browser title bar, click Vault.

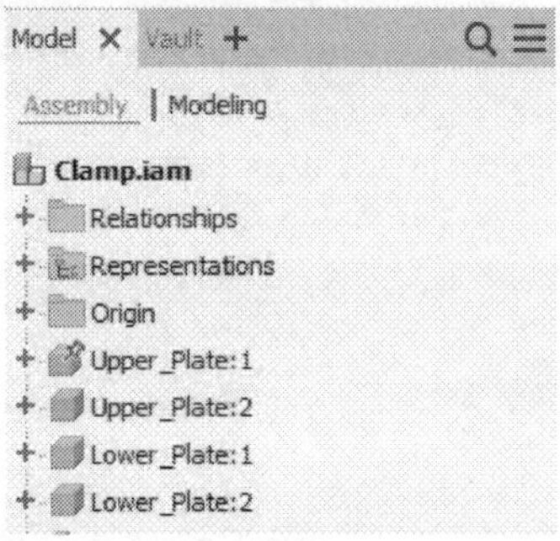

2. In the Vault browser, all part and assembly files are available for checkout.

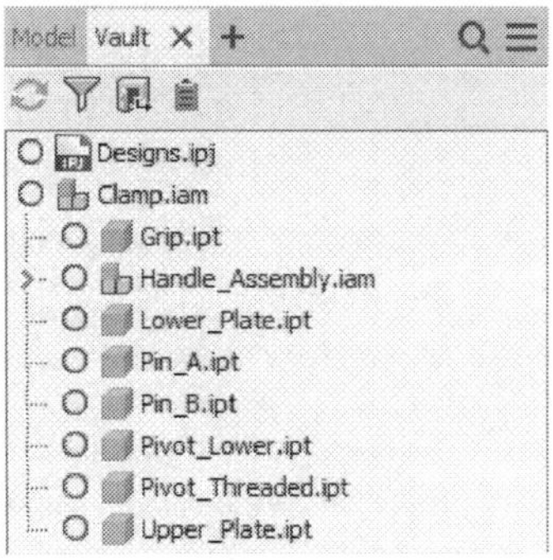

3. In the Vault browser, place the cursor over the filenames to display the tooltip and determine the status of each file. They should read Available for Check Out.

4. Start a new part using the metric Standard (mm).ipt template. Create a 6 mm diameter x 80 mm long cylinder with 0.5 mm chamfers on both ends.

5. Save the part in the Clamp folder, naming the file Handle.ipt.

6. Return to the Clamp.iam model.

7. In the Model browser, edit the Handle_Assembly subassembly.

8. Use the Place Component command to place Handle.ipt in the Handle_Assembly subassembly. Click Yes when prompted to check out the subassembly.

9. Constrain one instance of the handle to the hole. Check out Clamp.iam when prompted.

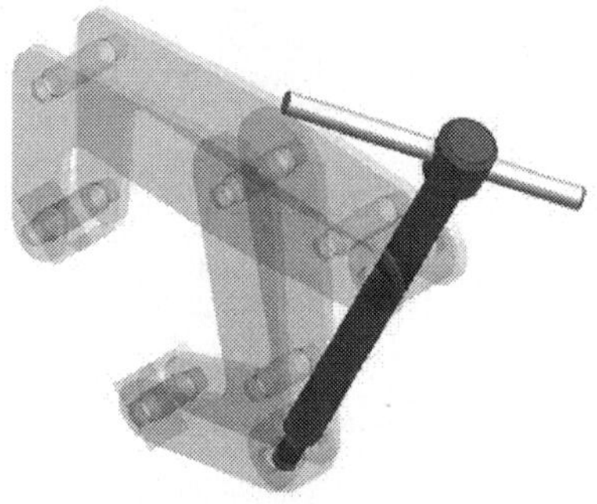

Note: The position of the handle in the hole does not matter.

10. Return to the top-level assembly.

11. Display the Vault browser. Move the cursor over the files to view the tooltips. The Clamp and Handle_Assembly.iam assemblies are both checked out. Both assemblies need to be saved. The Handle.ipt part is not in the vault so the vault status icon displays a circle with a small plus sign.

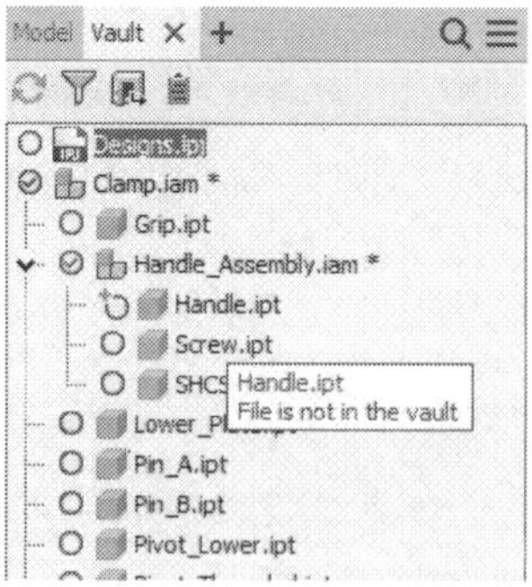

12. In Autodesk Vault, refresh the contents of the Clamp folder.

13. Confirm that Clamp.iam and Handle_Assembly.iam are reported as checked out.

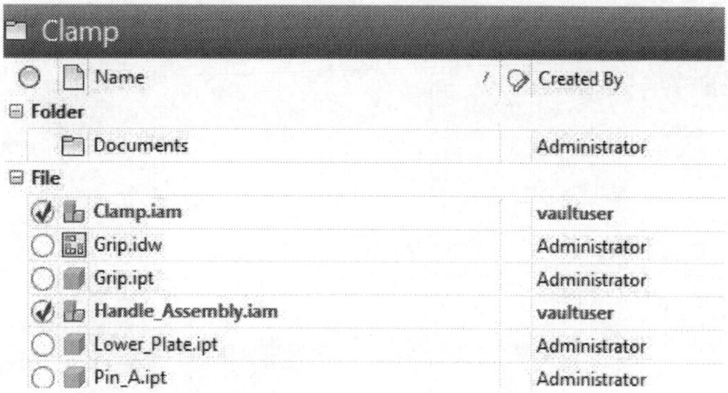

14. Return to Autodesk Inventor. Save Clamp.iam and Handle_Assembly.iam. Switch to the Vault browser. The icons for the two checked out files reflect the files are saved to the local working folder. Click  to show the vault status modifier.

15. The vault status modifiers display as a plus-sign in parentheses after the Clamp.iam and Handle_Assembly.iam filenames, indicating that there are modified local copies of the files.

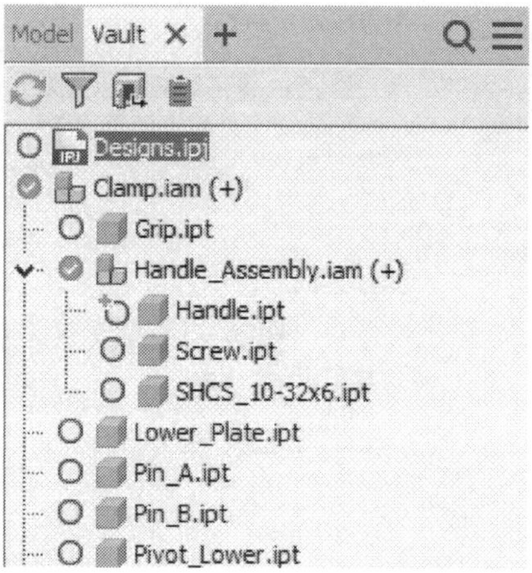

16. In the Vault browser, right-click Handle.ipt and select Check In.

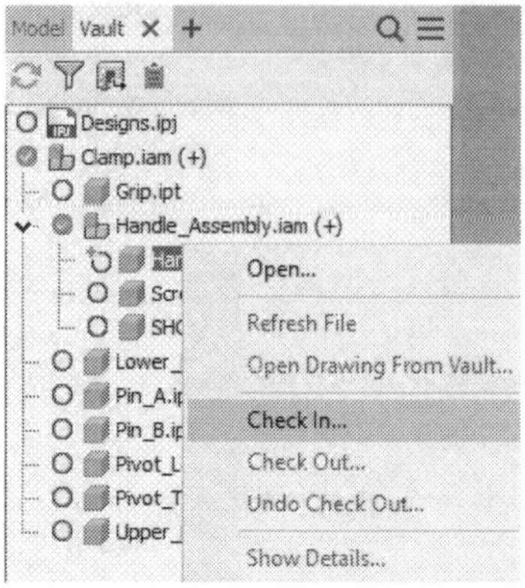

17. Click Settings. Confirm that the Create Visualization Attachment check box is checked. Click OK.

18. For Comment, enter **added to vault**.

19. Click OK. Review the browser and note that the vault status icon for Handle.ipt has changed and the tooltip reads Available for checkout.

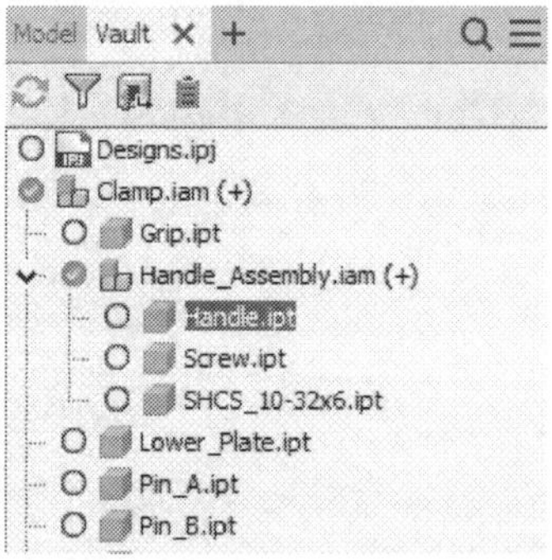

20. Right-click Clamp.iam and select Check In. The Check In 'Clamp.iam' dialog box opens.

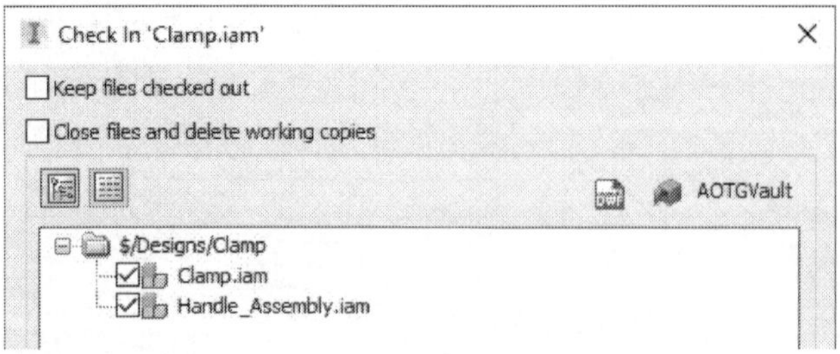

21. In the Check In dialog box, click Settings. Under Relationships, click the Include Children check box to toggle it off. Click OK.

22. Note that Handle_Assembly.iam is no longer displayed in the file list and will not be checked in.

23. Click Settings. Under Relationships, click the Include Children check box to toggle it on. Click OK. Handle_Assembly.iam is included again.

24. In the Comment field, enter **added handle.**

25. Click OK. Review the browser. Note that the checkmarks have been removed from the Clamp and Handle Assembly and their tooltip status reads Available for checkout.

26. In the Vault browser, right-click Clamp.iam and select Show Details. In the Details dialog box, you can now see there are two versions of the file. The first version does not show the Handle while the second does.

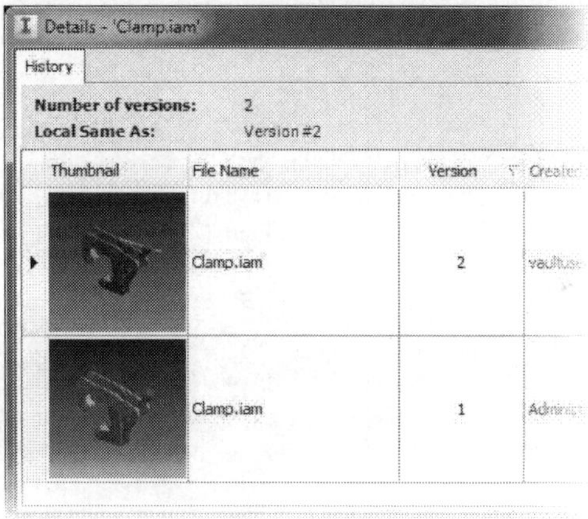

27. Close all files.

Task 3 - View the vault contents.

1. In Vault, click View menu>Refresh.
2. View the contents of the Clamp folder. Confirm that Handle.ipt is in the vault.
3. Click Handle.ipt.

4. Select the Where Used tab and confirm that the handle is used by Version 2 of the parent assemblies.

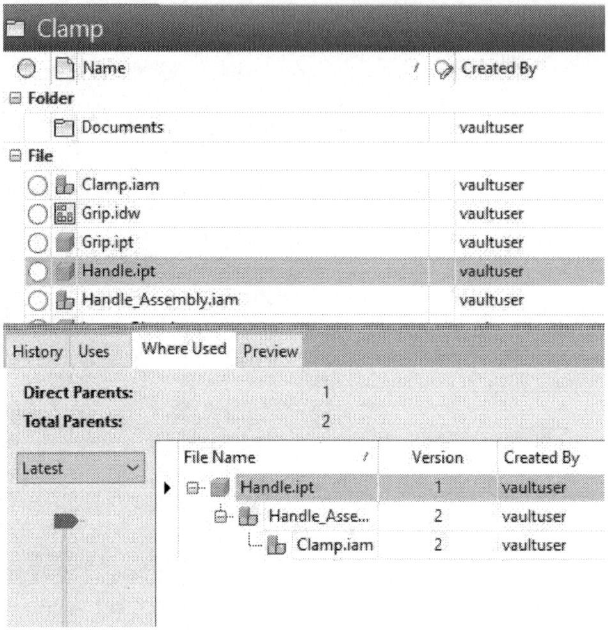

5. In the Main pane, select Clamp.iam. Click the Uses tab. Confirm that Version 2 of Clamp.iam uses Version 2 of Handle_Assembly.iam, which uses Version 1 of Handle.ipt.

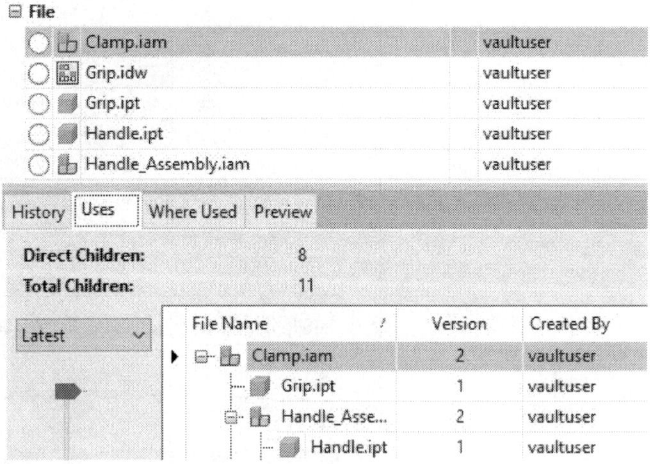

6. In the Versions drop-down list, select 1. Confirm that Version 1 of the clamp uses the Version 1 of Handle_Assembly, which does not include Handle.ipt.

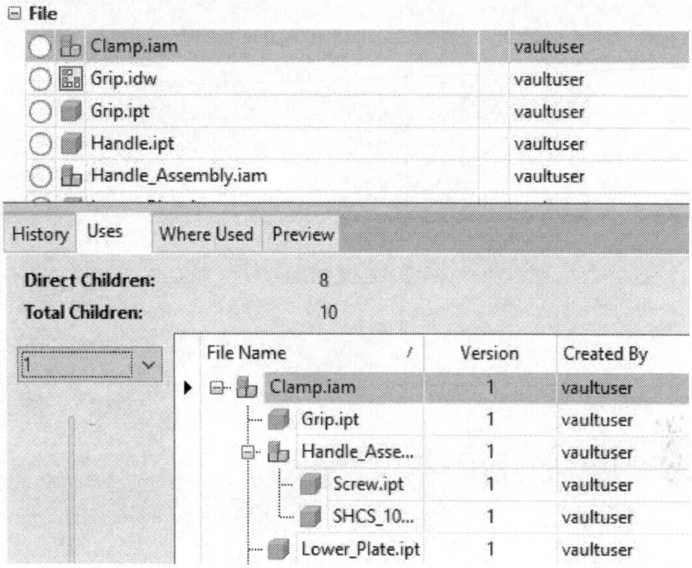

7. Click the Preview tab to view the clamp assembly. Select the Version 1 thumbnail image. Note that in Version 1 there is no handle.

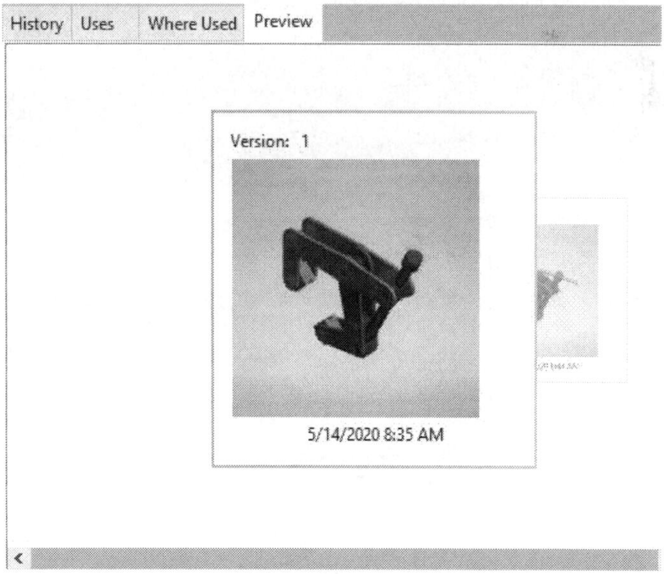

8. Select the Version 2 thumbnail image. The Handle part is displayed in the second version.

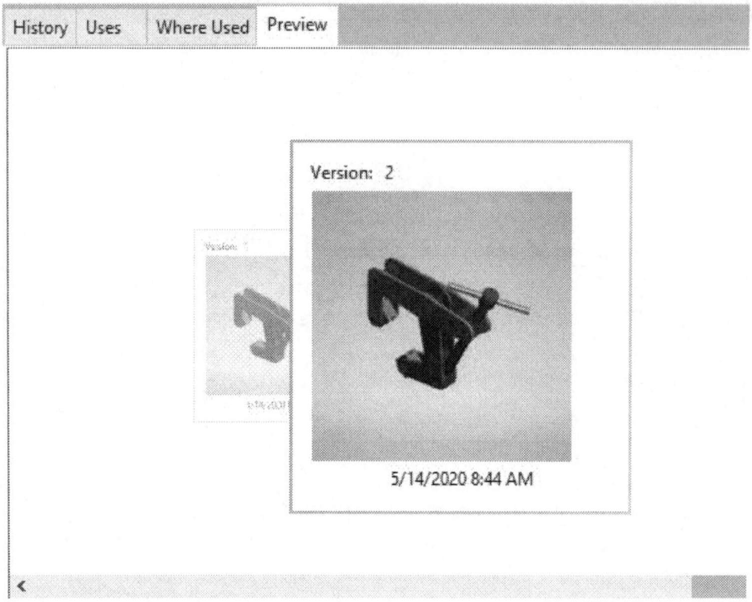

9. Close Vault.

3.3 Working With Vault in Autodesk Inventor

Overview

In this lesson, you learn how to manage designs and design versions using Autodesk Vault and the Autodesk Vault for Autodesk Inventor add-in.

Objectives

After completing this lesson, you will be able to:

- Place files from a vault directly in your designs.
- Update parent files after changes are made to child files.
- Add a new design to a vault from Autodesk Inventor.
- Streamline Vault workflows by controlling how Vault dialog boxes and prompts are displayed.

Placing Files from a Vault

If a file is in the vault and you want to place the file in your assembly, you can place the component from the vault without first manually retrieving a copy to your local computer.

About Placing Files from the Vault

You typically use the Place from Vault command to place common, shared parts in your assemblies. The vault is a central storage place for common components that are shared by many designs. These can include purchased parts or assemblies, such as motors and hydraulics, or in-house manufactured components that are unique to your company but shared by more than one design. These files can be in library folders in the vault, or in regular folders. Use the Place from Vault command to place these parts directly in your designs.

Place from Vault gets a copy of the file to your working folder and then places the component in your assembly.

Procedure: Placing Files from a Vault

The following steps describe how to place files from the vault directly in your designs.

1. On the ribbon, select the Vault tab and click Place on the Access panel. Optionally, on the ribbon, select the Assemble tab and click Place from Vault on the Component panel.

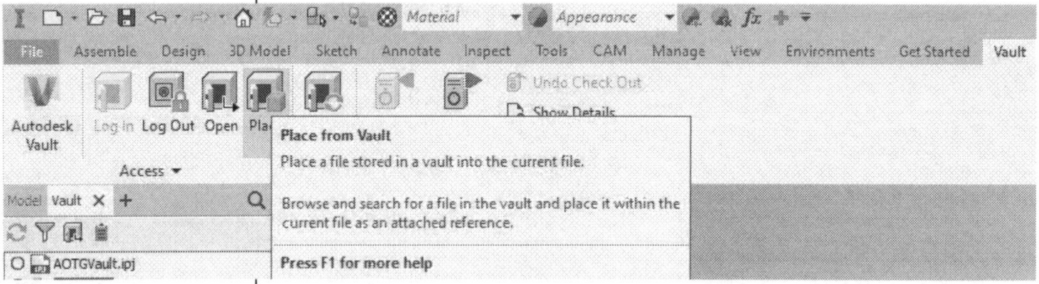

2. Navigate to a file in the vault. Use Shortcuts, Find, or saved searches to locate files in the vault..

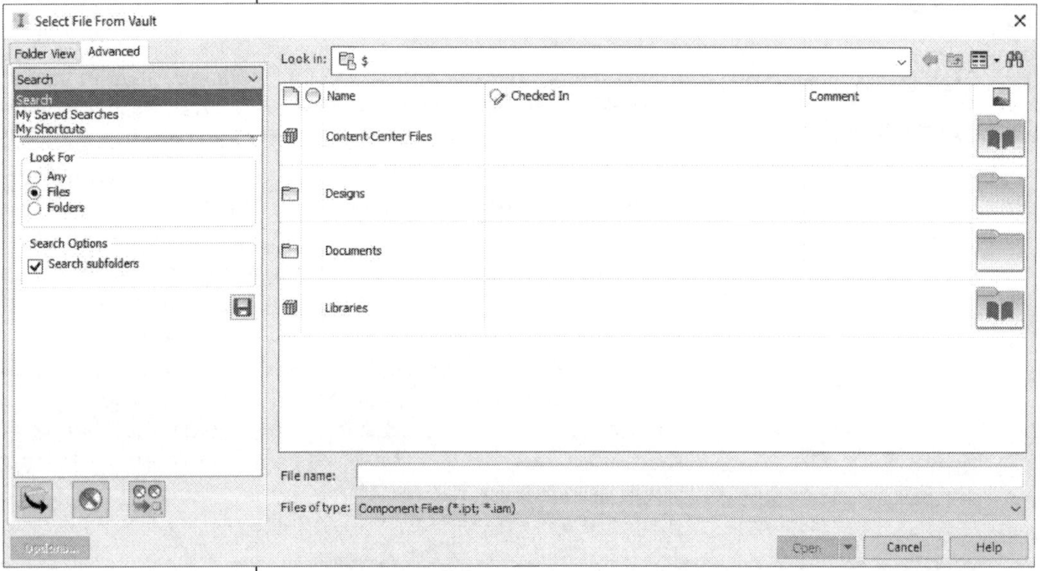

3. Select and open the file. The file is copied to your working folder.

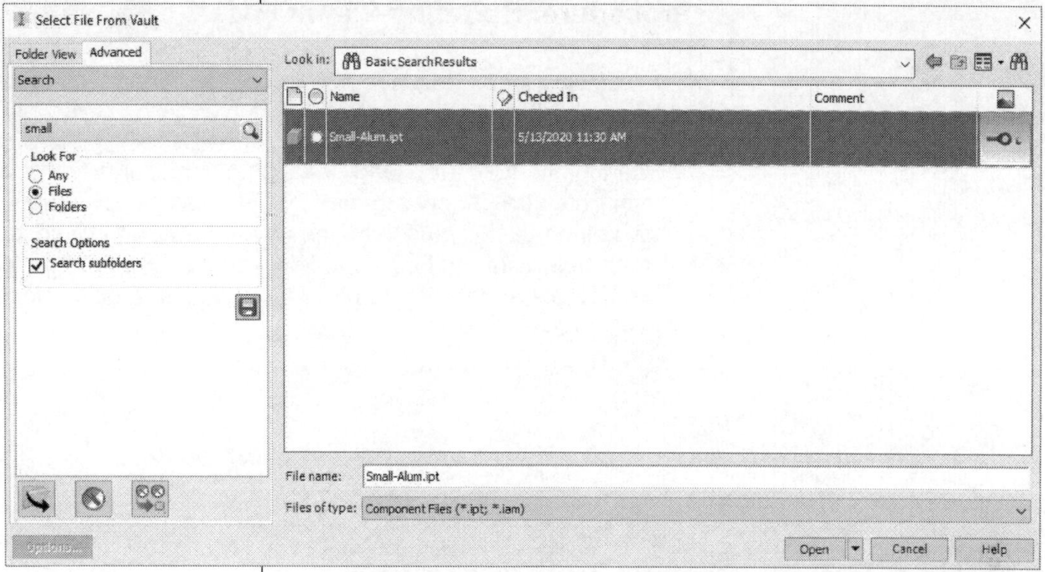

4. Place and position one or more instances of the local copy of the component in your assembly.

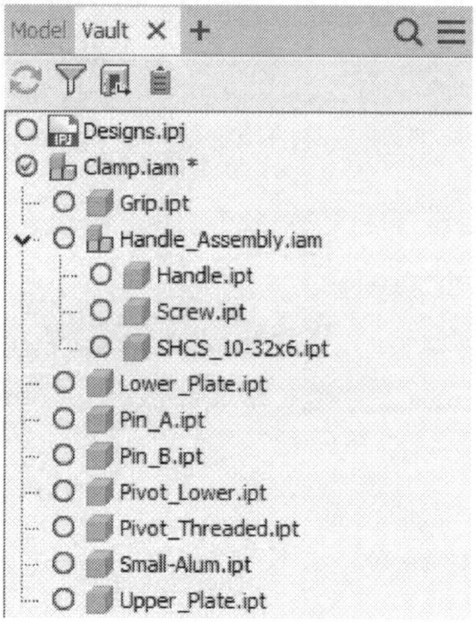

Updating Parent Files

In the course of a design, different designers can work on files at various levels in the model. One designer can check out a part, update it, and then check it back into the vault without checking out the assembly that contains the part. Another user can be working with the assembly and some of the other parts referenced in it. At some point in the design cycle, the parent assemblies, drawings, and presentation files must be updated to reflect the changes to their children.

Procedure: Updating Parent Files

The following steps describe how to update parent files to reflect changes made to their children.

1. Identify the files that need updating. In smaller models, this can be a straightforward task that you can perform manually by using the information on the Uses and Where Used tabs in Autodesk Vault. In larger models, you can use the Track File Status tool and the Status field in Autodesk Vault to identify which parent files are out of date.

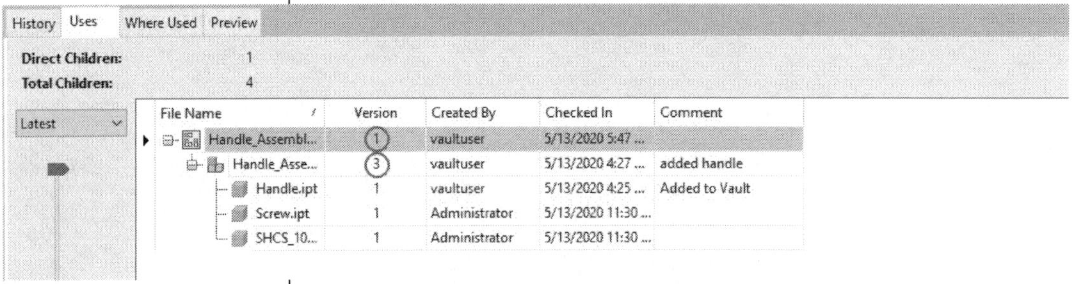

2. Use the Get command to get the latest version of the parent file and its children to the local working folder.

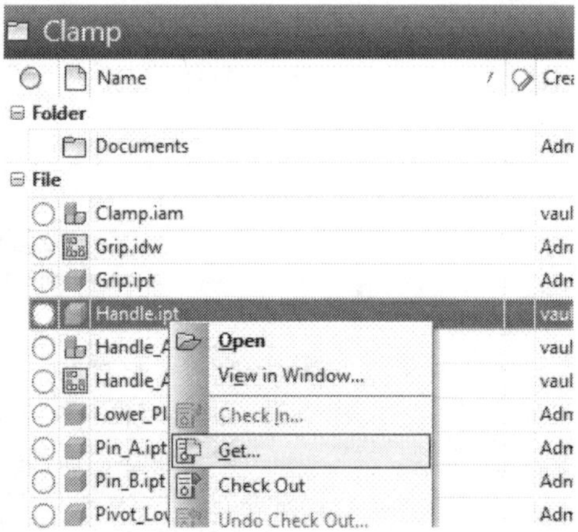

3. If you know which child file was modified, get the latest version of the child file and select the option to include all parents. Alternatively, check out the files and get the latest version simultaneously.

4. If you did not do so in the previous step, check out each parent file. If the model has a large number of parent files that need updating, check out all files rather than checking out individual files.

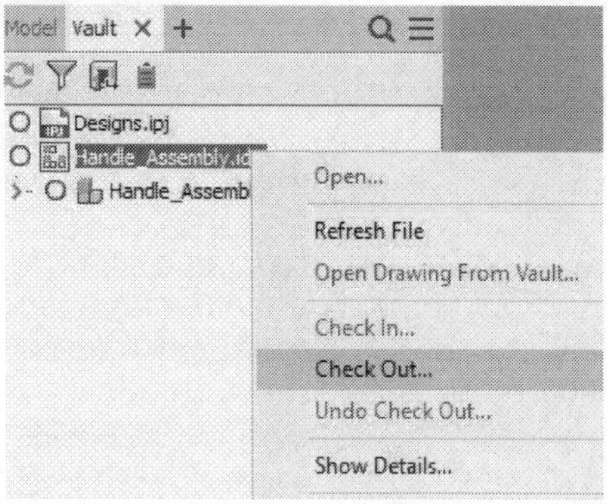

5. Check in the parent files. A new version of each parent file is added to the vault.

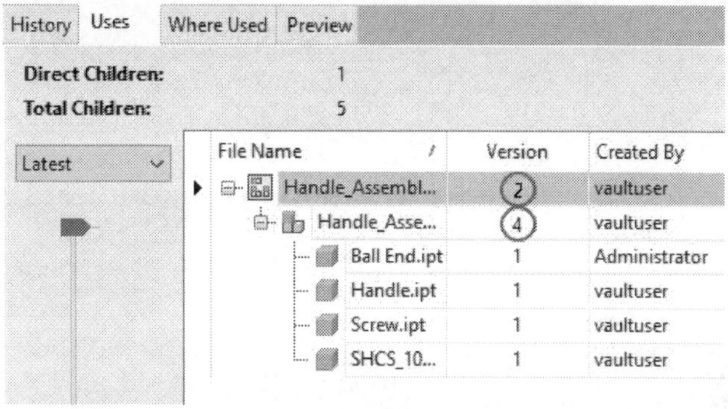

Adding a New Design

If you create a new design and need to add the design to the vault, you can upload all of the files at once to the vault.

About the Check In Project Command

The Check In Project command that is available in the Application Menu in Inventor, adds all the files associated with a project to the vault. Add Project finds all of the files in the search paths of the current project file and uploads the files to the vault, including non-model files, such as spreadsheets and documents. The relationships between Autodesk Inventor files are maintained when you add files to the vault using this method. Each time you use the Add Project command for the active project, the new files contained in the local project structure that are not yet in the vault are added to the vault.

When you use the Check In Project command, the active project must be a vault-type project and it must be set up correctly with the correct folder mapping. In addition, you should organize the project's files so that they are compatible with the vault, and you must set up the vault correctly to receive the files. Therefore, you typically use the Check In Project command to add new files to the vault after you have already set up and worked with the vault.

Check In Project versus Check In

You can use the Check In Project or Check In command to upload new files to the vault. The command you select depends on the workflow you prefer.

- The Check In command in Autodesk Inventor adds the files that are selected and currently open in Inventor. You can optionally select to check in children and parent files of the selected files. Therefore, use Check In to add new project files as you create them in Inventor.
- Use the Check In Project command after you have created a number of new files and want to add all of the files in the project file's paths to the vault.

Check In Project Versus Autodesk Autoloader

You can use the Check In Project command or Autodesk Autoloader to upload projects to the vault. The command you select depends on the state of the project file, the files to upload, and the vault.

- Autodesk Autoloader converts existing project files and organizes the model files and the vault for you. Use Autodesk Autoloader to upload existing designs to the vault, especially if the projects are not currently vault enabled or organized for the vault. Autoloader should also be used to populate an empty vault because it creates the correct folder structure and project file.
- The Check In Project command requires that the files are organized, the vault is correctly prepared, and the project file is correctly set up. Therefore, use the Check In Project command to add new projects to an existing, organized vault.

Check In a New Project to the Vault

The following steps describe how to add a new design to the vault using Check In Project.

1. From Autodesk Inventor, activate a vault-type project file. You must set up the project file correctly with the correct folder mapping.
2. Ensure that the files for the new project are located in the correct location in the working folder. For example, in the following image, the new project is located in the My New Design folder under the Designs folder in the local working folder.

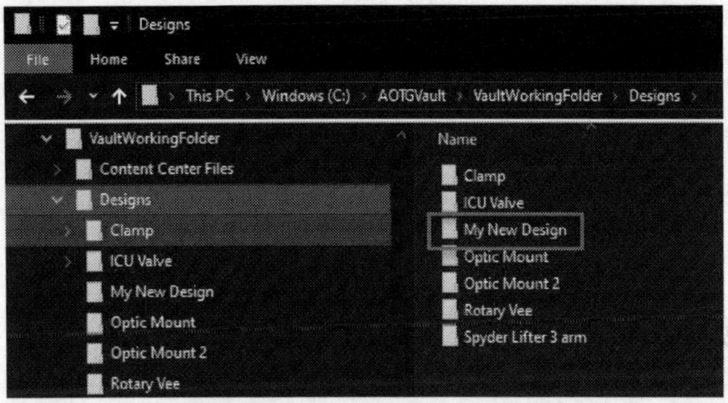

3. Click Inventor Application to the left of the Quick Access toolbar. Click Vault Server>Check In Project. You do not have to have any files open. The folders in the project file's search paths are scanned to locate files. Files that are not already in the vault are listed.

4. Add a comment if required and toggle visualization file publishing on or off. The files are added to the vault. The folder structure in the working folder is reproduced in the vault using the folder mapping from the project file.

Streamlining Vault Workflows

There are several ways to streamline your vault workflows. You can specify the default response for common dialog boxes and then suppress the dialog box so it is never displayed. You can also specify which commands are automatically performed without prompting you for input, reducing the number of times you need to directly interact with the vault prompts.

How to Control Vault Prompts

On the Vault tab, select Vault Options on the File Status panel to control prompts and dialog boxes in the Options dialog box.

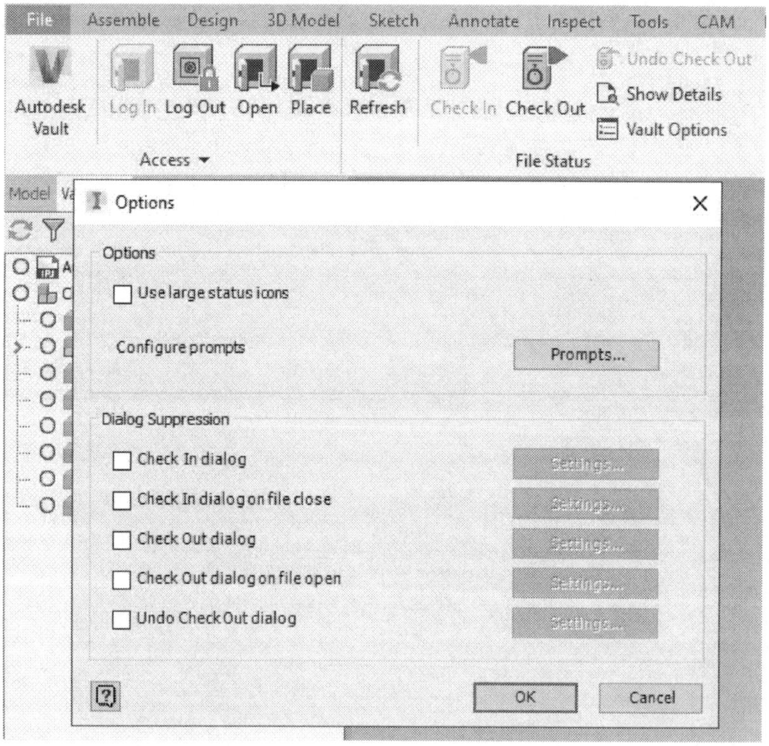

How to Set Suppressed Dialog Box Settings

You can set default responses for suppressed dialog boxes. When you check in files from Autodesk Inventor, click Settings when the list of files to check in is displayed. For example, in the Dialog Suppression group for Check In dialog selecting Settings… will display the Setting for Check In dialog. You can configure the options that best suit your workflow.

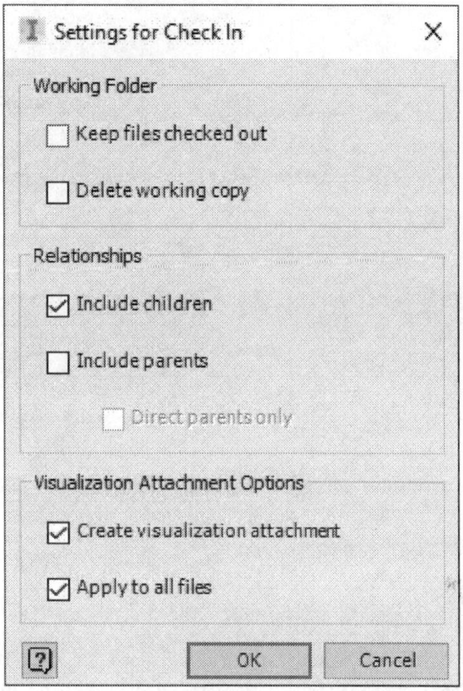

How to Manage Vault Prompts

Selecting Prompts… displays the Manage Prompts dialog box. This dialog enables extensive configuration of the prompts for the different commands, including the prompt text, the default response and the frequency of the prompt.

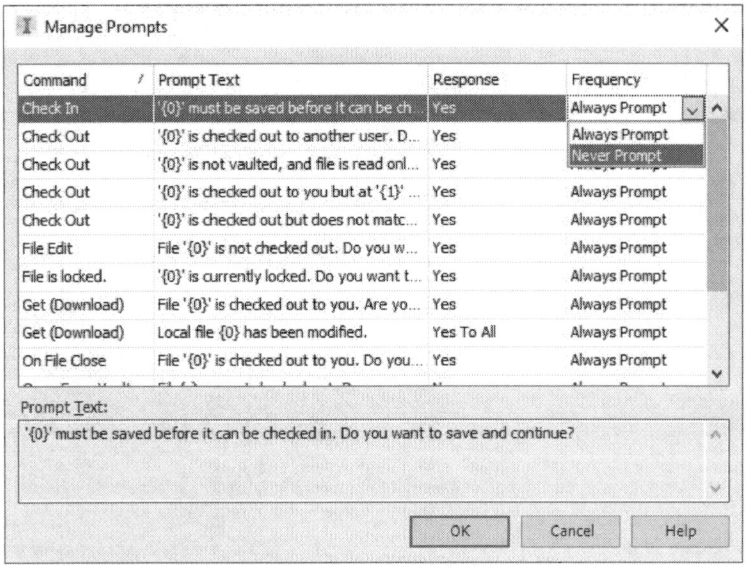

If you answer a prompt the same way every time the message box is displayed, set the response and then set the frequency to Never Prompt. You will not be prompted again.

Model States

Model States offer capabilities similar to those found in iParts/iAssemblies. However, all configurations are stored in a single file instead of multiple files. Each model state supports unique iProperties, Parameters, and Bill of Materials (BOM). You can open files with different model states from Vault while working with Inventor.

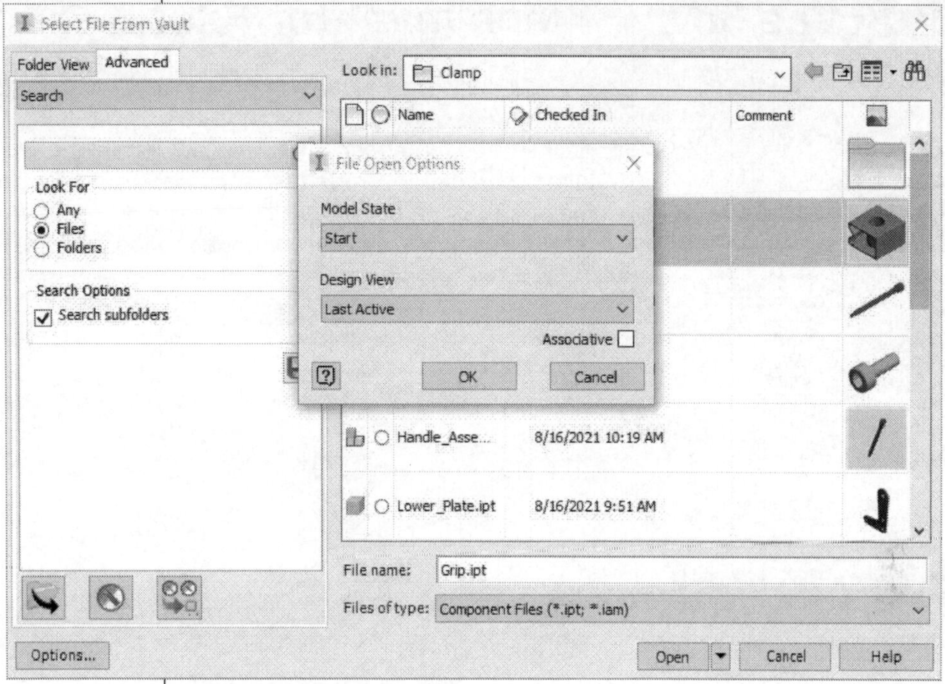

With Vault, you can:

- Check-in a model state file from the Inventor Vault add-in to the Vault client.
- Open and place a model state file from Vault.

Drawings with Mode States

While working on Inventor drawing files, you can:

- Automatically attach drawings of the specific model state to associated items.
- Open the drawing associated to a specific model state.
    - If a single drawing is associated to the model state file, the drawing file opens directly from Vault.
    - If there are multiple drawings associated to the model state, you can select and open one or more of the associated drawings from the "Select File from Vault" dialog.
    - If there is no associated drawing to the model state, you can open related drawings from other model states.

Practice 3c Place Inventor Files

In this practice, you learn how to place parts directly from the vault and how to update parent files to include the latest version of child files. You open a subassembly from the vault, place a library part directly from the vault, place a content center part, make a drawing of the new subassembly, and then update the parent assembly to reflect changes to the subassembly.

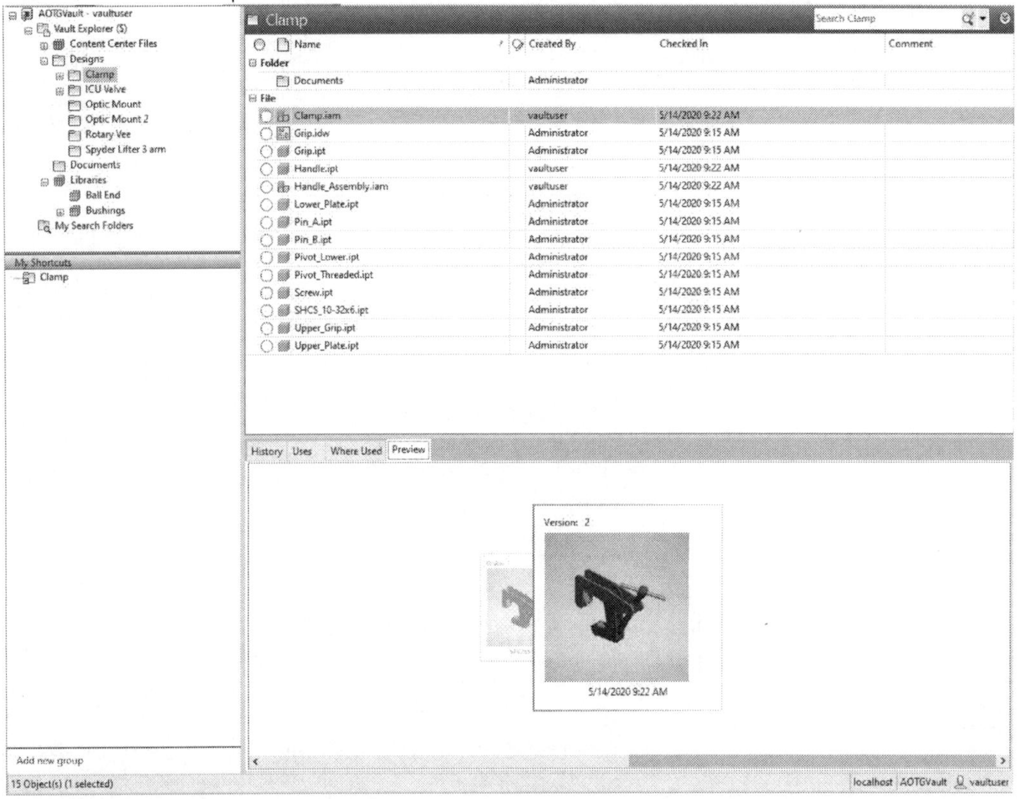

The completed practice

Task 1 - Place Inventor files.

1. Start Autodesk Vault. Log in using the following information:
    - For User Name, enter **vaultuser**.
    - For Password, leave the box empty.
    - For Vault, select AOTGVault.
2. In the Navigation Pane, expand the Designs folder.

3. Select Clamp from the Navigation Pane, and drag it to the My Shortcuts pane.

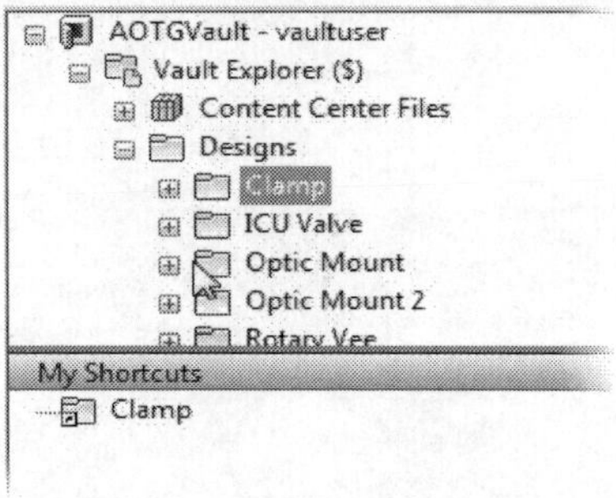

4. Start Autodesk Inventor. Activate the project file Designs.ipj if it is not already active.

5. On the ribbon, click the Vault tab. If you are not logged in to a vault, click Log In on the Access panel. Log in to AOTGVault.

6. Click Vault Options on the File Status panel.

7. In the Options dialog box, click Prompts. In the Manage Prompts dialog box, do the following:

   - For the Open from Vault command, where the prompt indicates the file is missing from the workspace, set the Response to Yes and the Frequency to Never Prompt.
   - For the Open from Vault command, where the prompt indicates the file is not checked out, set the Response to No and the Frequency to Never Prompt.
   - For the File Edit command, set the Response to Yes and the Frequency to Never Prompt.

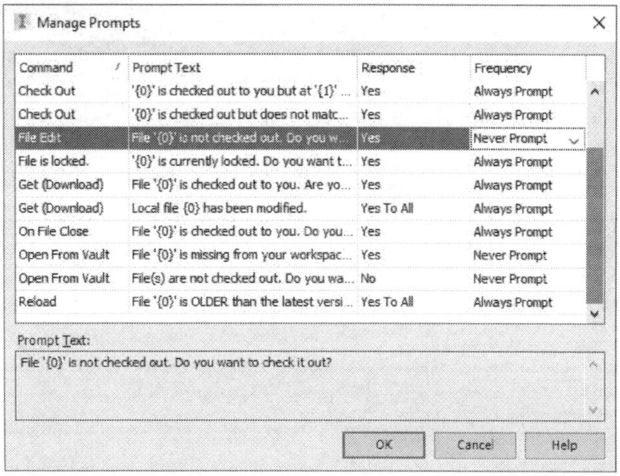

8. Click OK to close the Manage Prompts dialog box.
9. Click OK to close the Options dialog box.
10. Click Open on the Access panel.
11. Under My Shortcuts, click Clamp. Select Handle_Assembly.iam and click Open.

    Note: You are not prompted to check out the file because you specified that the prompt should never be displayed.

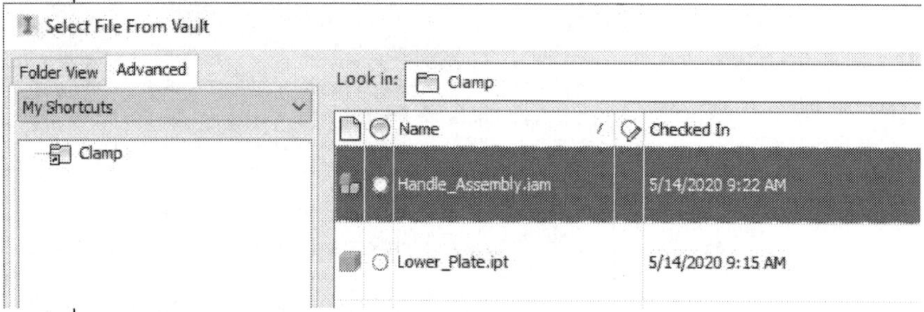

12. On the ribbon, select the Vault tab and click Place on the Access panel.
13. Open *Libraries\Ball End\Ball End.ipt.*
14. Place two copies of the part. Assemble the parts to the handle.

15. Place a cylindrical, ISO 13337 (or equivalent), 2.5 mm x 14 mm pin from the content center.

    You do not have to assemble the pin to the model.

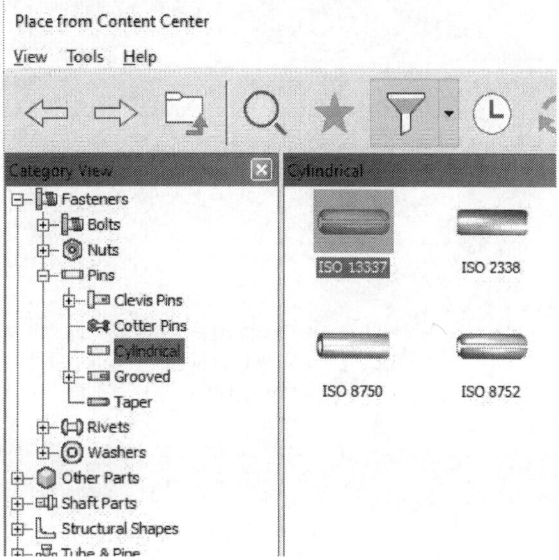

16. In the Vault browser, the pin that you placed from the content center is not in the vault so the vault status icon indicates that it is not in the vault.

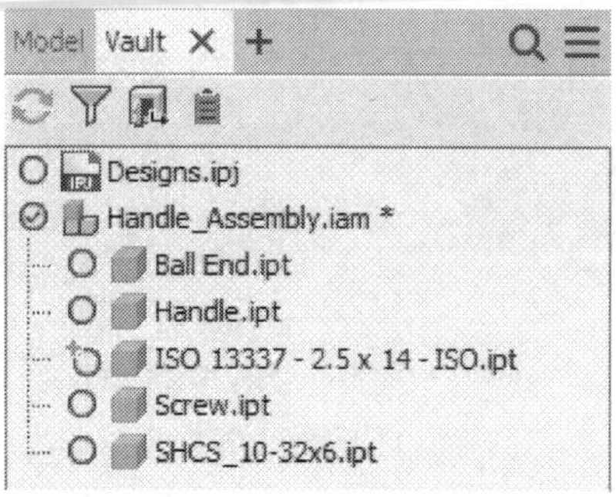

    Note that the parent assembly was automatically checked out for you because you set the default prompt response for file edits and specified that the prompt should not be displayed.

17. Save the file.

18. Click ▯ to show Vault Status Modifier. The (+) displays after the Handle_Assembly.iam filename.

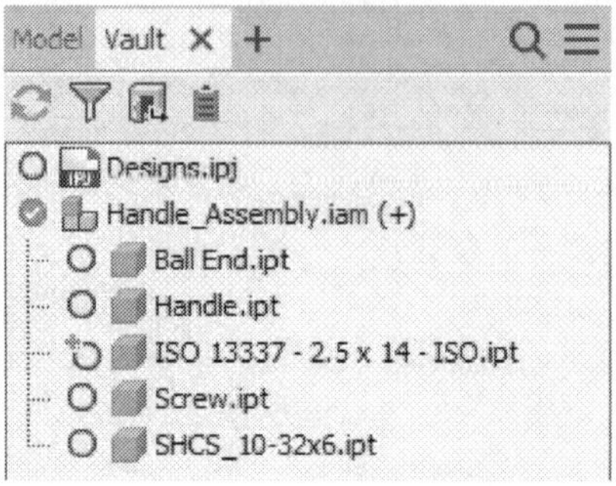

19. In the browser, right-click the pin you placed from the content center and select Check In. Click OK to add the pin to the vault.

20. In the browser, right-click Handle_Assembly.iam and select Check In.

21. For Comment, enter **added ball ends and pin**.

22. Click OK.

23. Close the file.

Task 2 - Create a drawing.

---

1. Start a new drawing based on the Metric\ANSI(mm).idw template.

2. Place a view of the handle assembly at a scale that fits the default sheet. The position and orientation of the handle do not matter.

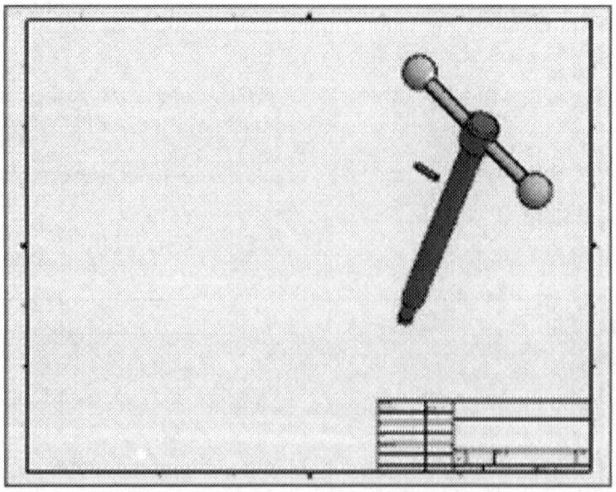

3. Save the drawing to the Clamp folder as Handle_Assembly.idw.

4. In the Vault browser, right-click the browser background. Click Expand All. The icon indicates that the drawing is not in the vault.

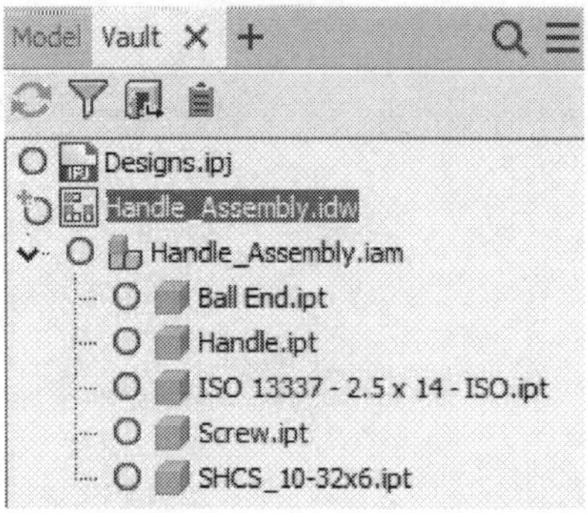

5. Right-click Handle_Assembly.idw and select Check In.

6. Click Settings. Click the Create visualization attachment check box to toggle it off. Click OK.

7. In the Comment box, enter **created and added to vault**. Click OK.

8. Close the drawing file.

9. In Vault, view the contents of the Clamp folder. You might need to refresh the view.

10. Click Handle_Assembly.idw. Select the Preview tab and click Version 1.

11. The drawing is not displayed because no visualization file was created for it.

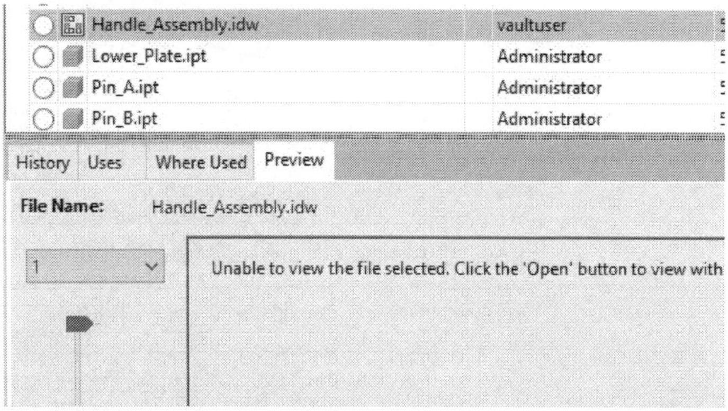

12. On the Preview tab, click Update. A visualization file is created and you can view the drawing (as long as Vault restrictions do not prevent it).

Task 3 - Update the main assembly.

1. In Vault, select Clamp.iam. Select the Uses tab. In the list of versions, select the highest number in the list. This should be 2 but might be different depending on where you started, etc.

   Note: The Latest option displays the latest versions of all files, although the latest versions of the children might not be associated with the latest version of the parent file.

2. This version of Clamp.iam should reference the previous version of Handle_Assembly.iam because Clamp.iam has not been updated.

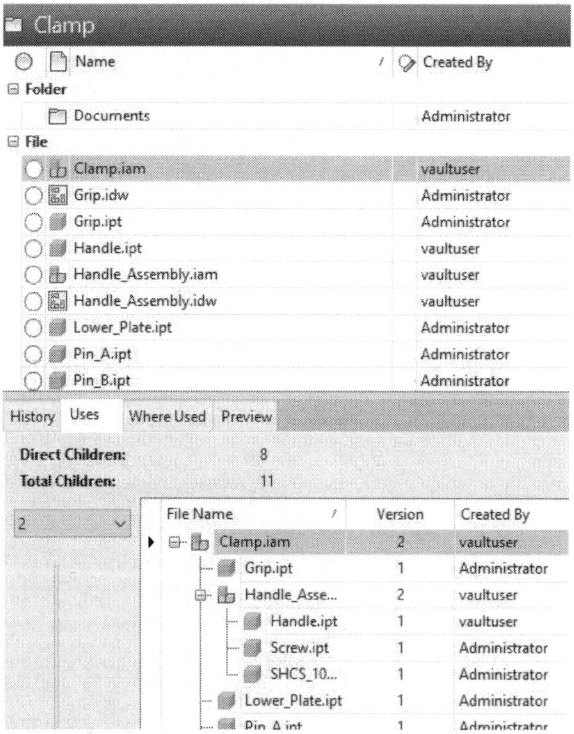

   Note: The Vault administrator can track file status to determine whether the parent files reference the latest versions of their children.

3. In Autodesk Inventor, on the ribbon, select the Vault tab and click Open on the Access panel.

4. Navigate to the Clamp folder. Select Clamp.iam but do not open the file.

5. Click the arrow next to Open. Click Open (Check Out).

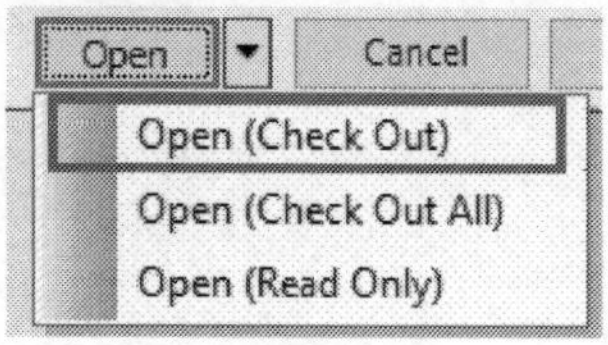

6. In the Check Out dialog box, click OK. If you are prompted to update the assembly, click Yes. If you are warned that Clamp.iam is read-only, click Yes.

7. In the Vault browser, the file icons should indicate that all files are up to date and that Clamp.iam is checked out.

8. Right-click Clamp.iam and select Check In. When prompted to save the assembly, click Yes.

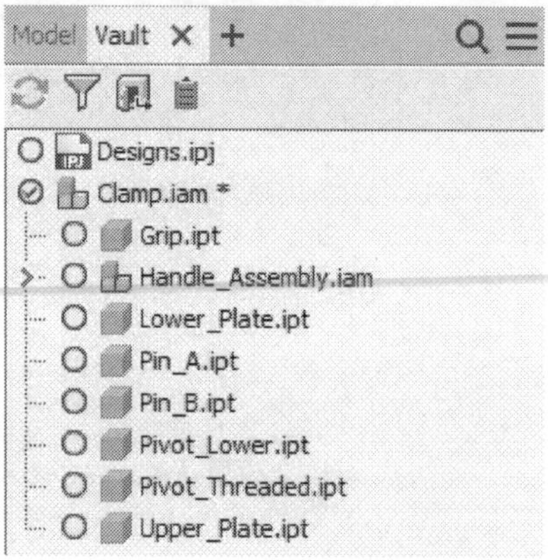

9. In the Comment box, enter **included latest handle**. Click OK.

10. In Vault, refresh the display.

11. On the Uses tab, confirm that the latest version of Clamp.iam uses the latest version of Handle_Assembly.iam.

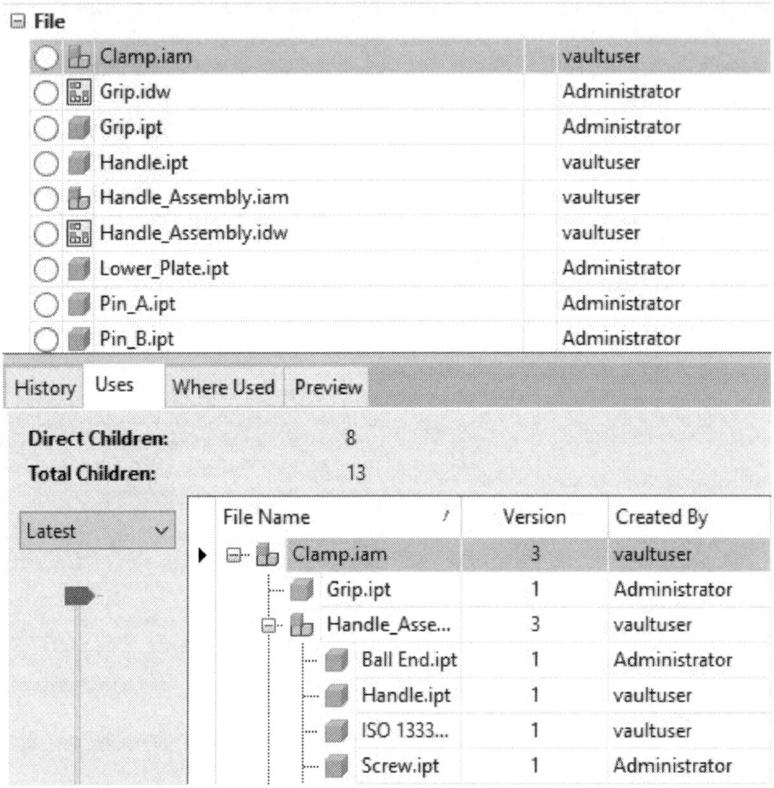

12. Close Vault.

13. Close all Inventor files.

3.4 Chapter Summary

Autodesk Inventor and Autodesk Vault are tightly integrated. In this chapter you learned how to use Autodesk Autoloader to populate a new vault with existing designs and library files. You also learned how to check files out of vault, edit them in Autodesk Inventor, and then check them back in to the vault. You also created new files in Inventor and checked them into the vault.

In order to streamline your vault workflows, you also learned how to specify the default response for common dialog boxes and suppress some of the dialog boxes so they are never displayed.

Having completed this chapter, you can:

- Use Autodesk Autoloader to add Autodesk Inventor files to a vault.
- Use common vault tasks in Autodesk Inventor.
- Manage Autodesk Inventor designs in a vault.

Chapter 4

Working with Vault and AutoCAD

In this chapter, you learn how to add existing AutoCAD® drawings to a vault and how to work with AutoCAD files from the vault.

Learning Objectives in This Chapter

- Open and access the vault from AutoCAD.
- Add AutoCAD drawings to a vault.
- Attach an XREF to a drawing and vault the host drawing and the XREF.

4.1 Opening and Accessing the Vault in AutoCAD

Overview

The AutoCAD Vault add-ins supply data management tools that work in AutoCAD, AutoCAD® Mechanical, AutoCAD® Architecture, AutoCAD® Map 3D, AutoCAD® Plant 3D, AutoCAD® P&ID, AutoCAD® MEP, AutoCAD® Electrical, Autodesk® Civil 3D®, and more. You can add files to a vault and check files in and out.

You can access the data management tools provided by the AutoCAD Vault add-in from a number of locations, including the File References palette.

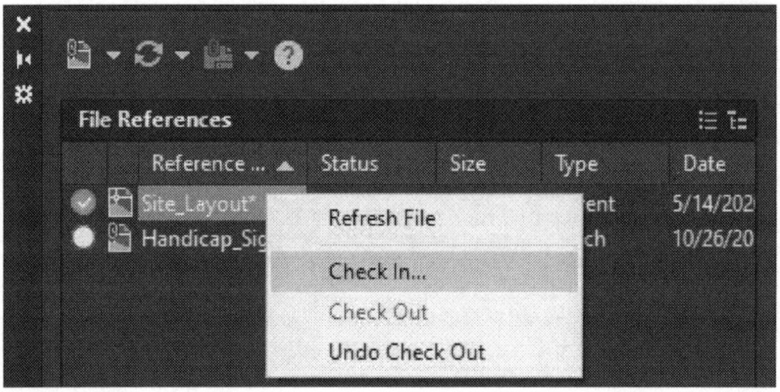

Objectives

After completing this lesson, you will be able to:

- Access Autodesk Vault from AutoCAD.

Opening and Accessing the Vault in AutoCAD

The first step in working with AutoCAD and Autodesk® Vault is to log in to the vault. This lesson covers how to access the vault from AutoCAD.

You log in to a specific vault through the vault Log In dialog box.

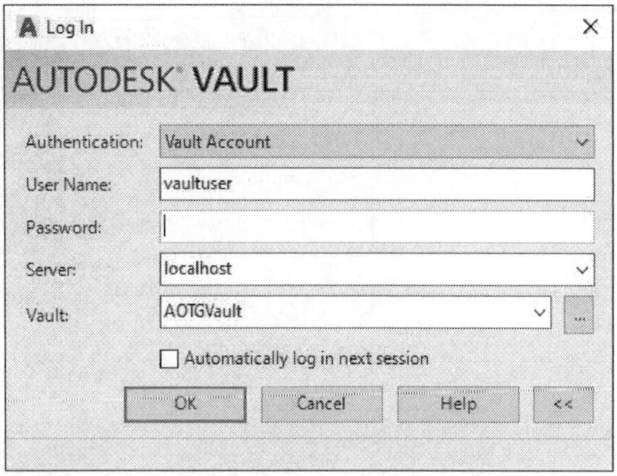

Procedure: Logging in to the Vault

You can access Autodesk Vault from AutoCAD using one of the following methods: the Vault tab on the ribbon, the Vault toolbar, the command line, or the Vault tray icon.

1. On the ribbon, select the Vault tab and click Log In on the Access panel.

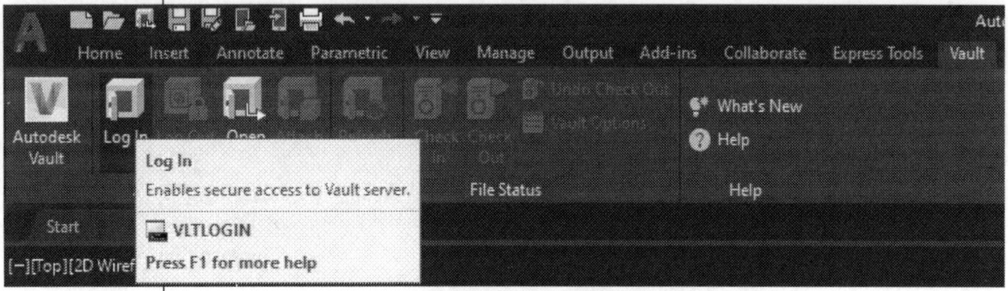

2. Click Log In on the Vault toolbar.

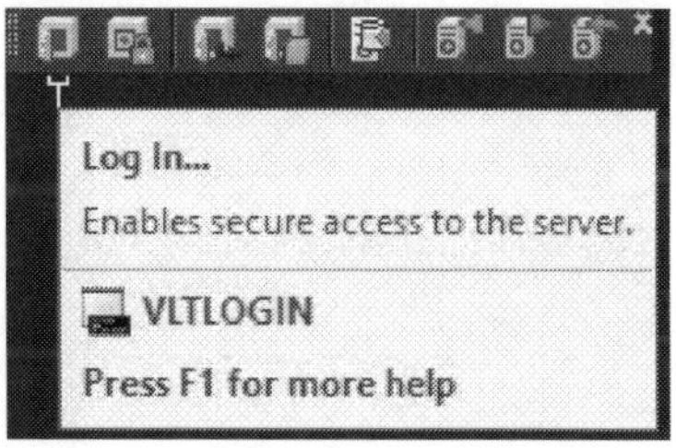

3. On the command line, enter **vault** or **vltlogin**.

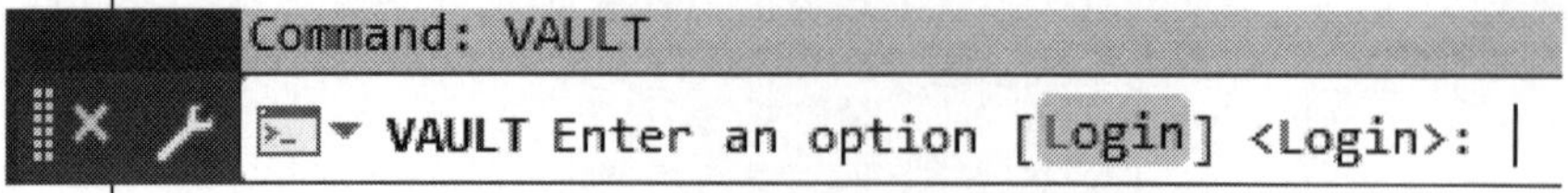

4. Right-click the Vault tray icon and then select Log In.

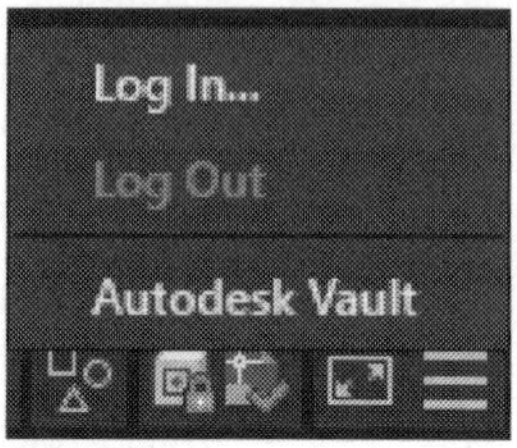

Status Bar Tray Icons

When you are not logged in to Autodesk Vault, the AutoCAD status bar tray icon is displayed as a locked vault. When you are logged in, the icon is displayed as an open vault door.

When logged in, rest the cursor over the Vault system tray icon to display the user login name, vault, and server.

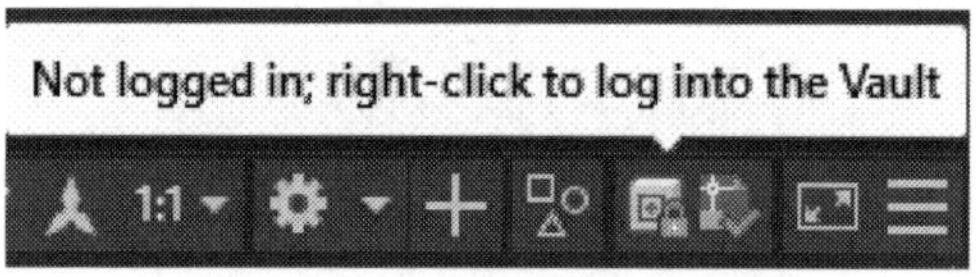

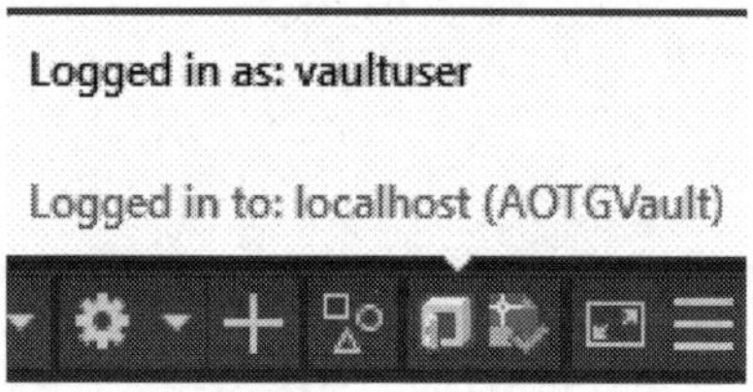

Practice 4a Access the Vault

In this practice, you log in to Autodesk Vault from AutoCAD. You also open Autodesk Vault, make two new folders for the practices in this chapter, and then set a working folder.

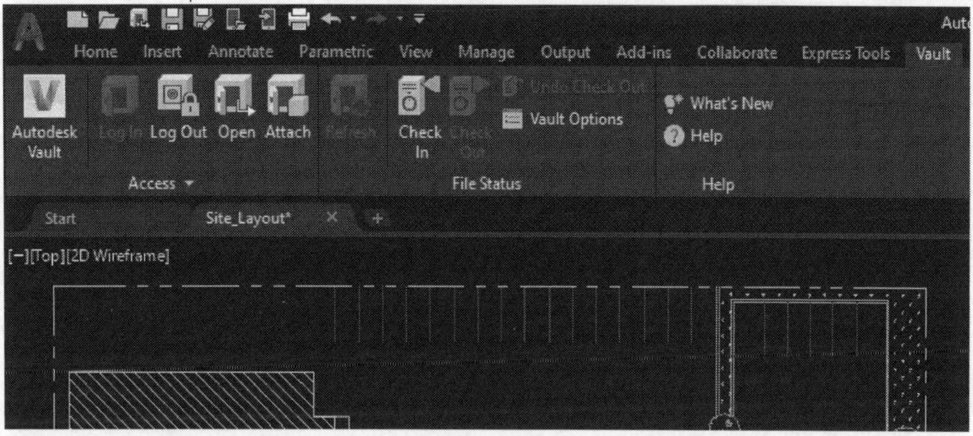

The completed practice

1. Start AutoCAD.
2. Open *C:\AOTGVault\Chapter4\AutoCAD DWG Files\Site_Layout.dwg*.
3. On the ribbon, select the Vault tab and click Log In on the Access panel.
4. Log in to the vault using the following information:
   - For User Name, enter **vaultuser**.
   - For Password, leave this box empty.
   - For Vault, select AOTGVault.
5. In the AutoCAD status bar tray, place the cursor over the Vault icon. The vault user name and vault name are displayed.

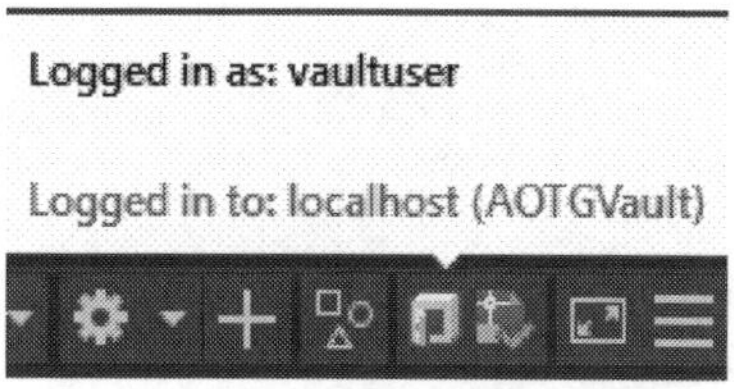

6. On the ribbon, select the Vault tab and click Autodesk Vault on the Access panel.
7. Log in to Autodesk Vault using the following information:
   - For User Name, enter **vaultuser**.
   - For Password, leave this box empty.
   - For Vault, select AOTGVault.
8. Right-click Vault Explorer ($). Click New Folder.
9. Name the new folder AutoCAD DWG Files.

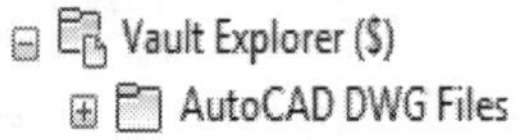

Note: Depending on the other practices you have done, the Navigation Pane folders might be different.

10. Repeat steps 8 and 9 to add another folder, this time a Library Folder, named AutoCAD Symbols to the root ($) folder in Vault.

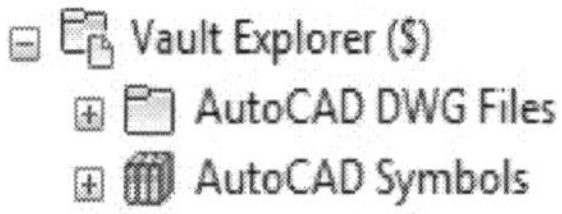

11. In Autodesk Vault click the File menu>Set Working Folder.
12. Browse to and select *C:\AOTGVault\VaultWorkingFolder.*

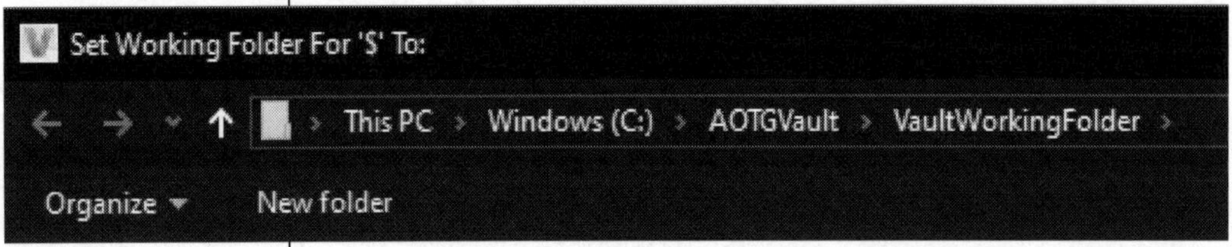

13. Click OK.
14. In AutoCAD save the file to ensure it is up to date.
15. Close the file.

4.2 Working with AutoCAD Files

Overview

The AutoCAD Vault add-in supplies data management tools that work in AutoCAD. You can add files to a vault, check files out of the vault to modify them, and check revised files in to the vault. The files can be DWG files, images, or any file associated with your design.

Objectives

After completing this lesson, you will be able to:

- Use a typical workflow for AutoCAD and Vault.
- Check drawings in and out of a vault.
- Open files from a vault.
- Attach files from a vault.

Typical Workflow for AutoCAD and Vault

In this lesson you will learn about a typical workflow using Autodesk Vault and AutoCAD.

The Vault tab on the ribbon includes a complete set of tools to manage drawings and other documents in your designs.

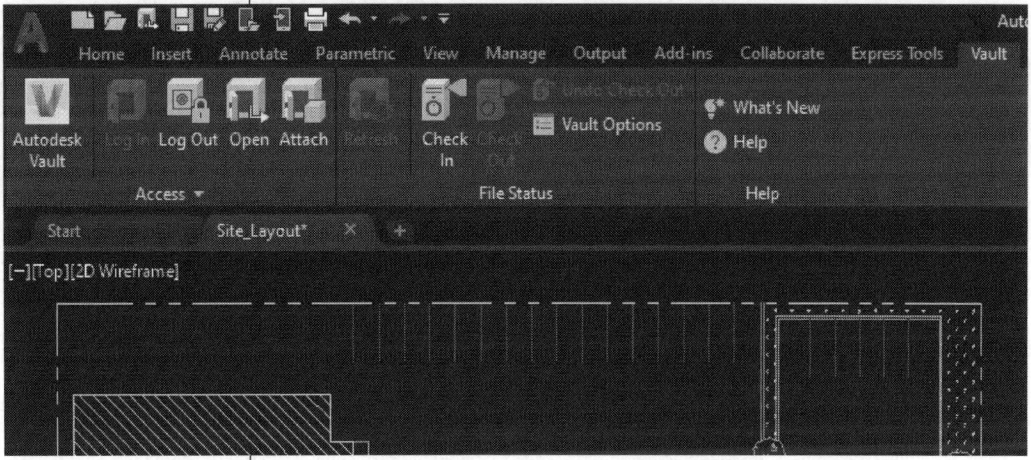

Procedure: Using AutoCAD and Autodesk Vault

Your workflow varies depending on where you are in the design cycle. The following steps describe a basic workflow for Autodesk Vault and AutoCAD.

1. Start Autodesk Vault, log in to the vault, and set the Working Folder.
2. Start AutoCAD.
3. In AutoCAD, open a file that you want to add to the vault.
4. Log in to the vault.

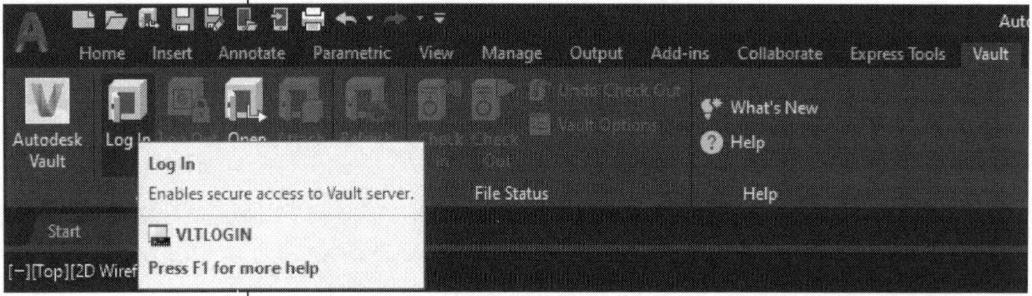

5. Attach any required external reference files (XREFs) to the open AutoCAD file, using either the Attach command or the Attach from Vault command.
6. In the File References palette, check the drawing in to the vault using the Check In command. The XREFs are also added to the vault.

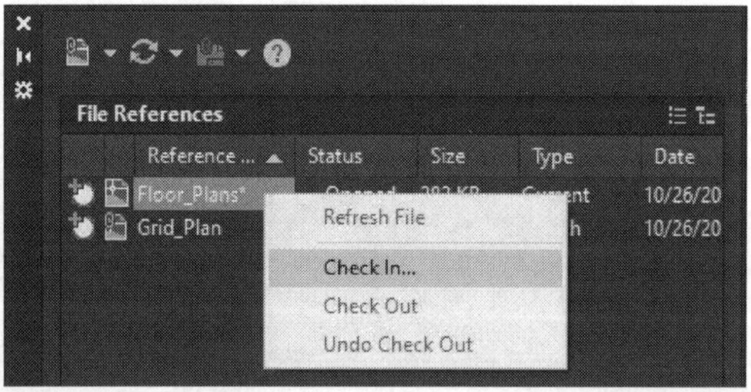

7. Open and check other files from the vault using the Open from Vault command.

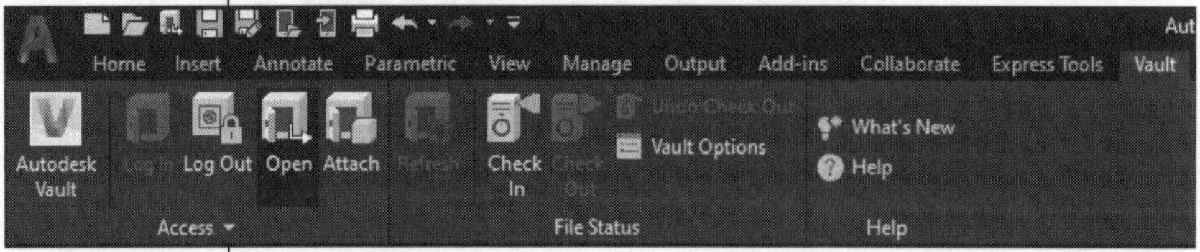

8. Check the modified files back in to the vault.

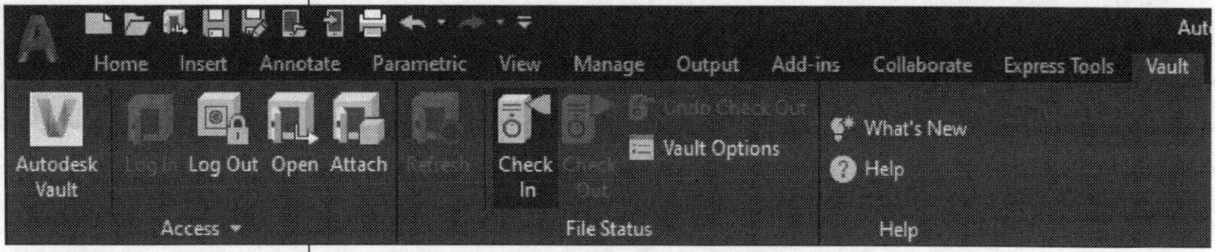

Check In and Check Out Drawings

Once you have completed work on a drawing and want to check the file into the vault, use the Check In command. You check a single drawing file at a time into the vault. If you are checking in a drawing file that contains external references (XREFs), all of the XREF drawings will be checked in at the same time. By adding files that use XREFs to the vault from AutoCAD, Autodesk Vault is able to keep track of the file relationships.

When you open a file from the vault you have the option to check the file out to yourself. The file is copied to the corresponding folder in or below the working folder. To modify a file that is in the vault, the file must first be checked out to you. You always edit the copy of the file in the working folder structure. The files in the vault are the master files and cannot be edited directly.

Check in Files to the Vault

You use the Check In command to store DWG and image files in a vault. The preferred workflow is to check in files from AutoCAD. The following procedure describes the methods you can use to check drawing and image files in to the vault.

1. On the ribbon, select the Vault tab and click Check In on the File Status panel.

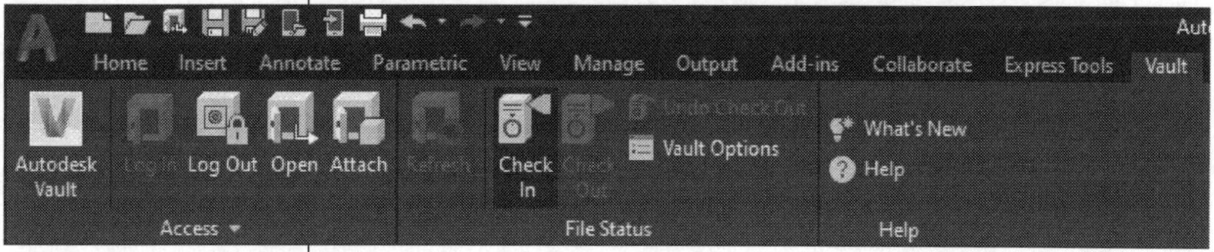

2. On the Vault toolbar, click Check In.

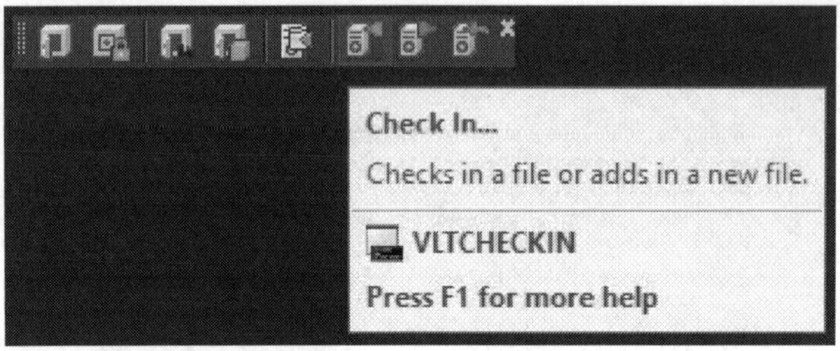

3. In the External References palette, right-click the file and select Check In.

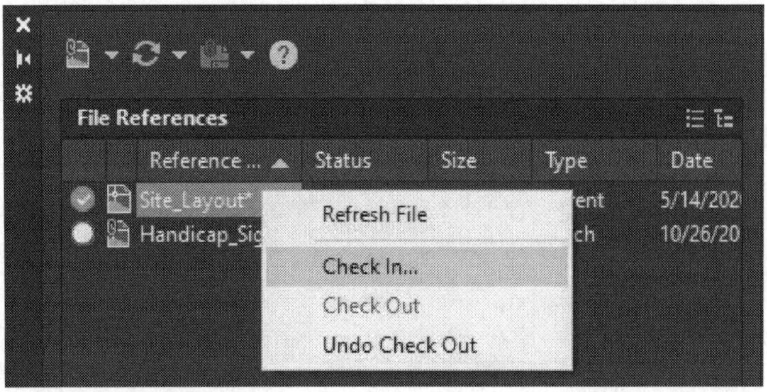

4. On the command line, enter **vault** or **vltcheckin**.

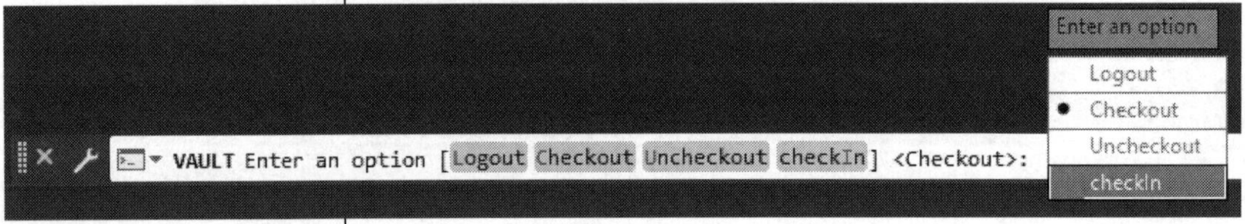

Check In

The Check In dialog box is used to control how the files are checked in.

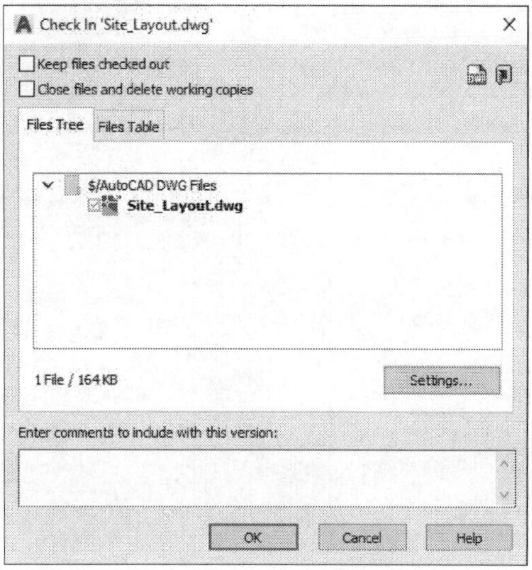

Check in Files Not in Working Folder

If the file you check in to the vault is not in the working folder or its subfolders, the Select Vault Location dialog box opens. You select the vault location for the drawing file in this dialog box.

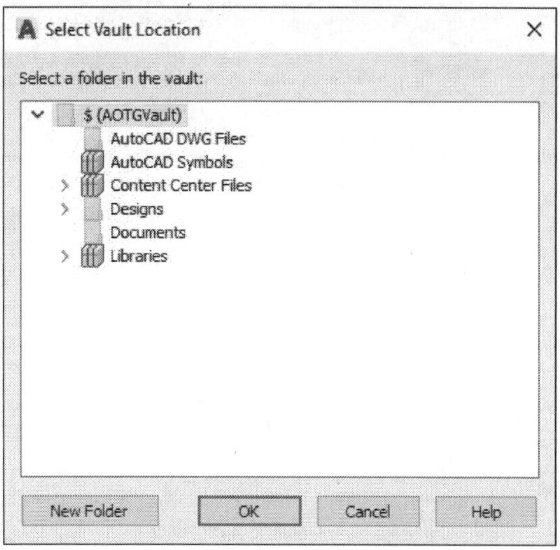

The Select Vault Location dialog box is always displayed if you do not set a working folder from Autodesk Vault.

When you next open this file from the vault, it is copied to the working folder structure.

Definition of Settings Dialog Box

The Settings buttons control organization of the files to be added to the vault and the visualization file options for each file.

Settings Options

The Settings dialog box has the following options.

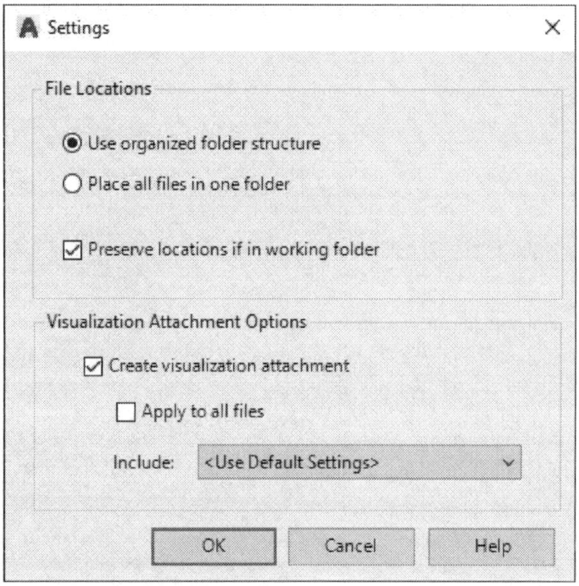

Setting	Description
File Locations - Use organized folder structure	The root folder is the top-level folder in a hierarchical folder tree. The folder structure is maintained for all folders that are at the same level or beneath the host file.
File Locations – Place all files in one folder	All XREFs and dependent files are flattened so that they exist at the same level as the host. All the files are located under the vault folder.
File Locations – Preserve locations if in working folder	Maintains the file structure of files being checked in from the local working folder. This is the preferred workflow.

Visualization Attachment Options – Create Visualization attachment	Creates and attaches a DWF™ or DWFx file for each drawing file being checked in.
Visualization Attachment Options – Apply to all files	Creates a visualization attachment for all files being checked in. This option must be toggled on to create DWF or DWFx files for external reference drawings.
Visualization Attachment Options - Include	Indicates which of the following tabs to include in the visualization attachment: Model Tab Only Layout Tabs Only Model and Layout Tabs <Use Default Settings> to use the settings specified on the Publish Options dialog in Autodesk Vault.

Current Visualization Settings

The Check In dialog box displays the current settings of the visualization Attachment options.

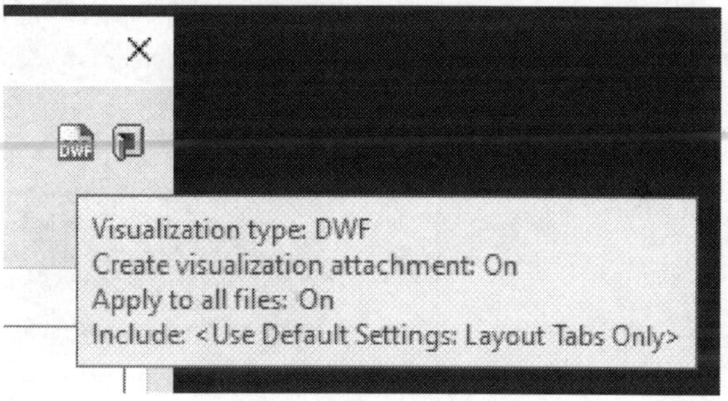

Check Out Files from the Vault

You can use the Check Out command to check out a file you have opened from your working folder if the file is currently checked in to the vault. You must check out a drawing from the vault before it can be edited. The following table outlines the methods you can use to check out a file from the vault.

1. On the ribbon, select the Vault tab and click Check Out on the File Status panel.

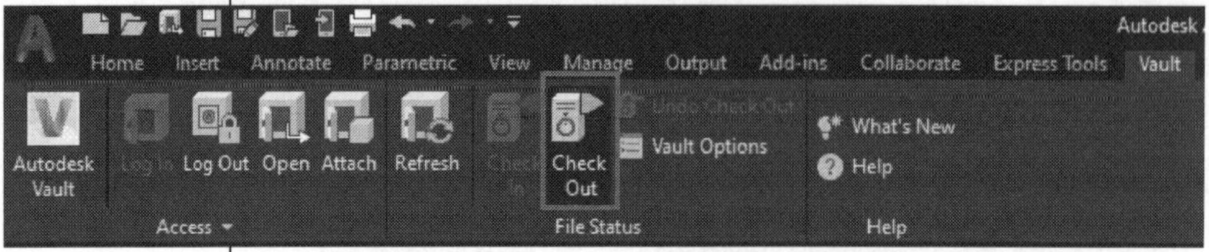

2. On the Vault toolbar, click Check Out.

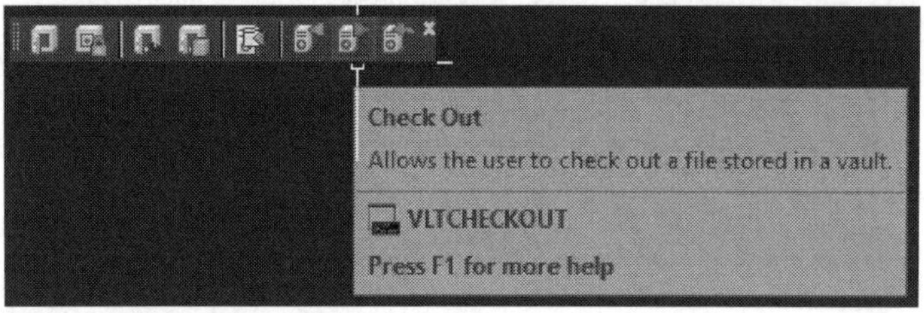

3. In the External References palette, right-click the file. Click Check Out.

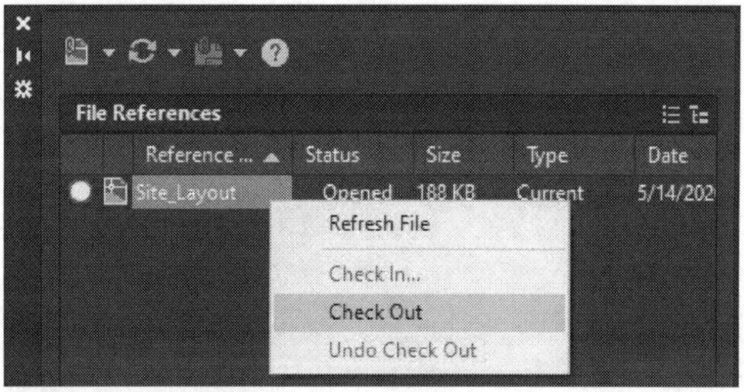

4. On the command line, enter **vault** or **vltcheckout**.

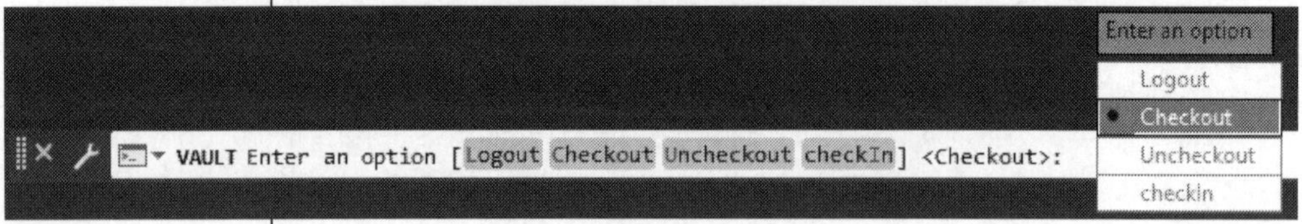

Open from Vault

You use Open from Vault to copy a file from the vault to your working folder and open the local copy. By default, the file is not checked out to you. Optionally, you can check out the local copy during the open process.

Opening a File from the Vault

Use any of the following commands to open a file from the vault.

1. On the ribbon, select the Vault tab and click Open on the Access panel.

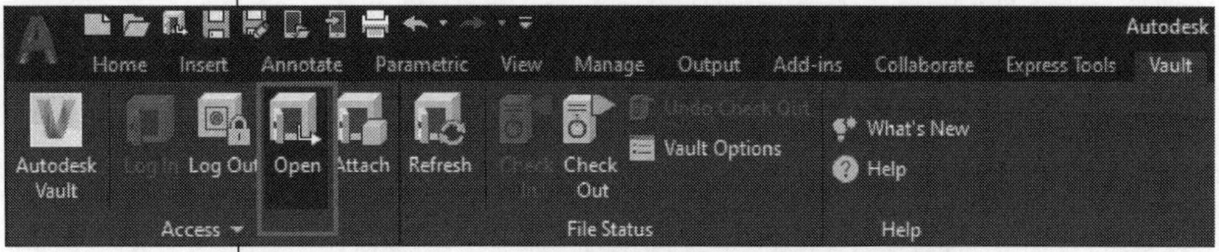

2. On the Vault toolbar, click Open from Vault.

3. On the command line, enter **vltopen**.

Open File Options

In the Select File dialog box, you can select to check out the file, check out the file and any external references, or open the file without checking it out.

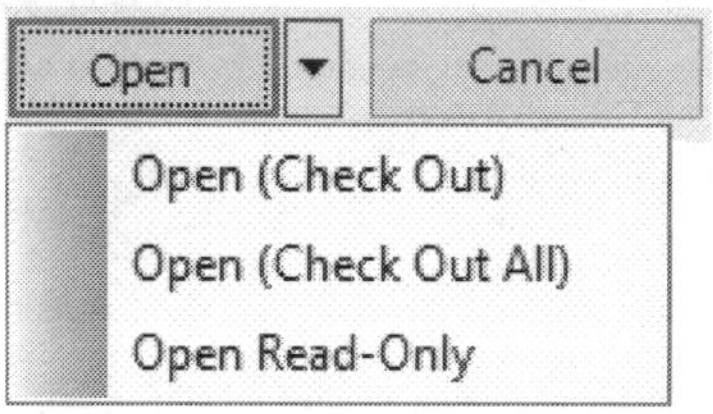

If you click Open without selecting one of the options, you are prompted for the check out behavior.

Attach from Vault

If a file is saved in the vault, you can attach it to an open AutoCAD file by using the Attach from Vault command. This works the same as the AutoCAD DWG Reference when you are working with external references, except that Attach from Vault searches the vault for files rather than searching your local drives.

Attaching a File from the Vault

Use any of the following methods to attach a file from the vault.

1. On the ribbon, select the Vault tab and click Attach on the Access panel.

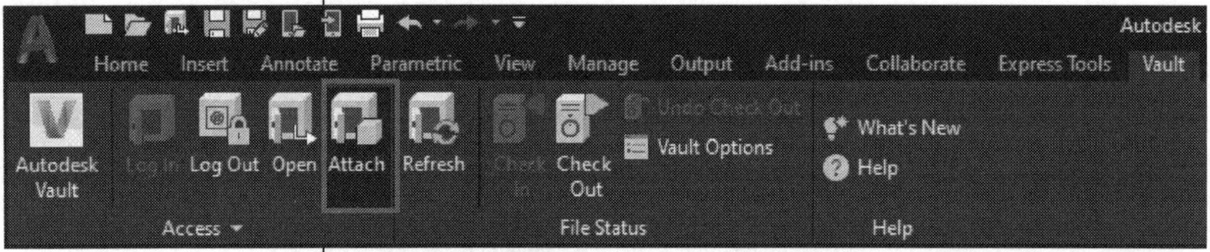

2. On the Vault toolbar, click Attach from Vault.

3. In the External References palette, select Attach from Vault from the list.

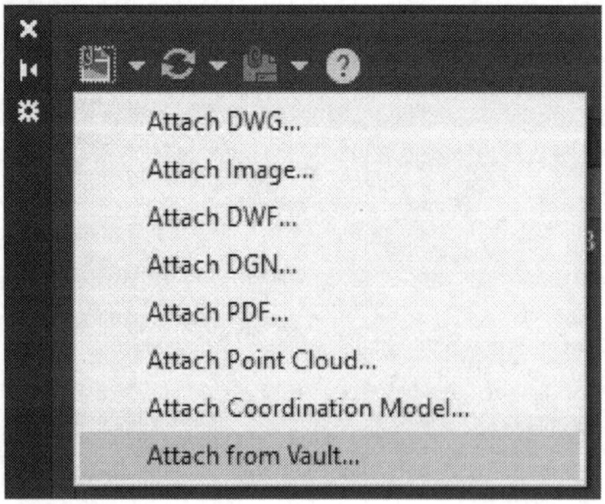

4. In the External References palette, right-click in the File References background. Click Attach from Vault.

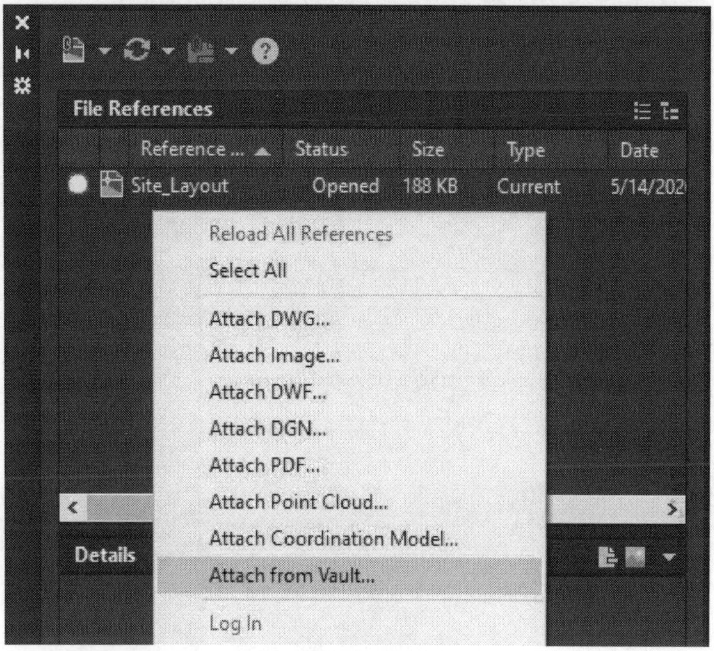

5. On the command line, enter **vltattach**.

If the file is a library file, the file is copied to your working folder in read-only format. For example, in the following image, Attach from Vault was used to attach the Handicap_Sign drawing.

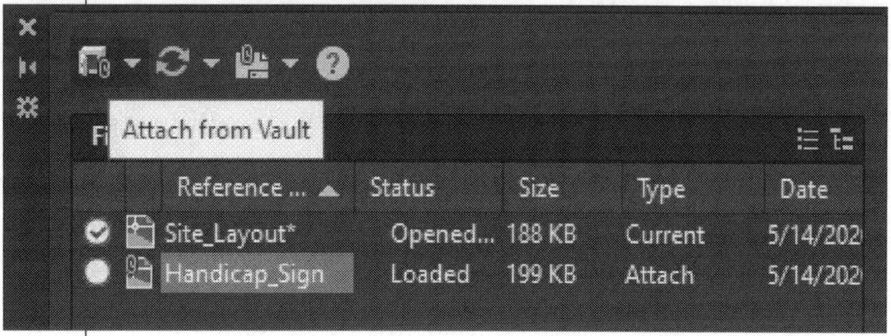

Practice 4b

Check Files In and Out of the Vault

In this practice, you check a drawing in to a vault library and a standard vault folder. You then attach a library drawing from the vault to an existing drawing and check in the combined file.

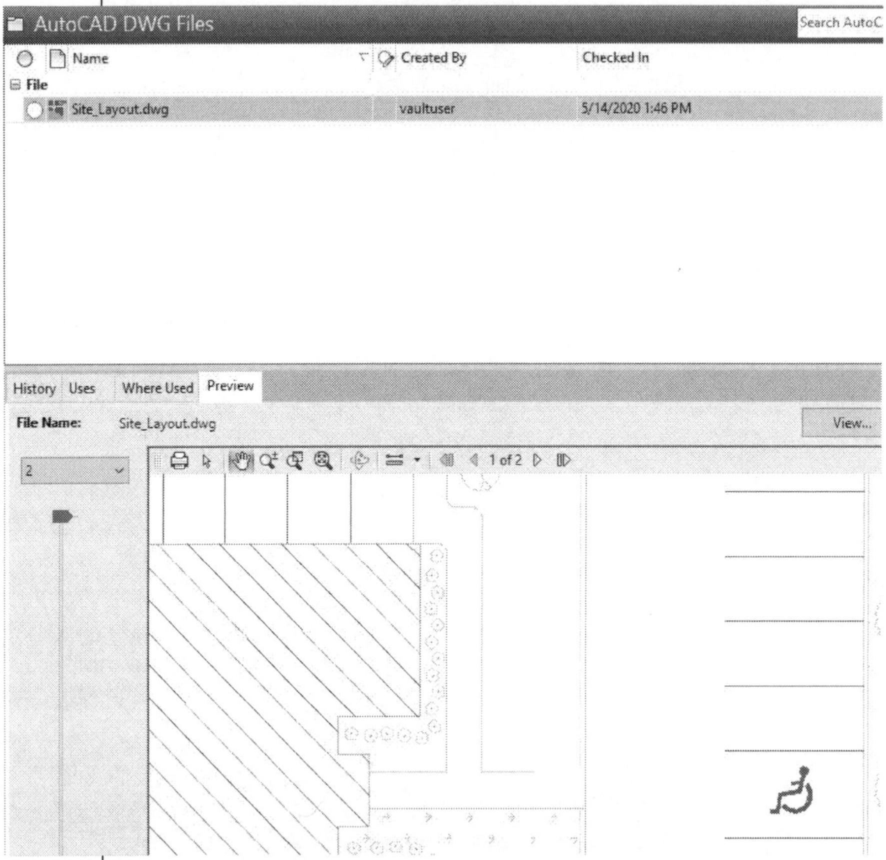

The completed practice

Task 1 - Check files into the vault.

1. In AutoCAD, open *C:\AOTGVault\Chapter 4\AutoCAD DWG Files\Site_Layout.dwg*.
2. Save the file.

3. If you are not already logged in to the AOTGVault, log in using the following information:
   - For User Name, enter **vaultuser**.
   - For Password, leave this box empty.
   - For Vault, select AOTGVault
4. On the ribbon, select the Vault tab and click Vault Options on the Access panel.

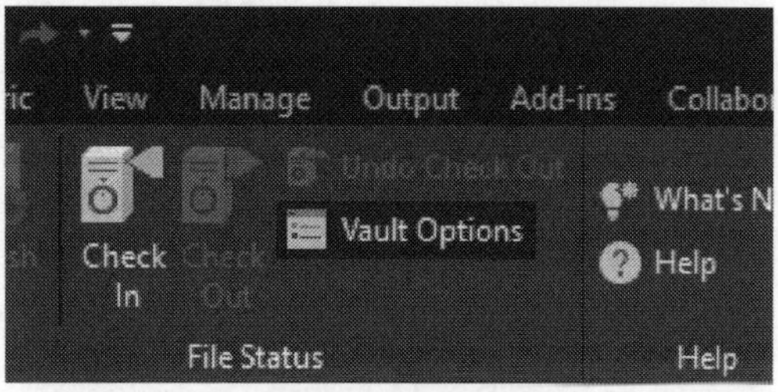

5. In the Options dialog box, ensure the Ignore AutoCAD View Only Changes check box is checked.

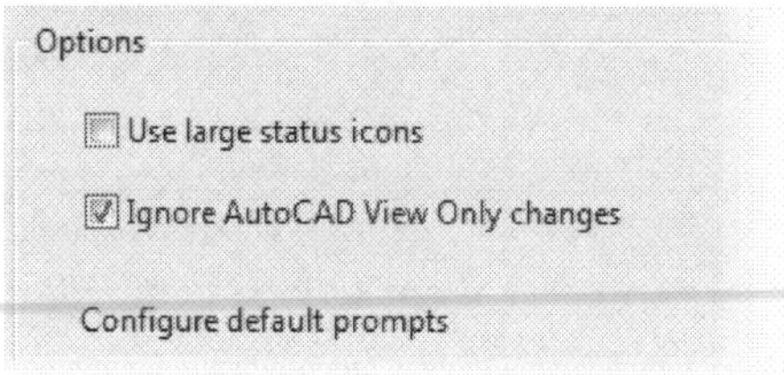

6. Click OK.
7. On the ribbon, select the Vault tab and click Check In on the File Status panel.
8. In the Select Vault Location dialog box, select the AutoCAD DWG Files folder.

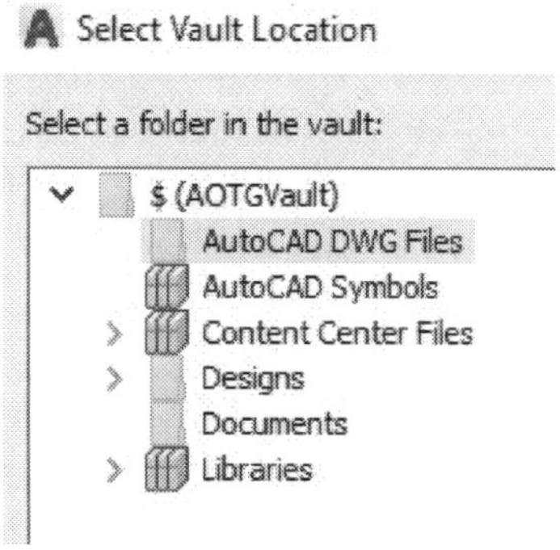

9. Click OK.

10. In the Check In dialog box, click Settings. In the Settings dialog box, ensure that your settings match the following image.

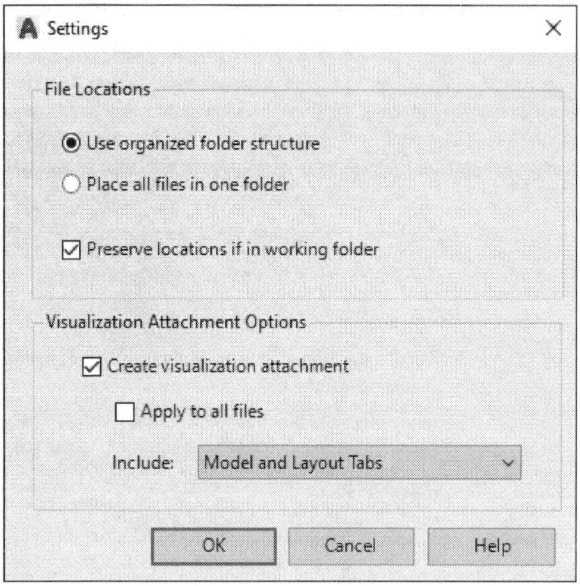

11. Click OK to dismiss the Settings dialog box and OK in the Check In dialog box to close it.

12. Click Yes if you are prompted to save the file. The drawing and visualization files are checked in to the vault.

13. Click OK when you are informed that you are now working on the vaulted copy of the file in the working folder.

    When you check in the drawing to the vault, it is automatically copied to the local working folder.

14. In AutoCAD, open *C:\AOTGVault\Chapter 4\AutoCAD Symbols\Handicap_Sign.dwg*.

15. Save the file.

16. On the Vault toolbar, click Check In.

17. In the Select Vault Location dialog box, select the AutoCAD DWG Files folder. Click OK.

18. In the Check In dialog box, click OK. Click Yes if you are prompted to save the file and click OK to dismiss the Vault Add-in message about the file now being in the working folder.

19. Close Site_Layout.dwg and Handicap_Sign.dwg.

Task 2 - Check files out of the vault.

1. In Autodesk Vault, click Refresh. Click the AutoCAD DWG Files folder.
2. Drag Handicap_Sign.dwg into the AutoCAD Symbols library folder.
3. Click the AutoCAD Symbols folder and verify that the file is in the folder.
4. In AutoCAD, on the Quick Access toolbar, click Open from the vault.

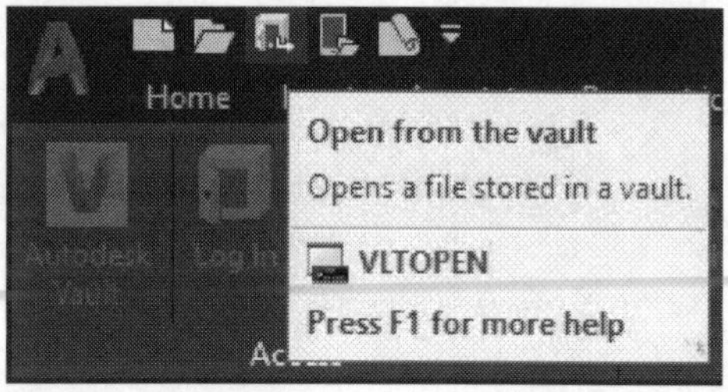

5. In the AutoCAD DWG Files folder, select Site_Layout.dwg. Click Open.
6. Click Yes to check out the file.

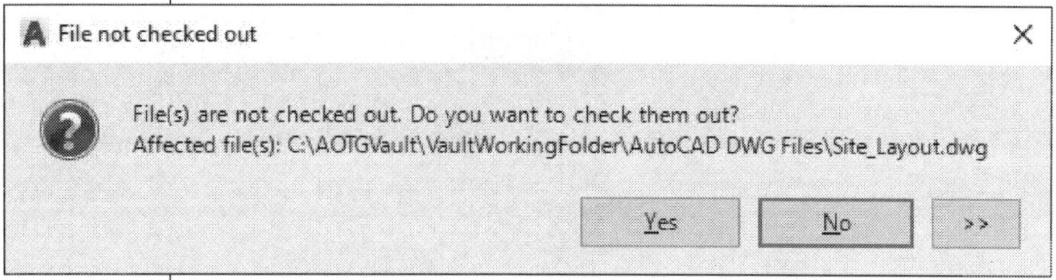

7. On the ribbon, select the Vault tab and click Attach on the Access panel.
8. Browse to the AutoCAD Symbols folder, select Handicap_Sign.dwg, and click Open.

9. For the insertion point, select Specify On-screen. Click OK.
10. Place the symbol in the larger parking space located in the lower-right corner of the drawing.

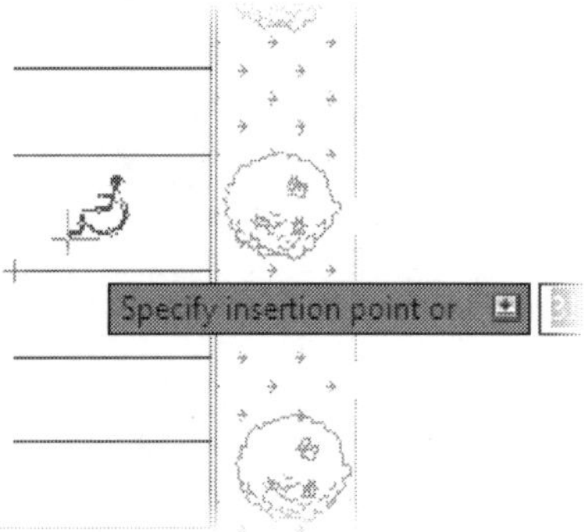

11. Save the file.
12. On the ribbon, select the View tab and click External References Palette on the Palettes panel.

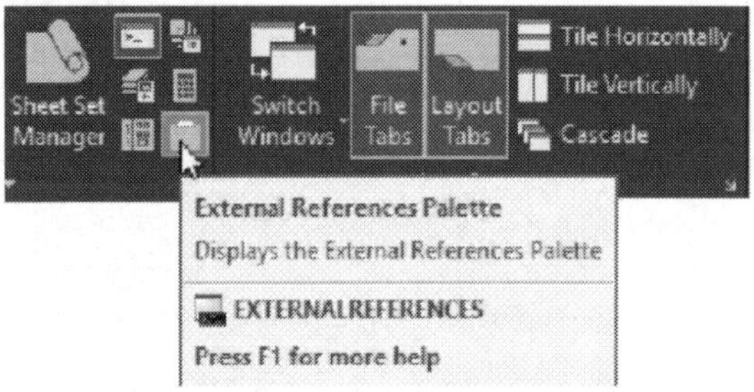

13. Move the cursor over the vault status icon to the left of Handicap_Sign. The status of the symbol is displayed as a library file that cannot be edited from inside AutoCAD.

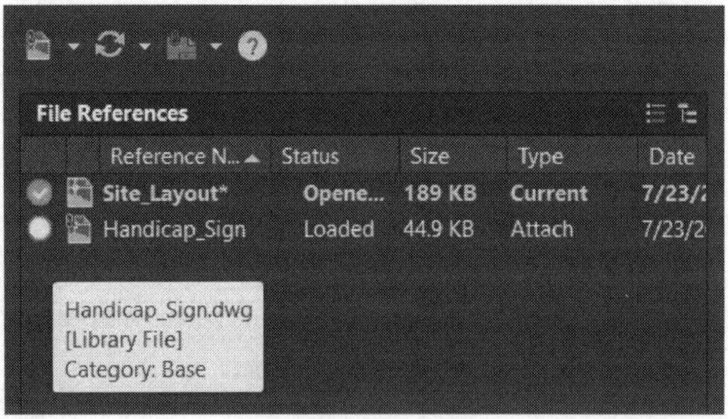

14. Check in Site_Layout.dwg.

15. In Autodesk Vault, select Site_Layout.dwg. Select the Preview tab, select Version 2, and review the visualization file. The handicap sign is displayed in the latest version.

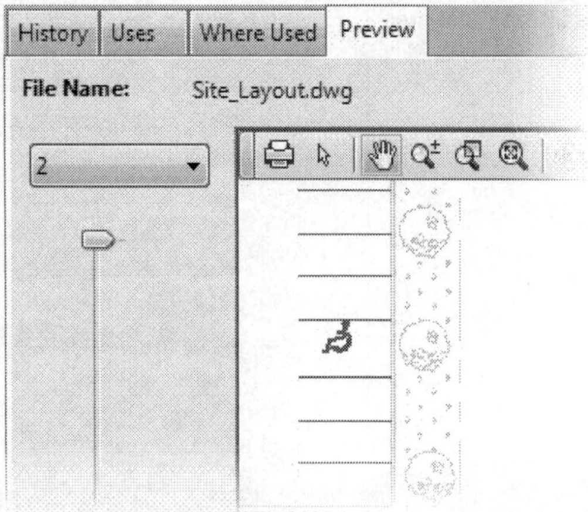

16. Select 1 from the version drop-down list. The version of the drawing without the XREF is displayed in the preview window.

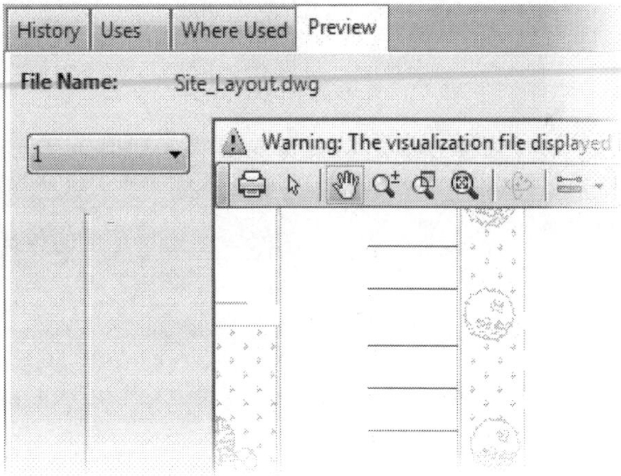

17. Close all AutoCAD files.

4.3 Working with External References in AutoCAD

Overview

You use the External References palette to work with external references in your designs. From the External References palette you can perform all AutoCAD XREF functions and Autodesk Vault commands. This lesson covers the user interface of the External References palette and its commands.

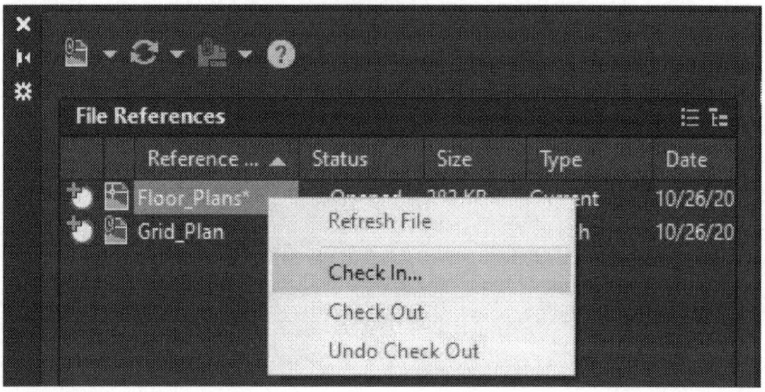

Objectives

After completing this lesson, you will be able to:

- View the external references in tree view or list view and toggle between details and a preview of the referenced file.
- Use the External References palette and Vault.

External References Palette

You can use the External References palette to control external references in AutoCAD and perform vault activities, such as checking files in and out and attaching files from the vault.

The External References palette is an enhanced standard window (ESW) that can be docked and used to help you manage attached files. You can manage references to drawing, image, DWF, DGN, and PDF files from this palette.

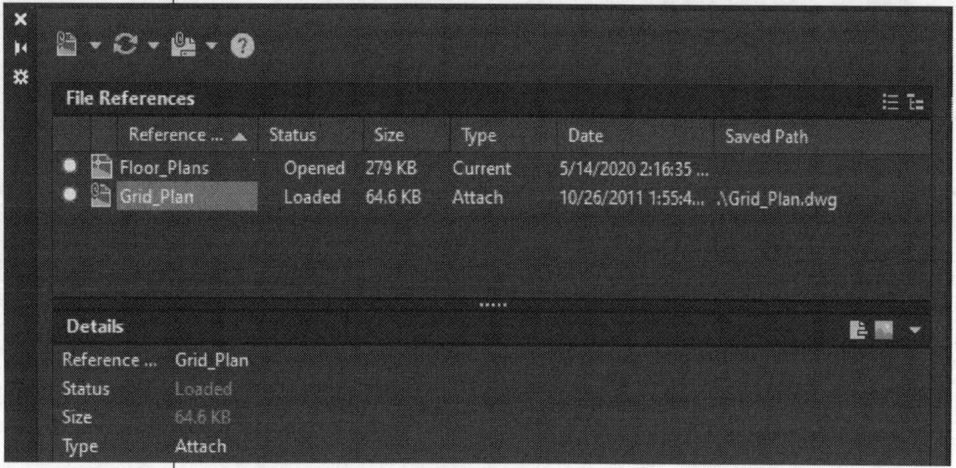

About the XREF Manager and the Vault

To use the External References palette with Vault commands, you must be logged in to the vault. In addition to all of the External References palette functionality that can be found elsewhere in AutoCAD, the Vault status icons are displayed. These icons indicate the status of your local copy of files as compared against the master copy of those same files in the vault.

The File References pane of the External References palette displays the current file, any attached drawings, images, and other reference files. You can view this area in either a list view or a tree view.

List View

The list view displays properties of the drawings used. These include status, size, and type.

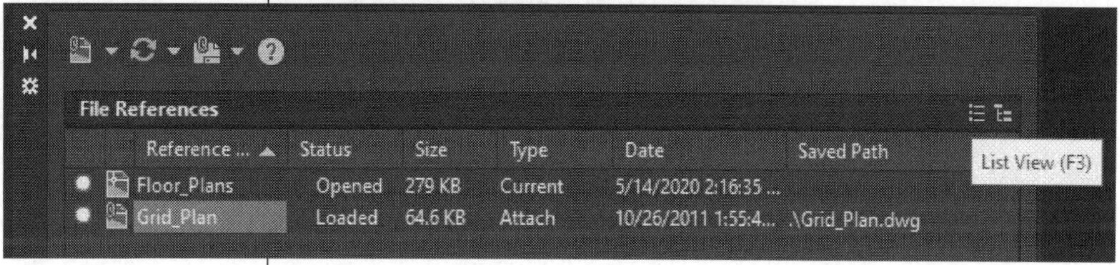

Tree View

The tree view displays the references between the open drawing and its file references.

Details Pane

The details pane of the XREF Manager ESW displays the properties of the file in a structured format. Properties displayed include the file version number. Autodesk Vault generates the version number and indicates the latest saved version of the file.

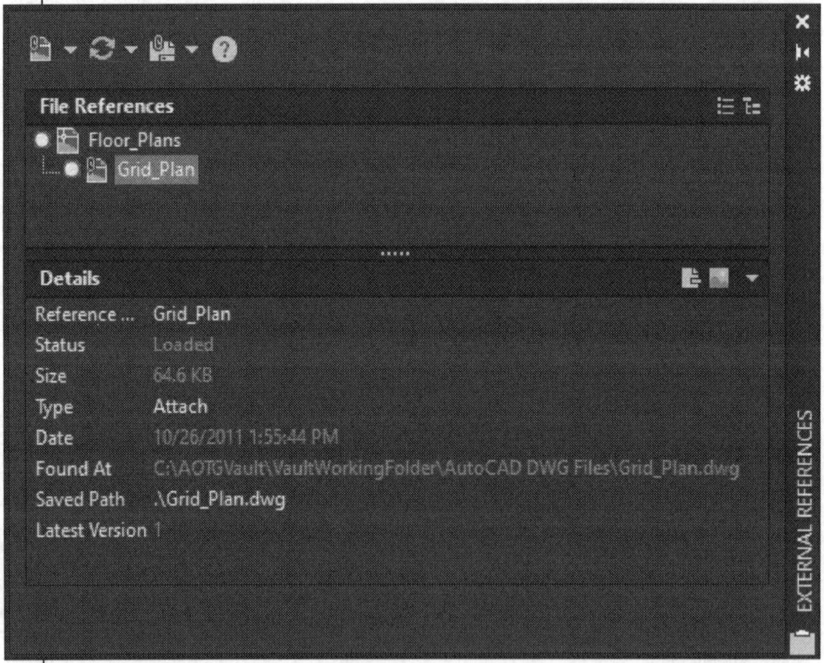

You can toggle the details pane to Preview mode. When you select a file in the File References pane, a preview image of it is displayed.

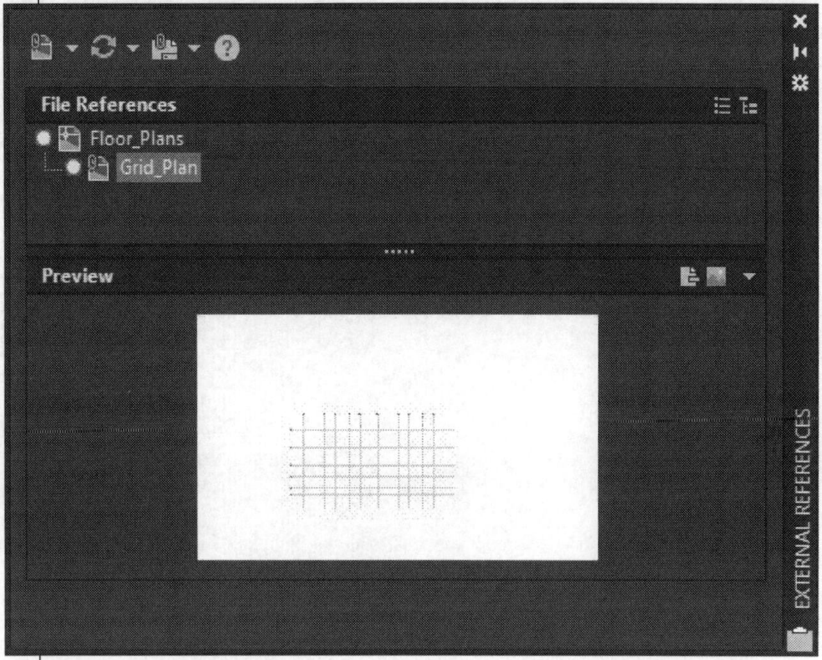

External References Palette and the Vault

The Autodesk Vault add-in enhances the functionality of the External References palette. In addition to the standard functionality of AutoCAD, you can use the External References palette to access many of the Vault commands. Using the External References palette improves your workflow between AutoCAD and the vault.

You can check referenced files in and out of the vault from the External References palette.

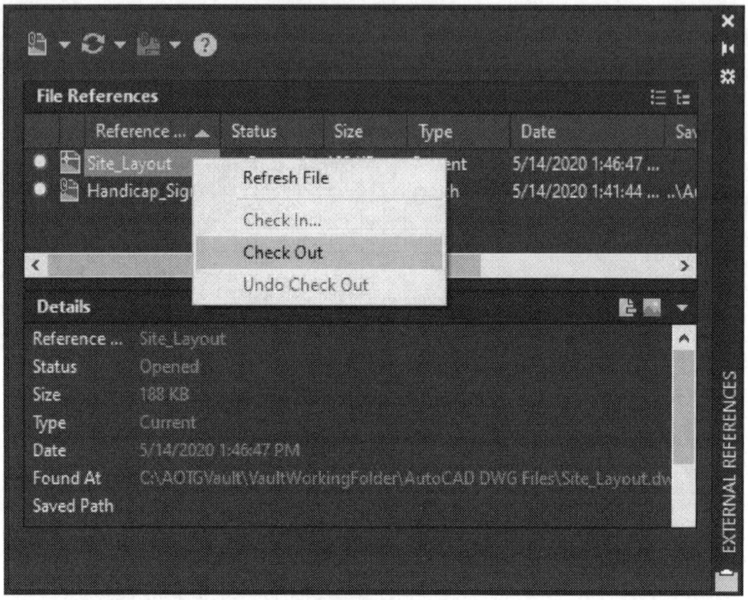

Procedure: Working with XREFs and the Vault

The following steps describe how to work with AutoCAD external references and the vault.

1. In AutoCAD, open the External References palette.

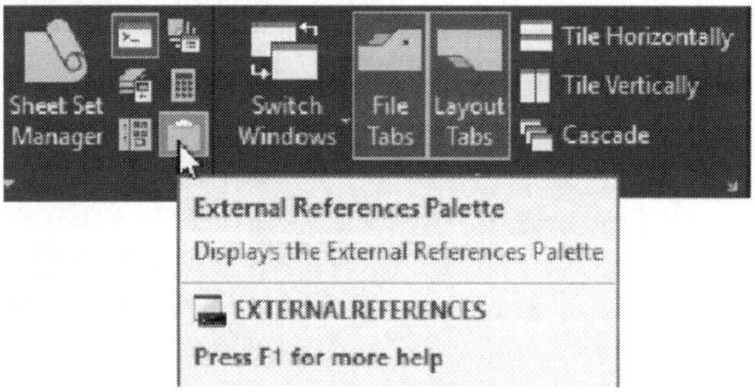

2. If the current drawing is not in the vault, the Vault status icon is displayed with a plus sign.

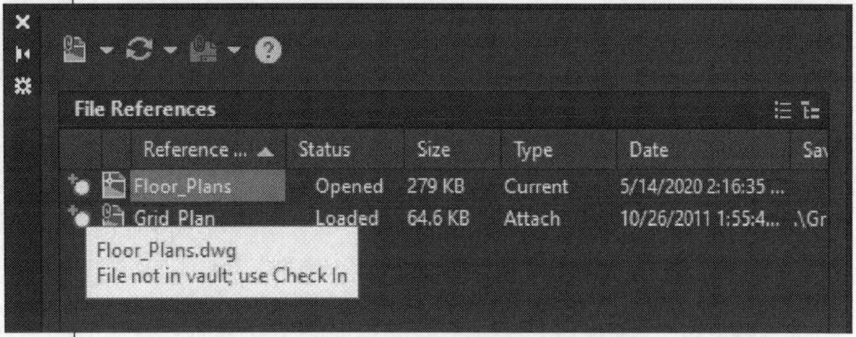

3. When you right-click in the File References background, a different shortcut menu is displayed. In addition to the AutoCAD commands, you have access to the Attach from Vault, Log In, and Log Out commands.

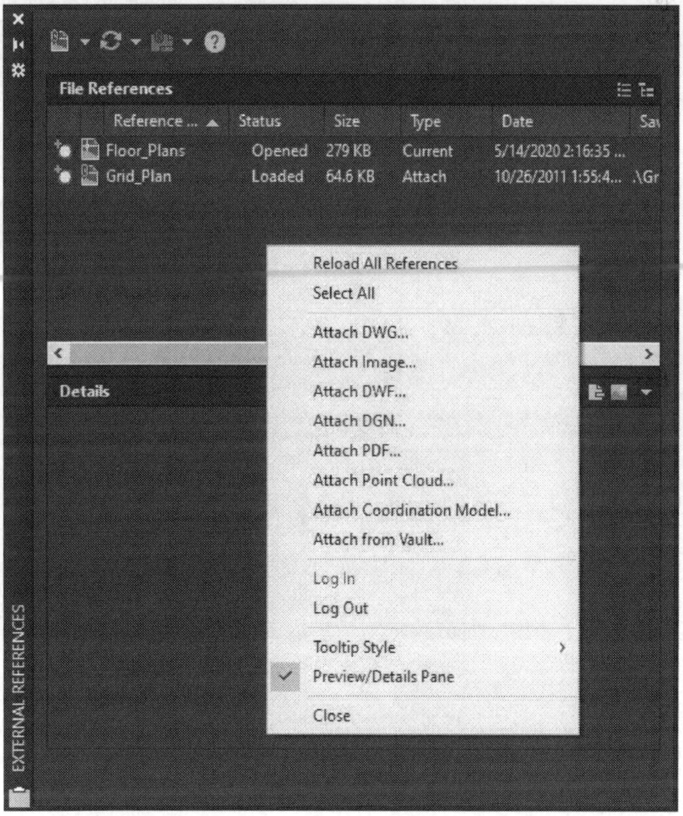

4. You attach another drawing as an XREF to the current file using the Attach DWG option.

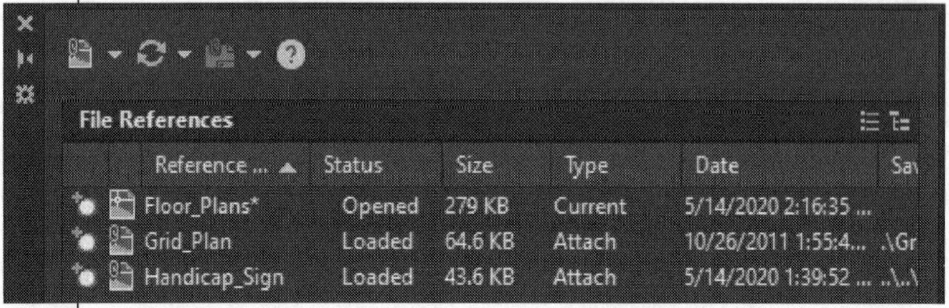

5. When you are ready to check in the files, in the File References list, right-click the host drawing. Select Check In.

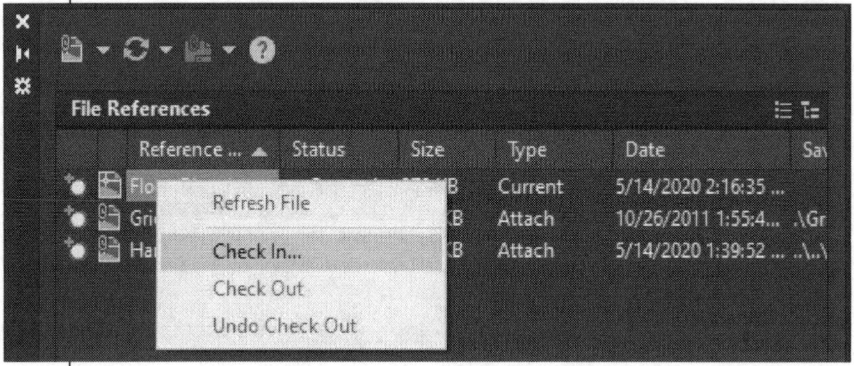

6. Vault recognizes that the Handicap_Sign.dwg and Grid_Plan files are XREF attachments and checks them in with the host file.
7. In the External References palette, the Vault status icons change to Available for Check Out icons.

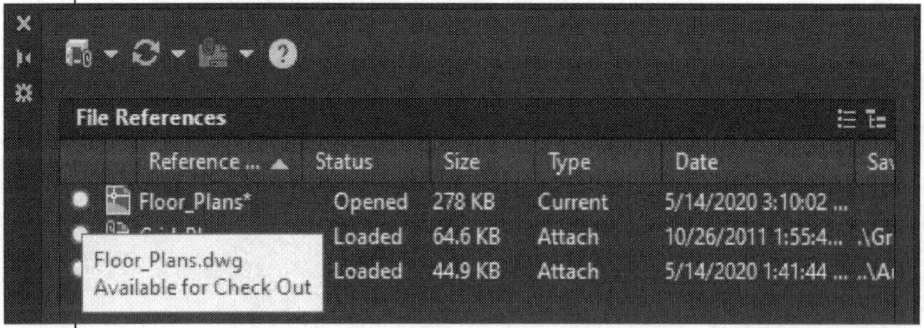

Practice 4c Use the External References Palette

In this practice, you check a drawing into the vault. You then attach a drawing from the vault to an existing drawing and check in the combined file.

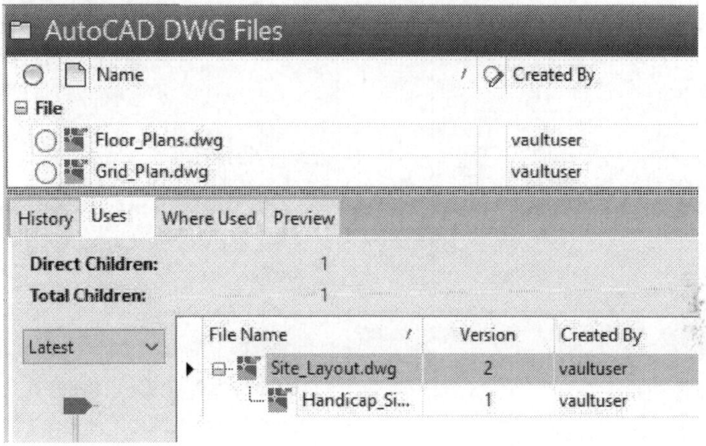

The completed practice

1. In AutoCAD, open *C:\AOTGVault\Chapter4\AutoCAD DWG Files\Floor_Plans.dwg*.
2. In the Proxy Information dialog box, click OK.

   This file is from a project that also uses data from AutoCAD Mechanical.
3. If you are not logged in to the vault, log in using the following information:
   - For User Name, enter **vaultuser**.
   - For Password, leave this box empty.
   - For Vault, select AOTGVault.

4. On the ribbon, select the View tab and click External References Palette on the Palettes panel.

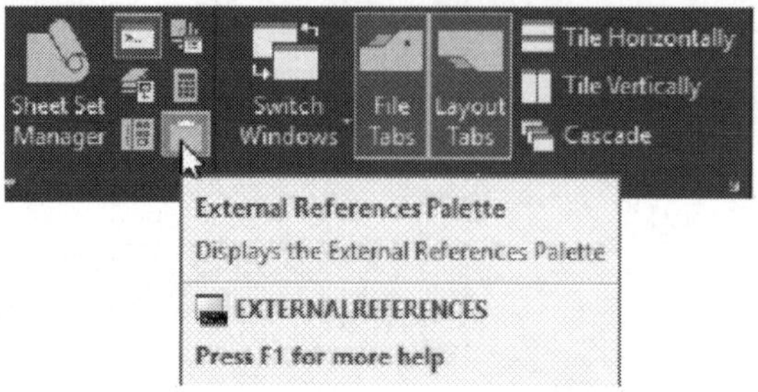

5. In External References, click Attach DWG. Do the following:

   - In the Select Reference File dialog box, select *C:\AOTGVault\Chapter 4\AutoCAD DWG Files\Grid_Plan.dwg*.
   - Click Open.
   - Specify the insertion point as 0,0,0.
   - Specify an X,Y,Z scale of 1.
   - Specify a rotation angle of 0.
   - Click OK.

   The grid plan is displayed in the drawing and added to the External References palette.

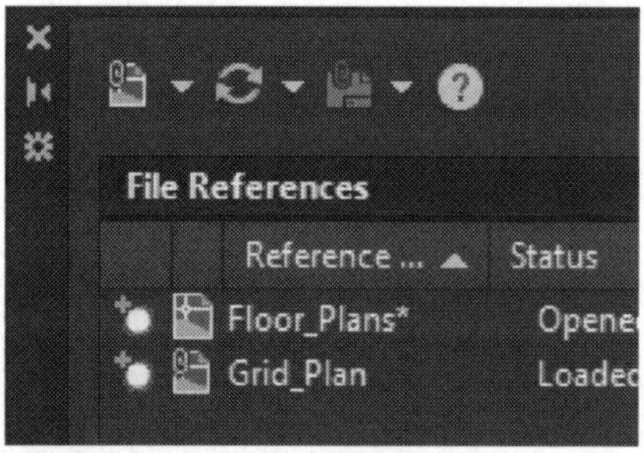

6. Place the cursor over the Vault icons and review the status of the files.

7. Save the file. The asterisk is removed from the filename.

8. On the External References palette, right-click Floor_Plans. Click Check In.

9. In the Select Vault Location dialog box, select the AutoCAD DWG Files folder. Click OK.

10. The Check In dialog box indicates that the attached Grid_Plan drawing is also added to the vault.

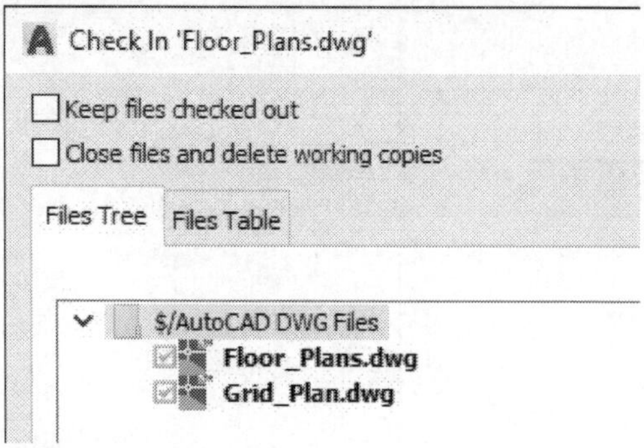

11. Enter **Added to Vault** as a comment and then click OK to close the Check In dialog box.

12. Click Yes if prompted to save the files. Click OK to dismiss the dialog box informing you that the file is now in the working folder.

13. The icons now show the files are checked in.

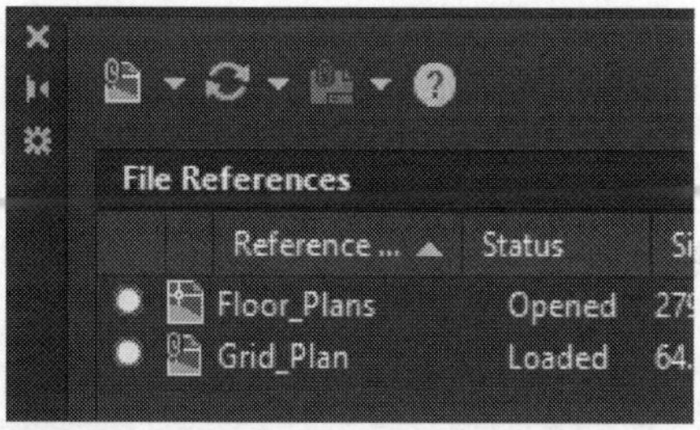

14. In Autodesk Vault, click Refresh. Click the AutoCAD DWG Files folder and review the status of the two files you checked in.

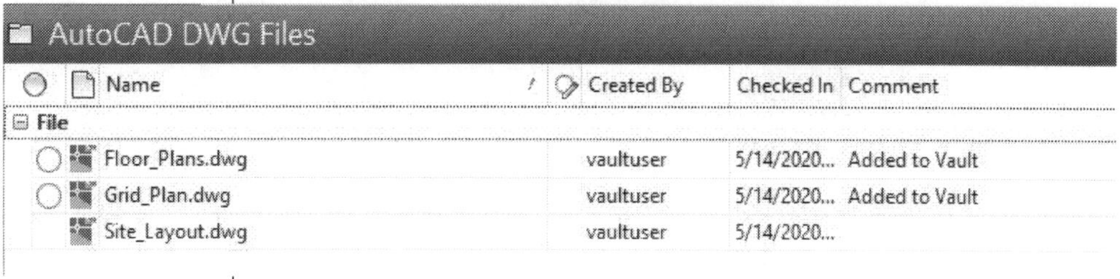

15. Switch to AutoCAD. On the ribbon, select the Vault tab and click Open on the Access panel. Complete the following:

- In the Select File dialog box, navigate to the AutoCAD DWG Files folder.
- Open Grid_Plan.dwg.

16. Click Yes to check out the file.

17. Delete the small horizontal line near the top of the vertical grid line C, which is located second from the right of the drawing.

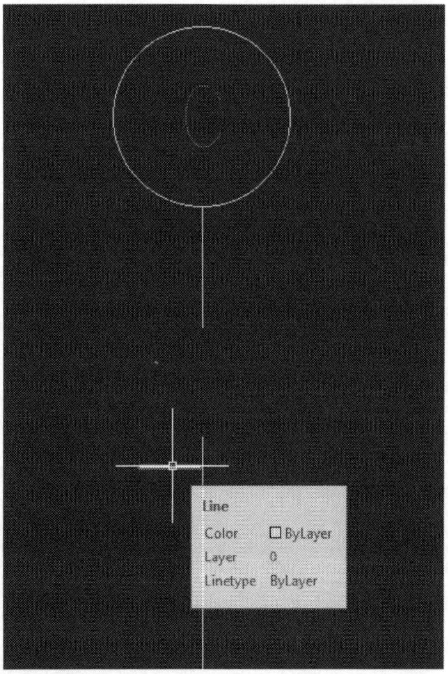

18. Save the file.

19. Check Grid_Plan.dwg in to the vault.

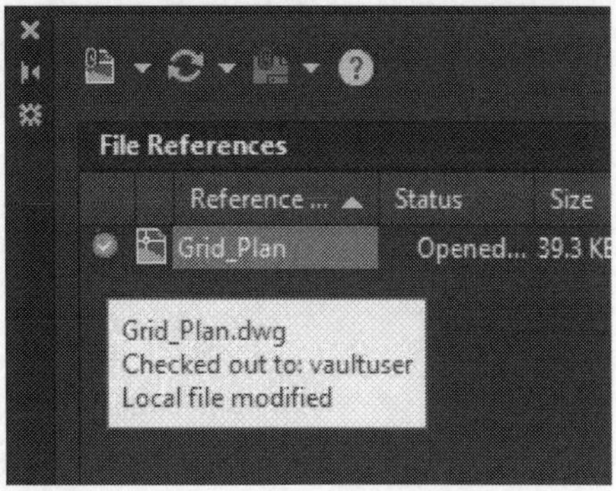

20. Close Grid_Plan.dwg.

21. Switch to the Floor_Plans drawing. On the External References palette toolbar, click Refresh. The modification to the Grid_Plan drawing has changed the Status detail.

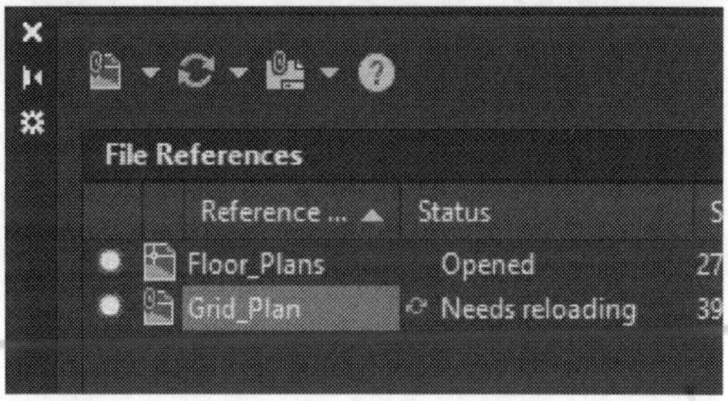

22. In the External References palette, right-click Grid_Plan and select Reload.

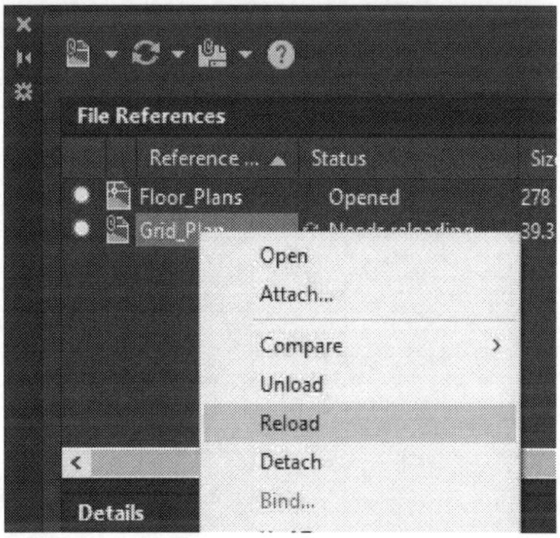

23. Click Yes to check out the Floor_Plans drawing file.

24. Save and Check in the Floor_Plans drawing.

25. Close all AutoCAD files.

26. In Autodesk Vault, click Refresh.

27. Select the Floor_Plans drawing. Select the Uses tab. Note that Version 2 of Floor_Plans.dwg uses Version 2 of Grid_Plan.dwg.

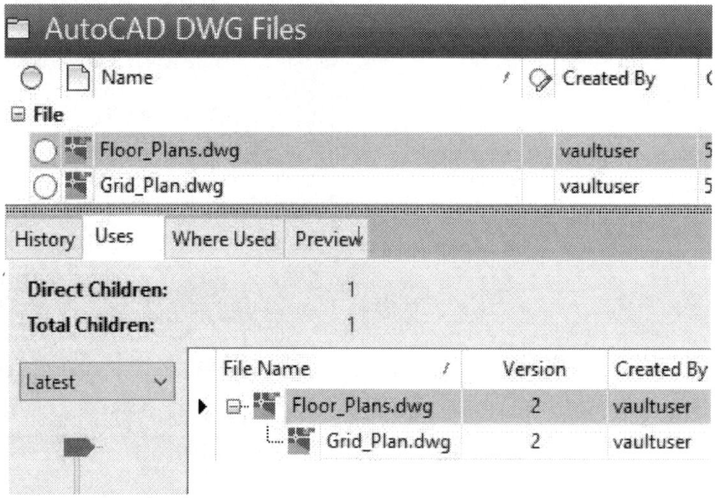

28. Close Autodesk Vault.

4.4 Chapter Summary

Autodesk Vault integrates with AutoCAD and provides an engineering data management system that offers file security, version control, and multiuser support. Logging in to the vault and then checking in and checking out AutoCAD drawings are examples of each of these functions.

Having completed this chapter, you can:

- Open and access the vault from AutoCAD.
- Add AutoCAD drawings to a vault.
- Attach an XREF to a drawing and vault the host drawing and the XREF.

Chapter 5

Working with Vault and AutoCAD Electrical

Autodesk® Vault integrates with AutoCAD® Electrical and provides an engineering data management system that offers file security, version control, and multiuser support.

Learning Objective in This Chapter

- Add AutoCAD Electrical projects to a vault.

5.1 Working with AutoCAD Electrical Files

Overview

The AutoCAD Vault add-in works in AutoCAD®, AutoCAD® Mechanical, AutoCAD® Electrical, and Autodesk® Civil 3D® among others, adding data management tools to the interface. You can add files to a vault and check files in and out. The files can be DWG™ files or images.

The vault add-in for AutoCAD Electrical adds vault status icons and data management tools to the Project Manager tool palette.

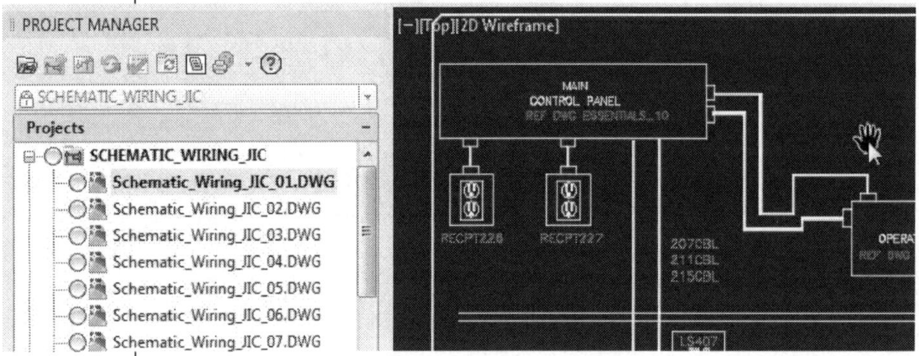

Objectives

After completing this lesson, you will be able to:

- Access Vault from AutoCAD Electrical.
- Use a typical workflow for AutoCAD and Vault.
- Check projects and drawings in to a vault.
- Check projects and drawings out of a vault.
- Open files from a vault.
- Attach files from a vault.

Opening and Accessing

The first step in working with AutoCAD Electrical and Autodesk Vault is to log in to the vault. This lesson covers how to access the vault from AutoCAD Electrical.

You can access Autodesk Vault from AutoCAD Electrical to check entire projects or individual drawings in and out of the vault.

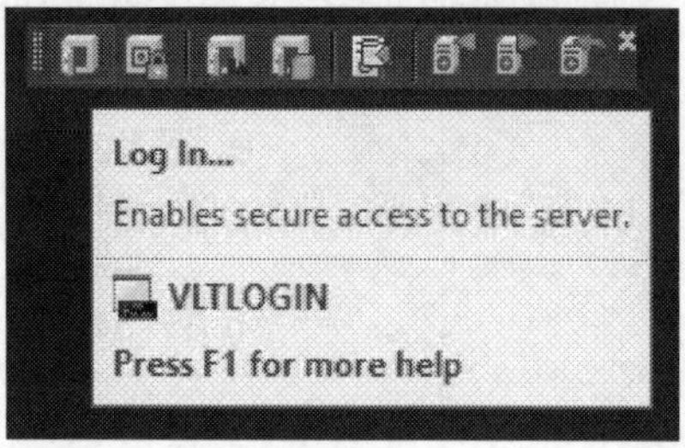

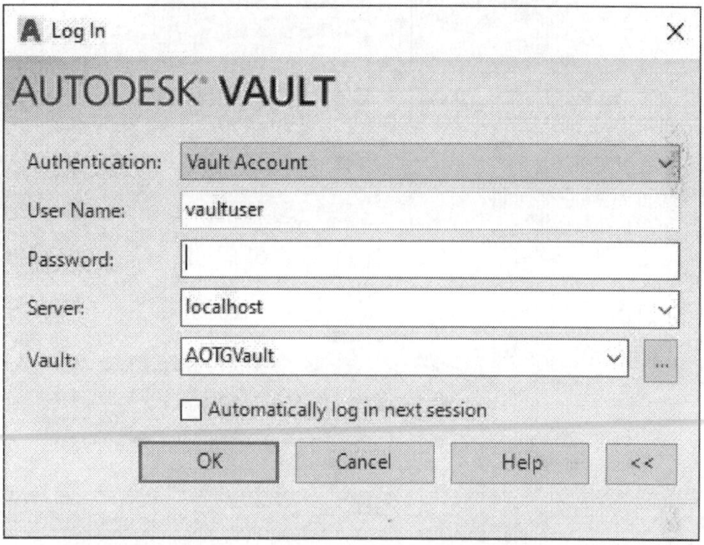

Procedure: Logging in to the Vault

You can access Autodesk Vault from AutoCAD Electrical using one of the following methods: the Vault tab on the ribbon, the Vault toolbar, the command line, or the Vault tray icon.

1. On the ribbon, select the Vault tab and click Log In on the Access panel.

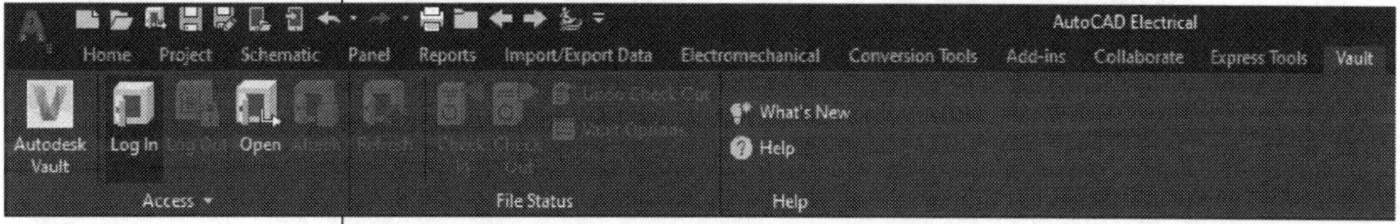

2. Click Log In on the Vault toolbar.

3. On the command line, enter **vault** or **vltlogin**.

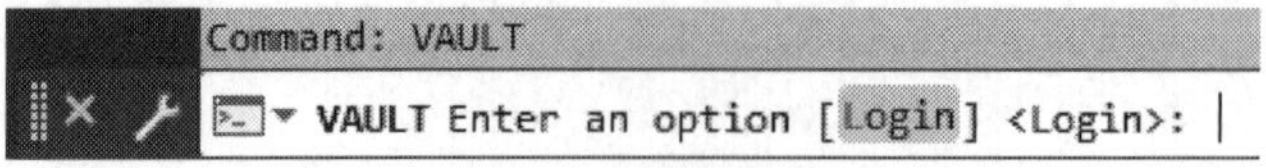

4. Right-click the Vault tray icon, and then select Log In.

Status Bar Tray Icons

When logged in, rest the cursor over the Vault system tray icon to display the user login name, vault, and server.

When you are not logged in to Autodesk Vault, the status bar tray icon is displayed as a locked vault. When you are logged in, the icon is displayed as an open vault door.

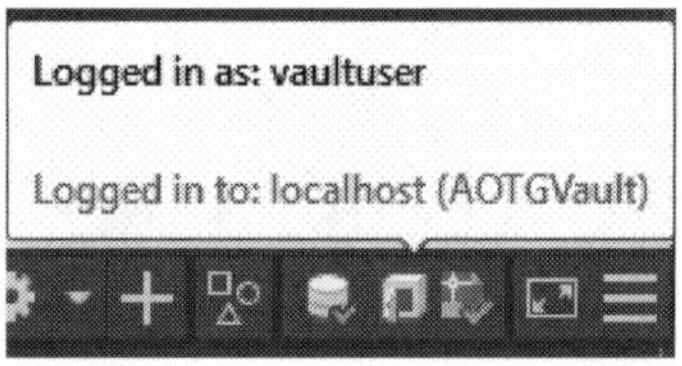

Typical Workflow

In this lesson, you learn about a typical workflow using AutoCAD Electrical and Autodesk Vault.

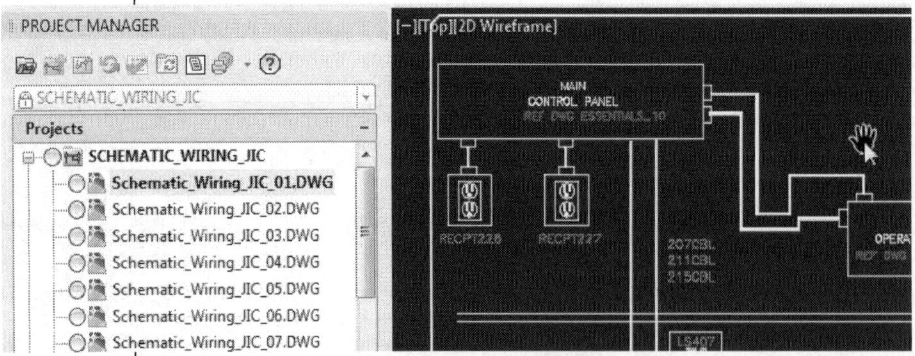

Procedure: Using Autodesk Vault and AutoCAD Electrical

In AutoCAD Electrical, you work on one project at a time. To maintain the relationship between the DWG files defined in the project file (WDP), you must check out the entire project to the working folder. You can then modify one or more files before checking the project back into the vault.

The following steps describe a typical workflow for using Autodesk Vault and AutoCAD Electrical.

1. Log in to Autodesk Vault as an administrator. Click Tools menu>Administration>Vault Settings. In the Vault Settings dialog box, under Working Folder, click Define. Enforce a single working folder for all members of your design team.

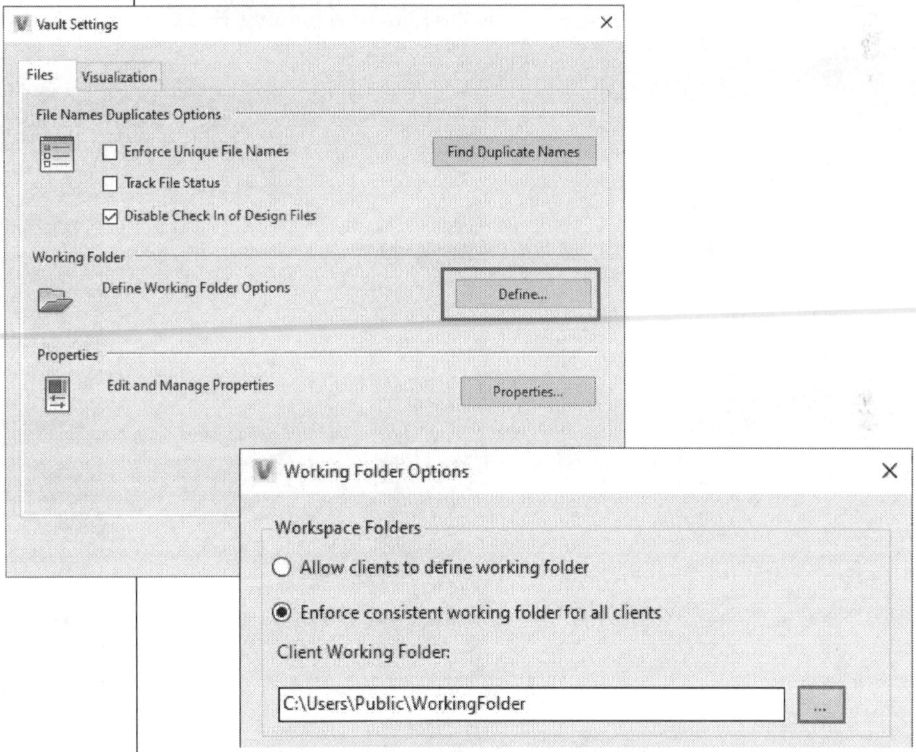

2. In AutoCAD Electrical, log in to the vault.

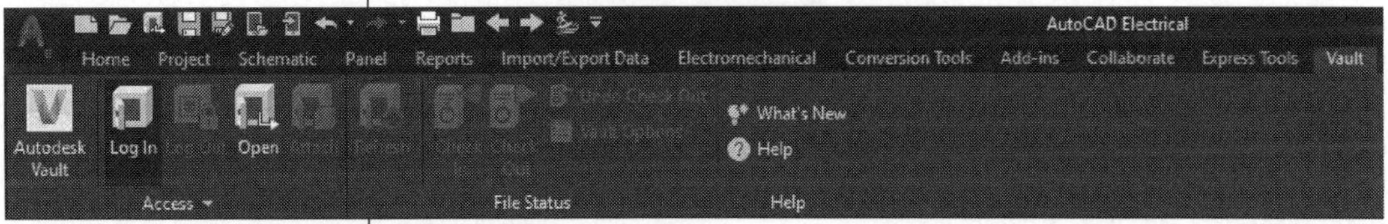

3. From the Project Manager, open the project you want to add to the vault.

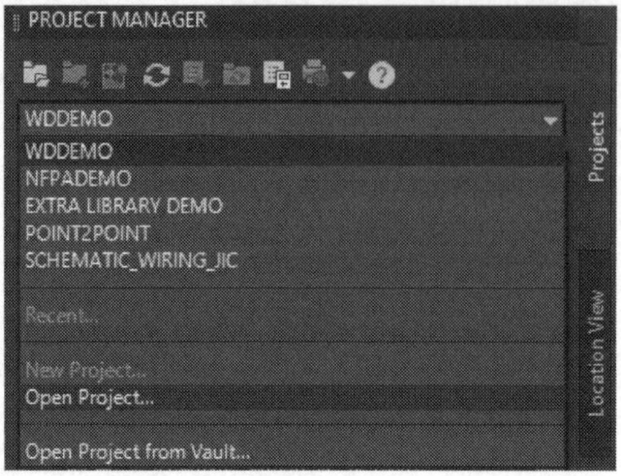

4. In the Project Manager palette, select a project file, and then select the Check In All command to add the project and drawing files to the vault. **Note:** A drawing must be open for this command to be available.

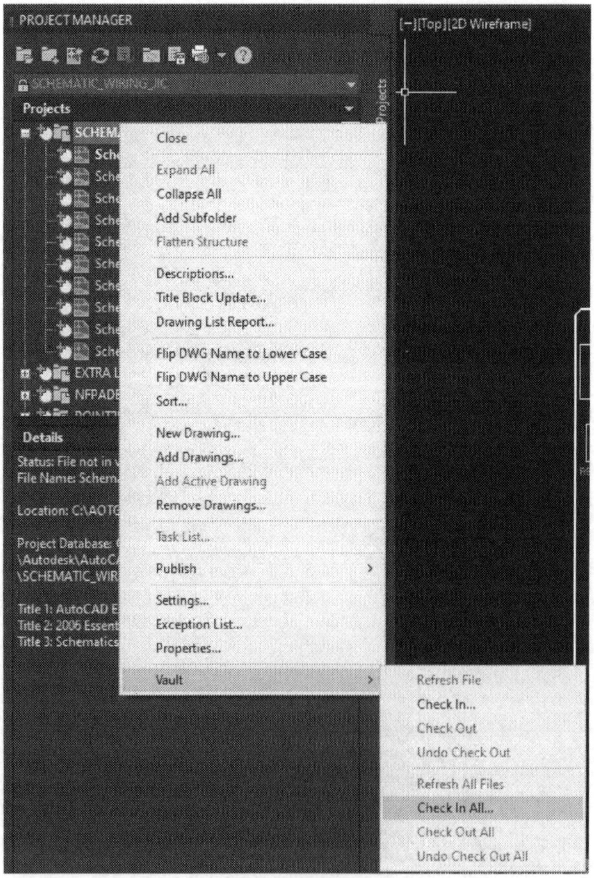

5. In the Check In dialog box, select the Keep Files Checked Out check box. This option adds the files to the vault and then checks them out to you for editing.

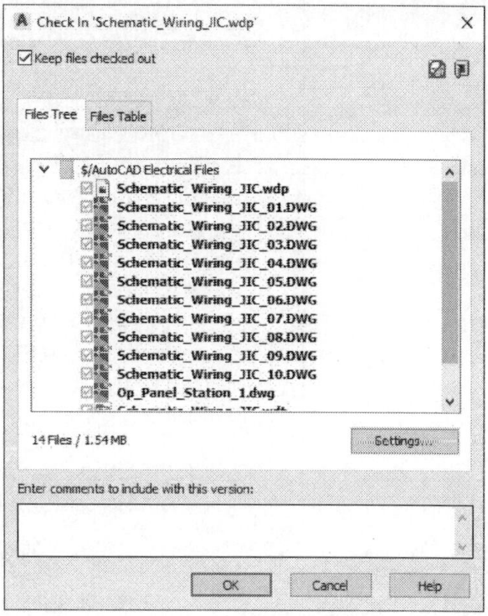

6. Modify the design as required, and then check the modified project back in to the vault by selecting the Check In All command. In the Check In dialog box, clear the Keep Files Checked Out check box to toggle it off. All files are checked in to the vault and are available to be checked out.

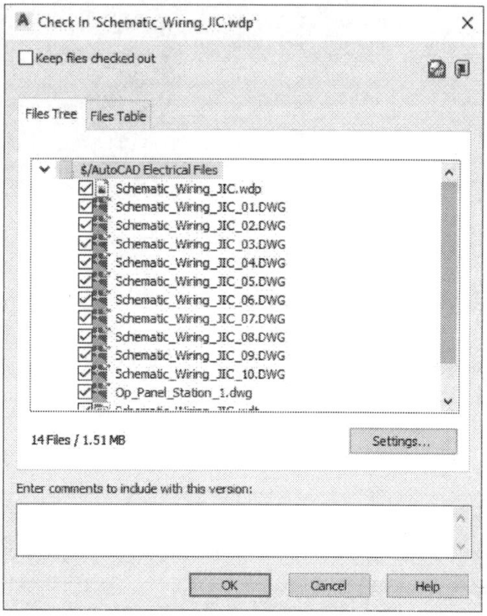

Check In Projects and Drawings

You can check files in and out of Autodesk Vault directly from AutoCAD Electrical. In this lesson, you learn the different ways to check in a project and DWG files from AutoCAD Electrical.

Procedure: Using Check In and Check In All

AutoCAD Electrical is project based. A project is a set of interrelated wiring diagram drawings. An ASCII text file, called the Electrical Project file, lists the AutoCAD drawing filenames that make up the wiring diagram set. You can have as many projects as you want, but only one project can be active at a time. Based on this workflow, you must check in the entire project to maintain the relationship between the DWG files defined in the project file.

Use one of the following methods to check in an individual file to the vault.

1. On the ribbon, select the Vault tab and click Check In on the File status panel.

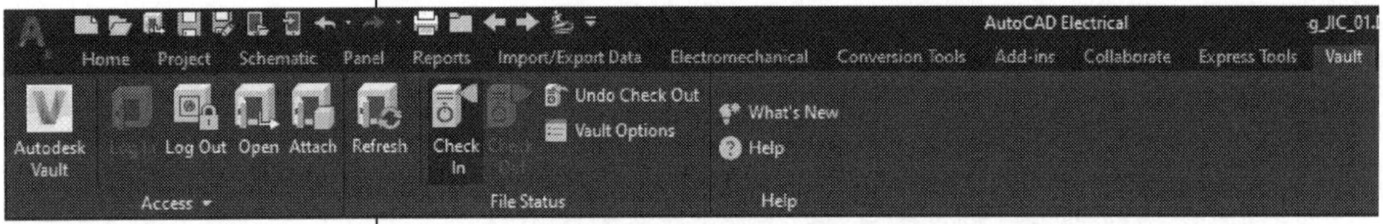

2. On the Vault toolbar, select Check In.

3. In the Project Manager palette, right-click the file and select Check In.

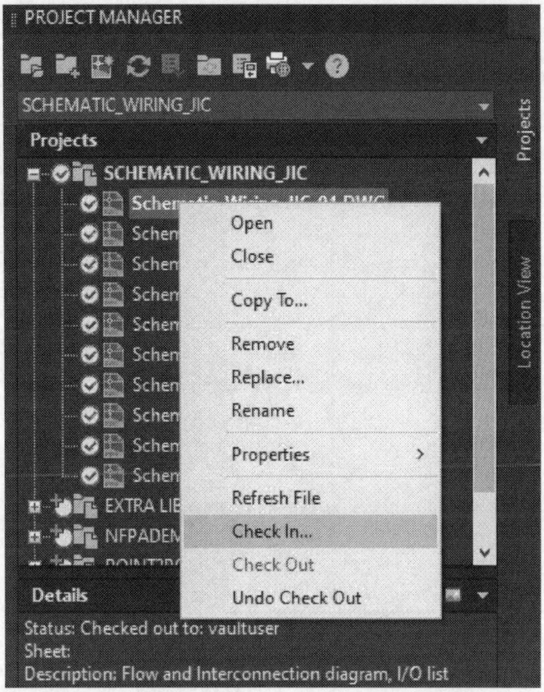

4. On the command line, enter vault or **vltcheckin**.

Use one of the following methods to check in all files in the active project to the vault.

1. In the Project Manager palette, right-click the project. Click Vault>Check In All.

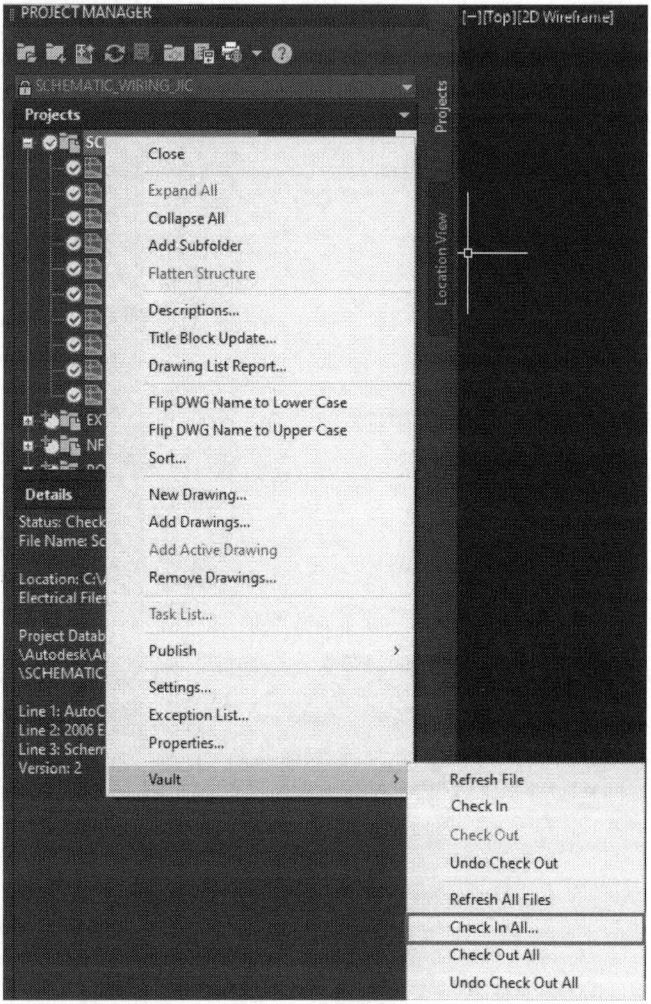

2. On the command line, enter **pchkin**.

Check in Files Not in Working Folder

If the file you check in to the vault is not in the working folder or its subfolders, the Select Vault Location dialog box displays. You select the vault location for the drawing file in this dialog box.

The Select Vault Location dialog box is always displayed if you do not set a working folder from Autodesk Vault.

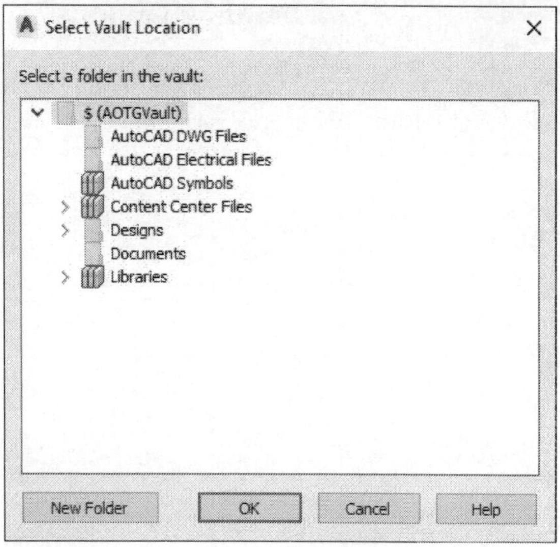

When you next open this file from the vault, it is copied to the working folder structure.

Definition of Settings Dialog Box

The Settings buttons control organization of the files to be added to the vault and the visualization file options for each file.

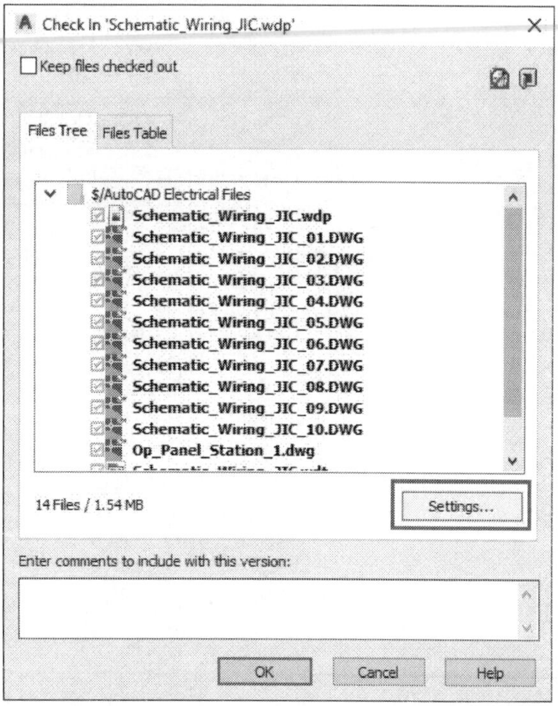

Settings Options

The Settings dialog box has the following Check In options.

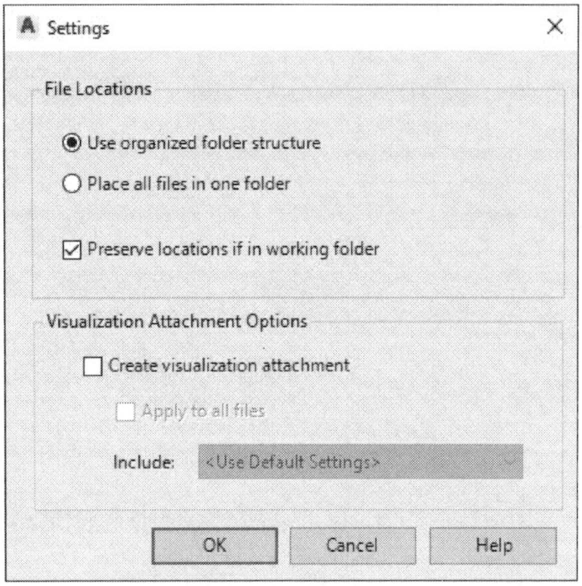

Setting	Description
File Locations - Use organized folder structure	The root folder is the top-level folder in a hierarchical folder tree. The folder structure is maintained for all folders that are at the same level or beneath the host file.
File Locations – Place all files in one folder	All XREFs and dependent files are flattened so that they exist at the same level as the host. All the files are located under the vault folder.
File Locations – Preserve locations if in working folder	Maintains the file structure of files being checked in from the local working folder. This is the preferred workflow.
Visualization Attachment Options – Create visualization attachment	Creates and attaches a DWF™ or DWFx file for each drawing file being checked in.
Visualization Attachment Options – Apply to all files	Creates a visualization attachment for all files being checked in. This option must be toggled on to create DWF or DWFx files for external reference drawings.

Visualization Attachment Options - Include	Indicates which of the following tabs to include in the visualization attachment: Model Tab Only Layout Tabs Only Model and Layout Tabs <Use Default Settings> to use the settings specified on the Publish Options dialog in the Autodesk Vault.

Current Visualization Settings

The Check In dialog box displays the current settings of the visualization Attachment options.

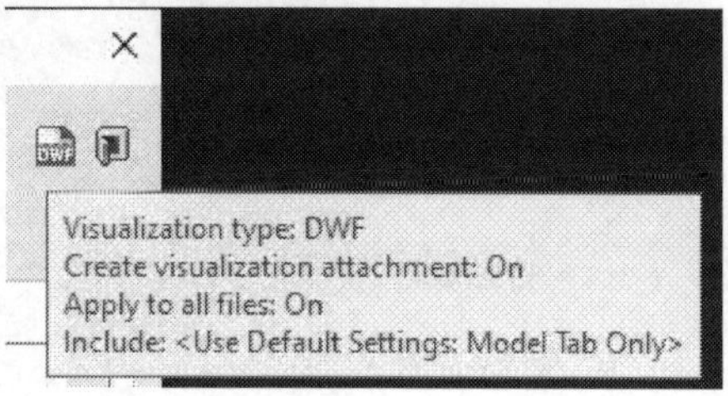

Check Out Projects and Drawings

You can check files in and out of Autodesk Vault directly from AutoCAD Electrical. In this lesson, you learn the different ways to check out a project and DWG files in AutoCAD Electrical.

Check Out Files from the Vault

AutoCAD Electrical is project based. To work on all files in the project, you use the Check Out All command. If you only have to modify a single file in a project, use the Check Out command to open and check out the file.

Use one of the following commands to check out an individual file from the vault.

1. On the ribbon, select the Vault tab and click Check Out on the File Status panel.

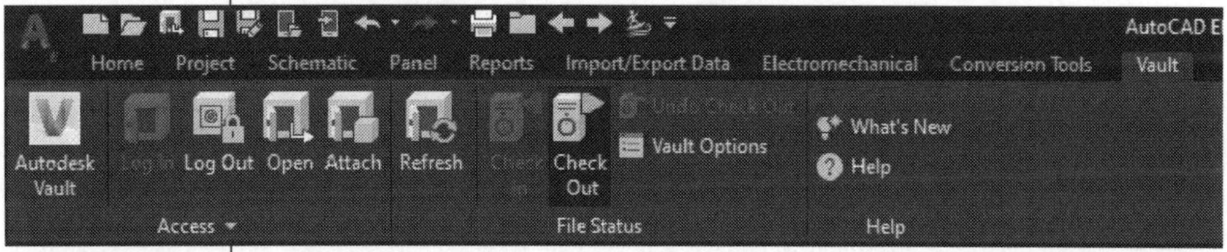

2. On the Vault toolbar, click Check Out.

3. In the Project Manager palette, right-click the file and select Check Out.

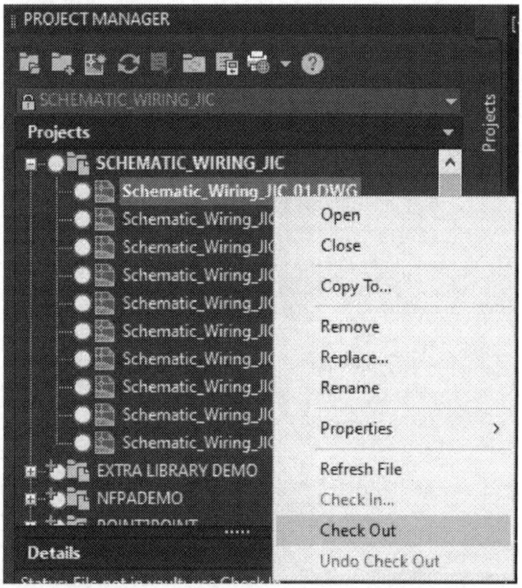

4. On the command line, enter **vault** or **vltcheckout**.

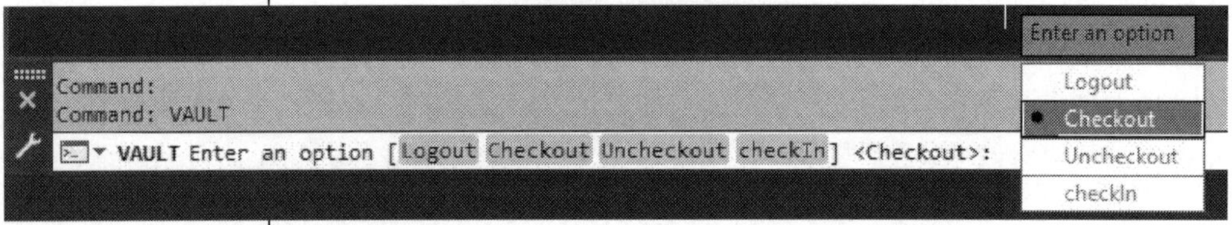

Check Out All Files

Use one of the following commands to check out all files in a project from the vault.

1. In the Project Manager palette, right-click the project. Click Vault>Check Out All.

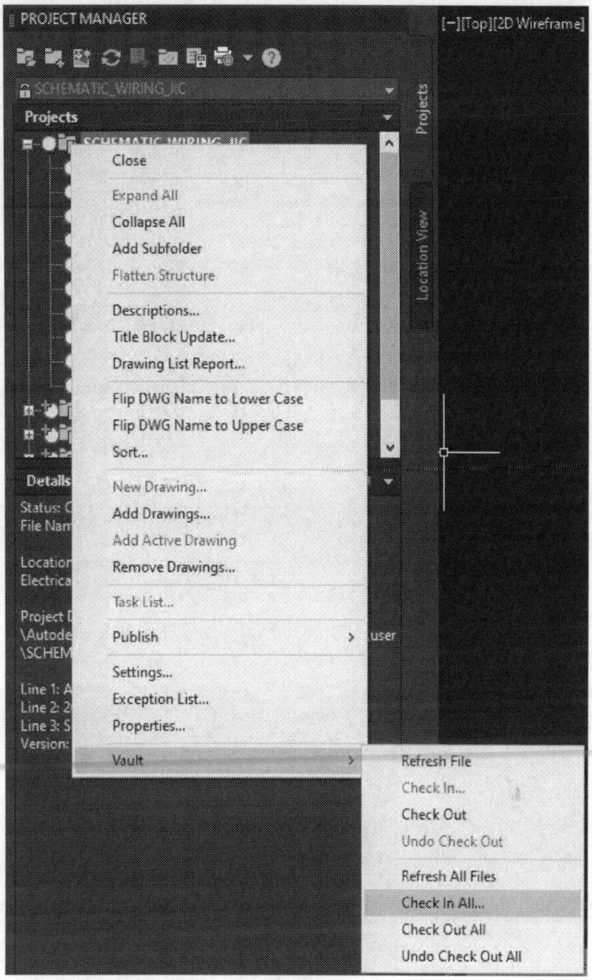

2. On the command line, enter **pchkout**.

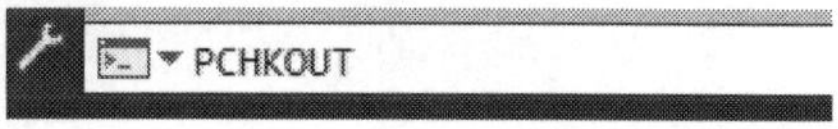

Open from Vault

You can also open files by browsing for them in the vault. If you do not have a copy of a file in the working folder, you can browse for the file in the vault and open it from there. The file in the vault file store is not opened directly. When you open a file from the vault, it is copied to the corresponding working folder and that file is opened. By default, this command opens the file in read-only mode to allow for viewing only. You can optionally check out the file when it is opened.

AutoCAD Electrical also provides an Open Project from Vault command on the Project Manager palette. You can use this command to open and check out the project and all files in the project at the same time.

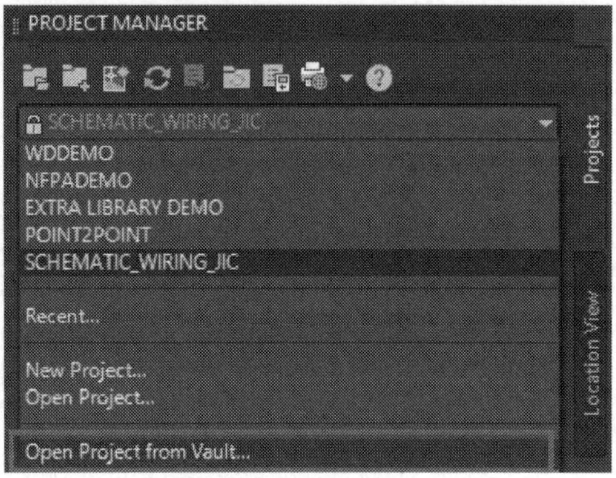

Opening a File from the Vault

Use any of the following commands to open a file from the vault.

1. On the ribbon, select the Vault tab and click Open on the Access panel.

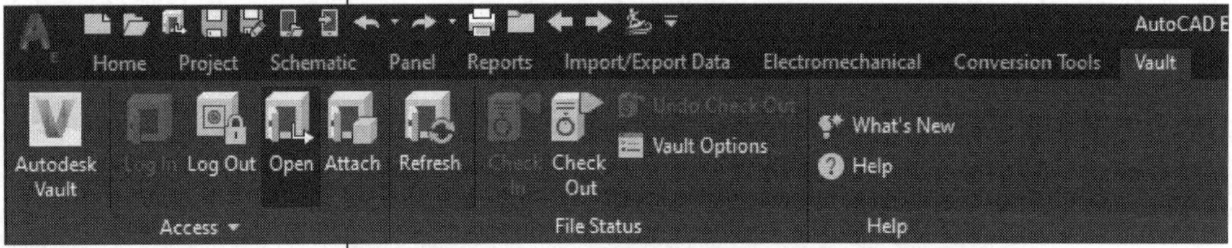

2. On the Vault toolbar, click Open from Vault.

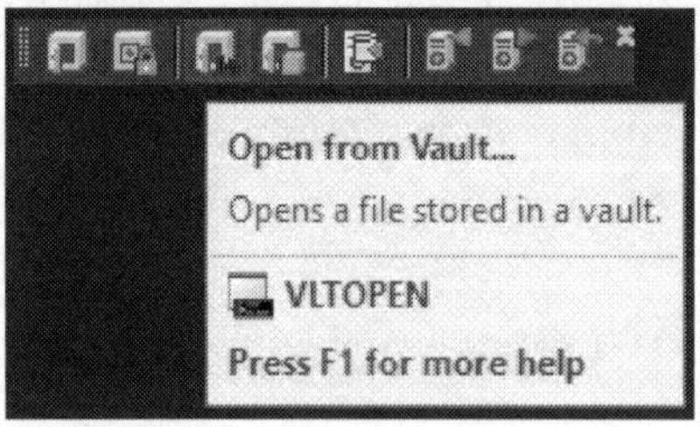

3. On the command line, enter **vltopen**.

Open File Options

From the Select File dialog box, you can choose to check out the file, check out the file and any external references, or open the file without checking it out.

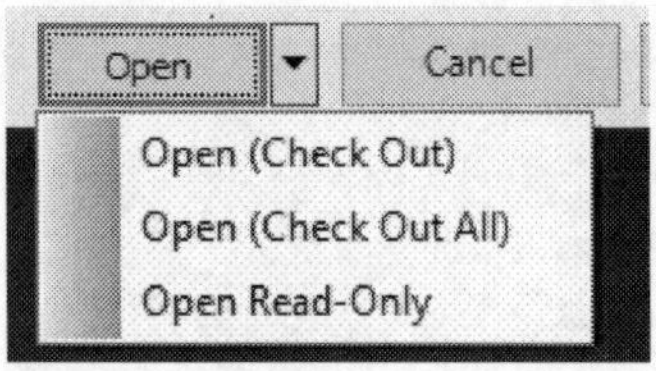

If you click Open without selecting one of the options, you are prompted for the check-out behavior.

For example, if you are working on a design and know that modifications are required, you can use the Open Project from Vault command with the Open (Check Out All) option.

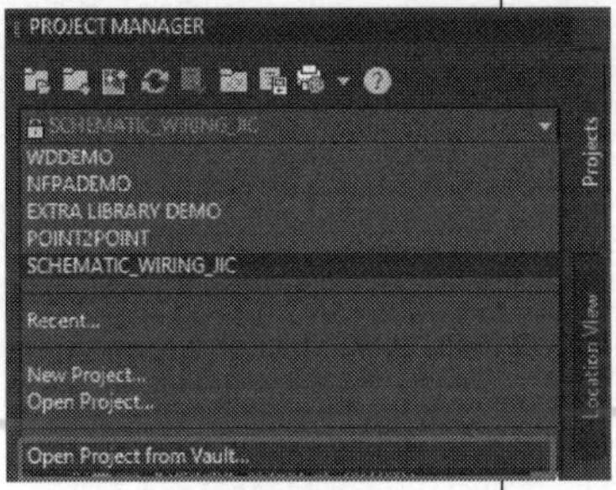

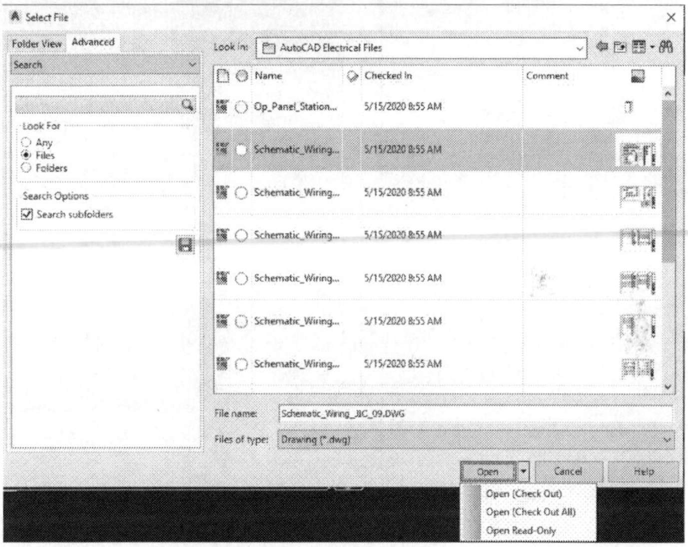

Attach from Vault

If a file is saved in the vault, you can attach it to an open AutoCAD Electrical file using the Attach from Vault command. This command works the same way as the Attach command when you are working with external references, except that Attach from Vault searches the vault for files rather than searching your local drives. The selected file is copied from the vault file store to the corresponding working folder, and that file is attached as an external reference.

Attaching a File from the Vault

Use any of the following methods to attach a file from the vault.

1. On the ribbon, select the Vault tab and click Attach on the Access panel.

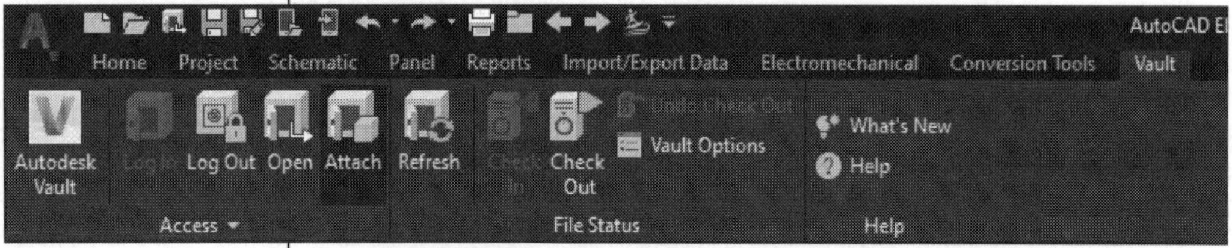

2. On the Vault toolbar, click Attach from Vault.

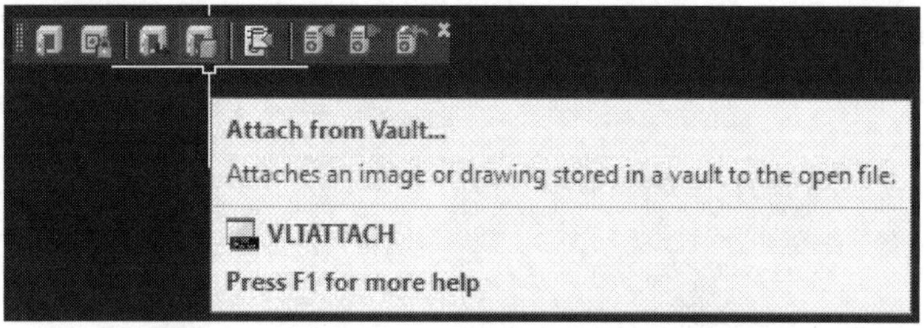

3. In the External References palette, select Attach from Vault from the list.

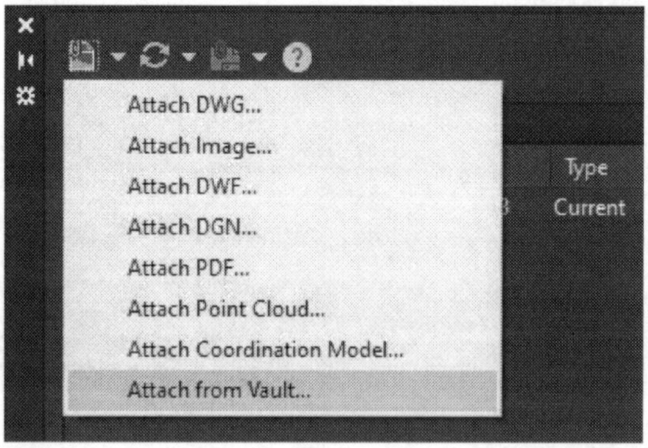

4. In the External References palette, right-click on the File References background and select Attach from Vault.

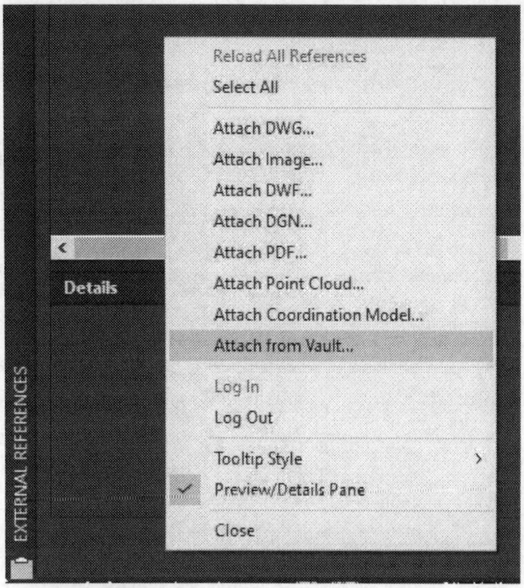

5. On the command line, enter **vltattach**.

If the file is a library file, the file is copied to your working folder in read-only format.

For example, in the following image, Attach from Vault was used to attach the Op_Panel_Station_1 drawing.

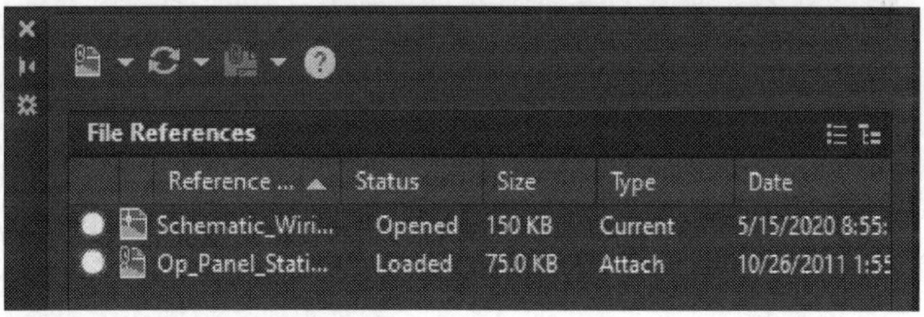

Practice 5a

Access the Vault

In this practice, you log in to Autodesk Vault from AutoCAD Electrical. You also open Vault Explorer, define a working folder, and then make two new folders for the practices in this chapter.

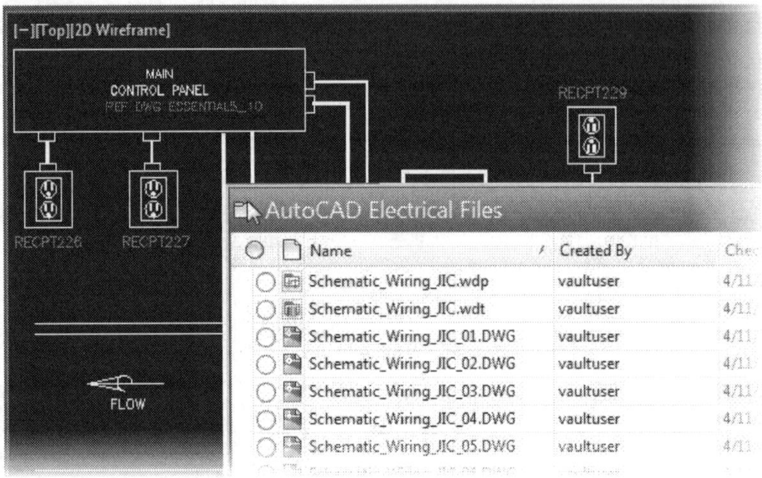

The completed practice

Task 1 - Vault setup.

1. Start AutoCAD Electrical.
2. If the Project Manager is not displayed, on the ribbon, select the Project tab and click Manager on the Project Tools panel. The Project Manager is displayed.
3. In the Project Manager palette, click the Open Project icon.

4. Open *C:\AOTGVault\Chapter 5\Schematic_Wiring_JIC.wdp*.

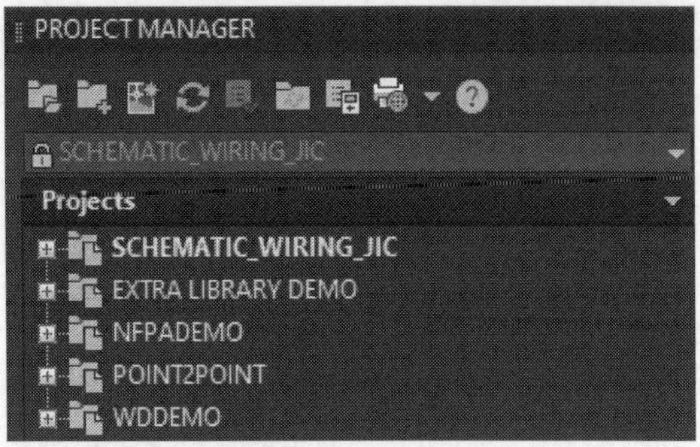

5. In the Project Manager, under Projects, double- click the project. The drawing files in the project are displayed.

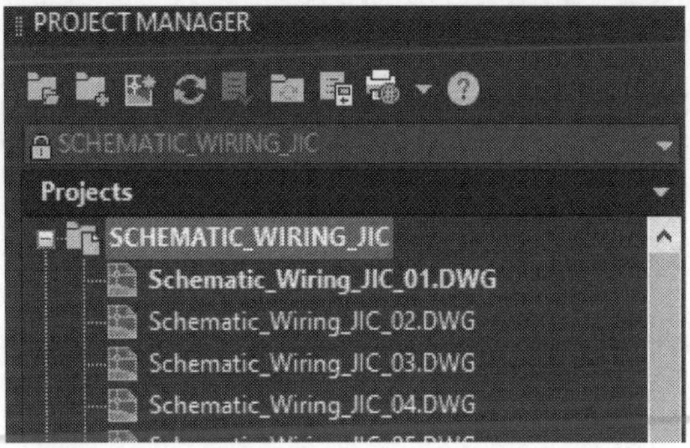

6. On the ribbon, select the Vault tab and click Log In on the Access panel.
7. Log in to the vault using the following information:
   - For User Name, enter **vaultuser**.
   - For Password, leave this box empty.
   - For Vault, select AOTGVault.
8. On the ribbon, select the Vault tab and click Autodesk Vault on the Access panel.
9. Log in to the vault using the following information:
   - For User Name, enter **administrator**.
   - For Password, leave this box empty.
   - For Vault, select AOTGVault.

   Note: You must have at least one file open to log in to the vault. You must log in to Autodesk Vault as an administrator to enforce a common working folder in the next step.

10. In Autodesk Vault, click Tools menu>Administration>Vault Settings.

11. In the Administration dialog box, under Working Folder, click Define. Under Working Folder Options, select Enforce Consistent Working Folder for All Clients. For Client Working Folder, browse to and select *C:\AOTGVault\VaultWorkingFolder*.

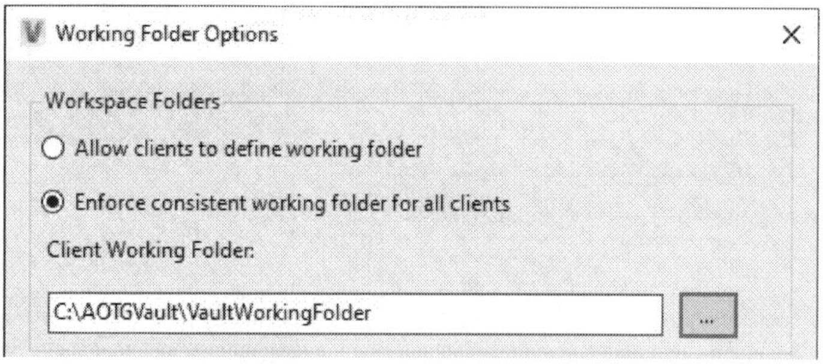

12. Click OK to dismiss the Working folder Options dialog and click Close to dismiss the Vault Settings dialog.

13. Right-click Vault Explorer ($).

14. Click New Folder.

15. Name the new folder AutoCAD Electrical Files.

16. Right-click Vault Explorer ($) and select New Library Folder.

17. Name the new folder AutoCAD Electrical Symbols.

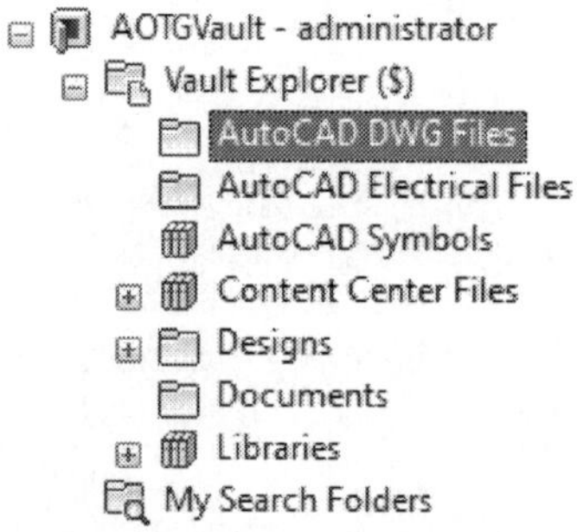

Note: If you have not completed other practices, your folder structure might be different from the image.

Task 2 - Access the vault.

1. Return to AutoCAD Electrical.
2. In the Project Manager, place the cursor over the vault icon next to the active project. The tooltip indicates that the file is not in the vault.

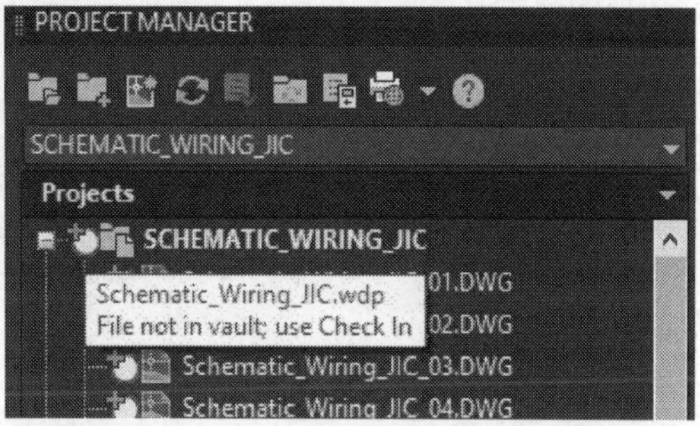

3. Right-click the project. Click Vault>Check In All.
4. In the Select Vault Location dialog box, select the AutoCAD Electrical Files folder. Click OK.

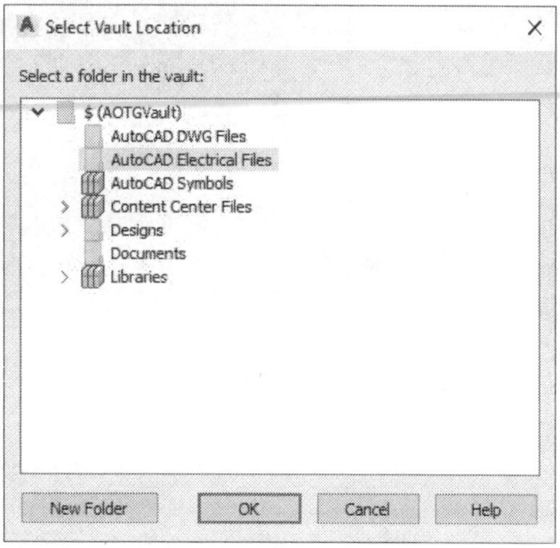

5. In the Check In dialog box, enter Added to Vault, and click OK.
6. In the Project Manager, double-click the Schematic_Wiring_JIC project to display the drawing files in the project.
7. Right-click Schematic_Wiring_JIC_01.dwg. Click Open.

8. Right-click Schematic_Wiring_JIC_01.dwg and select Check Out. The vault icon indicates the status of the checked-out drawing.

9. Zoom in to the main control panel located near the top-left corner of the drawing.

10. Double-click the REF DWG ESSENTIALS_09 attribute and change it to REF DWG ESSENTIALS_10.

11. Save the file.

12. In the Project Manager, the vault icon next to the drawing indicates that the file has been edited and saved locally.

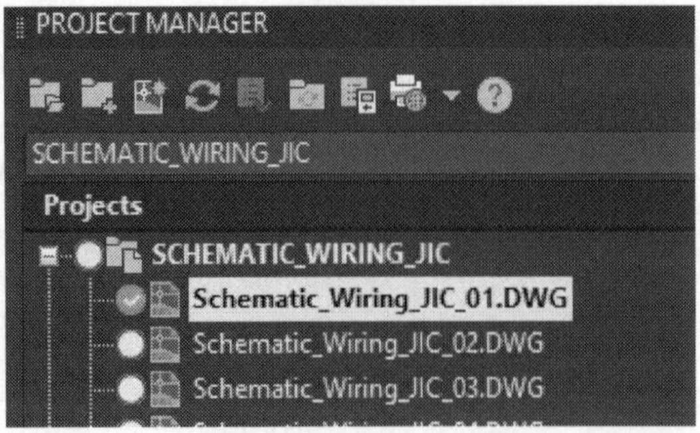

13. In the Project Manager, right-click Schematic_Wiring_JIC_01.dwg and select Check In.
14. In the Check In dialog box, enter a comment and click OK.
15. Close all AutoCAD Electrical files.
16. In Autodesk Vault, select the AutoCAD Electrical Files folder. Click Refresh.
17. The Schematic_Wiring_JIC_01.dwg file is set to Version 2.

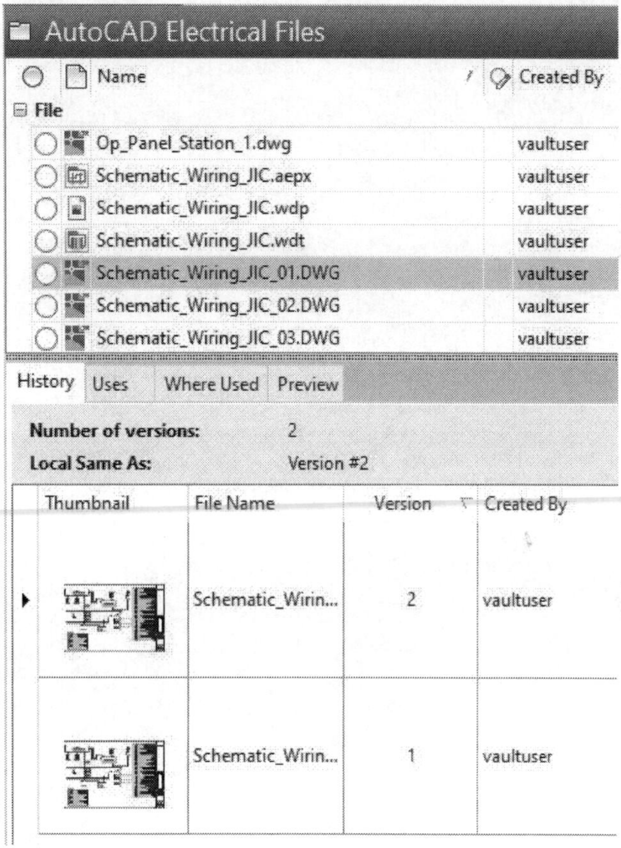

18. Close Autodesk Vault.

5.2 Chapter Summary

Autodesk Vault integrates with AutoCAD Electrical and provides an engineering data management system that offers file security, version control, and multiuser support. Logging in to the vault and then checking in and checking out AutoCAD Electrical projects and drawings are examples of each of these functions.

Having completed this chapter, you can:

- Add AutoCAD Electrical projects to a vault.

Chapter 6

Working with Vault and AutoCAD Mechanical

In this chapter, you learn how to add existing AutoCAD® Mechanical drawings to a vault and how to work with AutoCAD Mechanical files from the vault.

Learning Objectives in This Chapter

- Check AutoCAD Mechanical files in and out of a vault.
- Attach an XREF to a drawing and check in the host drawing and the XREF.

6.1 Working with AutoCAD Mechanical Files

Overview

You can configure Autodesk Vault to work in AutoCAD®, AutoCAD® Mechanical, AutoCAD® Electrical, Autodesk® Civil 3D® and more. The vault client adds data management tools to the interface of your AutoCAD-based software. You can add files to a vault and check files in and out. The vault maintains relationships between host drawings and external references.

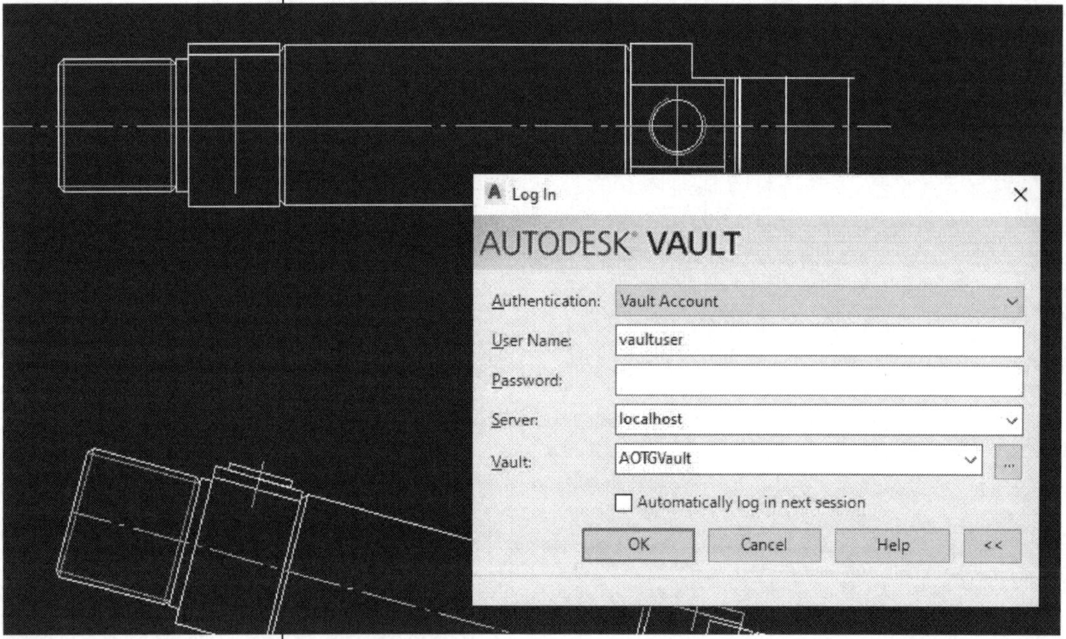

Objectives

After completing this lesson, you will be able to:

- Access Vault from AutoCAD Mechanical.
- Use a typical workflow for AutoCAD Mechanical and Vault.
- Check drawings in and out of a vault.
- Open files from a vault.
- Attach files from a vault.

Opening and Accessing

The first step in working with AutoCAD Mechanical and Autodesk Vault is to log in to the vault. In this lesson, you learn how to access the vault from AutoCAD Mechanical in order to check files in and out and keep track of attachments to files.

You can access Vault commands from a number of palettes, the Vault toolbar, and the Vault tab on the ribbon. The following image displays the Vault tab on the ribbon.

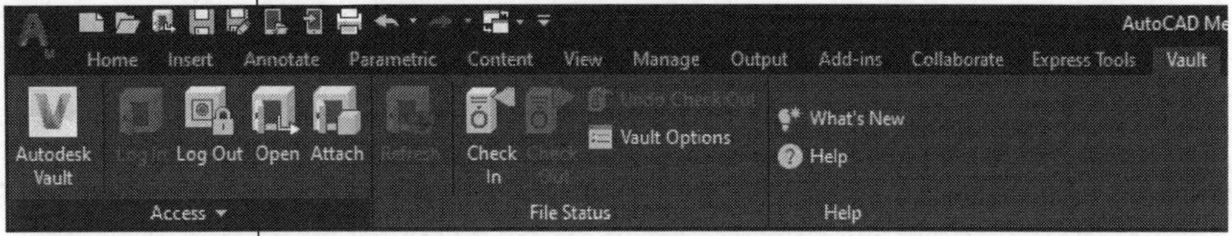

Procedure: Logging in to the Vault

You can access Autodesk Vault from AutoCAD Mechanical using one of the following methods: the Vault tab on the ribbon, the Vault toolbar, the command line, or the Vault tray icon.

1. On the ribbon, select the Vault tab and click Log In on the Access panel.

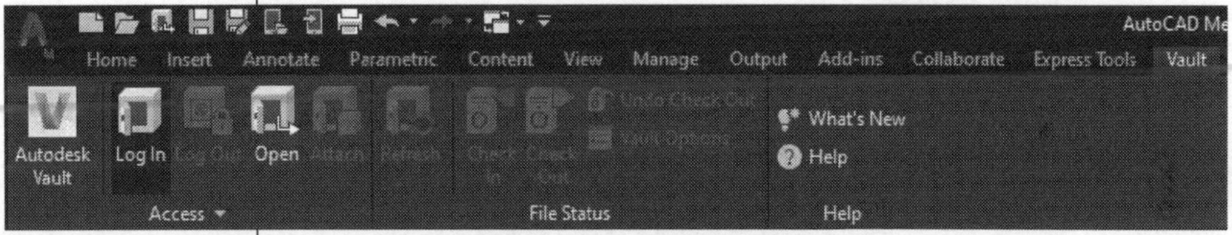

2. Click Log In on the Vault toolbar.

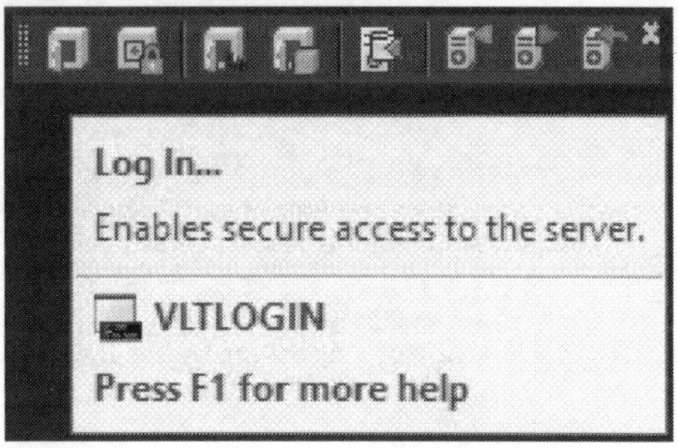

3. On the command line, enter **vault** or **vltlogin**.

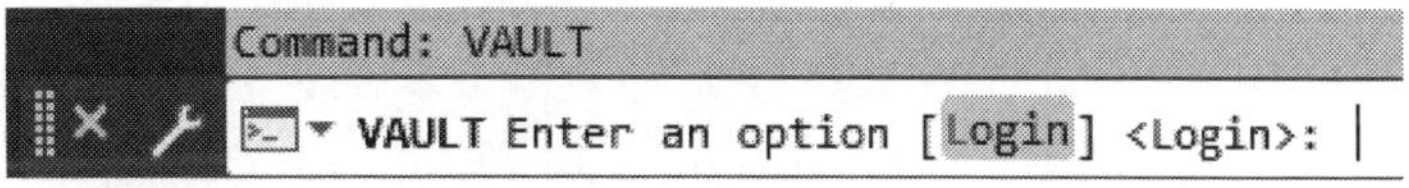

4. Right-click the Vault tray icon and then select Log In.

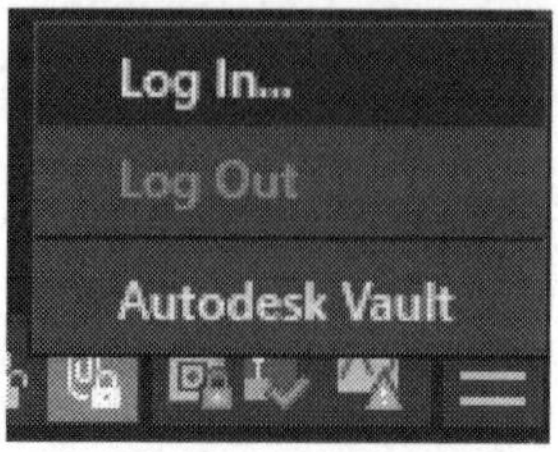

Status Bar Tray Icons

When you are not logged in to Autodesk Vault, the AutoCAD status bar tray icon is displayed as a locked vault. When you are logged in, the icon is displayed as an open vault door.

When logged in, rest the cursor over the Vault system tray icon to display the user login name, vault, and server.

Typical Workflow

In this lesson, you learn about the typical workflow for using Autodesk Vault and AutoCAD Mechanical. The following image displays a drawing in the process of being checked in to the vault.

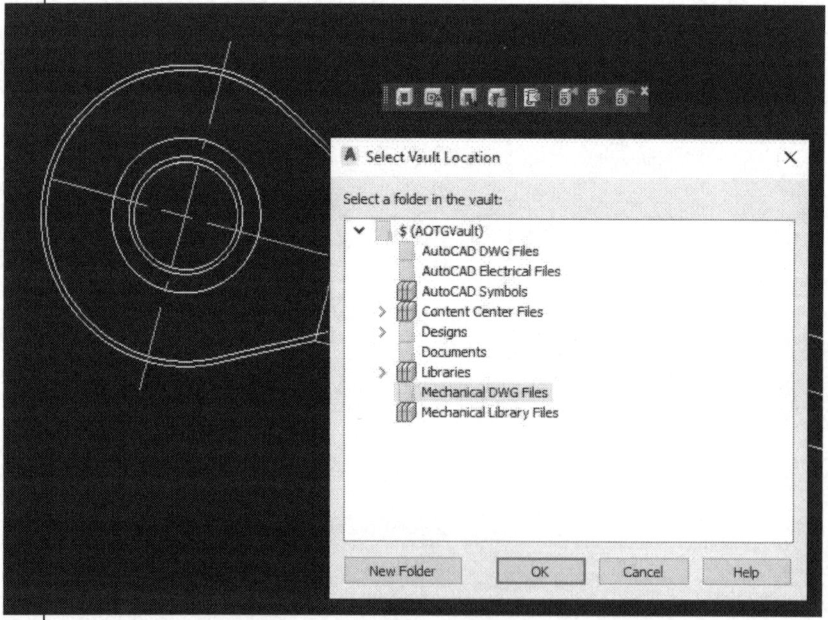

Procedure: Using Autodesk Vault and AutoCAD Mechanical

Your workflow varies depending on where you are in the design cycle. The following steps describe a basic workflow for Autodesk Vault and AutoCAD Mechanical.

1. Log in to Autodesk Vault. Set a working folder on your local drive.

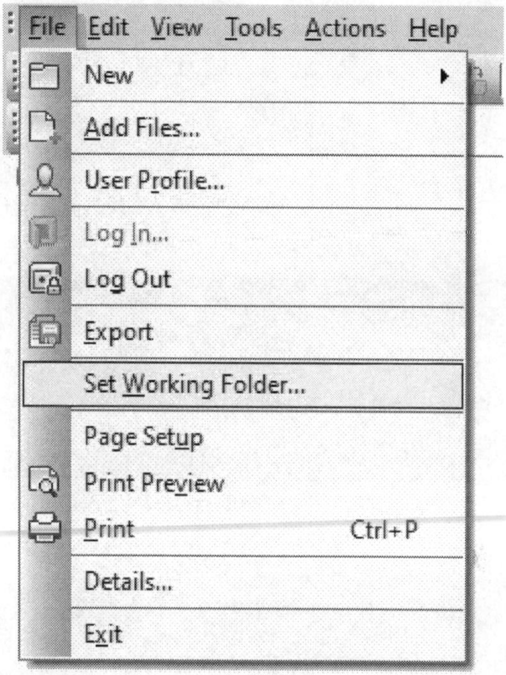

2. Start AutoCAD Mechanical, open a file that you want to add to the vault, and log in to the vault. Note that you cannot log into the vault until a drawing is opened or created.

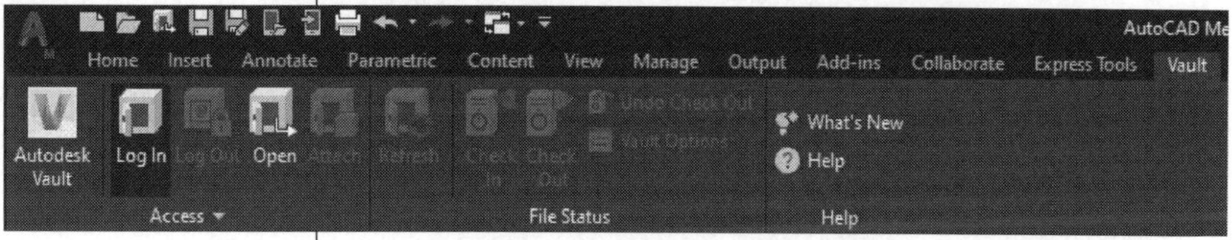

3. Attach any required external reference files to the open AutoCAD Mechanical file, using either the Attach command or the Attach from Vault command.

4. In the External References palette, check the drawing in to the vault using the Check In command. The XREFs are also added to the vault.

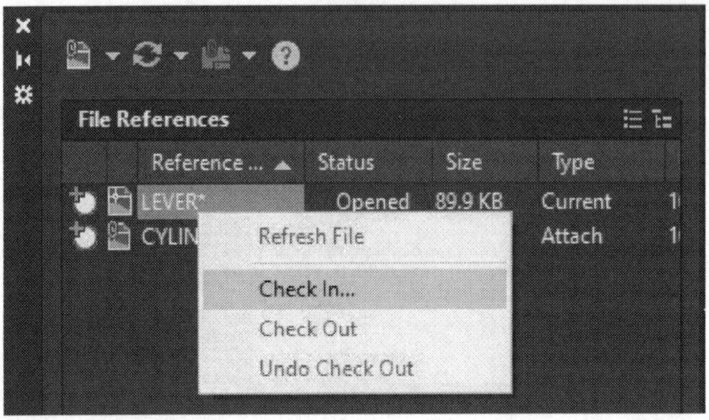

5. Open and check out other files from the vault using the Open from Vault command.

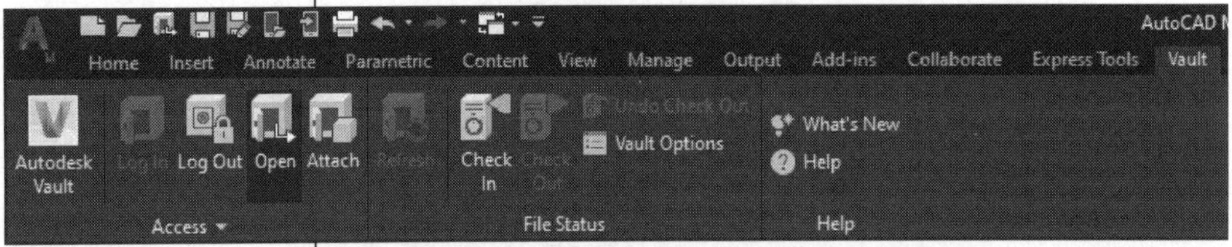

6. Check the modified files back in to the vault.

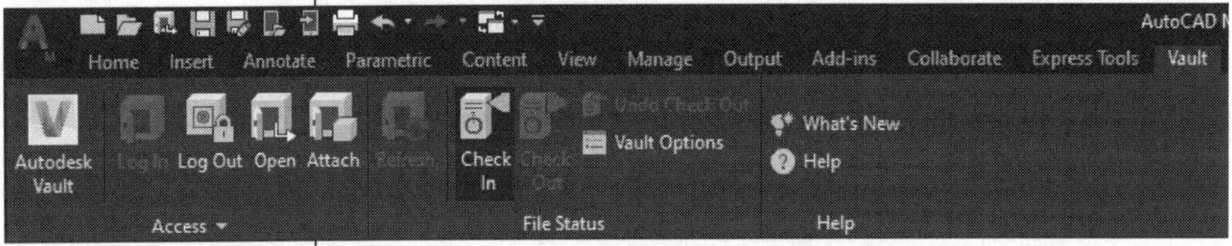

Check In Drawings

Once you have completed a drawing and want to check the file into the vault, use the Check In command. You check in a single drawing file at a time into the vault. If you are checking in a drawing file that contains external references (XREFs), all of the XREF drawings are checked in at the same time. By adding files that use external references to the vault from AutoCAD Mechanical, Autodesk Vault is able to keep track of the file relationships.

The following image displays a drawing being checked in to the vault.

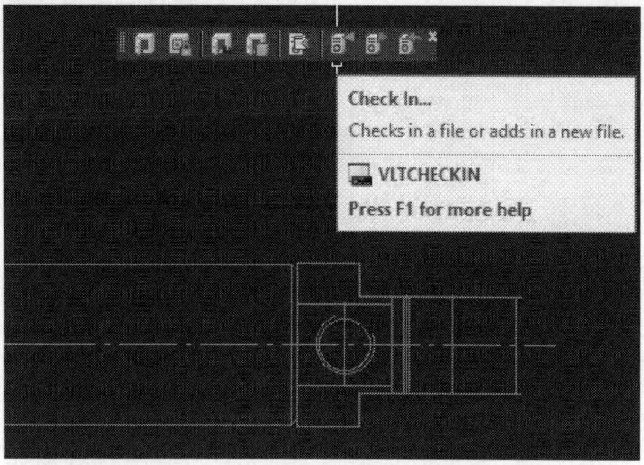

Check In Files to the Vault

You use the Check In command to store DWG™ and image files in a vault. The preferred workflow is to check in files from AutoCAD Mechanical. The following procedure describes the methods you can use to check drawing and image files in to the vault.

1. On the ribbon, select the Vault tab and click Check In on the File Status panel.

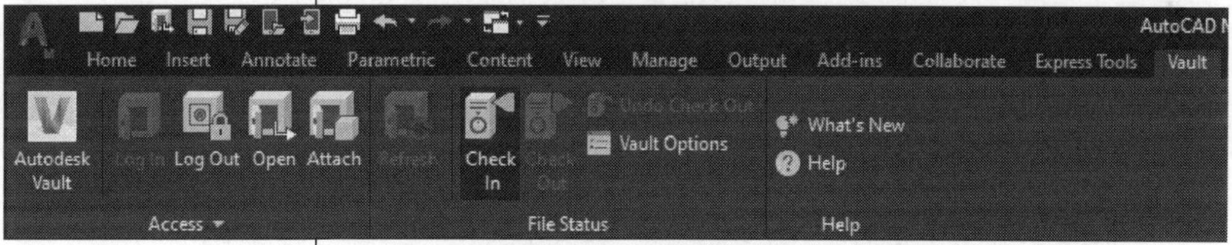

2. On the Vault toolbar, click Check In.

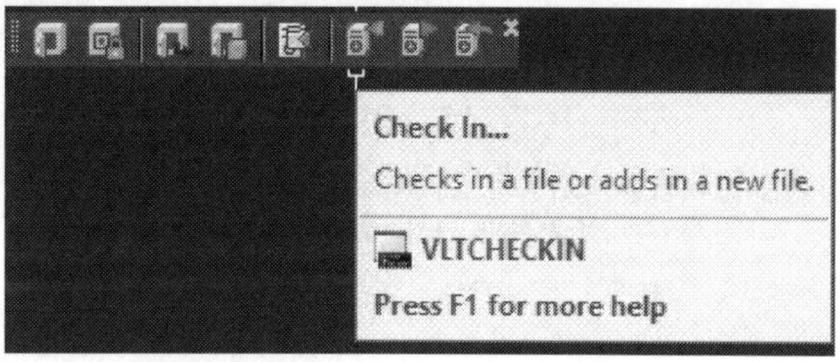

3. In the External References palette, right-click the file. Click Check In.

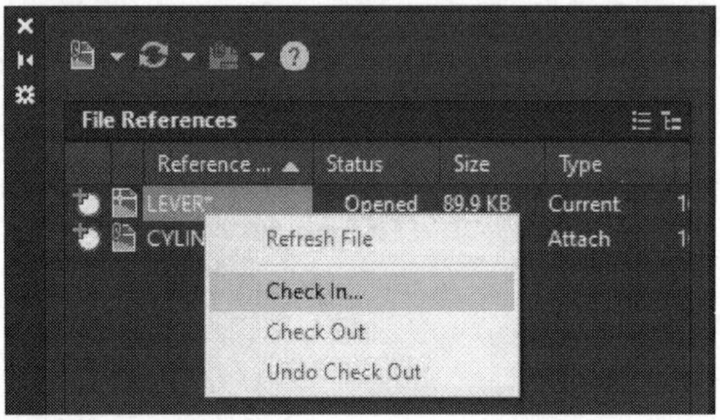

4. On the command line, enter **vault** or **vltcheckin**.

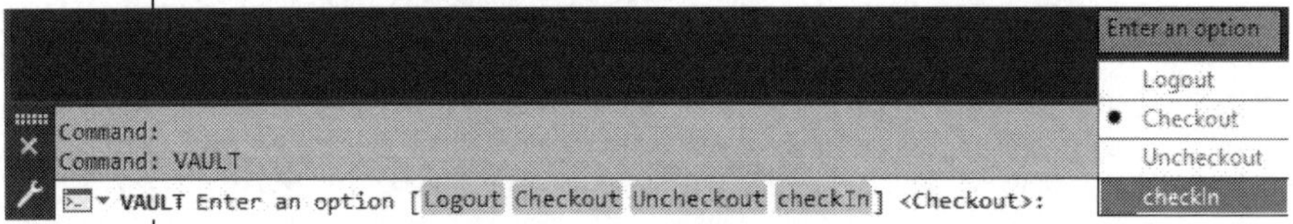

Check In Files Not in Working Folder

If the file you check in to the vault is not in the working folder or its subfolders, the Select Vault Location dialog box displays. You select the vault location for the drawing file in this dialog box.

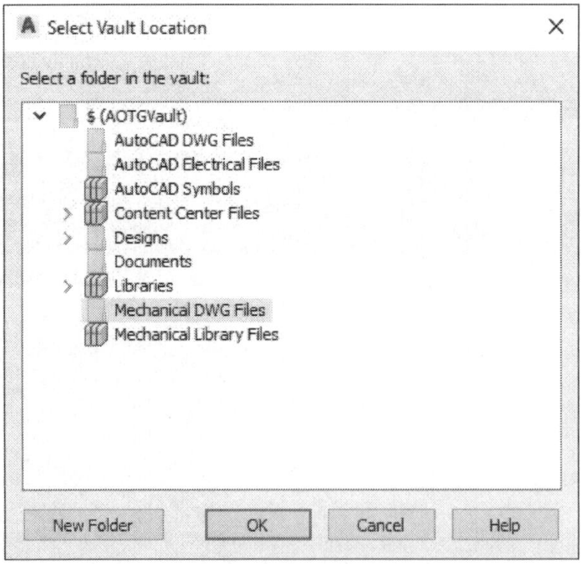

Definition of Settings Dialog Box

Settings control the organization of files to be added to the vault and visualization file options for each file.

Settings Options

The Settings dialog box has the following options.

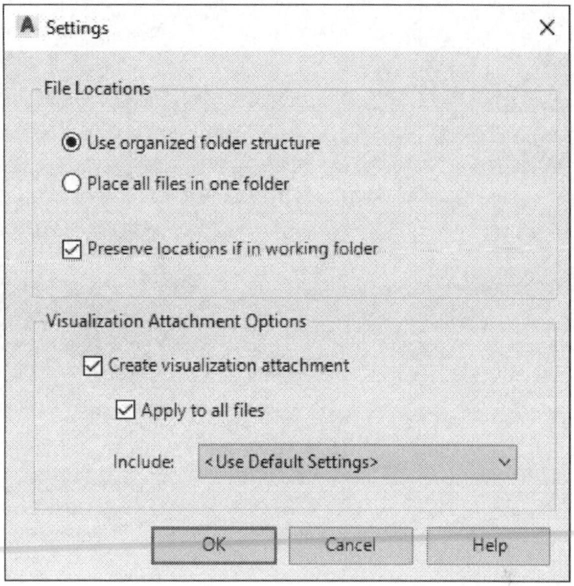

Setting	Description
File Locations - Use organized folder structure	The root folder is the top-level folder in a hierarchical folder tree. The folder structure is maintained for all folders that are at the same level or beneath the host file.
File Locations – Place all files in one folder	All XREFs and dependent files are flattened so that they exist at the same level as the host. All the files are located under the vault folder.
File Locations – Preserve locations if in working folder	Maintains the file structure of files being checked in from the local working folder. This is the preferred workflow.
Visualization Attachment Options – Create Visualization attachment	Creates and attaches a DWF™ or DWFx file for each drawing file being checked in.

Visualization Attachment Options – Apply to all files	Creates a visualization attachment for all files being checked in. This option must be toggled on to create DWF or DWFx files for external reference drawings.
Visualization Attachment Options - Include	Indicates which of the following tabs to include in the visualization attachment: Model Tab Only Layout Tabs Only Model and Layout Tabs <Use Default Settings> to use the settings specified on the Publish Options dialog in the Autodesk Vault.

Current Visualization Settings

The Check In dialog box displays the current settings of the visualization Attachment options.

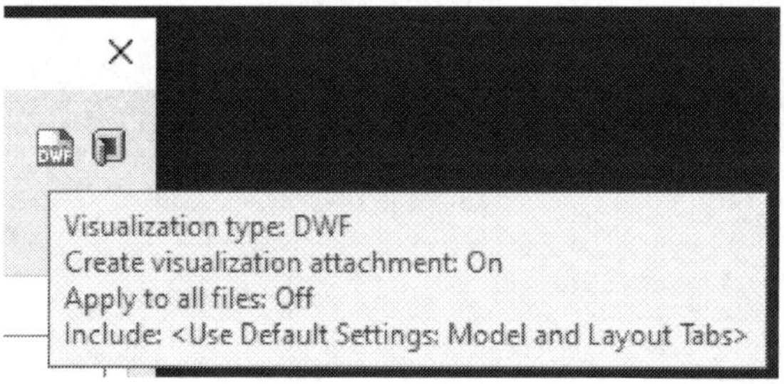

Check Out Files from the Vault

You can use the Check Out command to check out a file you have opened from your working folder if the file is currently checked in to the vault. You must check out a drawing from the vault before it can be edited. The following are various methods that you can use to check out a file from the vault.

1. On the ribbon, select the Vault tab and click Check Out on the File Status panel.

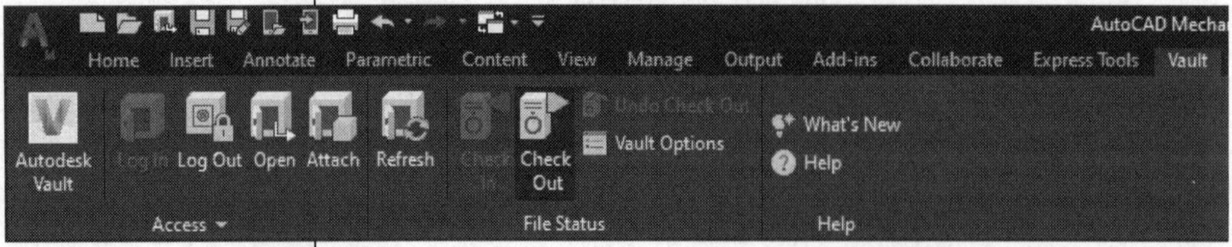

2. On the Vault toolbar, click Check Out.

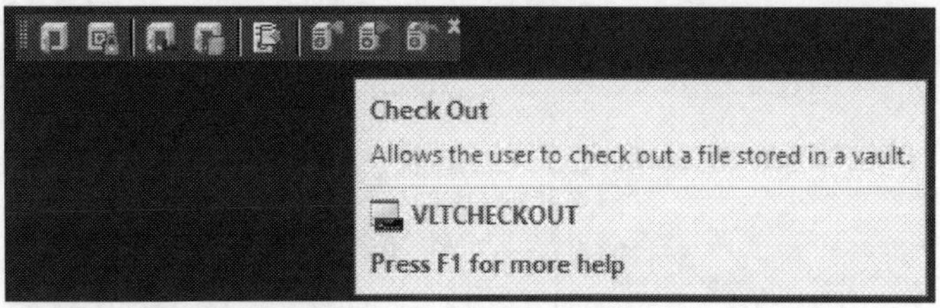

3. In the External References palette, right-click the file and select Check Out.

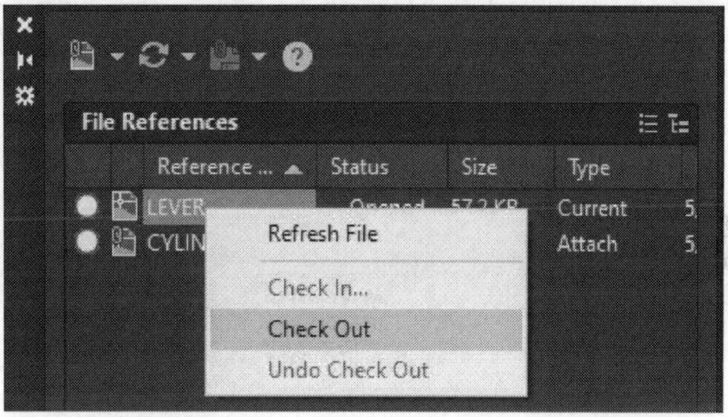

4. On the command line, enter **vault** or **vltcheckout**.

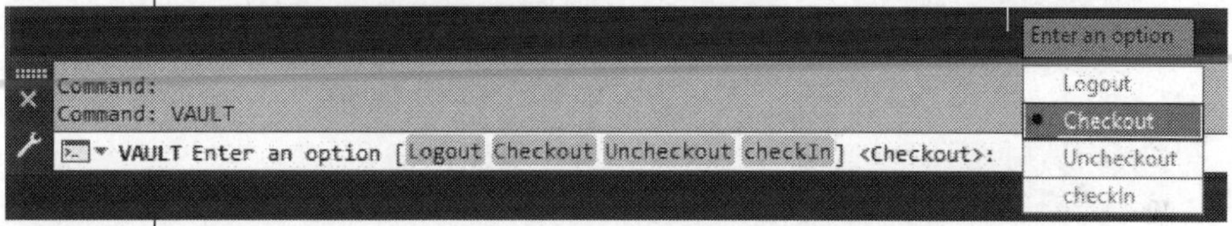

Open from Vault

You use Open from Vault to copy a file from the vault to your working folder and open the local copy. By default, the file is not checked out to you. Optionally, you can check out the local copy during the open process.

Opening a File from the Vault

Use any of the following commands to open a file from the vault.

1. On the ribbon, select the Vault tab and click Open on the Access panel.

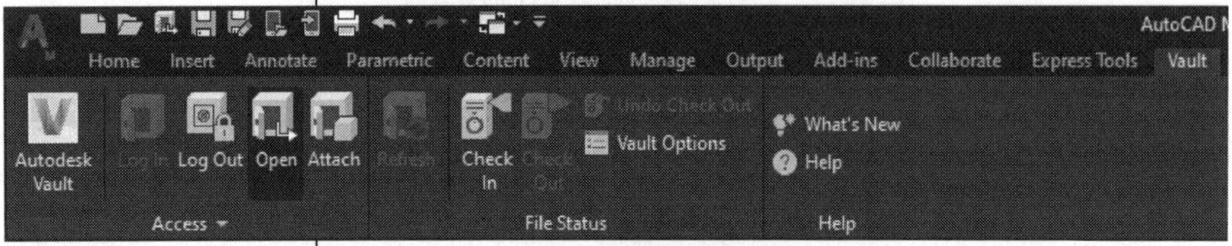

2. On the Vault toolbar, click Open from Vault.

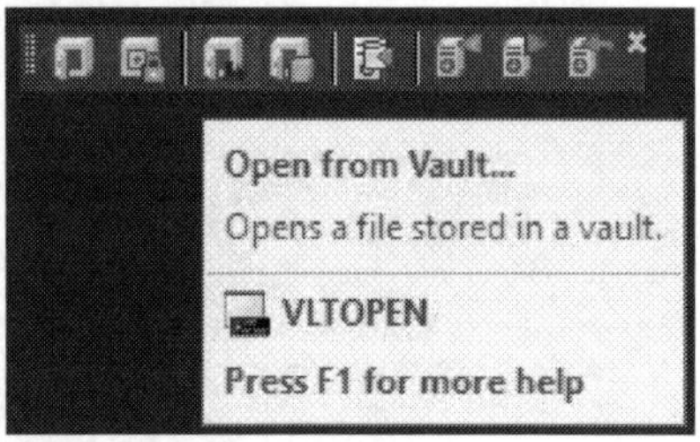

3. On the command line, enter **vltopen**.

Open File Options

In the Select File dialog box, you can select to check out the file, Check out the file and any external references, or open the file without checking it out.

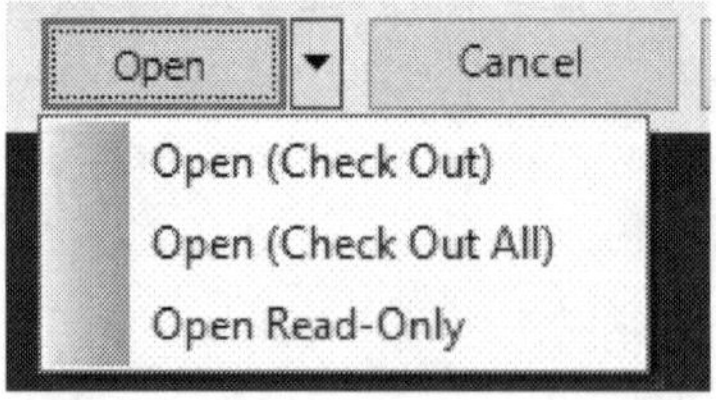

If you click Open without selecting one of the options, you are prompted for the check-out behavior.

Attach from Vault

If a file is saved in the vault, you can attach it to an open AutoCAD Mechanical file using the Attach from Vault command. This command works the same way as the Attach command when you are working with external references, except that Attach from Vault searches the vault for files rather than searching your local drives. The selected file is copied from the vault file store to the corresponding working folder, and that file is attached as an external reference.

Attaching a File from the Vault

Use any of the following methods to attach a file from the vault.

1. On the ribbon, select the Vault tab and click Attach on the Access panel.

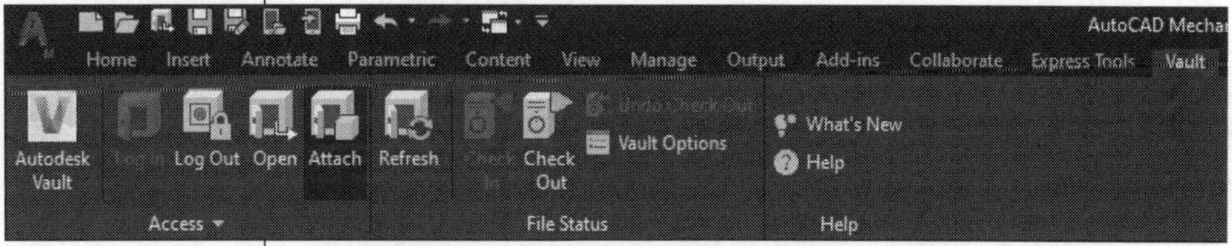

2. On the Vault toolbar, click Attach from Vault.

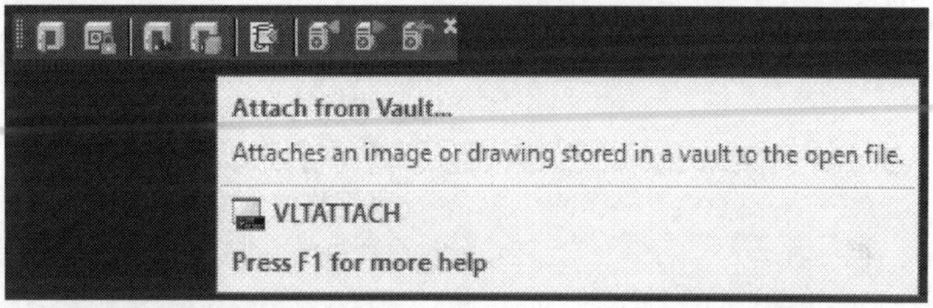

3. In the External References palette, select Attach from Vault from the list.

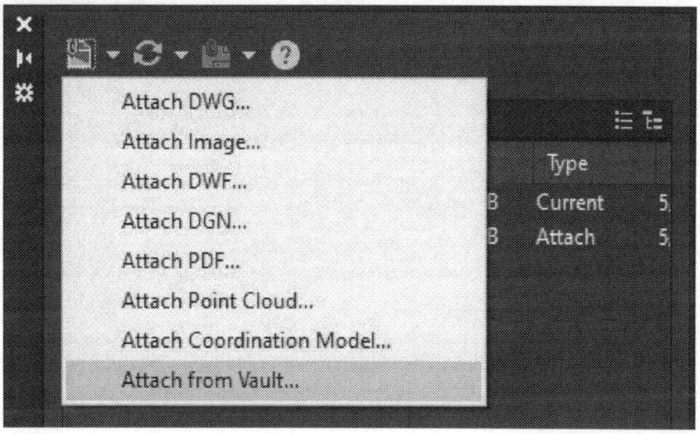

4. In the External References palette, right-click in the File References background. Click Attach from Vault.

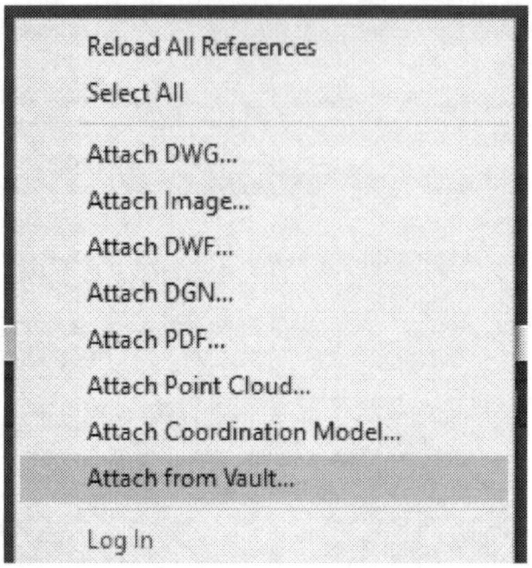

5. On the command line, enter **vltattach**.

If the file is a library file, the file is copied to your working folder in read-only format.

For example, in the following image, Attach from Vault was used to attach the CYLINDER drawing.

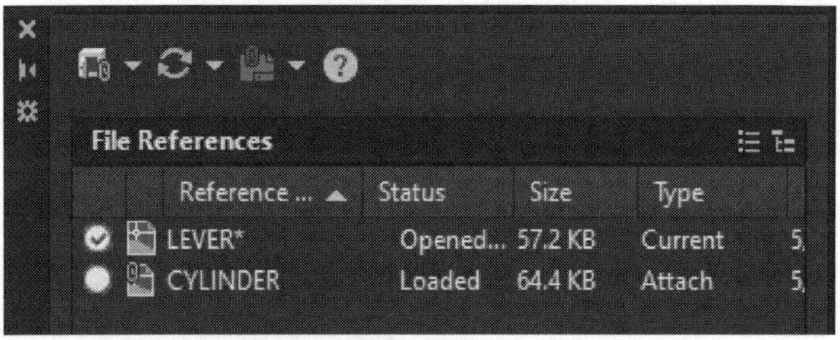

Practice 6a

Check Files In to the Vault

In this practice, you log in to Autodesk Vault from AutoCAD Mechanical. You also launch Vault from AutoCAD Mechanical and make two new folders for storing data.

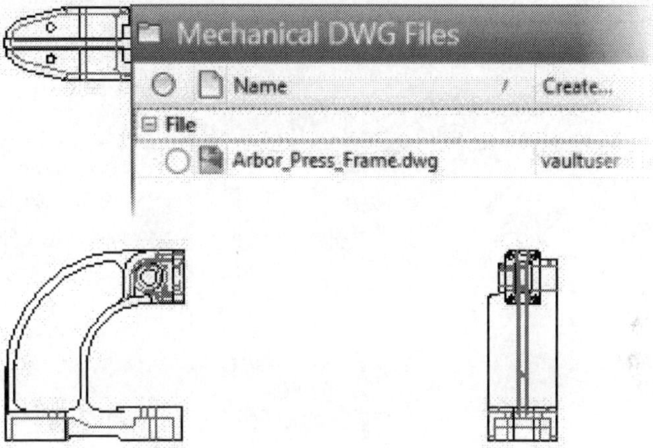

The completed practice

Task 1 - Check files in to the vault.

1. Open AutoCAD Mechanical.
2. In AutoCAD Mechanical, open *C:\AOTGVault\Chapter6\AutoCAD Mechanical Files\TitleBlock.dwg*.

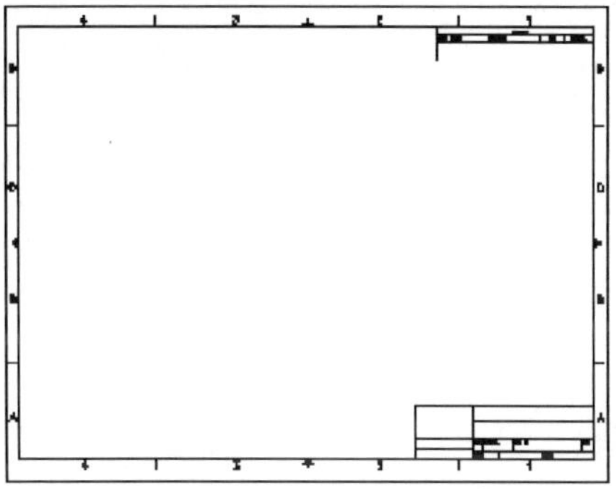

3. On the ribbon, select the Vault tab and click Log In on the Access panel.
4. Log in to the vault using the following information:
    - For User Name, enter **vaultuser**.
    - For Password, leave this box empty.
    - For Vault, select AOTGVault.
5. On the ribbon, select the Vault tab and click Autodesk Vault on the Access panel.
6. Log in to the vault using the following information:
    - For User Name, enter **administrator**.
    - For Password, leave this box empty.
    - For Vault, select AOTGVault.
7. Right-click Vault Explorer ($) and select New Folder. Name the new folder Mechanical DWG Files.
8. Right-click Vault Explorer ($) and select New Library Folder.
9. Name the new folder Mechanical Library Files.

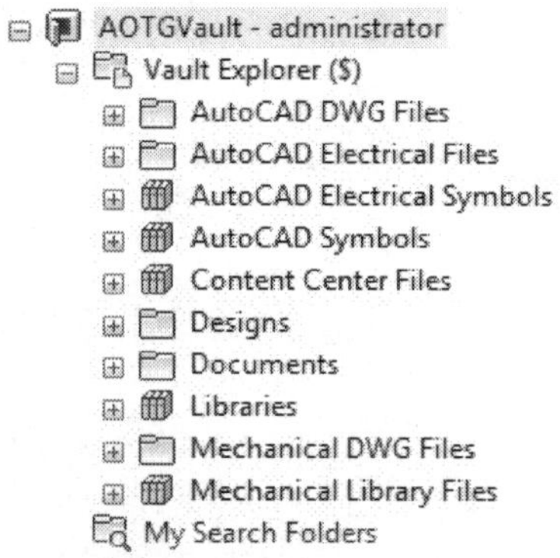

10. Click Tools menu>Administration>Vault Settings.
11. On the Files tab, under Working Folder, click Define.
12. In the Working Folder Options dialog box, click Enforce Consistent Working Folder for All Clients. Click the browse button.
13. In the Browse for Folder dialog box, browse to and select *C:\AOTGVault\ VaultWorkingFolder*. Click OK>Close.

14. In AutoCAD Mechanical, save the file to ensure that the file is up to date.

15. On the ribbon, select the Vault tab and click Check In on the File Status panel.

16. In the Select Vault Location dialog box, select Mechanical Library Files. Click OK.

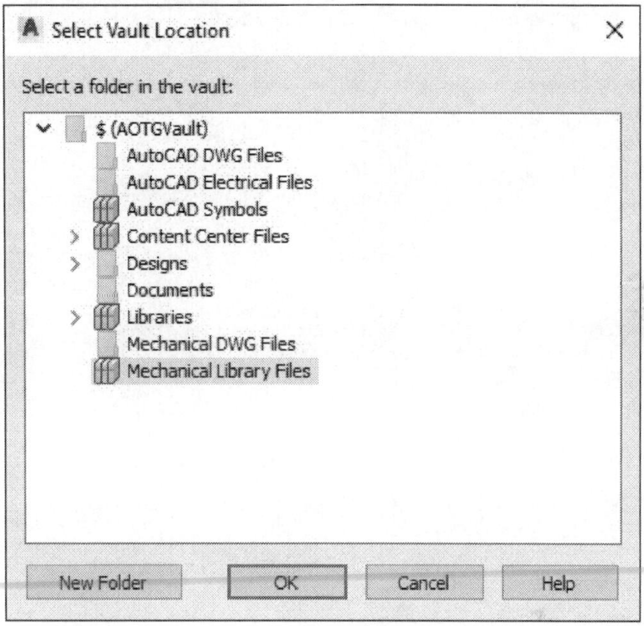

17. Enter Added to Vault in the Check In dialog and select OK to dismiss it and check in the file.

18. Select Yes if prompted to save the file.

19. A message indicates that you are now working with the local copy of the file from the working folder structure. Select OK to dismiss the dialog and finish the check in process.

20. Close the Title Block.dwg file.

21. In AutoCAD Mechanical, open *C:\AOTGVault\Chapter6\AutoCAD Mechanical Files\Arbor_Press_Frame.dwg*.

22. Save the file.

23. Check in the Arbor_Press_Frame.dwg file to the Mechanical DWG Files folder. Enter Added to Vault in the Check In dialog and select OK.

24. In Autodesk Vault, click Refresh.

25. Click the Mechanical DWG Files folder. Note that the Arbor_Press_Frame drawing is available for checking out.

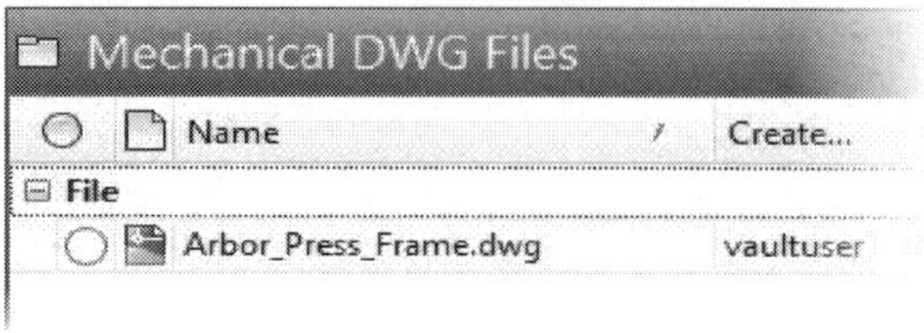

26. In AutoCAD Mechanical, close all files.

6.2 Working with External References in AutoCAD Mechanical

Overview

You use the External References palette to work with external references (XREFs) in your designs. On the External References palette, you can perform all AutoCAD Mechanical XREF functions and use Vault commands. This lesson teaches you how to use the External References palette with Vault.

The following image displays some of the Vault features you can access from the External References palette. Each file has a Vault status icon, and the File References pane includes tools that help you to work with files in the vault.

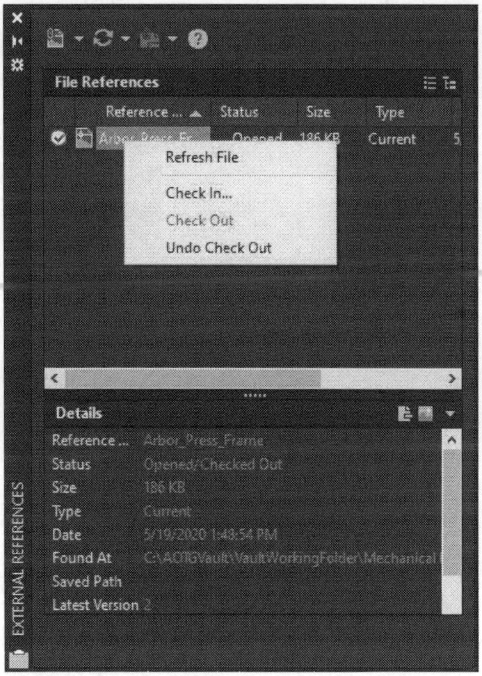

Objectives

After completing this lesson, you will be able to:

- Use the External References palette and Vault.
- Attach an external reference drawing from the vault.

External References Palette

You can use the AutoCAD Mechanical External References palette to control external references in AutoCAD Mechanical and perform Vault tasks such as checking files in and out and attaching files from the vault.

The External References palette supports drawing, DWF, DGN, PDF, and image file external references in the same window.

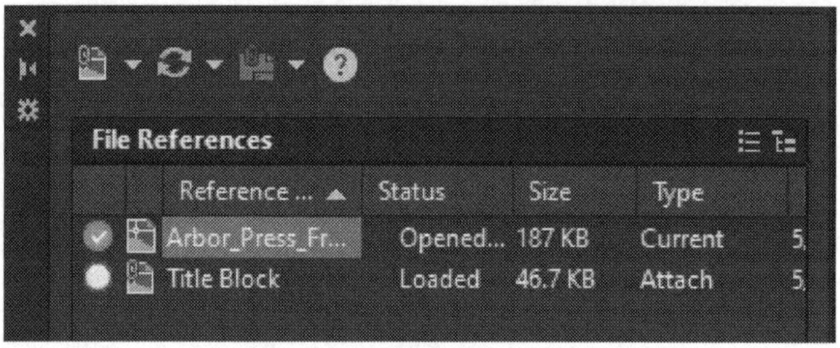

External References Palette and the Vault

To use the External References palette with Vault commands, you must be logged in to the vault. In addition to all of the External References palette functionality that can be found elsewhere in AutoCAD Mechanical, the Vault status icons are displayed. These icons indicate the status of your local copy of files as compared to the master copies of those same files in the vault.

The File References pane of the External References palette displays the current file, any attached drawings, images, and other reference files. You can view this area in either a list view or a tree view.

List View

The list view displays properties of the drawings. Properties include the status, size, and type.

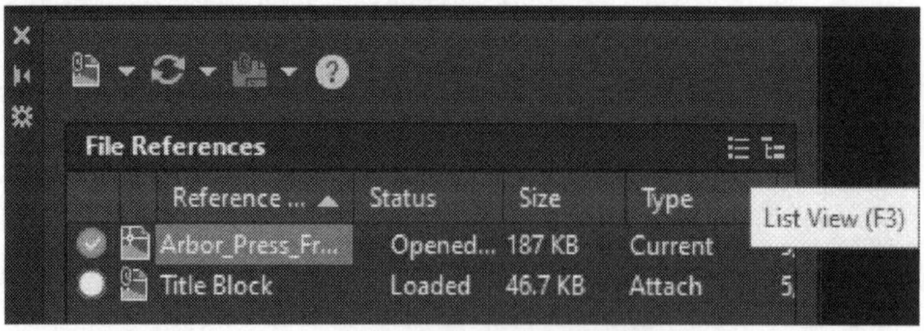

Tree View

The tree view displays the filenames and their relationships. External references are shown as child files in the File References pane.

Details Pane

The details pane of the External References palette displays the properties of the file including the vault status. The file in the following image is checked out from the vault.

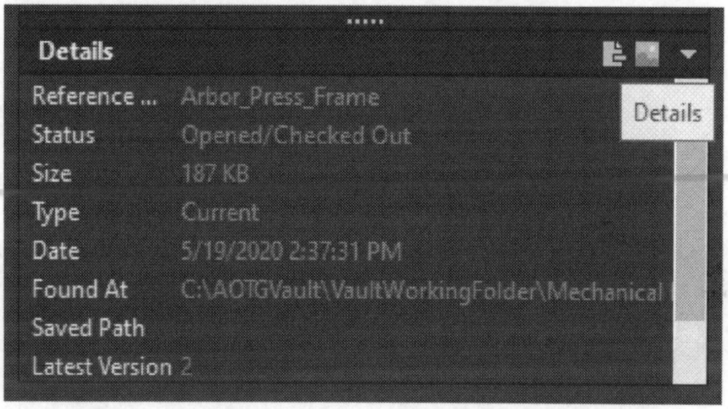

You can toggle between the details pane and Preview mode. When you select a file in the File References pane, a preview of the selected file reference is displayed.

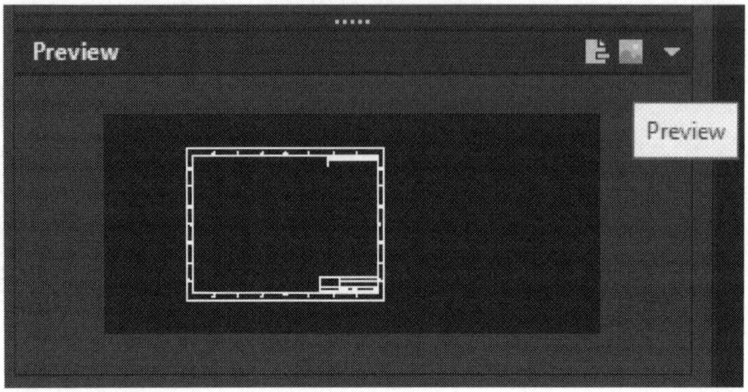

Hint: Structured Components

In files that contain structured components, use the Externalize command to create XREFs of components that you want to exist in separate files.

External References Palette and the Vault

The Autodesk Vault add-in enhances the functionality of the External References palette. In addition to the standard functionality of AutoCAD Mechanical, you can use the External References palette to access many of the Vault commands. Using the External References palette improves your workflow between AutoCAD Mechanical and the Vault.

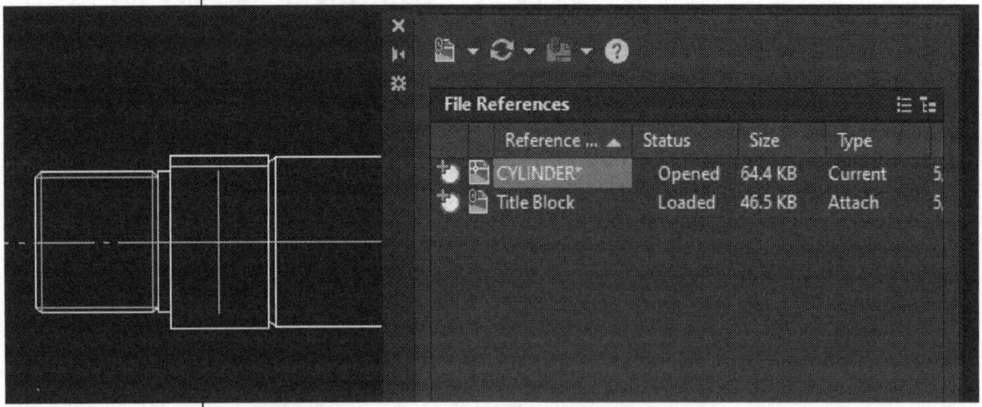

Procedure: Working with the External References Palette and Vault

The following steps describe a standard workflow for working on an AutoCAD Mechanical file with XREFs.

1. On the ribbon, click the Insert tab>Reference panel>External References. If the current drawing or its external references are not in the vault, the Vault status icon is displayed as a circle with a plus sign.

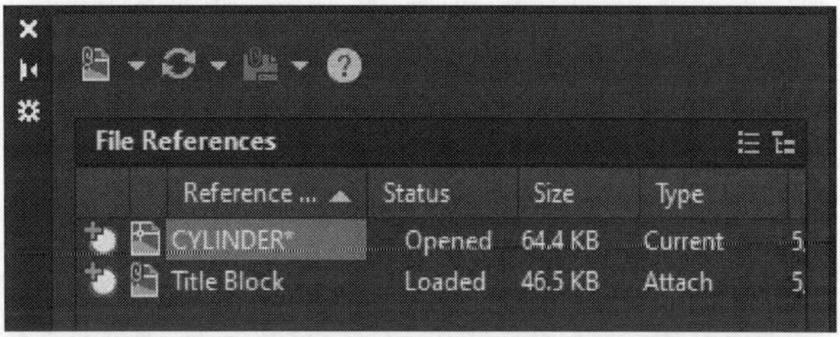

2. To add the drawing to the vault, save the file. Right-click the file in the External References palette and select Check In.

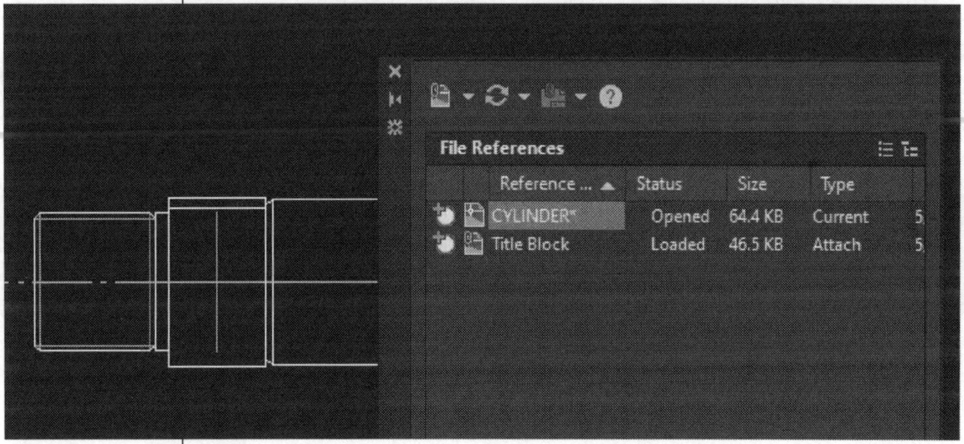

3. Select the folder location in the vault. Click OK.

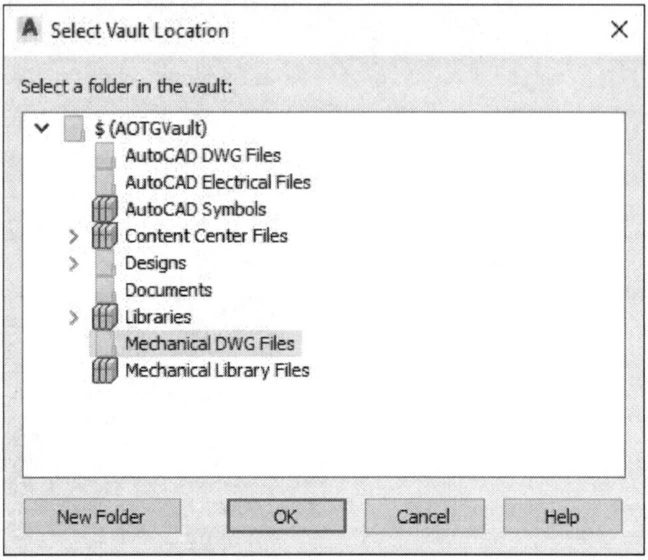

4. The Check In dialog box is displayed. The selected drawing and all external references are automatically selected to be checked in. Enter a comment. Click OK.

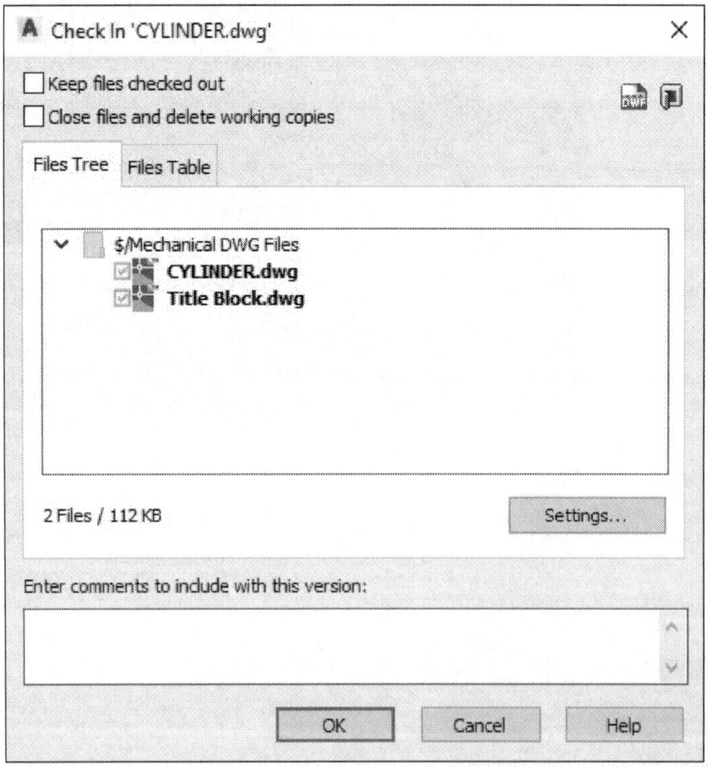

5. To modify a drawing, check out the file from the vault. You make modifications to the checked- out file in your working folder. You can select multiple files to be checked out at the same time.

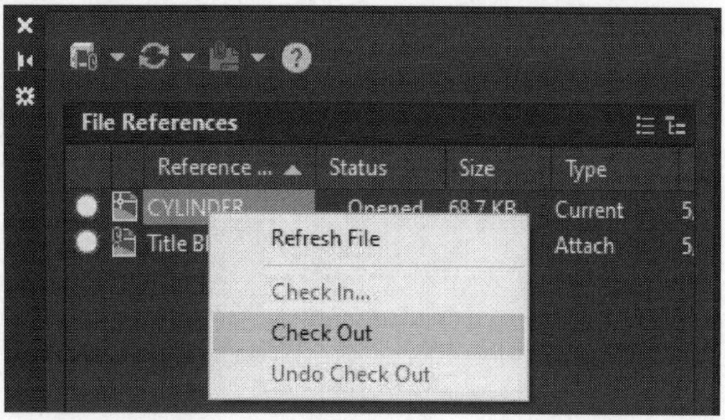

6. To attach a drawing in the vault as an XREF to the current drawing, use the Attach from Vault option. You can also add new external references to files that are not in the vault.

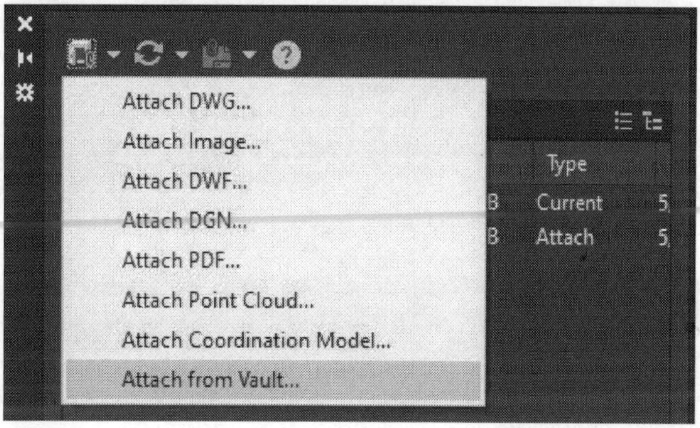

7. Save your revised drawing and check it in to the vault so the latest revisions will be available to all team members. If you want to continue to work on a drawing, you have the option to keep the file checked out.

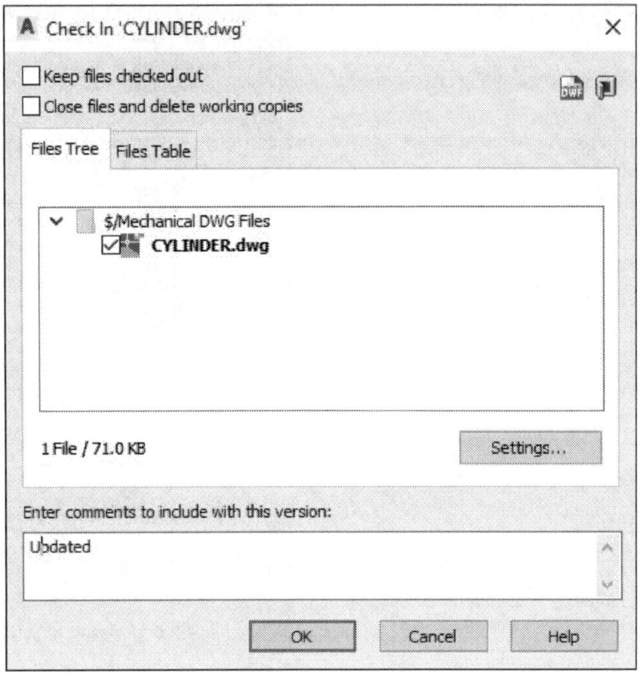

Practice 6b Attach a Drawing from the Vault

In this practice, you check a drawing in to the vault. You then attach a drawing from the vault to an existing drawing and check in the combined file.

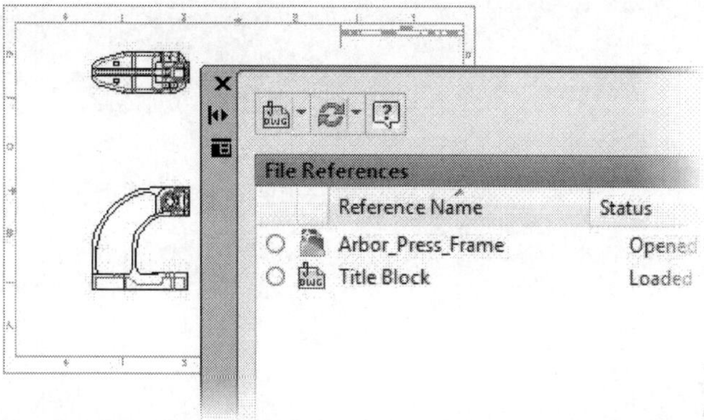

The completed practice

1. In AutoCAD Mechanical, close all drawings.
2. On the Quick Access toolbar, click Open from Vault.

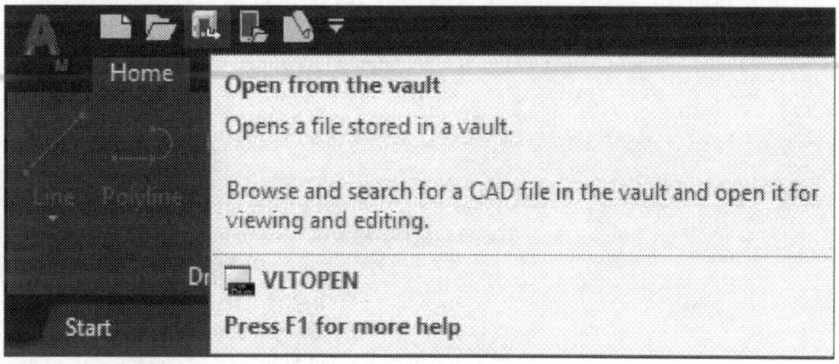

3. If you are not logged in from the previous practice, log in to the vault using the following information:
   - For User Name, enter **vaultuser**.
   - For Password, leave this box empty.
   - For Vault, select AOTGVault.

4. In the Mechanical DWG Files folder, open *Arbor_Press_Frame.dwg*.

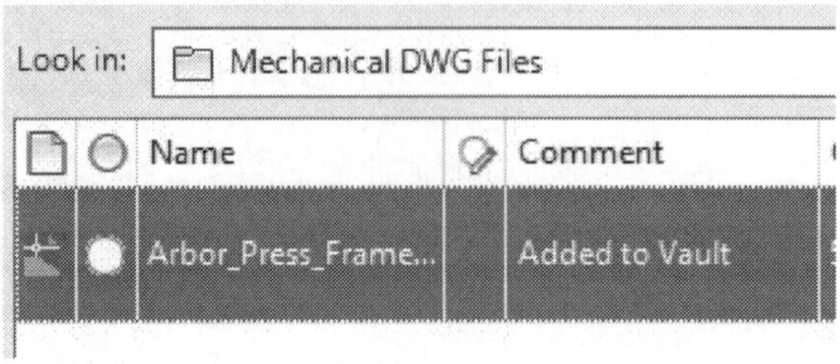

5. In the File not checked out dialog box, click Yes.

   The file is opened and checked out to you. Your view should match the following image.

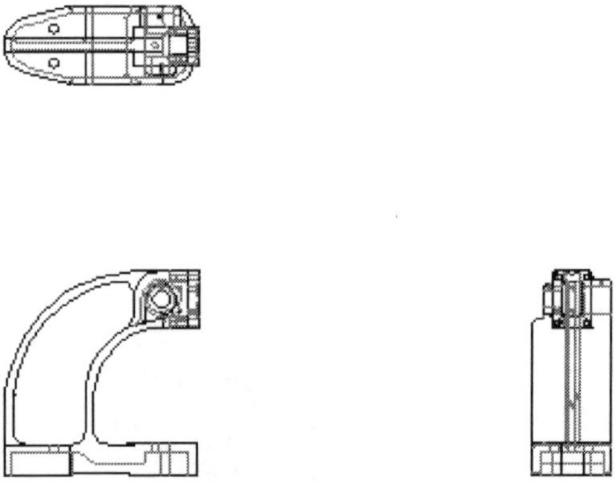

6. On the ribbon, click the View tab>Palettes panel>External References to display the external references palette.

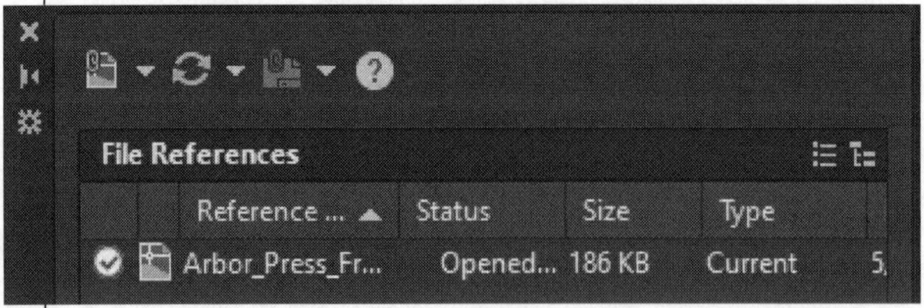

7. Right-click on the External References palette. Click Attach from Vault.

8. In the Mechanical Library Files folder, open *Title Block.dwg*.

9. In the Attach External Reference dialog box, under Insertion Point, ensure that the Specify On- Screen check box is not checked.

10. Click OK. The file is opened and loaded into the current drawing.

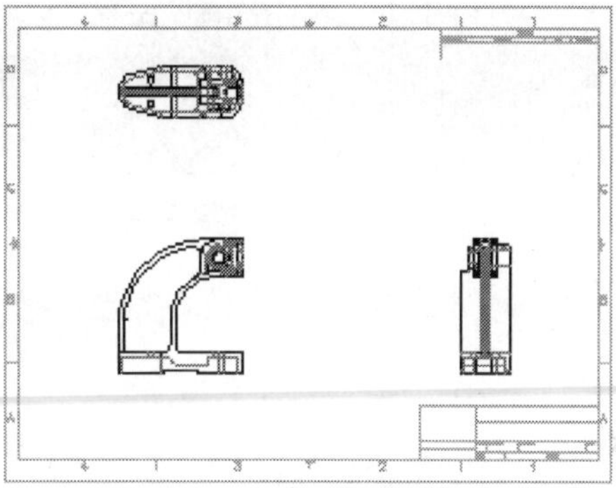

11. Zoom in to the right elevation. Delete the extra line shown.

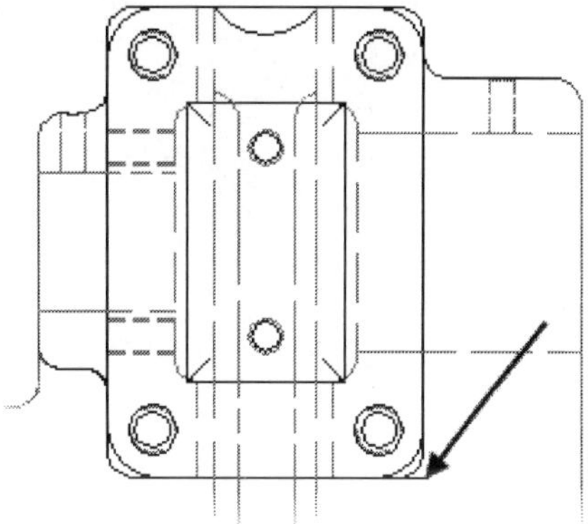

12. Review the status of both files on the External References palette.

13. Save the Arbor_Press_Frame.dwg file.

14. Review the file status on the External References palette. The icon status changes to indicate that the file has been edited and should be checked in.

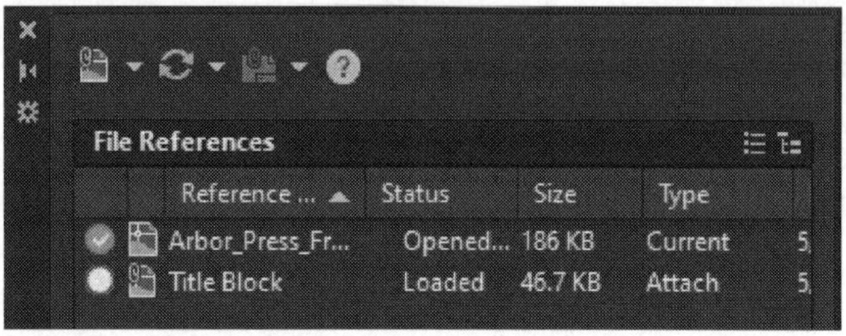

15. On the External References palette, right-click the Arbor_Press_Frame file and select Check In.

16. In the Check In dialog box, enter **Added title block to drawing + minor edit.**

17. Click OK. Click Yes if prompted to save the file.

18. Close all AutoCAD Mechanical files.

6.3 Chapter Summary

Autodesk Vault integrates with AutoCAD Mechanical and provides an engineering data management system that offers file security, version control, and multiuser support. Logging in to the vault and then checking in and checking out AutoCAD Mechanical drawings are examples of each of these functions.

Having completed this chapter, you can:

- Check AutoCAD Mechanical files in and out of a vault.
- Attach an XREF to a drawing and check in the host drawing and the XREF.

Working with Vault and Autodesk Civil 3D

In this chapter, you learn how to add existing Autodesk® Civil 3D® drawings to a vault and how to work with Autodesk Civil 3D files from the vault. Autodesk Civil 3D works like AutoCAD when interfacing with Autodesk® Vault Basic.

Learning Objectives in This Chapter

- Open and access the vault from Autodesk Civil 3D.
- Add Autodesk Civil 3D drawings to a vault.
- Attach an XREF to a drawing and vault the host drawing and the XREF.

7.1 Accessing the Vault in Autodesk Civil 3D

Overview

The Autodesk Vault add-in supplies data management tools that work in AutoCAD®, AutoCAD® Mechanical, AutoCAD® Electrical, Autodesk® Civil 3D® and more. You can add files to a vault and check files in and out. The files can be DWG™ or images.

You can access the data management tools provided by the Autodesk Vault add-in from a number of locations, including the XREF manager and the Vault tab in the ribbon.

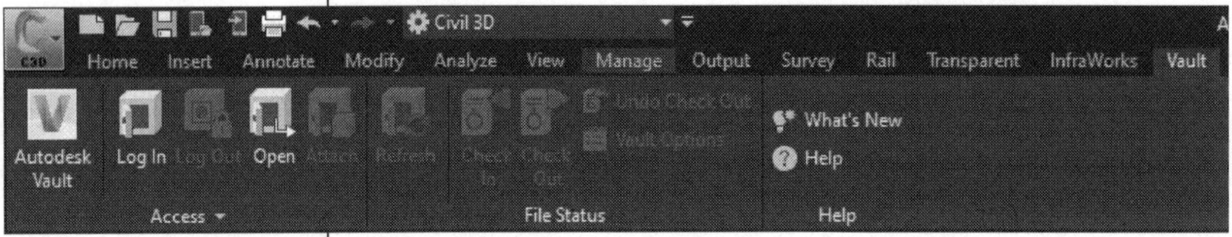

Objectives

After completing this lesson, you will be able to:

- Access the vault from Autodesk Civil 3D.
- Use a typical workflow for Autodesk Civil 3D and Autodesk Vault.

Opening and Accessing the Vault in Autodesk Civil 3D

The first step in working with Autodesk Civil 3D and Autodesk Vault is to log in to the vault. This lesson covers how to access the vault from Autodesk Civil 3D.

You log in to a specific vault through the vault Log In dialog box.

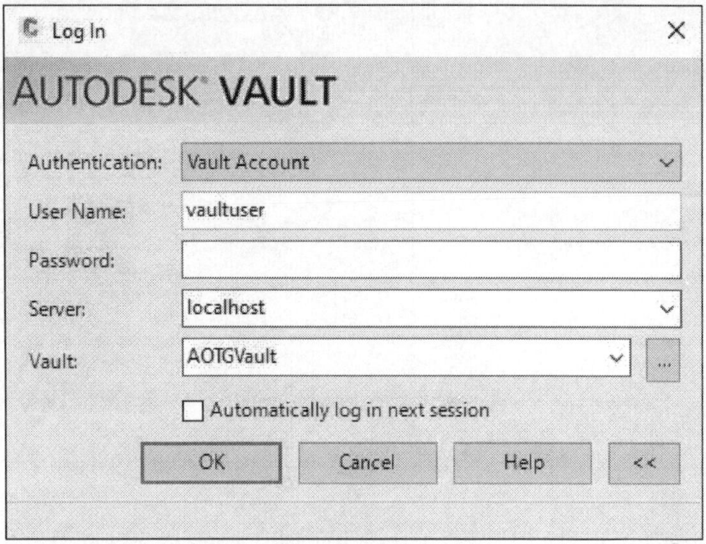

Procedure: Logging in to the Vault

You can access Autodesk Vault from Autodesk Civil 3D using one of the following methods: the Vault tab on the ribbon, the Vault toolbar, the command line, or the Vault tray icon.

1. On the ribbon, select the Vault tab and click Log In on the Access panel.

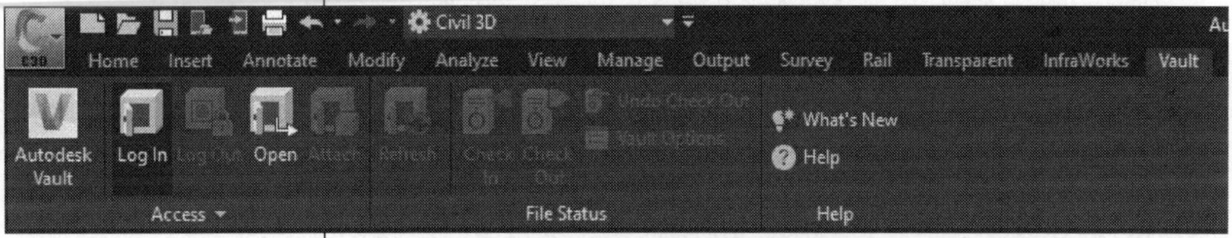

2. Click Log In in the Vault toolbar.

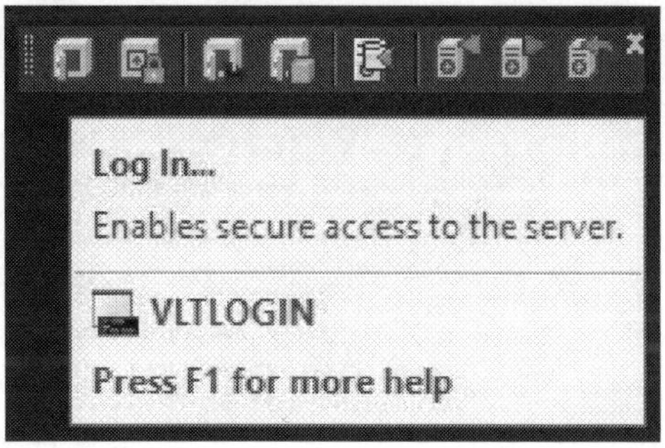

3. On the command line, enter **vault** or **vltlogin**.

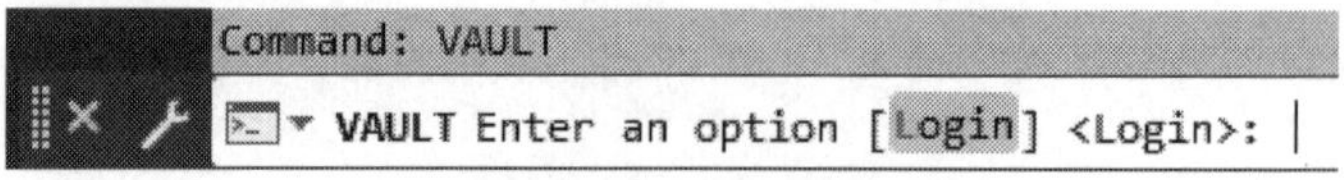

4. Right-click on the Vault tray icon and select Log In.

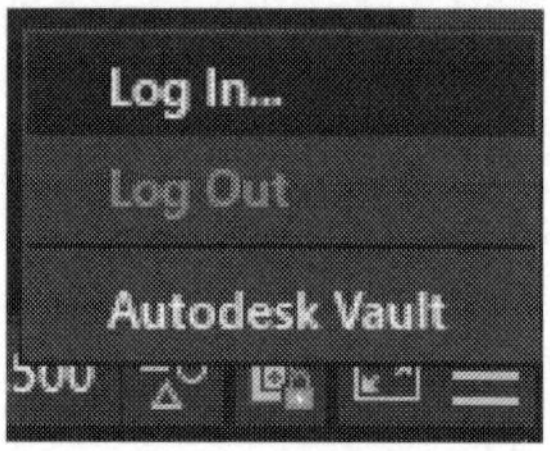

Status Bar Tray Icons

When logged in, rest the cursor over the Vault system tray icon to display the user login name, database, and server.

When you are not logged in to Autodesk Vault, the AutoCAD status bar tray icon is displayed as a locked vault. When you are logged in, the icon displays as an open vault door.

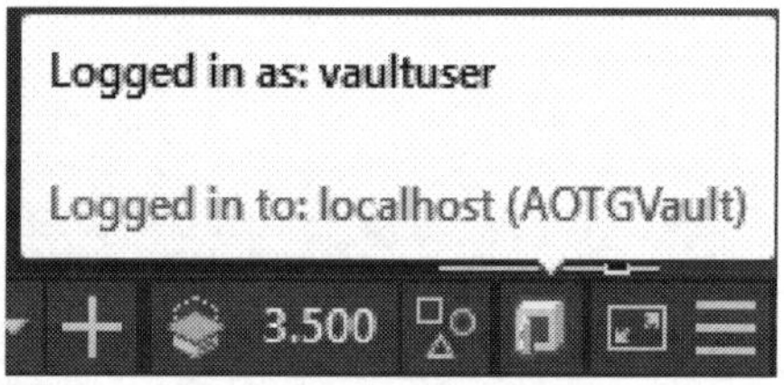

Typical Workflow for Autodesk Civil 3D and Autodesk Vault

In this lesson you learn about a typical workflow using Autodesk Vault and Autodesk Civil 3D.

The Vault tab on the ribbon includes a complete set of tools to manage drawings and other documents in your designs.

Procedure: Using Autodesk Civil 3D and Autodesk Vault

Your workflow varies depending on where you are in the design cycle. The following steps describe a basic workflow for Autodesk Vault and Autodesk Civil 3D.

1. Start Autodesk Civil 3D and click Autodesk Vault on the Vault tab of the ribbon.
2. Log in to the vault and set the working folder.

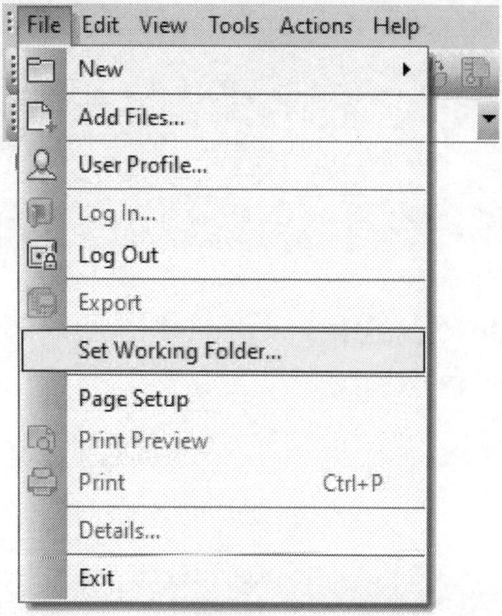

3. Add any Vault folders that are required for your project type.
4. In Autodesk Civil 3D, select the Vault tab and click Log In on the Access panel.

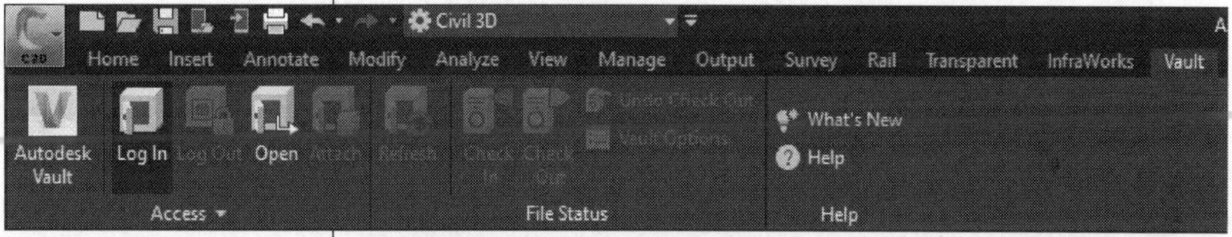

5. Open a file that you want to add to the vault or start a new drawing.
6. Attach any required external reference files (XREFs) to the open Autodesk Civil 3D file using the Attach command or the Attach from Vault command.
7. Save the drawing to the current working folder under the project you created.
8. Click Check In on the Vault tab to add the files to the Vault.
9. Open and check out other files from the vault using the Open from Vault command.

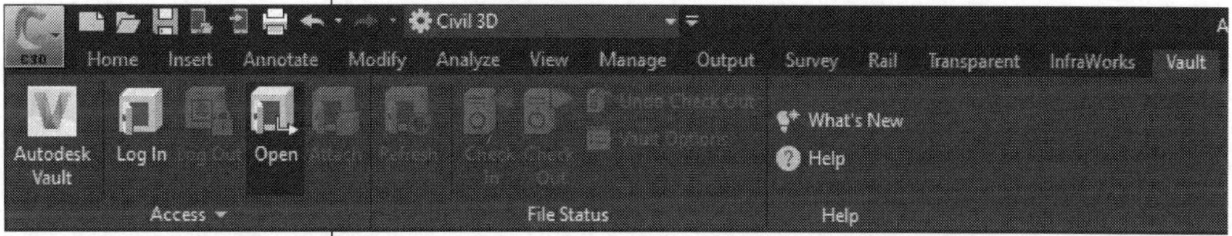

10. Check the modified files back in to the vault.

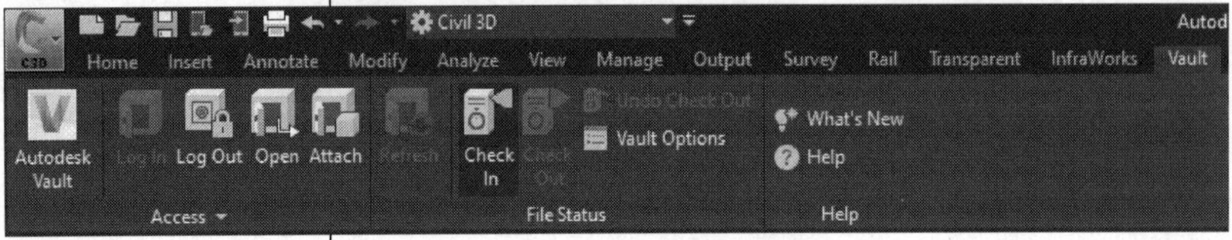

Adding Vault Folders

In this lesson, you will learn how to add Vault Folders to help organize files in the Vault. Two types of folders can be created:

1. Vault Folder
2. Library Folder

Vault folders add structure to the Vault permitting various types of files to be saved separately. A typical workflow in Civil Engineering projects would include having source drawings (housing design objects) and production drawings (in which the labeling would occur) in separate folders. Each folder in the Vault structure would contain specific types of files. A sample project folder structure is shown in the following image.

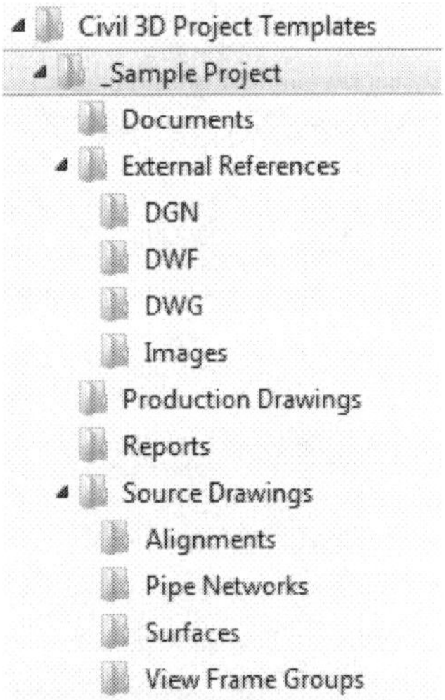

Typical Civil Folder Structure

Library folders are used to keep symbols and other read-only files safe from being changed. Library files are meant to be static, reused, and part of a company standard. For example, survey monuments and other symbols are files that you might want to store in library folders.

Practice 7a

Setting up the Vault

In this practice, you will log in to the Autodesk Vault software from the Autodesk Civil 3D software. You will also create two new folders for the practices in this chapter, and then set a working folder.

The completed practice

1. Start Autodesk Civil 3D.
2. Open *C:\AOTGVault\Chapter7\V-Original Topo.dwg*. If the Open Drawing - Previous Version AEC Objects Detected, click Close.

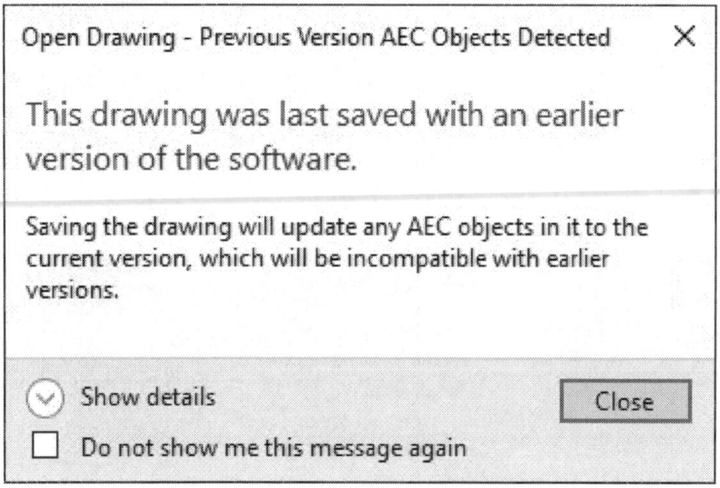

3. On the ribbon, select the Vault tab and click Log In on the Access panel.
4. Log in to the vault using the following information:
   - For User Name, enter **vaultuser**.
   - For Password, leave this box empty.
   - For Vault, select AOTGVault.

5. In the status bar tray, place the cursor over the Vault icon. The vault user name and vault name are displayed.

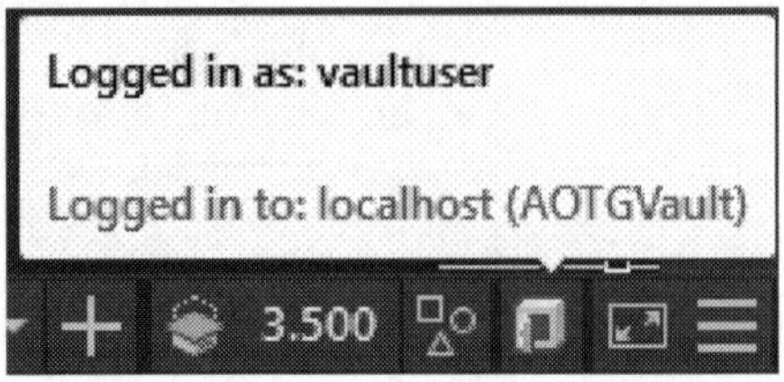

Next you will set the working folder. This will set the location in which to store Vault projects. The default working folder for Civil 3D projects is: *C:\Civil 3D Projects*.

6. On the ribbon, select the Vault tab and click Autodesk Vault on the Access panel.
7. Log in to Autodesk Vault using the following information:
    - For User Name, enter **administrator**.
    - For Password, leave this box empty.
    - For Vault, select AOTGVault.
8. Right-click on Vault Explorer ($) and click New Folder.
9. Name the new folder Civil 3D DWG Files.

Note: Depending on which practices you have completed, the Navigation Pane folders might be different.

10. Repeat Step 8 and 9 to add another folder, this time a Library Folder named Civil 3D Symbols, to the root ($) folder in Vault.

11. In the Autodesk Vault software, click the File menu>Set Working Folder. If you receive a message indicating that the working folder cannot be changed since the location has been preset by your system administrator, skip to step 14.

12. Browse to and select *C:\AOTGVault\VaultWorkingFolder.*

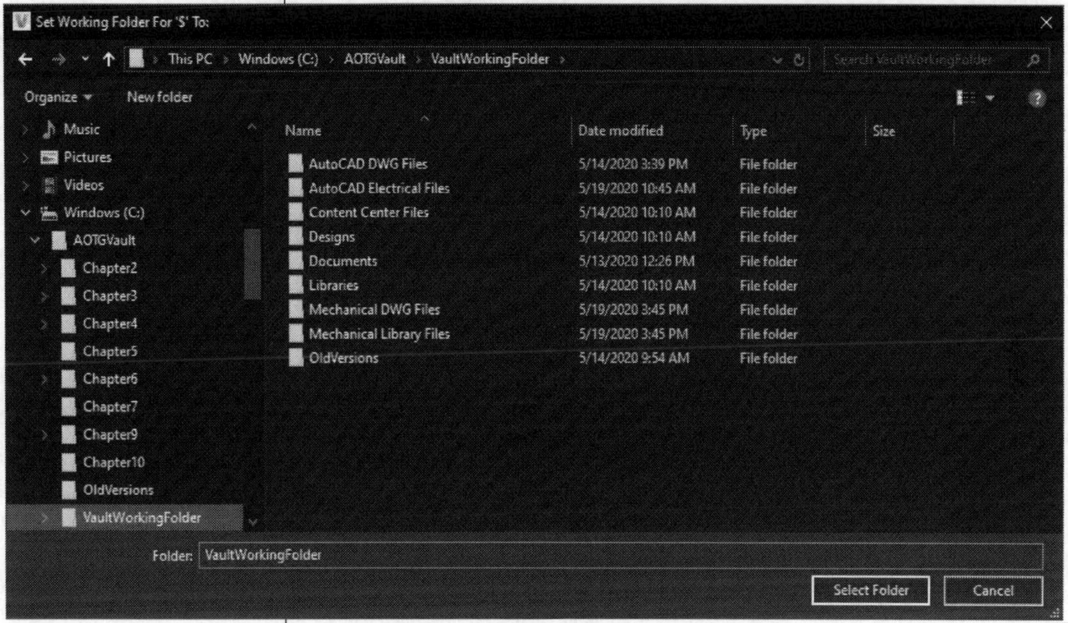

13. Click OK.

14. Close Autodesk Vault.

15. In Autodesk Civil 3D, save the file to ensure it is up to date.

16. Close the file.

7.2 Working with Autodesk Civil 3D Files

Overview

The Autodesk Civil 3D Vault add-in supplies data management tools that work in Autodesk Civil 3D. You can add files to a vault, check files out of the vault to modify them, and check modified files in to the vault. The files can be DWG files, images, or any file associated with your design.

Objectives

After completing this lesson, you will be able to:

- Check drawings in and out of a vault.
- Open files from a vault.
- Attach files from a vault.

Check In and Check Out Drawings

Once you have completed work on a drawing and want to check the file into the vault, you can use the Check In command. You can check a single drawing file at a time into the vault. If you are checking in a drawing file that contains external references (XREFs), all of the XREF drawings are checked in at the same time. By adding files that use XREFs to the vault from Autodesk Civil 3D, Autodesk Vault can keep track of the file relationships.

When you open a file from the vault, you have the option of checking out the file. The file is copied to the corresponding folder in or below the working folder. To modify a file that is in the vault, the file must first be checked out to you. You always edit the copy of the file in the working folder structure. The files in the vault are the master files and cannot be edited directly.

Check in Files to the Vault

You use the Check In command to store DWG and image files in a vault. The preferred workflow is to check in files from Autodesk Civil 3D. The following procedure describes the methods you can use to check drawing and image files in to the vault.

1. On the ribbon, select the Vault tab and click Check In on the File Status panel.

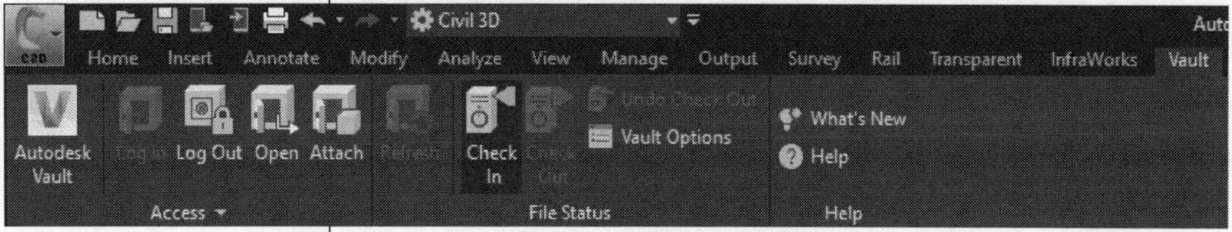

2. On the Vault toolbar, click Check In.

3. In the External References palette, right-click the file and select Check In.

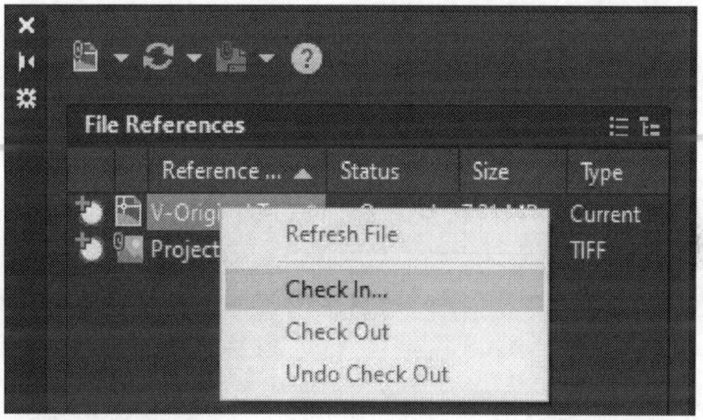

4. On the command line, enter **vault** or **vltcheckin**.

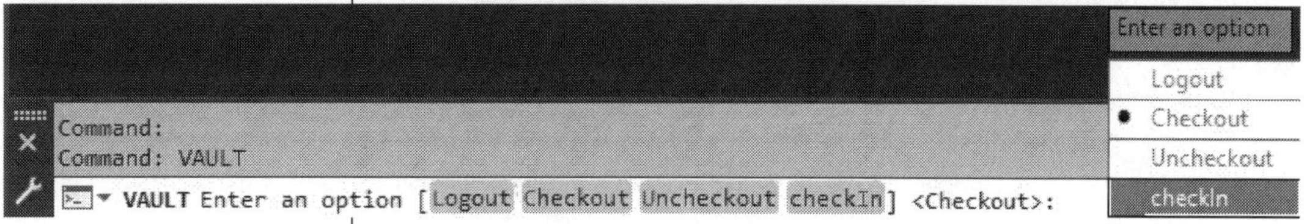

Check In

The Check In dialog box is used to control how the files are checked in.

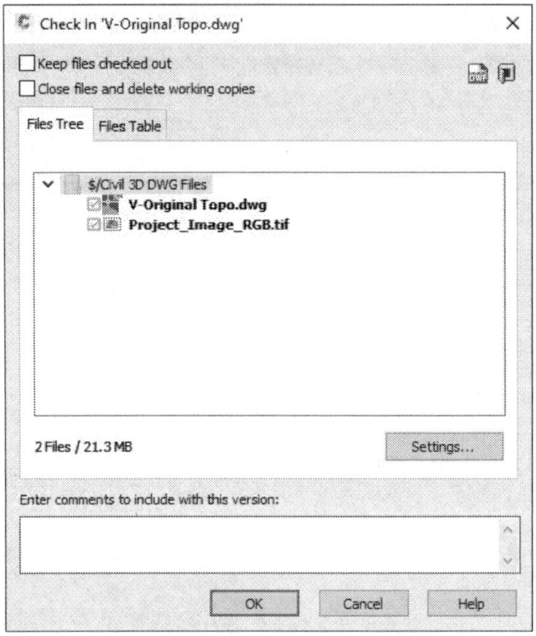

Check in Files Not in Working Folder

If the file you check in to the vault is not in the working folder or its subfolders, the Select Vault Location dialog box opens. You select the vault location for the drawing file in this dialog box.

The Select Vault Location dialog box is always displayed if you do not set a working folder from Autodesk Vault.

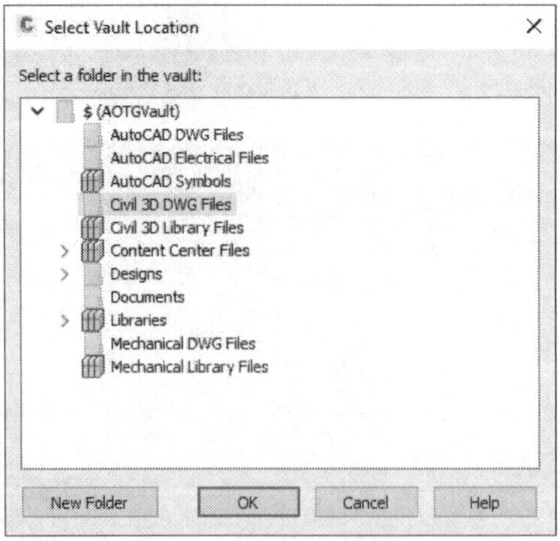

When you next open this file from the vault, it is copied to the working folder structure.

Definition of Settings Dialog Box

The Settings buttons control organization of the files to be added to the vault and the visualization file options for each file.

Settings Options

The Settings dialog box has the following options.

Setting	Description
File Locations - Use organized folder structure	The root folder is the top-level folder in a hierarchical folder tree. The folder structure is maintained for all folders that are at the same level or beneath the host file.
File Locations – Place all files in one folder	All XREFs and dependent files are flattened so that they exist at the same level as the host. All the files are located under the vault folder.
File Locations – Preserve locations if in working folder	Maintains the file structure of files being checked in from the local working folder. This is the preferred workflow.
Visualization Attachment Options – Create Visualization attachment	Creates and attaches a DWF™ or DWFx file for each drawing file being checked in.
Visualization Attachment Options – Apply to all files	Creates a visualization attachment for all files being checked in. This option must be toggled on to create DWF or DWFx files for external reference drawings.
Visualization Attachment Options - Include	Indicates which of the following tabs to include in the visualization attachment: Model Tab Only Layout Tabs Only Model and Layout Tabs <Use Default Settings> to use the settings specified on the Publish Options dialog in the Autodesk Vault.

Current Visualization Settings

The Check In dialog box displays the current settings of the visualization Attachment options.

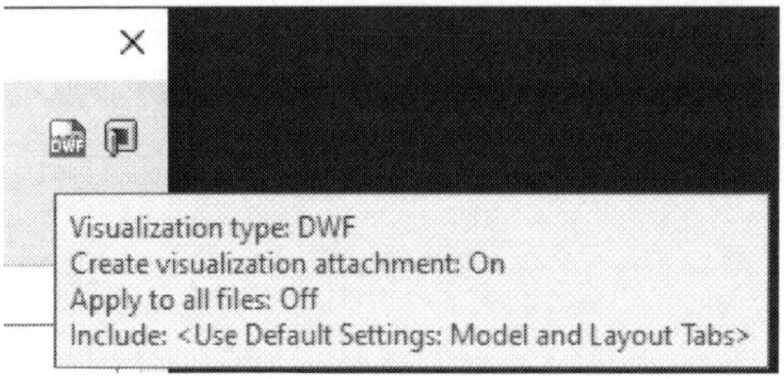

Check Out Files from the Vault

You can use the Check Out command to check out a file you have opened from your working folder if the file is currently checked in to the vault. You must check out a drawing from the vault before it can be edited. The following are various methods that you can use to check out a file from the vault.

1. On the ribbon, select the Vault tab and click Check Out on the File Status panel.

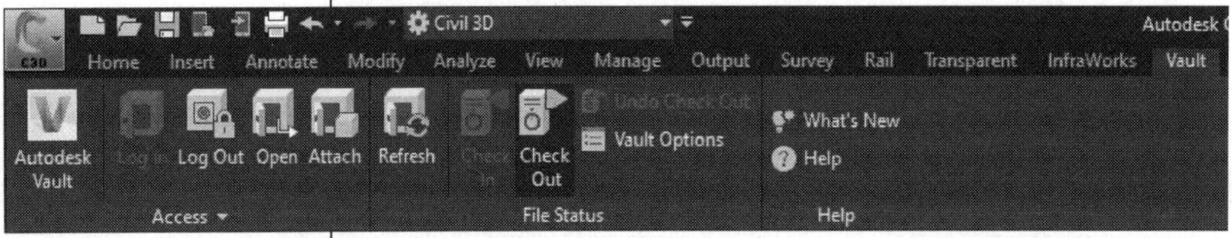

2. On the Vault toolbar, click Check Out.

3. In the External References palette, right-click the file. Click Check Out.

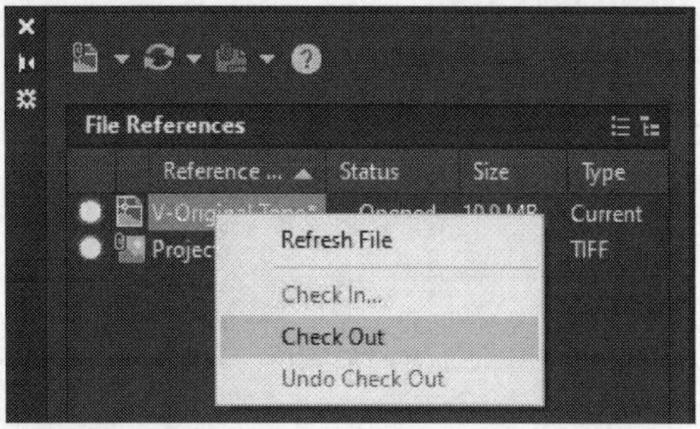

4. On the command line, enter **vault** or **vltcheckout**.

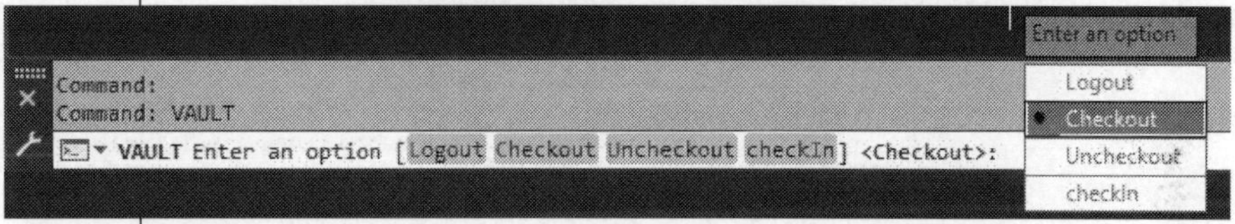

Open from Vault

You use Open from Vault to copy a file from the vault to your working folder and open the local copy. By default, the file is not checked out to you. Optionally, you can check out the local copy during the open process.

Opening a File from the Vault

Use any of the following commands to open a file from the vault.

1. On the ribbon, select the Vault tab and click Open on the Access panel.

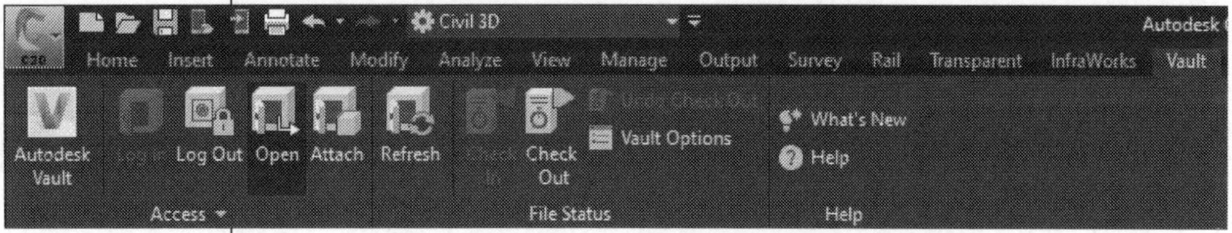

2. On the Vault toolbar, click Open from Vault.

3. On the command line, enter **vltopen**.

Open File Options

In the Select File dialog box, you can select to check out the file, check out the file and any external references, or open the file without checking it out.

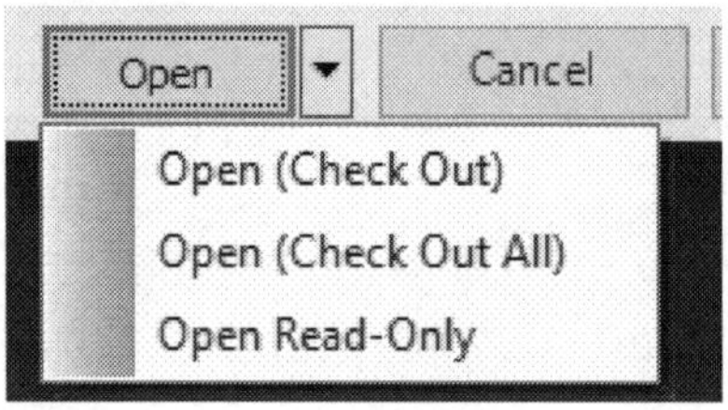

If you click Open without selecting one of the options, you are prompted for the check-out behavior.

Attach from Vault

If a file is saved in the vault, you can attach it to an open Autodesk Civil 3D file by using the Attach from Vault command. This works the same as the AutoCAD DWG Reference when you are working with external references, except that Attach from Vault searches the vault for files rather than searching your local drives.

Attaching a File from the Vault

Use any of the following methods to attach a file from the vault.

1. On the ribbon, select the Vault tab and click Attach on the Access panel.

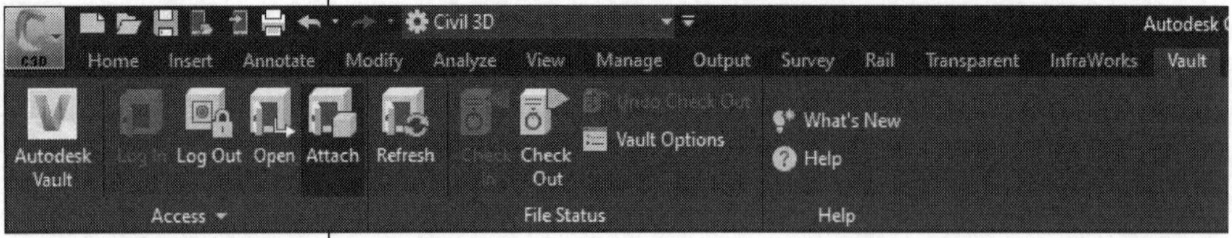

2. On the Vault toolbar, click Attach from Vault.

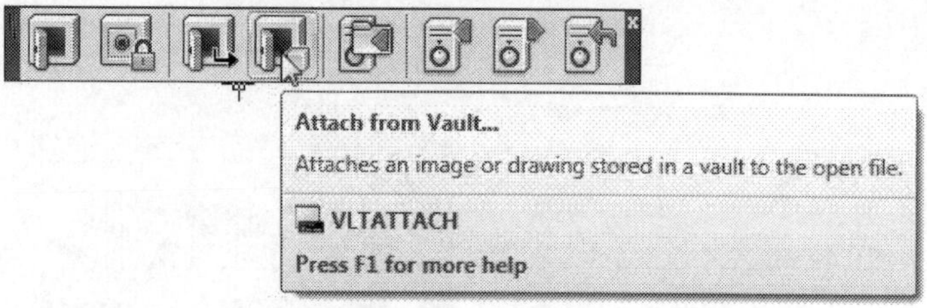

3. In the External References palette, select Attach from Vault from the list.

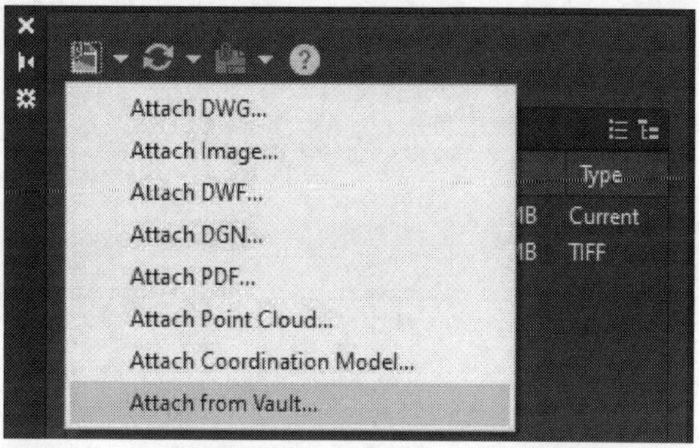

4. In the External References palette, right-click in the File References background. Click Attach from Vault.

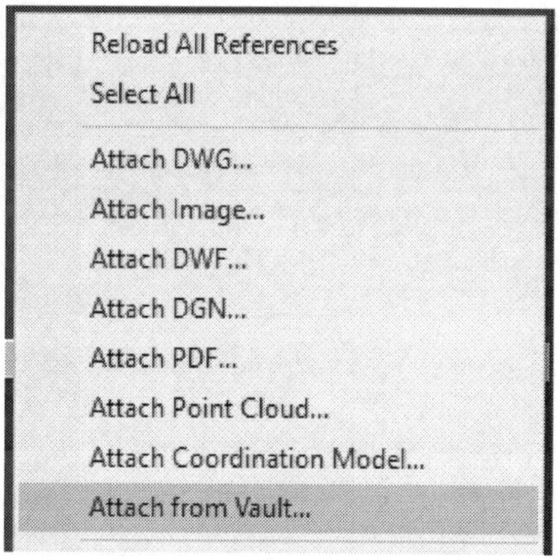

5. On the command line, enter **vltattach**.

If the file is a library file, the file is copied to your working folder in read-only format. For example, in the following image, Attach from Vault was used to attach the Project_Image_RGB.tif drawing.

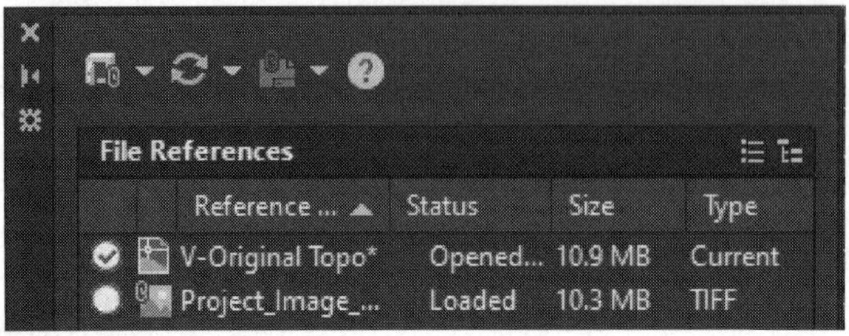

Practice 7b

Check Files In and Out of the Vault

In this practice, you check a drawing in to a vault library and a standard vault folder. You will then attach a drawing from the vault to an existing drawing and check in the combined file.

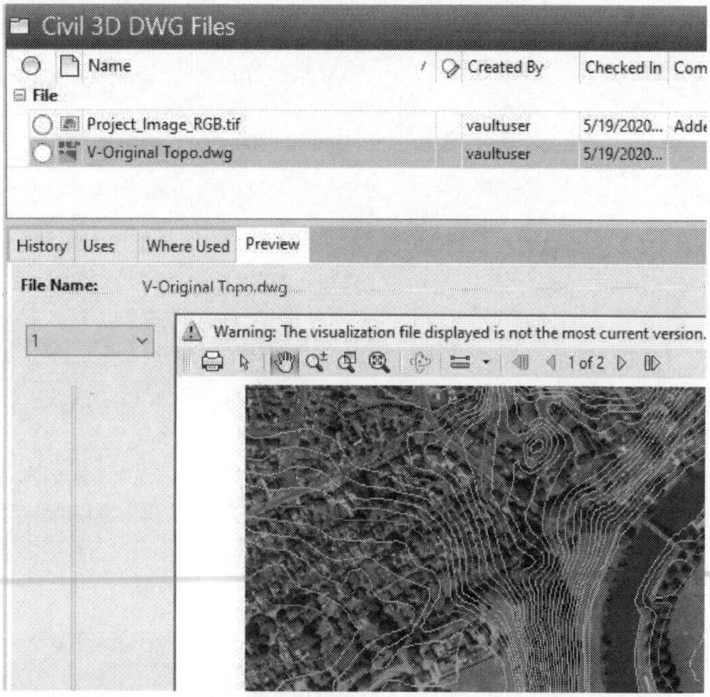

Task 1 - Check files into the vault.

1. If required, start Autodesk Civil 3D.
2. Open *C:\AOTGVault\Chapter7\V-Original Topo.dwg*.
3. Save the file.
4. If you are not already logged in to the AOTGVault, log in using the following information:
    - For User Name, enter **vaultuser**.
    - For Password, leave this box empty.
    - For Vault, select AOTGVault.

5. On the ribbon, select the Vault tab and click Vault Options on the Access panel.

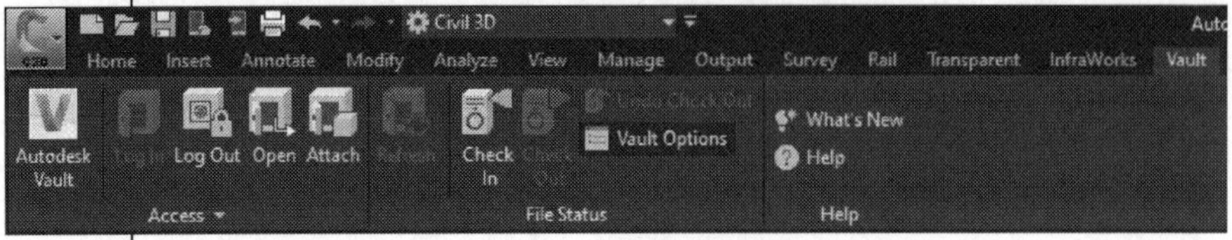

6. In the Options dialog box, ensure that the Ignore AutoCAD View Only Changes check box is checked.

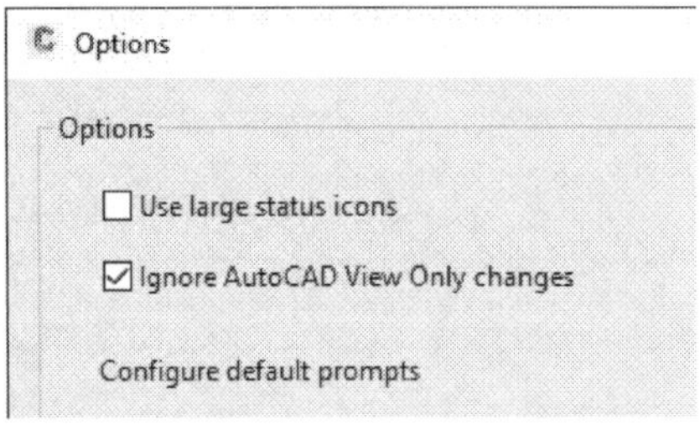

7. Click OK.

8. On the ribbon, select the Vault tab and click Check In on the File Status panel.

9. In the Select Vault Location dialog box, select the Civil 3D DWG Files folder.

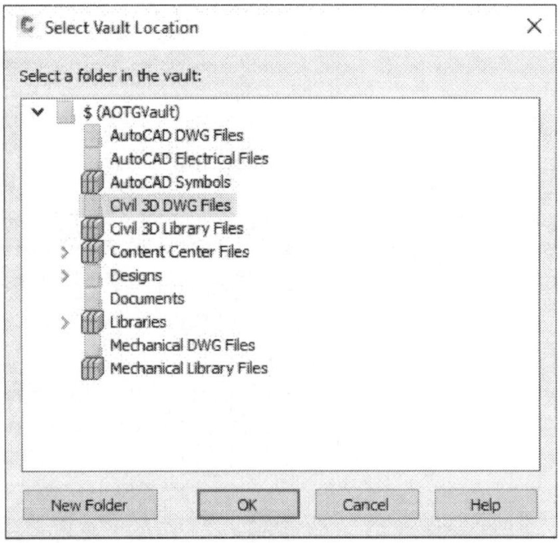

10. Click OK.

11. In the Check In dialog box, click Settings. In the Settings dialog box, ensure that your settings match the following image.

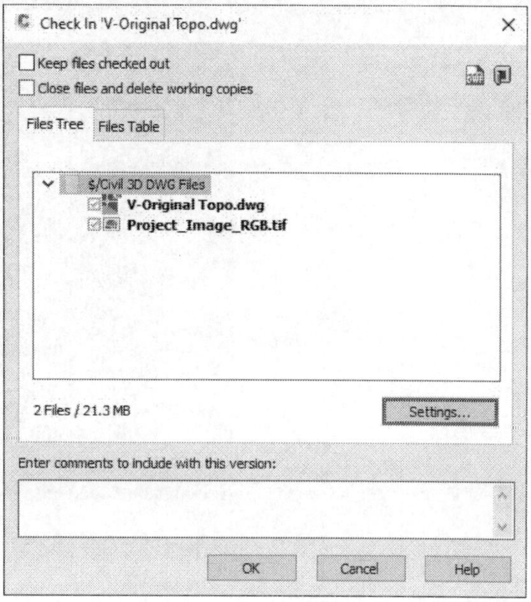

12. Click OK to close the Settings dialog box. Enter Added to Vault and click OK in the Check In dialog box to close it.

13. Click Yes if you are prompted to save the file. The drawing and visualization files are checked in to the vault.

14. Click OK when you are informed that you are now working on the vaulted copy of the file in the working folder.

15. Open *C:\AOTGVault\Chapter7\Section-Monument.dwg*.

16. Save the file.

17. On the Vault toolbar, click Check In.

18. In the Select Vault Location dialog box, select the Civil 3D Symbols folder. Click OK.

19. In the Check In dialog box, enter Added to Vault and click OK. Click Yes if you are prompted to save the file and dismiss the Vault.

20. Click OK when you are informed that you are now working on the vaulted copy of the file in the working folder.

21. Close V-Original Topo.dwg and Section-Monument.dwg.

Task 2 - Check files out of the vault.

1. From the application icon, click Open>Open from the vault.

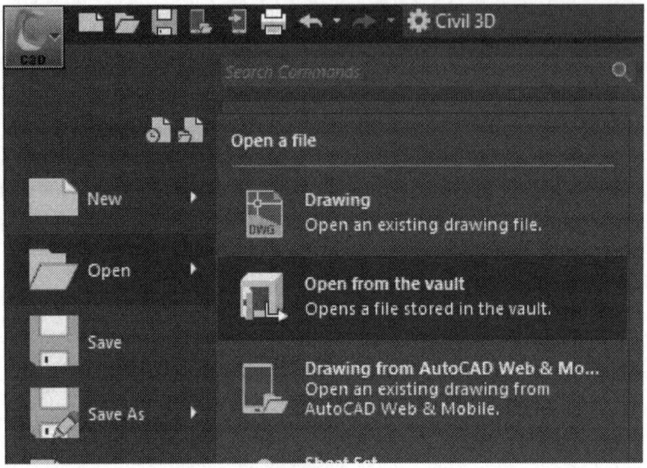

2. In the Civil 3D DWG Files folder, select V-Original Topo.dwg. Click Open.
3. Click Yes to check out the file.

4. On the ribbon, select the Vault tab and click Attach from the Access panel.
5. Browse to the Civil 3D Symbols folder and select Section-Monument.dwg to open the file.
6. For the insertion point, select Specify On-screen. Click OK.
7. Place the symbol by entering **348516.697,312386.520**.
8. Save the file.

9. On the ribbon, select the View tab and click External References Palette from the Palettes panel.

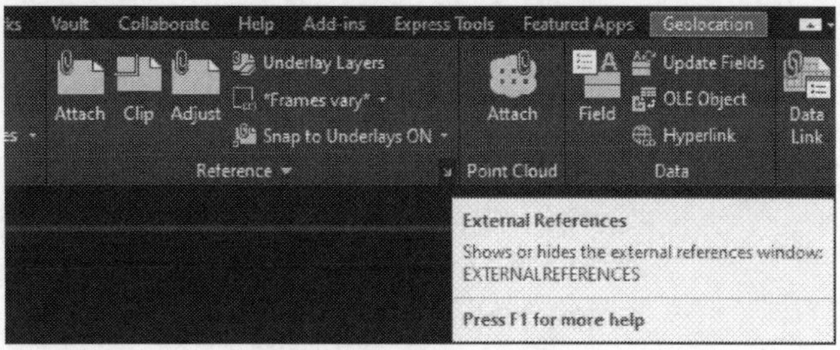

10. The status of the files is displayed.

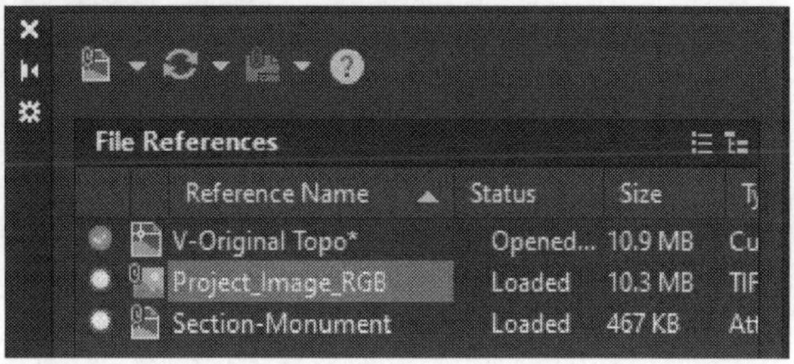

11. Select the V-Original Topo.dwg, right-click and select Check in and click OK. Click Yes if you are prompted to save.

12. In Autodesk Vault, select V-Original Topo.dwg. Select the Preview tab and select Version 2. Review the visualization file. Note that on the second page, the section monument symbol is displayed in the latest version.

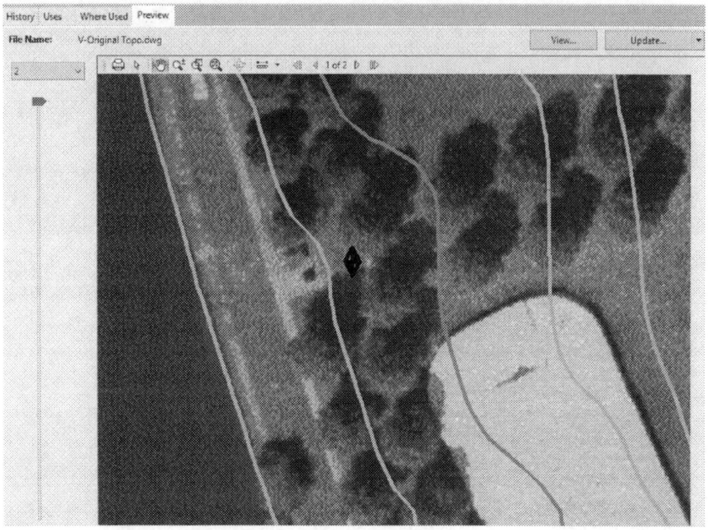

13. Select 1 in the version drop-down list. The version of the drawing without the XREF is displayed in the preview window.

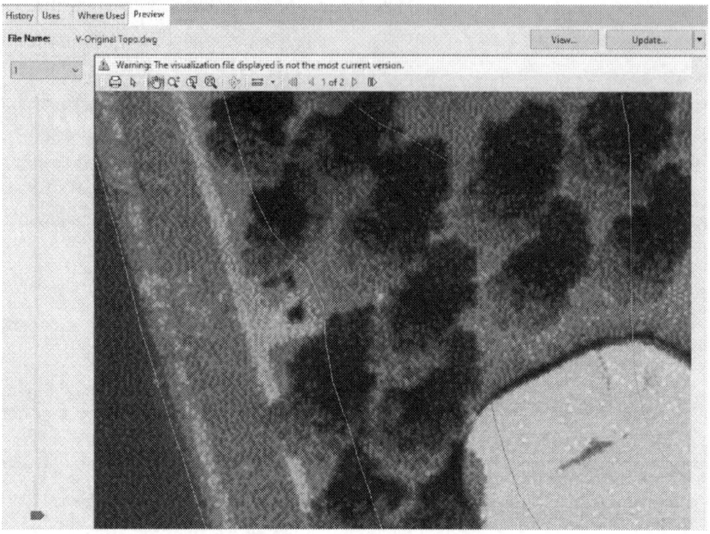

14. Close all of the Autodesk Civil 3D software files.

7.3 Working with External References in AutoCAD

Overview

You use the External References palette to work with external references in your designs. From the External References palette you can perform all AutoCAD XREF functions and Autodesk Vault commands. This lesson covers the user interface of the External References palette and its commands.

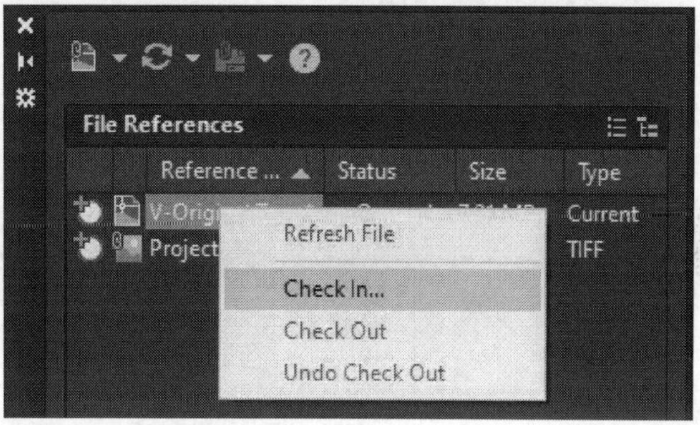

Objectives

After completing this lesson, you will be able to:

- View the external references in tree view or list view and toggle between details and a preview of the referenced file.
- Use the External References palette and Vault.

External References Palette

You can use the External References palette to control external references in Autodesk Civil 3D and perform vault activities, such as checking files in and out and attaching files from the vault.

The External References palette is an enhanced standard window (ESW) that can be docked and used to help you manage attached files. You can manage references to drawing, image, DWF, DGN, and PDF files from this palette.

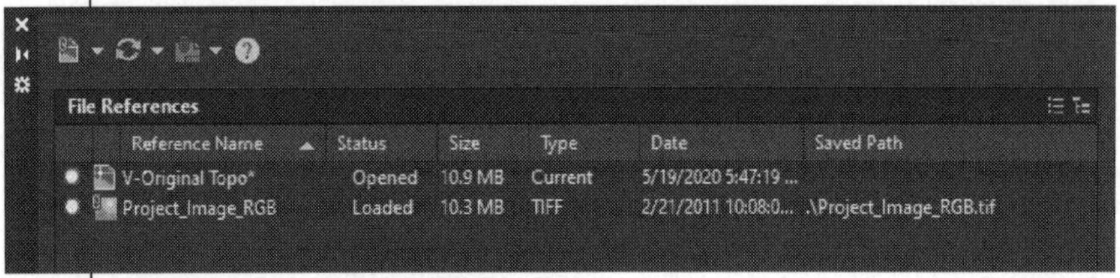

About the XREF Manager and the Vault

To use the External References palette with Vault commands, you must be logged in to the vault. In addition to all of the External References palette functionality that can be found elsewhere in the Autodesk Civil 3D software, the Vault status icons are displayed. These icons indicate the status of your local copy of files as compared against the master copy of those same files in the vault.

The File References pane of the External References palette displays the current file, any attached drawings, images, and other reference files. You can view this area in either a list view or a tree view.

List View

The list view displays properties of the drawings used. These include status, size, and type.

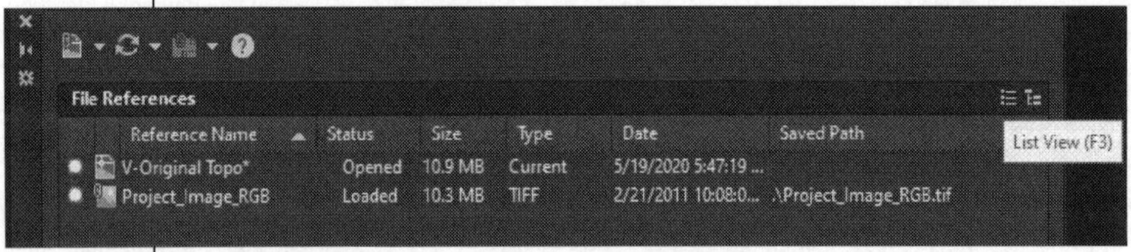

Tree View

The tree view displays the references between the open drawing and its file references.

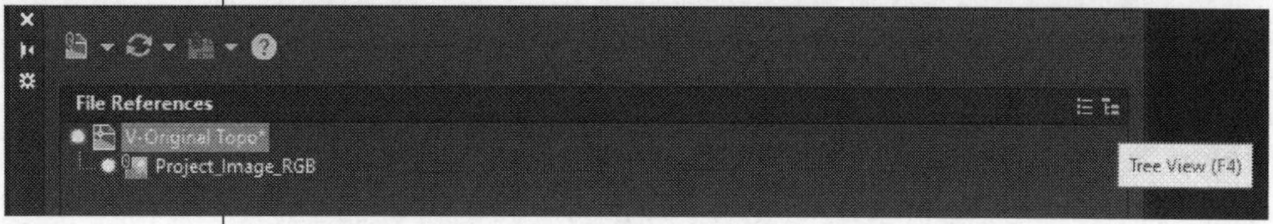

Details Pane

The details pane of the XREF Manager ESW displays the properties of the file in a structured format. Properties displayed include the file version number. Autodesk Vault generates the version number and indicates the latest saved version of the file.

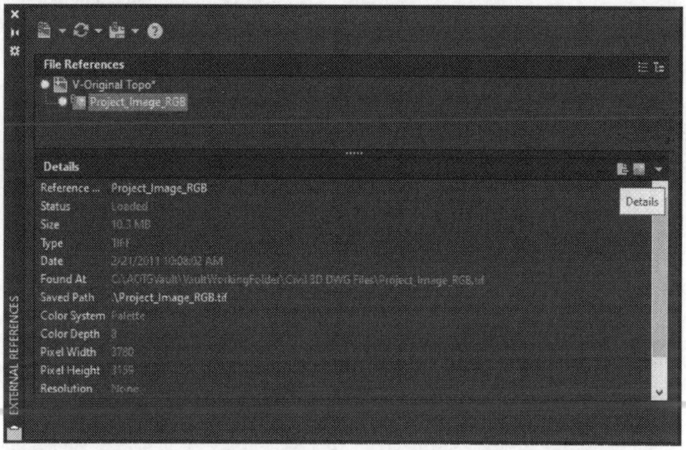

You can toggle the details pane to Preview mode. When you select a file in the File References pane, a preview image of it is displayed.

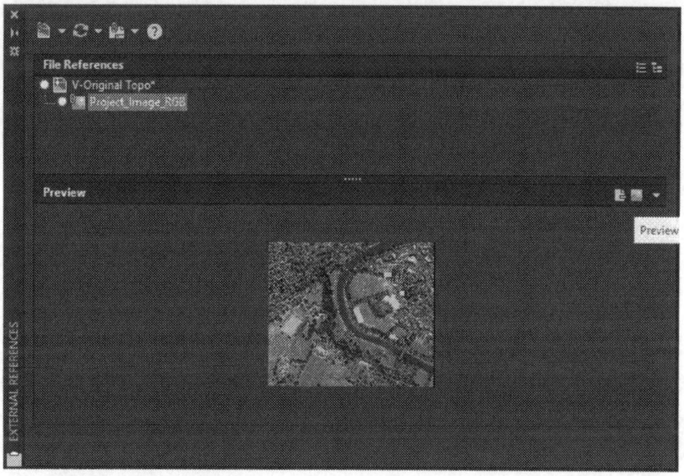

External References Palette and the Vault

The Autodesk Vault add-in enhances the functionality of the External References palette. In addition to the standard functionality of Autodesk Civil 3D, you can use the External References palette to access many of the Vault commands. Using the External References palette improves your workflow between Autodesk Civil 3D and the vault.

You can check referenced files in and out of the vault from the External References palette.

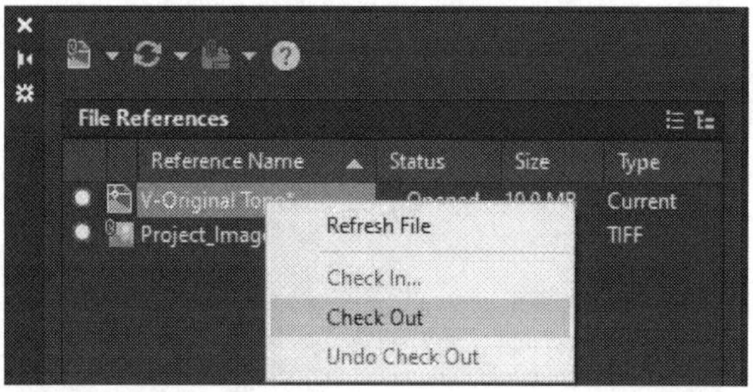

Procedure: Working with XREFs and the Vault

The following steps describe how to work with the Autodesk Civil 3D software's external references and the vault.

1. In the Autodesk Civil 3D software, open the External References palette.

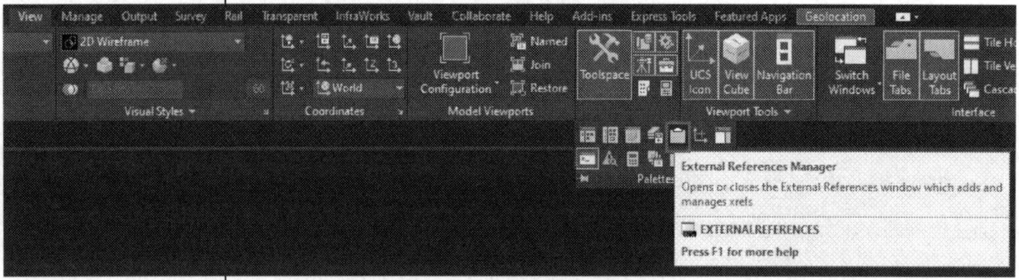

2. If the current drawing is not in the vault, the Vault status icon is displayed with a plus sign.

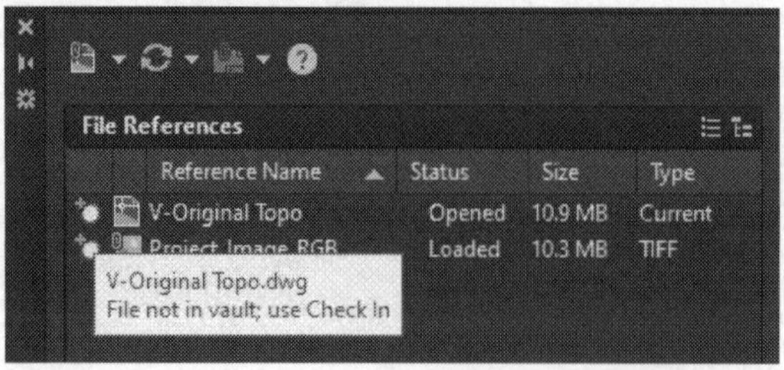

3. When you right-click in the File References background, a different shortcut menu is displayed. In addition to the AutoCAD commands, you have access to the Attach from Vault, Log In, and Log Out commands.

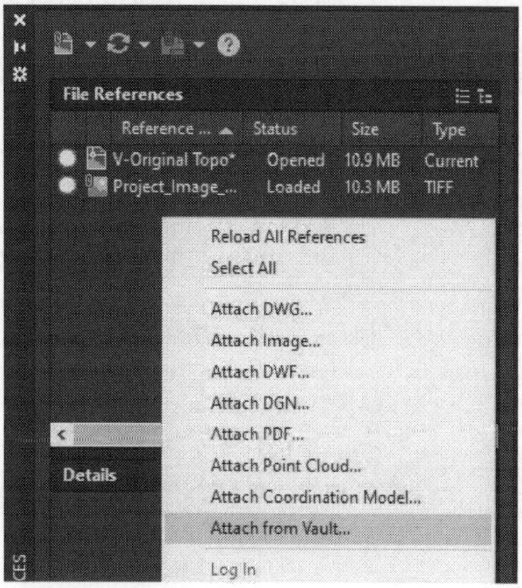

4. You attach another drawing as an XREF to the current file using the Attach DWG option.

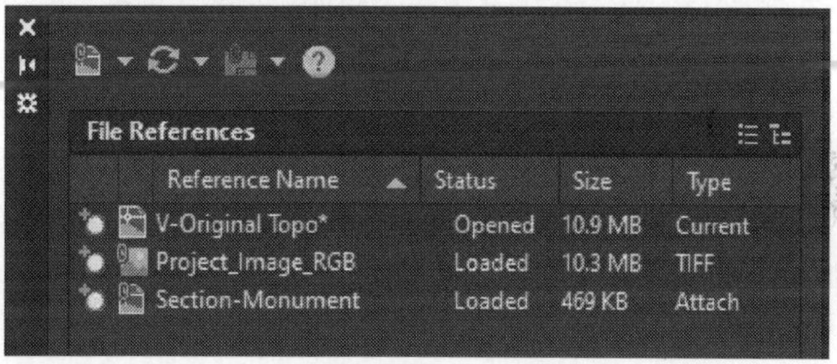

5. When you are ready to check in the files, in the File References list, right-click the host drawing. Select Check In.

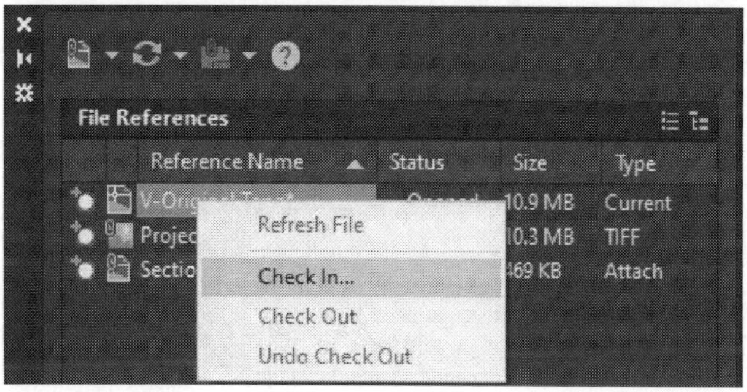

6. Vault recognizes that the Handicap_Sign.dwg file is an XREF attachment and checks it in with the host file.
7. In the External References palette, the Vault status icons change to Available for Check Out icons.

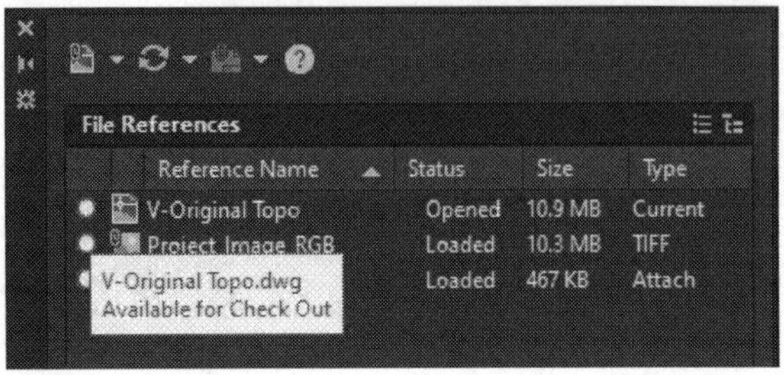

Practice 7c

Use the External References Palette

In this practice, you will check a drawing into the vault. You will then attach a drawing from the vault to the new drawing, make changes, and check in the combined file.

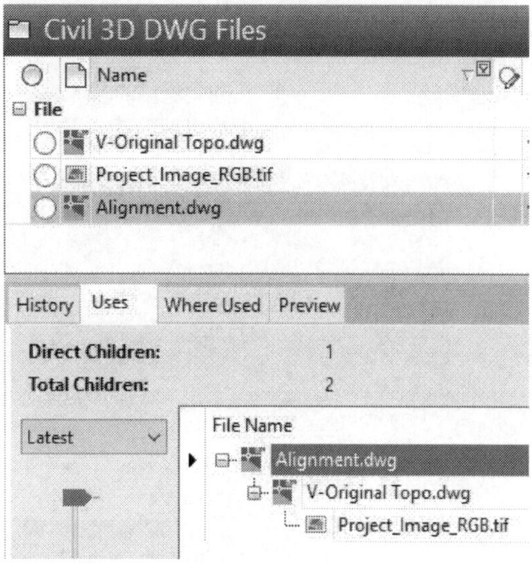

The completed practice

1. In Autodesk Civil 3D, start a new drawing from the _Autodesk Civil 3D (Metric) NCS.dwt.

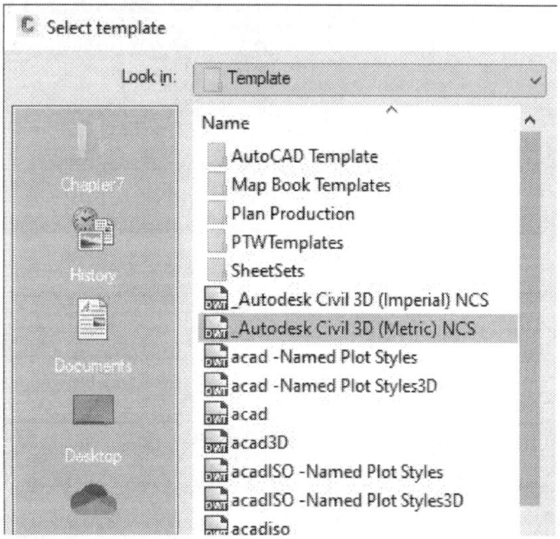

2. Save the file as Alignment.dwg and place it in the *C:\AOTGVault\VaultWorkingFolder\Civil 3D DWG Files* folder.

3. If you are not logged in to the vault, log in using the following information:

   - For User Name, enter **vaultuser**.
   - For Password, leave this box empty.
   - For Vault, select AOTGVault.

4. On the ribbon, select the View tab and click External References Palette on the Palettes panel.

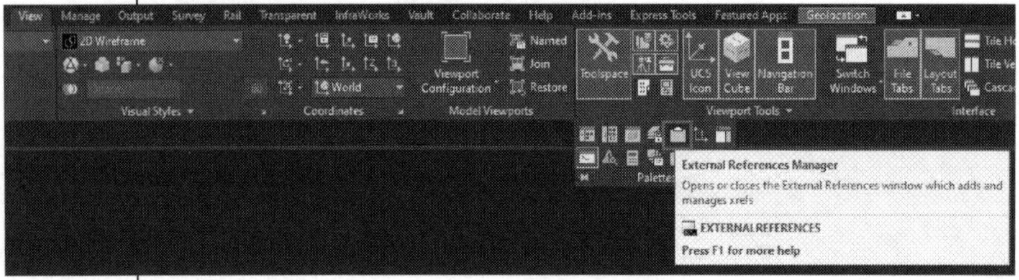

5. In External References, right-click Attach from Vault. Do the following:

   - In the Select File dialog box, select V-Original Topo.dwg from the Civil 3D DWG Files folder.
   - Click Open.
   - Click No to checking out prompt.
   - Specify the insertion point as 0,0,0.
   - Specify an X,Y,Z scale of 1.
   - Specify a rotation angle of 0.
   - Click OK.

6. Zoom Extents.

   The Section-Monument drawing and Project_Image are both displayed in the V-Original Topo.dwg drawing and added to the External References palette.

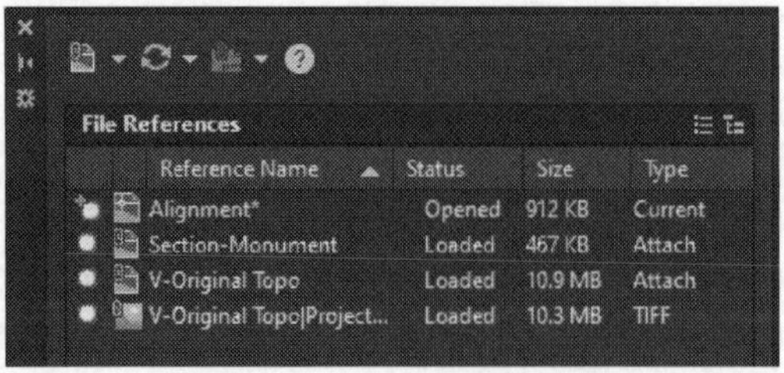

7. Hover the cursor over the Vault icons and review the status of the files.

8. Save the file.

9. On the External References palette, right-click on Alignment and click Check In.

10. Enter **Added to Vault** as a comment and then click OK to close the Check In dialog box.

11. Click Yes if prompted to save the files. Click OK to dismiss the dialog box prompting you that the file is now in the working folder.

12. The icons now indicate that the files are all checked in.

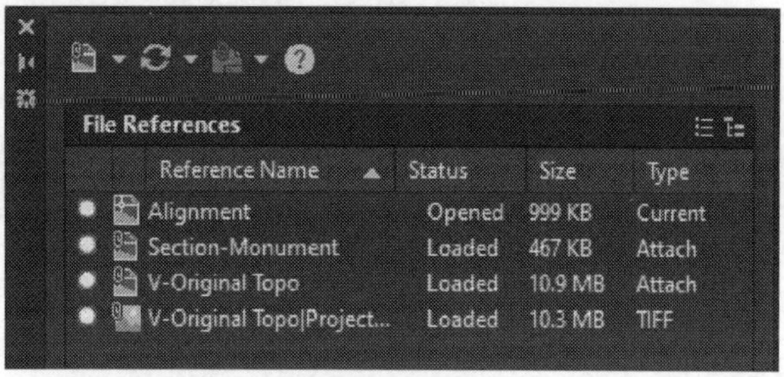

13. In Autodesk Vault, click Refresh.

14. Click the Civil 3D DWG Files folder and review the status of Alignment.dwg that you checked in.

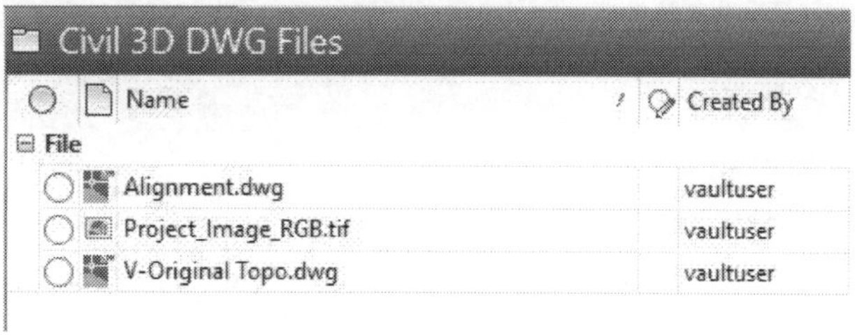

15. Switch to the Autodesk Civil 3D software. On the ribbon, select the Vault tab and click Open on the Access panel. Complete the following:
    - In the Select File dialog box, navigate to the Civil 3D DWG Files folder.
    - Open *V-Original Topo.dwg*.

16. Click Yes to check out the file.

17. In the XREF manager, right-click on Section-Monument and select Detach to remove it from the file.

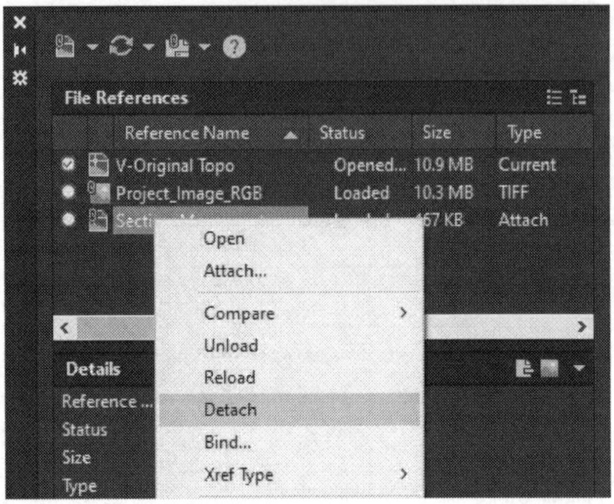

18. Save the file.

19. Check V-Original Topo.dwg in to the vault.

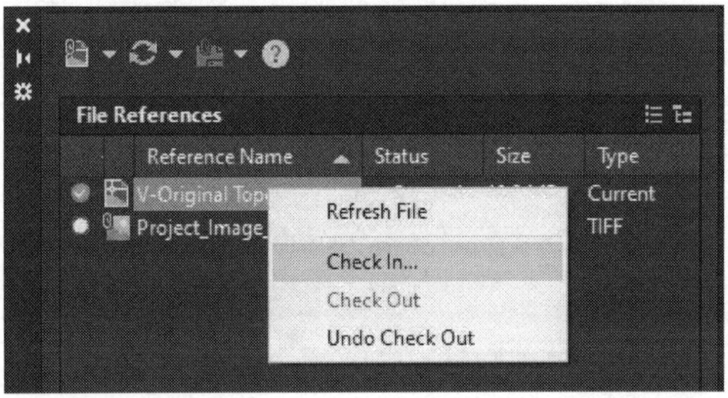

20. Close V-Original Topo.dwg.

21. Switch to the Alignment drawing. Note that V-Original Top.dwg requires reloading since it has changed.

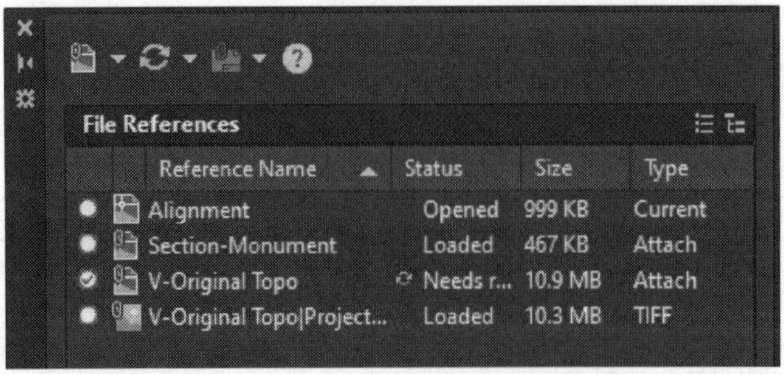

22. In the External References palette, right-click on V-Original Topo and select Reload.

    The modification to the V-Original Topo drawing has changed the icon display and the Status detail.

23. Click Yes to check out the Alignment file.

24. Save the file.

25. Check in the Alignment drawing.

26. Close all of the Autodesk Civil 3D files.

27. In Autodesk Vault, click Refresh.

28. Select the Alignment drawing. Select the Uses tab. Note that the latest version of Alignment.dwg does not use the Section-Monument.dwg but Version 1 does.

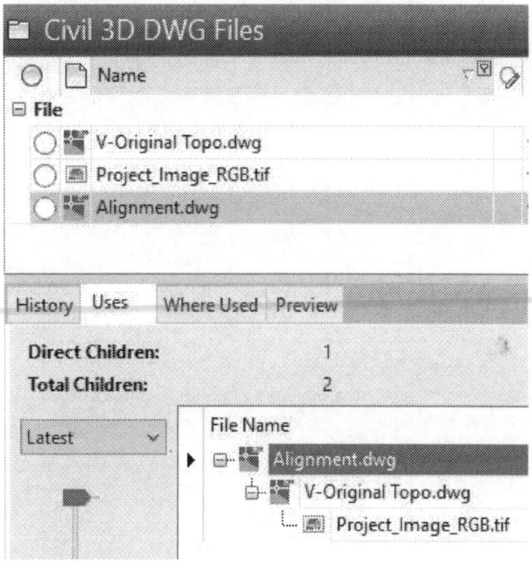

29. Close Autodesk Vault.

7.4 Chapter Summary

Autodesk Vault integrates with Autodesk Civil 3D and provides an engineering data management system that offers file security, version control, and multiuser support. Logging in to the vault and then checking in and checking out Autodesk Civil 3D drawings are examples of each of these functions.

Having completed this chapter, you can:

- Open and access the vault from the Autodesk Civil 3D software.
- Add Autodesk Civil 3D drawings to a vault.
- Attach an XREF to a drawing and vault the host drawing and the XREF.

Chapter 8

Common Vault Tasks

In this chapter you learn how to perform common everyday tasks using Autodesk® Vault. You create customized views in the main and preview panes, move, copy, rename, and replace files in designs, edit file properties, and pack files for use outside the vault.

The concepts, workflows, and techniques in this chapter apply to all applications associated with Autodesk Vault, but the practices are specific to Autodesk® Inventor®. The files that you use in this chapter's practices were loaded into the vault in a previous practice. If you have not completed the practice in Chapter 3 on adding Autodesk Inventor files to the vault using Autodesk Autoloader, complete it before you start this chapter's practices.

Learning Objectives in This Chapter

- Customize the Main pane in Autodesk Vault.
- Use find tools to find files and save searches, the Custom Filter tool to filter file lists, and shortcuts to quickly navigate to a file or folder.
- Manage file versions to preview versions, get a previous version, get the latest version, and work with labels.
- Move and rename files in Vault while maintaining file dependencies.
- Create new designs from existing ones with the Copy Design command in Autodesk Vault.
- Use Pack and Go to archive or copy a complete set of files from Vault.
- View and edit file properties in the vault.
- Replace files in the vault.

8.1 Customizing Views

Overview

In this lesson, you learn how to customize and rearrange the field columns in Autodesk Vault so that you can view important information about files.

You can customize the views in Autodesk Vault so that you can look at the data in many different ways. For example, you can view the thumbnails for the files, or you can group the files by file properties, such as the designer or engineer. In a large project, you might want to customize the view to show who has the files checked out.

Customizing views increases your efficiency by displaying the data that you need and removing and filtering out data that is not required.

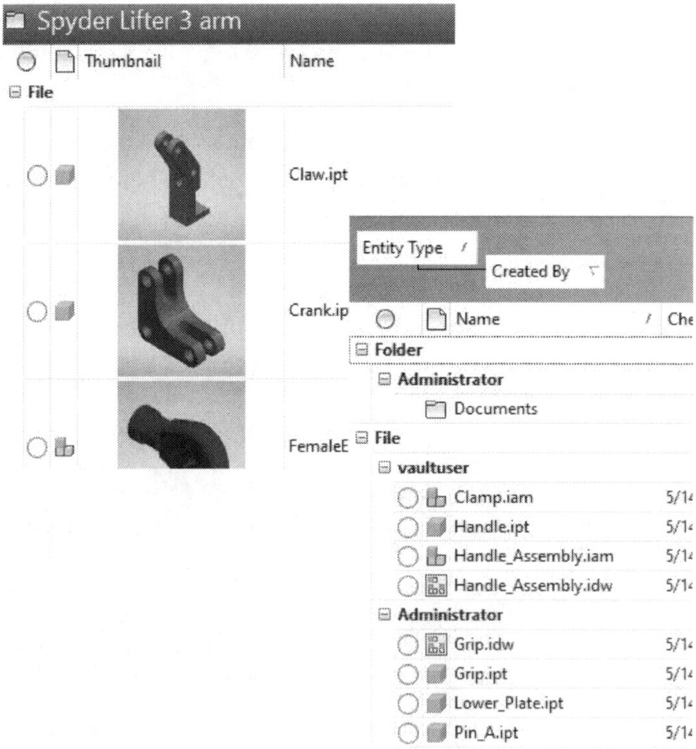

Objectives

After completing this lesson, you will be able to:

- Customize views for the main and preview panes in Autodesk Vault to view the data you want.
- Use file properties to sort, view, and manage files in the vault.
- View file properties by adding and removing the fields you want to see, sorted by the required data column.
- Save your customized views to reuse them when required.

Customizing the Panes

In addition to managing files, the vault stores information about each file that the native application generated. This information can include the creation date, document title, design status, and part number. To display the information, you add field columns in either the Main or Preview pane of Autodesk Vault. In the Preview pane, you can customize each tab separately so that only the information you want is displayed.

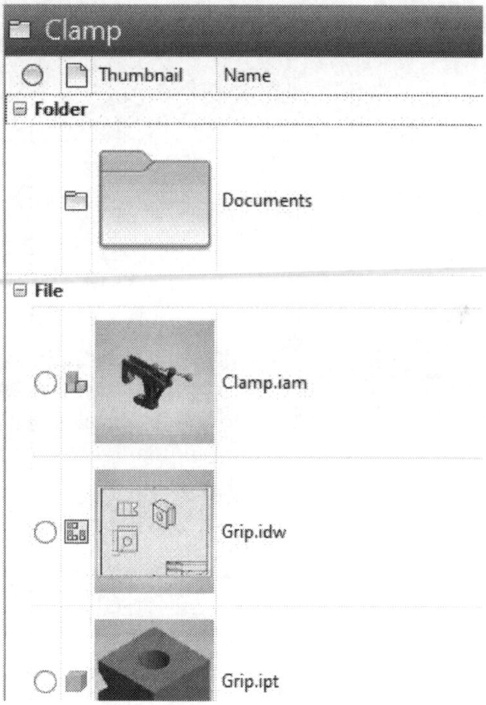

Definition of Customizing Views

In the main and preview panes, each column represents a field. These columns can be resized and rearranged or grouped. The contents of any column can be easily sorted into ascending or descending order. By customizing the panes to display what you need, you can quickly view important information without extensive searching.

Example of a Customized Main Pane

Members of the design team are working on an assembly. To display which members of the team have files checked out, the Main pane is customized to show the Checked Out By field. In the following example, vaultuser is logged in and has three files checked out. The Administrator also has a file checked out.

File Properties

Autodesk Vault helps you manage your data by maintaining a relational database. The files added to the vault are processed, and the file properties are placed in the relational database. The data in this database can be used to view and manage the files in the vault.

Facts

There are two types of properties for files in the vault:

- Vault has many common properties for all the files in the vault, such as Vault Status, Version, and Checked In. These are automatically updated by the vault as the files are being checked out and in.
- Vault also reads the standard and custom properties in the files when they are added to the vault. In Autodesk Vault, these properties are added to the available fields list and can be used to customize a view.

Viewing File Properties

Columns in the main and preview panes represent file properties (these are fields in Vault's database). There are many fields, and you can customize the number of columns (properties) displayed in the list.

Procedure: Adding, Removing, and Rearranging Columns in the Item List

The following steps describe how to add, remove, or rearrange a column in the list.

1. In the file list, right-click on a column header.
2. Click Customize View.
3. Click Fields.
4. Add, remove, and rearrange columns, as required.

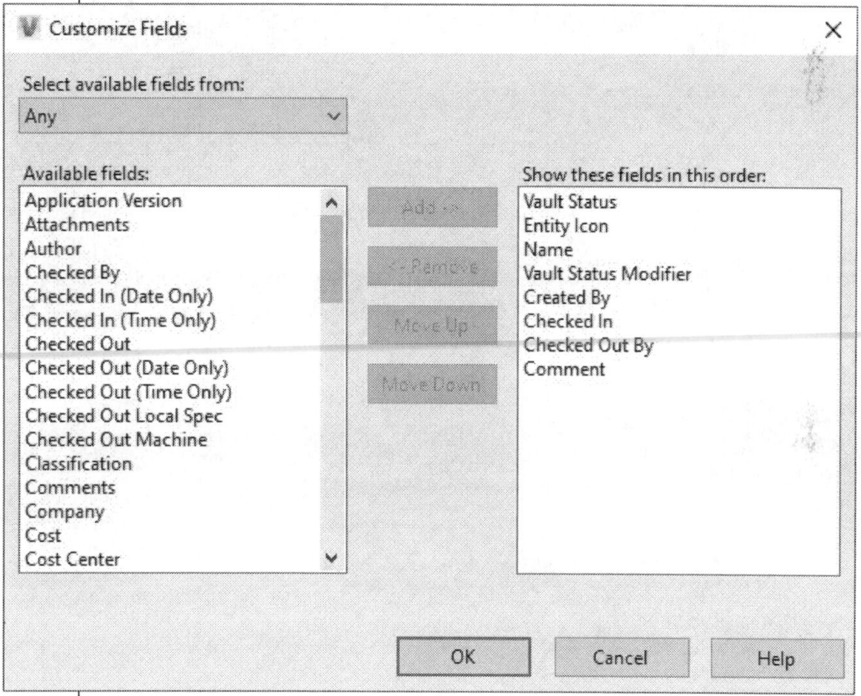

Procedure: Removing and Rearranging Columns in the Item List

The following steps describe how to remove a column in the list.

1. In the file list, right-click on the column header that you want to remove, and select Remove This Column.

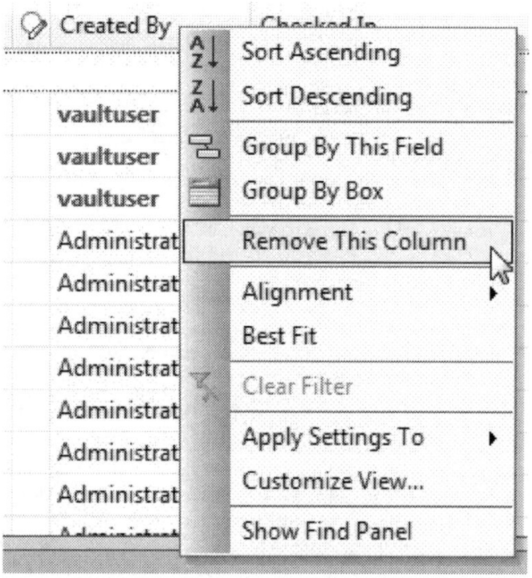

If you only want to customize the order of the fields (columns), drag the column headers to rearrange them in the list.

2. Drag the column headers to rearrange the columns.

Procedure: Resizing and Rearranging Columns

The following steps show how to resize and rearrange columns in Autodesk Vault's main and preview panes.

1. Move the cursor over the edge of a column label until the cursor changes to a double arrow.

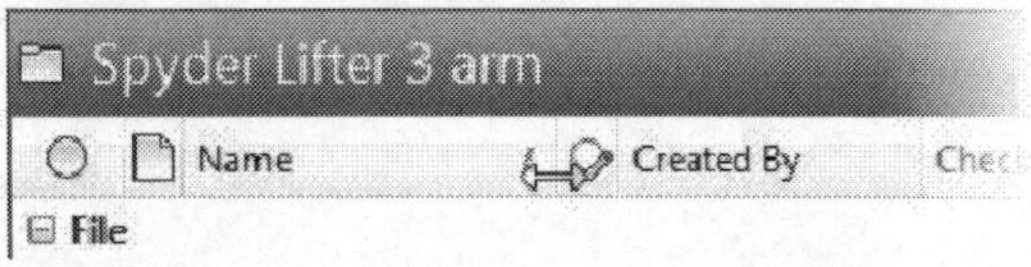

2. Click and drag to the required column width.
3. To automatically adjust a column to the best fit, right-click on the column label and select Best Fit.

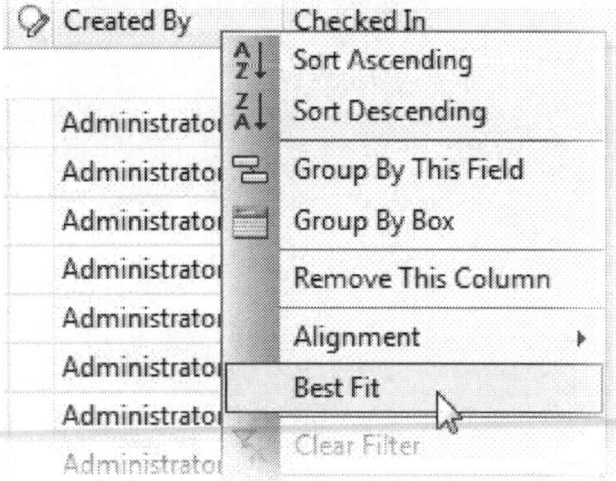

4. To rearrange columns, click a column label and drag it to the required position. You can also rearrange columns in the Customize Fields dialog box.

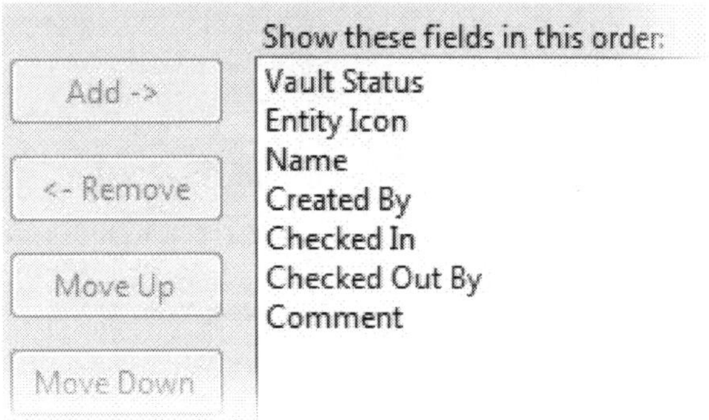

Procedure: Grouping Items by Column Header

The following steps show how to group fields in Autodesk Vault's main and preview panes.

1. Right-click on the column label and select Group By This Field. Repeat this to group by more than one field.
2. Click the plus sign in front of a group to expand its contents.

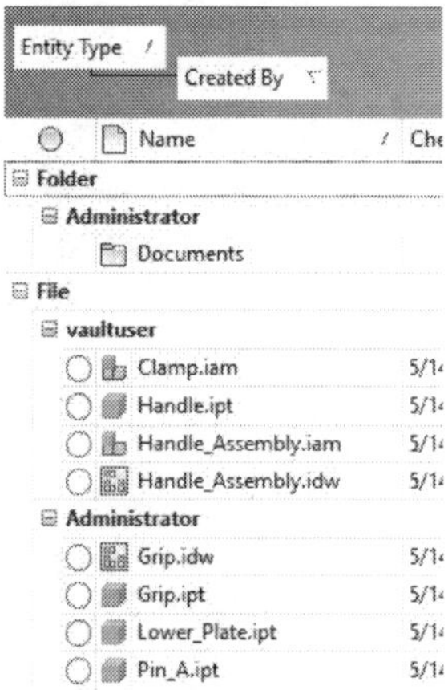

3. To expand or collapse all groups, right-click on Group By Box. Click Full Expand or Full Collapse.

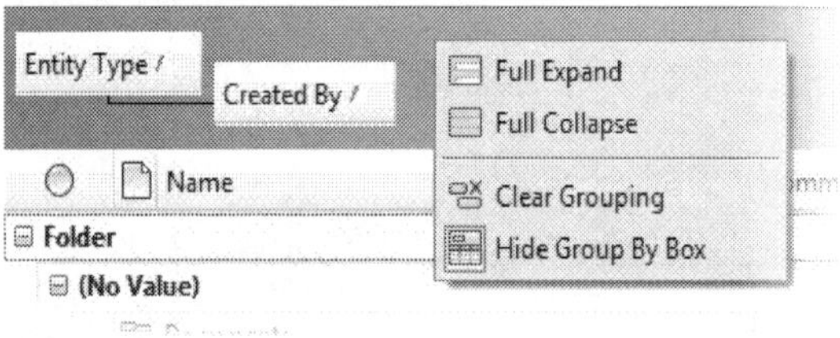

4. To clear all groups, right-click on Group By Box. Click Clear Grouping.

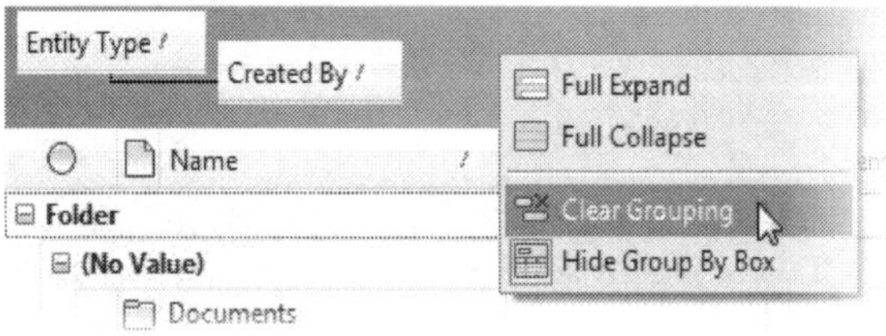

Hint: Drag and Drop Method

You can drag and drop the column label to the Group by Box area. If the Group by Box area is not displayed, right-click on any column label and click Group by Box.

Saving Customized Views

Customized views help you to manage your data in Autodesk Vault. These views can be saved and reused and are stored individually for each user.

Procedure: Saving Customized Views

The following steps describe how to save a customized view.

1. In the Advanced toolbar, from the views list, select Define custom views.

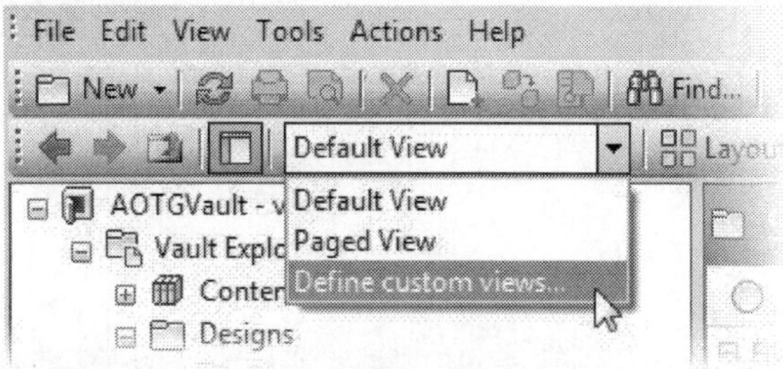

2. In the Manage Custom Views dialog box, click New.
3. In the Create Custom View dialog box, enter the required view name. Click OK.
4. Select the new view in the Manage Custom Views dialog box and click Modify. Use the Customize View dialog box to customize the view, as required. Close the dialog box.
5. Click Close to exit the Manage Custom Views dialog box.

Procedure: Managing Custom Views

The following steps show how to manage customized views.

You cannot rename or delete the default custom view (All Files). It is possible to add additional custom filter criteria to this custom view, but this is not recommended; the built-in filter is meant to show all files.

1. On the Advanced toolbar, from the views list, select Define custom views.

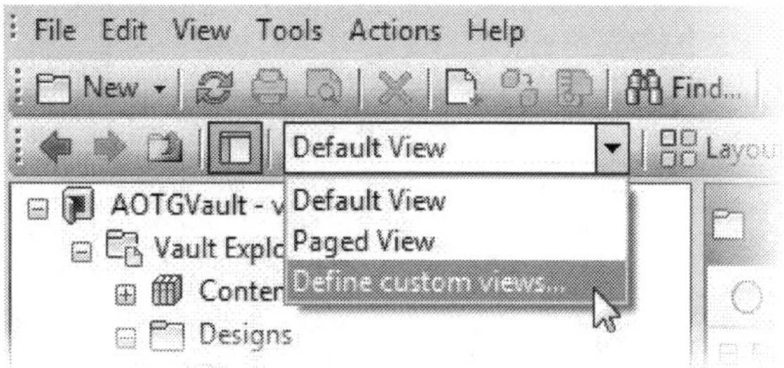

2. In the Manage Custom Views dialog box, select the required view name.
3. Click Modify, Copy, Rename, or Delete, as required.
4. Complete the required operation. Close all dialog boxes.

Practice 8a

Customize Vault Explorer Views

The files that you use in this chapter's practices were loaded into the vault in a previous practice. If you have not completed Practice 3a, complete it before you start this chapter's practice.

In this practice, you create a custom view showing the thumbnails for each file, and you automatically generate the corresponding DWF™ files that you can then use in Autodesk Vault. Creating customized views for the Main pane in Autodesk Vault simplifies the management of your vault data.

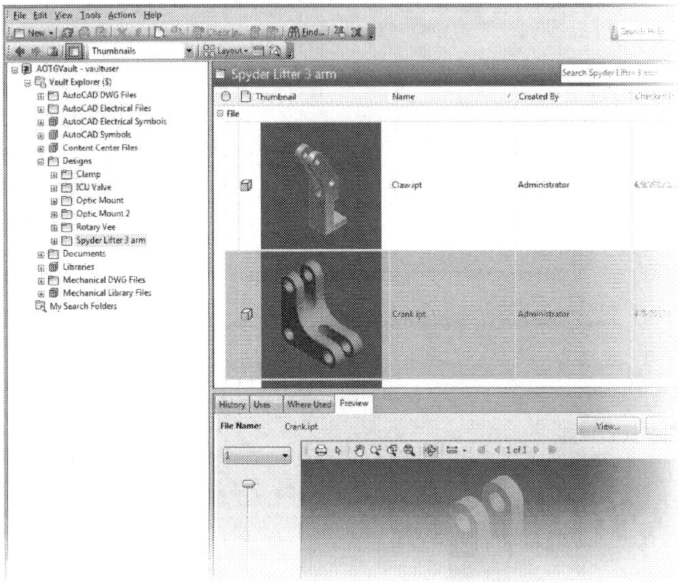

The completed practice

Task 1 - Set the working folder.

You can skip this task if your working folder is already set to *C:\AOTGVault\VaultWorkingFolder.*

1. Start Autodesk Vault. Log in using the following information:
   - For User Name, enter **Administrator**.
   - For Password, leave it blank.
   - For Vault, select AOTGVault
2. Click the Tools menu>Administration>Vault Settings.
3. In the Vault Settings dialog box, under Working Folder, click Define.
4. In the Working Folder Options dialog box, click Allow clients to define working folder. Click OK. Click Close.

5. Click the File menu>Log Out.

6. Log in to Autodesk Vault using the following information:

   - For User Name, enter **vaultuser**.
   - For Password, leave it blank.
   - For Vault, select AOTGVault.

7. Click Vault Explorer ($) then click File menu>Set Working Folder. In the Browse for Folder dialog box, select *C:\AOTGVault\VaultWorkingFolder.*

8. Click OK.

Task 2 - View attached DWFs.

1. Login to Vault as vaultuser, if you haven't already done so.

2. In the Navigation pane, navigate to *Designs/Spyder Lifter 3 arm.*

3. In the Main pane, review the file list. Note that there are part and assembly files listed, but no DWF files.

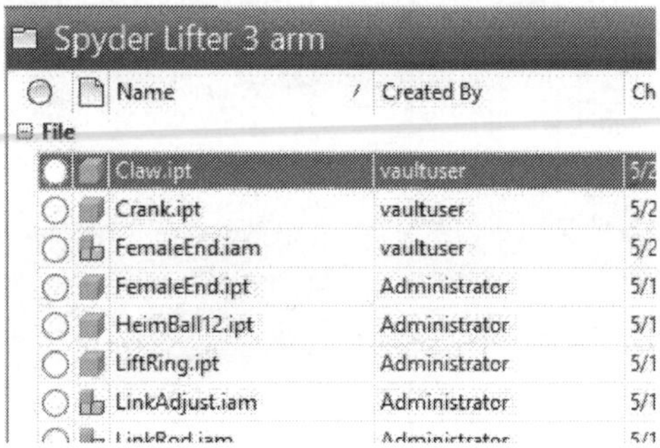

4. Click Tools menu>Options.

5. In the Options dialog box:

   - Select Show hidden files.
   - Click OK.

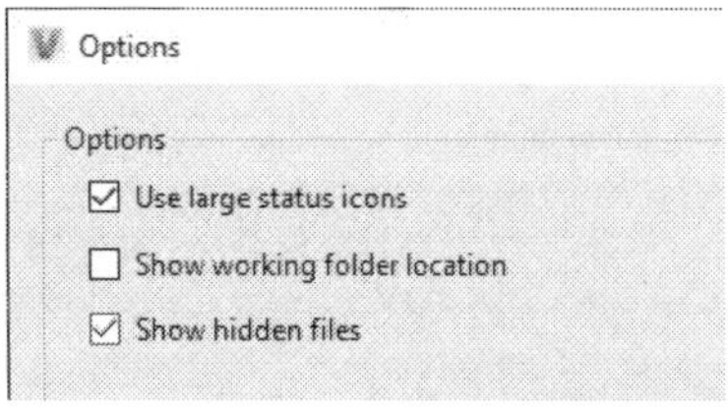

6. In the Main pane, view the list of files. A DWF file is listed for each of the CAD files.

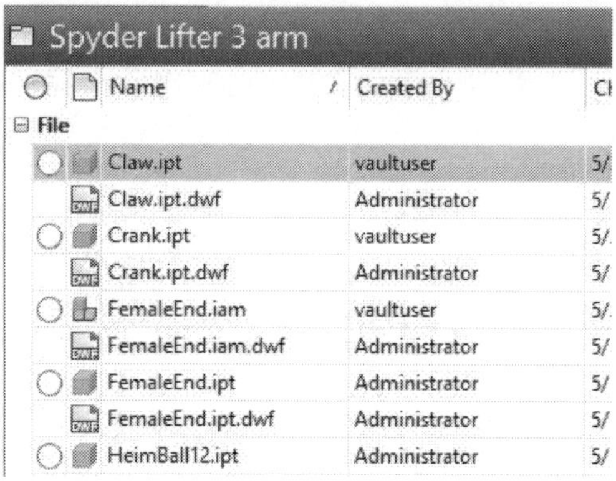

7. Click one of the CAD (not DWF) files in the Main pane.

8. In the Preview pane, click the Uses tab. The DWF file is shown attached to the CAD file.

9. In the Preview pane, click the Preview tab.

10. Select the Version 1 image. Use the tools to view the model. The DWF file is attached to the file you selected. The same DWF you are viewing is used to create thumbnails of the files.

11. Click Tools menu>Options.

12. In the Options dialog box:

   - Clear Show hidden files.
   - Click OK.

Task 3 - Create a custom view showing the thumbnails for each file.

1. On the Advanced toolbar, select Define custom views.

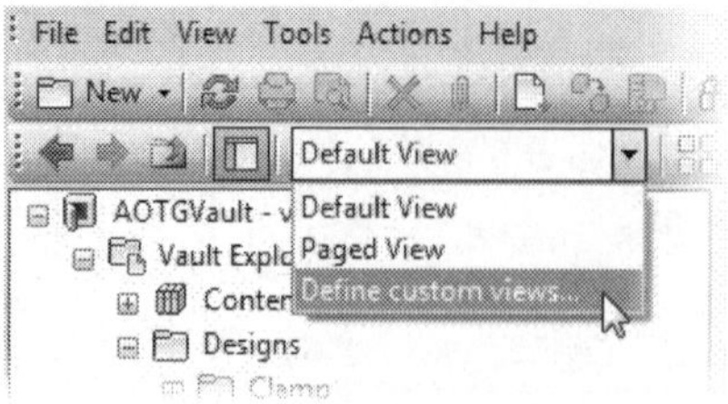

2. Create the new view. In the Manage Custom Views dialog box, do the following:
   - Click New.
   - Under View Name, enter **Thumbnails**.
   - Click OK.
3. In the Manage Custom Views dialog box, select the Thumbnails view. Click Modify then click Fields.
   - Under Select available fields from, select Any.
   - In the Available fields list, select Thumbnail. Click Add.
   - Under Show these fields in this order, select Comment. Click Remove.
   - Under Show These Fields in This Order, select Thumbnail. Click Move Up until Thumbnail displays above Name.
   - Click OK.

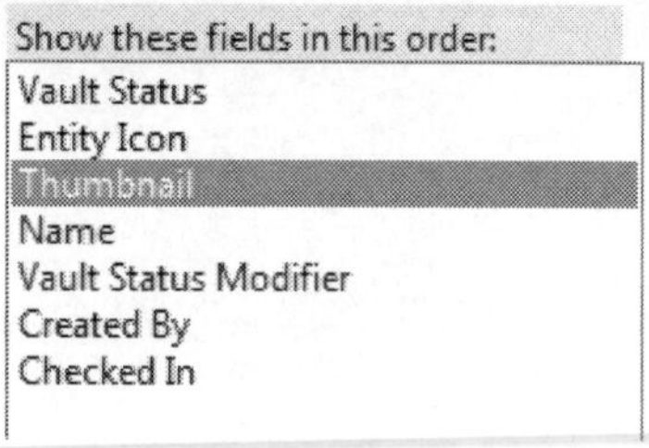

4. Click Close twice to close the other dialog boxes. The Main pane displays thumbnails (generated from the DWF files) of the files.

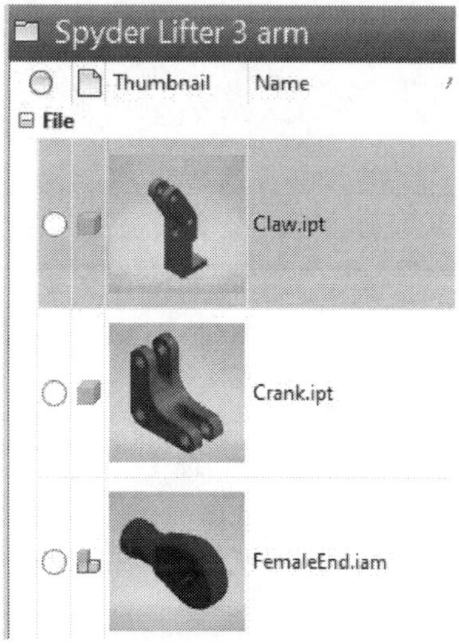

5. To adjust the size of the thumbnails, resize the Thumbnail column.

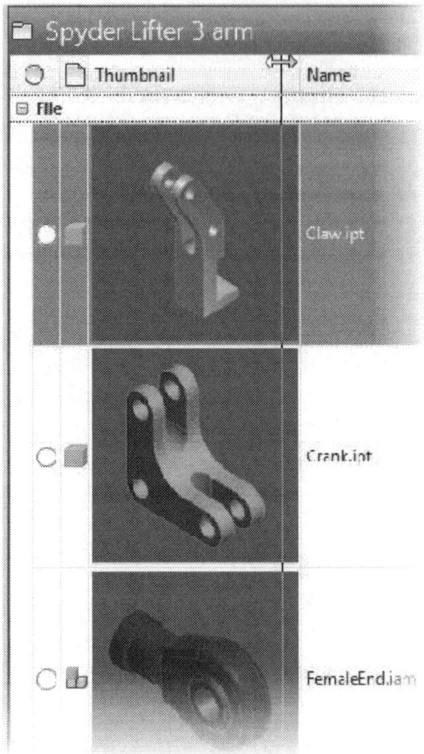

8.2 Finding Files

Overview

In this lesson you learn how to use the Autodesk Vault search capabilities to quickly locate files.

As the number of files in the vault grows, you might find that tracking down a file is more difficult. By leveraging the file properties stored in the Vault relational database, you can quickly filter out files and narrow your search.

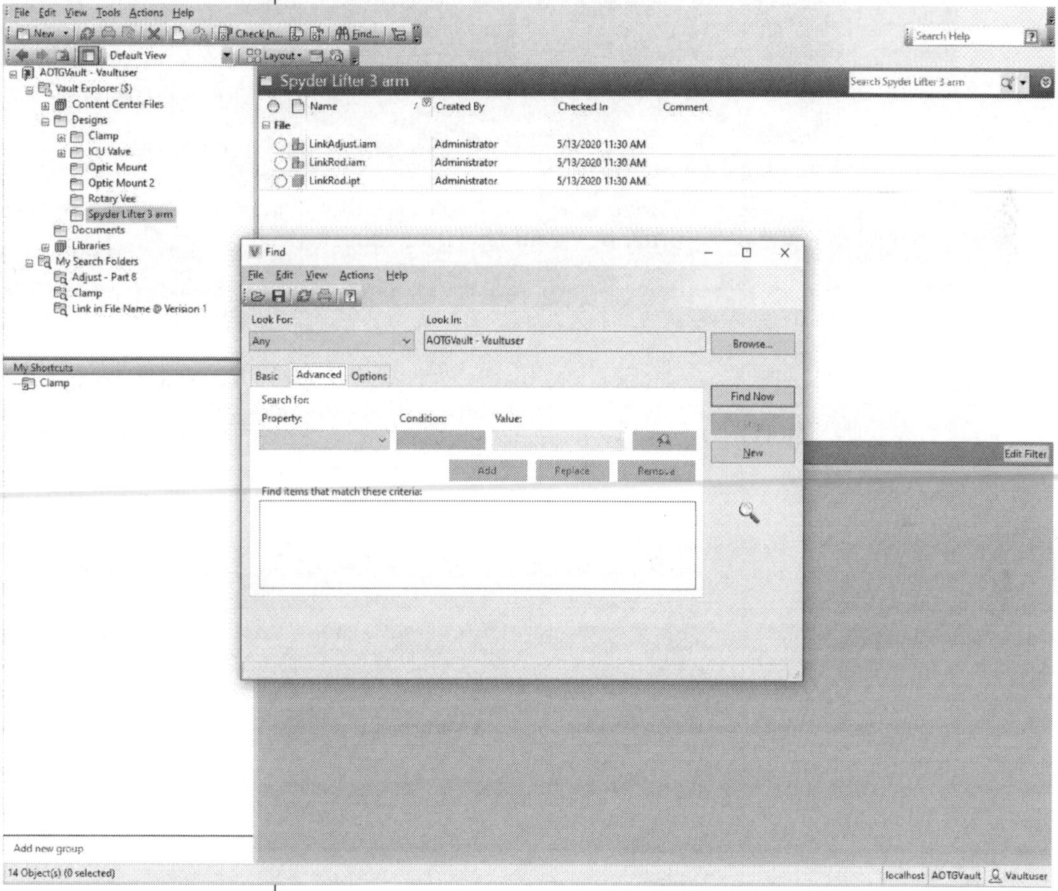

Objectives

After completing this lesson, you will be able to:

- Use Find tools and custom filters to find and display files in the vault.
- Use the Basic tab of the Find tool to find files using a single search string.
- Use the Advanced tab of the Find tool to search for files with one or more specific search criteria.
- Use the Search box to quickly find a text string in the properties of the files and display them in the Main pane.
- Use custom filters to filter the Main pane file list.
- Save searches and reuse them when required to effectively manage your files in Autodesk Vault.
- Navigate to specific folders or files using shortcuts.

Finding Files

Engineering projects typically contain a large number of files of many types with a variety of information. When you need to meet a project deadline, performing searches in Autodesk Vault helps you to locate your design information quickly, reduce design duplication, and improve reuse.

Definition of Finding Files in Autodesk Vault

The Basic and Advanced tabs of the Find tool are used to search locations in Vault, to find files based on search criteria.

Search and Custom Filters are similar tools. The main difference is that while Find searches any location and might report several files located in different folders, Custom Filters applies to the list of files in the Main pane and filters that list alone.

Both types of tools can be useful for finding files.

Hint: Searchable Properties

The search engine searches only properties that are marked searchable. These can be set by the Vault administrator.

Examples of Finding Files in Autodesk Vault

Use of the Advanced Tab in the Find Dialog Box

The following image displays an advanced search on a large vault. The filename contains the word link; however, this would not narrow the search by much because many of filenames contain the word link. So, a second criteria is added: The Checked Out By property contains vaultuser. This narrows the search.

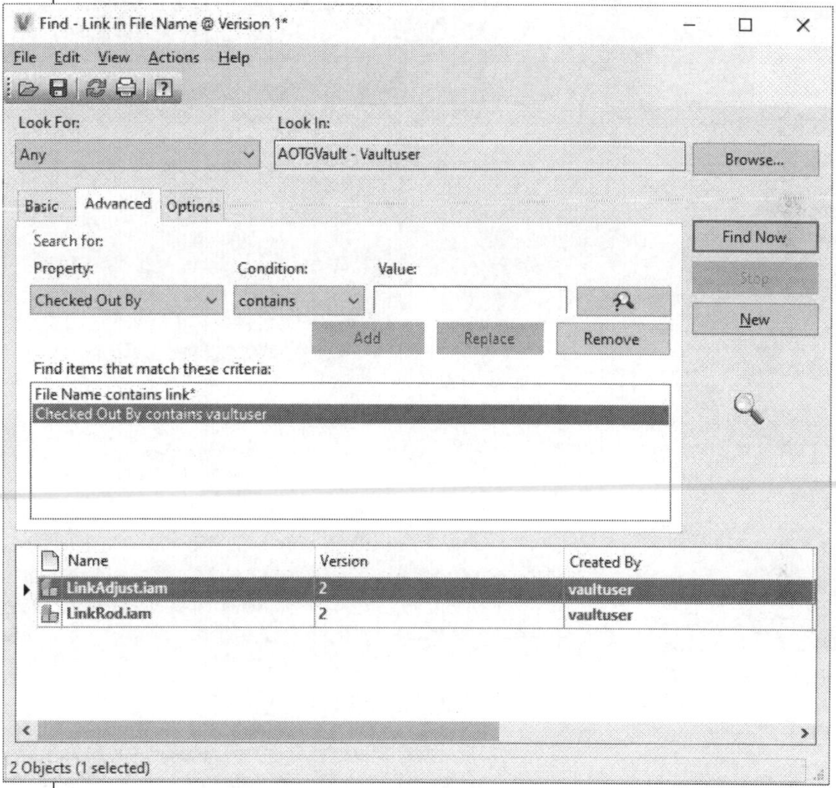

Use of the Basic Tab in the Find Dialog Box

In the following image, the results of Find using the Basic tab are shown. Many files matched the search text AIV1_M07_01.

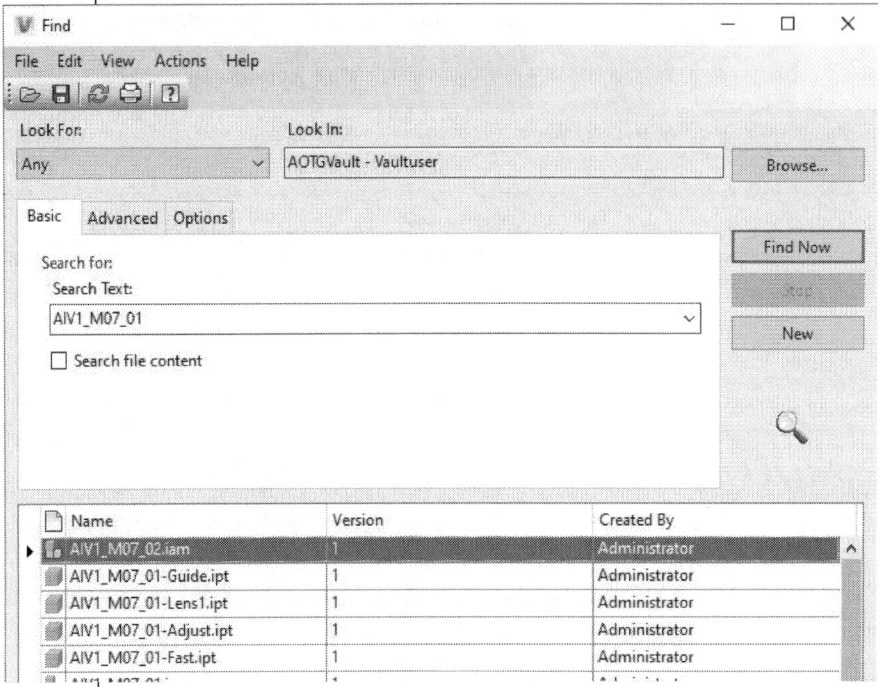

Note that for some files, it is not obvious how Basic Find located the files. For example, the AIV1_M07_02.iam file has the search string AIV1_M07_01 in the Part Number which matches the search string. Basic Find searches all searchable file properties for the text.

Use of a Customized Filter

The following image displays the files in the Spyder folder. This is a customized view using custom filters; the list of files is filtered by searching for files with Rodney in the Created By property.

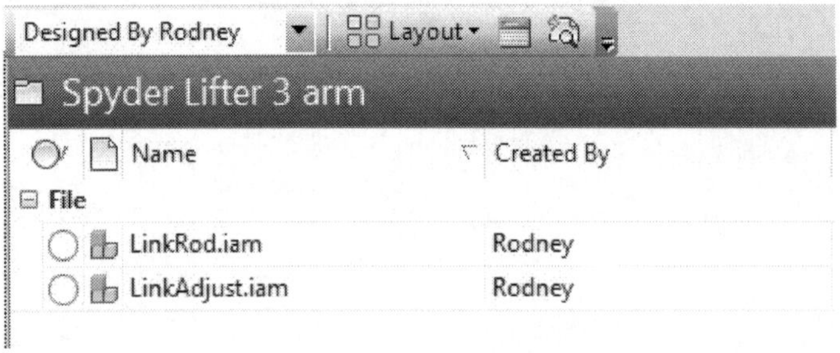

Use of Searching

By using the search text box and entering the word **link***, you narrow the list of files in the Main pane to files that have a word starting with link anywhere in the file properties in the Spyder Lifter 3 arm folder and subfolders.

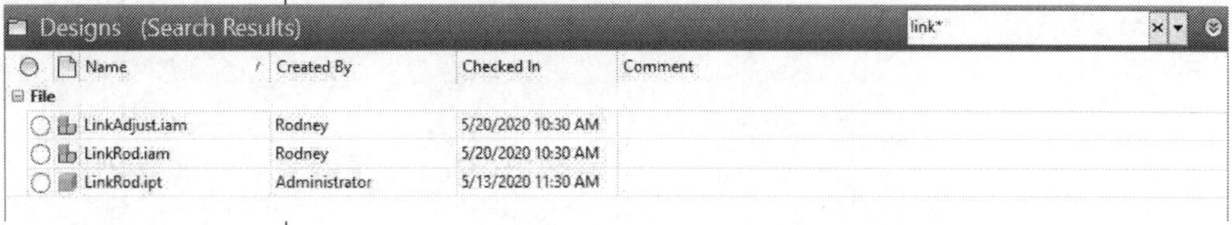

Basic Find

Basic Find searches through the specified Vault location for files whose properties match the specified criteria. Using Basic Find to search for "*rod*" in a vault can result in a file with the name "link-rod.ipt", or in a file that has an author named "Rodney" for example.

Procedure: Searching for Files Using Basic Find

The following steps show you how to locate files with the Basic tab in the Find dialog box.

1. To start a basic search in Autodesk Vault, click Tools menu>Find. You can also click Find in the Standard toolbar.

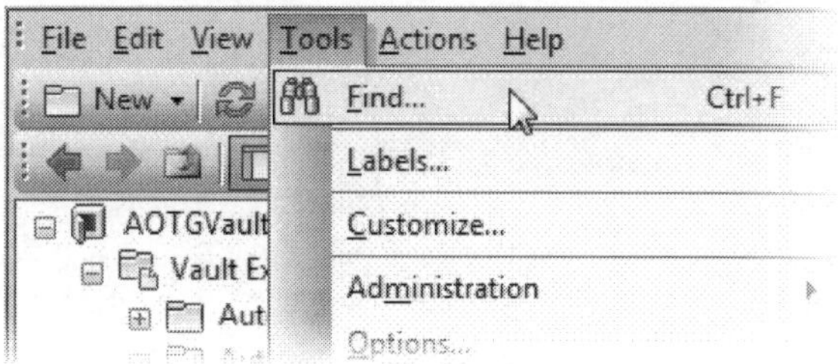

2. In the Find dialog box, on the Basic tab, enter a text string for the search criterion.

3. Click Find Now to begin the search.

4. The bottom pane of the Find dialog box displays the results.
5. Right-click a file. Click to view the file. Alternatively, click Go To Folder to open its folder in the Main pane.

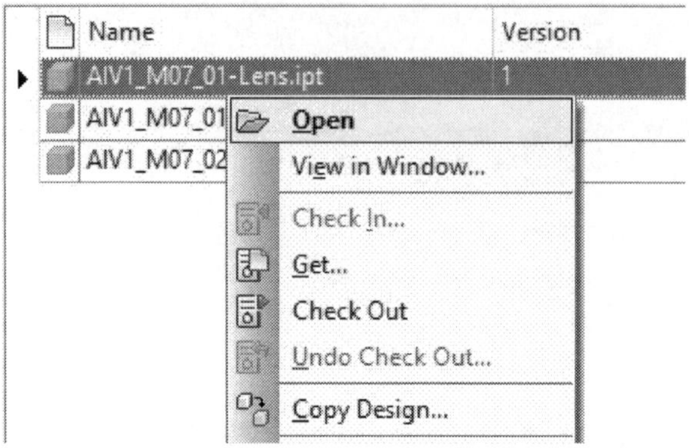

Searching for Incomplete Words

You can enter the first few letters of a word and add a wild card to have Autodesk Vault search for all words that begin with those letters. You can search for link* and find all of the text that has words starting with "link" as well as the word "link" itself, for example.

You can use wild cards and Boolean operators in your search. For example, searching for *adj* looks for text that contains the letters "adj" with any combination of letters before and after.

Searching for File Contents

You can search the file contents using Find if your Vault administrator enabled the content indexing service on the vault.

Defining Search Locations

You can narrow your search by choosing which folders to look in. In the Find dialog box, click Browse and check the folders you want to search.

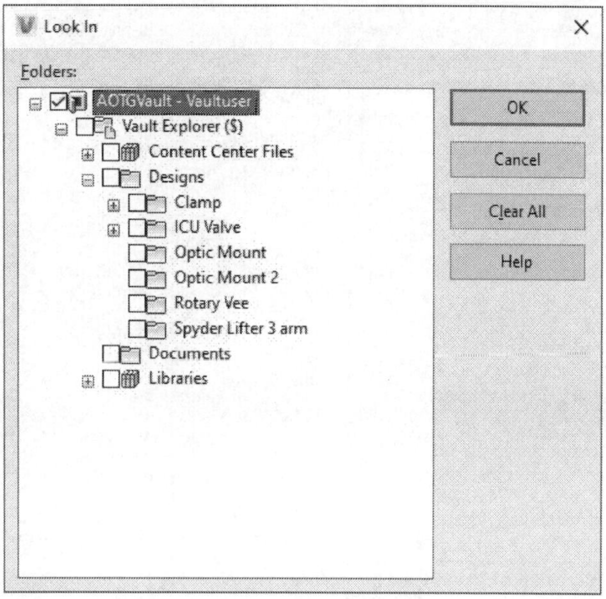

Options

By default, Find searches for the latest versions of a file and searches subfolders. This can be changed on the Options tab in the Find dialog box.

Just as you can with the panes in Autodesk Vault, you can customize, rearrange, group, and sort the field columns in the lower pane of the Find dialog box.

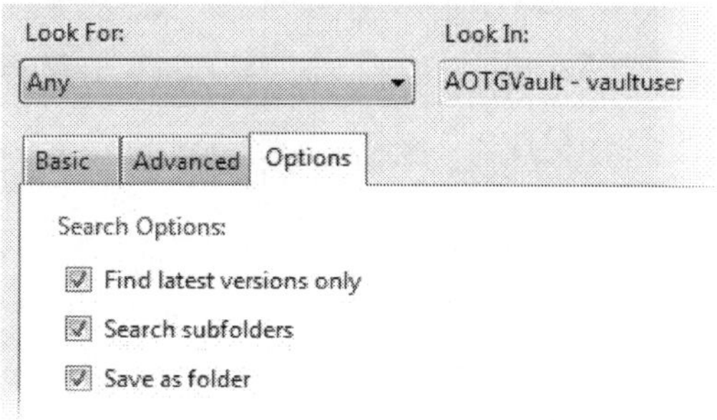

Advanced Find

To find a file that has properties that meet one or more specific criteria use the Advanced Find tab. Searches include File Name Contains "Rod" and Author Contains "Phil" for example.

Procedure: Searching for Files Using Find, Advanced Tab

The following steps describe how to locate files by narrowing your search with the Find tool's Advanced tab in Autodesk Vault.

1. To start an advanced search in Autodesk Vault, click Tools menu>Find. You can also click Find in the Standard toolbar.

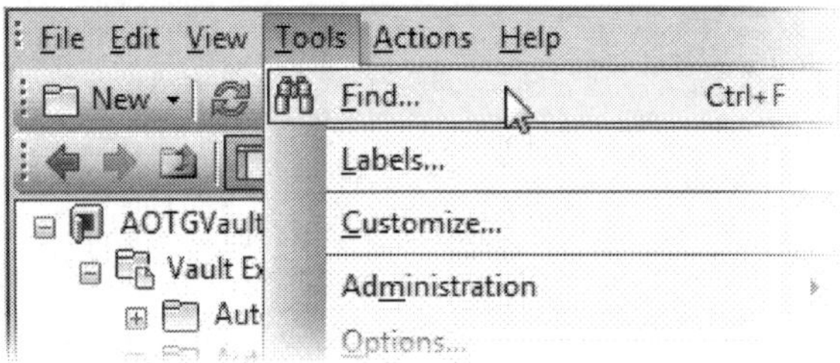

2. In the Find dialog box, select the Advanced tab.
3. Select the first Property you want to search on, specify the Condition and enter the value.

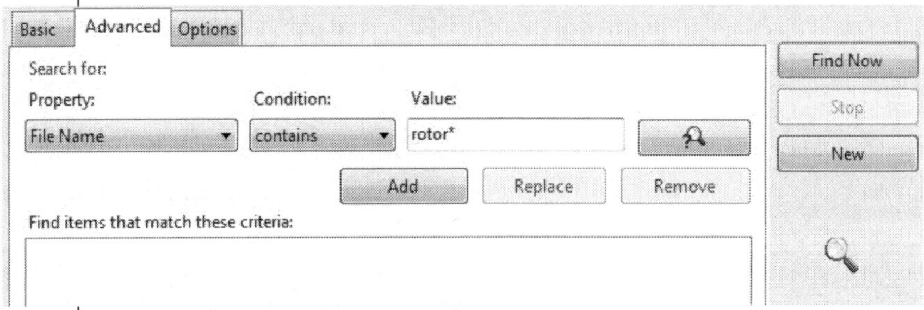

4. Select Add to add the first criteria to the list..

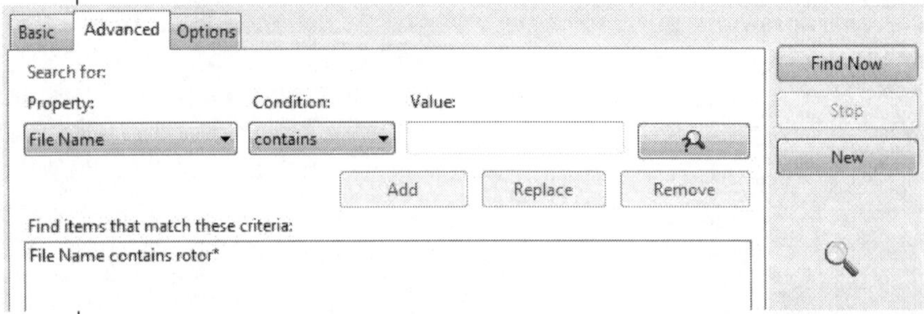

5. Repeat Steps 3 and 4 to add additional criteria to the list.

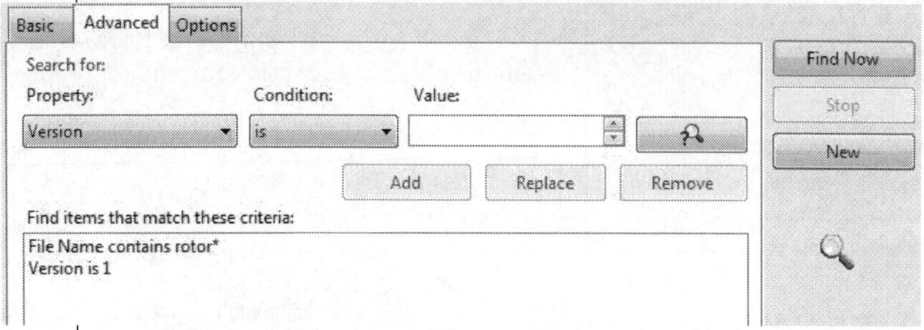

6. Click Find Now to begin the search. The bottom pane of the Find dialog box displays the results.

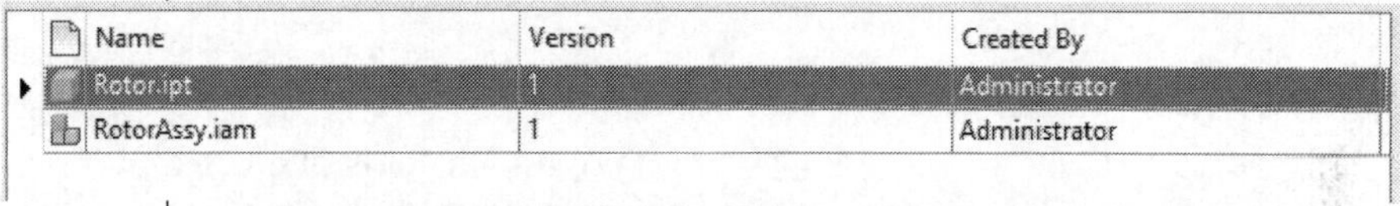

7. Right-click a file. Click an option to view the file, get the file, or go to the Vault folder that contains it.

Just as you can with the panes in Autodesk Vault, you can customize, rearrange, group, and sort the field columns in the lower pane of the Find dialog box.

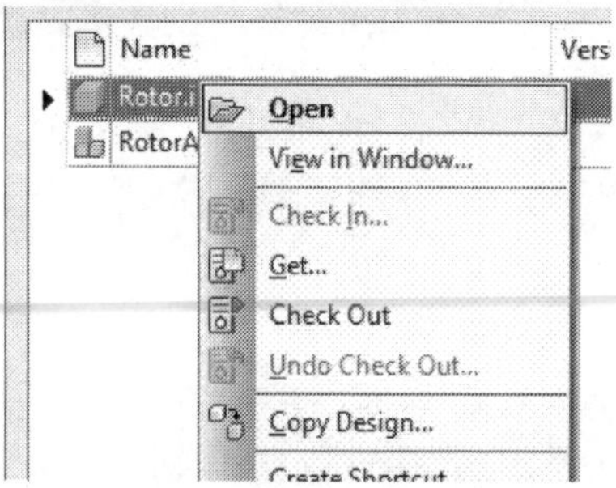

Using Search

The Basic and Advanced tabs of the Find tool enable you to search the entire vault or any portions of it for files matching the criteria. The files are searched using the text entered into the search box and the files are displayed in the Autodesk Vault Main pane.

By default, Search looks in the folder selected in the Navigation pane and any subfolders.

In cases where the size of an assembly (the number of files) is not trivial, using the search can be a simple and effective method for filtering the files list in the Main pane.

Procedure: Finding Files Using Search

The following steps search the folder selected in the Navigation pane for files and display the results in the Main pane.

1. In the Search field, enter the text string to search for. Click Search.

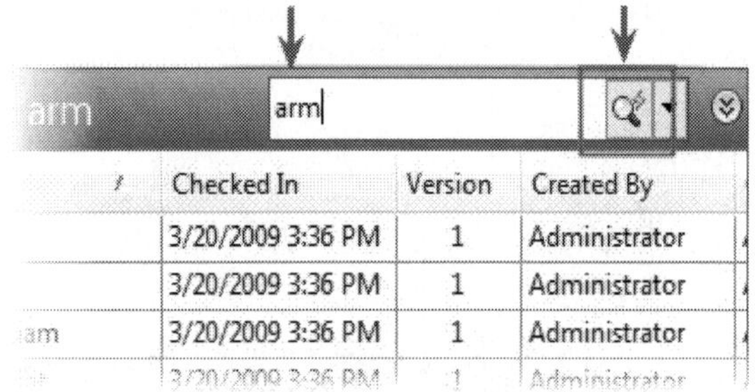

2. The Main pane file list is filtered, and the Clear or Cancel Search icon display in place of the Search icon.

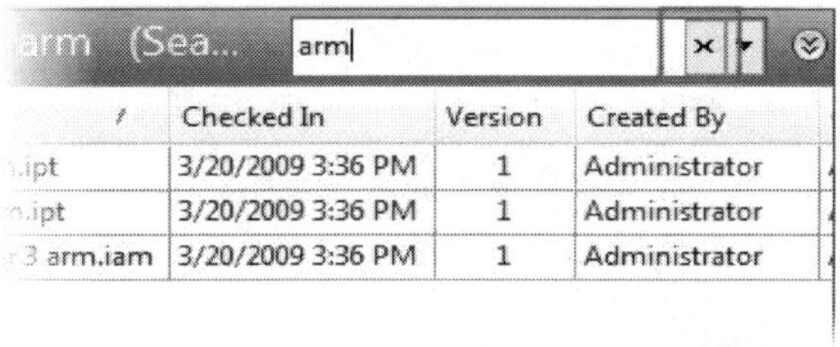

3. Click Clear or Cancel Search to remove the search results, or click Expand the Query Builder to do a more advanced search.

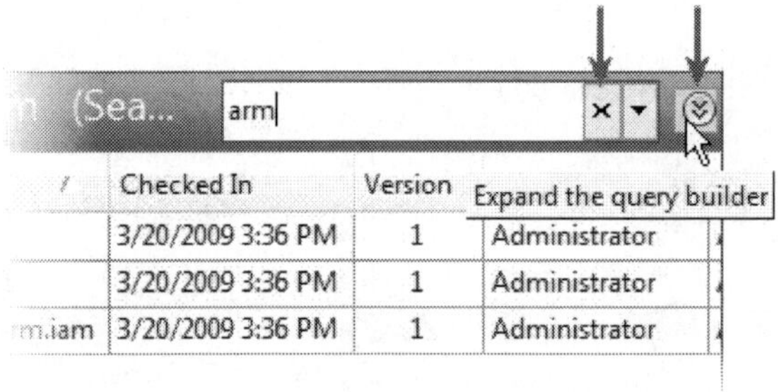

4. Select specific properties and enter more search criteria in the expanded search box.

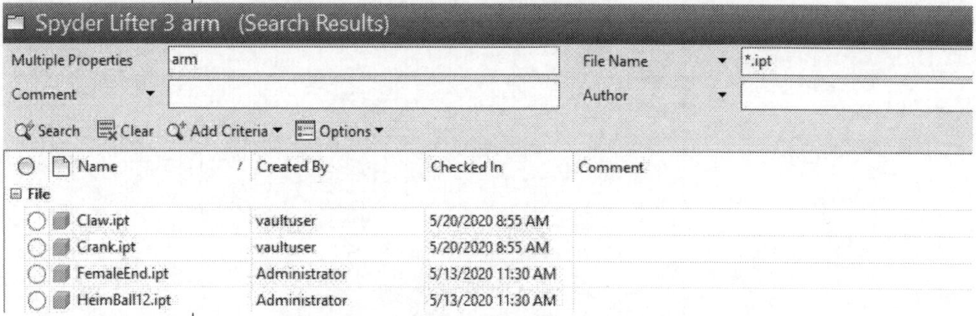

Defining Custom Filters

The Custom Filters feature is similar to Find except that custom filters apply to the Main pane in Vault Explorer.

Custom filters are frequently used to create customized views. You could set up a customized view that displays "all files checked out by me" or "all files but idw files" for example.

Procedure: Defining a Custom Filter in the Main Pane

The following procedure teaches you how to create a filtered custom view.

1. In the Main pane list, right-click a column header. Click Customize View.
2. In the Customize View dialog box, click Custom Filters.

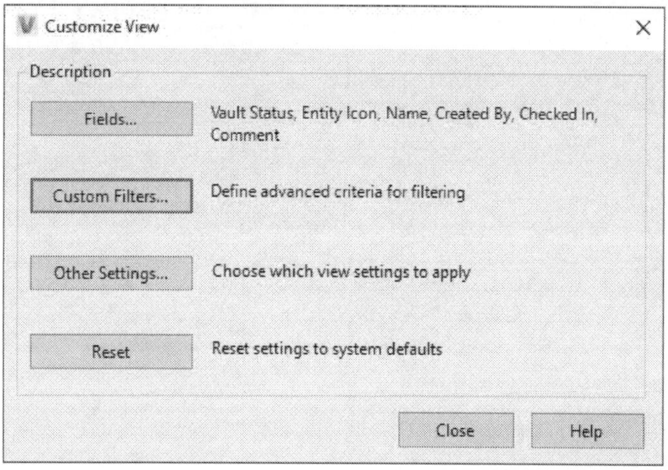

3. Similar to Advanced Find, in the Custom Filters dialog box select the Advanced tab and then select a file property, condition, and required value.
4. Click Add to add the first criteria.

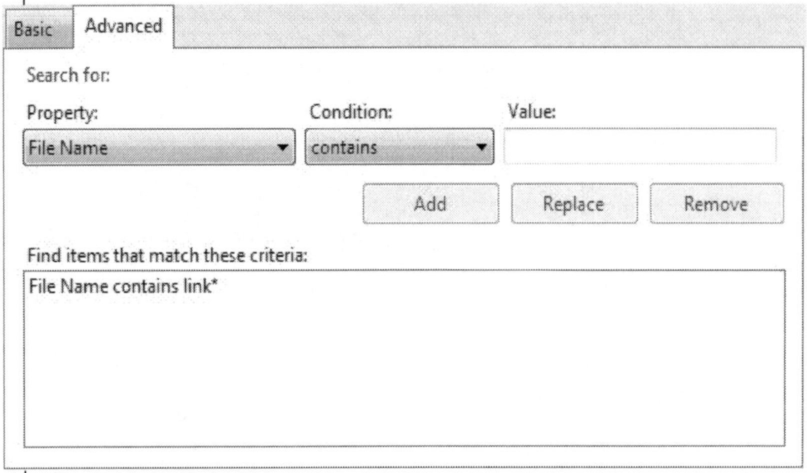

5. Repeat Steps 3 and 4 to add any additional criteria.

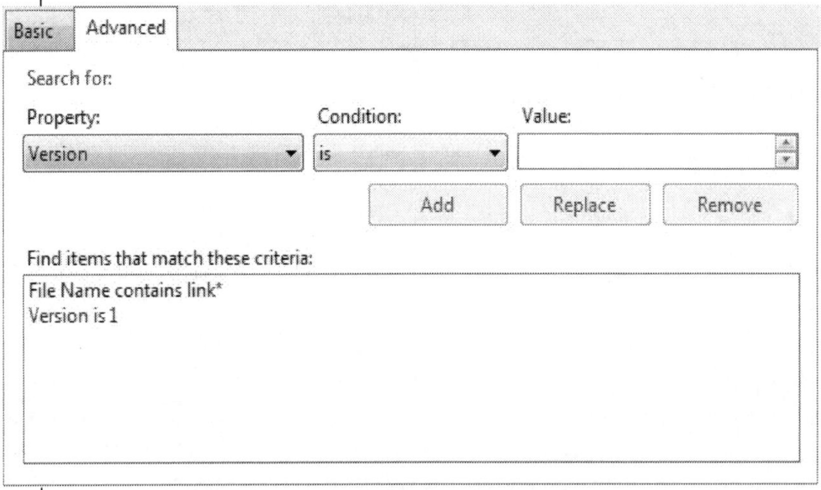

6. Click OK to dismiss the Custom Filters dialog box and Close to dismiss the Customize View dialog.

The Main pane file list is filtered, and a small filter symbol displays on the right side of the Main pane title bar.

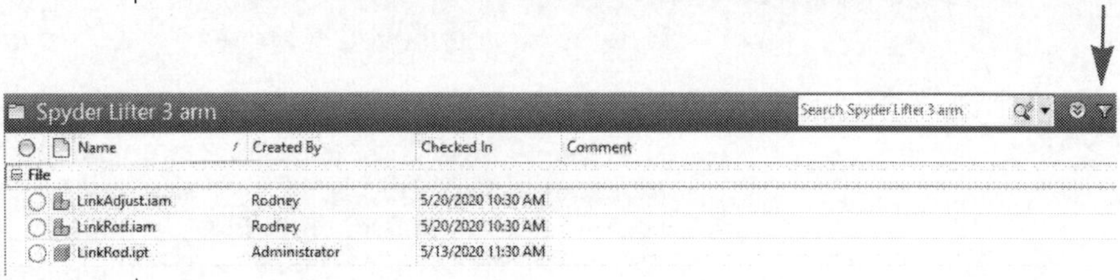

Procedure: Editing or Clearing Custom Filters in the Main Pane

The following procedure teaches you how to quickly edit or clear a custom view applied to the Main pane.

1. In the Main pane, right-click on the Custom Filter Applied icon.

2. Click Edit Custom Filters to modify the custom filters applied, or click Clear Custom Filters to remove the filter and return to the original view.

By having multiple criteria, the Advanced tab in Custom Filters finds files that match all the criteria in the same way as an AND condition.

Saving Searches

Reentering search criteria again and again to find files in Vault is a repetitive and unnecessary task. Searches can be saved and used again when required. Searches are saved per user account, so your saved searches are accessible only to you.

Any search using Find or the Search box can be saved. The search criteria will be saved as a simple search that can be reused in the Find dialog box, or saved as a search folder that displays under My Search Folders in the Navigation pane. Clicking these search folders causes the search results to be displayed in the Main pane.

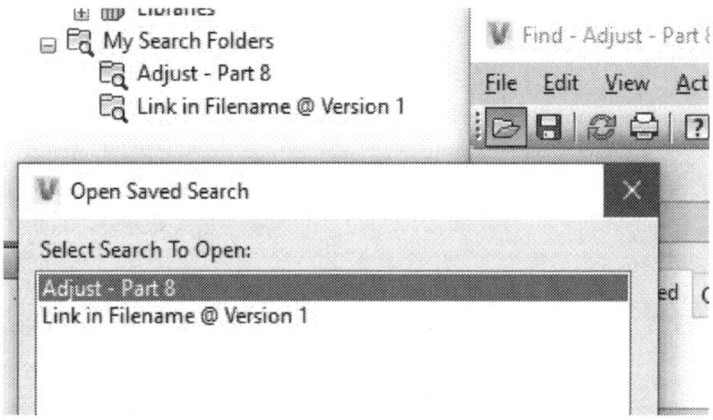

In the image above, the Find dialog box has been opened and Open Search clicked on the toolbar. Note that the saved searches are visible in the Open Saved Search dialog box. They are also displayed as Search folders in the Navigation pane as shown in the upper left portion of the image.

Procedure: Saving Your Searches

The following steps show the procedure for saving a search.

1. To start an advanced search in Autodesk Vault, click Tools menu>Find. You can also click Find in the Standard toolbar.

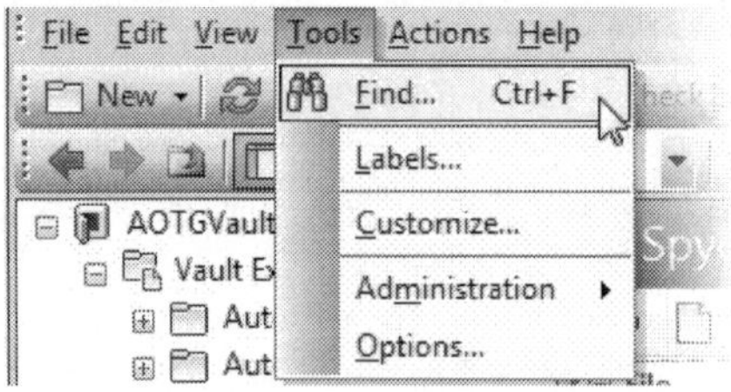

2. In the Find dialog box, on the Advanced tab, specify the search criteria.
3. Click Find Now to begin the search.

The bottom pane of the Advanced Find dialog box displays the results.

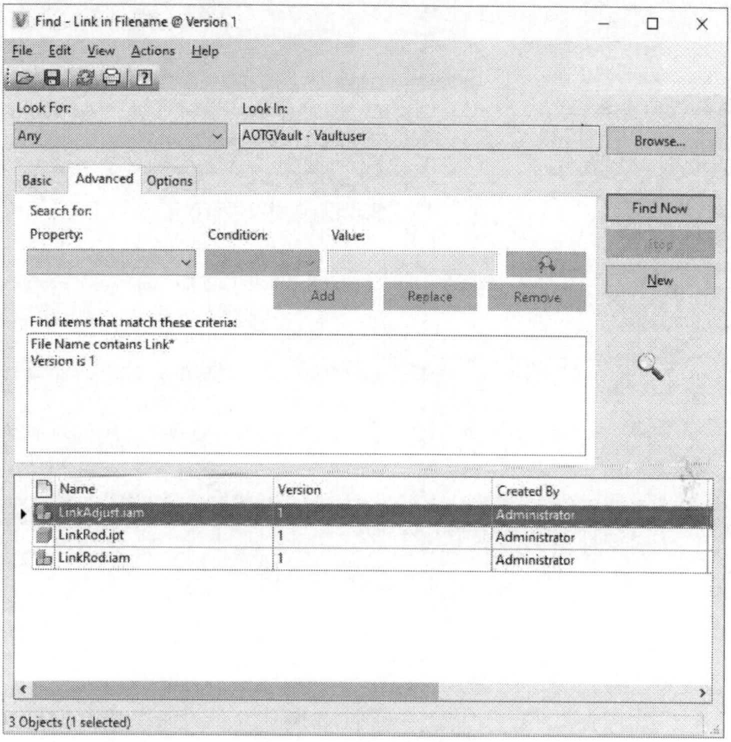

4. On the toolbar, click Save Current Search.

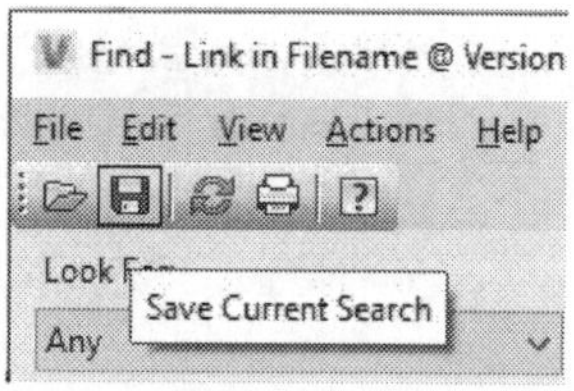

5. In the Save Search dialog box, enter a name for the search. If required, clear Save As Folder. By clearing this option, the search is still created; however, it is not listed in the My Search folder. To later add the search to the folder or delete it, you can right-click on the My Search folder and click Manage Saved Searches.

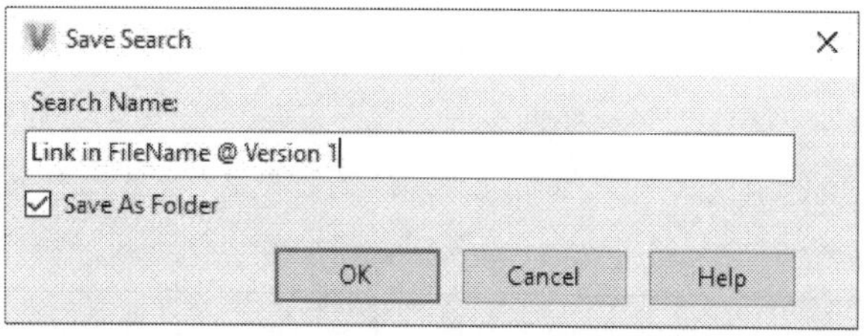

6. Click OK. Your search is now saved and can be reused.

7. Close the Find dialog box.

Procedure: Reusing Your Saved Searches in My Search Folders

The following steps show the procedure for reusing a saved search under My Search Folders.

1. In the Navigation pane, under My Search Folders, click the saved search.
2. The search results show in the Main pane.

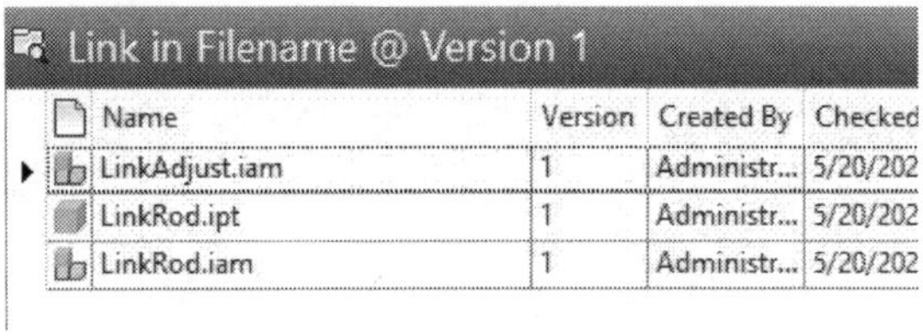

Procedure: Opening Your Saved Searches in the Find Dialog Box

The following steps show the procedure for reusing a saved search in the Find dialog box or making changes to it.

1. To start an advanced search in Autodesk Vault, click Tools menu>Find. You can also click Find in the Standard toolbar.

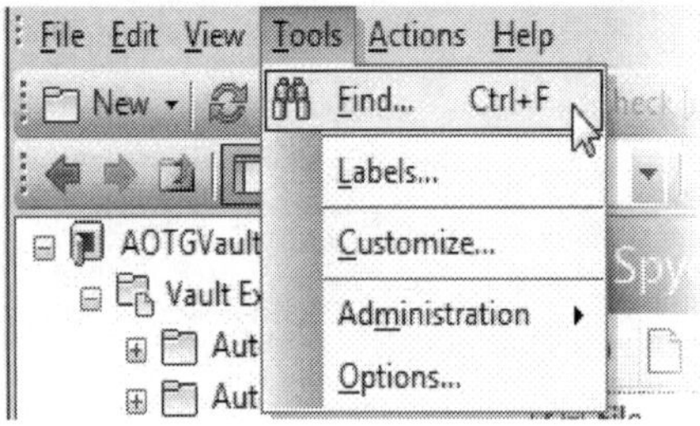

2. In the Find dialog box, click Open Search.

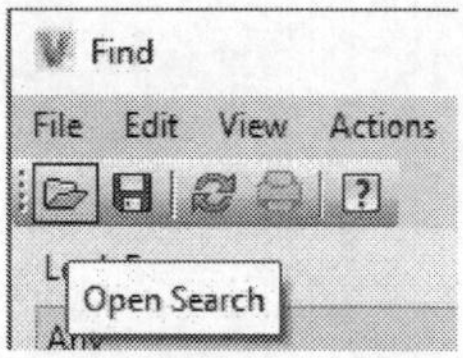

3. In the Open Saved Search dialog box, select the saved search from the list. Click Open.

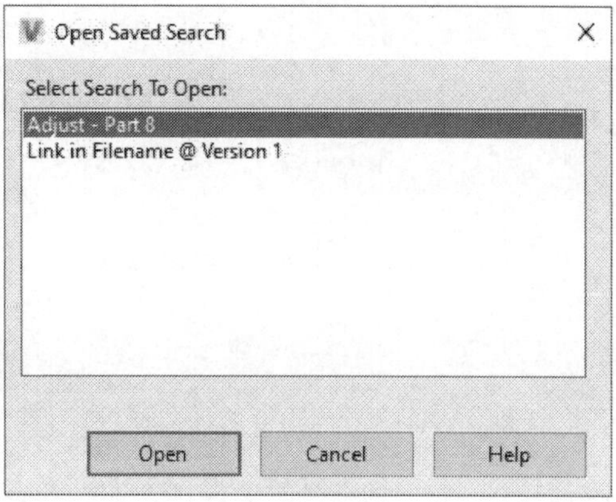

4. The bottom pane of the Find dialog box displays the results. You can edit or use this as the starting point for a new search.

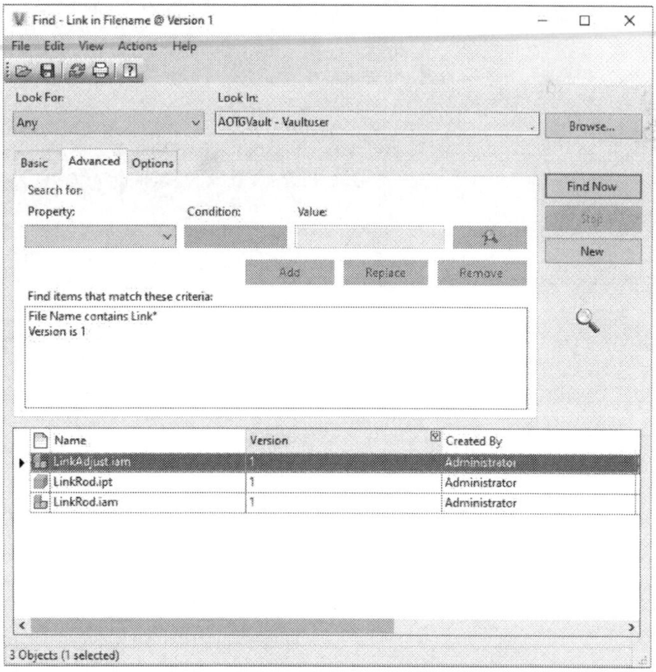

Shortcuts

Another way to find files and keep them organized is by creating shortcuts pointing to a file or a folder. Shortcuts can be organized into groups, and can make navigating to a file or folder very simple.

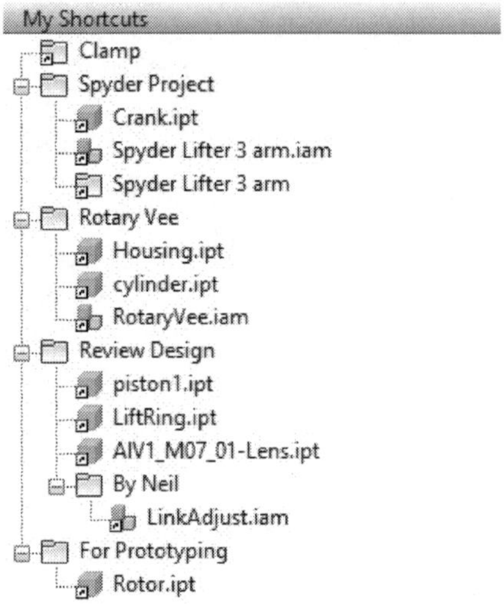

Shortcuts are user specific: users create their own shortcuts and groups.

Procedure: Creating Shortcuts

The following steps show how to create shortcuts.

1. In the Navigation pane or the Main pane, select the folder or file, respectively.
2. Drag the folder or file to My Shortcuts.

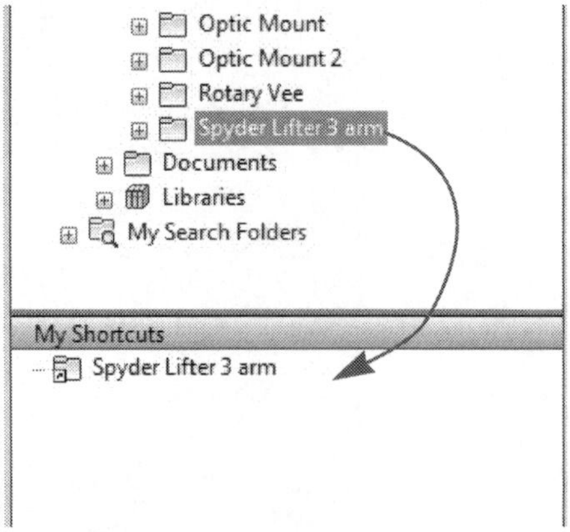

3. The shortcut is added to the list.

Procedure: Creating Groups

The following steps show how to create groups.

1. At the bottom of My Shortcuts, click Add New Group.

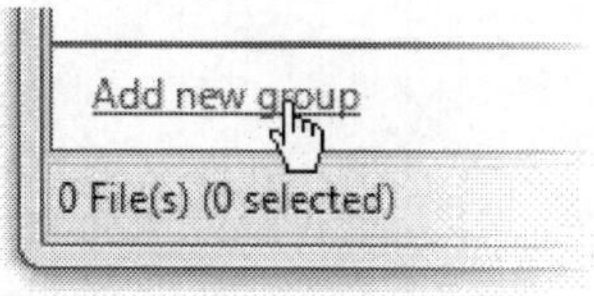

2. Enter a group name.

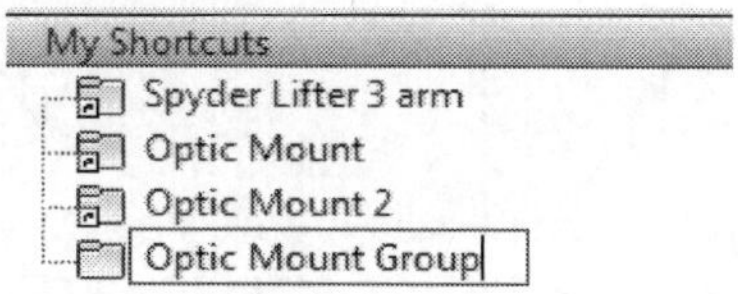

3. Drag shortcuts or other groups into this group.

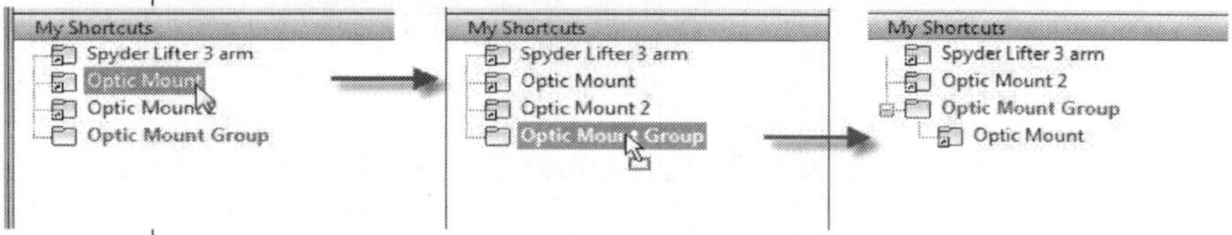

Hint: Accessing Shortcuts and Saved Searches in Inventor

Shortcuts and saved searches can be used in Inventor when opening a file from Vault; the following example displays the My Shortcuts pane that is available when opening a file in Inventor. Saved Searches from Vault are displayed here as well. A Find button is also available on the Select File From Vault dialog box to create a new search.

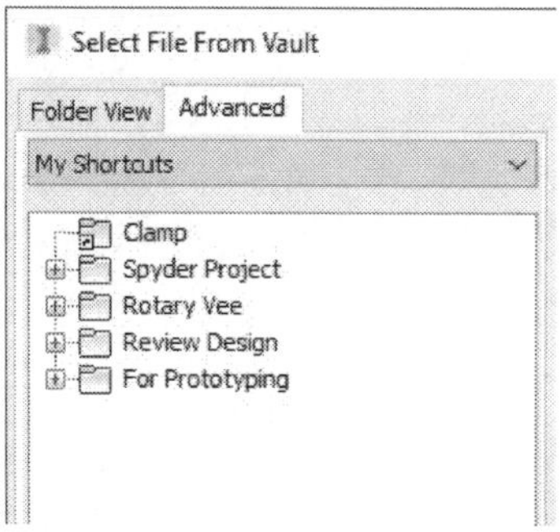

Practice 8b Find Files in the Vault

In this practice, you find the Bend Calculation document and the Adjuster file. Additionally you will organize your shortcuts.

Example

In a typical scenario, for one project, you might want to look up a document containing the calculation for a bend allowance, and for another project, you might be looking for an Adjuster assembly that was done by another designer. Because you are not sure what the name of the bend calculation file is, you use the Basic tab on Find to search for the "bend" text. This finds "bend" in any property of the files. For the Adjuster parts, you use Find, and on the Advanced tab, you search for "adjust" in the filename and for the part number. Once you find the two files, you create shortcuts to them so that you can find them again easily. You also save the Advanced search for reuse later.

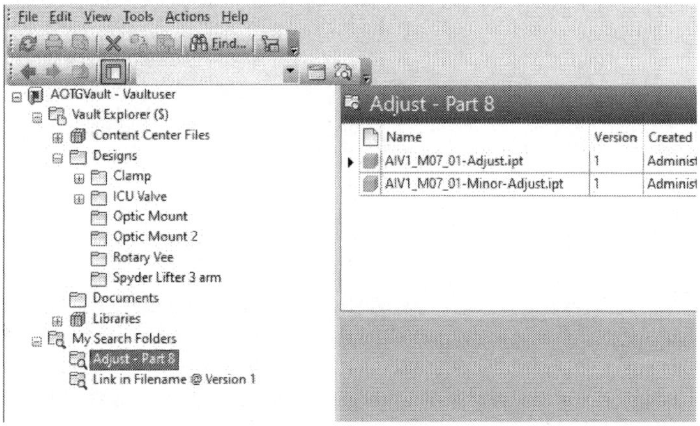

The completed practice

Task 1 - Find the bend calculation document.

Note: This practice uses the documents added to the vault in Chapter 2 Basic Vault Tasks.

1. Start Autodesk Vault. Log in using the following information:
   - For User Name, enter **administrator**.

- For Password, leave this box empty.
- For Vault, select AOTGVault.

2. Click Tools menu>Find.
3. In the Find dialog box, click the Basic tab.
4. For Search Text, enter **bend**.
5. Click Find Now.

   The results of the search are displayed in the bottom pane of the dialog box.

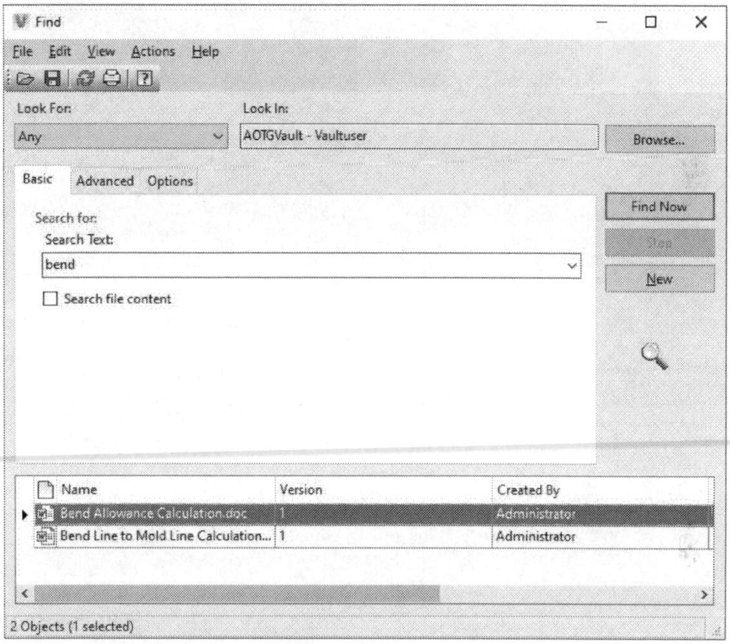

6. Right-click Bend Allowance Calculation.doc.
7. Click Create Shortcut.
8. Right-click Bend Allowance Calculation.doc.
9. Click View in Window.

   Select No if prompted to check out the file. The file opens in Microsoft Word.

10. Close the Word document, and close the Find dialog box.

Task 2 - Find the adjuster files.

1. Click Tools menu>Find.
2. On the Advanced tab, add the first criteria as follows:
   - For Property, select File Name.
   - For Condition, select contains.
   - For Value, enter **Adjust**.
   - Click Add.

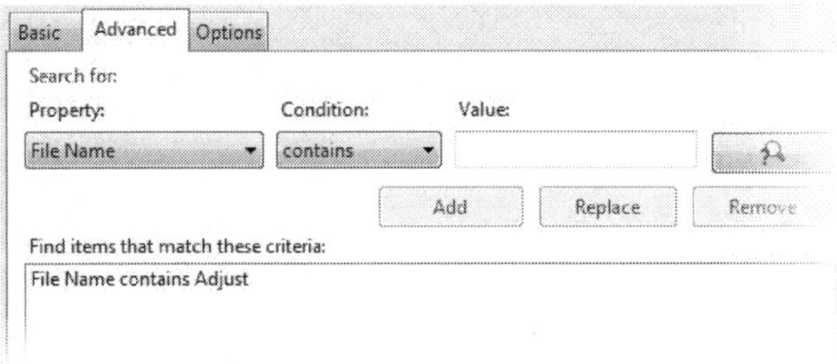

   Add the second criteria, as follows:
   - For Property, select Part Number.
   - For Condition, select contains.
   - For Value, enter **8-***.
   - Click Add.

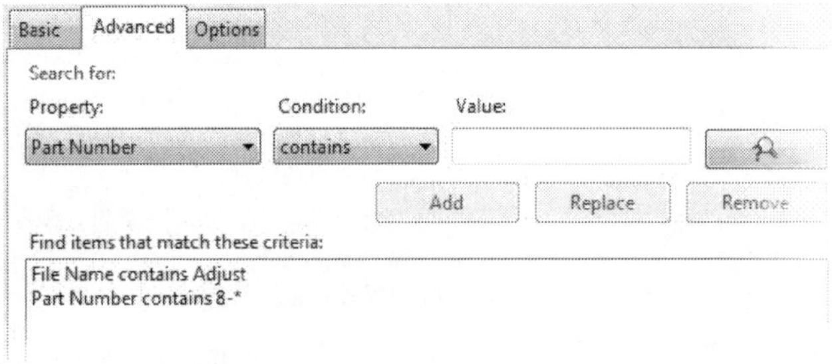

3. Click Find Now.

   The results are displayed in the bottom pane of the dialog box. Note that the columns in the result field were customized to show the part number.

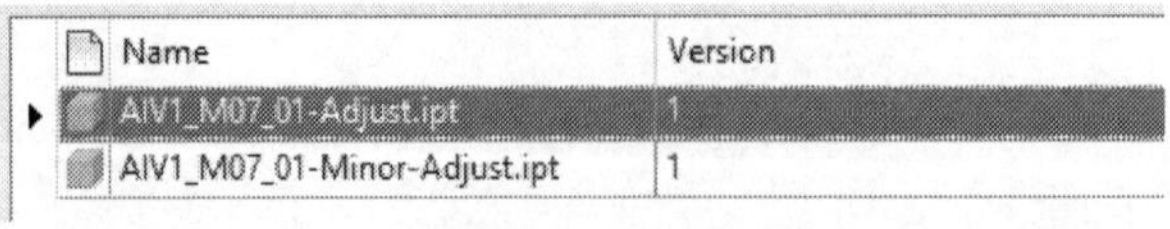

4. On the toolbar, click Save Current Search.

5. In the Save Search dialog box, do the following:

   - For Search Name, enter **Adjust - Part 8**.
   - Ensure that the Save As Folder box is checked.
   - Click OK.

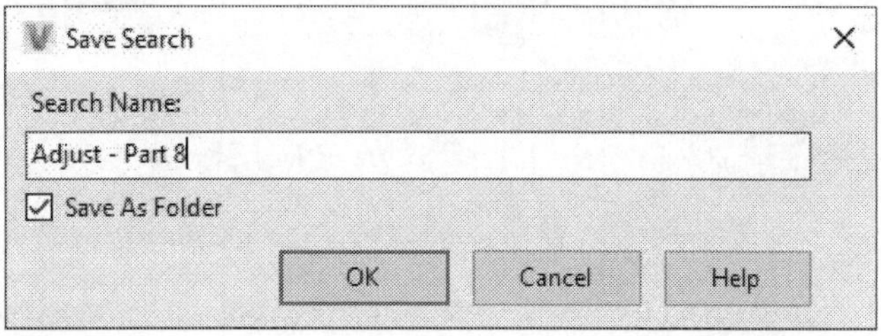

6. Right-click AIV1_M07_01-Adjust.ipt. Click Create Shortcut.

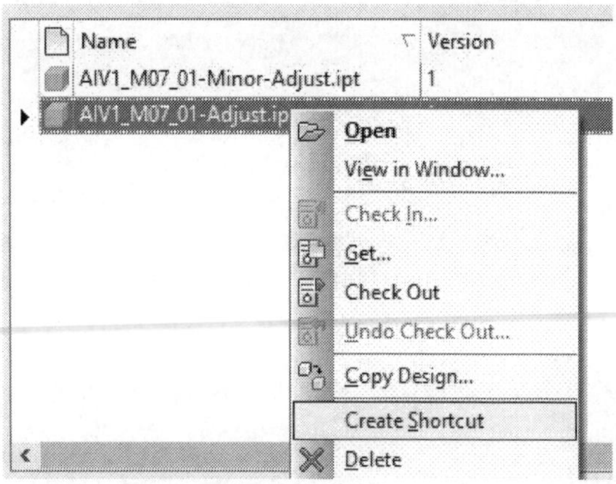

7. Close the Find dialog box.

Task 3 - Organize shortcuts.

1. In the My Shortcuts pane, click Add new group at the bottom of the pane or right-click and select New Group.

2. Enter **Optic Mount**. Press Enter.

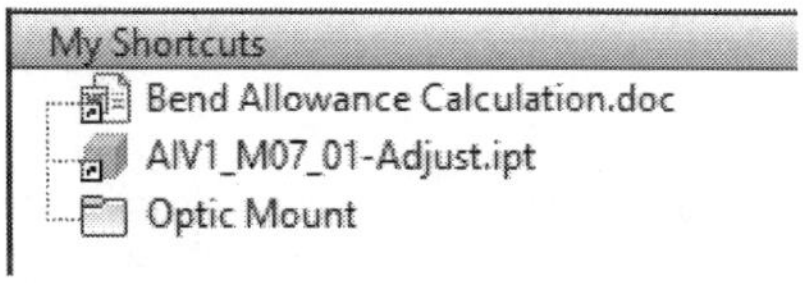

3. In the Navigation pane, drag the Optic Mount folder into the Optic Mount group you just created.

4. Expand the Optic Mount group.

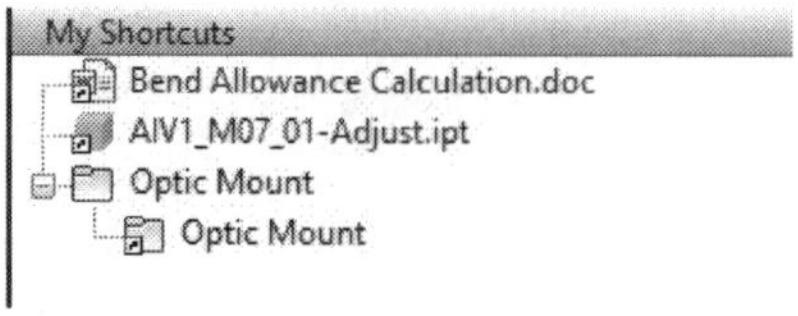

5. Under My Shortcuts, drag the AIV1_M07_01- Adjust.ipt shortcut to the Optic Mount group.

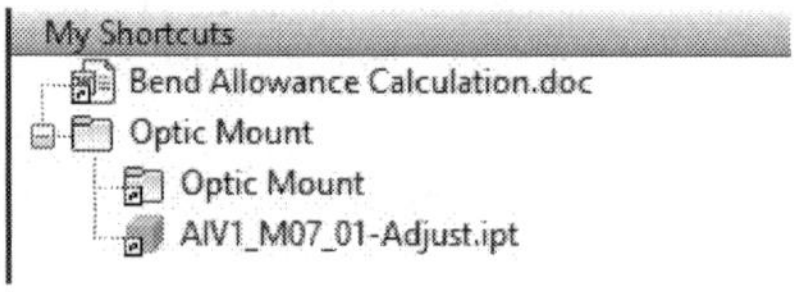

Under My Shortcuts, right-click AIV1_M07_01- Adjust.ipt. Click Rename.

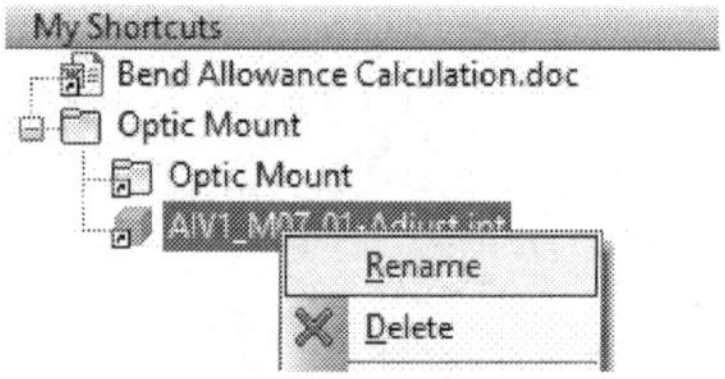

6. Rename the shortcut Adjuster Part.

7. In the Navigation pane, under My Search Folders, click the Adjust - Part 8 folder. The search displays in the Main pane.

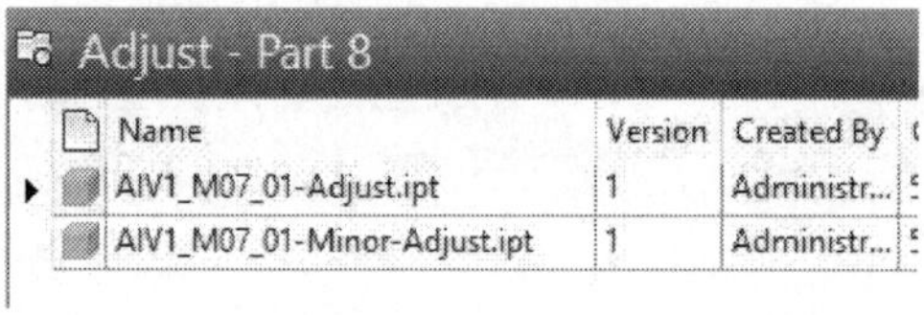

8.3 Managing Versions

Overview

In this lesson you learn how Autodesk Vault manages versions of files that have been checked in. The lesson also covers the tools that you use to view and retrieve a previous version or the latest version of a file.

As designs are created and files are checked in and out of the vault, different versions of the files are maintained by Vault. In case of an error in a design, these versions can be retrieved.

Objectives

After completing this lesson, you will be able to:

- Manage file versions to view the history of a file.
- View file history to determine the file version you want to retrieve.
- Get a previous version of a file from Vault when required.
- Use Get Latest Version to keep your local copies of files up to date with the vault.
- Make a previous version of a file the latest version.
- Create labels to mark milestones in the progress of a design.

File Versions

In the life of a product, from conception through development to supporting the design, it is important to maintain a history of all the files and any engineering-related documents. Autodesk Vault automatically manages versions as files are modified and checked back in. Vault keeps a history of the files, so that you can retrieve any version of a file at any time. This means that if the current design fails, you can go back to a previous design. You can also view file properties such as comments about the version, who checked it out, when it was revised, and so on.

Definition of File Versions

When you initially add a file to the Vault, it becomes version 1. When the file is checked out, it is temporarily assigned the next version number; the previous version remains unchanged. The permanent version number is not assigned until the modified file is checked back in. If the file is unchanged when it is checked back in, it is not assigned a new version number.

The following image displays the history of a file in Vault Explorer.

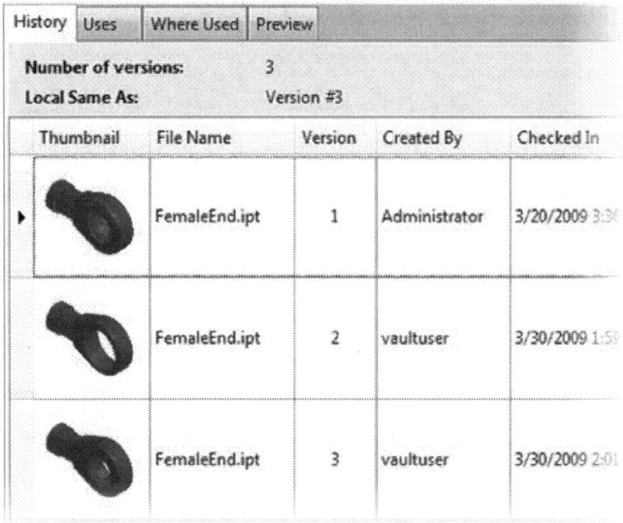

If a file is a parent of other files, such as an Autodesk Inventor assembly file or a DWG™ file with external references (XREF), each version of the parent file maintains a list of the child files and their versions. When you check out a previous version of the host file, Vault determines the correct version of the files to retrieve.

The following image indicates where the file is being used on the Where Used tab of Autodesk Vault.

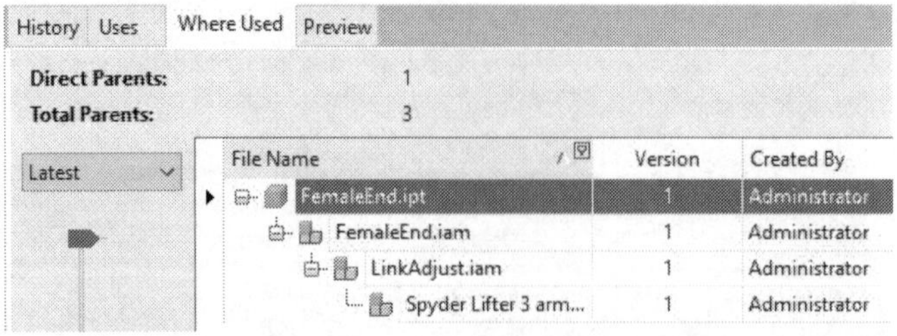

When you retrieve a previous version of a file, Vault does not check the file out. Instead, it places a read-only copy of the file in your working folder. You can either view the copy or use it to roll back to a previous version.

If you want to view the latest version of a file to see if the changes will affect your design, you can get a read-only copy even if someone else has the file checked out. You can view the file but not edit it, because it is not checked out to you.

Example

The following image displays four versions of the MaleEnd part. As the design cycle progressed, the part was modified: the material was changed and small changes were added to the threads and the holes. The latest version is displayed in the Main pane, and all the versions are shown in the Preview pane on the History tab.

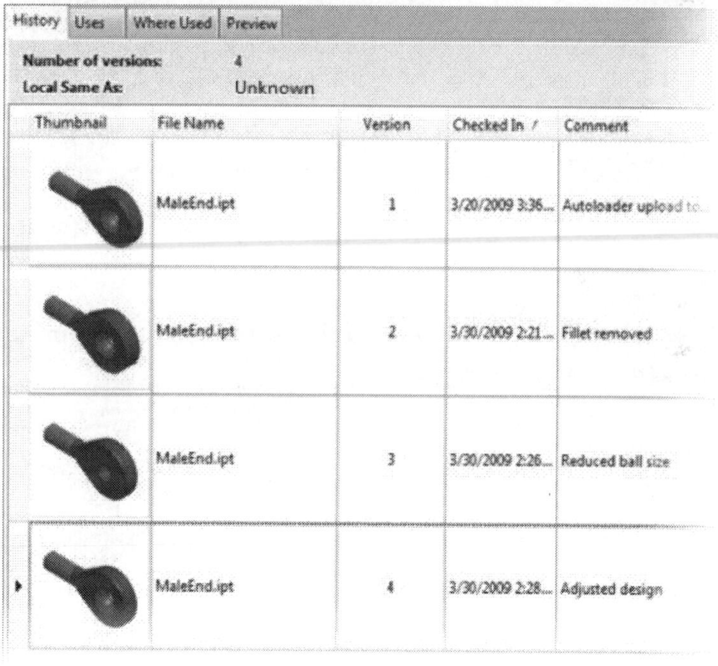

Viewing File History

Introduction to Viewing a File History

Vault keeps track of previous file versions, and you can view these versions at any time.

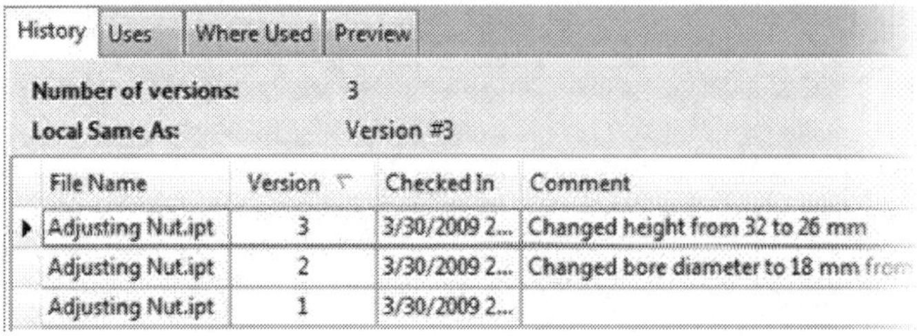

Procedure: Viewing File History in Autodesk Vault

The following steps show how to view a file's history in the Preview pane.

1. In the Main pane of the Autodesk Vault, select the file.
2. Select the History tab in the Preview pane to display all versions of the selected file.

   In the Preview pane, right-click any column header and click Customize View to customize the History tab.

Procedure: Viewing a File History in Autodesk Inventor

The following steps show how to view a file's history in Inventor.

1. Display the Vault browser.
2. Right-click the required file and select Show Details.

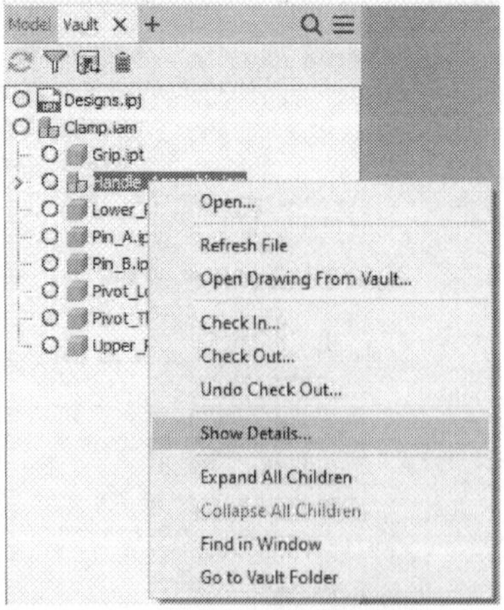

3. View the different versions of the handle assembly.

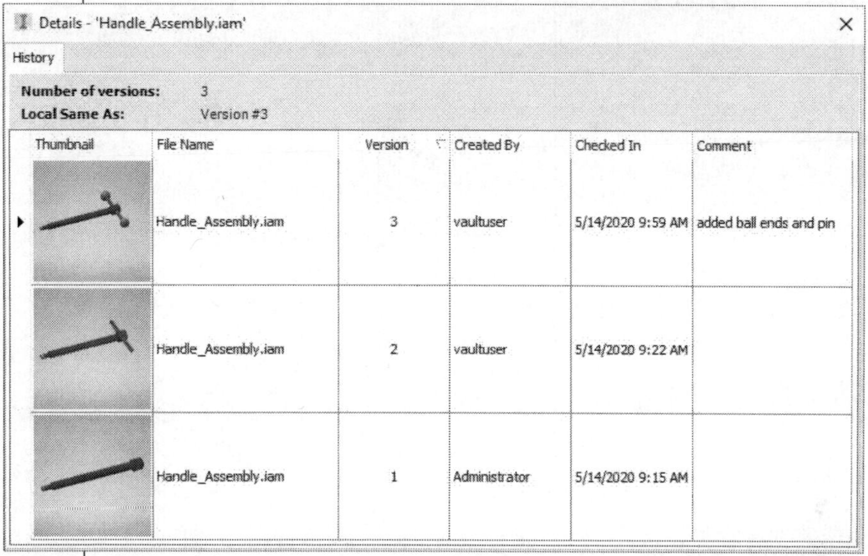

Getting a Previous Version

As a design changes and evolves, Vault keeps track of the different versions of the file. You can use Get in Autodesk Vault in case you need a previous version of a design file.

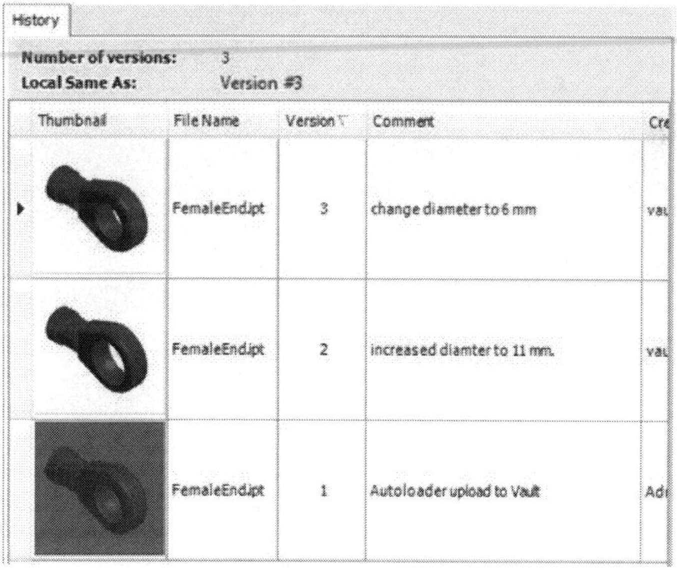

Procedure: Getting a Previous Version

The following procedure teaches you how to get a previous version of a file.

1. In the Main pane of Autodesk Vault, right-click a file and select Get.

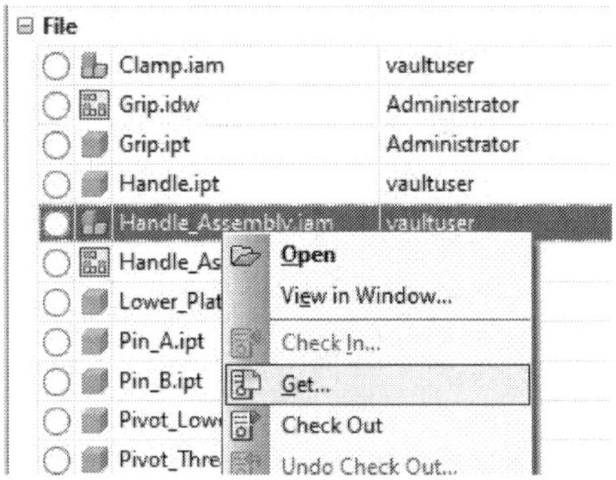

2. The Get dialog opens. Select Expand to examine where the file will be downloaded. If you do not want to overwrite the current copy, change the default location. Specify the version to get from the Select Version drop-down list.

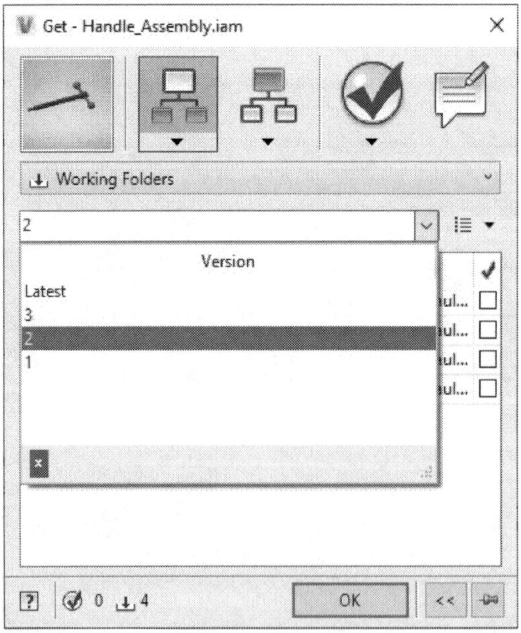

3. Select OK to download the selected version to the specified location.

Previous Version

When you get a previous version using Autodesk Vault in the same location as the original file, this previous version is now copied to the local computer. The local copy is now an older version, and the following warning is shown in Autodesk Vault.

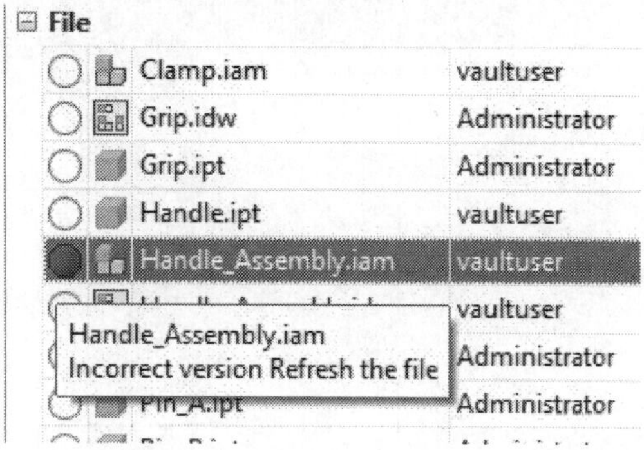

Getting the Latest Version

When working on a design, other members of the design team can check out a file, edit it, and check it back in. Or they can restore an older version of a file. In either case, to see the latest version of the checked-in files you need to get the Latest Version.

This synchronizes the local copy of the file with the one in the vault; but the data in the local file cannot be modified until it is checked out.

Procedure: Getting the Latest Version

The following procedure teaches you how to see the latest version of a file.

1. In the Main pane of Autodesk Vault, right-click a file. Click Get.

2. In the Get dialog, select the latest version from the Select Version drop-down list. Ensure that the file is downloaded to the required location.

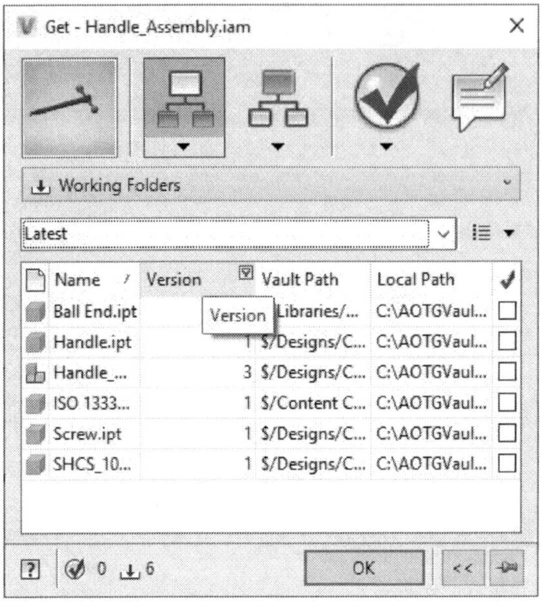

3. Select OK to download the file.
4. Note the file status in the in the Main pane.

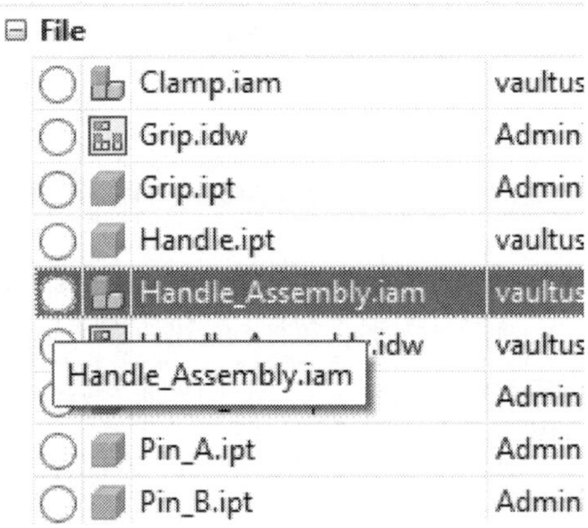

Get Latest Version

You can also get the Latest Version in the client application. For example, in Inventor you can get the most current version by right-clicking a file and clicking Refresh File.

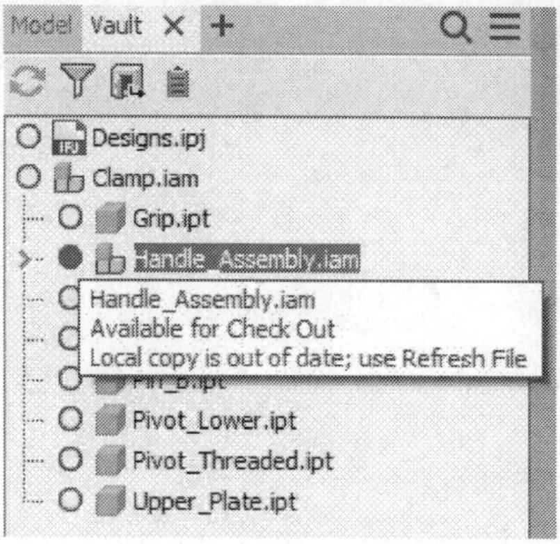

Reverting to a Previous Design

At times in a design cycle, you can make changes to files, check them into the vault for other team members to review, and then decide to cancel the changes and revert to a previous version. The vault stores all previous versions so you can revert to a previous version at any time.

Process: Reverting to a Previous Version

If you change a file and check it in to the vault, the copy in the vault is updated with the new version. If you decide that you want to revert to a previous version of a design, you can follow this process.

1. Close the model in Autodesk Inventor.
2. In Autodesk Vault, get a previous version of the model from the vault, replacing the local copies.
3. Open the model in Autodesk Inventor. The Vault browser indicates that some local files have new edits because there are newer versions of the same files in the vault.

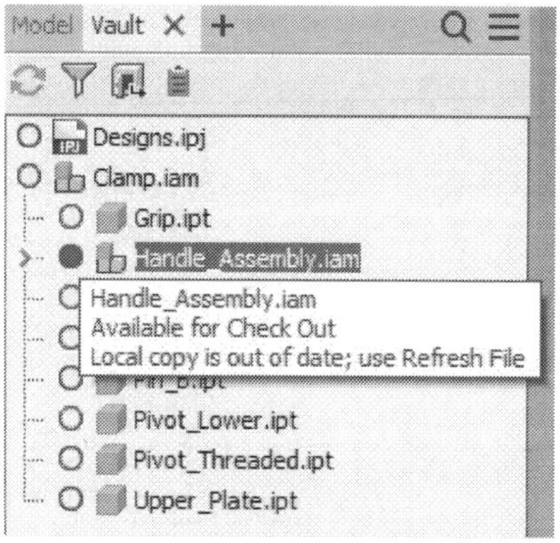

4. Check out the files. You can check out just the files that have new edits available, or, if the model has several files with new edits, select the option to include children and check out all of the files at once.

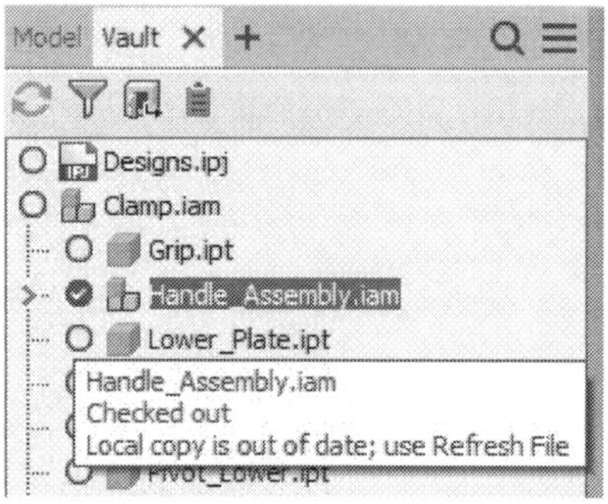

5. Check the files back in to the vault. The old versions of the files are copied to the vault and become the latest version. If the create visualization files setting is checked, new visualization files are generated. If you want to remove the previous version from the vault, purge the files.

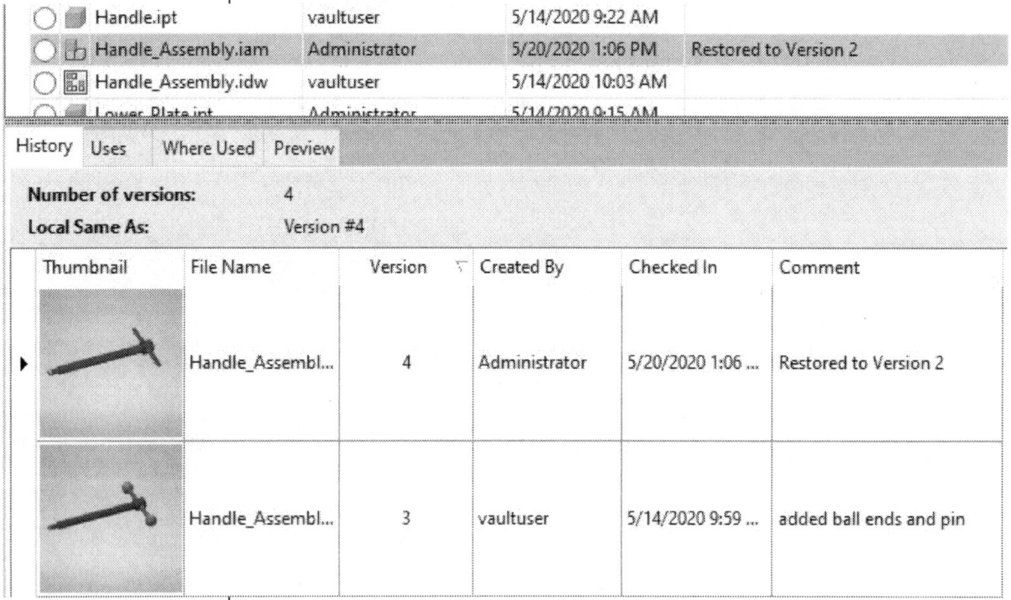

Labeling Designs

Labels define a snapshot in time of a design while under work in progress. Labels are applied at the Vault folder level and are stored with a unique, user-specified name.

Labels can be used to mark any point in the evolution of a design: the preliminary customer proposal, different variations in the design, reviews, approvals, and so on.

Labels can be created, deleted, renamed, archived, and restored all from the Labels dialog box. The Labels dialog box also displays details about labels, such as who created it, when it was created, how many files are assigned to the label, and the comment associated with the label. You access the Label dialog box from Tools menu>Labels.

Assigning a label to a project creates a dependency between the project files and the corresponding label. Files associated with labels cannot be deleted from the vault unless the label is deleted first. When you delete a label, only the label is removed. The associated files remain in the vault.

Procedure: Creating a New Label

The following procedure teaches you how to create a new label.

1. In the Autodesk Vault Navigation pane, right-click the folder you want to label. Click New Label.
2. Under Label Name, enter the label name. It must not contain the characters \ / : * ? " < >|.
3. Enter any required comments. The more comments you enter, the easier others can learn about the milestone event you are labeling.

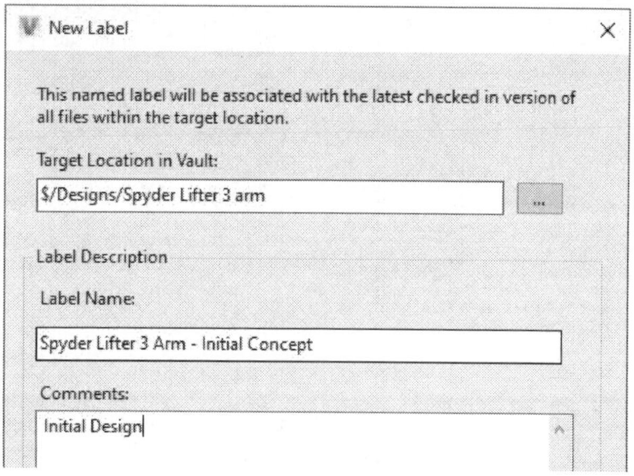

Procedure: Working with Labels

The following procedure teaches you how to work with existing labels.

1. To view the list of active labels, click Tools menu>Labels.

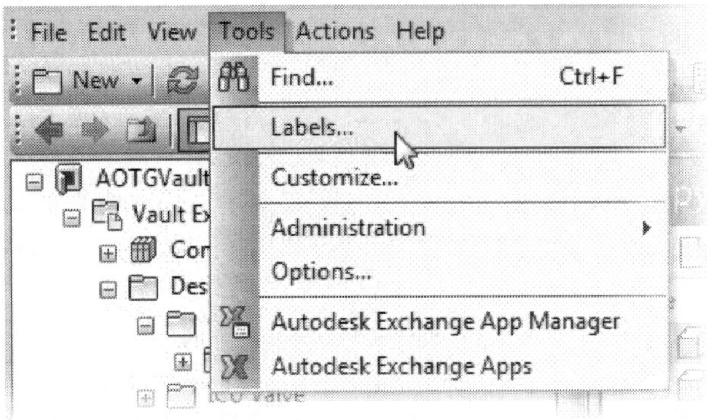

2. The Labels dialog box displays the current labels using the Created By and Create Date fields.

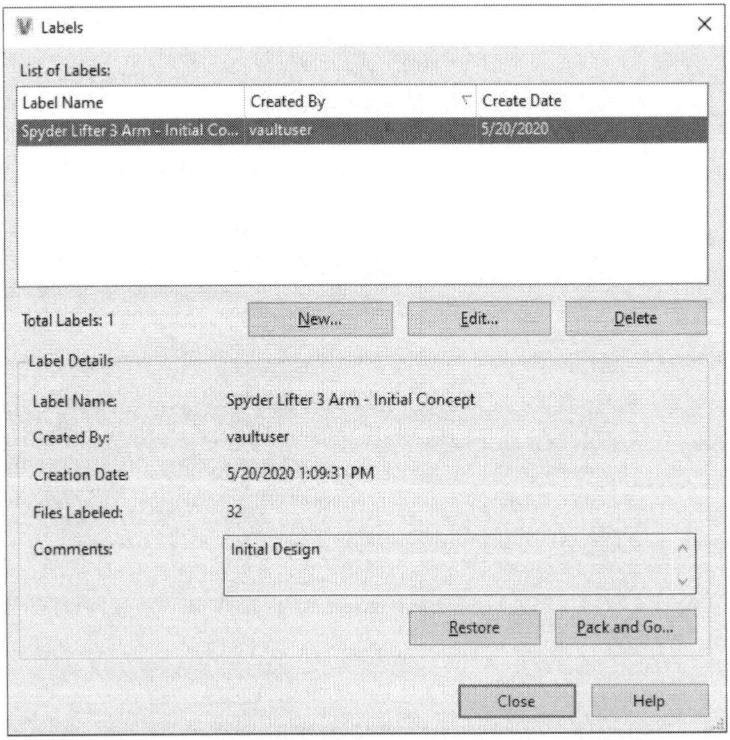

3. Edit... enables you to rename the label or change its comments.

4. Pack and Go archives the label. Options include:
    - Set Destination Folder
    - Package Type (*.zip or folders)
    - Output Structure Flattened or Keep Hierarchy
5. Click Restore to revert to the initial snapshot of the design. This is similar to getting a previous version, only it is more global in nature, and multiple files will be restored to a previous version.
6. You will be prompted to confirm restoring the label. Restoring a label in Vault changes the versions of the files numerically forward, not backward (so, while working with the current Version 6, you restore a label from Version 2, the latest version will carry the number 7)).

Practice 8c Manage File Versions

In this practice, you learn how to capture design intent by creating and restoring labels.

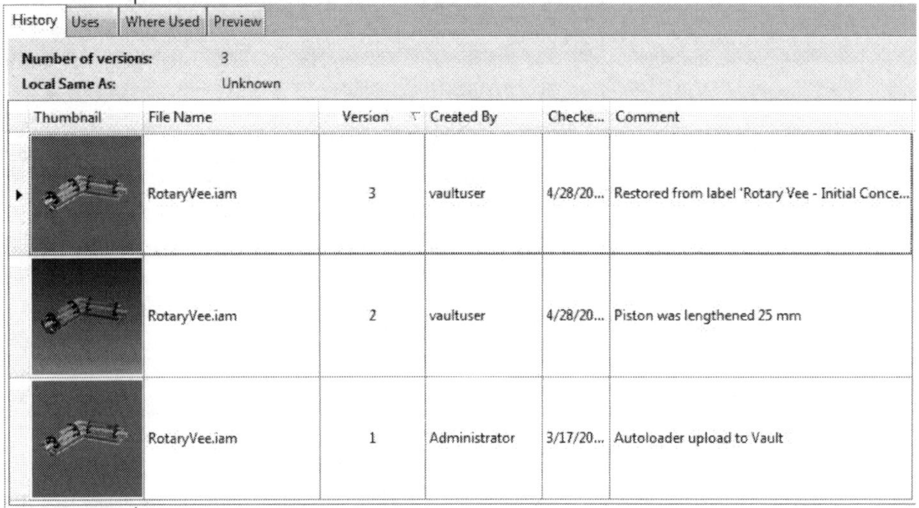

The completed practice

Task 1 - Create a label.

1. Start Autodesk Vault. Log in using the following information:
    - For User Name, enter **vaultuser**.
    - For Password, leave this box empty.
    - For Vault, select AOTGVault.
2. In Autodesk Vault, in the Navigation pane, expand the Designs folder. Right-click Rotary Vee. Click New Label.
3. For Label Name, enter **Rotary Vee – Initial Concept.**

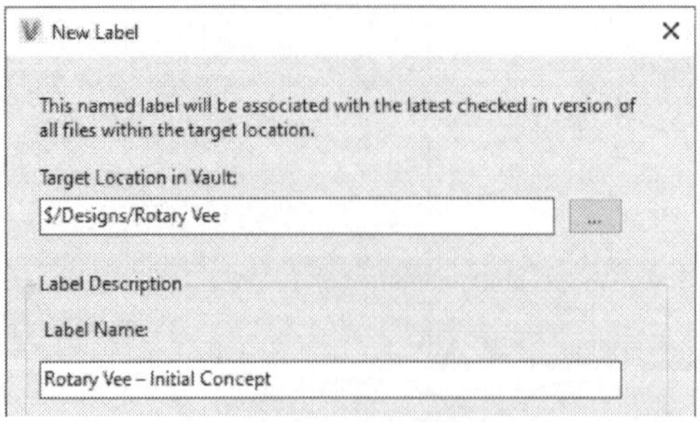

4. Under Comments, enter **Initial Design**. Click OK.
5. Click Tools menu>Labels.
6. View the label details.
7. Close the Labels dialog box.

Task 2 - Modifying a component in the design.

1. Open Autodesk Inventor. Do the following:
   - On the ribbon, click the Vault tab. If you are not logged in to a vault, click Log In. Log in to AOTGVault.
   - On the Vault tab, click Open.
   - Expand Designs and browse to the Rotary Vee folder.
   - Select RotaryVee.iam and click the list next to Open.
   - Select Open (Check Out All).

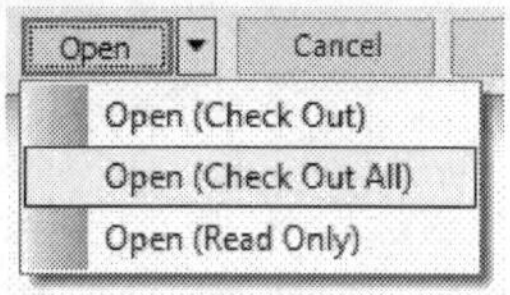

   - Click OK in the Check Out dialog box.
2. In the Model browser, right-click pistonAssy:1. Click Edit.
3. Once pistonAssy:1 is activated, right-click piston1:1. Click Edit.
4. Right-click Revolution1 and select 3D Grips.

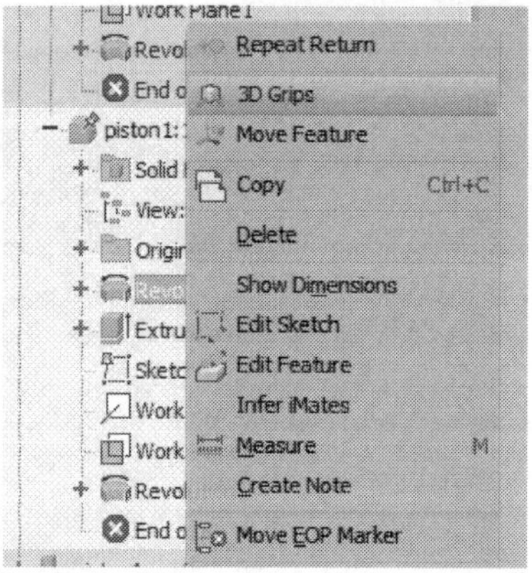

5. Zoom in on the left end of the piston as shown.

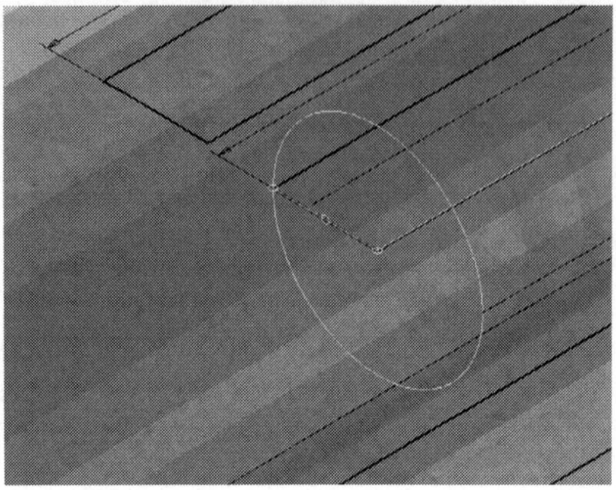

6. Rest the cursor at the midpoint until the arrow is displayed as shown.

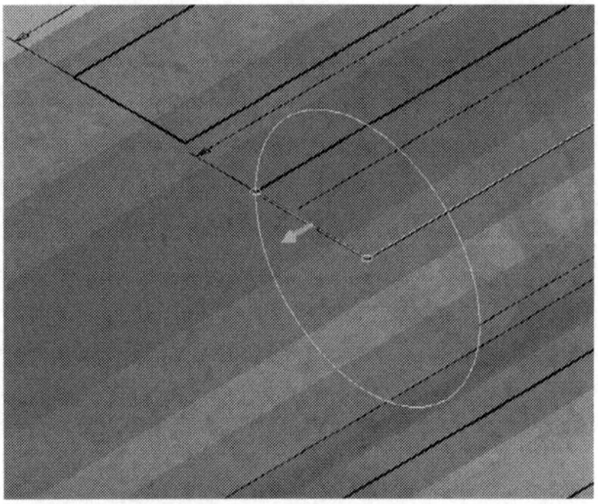

7. Right-click and select Edit Offset.

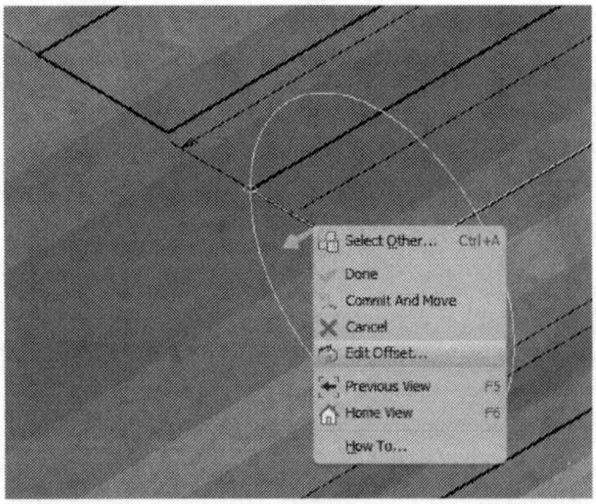

8. In the Edit Offset dialog box:

   - Under Edit Offset Distance, enter **25 mm**.
   - Click OK.
   - Right-click in the window. Click Done.

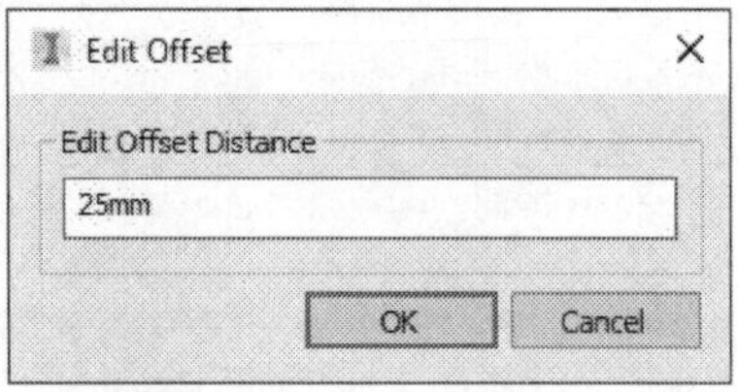

9. Right-click in the window. Click Done.

   The pistonAssy:1 subassembly is activated again

10. Right-click in the window. Click Finish Edit.

11. The RotaryVee.iam assembly is active.

12. In the browser, click Vault. Note the effect the edit had on other files.

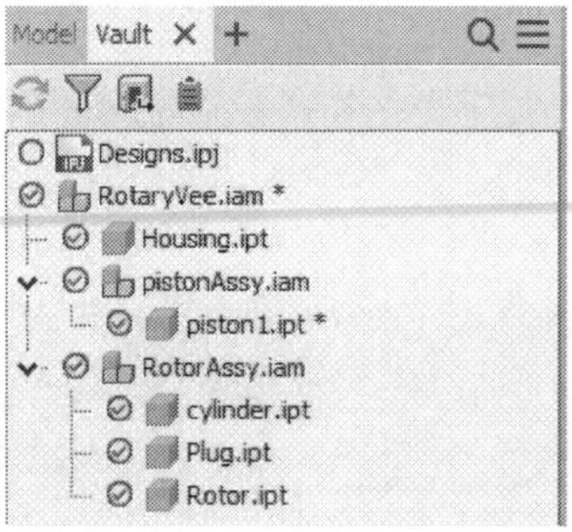

13. Save RotaryVee.iam. Do not save any files that have not been modified.

14. Right-click RotaryVee.iam and select Check In.

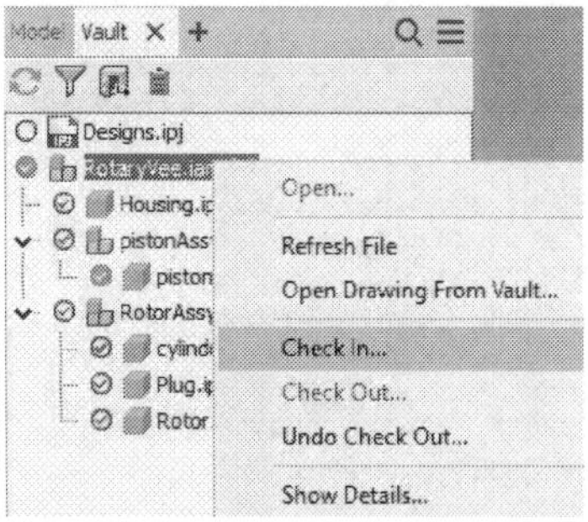

15. In the Check In dialog box, click Settings.

16. In the Settings dialog box, verify that Include Children, Create Visualization Attachment, and Apply to All Files are selected. Click OK.

17. In the Check In dialog box:

- Select Close files and delete working copies.
- Enter a comment that the piston was lengthened 25 mm.
- Click OK.
- If you are warned that the local files will be deleted, click Yes.

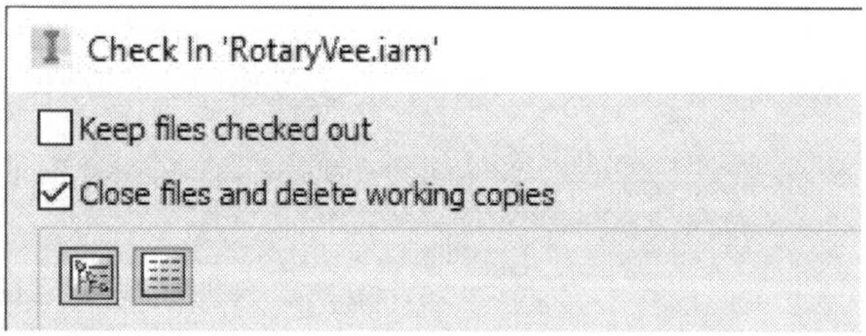

18. Switch to Autodesk Vault. Do the following:

    - Click View menu>Refresh. Alternatively, you can click Refresh in the Standard toolbar.
    - Click the Rotary Vee folder. Click RotaryVee.iam.
    - In the Preview pane, on the History tab, note that there are two versions of the RotaryVee.iam assembly.

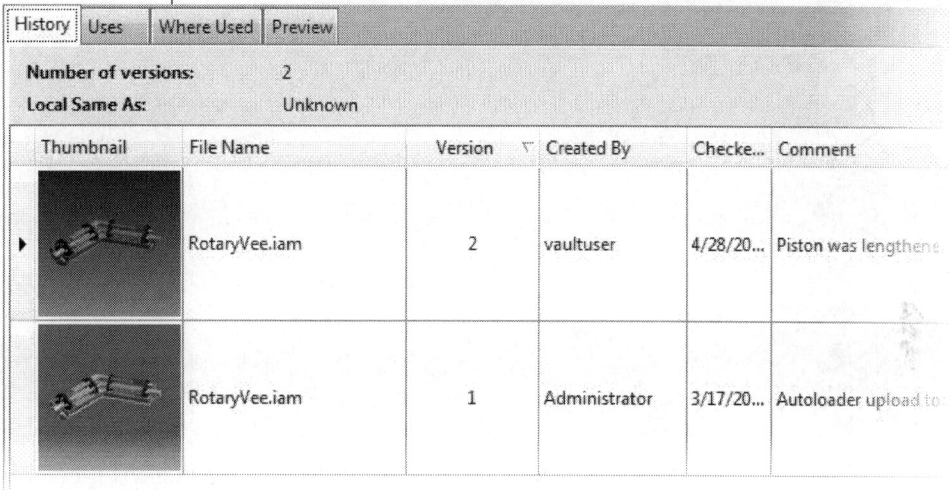

Task 3 - View file history and restore a label.

1. In Autodesk Vault, click Tools menu>Labels.
2. In the Labels dialog box, select the Rotary Vee- Initial Concept label you created earlier.
3. Click Restore. You will be warned that a new file version will be created for all files associated with the label. Click Yes.

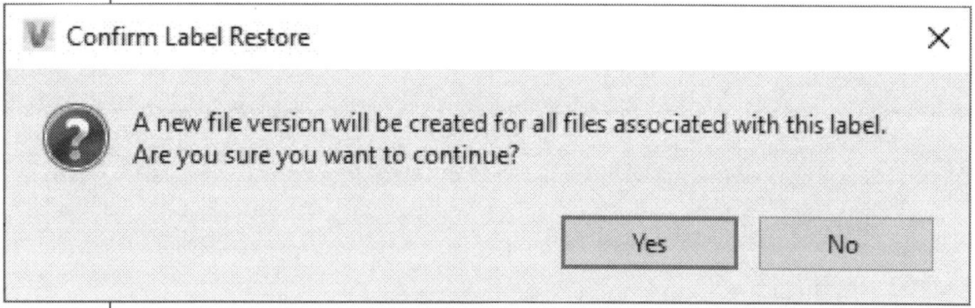

4. Close the Labels dialog box. The Rotary Vee assembly is restored to its original state as defined in the label.

5. In the Preview pane, History tab, examine the version numbers of the files.

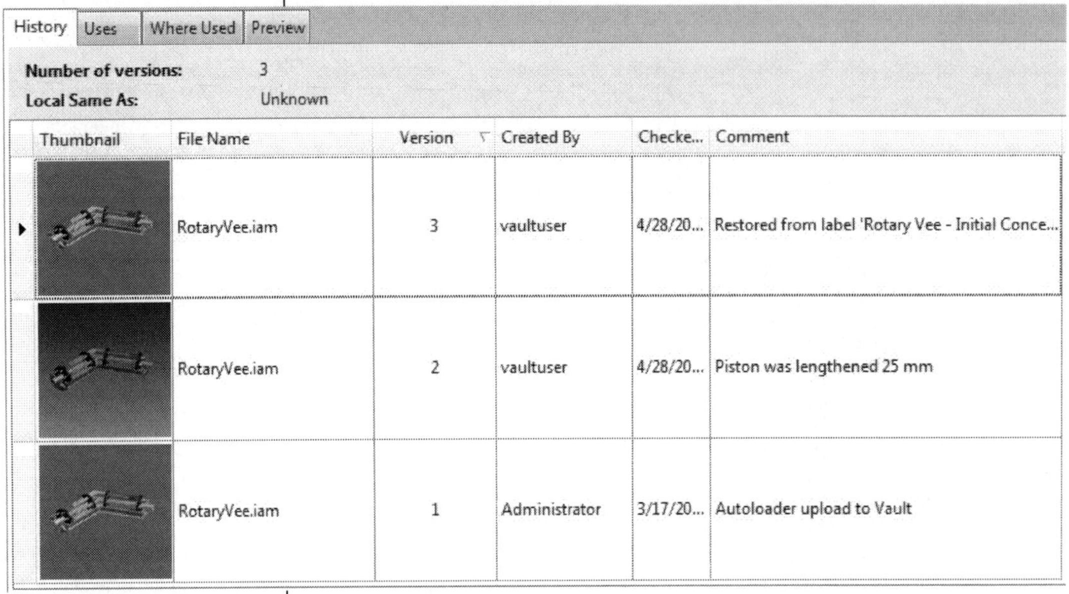

Note that the file versions have incremented forward on all files that were different from the files associated with the label.

8.4 Renaming and Moving Files

Overview

In this lesson, you learn about moving and renaming files in Vault.

As a design evolves and changes, the design's file structure and naming can also change. New components can be added that require some files to be renamed. Files shared between multiple designs can be placed in a shared folder instead of being in one design's folder or another.

Objectives

After completing this lesson, you will be able to:

- View file dependencies in order to correctly move and rename files.
- Use the Rename wizard in Vault to rename files and check their dependencies.
- Move files in Vault to organize folder structures without breaking file dependencies.

File Dependencies and Vault

In most CAD systems the concept of linked or dependent files is important. Instead of building the entire model in one file, the model is built with components in several files that are linked together. This makes loading the model easier and more efficient, and creates smaller files.

The only drawback to this approach is the links or dependencies between the files. The files must maintain their links, which makes changing the file names or their location on the computer more difficult.

Definition of File Dependencies

A file dependency is a way to describe a link from one file to another. Different CAD systems use various names and workflows for this; in some it is entirely automatic, while in other systems, the user creates the links.

AutoCAD uses external references to link files. Drawing (DWG) files are attached as external references to another drawing. The attached drawings can either be in the same folder as the one they are attached to so that they can be found when loading the drawing. Alternatively, search paths can be set up so the cross-referenced files can be found.

Linking files in AutoCAD is a manual process. The user creates links between the drawing files, and maintains the links.

Other AutoCAD-based systems such as AutoCAD® Mechanical, AutoCAD® Electrical, and Autodesk® Civil 3D® use the same external reference system, but it can be more transparent and automated. In some cases the user still has to set up search paths for the referenced files.

Autodesk Inventor also uses file dependencies, but in a totally transparent way. For example when you create an assembly file and add components, the assembly file contains references to the files containing these components. This is done transparently and the user rarely has to intervene except in the case where files are moved or renamed. In those cases, Inventor prompts for the missing files.

File Dependencies and Vault

Autodesk Vault is capable of analyzing and understanding file dependencies and can take them into account when moving, renaming, or checking files in and out.

File dependencies can be viewed in the Preview pane on the Uses and Where Used tabs.

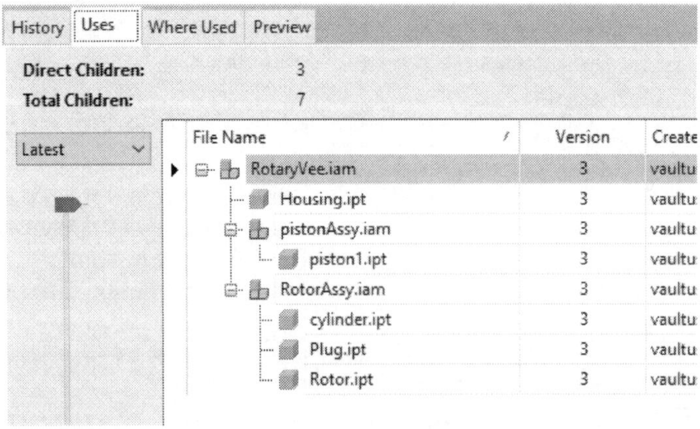

Example of File Dependencies

The Optic Mount shown below has three Adjuster subassemblies. The Adjuster subassembly has three components.

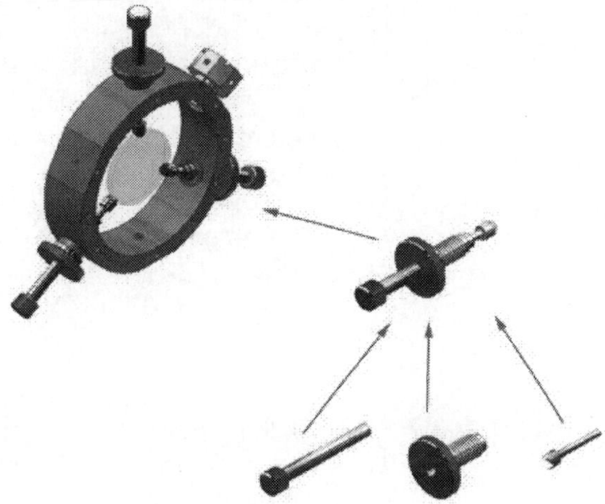

In Autodesk Vault, in the Preview pane, the Where Used tab indicates that the Adjuster subassembly has two parents: the Main assemblies for Optic Mount and Optic Mount 2.

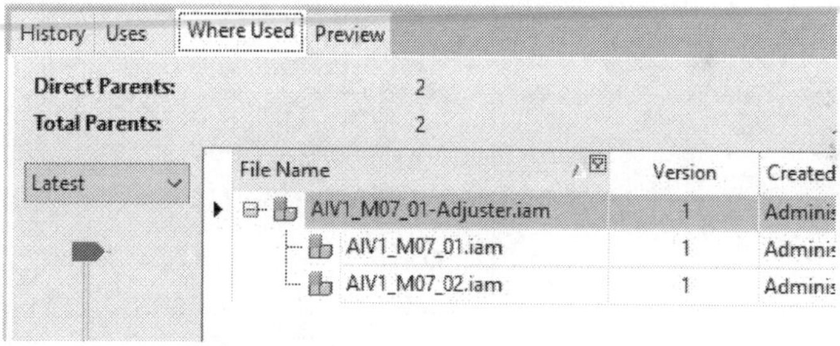

The Uses tab indicates that the Adjuster subassembly has three children (or dependents).

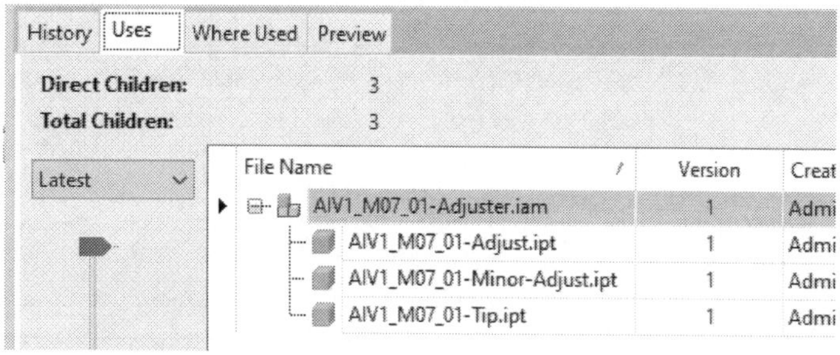

Renaming Files

The Rename wizard in Autodesk Vault enables you to rename single or multiple files. It maintains relationships between files by repairing links as required to maintain existing file dependencies.

The wizard indicates what models are affected by the rename operations, and suggests a naming scheme. Optionally, it can also update part numbers.

Guidelines for Renaming Files

When renaming files in Autodesk Vault, it is recommended you follow these guidelines:

- Use the Rename wizard to rename files in the vault.
- Files being renamed and all related files must be checked in to the vault.
- Update the file reference information for migrated files. When adding a file to the vault from a CAD application, reference information, which is used for updating files renamed or moved in Vault is automatically created. However, the files migrated from previous releases might be incomplete and might cause unresolved links when opening in an authoring application. You can see the parent or child in the Uses or Where Used tab, but a rename or move action is blocked to protect the data. To resolve this issue, you can update file references before renaming or moving migrated files. To update file references, select the files(s) in the Actions menu and select Update File Reference. Note that the corresponding authoring application is required to run this command.

Note: The project specified in Autodesk Inventor Project Settings is used for file resolving. An Autodesk Inventor project file to be used for all clients can be set by your administrator. Otherwise, you can specify the Autodesk Inventor project file in Autodesk Vault using the Tools menu>Options dialog box or by right-clicking the project file and selecting Set Inventor Project File.

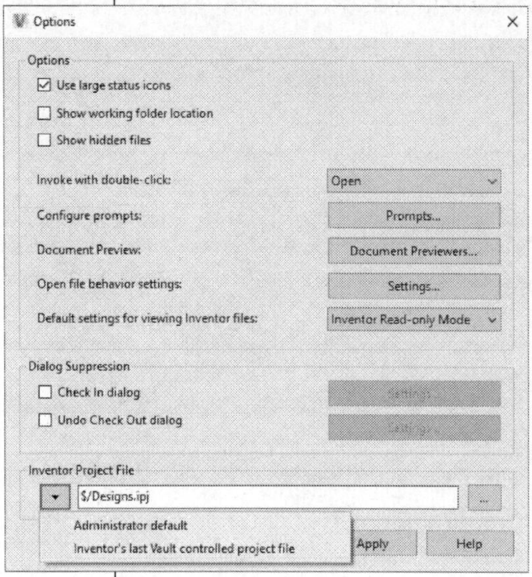

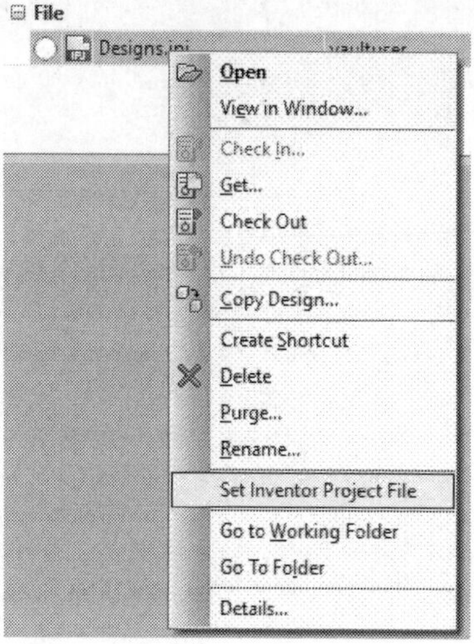

Procedure: Renaming Files Using the Rename Wizard

The following procedure teaches you how to rename files using the Rename wizard.

1. Right-click a file or a selection of files in the Main pane and select Rename.

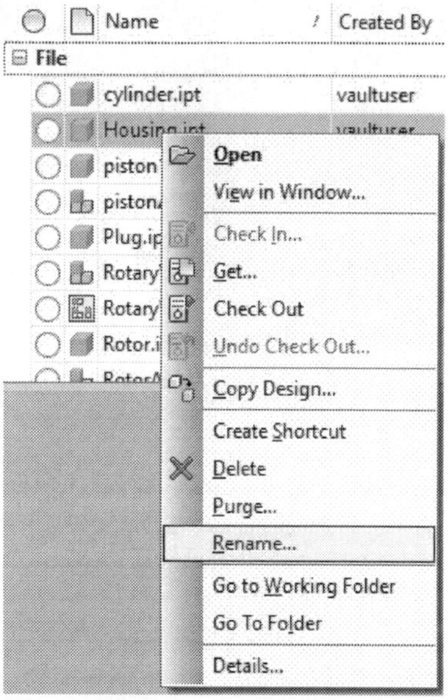

2. The Rename wizard is displayed. The wizard lists the file or files that were selected from the Main pane. Click Add Files to include other files from the vault.

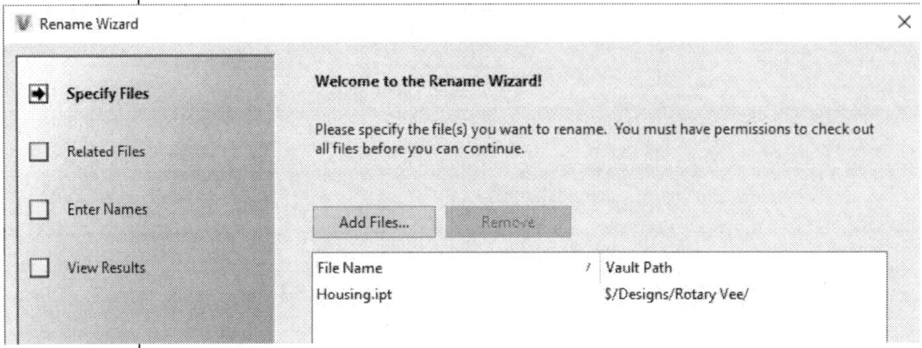

3. Click Next. The Rename wizard determines the related files that are affected by the name change. The reference to the renamed file or files is updated.
4. The files to be renamed are listed. Click in the New Name field for each file to enter a new filename. You can also click Numbering Scheme and specify a naming scheme to follow. Click Next.

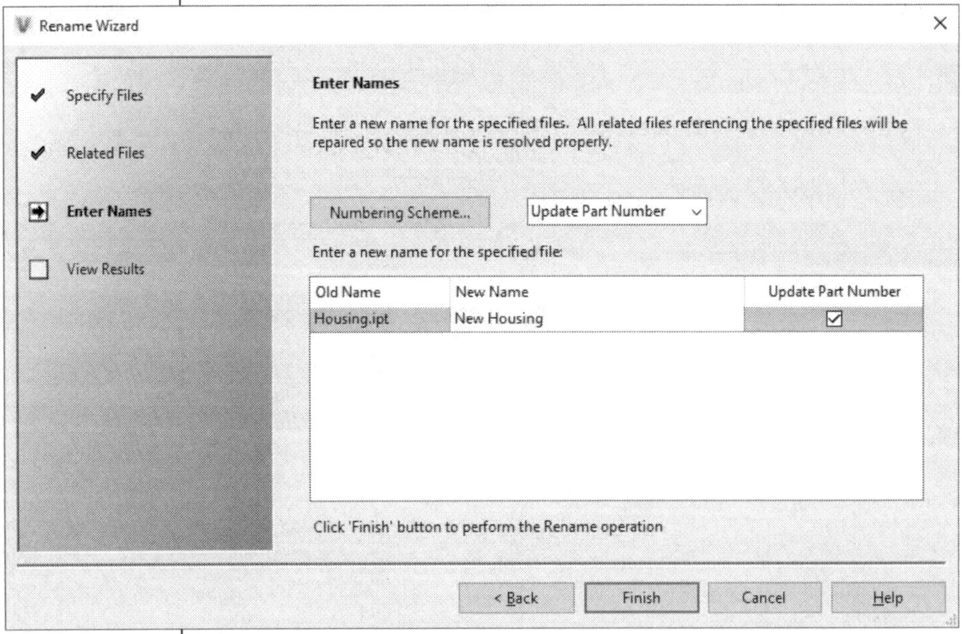

5. Click Finish. The wizard displays a summary of the files that were renamed.

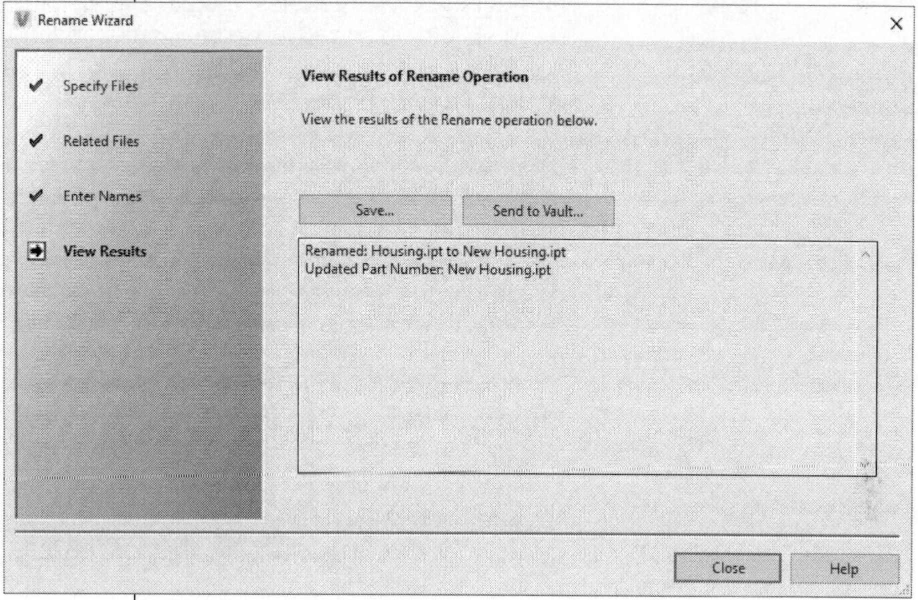

Moving Files

The Move tool moves files from one folder to another. This tool enables you to rearrange how the files are stored in the vault while maintaining file dependencies.

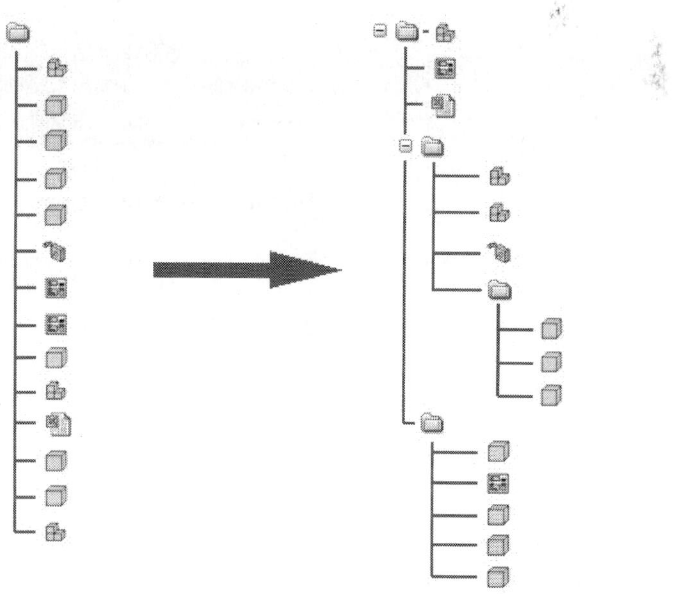

Autodesk Inventor and File Dependencies

For Autodesk Inventor files, the advantage of moving files is being able to do so without breaking dependencies.

AutoCAD and File Dependencies

While Vault is aware of file dependencies and can track them, it might not be able to keep those dependencies once the files are checked out of the vault and opened. For example, AutoCAD relies on search paths to find externally referenced files; this data is stored in the application and not in the vault. Another example is a relative or absolute path embedded in a file; these links can break.

Moving Files Using Windows Explorer

When you move files on your local computer using Windows Explorer, you break file dependencies. For example, after moving Inventor files, you have to open the files in Inventor and fix the file links.

A good example of using Move in Autodesk Vault is to move shared files to a common folder. Move maintains the file links and repairs files as required to keep the correct dependencies.

Rules for Moving Files

When you move CAD files, you risk breaking the dependencies between the files. The following rules apply:

- Always use Move in Autodesk Vault to restructure your files.
- Ensure that all files to be moved are checked in to the vault.
- Avoid using Windows Explorer to move files.

Procedure: Moving Files

The following procedure teaches you how files can be moved from one folder to another.

1. In Autodesk Vault, create new folders if required.
2. Navigate to the folder that contains the files you want to move.
3. In the Main pane, select the file or files you want to move.
4. Drag the selected files to the required folder destination in the Navigation pane.

Practice 8d

Rename and Move Files

In this practice, you rename and move files to better capture design intent. First, you rename the Optic Mount adjuster subassembly and two of its components. Then, you create a new common folder and move the subassembly and the two components to this folder.

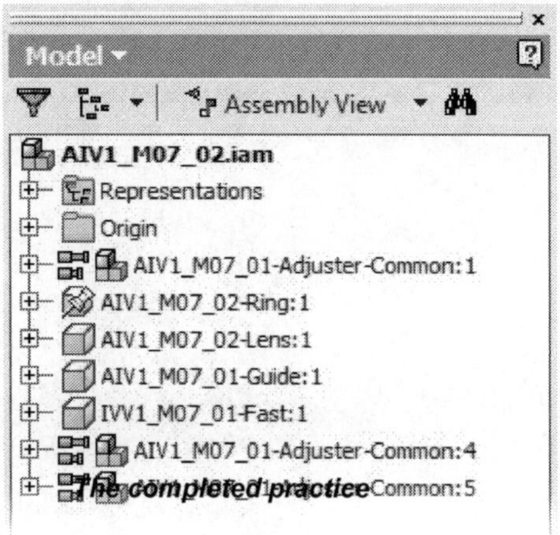

The completed practice

Task 1 - Rename a subassembly.

1. Start Autodesk Vault. Log in using the following information:
   - For User Name, enter **vaultuser**.
   - For Password, leave the box empty.
   - For Vault, select AOTGVault.
2. In Vault, click Tools>Options and in the Options dialog box, do the following:
   - In the Inventor Project File field, browse to and select $/Designs.ipj.
   - Click Open.
   - Click OK.
3. Navigate to the Designs\Optic Mount folder.

4. In the Main pane, select AIV1_M07_01- Adjuster.iam. In the Preview pane, click the Where Used tab.

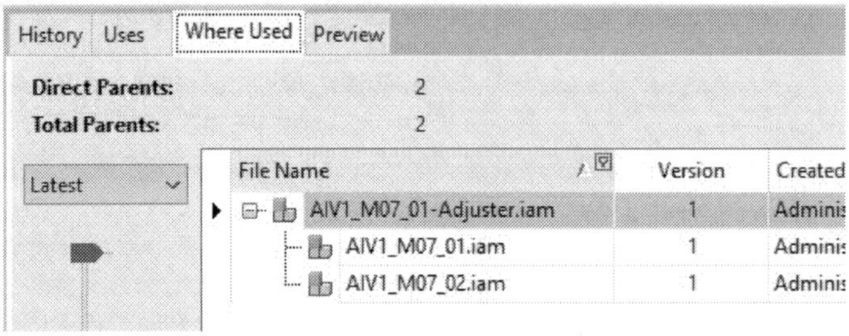

The file's parents have already been checked in to the vault

5. In the Main pane, select AIV1_M07_01- Adjust.ipt. In the Preview pane, click the Where Used tab. The file's parents have been checked in to the vault.

6. Repeat the previous step for the file AIV1_M07_-1-Minor-Adjust.ipt. This way you can check for possible errors before starting the Rename wizard.

7. In the Main pane, select AIV1_M07_01- Adjuster.iam, AIV1_M07_01-Adjust.ipt, and AIV1_M07_01-Minor-Adjust.ipt.

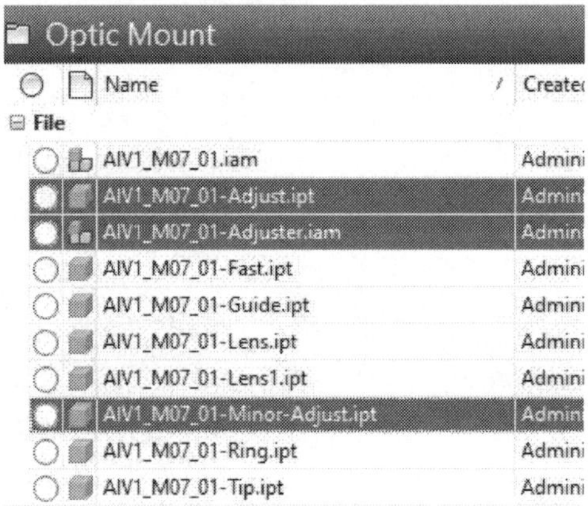

8. Right-click one of the selected files. Click Rename.

9. In the Rename Wizard dialog box, verify that you selected the correct files. Click Next.

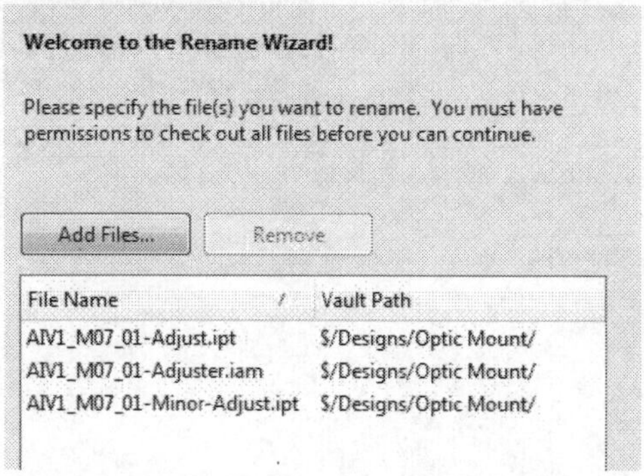

10. In the Rename Wizard dialog box, under Enter Names, click Numbering Scheme.

11. In the Numbering Scheme dialog box, do the following:

    - Clear Prefix.
    - Select Suffix.
    - In the Suffix box, enter **-Common**.
    - Click Apply.

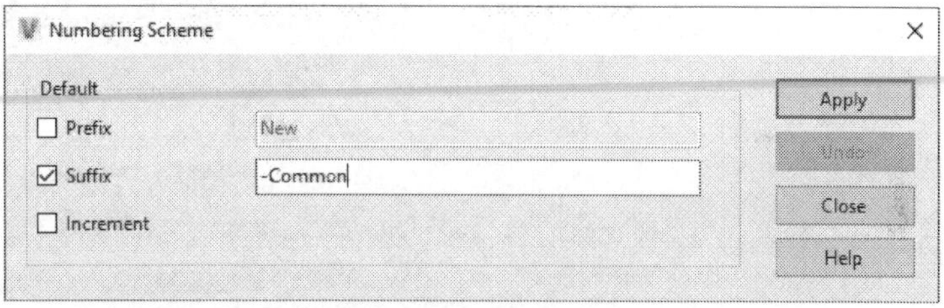

12. Click Close. Examine the New Name field in the Wizard to see the results of the Numbering Scheme.

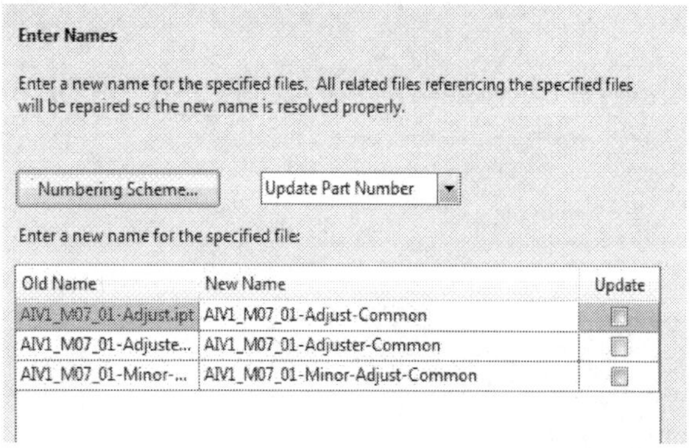

13. Click Finish. The results of the rename operation are shown.

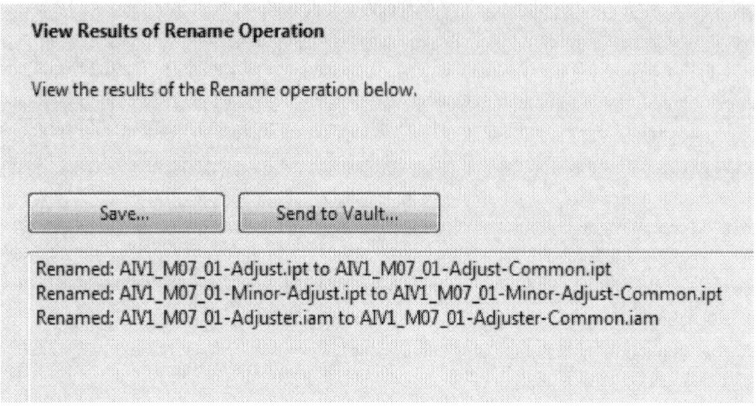

14. Select Close to dismiss the dialog.

15. Examine the Optic Mount files in the Main pane. Three of the files now have -Common suffixed to their names.

Task 2 - Move the subassembly to a new shared folder.

1. In the Navigation pane, right-click Designs and select New Folder. In the New Folder dialog box, do the following:
   - Enter **Optic Mount - Shared Parts.**
   - Click OK.

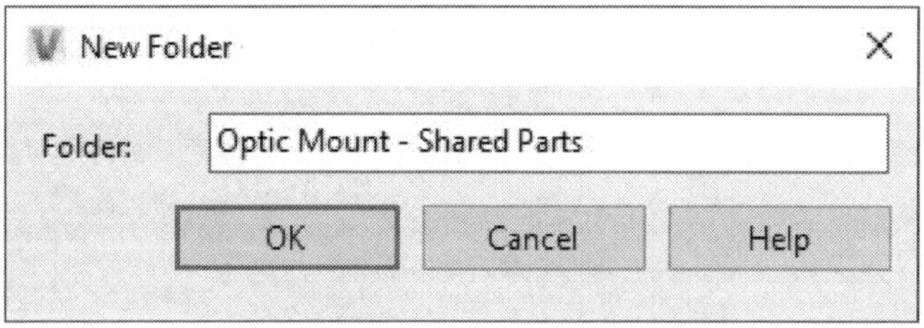

2. Re-select the Optic Mount folder then in the Main pane, select:
   AIV1_M07_01- Adjuster-Common.iam
   AIV1_M07_01-Adjust- Common.ipt
   AIV1_M07_01-Minor-Adjust- Common.ipt.

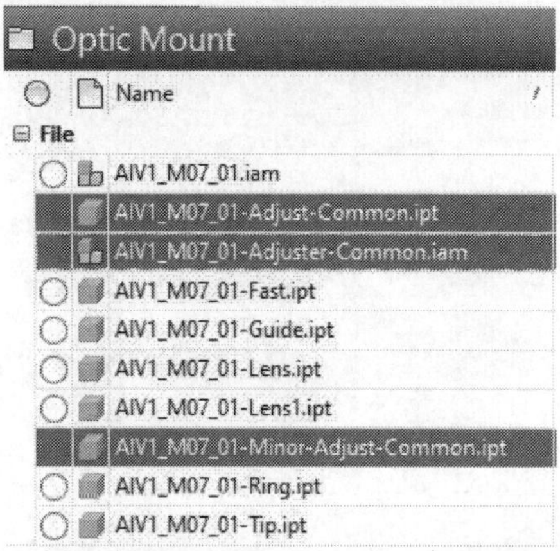

3. Drag all three files to the Optic Mount – Shared Parts folder.

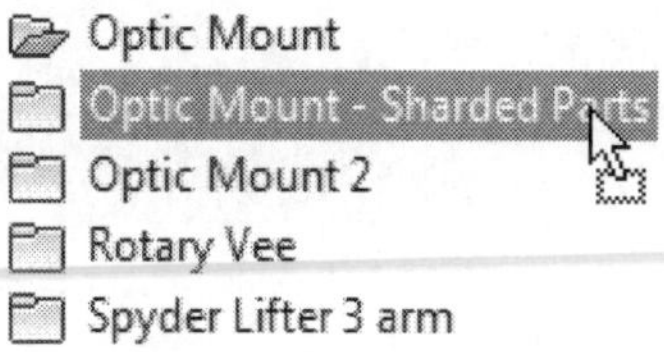

4. If asked if you want to update the file references for the moved files, click Yes.

5. In the Main pane, click the AIV1_M07_01-Adjuster-Common.iam file. Do the following:

   - In the Preview pane, click the Where Used tab.
   - Note that Vault correctly adjusted the dependencies.

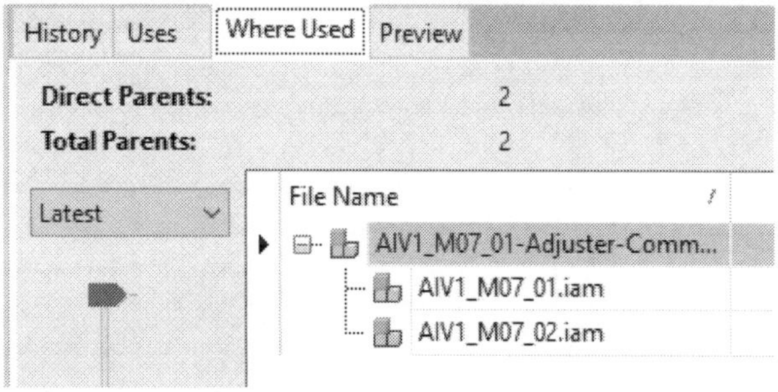

6. Start Autodesk Inventor. On the ribbon, click the Vault tab. If you are not logged in to AOTGvault, click Log In. Do the following:
    - For User Name, enter **vaultuser**.
    - For Password, leave the box empty.
    - For Vault, select AOTGVault.
7. On the Vault tab, click Open.
8. Browse to the Optic Mount 2 folder. Select AIV1_M07_02.iam. Click Open.
9. The renamed files are in the browser.
10. Close all files.

8.5 Reusing Designs

Overview

In this lesson, you learn how to use the Copy Design tool to copy Inventor designs in the vault. Many new engineering designs are based on existing designs. The traditional method is to copy the entire design to a new folder, rename files and delete some files as required, open the files in the CAD application to fix any links between files, and then start working on the new design. When you use the Copy Design command, you save engineering time by creating new products based on existing designs.

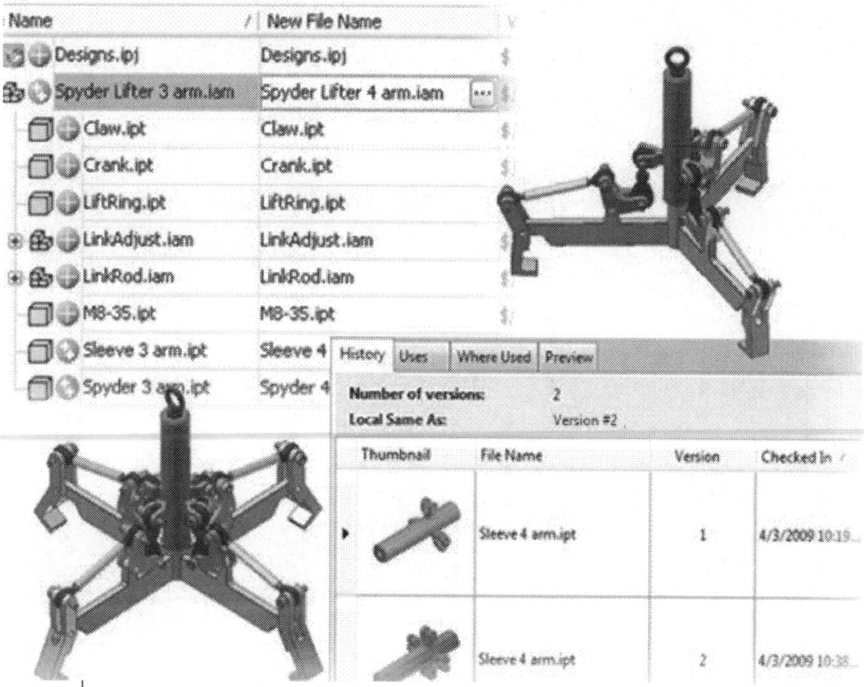

Objectives

After completing this lesson, you will be able to:

- Determine which files need to be copied, reused, or replaced before copying a design in the vault.
- Use Copy Design to copy Inventor designs in the vault.

About Copy Design

You can create new products by copying files of existing models and their drawings in the vault. The files can be copied to a new design structure, and files can reference new files or reference (reuse) the old files. You can use the Copy Design command to create new products based on existing designs while retaining all structure, including drawings, parts, assemblies, and presentations.

Copy Design Options

Option	Icon	Description
Copy		Generates a new file. You can rename and change the destination folder. The new file is initially identical to the original, but you can make changes without affecting the source file.
Reuse		Retains the original file in the new design while maintaining all links. By default, library components, content center files, and shared files are set to Reuse during the Copy process.
Exclude		Omits a file from the new design. Inventor files can be excluded from the Where Used view in the Copy Design dialog box.
Replace		Enables the user to substitute a part or assembly with another.

Example of Copy Design

The following image displays the Copy Design dialog box. Most of the files will be reused, but the top level part is copied and the Handle Assembly is replaced, excluding all of its children.

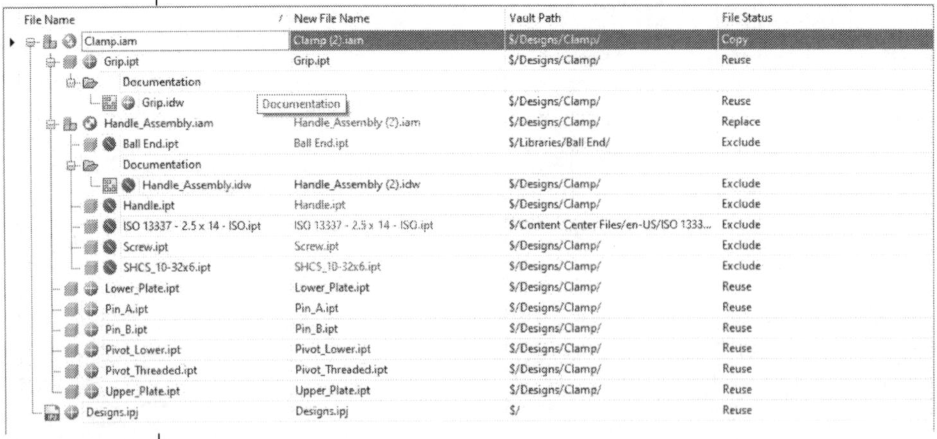

File Name	New File Name	Vault Path	File Status
Clamp.iam	Clamp (2).iam	$/Designs/Clamp/	Copy
Grip.ipt	Grip.ipt	$/Designs/Clamp/	Reuse
Documentation			
Grip.idw		$/Designs/Clamp/	Reuse
Handle_Assembly.iam	Handle_Assembly (2).iam	$/Designs/Clamp/	Replace
Ball End.ipt	Ball End.ipt	$/Libraries/Ball End/	Exclude
Documentation			
Handle_Assembly.idw	Handle_Assembly (2).idw	$/Designs/Clamp/	Exclude
Handle.ipt	Handle.ipt	$/Designs/Clamp/	Exclude
ISO 13337 - 2.5 x 14 - ISO.ipt	ISO 13337 - 2.5 x 14 - ISO.ipt	$/Content Center Files/en-US/ISO 1333...	Exclude
Screw.ipt	Screw.ipt	$/Designs/Clamp/	Exclude
SHCS_10-32x6.ipt	SHCS_10-32x6.ipt	$/Designs/Clamp/	Exclude
Lower_Plate.ipt	Lower_Plate.ipt	$/Designs/Clamp/	Reuse
Pin_A.ipt	Pin_A.ipt	$/Designs/Clamp/	Reuse
Pin_B.ipt	Pin_B.ipt	$/Designs/Clamp/	Reuse
Pivot_Lower.ipt	Pivot_Lower.ipt	$/Designs/Clamp/	Reuse
Pivot_Threaded.ipt	Pivot_Threaded.ipt	$/Designs/Clamp/	Reuse
Upper_Plate.ipt	Upper_Plate.ipt	$/Designs/Clamp/	Reuse
Designs.ipj	Designs.ipj	$/	Reuse

Using Copy Design

With Copy Design you specify what parts of a design you want to copy, reuse, exclude, or replace. You also specify the location of the copied files.

Guidelines for Using Copy Design

- Plan your strategy ahead of time; look at your design and decide which files will be copied, reused, or replaced.
- It is recommended that you view the Where Used information in the Preview pane for each affected file so you do not accidentally change other designs.

Procedure: Using Copy Design

The following steps outline the procedure for using Copy Design.

1. Select a file in either the Main pane or the Preview pane. This is typically a top-level document (assembly or drawing).
2. Right-click and select Copy Design. The project file and all children of the design are located and listed in the Copy Design dialog box. This list represents the starting dataset for the design to be copied.
3. Choose one of the following three view options:
   - Folder view displays files grouped by folder location.
   - List view provides a flat list of files that are part of the design.
   - Design view displays a list of the target file and its children in an assembly tree structure.
4. Click Settings. Specify the file relationships to include in the copy process. Relationship options are either only the children or the children and all related documentation files. This feature is only available for Autodesk Inventor files.
5. To change the action performed on a selected file, right-click and click the action required.

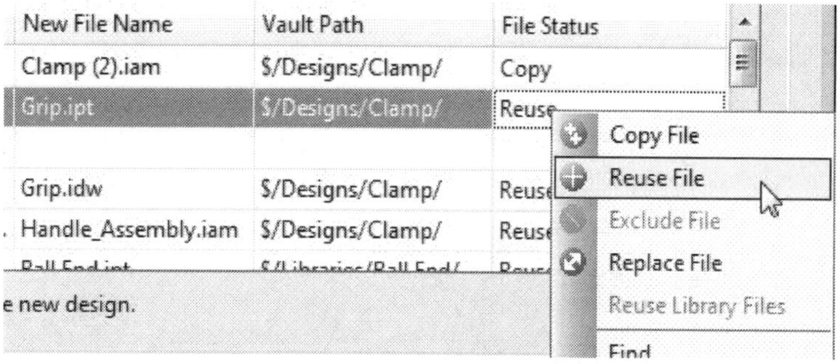

6. If a file is set to Copy, click Browse in the Vault Folder column for that file to specify a location in the vault for the new design. You can set a global folder location for all copied files with Browse to Folder in the upper-right corner of the Copy Design dialog box.
7. If a file is set to Replace, click Browse in the New File Name column for that file to specify a replacement file from the vault. Use the following guidelines for replacement:
    - You can replace Autodesk Inventor part files (IPT) and assembly files (IAM). An existing assembly can replace a part file and an existing part file can replace an assembly file.
    - You can only replace AutoCAD DWG files with other DWG files.
8. Specify a naming scheme for the files that you create. You can also set the following options:
    - Set a prefix or a suffix to append to the new files.
    - Select the Increment check box to sequentially update any filenames that end in an integer.
    - Click Match Name to match the filenames of presentation and drawing files with the name of their direct child.

Use the shortcut menu to access the Find and Replace options to change character strings quickly in the filenames or folder paths.

9. Click Apply to preview the naming scheme. To return to the original naming scheme, click Revert.
10. Click OK to begin copying the design.

Practice 8e

Copy Designs with Autodesk Vault

In this practice, you create a new design by copying an existing design. Use Copy Design to both copy and reuse components from one design into another.

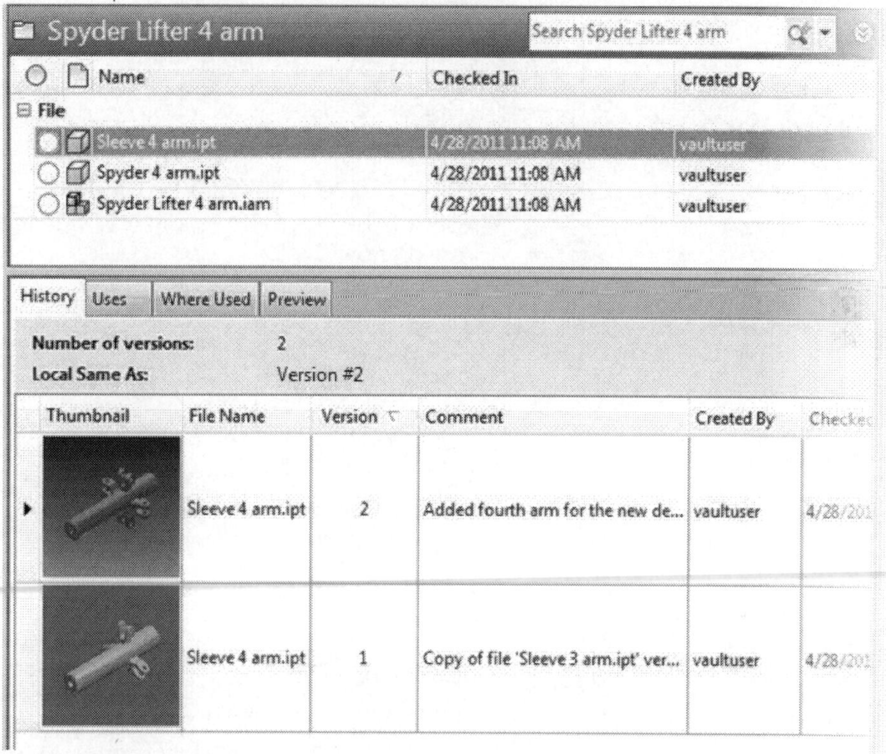

The completed practice

Task 1 - Copy designs in Autodesk Vault.

1. Start Autodesk Vault. Log in using the following information:
   - For User Name, enter **vaultuser**.
   - For Password, leave this box empty.
   - For Vault, select AOTGVault.
2. Select the Spyder Lifter 3 arm folder. Do the following:
   - Right-click Spyder Lifter 3 arm.iam.
   - Select Copy Design.

3. In the Copy Design dialog box, click Spyder Lifter 3 arm.iam. In the Vault Folder column, click Browse.

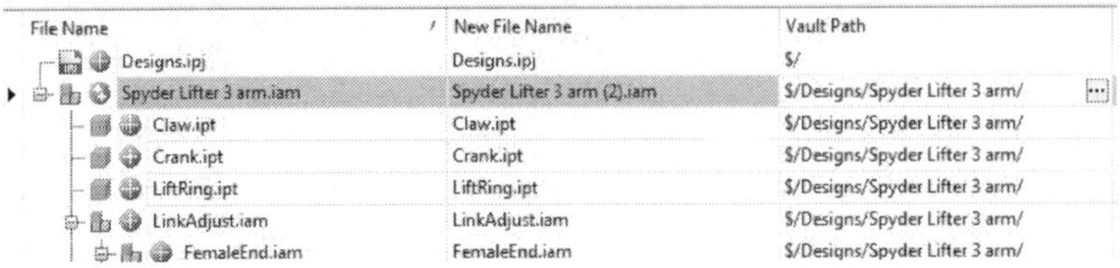

4. Expand Designs. Do the following:

   - Select the Designs folder.
   - Click New Folder.
   - Enter Spyder Lifter 4 arm.
   - Click OK. Click OK again to return to the Copy Design dialog box.

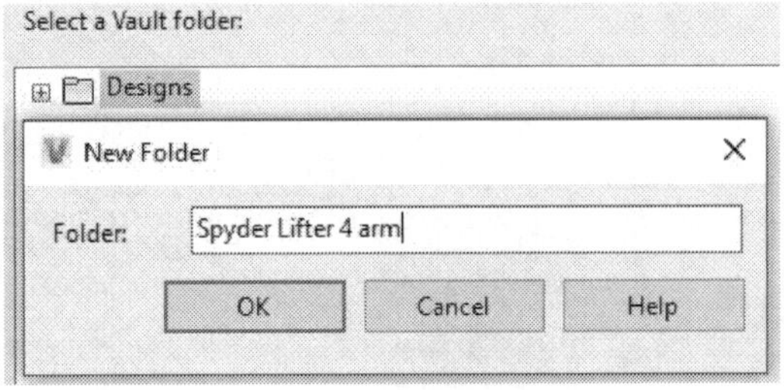

5. For Sleeve 3 arm.ipt, right-click the File Status cell. Do the following:

   - Click Copy File.
   - Repeat this for Spyder 3 arm.ipt.

6. In New File Name column, enter new names for the following files:

   - For Spyder Lifter 3 arm.iam, enter **Spyder Lifter 4 arm.iam**.
   - For Sleeve 3 arm.ipt, enter **Sleeve 4 arm.ipt**.
   - For Spyder 3 arm.ipt, enter **Spyder 4 arm.ipt**.

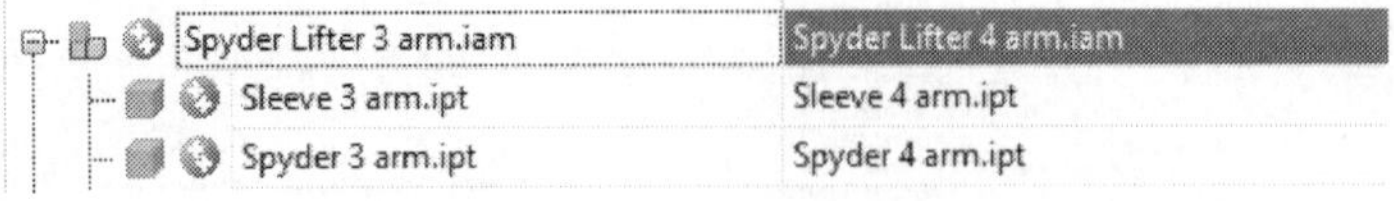

7. Click Sleeve 3 arm.ipt . Do the following:
   - In the Vault Path column, click Browse.
   - Expand Designs.
   - Click the Spyder Lifter 4 arm folder.
   - Click OK to return to the Copy Design dialog box.

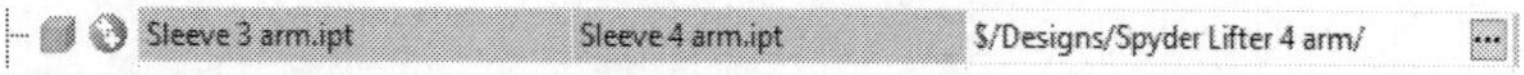

8. Repeat the previous step for Spyder 3 arm.ipt.

9. Click OK to complete the copy design.

10. Select the Spyder Lifter 4 arm folder and note the copied assembly and part files.

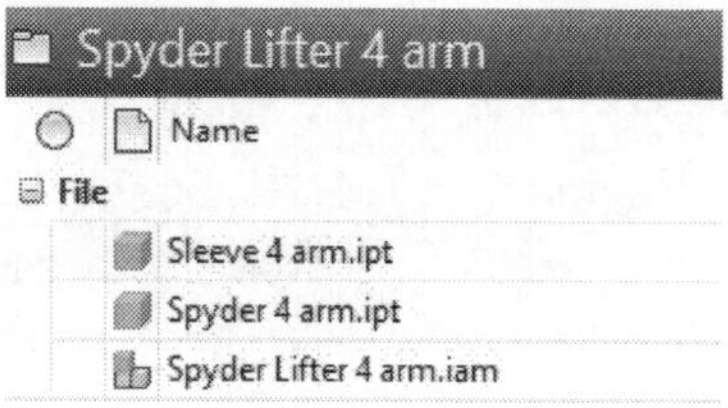

Task 2 - Edit new design files.

1. Open Autodesk Inventor and log in to Vault if you are not already logged in. Do the following:
   - On the ribbon, on the Vault tab, click Open.
   - Expand *Designs\Spyder Lifter 4 arm*.
   - Select Spyder Lifter 4 arm.iam.

2. Click the list next to Open. Do the following:
   - Select Open (Check Out All).
   - In the Check Out dialog Click OK.
   - If asked to update the assembly, click Yes.

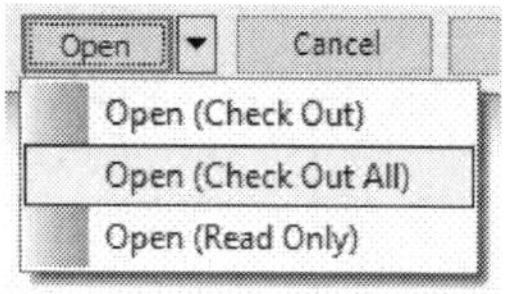

3. In the browser, double-click Sleeve 4 arm:1 to activate it.

4. In the browser, right-click PolarArray1. Click Edit Feature.

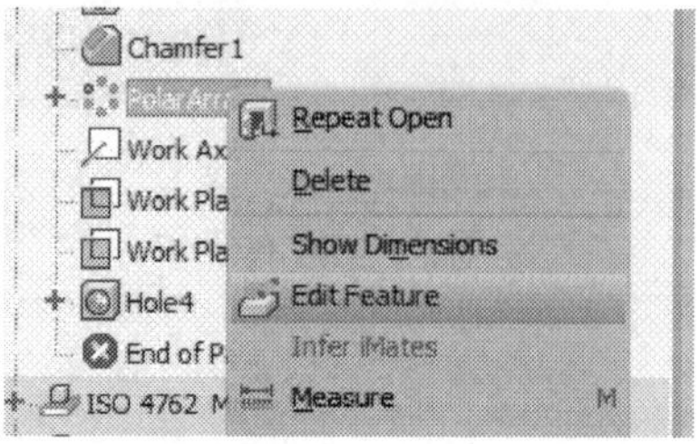

5. Under Placement, Occurrence Count, enter **4**.

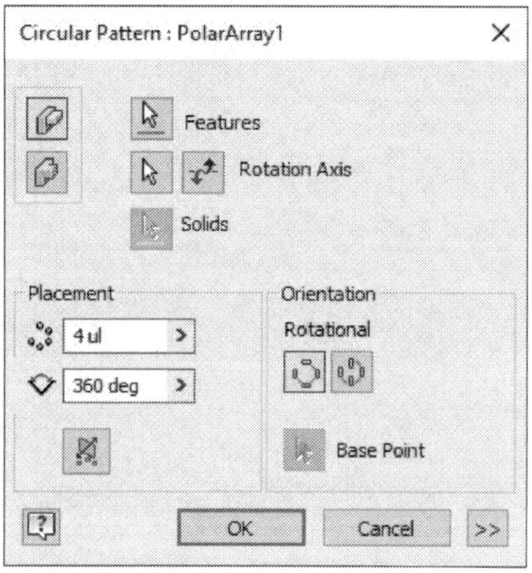

6. Click OK.

7. In the browser, double-click Spyder 4 arm:1 to activate it.

8. In the browser, right-click PolarArray1. Click Edit Feature.

9. Under Placement, Occurrence Count, enter **4**.

10. Click OK.

11. On the ribbon, click Return to return to the top-level assembly. Switch to the Vault browser and note that the modified files must be saved.

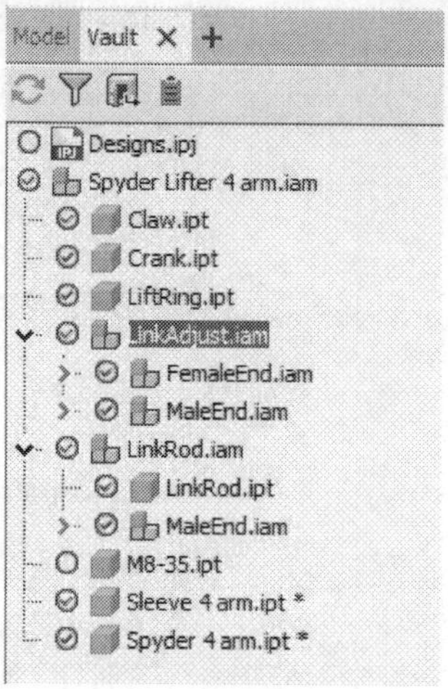

12. Save the assembly and all dependents. Do the following:

- In the Save dialog box, click Yes to All.
- Click OK.

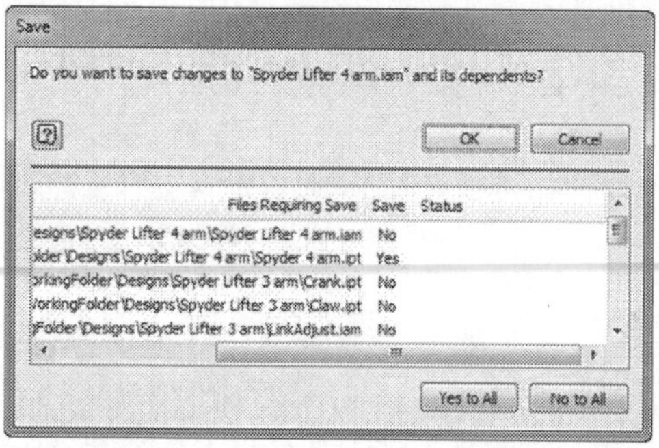

13. Note that the Vault browser indicates that the parts are ready to be checked in.

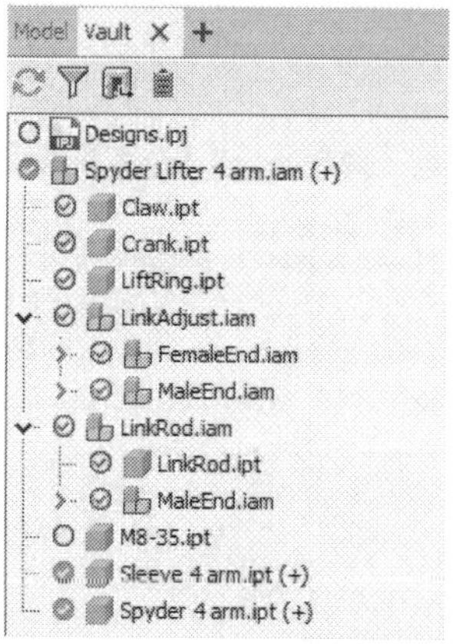

14. Right-click Spyder Lifter 4 arm.iam. Do the following:

- Click Check In.
- In the Check In dialog box, clear Close files and delete working copies.
- Enter a comment Added fourth arm for the new design
- Click OK.

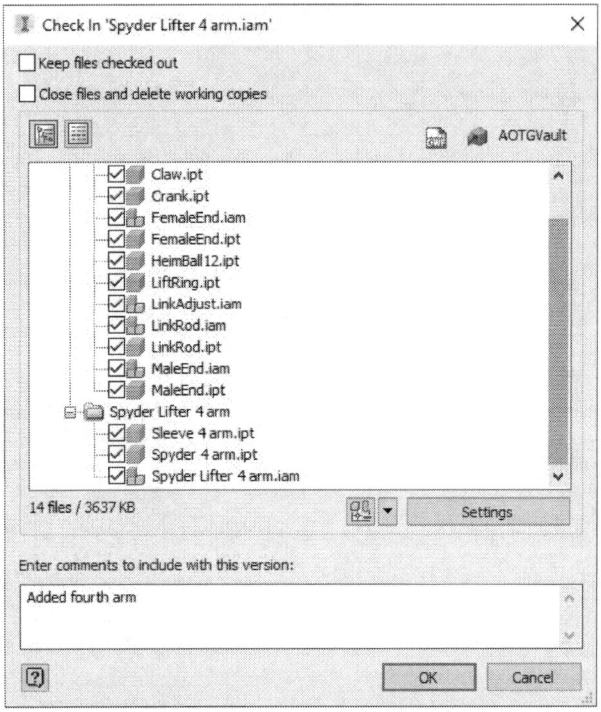

Task 3 - View file version in Autodesk Vault.

1. In Autodesk Vault, navigate to the Spyder Lifter 4 arm folder. Click View menu>Refresh.

2. Select Spyder Lifter 4 arm.iam. Do the following:

- In the Preview pane, click the Uses tab.
- Note that Version 2 of Spyder Lifter 4 arm.iam uses Version 2 of both Spyder 4 arm.ipt and Sleeve 4 arm.ipt.

3. Click Sleeve 4 arm.ipt. On the History tab. The thumbnail for Sleeve 4 arm.ipt reflects the changes made to the part.

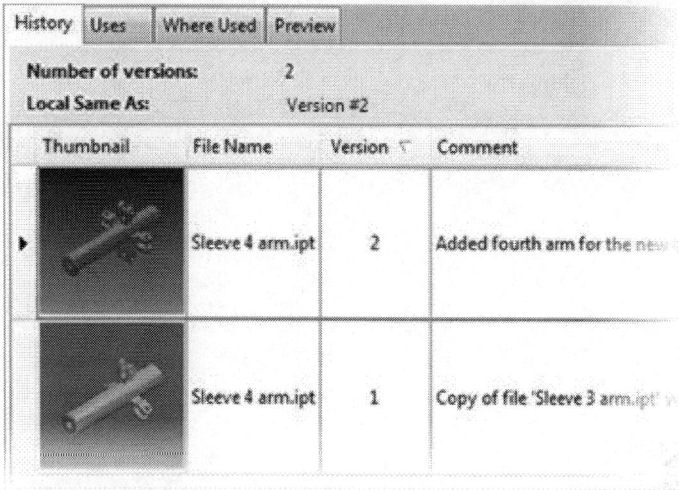

8.6 Using Vault Files Outside of the Vault Environment

Overview

This lesson describes how to use Pack and Go in Autodesk Vault. You use Pack and Go to save designs in a single location outside the vault.

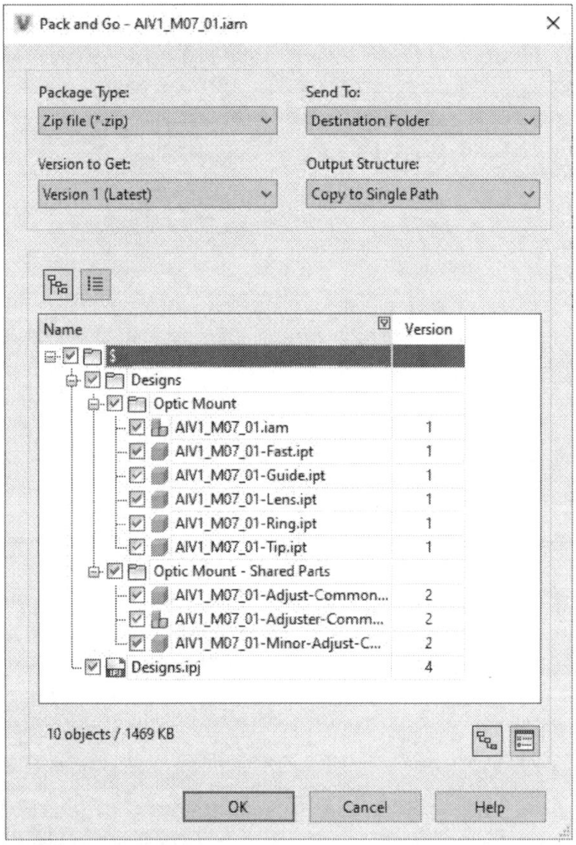

The Pack and Go dialog box

Objectives

After completing this lesson, you will be able to:

- Set Pack and Go options to correspond to the required task.
- Use Pack and Go to copy a file and all related files to a location outside the vault.

About Pack and Go

In some cases it is required to copy all files for a design and work on these files outside the vault.

For example, you can send a copy of the design to another colleague who cannot access the vault. Or you can copy the design files to a laptop and work on the files offline.

Pack and Go will package the files in the vault in a single location outside the vault.

Pack and Go Dialog Box

Pack and Go packages a file and all of its referenced files in a single location outside the vault. All files that are referenced by a selected file are included in the package unless you specify otherwise in the Pack and Go dialog box.

The following image displays the Pack and Go dialog box.

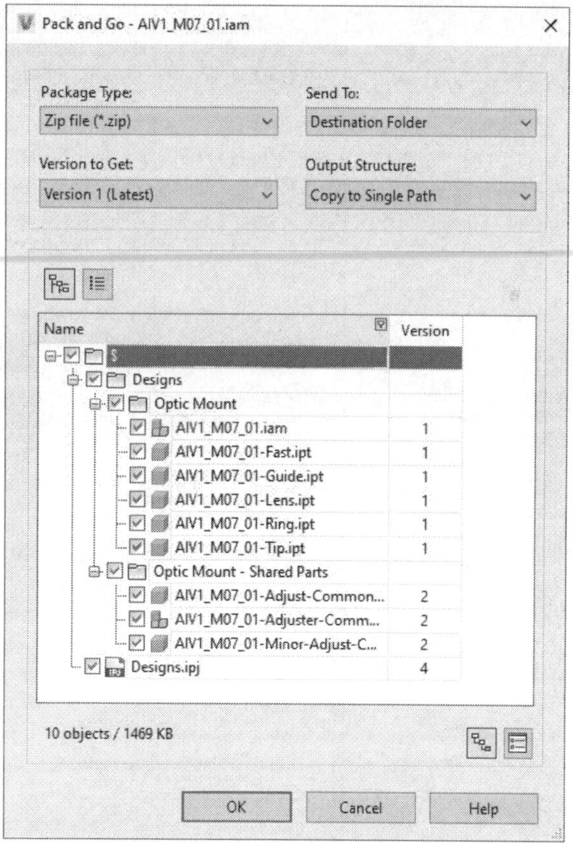

The Pack and Go dialog box contains the following options:

Option	Description
Package Type	Unzipped: Creates a folder containing a copy of the files in uncompressed format. Zip File (*.zip): Creates a copy of the files compressed into one file. DWF Package: Creates a single multisheet DWF that contains all the DWF files selected. DWFx Package: Creates a single multisheet DWFx that contains all of the selected DWFx files.
Send To	Destination Folder: Specifies the location on the local computer or a network drive where you want to save the Pack and Go file. Mail Recipient: Packages the files and sends them as an attachment by email.
Versions to Get	Specifies the version of the files to retrieve from the vault.
Output Structure	Specifies whether the packed file retains the folder structure of the vault or is a single directory that contains all of the files at the same level.
Settings - Relationships	Click Settings. Options for packing related files: Include dependents: Applies the Pack and Go operation to all of the files on which the selected file depends. Include attachments: Applies the Pack and Go operation to all of the attachments to the files. Include library files: Applies the Pack and Go operation to all library files on which the selected file depends. Include related documentation: Applies the Pack and Go operation to all other files related to the selected file, including the drawing files. 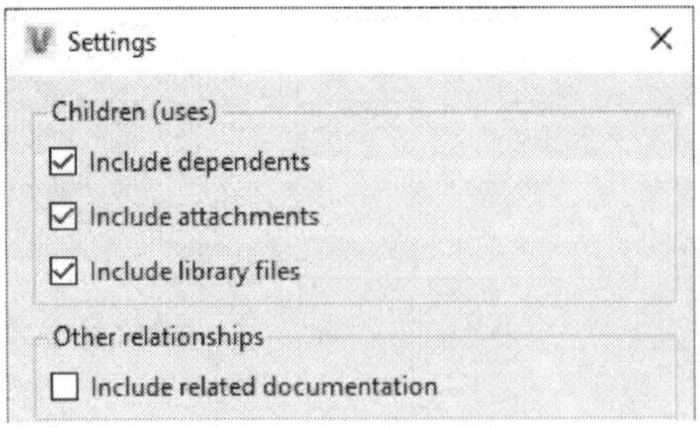

Settings – Visualization Filter	Click Settings. Options: Include Visualization Files: Applies the Pack and Go operation to all visualization files. Exclude Visualization Files: Does not include the visualization files in the Pack and Go operation (except for those DWF or DWFx files that are attached to a file). Visualization Files Only: Creates a DWF or DWFx package with only the visualization files. 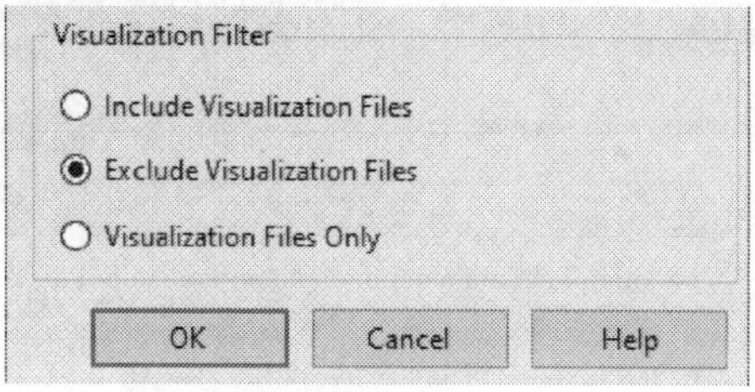

Example of Pack and Go Options

To copy a design and send it to a designer in another company:

Option	Chosen Option	Reason
Send To	Destination Folder	Since the design is typically too large in size to send via email, save the design to a destination folder.
Package Type	Zip file (*.zip)	Compress all the design files into a zip file to then share with a browser application, for example.
Version	Latest	Latest versions of the files will be copied.
Output Structure	Copy to Single Path	Other companies might not use complex folder hierarchies in their designs. To simplify the design, all files will be copied into one folder.

To archive a design:

Option	Chosen Option	Reason
Send To	Destination Folder	The design is not going to be sent by email.
Package Type	zip file	The design files will be compressed and placed in a zip file to save storage space
Version	Latest	Latest versions of the files will be copied

Output Structure	Keep Folder Hierarchy	Enables you to keep the design folders (including library and content center folders) intact so they can be restored easily
Settings	Include related documentation	This archives all files that are related to the selected file such as drawing and presentation files.

Using Pack and Go

Introduction to Pack and Go

Pack and Go packages a file and all of its referenced files in a single location outside the vault. You use Pack and Go to:

- Create a complete set of files in one folder while maintaining file relationships.
- Create a copy of a set of files in the vault complete with the folder hierarchy.
- Create an archive of a design.
- Create a zipped file of a design and send the file by email.
- Create a set of files from a specific version or label.

Procedure: Using Pack and Go

The following steps show how to create a Pack and Go package from Autodesk Vault.

1. In Autodesk Vault, select a file from the Main pane.
2. Click File menu>Pack and Go.
3. In the Pack and Go dialog box, select the type of package to create from the Package Type list.
4. Specify the destination folder.
5. In the Version to Get list, select the version of the files to pack.
6. In the Output Structure list, select either Keep Folder Hierarchy or Copy to Single Path.
7. Click Settings. Select the related files that you want to include.
8. Click OK.
9. Specify the destination folder and click Save.

Making Project Files with Pack and Go

When you use the Pack and Go command, the project file is included with any Inventor part or assembly. Use this project file when you open an assembly to ensure correct file resolution.

The project file created by the Pack and Go command is a single-user project and not a Vault project. Therefore, you can send a design to team members who might not have access to the vault.

If you use Pack and Go to create a copy of the files for design experimentation, it is recommended that you rename the project file created by the Pack and Go command. This way you don't end up with two projects with the same name in your projects list: one for the Vault files and one for the single-user project created by Pack and Go.

Procedure: Changing a Single-User Project to a Vault Project

The following steps describe how to change a Pack and Go single-user project to a Vault project.

1. In Inventor, click Application menu>Get Started>Projects. Ensure that the assembly and any parts used in the project that you are changing are not open.
2. Select the project that you want to edit.
3. Right-click Type: Single User and select Vault.

Practice 8f

Pack and Go

In this practice, you pack an Inventor assembly in a zip file and place it in a specific location on your local drive.

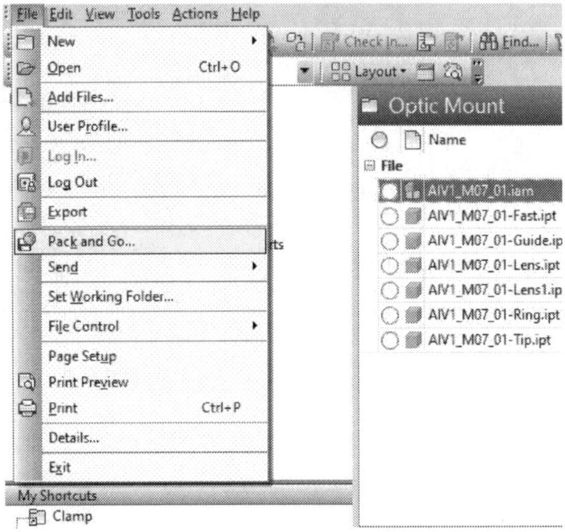

The completed practice

1. Start Autodesk Vault. Log in using the following information:
   - For User Name, enter **vaultuser**.
   - For Password, leave this box empty.
   - For Vault, select AOTGVault.
2. In Autodesk Vault, navigate to the Designs/Optic Mount folder.
3. In the Main pane, select AIV1_M07_01.iam.
4. Click File menu>Pack and Go.

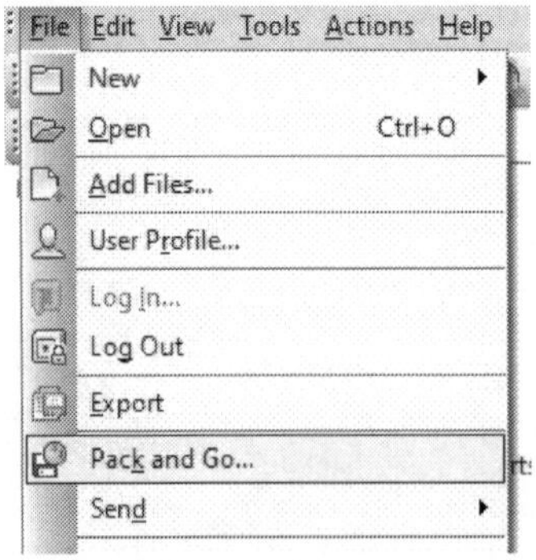

5. In the Pack and Go dialog box, do the following:

   - For Package Type, select Zip file (*.zip).
   - For Send To, verify that Destination Folder is selected.
   - For Version to Get, select the latest version.
   - For Output Structure, select Copy to Single Path.

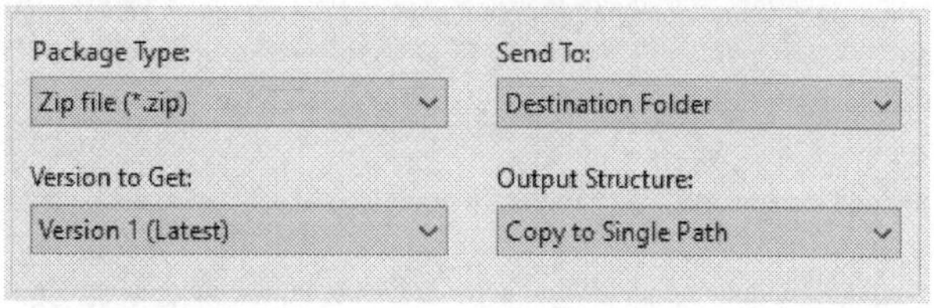

6. In the Pack and Go dialog box, click Settings. Do the following:

   - For Other Relationships, click Include Related Documentation.
   - Under Visualization Filter, click Include Visualization Files.
   - Click OK to dismiss the Settings dialog box.

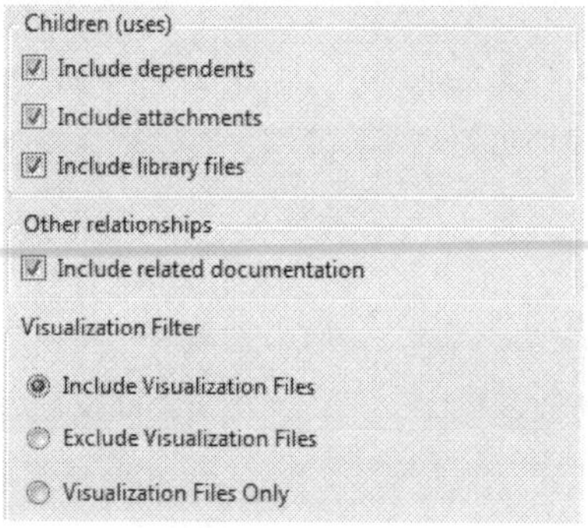

7. Inspect the list of files to be included. Ensure that all checkboxes are selected. Click OK.

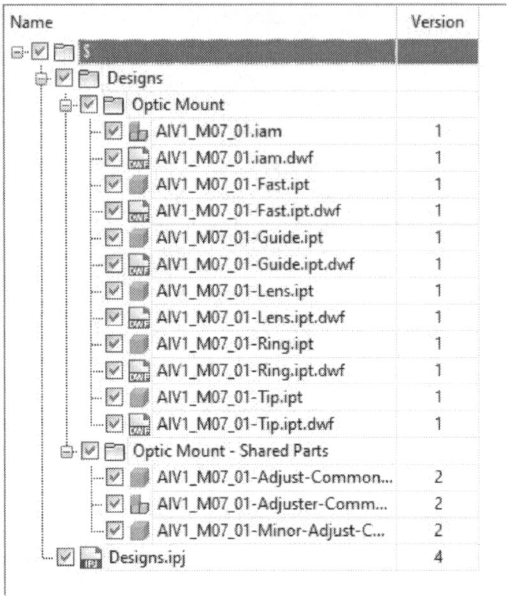

8. In the Select a zip package file dialog box, do the following:

- Navigate to a temporary folder on your hard drive.
- Verify that the filename is AIV1_M07_01.zip.
- Click Save.

9. In Windows Explorer, verify that the zip file is now in the temporary folder. Double-click the file to open it.

Examine the files and folder structure in the zip file.

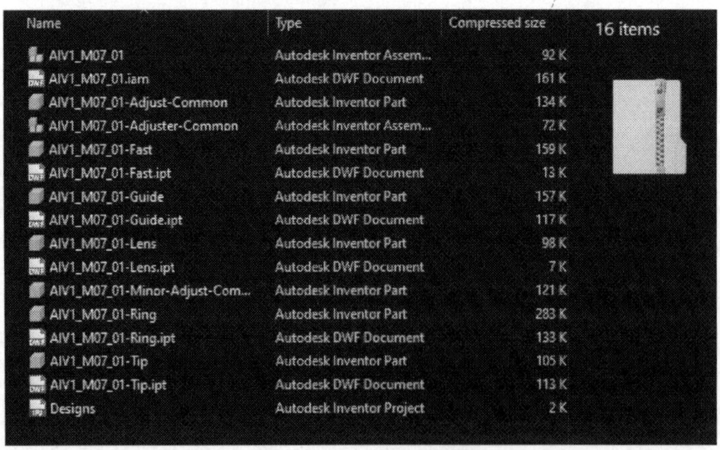

8.7 Managing Properties

Overview

This lesson describes how to view and edit file properties in Autodesk Vault.

Objectives

After completing this lesson, you will be able to:

- Use the Property Editing Wizard in Autodesk Vault to edit file property values.

Editing File Properties

File properties are used to view, filter, and search for files in the vault. They are also used in drawing title blocks and BOMs.

You edit file properties in Autodesk Vault using the Property Editing Wizard.

Process: Editing File Properties

With the Property Editing wizard you edit the properties of one or more files. You can edit values directly, copy and paste them, or paste them across a range.

The general process for the Property Editing wizard is as follows:

Step	Action
Specify files	You specify the files that contain the properties you want to edit.
Add or remove properties	Use the column customization or Select Properties to add or remove the properties you want to edit.
Edit values	Select the cells and edit and existing value or add a missing one.
View Results	You can view the results of the editing, and optionally save the summary to an Excel or comma-delimited file

Procedure: Using the Property Editing Wizard

The following steps describe how to use the Property Editing wizard:

1. Select one or more files in the Main pane.
2. Select the Edit menu>Edit Properties…

3. In the Property Edit dialog box, check the list of files. Add or remove files if required.
4. If the file properties you want to edit are not displayed, click Select Properties and select the fields (editable file properties) you want to edit.
   - Enter or edit the values and select OK to confirm the changes.
   - Right-click a cell to copy or paste.
   - Double-click a cell to edit its value.
   - Click and drag the black square at the lower-right corner of a cell to fill multiple cells with the same value

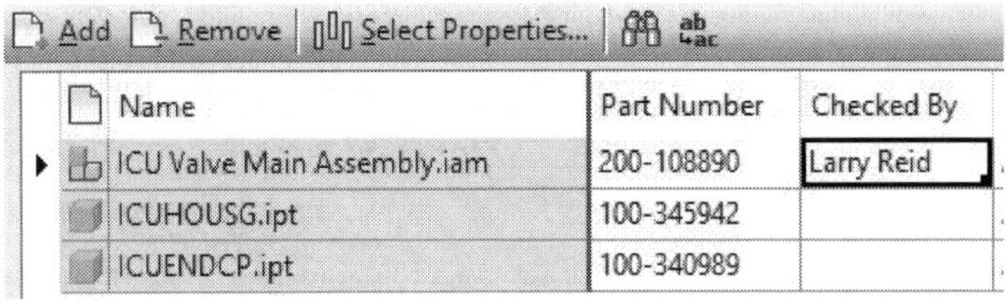

The following image displays the results after dragging the cell.

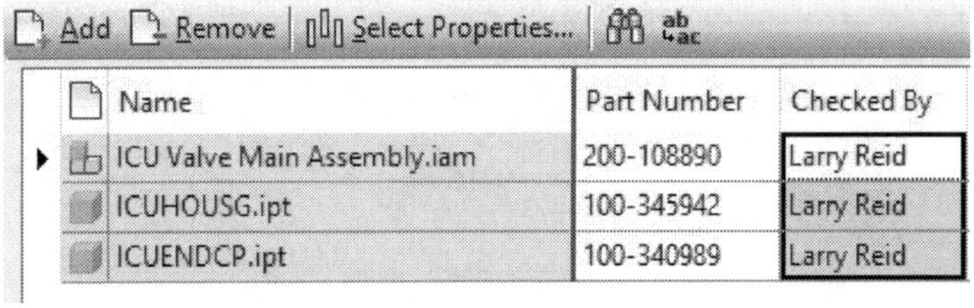

   - Right-click on a cell and use Find or Replace to find another identical value or replace it. You can replace all identical values with another.
5. The Property Edit Results dialog box summarizes the editing operation.
   - Click Report to save the summary of the results to an Excel or to a comma-delimited text file or send the results to the vault.
   - Click Send to Vault to save the report to the vault.

Guidelines for Editing Properties

In order for properties to be edited:

- Your role in the vault must be editor or administrator to perform this action.
- The files to be edited must be checked in to the vault.
- It is recommended that you start by looking at the files in the Preview pane, Where Used tab, to see if the operation will affect other designs. Some files can be used in more than one design, and you might want to exclude them from editing.

Practice 8g Edit File Properties

In this practice, you edit the file properties for a design using the Property Editing Wizard in Autodesk Vault.

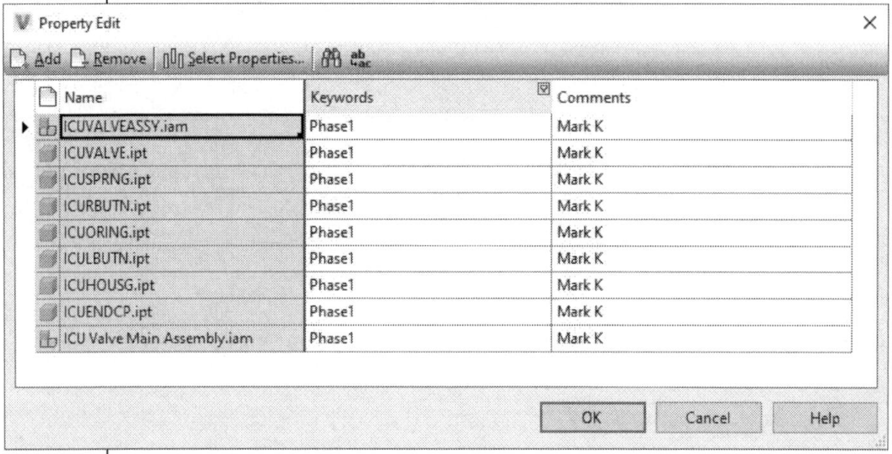

The completed practice

1. Start Autodesk Vault. Log in using the following information:
   - For User Name, enter **vaultuser**.
   - For Password, leave this box empty.
   - For Vault, select AOTGVault.
2. Click the ICU Valve folder. Do the following:
   - Click ICUENDCP.ipt.
   - In the Preview pane, on the Where Used tab, review where the file is used.

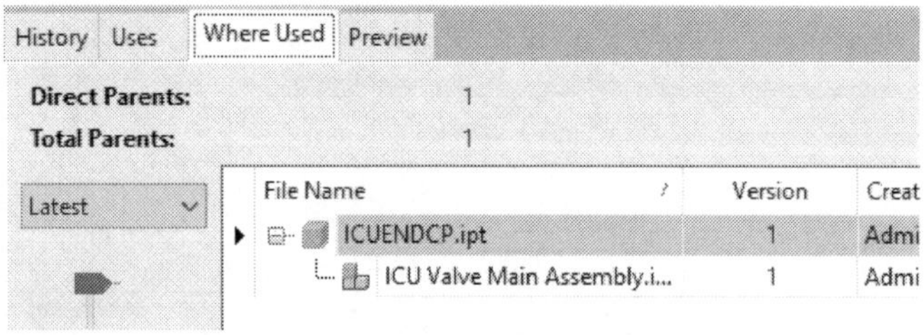

3. Repeat the previous step for all the files in the ICU Valve folder. Note that all the files are used in the ICU Valve design only.
4. Click in the Main pane. Do the following:
   - Click ICUENDCP.ipt.

- Click Edit menu>Select All.
- The files for the ICU Valve Design are selected.

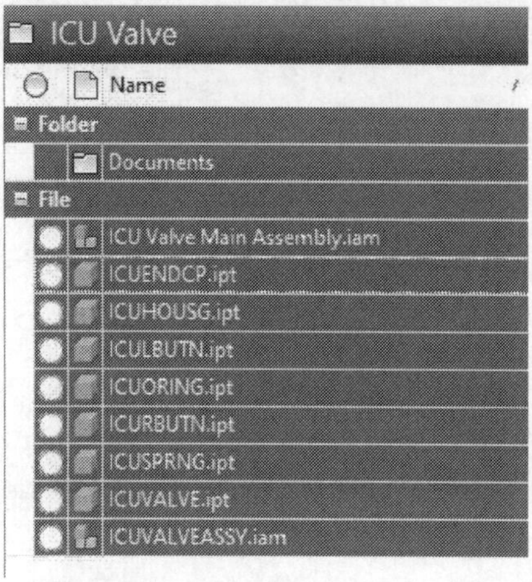

5. Click Edit menu>Edit Properties.

6. In the Property Edit dialog box, verify that all the files in the ICU Valve design are listed. If any files are missing, click Add Files and add them.

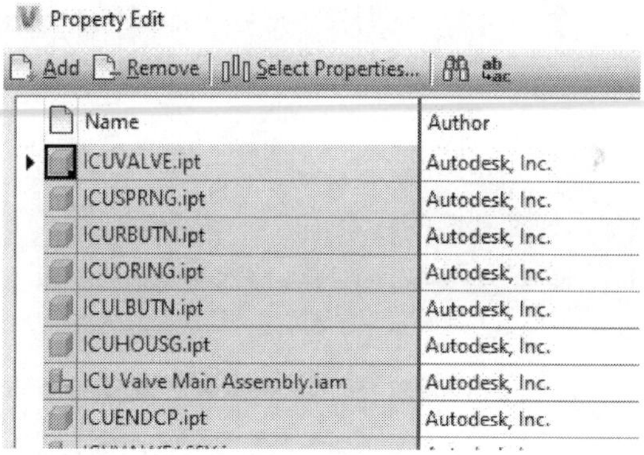

Note: Your dialog box might have properties displayed in addition to Name and Author as shown.

7. Click Select Properties to display the Customize Fields dialog box.

8. In Select available fields from: drop-down list, select All fields to display the complete list of fields.

9. Do the following to add Available fields to the list:
    - Select Comments.
    - Click Add -> to add the field to the Show these fields in this order list.
    - Add Keywords, if not already listed.

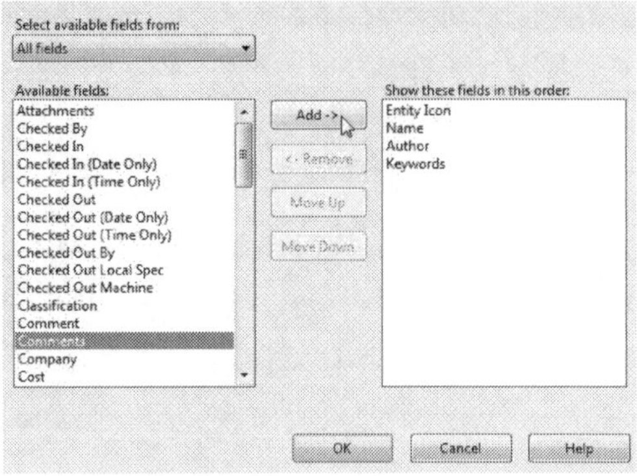

10. In the Show these fields in this order list, select Author and click <- Remove to remove the field from the list.

11. Select any additional fields other than Entity Icon, Name, Keywords, and Comments in the show these fields in this order list and remove them.

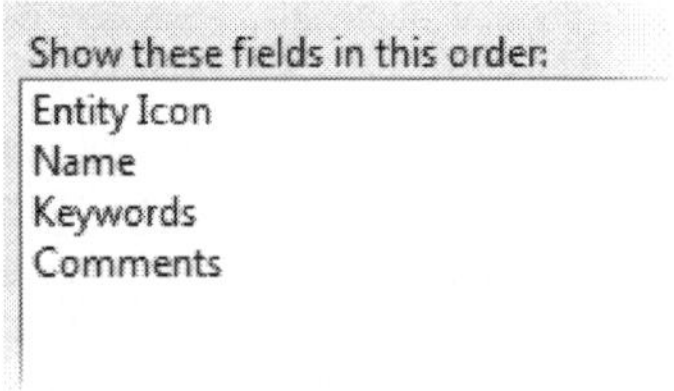

12. Click OK to dismiss the Customize Fields dialog box.

13. Edit the property values. Do the following:
    - In the top row, for Keywords, enter **Phase 1**.
    - Fill all the cells with the same value by selecting and dragging the black square at the lower-right corner of the cell.

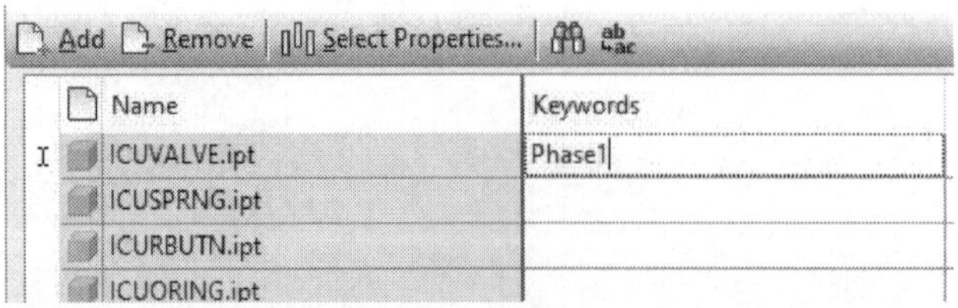

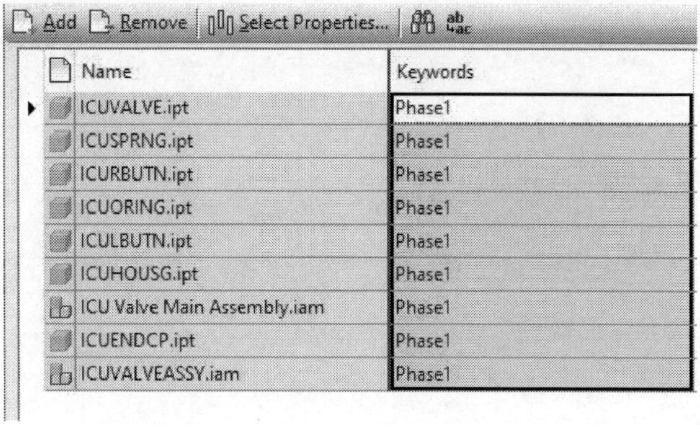

14. Double-click the Comments cell. Enter your name.

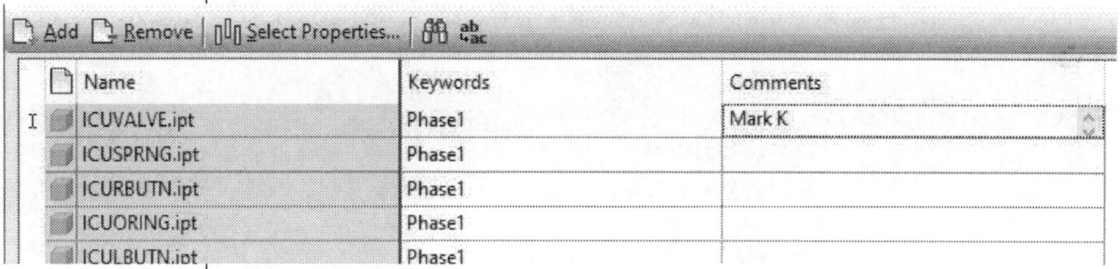

15. Select the last cell you edited. Right-click the cell and select Copy.

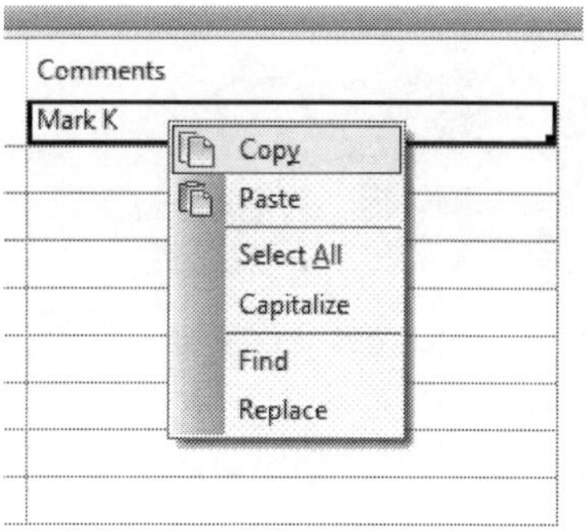

16. Select the rest of the cells under Comments.

17. Right-click and select Paste.

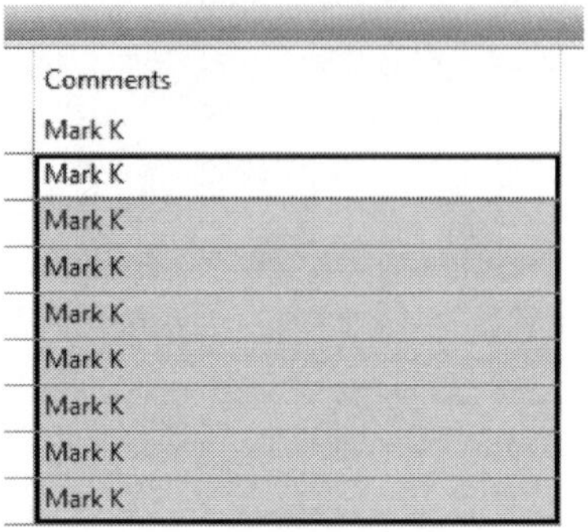

18. Click OK. Vault checks the files out of the vault, edits their properties, and checks them back in. The results of the property editing operation are displayed.

19. Review the results. Click Close.

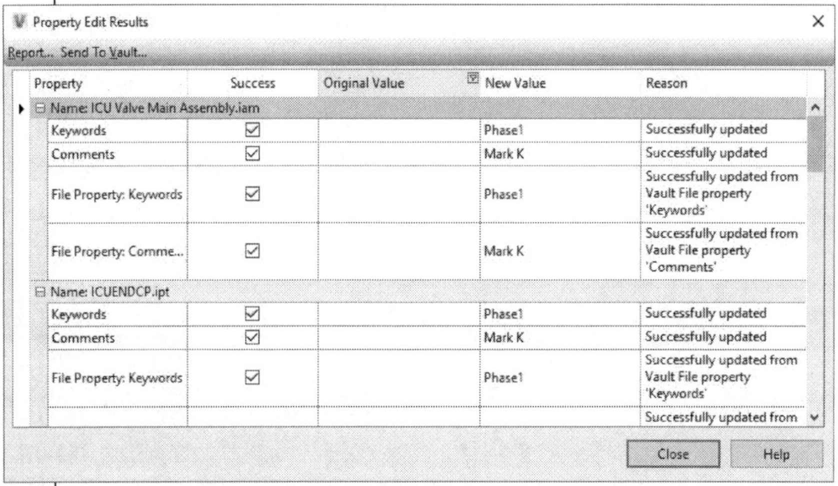

20. Review the updated versions in the Preview pane.

8.8 Replacing Files

Overview

This lesson describes how to replace files in the vault.

Replacing files in the vault maintains file relationships with the new files.

Objectives

After completing this lesson, you will be able to:

- Replace files in the vault using the Replace Wizard while maintaining file dependencies.

Replacing Files

In most CAD systems, the concept of linked or dependent files is important. CAD models are built with components in several files that are linked together. This makes loading the model easier and more efficient and creates smaller files.

The only drawback to this approach is the links or dependencies between the files. The files must maintain their links, which makes replacing a file with another more difficult.

The Replace wizard in Vault Explorer can replace files and repair relationships between files.

Guidelines for Replacing Files

- The status of the replacement file is not important. The file can be checked out or locked and the replacement will still work.
- You must have permission to check out and check in the files you are replacing and their parent files.

You must have the Vault add-in for the application installed; for example, if you are replacing Inventor files, then the Vault add-in for Inventor should be installed.

- It is recommended that you view the information on the Where Used tab in the Preview pane for each affected file so that you do not accidentally change other designs. In case you miss any parent files, this information is also listed in the Replace Wizard command.
- You can only replace a file with one of the same type; for example, you cannot replace an assembly file with a part file.

Procedure: Replacing Files

The following procedure teaches you how to replace a file in the vault.

1. In Vault Explorer, select a file or files. Click Edit menu>Replace.
2. In the Replace Wizard, review the list of files. Add or remove files if required.

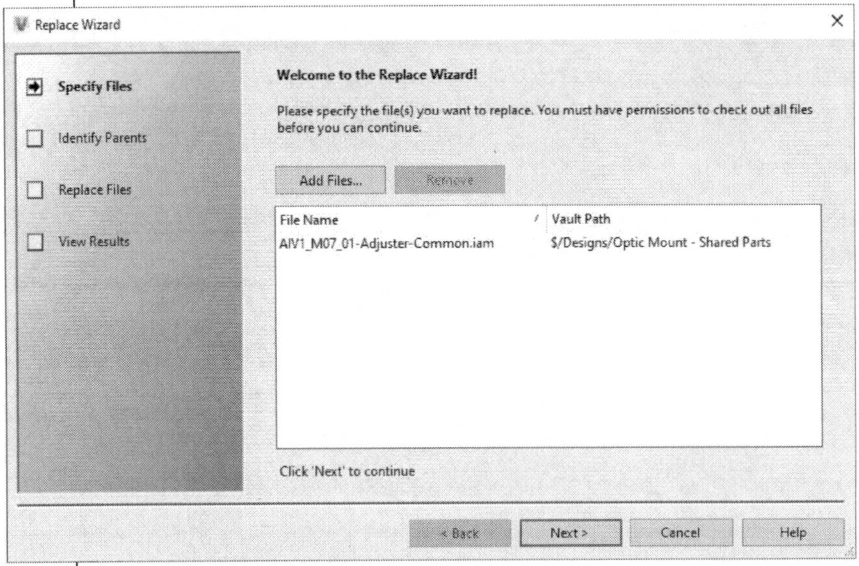

3. Click Next.
4. The Related Files page displays the immediate parents of the selected files. Each of the parents is selected (indicated by a checkmark), which means that Vault will repair the parent, and the file relationship will point to the new reference. Clear the parent files you do not want repaired.

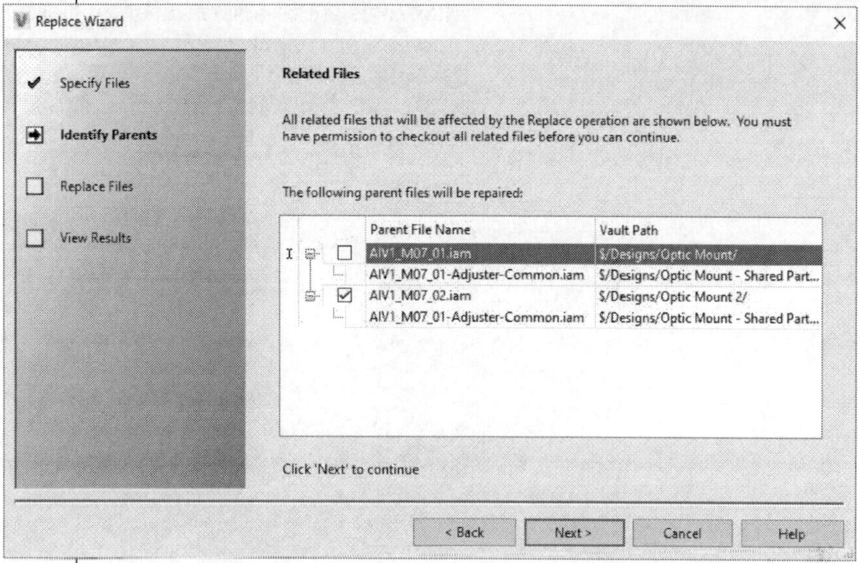

5. Click Next.

6. The Specify Replacement Files page lists the files to be replaced. Click the browse button next to each of the files and select the replacement file.

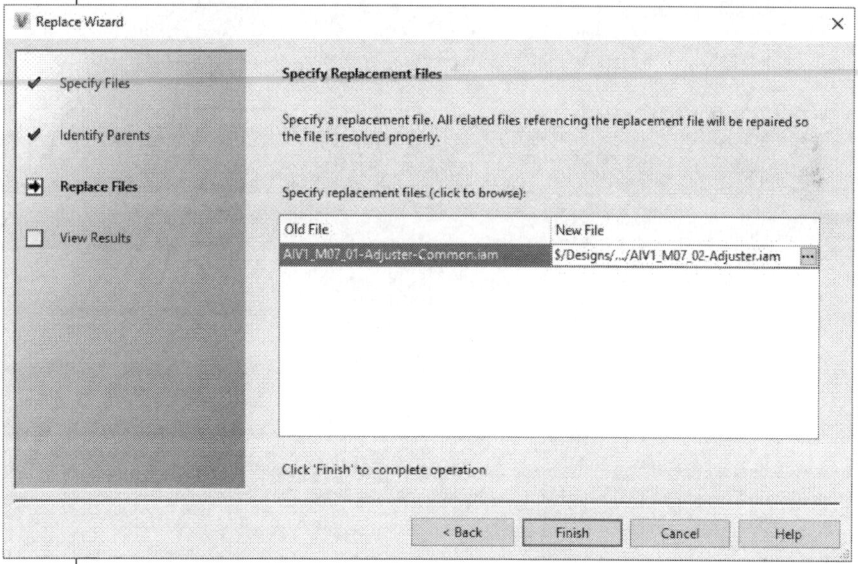

7. Click Finish. The selected parent files and the files to be replaced are checked out, repaired, and checked back in to the vault. The final page displays a summary of the Replace operation. The files that were replaced and the parents that were repaired are listed.

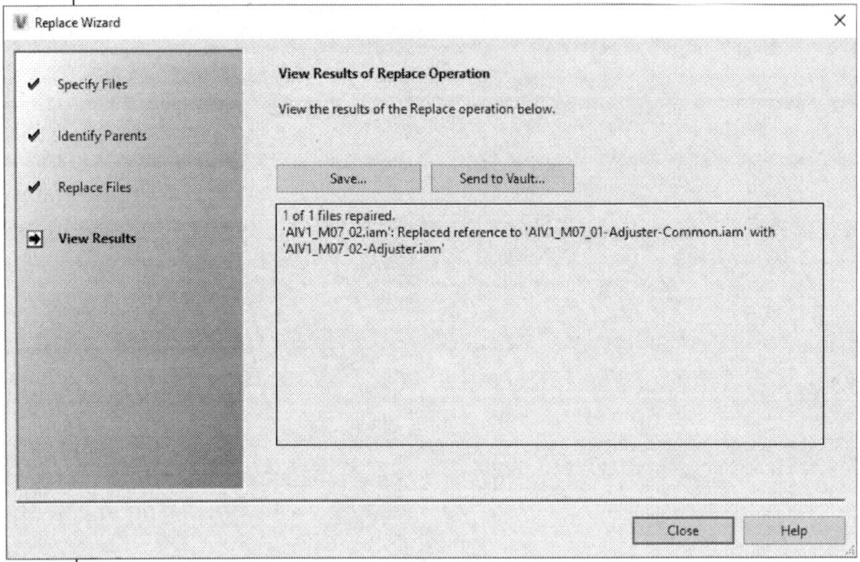

Practice 8h

Replace Files

In this practice, you copy a file in the vault and then replace files in the vault. In order to complete this practice, you must have completed Practice 8e in this chapter.

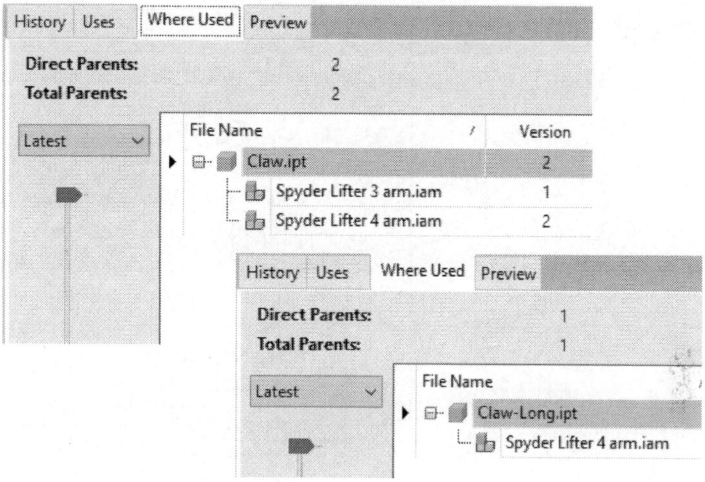

The completed practice

1. Start Autodesk Vault. Log in using the following information:
   - For User Name, enter **vaultuser**.
   - For Password, leave the box empty.
   - For Vault, select AOTGVault.t.
2. Navigate to the Spyder Lifter 3 arm folder.
3. Click Claw.ipt. In the Preview pane, on the Where Used tab, review the Claw parent files.

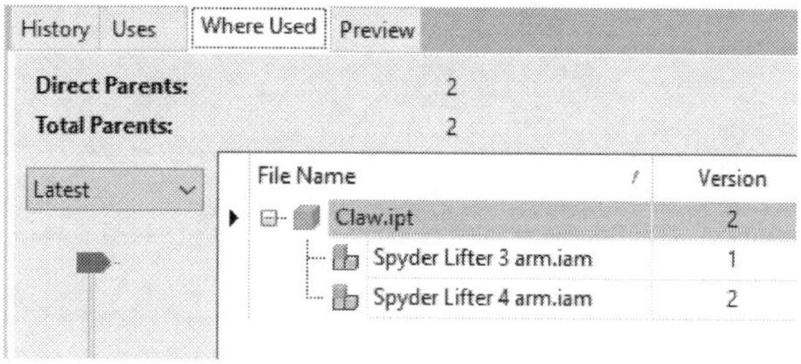

   You replace Claw.ipt with Claw-Long.ipt for the Spyder Lifter 4 arm.iam parent only.

4. Right-click Claw.ipt. Click Copy Design.

5. In the Copy Design dialog box, for Claw.ipt, in the New File Name cell, enter **Claw-Long.ipt**.

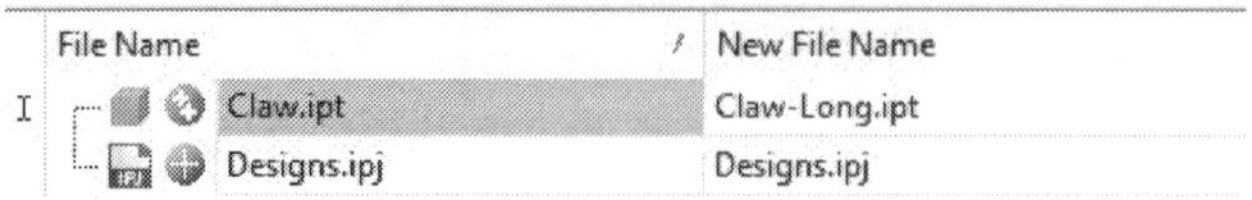

6. Click OK. The new file is displayed in the Main pane.

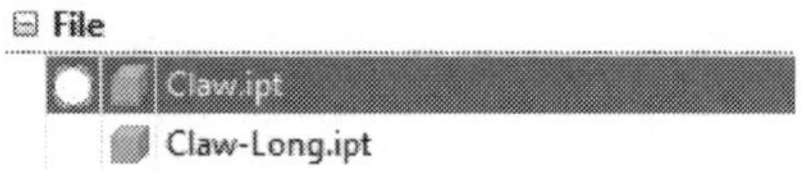

7. Click Claw.ipt.

8. Click Edit menu>Replace.

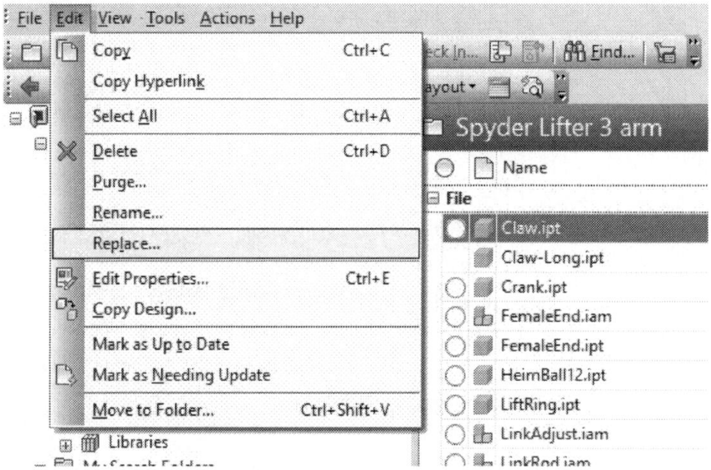

9. In the Replace Wizard dialog box, click Next.

10. On the Identify Parent Files page, do the following:
    - Clear the Spyder Lifter 3 arm.iam check box.
    - Click Next.

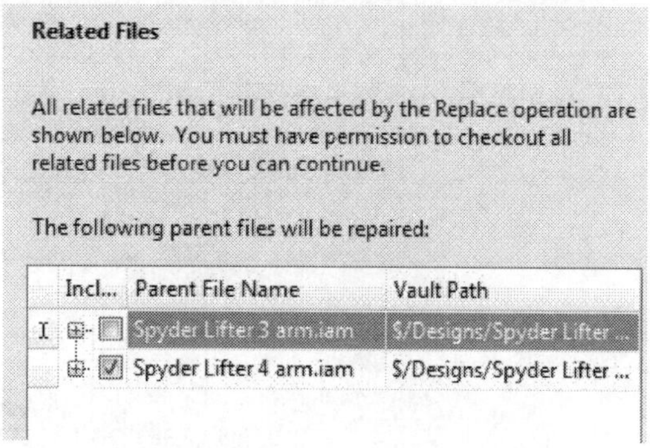

11. On the Specify Replacement Files page, do the following:
    - Click the browse button.
    - Select Claw-Long.ipt.

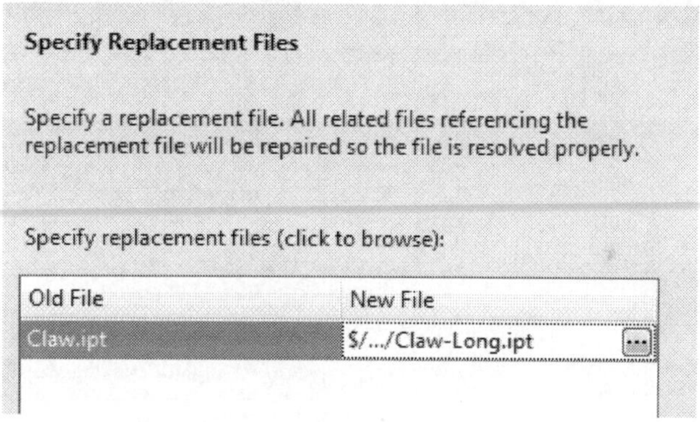

12. Click Finish. In the Warning: Potential Data Loss dialog box, click Yes.

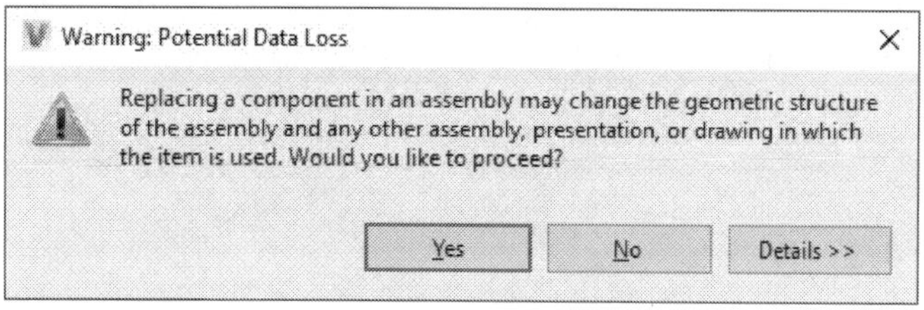

13. View the results of the Replace operation. Click Close.

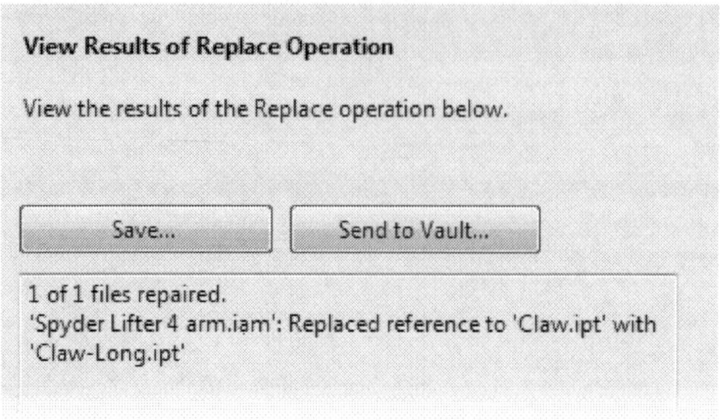

14. In the Main pane, click Claw.ipt. Do the following:

- In the Preview pane, on the Where Used tab, verify that its parent is Spyder Lifter 3 arm.iam.
- In the Main pane, click Claw-Long.ipt.
- In the Preview pane, on the Where Used tab, verify that its parent is Spyder Lifter 4 arm.iam.

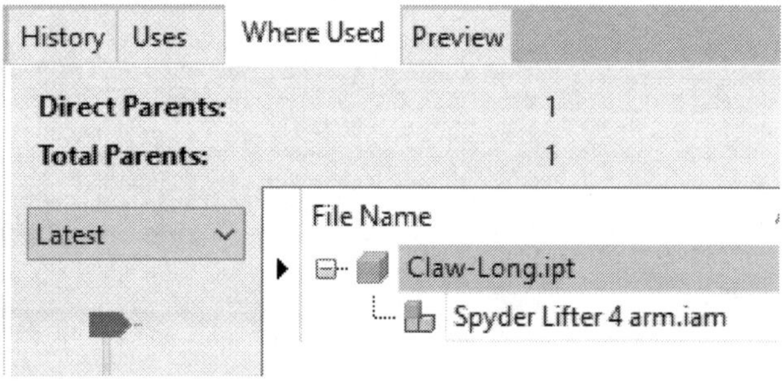

8.9 Chapter Summary

In this chapter you learned how to perform common tasks using Autodesk Vault. You created customized views in the main and preview panes, moved, copied, renamed, and replaced files in designs, edited file properties, and packed files for use outside Vault.

Having completed this chapter, you can:

- Customize the Main pane in Autodesk Vault.
- Use find tools to find files and save searches, the Custom Filter tool to filter file lists, and shortcuts to quickly navigate to a file or folder.
- Manage file versions to preview versions, get a previous version, get the latest version, and work with labels.
- Move and rename files in Vault while maintaining file dependencies.
- Create new designs from existing ones with the Copy Design command in Autodesk Vault.
- Use Pack and Go to archive or copy a complete set of files from Vault.
- View and edit file properties in the vault.
- Replace files in the vault.

Organizing and Populating a Vault

In this chapter, you learn how Autodesk® Inventor® files are organized for best results with Autodesk® Vault. You then learn how to prepare existing projects and upload them to a Vault using Autodesk Autoloader, which is an application that builds the recommended vault structure for you.

Learning Objectives in This Chapter

- Describe how Inventor project and model files are organized for the best results with Vault.
- Add existing models to a vault using Autodesk Autoloader.

9.1 How Autodesk Inventor Files Are Organized

Overview

In this lesson, you learn how Autodesk Inventor project files, model files, and library files are organized for the best performance with Vault. A typical Autodesk Inventor design includes a large number of files. You can use Autodesk Autoloader to help organize your existing models before uploading them to the vault, or you can organize the files manually before you upload them. Whichever method you use, you should know how Autodesk Inventor uses the project file to find files and how regular model files and library files are organized.

The following image displays a number of designs added to a vault. The files are organized in the vault to match the folder structure in place when the files were uploaded to the vault.

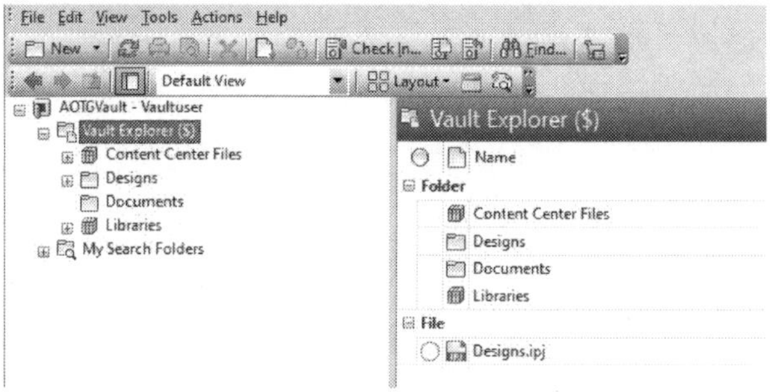

Objectives

After completing this lesson, you will be able to:

- Describe how Autodesk Inventor project files work with a vault.
- Describe how Autodesk Inventor model files are organized for best results with Autodesk Vault.
- Describe how library files are organized for best results with Vault.
- Describe how content center files are organized for best results with Vault.View file properties by adding and removing the fields you want to see, sorted by the required data column.

About Project Files

Autodesk Inventor uses project files to organize and locate related files. Before you upload files to a vault or try to fix resolution issues, you must learn how Autodesk Inventor uses the project file to locate the files in a design.

Project Files Defined

Autodesk Inventor uses project files to organize storage locations for related files in a design. For example, when you open an assembly in Autodesk Inventor, it looks for the component files relative to the locations specified in the project file. When you place a part from the content center, the generated part is stored in a folder relative to the top-level folder specified in the project file. A project file is set up to correspond with the way the files are organized in the vault.

You must create a Vault project file when you want to work with designs that will be managed using Autodesk Vault. This project file format is only available if you have Autodesk Vault installed. The workspace, libraries, and content center files entries specify where Inventor searches for files. All paths are defined relative to a project file location.

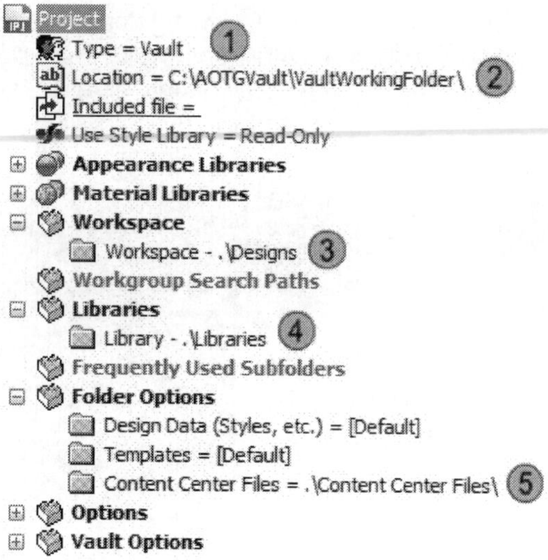

1. A Vault project file is required for managing designs stored in the vault.

2. The local working folder is mapped to the root folder in the vault. All files in the design are typically located under this folder.

3. The Workspace folder is the top-level folder for the models and drawings you create for all designs stored in the vault. You create subfolders under here to organize your designs.

4. Library files in the vault are copied to folders under this local folder. Files in these folders cannot be edited.

5. Files generated from the content center are stored under this folder when copied from the vault.

Autodesk Inventor uses the copy of the project file in the local working folder when you work with files you have checked out from the vault. Therefore, the paths in the project file must correspond to the way that files are organized in the local working folder. When you get files from the vault, the vault structure is reproduced in the local working folder.

Project File Location

The project file should be located one folder above all other model and library file folders. A folder beneath the project file folder holds all designs with folders for each design.

The following image displays the layout of a typical vault working folder. The project file, Designs.ipj, is located in the root folder (VaultWorkingFolder). The Designs folder is the workspace folder in the project file and is located under the project file. It contains folders for different designs. The Content Center Files and Libraries folders are also located under the project file but outside of the workspace folder.

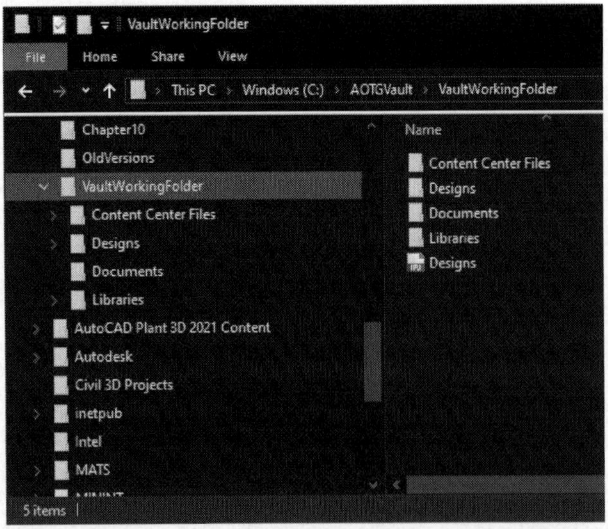

Use a Single Project File

There are many ways to organize Autodesk Inventor project and model files. Some users have one project file for all designs; other users have one project file for each design. With Vault, a single project file should be used so you need to manage just one project file and do not have to switch project files when moving from one design to another.

Frequently Used Subfolders

Frequently Used Subfolders are shortcuts defined in the project file to give you quick access to designs and library parts in your local working folders. In the following image, a project file is displayed in the project file editor. The Frequently Used Subfolders entry of the project file contains paths to frequently used design and library folders.

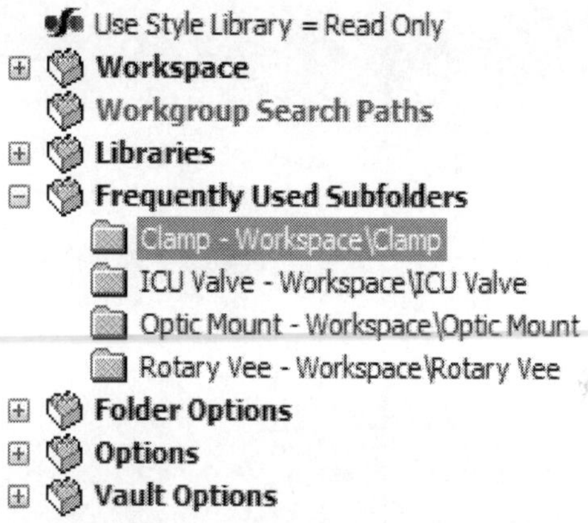

Frequently used subfolders are displayed when you browse for a file in Autodesk Inventor, making it easier to navigate to specific designs or libraries.

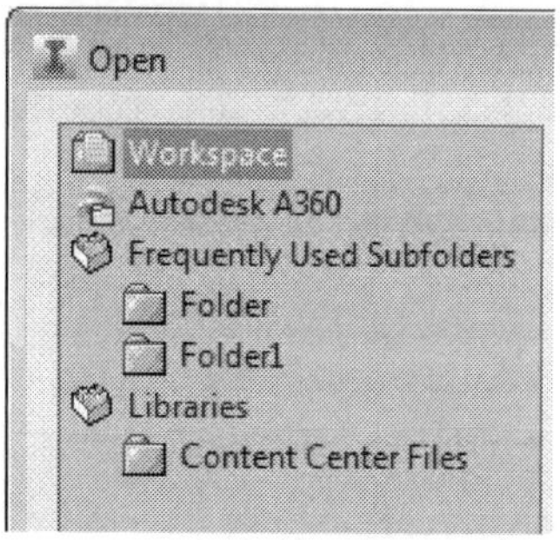

Mapping Project Folders

When you check in files or add new files to the vault, the files are copied from the local working folder to folders in the vault. Inventor determines where to copy the files by looking in the project file. The vault folders are specified by mapping each local search path to a vault folder.

A typical folder mapping is shown in the following image. The Project Root folder is where the project file is stored. In the example shown, the local Project Root folder is mapped to the root folder of the vault. Therefore, the project file is copied to the root of the vault, and model files will be copied to their respective folders relative to the root folder in the vault. Each library path in the project file is also mapped to a vault folder. In the following image, files in the local path named Library are copied to the Libraries folder in the vault, and files in the local Content Center Files path are copied to the Content Center Files folder in the vault.

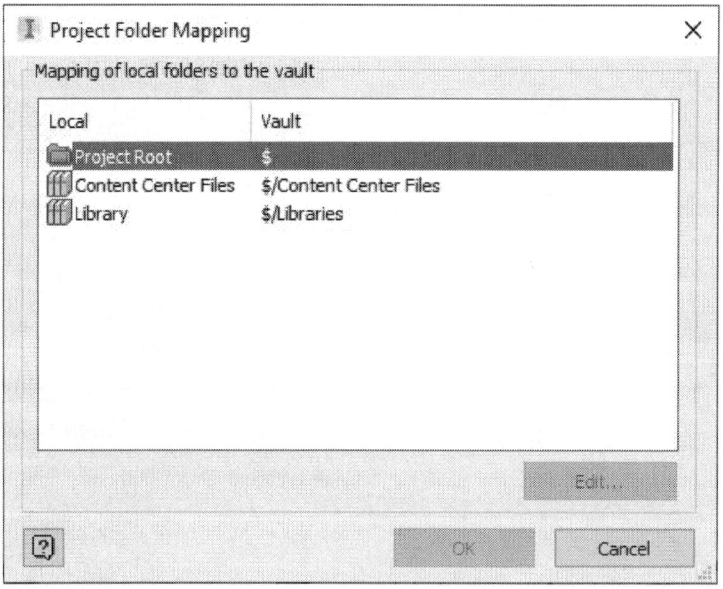

The mapping information is stored as XML data in the project file. For example, the mapping for the Library folder corresponding to the previous image is displayed in the following image. The local path and the vault path are both specified.

```
<ProjectPath pathtype="Library">
  <PathName>Library</PathName> (1)
  <Path>.\Libraries</Path> (2)
  <VaultPath>$/Libraries</VaultPath> (3)
</ProjectPath>
```

1. Path name in project file.
2. Local folder path. This folder is relative to the folder containing the project file.
3. Corresponding vault folder path. The folder structure under this folder matches the folder structure under the local folder path.

About Model Files

There are many ways to organize model files. The method you select must be compatible with the project file and with Vault. In this section, you learn how model files are organized for the best results with Autodesk Vault.

How Inventor Model Files Are Organized

For best results, model files are organized in folders under a single project file.

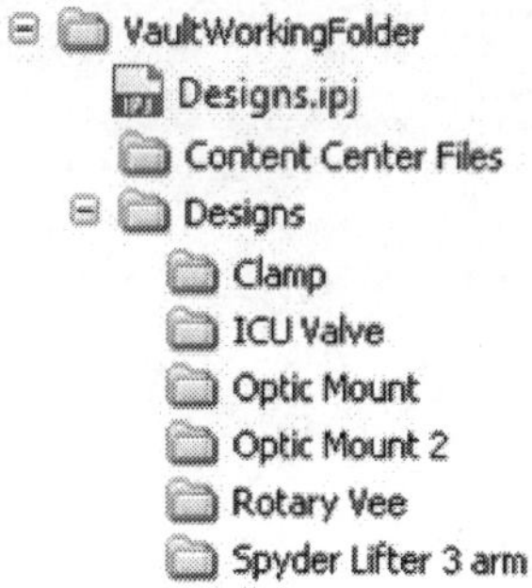

The same folder structure is used in the vault. When you retrieve files to your local working folder, they are copied to the same relative location and they open successfully in Inventor. For example, the corresponding vault is organized as shown. A single project file is located in the root of the vault.

Folders for the designs, libraries, and content center parts are one level below. You can further organize your files using subfolders under these top-level folders. When you get files from the vault, they are copied to the local working folder with the same structure and can be opened successfully.

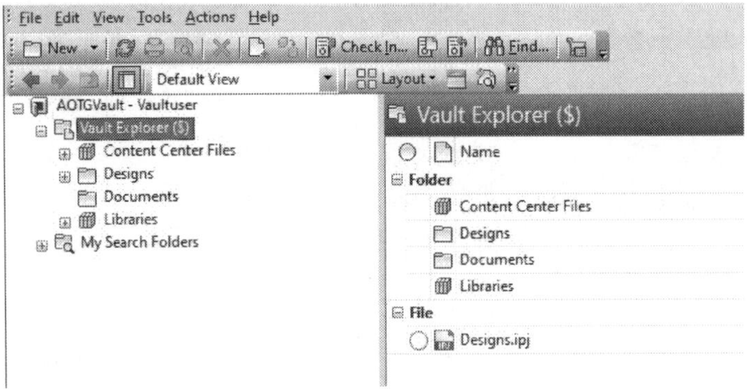

Project File Settings for Model Files

The Workspace path specifies the location of a top-level folder for all non-library model files. Files for different designs are stored in folders under the Workspace folder. If model files are saved outside of the Workspace folder, Autodesk Inventor will not find them.

In the project file, the Workspace is set as a relative path to the folder that contains the project file.

How Common Parts Are Organized

If a part or subassembly is used in more than one design, the file should be stored in a separate folder from the designs in which the part is used, and then it should be referenced in each design. If the part or assembly rarely or never changes, the file can be stored in a library folder so that it cannot be modified by users.

The vault is used as a centralized storage area for all of your files including common parts and library parts and assemblies. Upload all of your library and common components to the vault so that Inventor users can place them in their designs using the Place from Vault command. The following image displays a folder named Common Parts, which contains parts that are included in a number of designs.

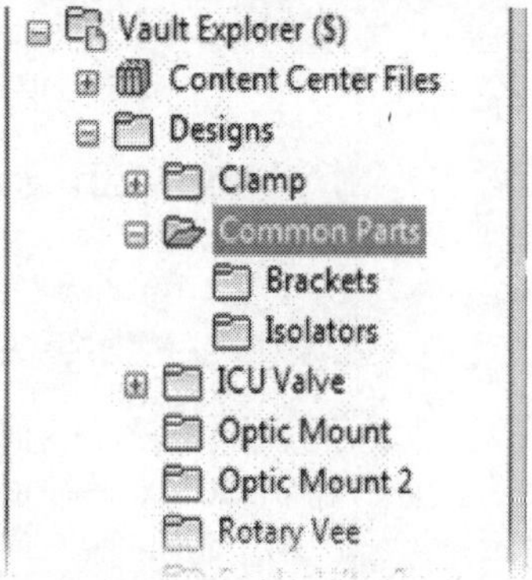

About Library Files

Library files are parts or subassemblies that do not normally change. In Autodesk Inventor, library files are treated as read-only files that are not normally versioned.

Typically, library files are used in more than one design. Common purchased components, content center files, and iParts are typical library components. Autodesk Inventor includes a wide selection of library parts in the content center libraries. You can also get library parts and assemblies from component manufacturers or create them yourself. Some library components are available as iPart or iAssembly factories, which contain multiple sizes or configurations of a given component in a single file. You must set up and organize library components correctly so that they work with the vault.

About Library Files

Library files are parts or subassemblies that do not normally change and are used in more than one design. You store library files in library folders. Files stored in library folders are treated as read-only and cannot be modified by users. Any file can be designated as a library file including regular Inventor parts and assemblies, iParts, iAssemblies, and AutoCAD® drawing files.

About iParts and iAssemblies

An iPart or iAssembly contains multiple part or assembly definitions in one file, called a factory. When you place an iPart or iAssembly in a design, you select one of the definitions and a part or assembly file is created. By default, the file is saved in a folder under the factory.

iParts and iAssemblies are usually stored in library folders because they represent common parts that do not change.

About Library Folders

Files that are stored in library folders in the vault are designated as library files. Library folders are similar to regular folders except that files in library folders are treated as library files and cannot be modified while stored in a library folder. Library folders must be created directly under the root of the vault, because you cannot create them under a regular folder.

Library folders use a different icon than regular folders. Note that subfolders are used to group library parts into meaningful categories. You can create any level of nested library folders to help organize the files.

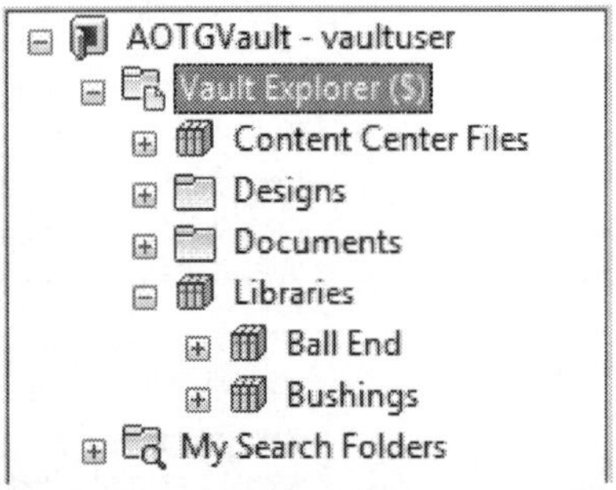

When a user retrieves a design from the vault and the design contains library files, the library files are copied into the working folder to the same relative location and folder as in the vault.

iParts in the Vault

The following image displays an iPart factory, Heim Bushing.ipt, in a library folder. Note that a unique icon is used to distinguish a factory from other file formats. iPart children also have unique icons.

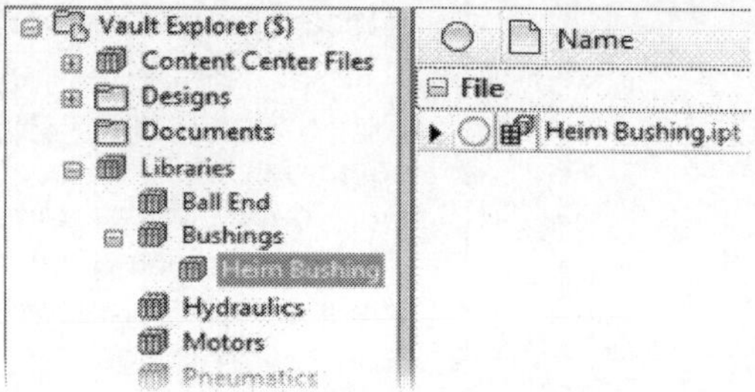

Project Files Settings for Library Parts

When you open a model, Autodesk Inventor looks for library files in the locations specified in the project file. The following image displays a project file with a single library path that points to the top-level library folder. The library path is relative because the library folder is beneath the folder containing the project file.

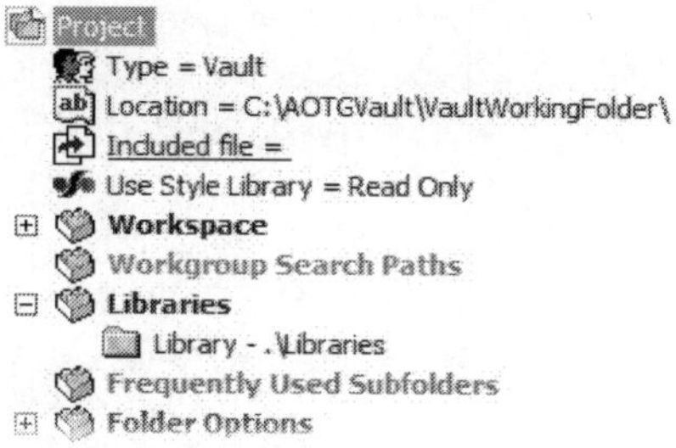

Importance of Relative Paths

Because all files, including library files, are stored in the vault, all paths in a vault project file should be defined relative to the folder containing the project file. When you use relative paths, the entire local working folder structure is portable; it can be located in any location on a user's computer. If you use absolute paths to local folders such as *G:\Libraries*, or UNC names such as *\\PartServer\Libraries*, each user must have the same setup on their computer if they want to share the same project file from the vault.

About Content Center Files

Content center files are parts that you often use in more than one design. They are similar to other library files and you need to set them up correctly to work with Autodesk Vault.

About Content Center Files and Vault

Content center files are parts that are placed from the content center libraries. The content center libraries are databases that store definitions of parts. A part file is not created until you first place the selected part in your design. Because many designs use identical instances of a part (for example, a common fastener), you normally store the resulting part file in a common folder that is outside of your designs so that many designs can reference one copy of the library part. When you place the part from the content center in another model, the folder in which you store content center parts is checked before a new part file is created. If the part already exists, the design references the existing part instead of creating another.

When you use Autodesk Vault to manage documents for a design team, you should install the content center libraries with the Autodesk Data Management Server (ADMS) rather than as Inventor Desktop Content.

How Content Center Files Are Organized

As with user-defined library components, you share content center files between designs but you do not modify them. In the same way that you use the top-level Libraries folder, you specify a storage location for content center parts in the project file that is outside the Designs folder. Because you cannot modify parts generated from the content center, you store them in library folders in the vault. When you store a design in the vault or get versions of a design, parts placed from the content center act in a similar manner to other library parts.

You can organize content center files in many ways. However, for best results when using the vault, you should organize these files in the same way that you organize library files. The following image displays the recommended folder structure for storing content center files. The Content Center Files folder is located directly under the project file but outside of the folder where regular design files are stored.

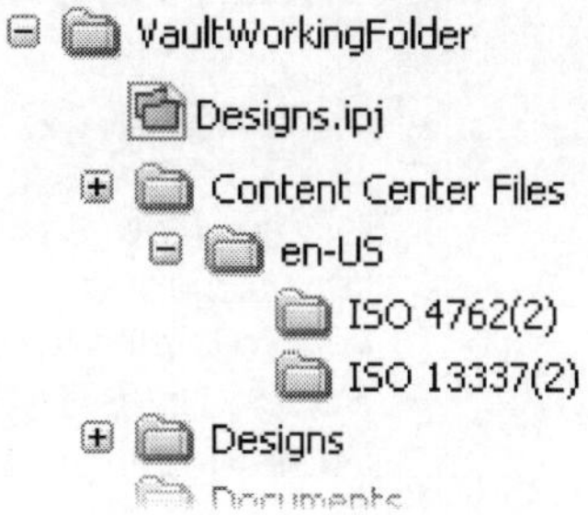

Content Center Files in the Vault

Parts generated from the content center libraries are stored in the vault using the same folder structure below your working folder. When you create a part from the content center, the part is placed in a folder below the Content Center Files folder. The folder name reflects the family name of the part in the content center. In the vault, the local Content Center Files folder is mapped to a library folder one level below the root folder in the vault.

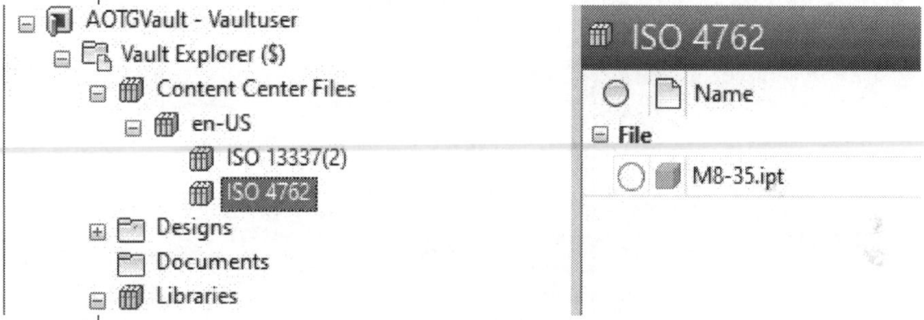

Project File Settings for Content Center Parts

In the Autodesk Inventor project file editor, the Content Center Files path is set to the folder that you created for the content center files. Because the Content Center Files folder is beneath the project file, the path is relative to the project file as shown in the following image. The Content Center Files folder should be located outside the folder specified for user-defined library components.

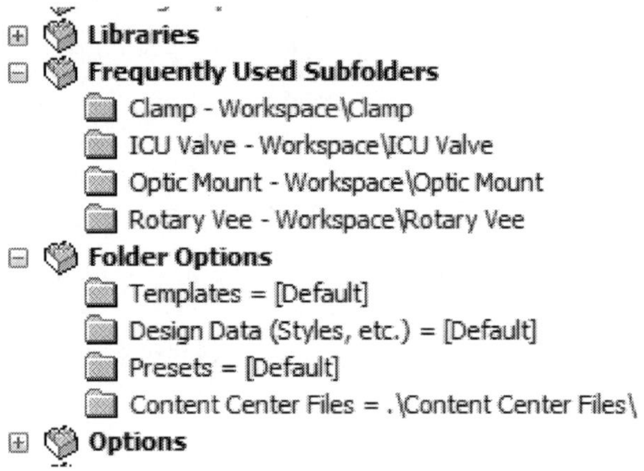

9.2 Adding Existing Models to a Vault

In this lesson, you learn how to prepare existing designs and add them to a vault using Autodesk Autoloader, a software that prepares, analyzes, and uploads Autodesk Inventor files to a vault. Many companies have existing Inventor designs that they need to add to the vault. You can use several methods to add your existing designs to the vault, depending on whether you want to manually prepare and upload the designs or use a more automated method such as Autodesk Autoloader.

Objectives

After completing this lesson, you will be able to:

- Prepare existing models to use Autodesk Autoloader.
- Upload models to a vault using Autodesk Autoloader.

Preparing Models

The method you use to prepare data depends on the method you use to upload data to the vault. When you use Autodesk Autoloader to upload data, there is little preparation required because Autoloader reorganizes the files for you. If Autodesk Autoloader finds problems with some file relationships, you are required to fix the problems before using Autoloader to upload the files to the vault.

Planning the Vault Structure

Before you upload existing model data, you must plan how you want to store your model files, library files, content center files, non-model files, and other data in the vault. If you use Autodesk Autoloader to upload your data, the software creates a single project file and the top-level vault folders for you. All that you need to create are subfolders to organize the files for each design. The structure and project file that Autoloader creates ensures that you can successfully work on your designs in Autodesk Inventor.

It is not a requirement that you have a single project file for all your designs before uploading files to a vault with Autodesk Autoloader. You can run Autoloader for each project file to upload the designs managed by the project file. It is highly recommended that you place all designs uploaded to the vault under the single vault project file created when you first upload files to a new vault using Autoloader.

Preparing Project Files

When you run Autodesk Autoloader, you select an existing folder to upload. You then select a project file associated with the designs in the selected folder and its subfolders. The selected project file is used to validate file references in the designs in the selected folder before they are uploaded to the vault. Autodesk Autoloader reads any type of project file including Single-User, Shared, Semi-Isolated, and Vault.

Autoloader uses all defined paths in the project file to determine which files to upload. Each design in the selected folder and its subfolders is examined for dependent files. Autoloader checks that all dependent files can be found in the scope of the search paths so that models correctly resolve after uploading to the vault. All dependent files are added to the list of files to upload. Because Autoloader supports all project file formats, it locates all referenced files in the Workspace, Workgroup, Libraries, and Content Center Files search paths.

Existing projects can be organized in many different ways. Because Autoloader works with one project file at a time, run Autoloader once for each project file. If you already use a single project file for all of your designs, all designs can be uploaded at once using Autoloader. If you use multiple project files, you must run Autoloader for each project file.

You do not need to convert your existing project files to a Vault-type project file before you work with Autoloader. Autoloader creates a new Vault project file for you and adds it to the vault. The new project file is ready to use, including the correct search paths and folder mappings.

Common Project File Problem

Although your existing projects can resolve correctly when you open the file in Autodesk Inventor, you might have to add additional search paths if Autodesk Autoloader cannot find files. For example, in the following image, the project file is located in the same folder as the main assembly, Winch.iam. The project file has Workgroup search paths to the Motors and Hydraulics folders, which are not located below the project file location. The project file does not contain a Workspace path. The main assembly opens successfully in Autodesk Inventor. However, when Autodesk Autoloader searches for files, the main assembly is not found because none of the search paths in the project file include the location of the main assembly file.

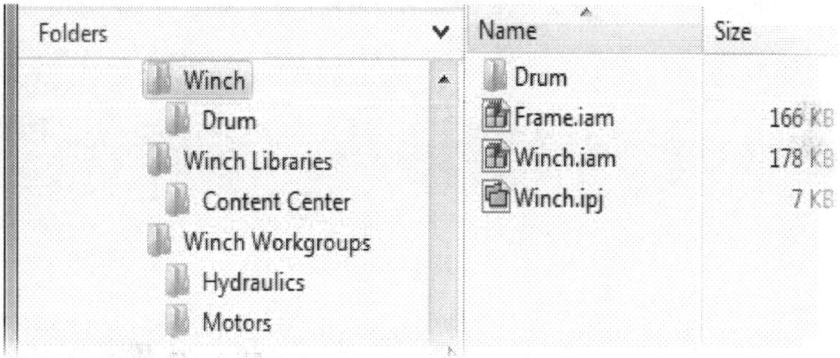

To fix the project file, add a Workspace path to the existing project file, and then run Autodesk Autoloader again.

Solving File Resolution Problems

You cannot upload designs that fail to fully resolve. If Autoloader cannot find child files, you must either locate them and resolve the problem or remove the child part's reference from the parent file.

You can check your designs by opening each master assembly, drawing, and presentation file in Autodesk Inventor to ensure that all files are found. This can be a lengthy process, especially for large designs with many parent files. Alternatively, use Autodesk Autoloader to find resolution problems because it identifies just the issues that you need to resolve. Resolve the problem files and then run Autoloader again to recheck the data.

Duplicate File Names

Although you can store files with the same name in the vault, it is recommended that you use unique filenames. If files are different, they should have different names. If the same file is used in more than one model, place the file in a common folder from which you can use the file in many designs, as shown in the following image. If the file is used by many designs and is rarely or never modified, move the file to a library folder so that it is protected from unintended changes.

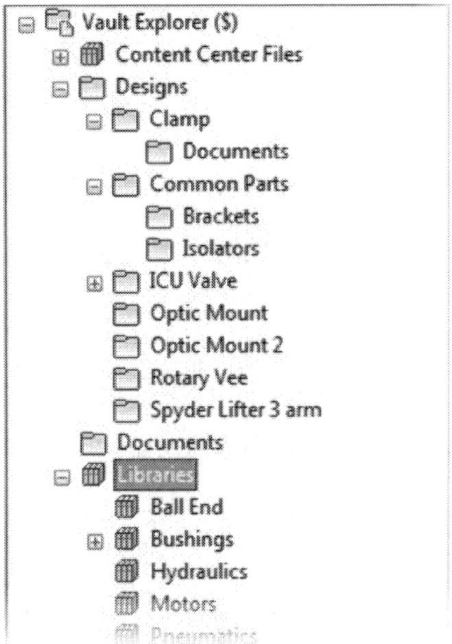

If you need to rename files, upload the files to the vault and then use the Vault renaming utility to rename the files rather than renaming the files in Windows Explorer and manually repairing the references. To add files with duplicate names to the vault, toggle off the Enforce Unique File Names setting in the vault and then add the files. In Vault, search for duplicate filenames. If the files are different, rename them. After renaming, toggle on Enforce Unique File Names. The option to enforce unique filenames in a vault is located on the Files tab in the Administration dialog box (Tools> Administration>Vault Settings). If using Autoloader the Enforce Unique File Names must be disabled.

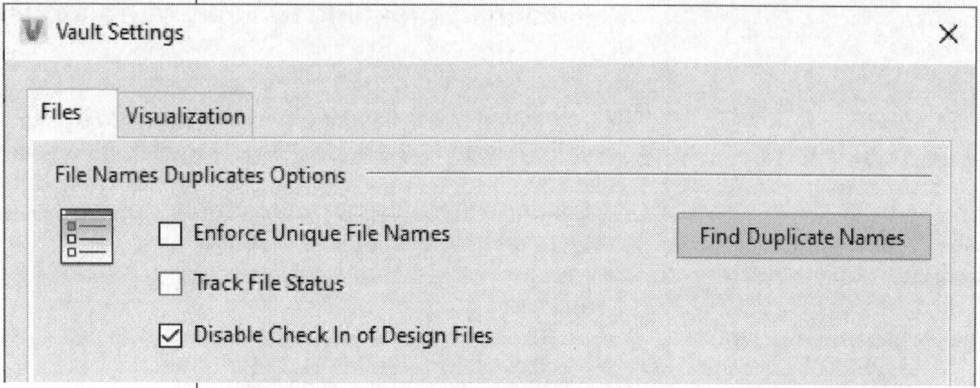

To consolidate duplicate files into one shared file, add your designs to the vault and then reorganize the files. Vault understands file relationships; therefore, you can move files without breaking links. To find where a file is used, view the Where Used information in Vault Explorer and record where each file is used. Delete all but one copy of the file, move the one copy from its current folder to a common folder, and then check out each dependent file and resolve the links. Use the File Replace operation where appropriate.

Migrating Files

If you want to migrate your design files to the latest release of Autodesk Inventor, you can migrate the files before or after you add them to the vault. To migrate files, schedule a migration task using the Task Scheduler in Inventor. The scheduled task opens all files from a local or vault folder, migrates the files, and saves them back to the same local or vault location.

You are not required to migrate Autodesk Inventor files before uploading them to the vault; however, Autoloader will not upload Inventor files older than R10 (must be migrated first) and AutoCAD files older than R14.

Uploading Models

When you have prepared your data for uploading, you use Autodesk Autoloader to upload the models to the vault. Autoloader checks file dependencies, consolidates files, creates the vault folder structure, uploads the files, and creates a vault project file. The resulting vault folder structure and project file ensure that you can successfully work with Autodesk Inventor and Vault.

Procedure: Uploading to Vault with Autodesk Autoloader

The following steps describe how to upload an existing Autodesk Inventor design to the vault using Autodesk Autoloader.

1. Organize the folder structure of your existing designs as you want them to display in the vault.

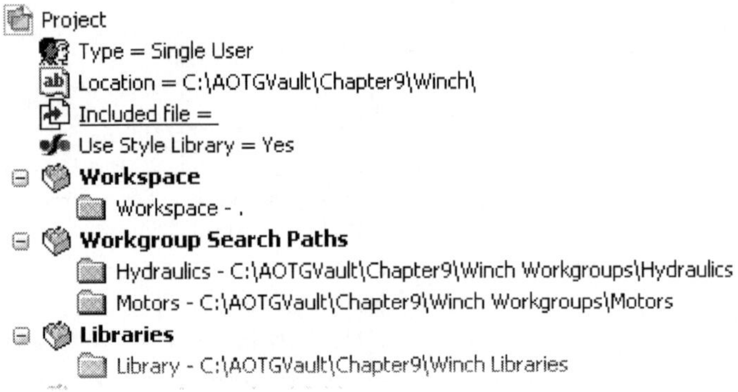

2. Start Autodesk Autoloader.
3. Select the top-level folder containing the designs you want to upload to the vault.

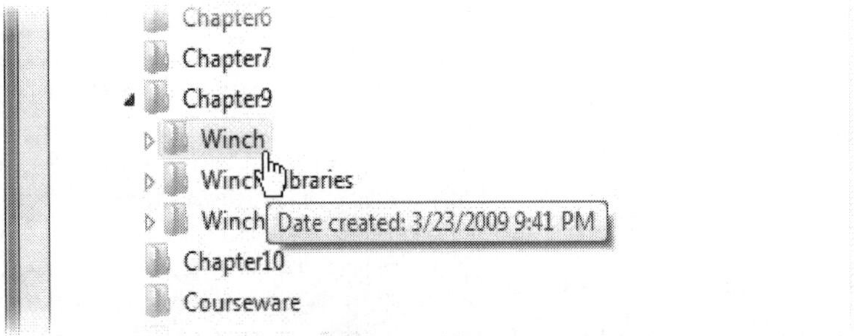

4. Select the project file that manages the files to be uploaded.

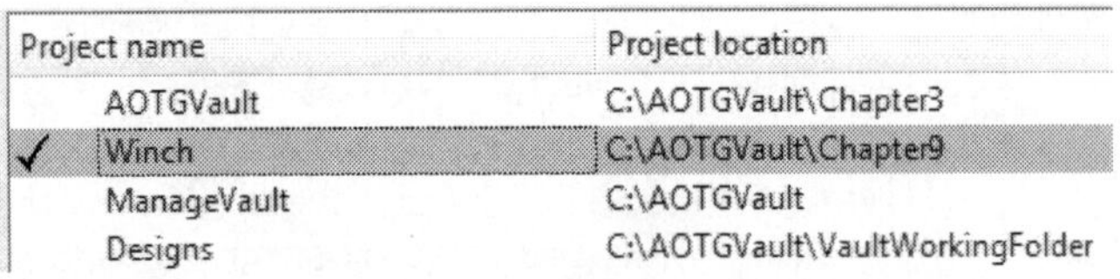

5. Click Scan to scan all files in the project folders and confirm file relationships.

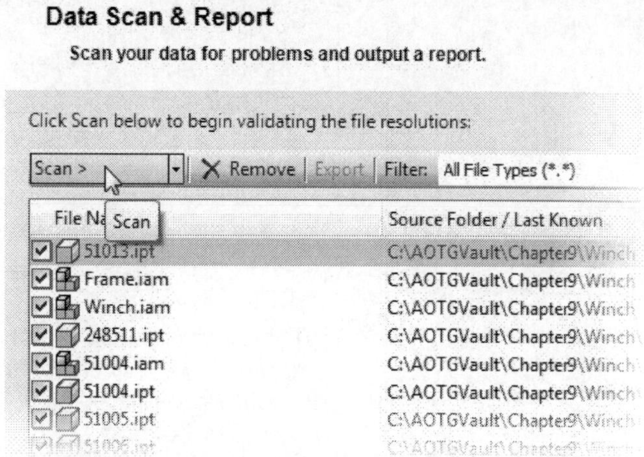

6. If required, fix any reported problems. Missing files and file resolution issues are reported. You are not required to abandon the Autoloader session. Open the files in their associated CAD application and repair the reported issues.

7. Return to Autoloader and rescan the files. You can only proceed when all reported issues have been resolved. The problem files can also be excluded from the selection set and loaded by hand later.
8. In the drop-down list, select Find duplicates. This will help identify any identical files that might cause confusion later in the process.

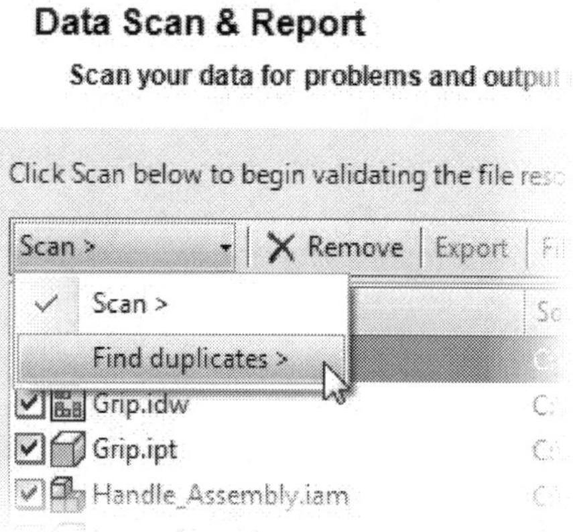

9. Once all issues have been resolved, click Next.
10. Log in to the vault.
11. Map the generated folders in the vault to the corresponding folders in the existing project folder. If your project file contains multiple workgroup or library search paths, you must map each one to a corresponding folder in the vault. You can create additional vault folders below the three Autoloader-generated folders to help organize the data in the vault. Click Next.

    Note: During the mapping step, selecting to map 'Winch' to 'Products' in the vault will put 'Winch' under 'Products'. If mapping the 'Winch' folder to a 'Winch' folder in the vault, select the Direct Mapping option at the bottom of the Browse Vault For Folder dialog box.

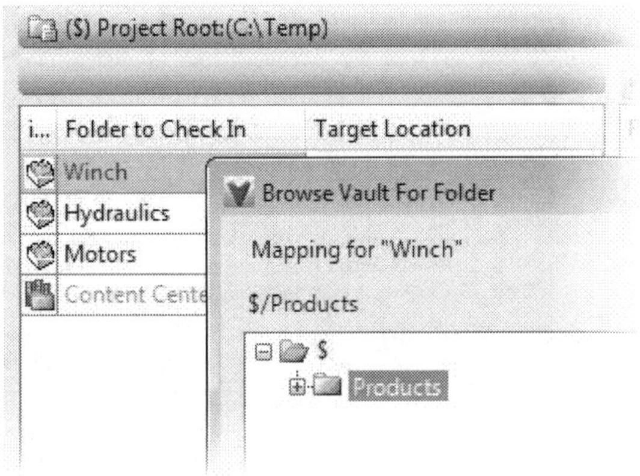

12. On the Copy & File Redirection Progress Page, wait until the operation is complete and click Next.
13. Upload the files to the vault. You can optionally generate a visualization file of each CAD file before it is uploaded to the vault. Once uploaded the Autoloader Progress and Report page notes, the report location and filename to review the details of the upload.

Autoloader Results

When you use Autoloader to upload files to a new vault, Autoloader organizes the files based on the recommended vault structure. The following image displays the results of using Autoloader to upload several designs. Autoloader creates a new Vault project file, and creates two top-level library folders, Content Center Files and Libraries, along with a single top-level Designs folder. The project file contains the correct search paths and folder mappings. You should not have to edit the project file unless you want to add frequently used subfolders. You can get a copy of the project file to your working folder and immediately start working with the model files.

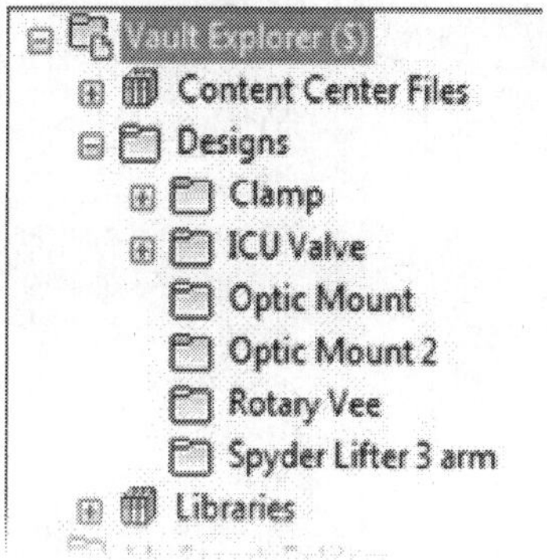

Uploading Non-Inventor Data

By default, all files in and below the selected folder are uploaded to the vault. File relationships between Autodesk Inventor documents are maintained, as are external reference relationships between DWG™ files. Other files, such as images, documents, and spreadsheets are also uploaded, but are not automatically attached to other documents in the vault. If required, you must manually attach them to the appropriate file after you upload the files to the vault.

In Autoloader, you can upload all files found in or below the selected folder or limit the upload to Autodesk Inventor files or DWG-based files. You can also control the upload status for each file.

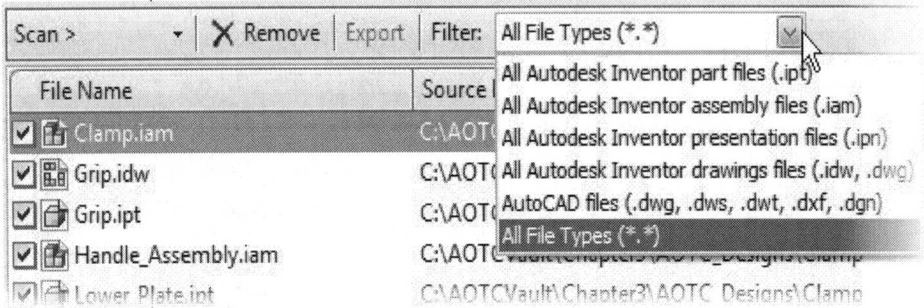

Adding Visualization Files

You can also generate DWF™ or DWFx files for all CAD files uploaded to the vault. This can take a considerable amount of time for large datasets. You can run Autoloader multiple times with subsets filtered by file format to reduce the time for any one upload.

Another approach is to use the Task Scheduler to check out and then immediately check in all files after you have uploaded all files without DWF attachments. DWF files are created when the files are checked back in to the vault.

Practice 9a

Add Existing Projects to a Vault

In this practice, you prepare a project for uploading and then upload the design to an empty vault using Autodesk Autoloader.

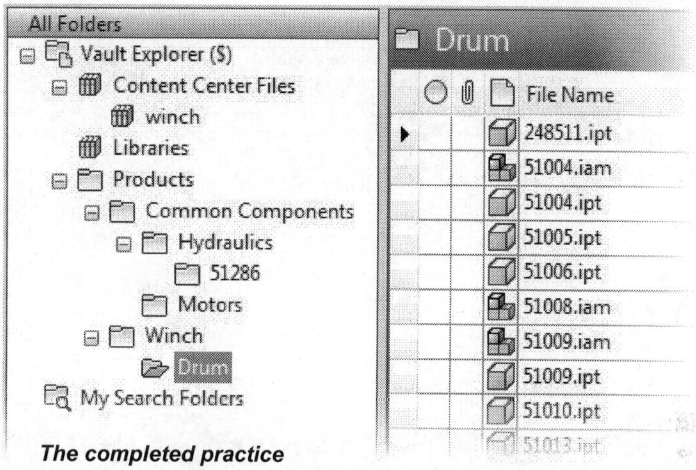

The completed practice

Task 1 - Add existing projects to a vault.

1. Exit Autodesk Inventor if it is running.
2. Start Autodesk Data Management Server Console. Log in as administrator.
3. The password is blank.
4. Right-click the Vaults folder and select Create.

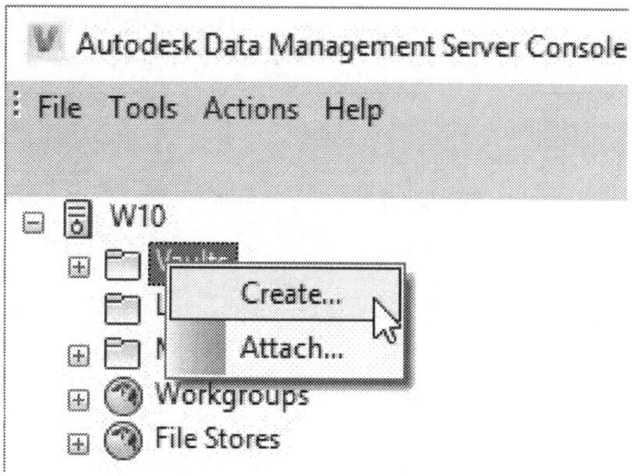

5. In the Create Vault dialog box, under New Vault Name, enter **UploadVault**. Click OK. When the vault is created, click OK to close the message box.

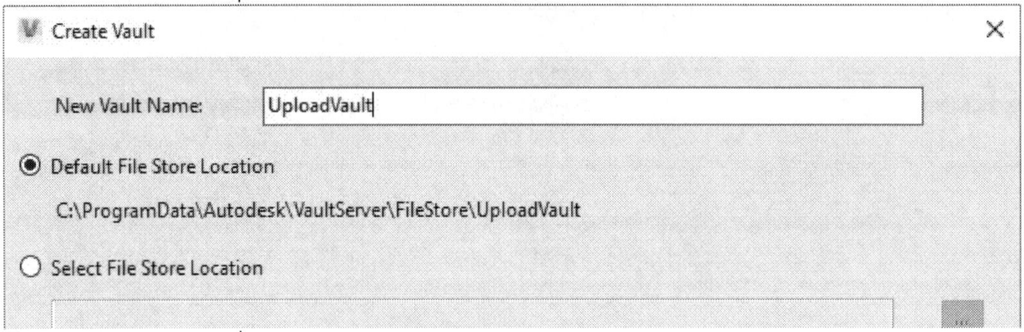

6. Exit Autodesk Data Management Server Console.

7. In Windows Explorer, click the folder *C:\AOTGVault\Chapter9*. Right-click Winch.ipj. Click Edit. View the project file's entries for Workgroup Search Paths. The Hydraulics and Motors workgroup folders are located below the folder containing the project folder.

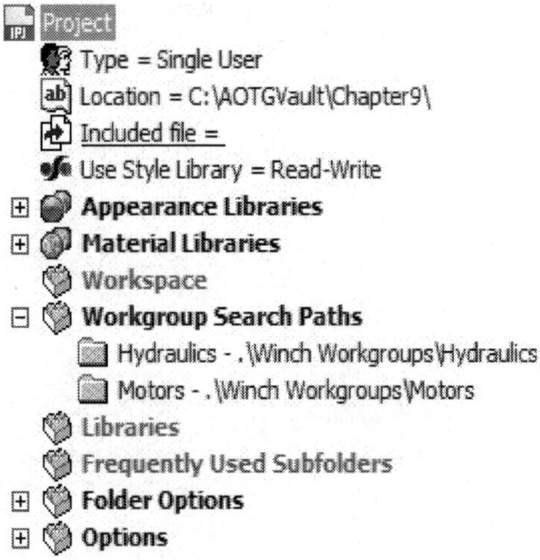

8. In the Inventor Project Editor dialog box, right- click Workspace. Click Add Path. In the location, enter **.\Winch** (a period, followed by \Winch). Press ENTER.

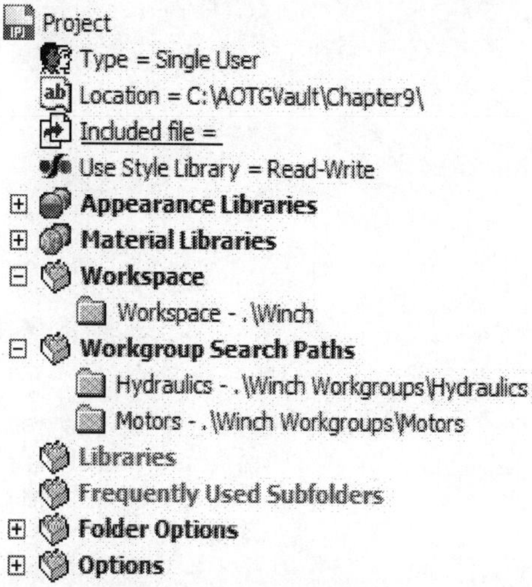

9. Click the plus sign (+) to expand Folder Options.

10. View the content center files path.

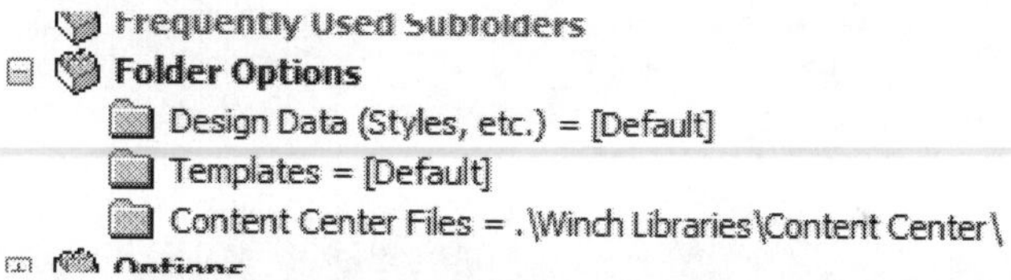

Note: If the supplied data folders were not installed to their default location, you might have to select a new path for the content center files.

11. Click Save. Click Close to close the Project File Editor.

Task 2 - Check file dependencies.

1. Start Autodesk Autoloader. On the Welcome page, click Next.
2. On the Select Data Source page, click Select Folder. Browse to and select the *C:\AOTGVault\Chapter9\Winch* folder.
3. Click OK.
4. In the Select Project dialog box, ensure that the Winch project file is shown as the active project file. If not, activate it.

5. Click OK.

	Project name	Project location
	AOTGVault	C:\AOTGVault\Chapter3
✓	Winch	C:\AOTGVault\Chapter9
	ManageVault	C:\AOTGVault
	Designs	C:\AOTGVault\VaultWorkingFolder

6. Click Next.

7. On the Data Scan & Report page, click Scan.

8. When the scan is complete, click OK to close the message box.

9. Note that Next is unavailable, indicating that there was a problem in one or more files. Click the Status column header to sort by status, and then scroll through the files and view the Status column.

File Name	Source Folder / Last Known	Status
51013.ipt	C:\AOTGVault\Chapter9\Winch	Duplicates found
51013.ipt	C:\AOTGVault\Chapter9\Winch\Drum	Duplicates found
P31A.iam	C:\AOTGVault\Chapter9\Winch Workgroups\Motors	File resolutions not validated
Winch.iam	C:\AOTGVault\Chapter9\Winch	Issue(s) in children
Frame.iam	C:\AOTGVault\Chapter9\Winch	Successfully opened
248511.ipt	C:\AOTGVault\Chapter9\Winch\Drum	Successfully opened

10. Under File Name, click Winch.iam. Click >> to expand the Autoloader dialog box, if not already expanded.

    In the File Dependencies tab, scroll down to P31A.iam. The file resolution issue for Winch.iam is that P31A.iam cannot be found.

File Name	Status
51139.ipt	Successfully Opened
51157.ipt	Successfully Opened
51009.iam	Successfully Opened
51013.ipt	Successfully Opened
51010.ipt	Successfully Opened
51013.ipt	Successfully Opened
P31A.iam	File can't be found(missing)

Task 3 - Solve file resolution problem.

1. Start Autodesk Inventor.
2. Ensure that Winch.ipj is the active project file.
3. Open *Winch.iam.*
4. In the Resolve Link dialog box, resolve the link error by selecting the P31B.iam file from the Winch Workgroups\Motors folder. Click Open. Click Yes if you are prompted to update the assembly.

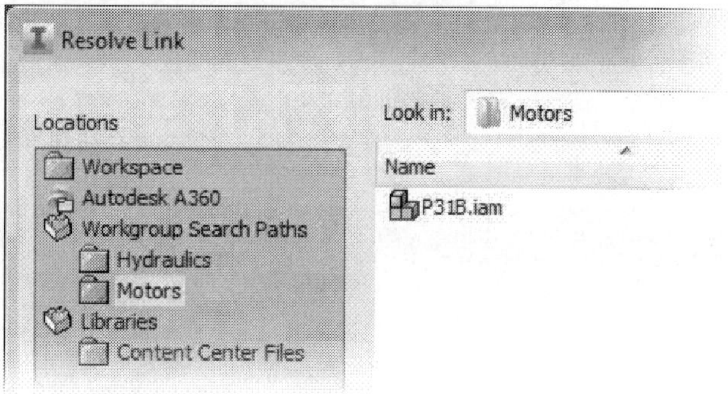

5. Click Save. In the Save dialog box, click Yes to All>OK. Update the data format if prompted.
6. Close the file.

Task 4 - Solve duplicate files problem.

1. Switch to Autodesk Autoloader. Click Scan. If you cannot restart the scan, click Back and Next again to return to the Data Scan & Report page. Click Scan to rescan the files. The Winch.iam file is now resolved without errors.

   The scan reports that two different 51013.ipt files are referenced in the examined files.

File Name	Source Folder / Last Known	Status
51013.ipt	C:\AOTGVault\Chapter9\Winch	Duplicates found
51013.ipt	C:\AOTGVault\Chapter9\Winch\Drum	Duplicates found
Frame.iam	C:\AOTGVault\Chapter9\Winch	Successfully opened
Winch.iam	C:\AOTGVault\Chapter9\Winch	Successfully opened
248511.ipt	C:\AOTGVault\Chapter9\Winch\Drum	Successfully opened
51004.iam	C:\AOTGVault\Chapter9\Winch\Drum	Successfully opened

2. Under File Name, click the first 51013.ipt row. In the details pane at the bottom of the dialog box, click the Duplicate Files tab. The location of each 51013.ipt file is displayed.

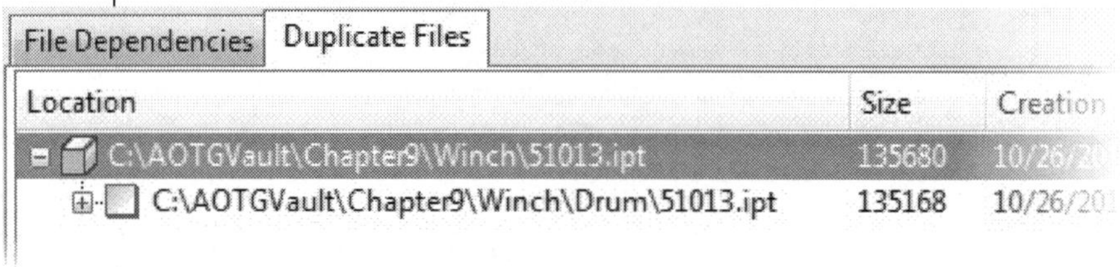

3. Switch to Autodesk Inventor. Open ...*Winch \Frame.iam*.

4. In the browser, select 51013:3. On the ribbon, click the Assemble tab>Component> Replace>Replace All.

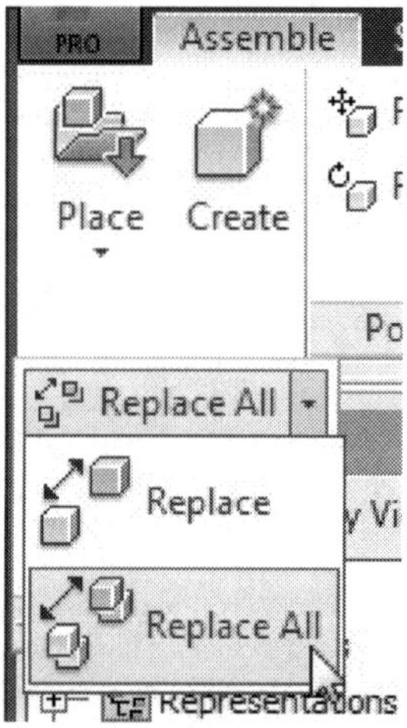

5. In the Place Component dialog box, browse to the Drum folder. Select 51013.ipt. Click Open.

6. Save the file. Close Frame.iam. Update the data format if prompted.

   The original ...\Winch\51013.ipt file is no longer referenced in the assembly.

7. In Windows Explorer, browse to the *C:\AOTGVault\Chapter9\Winch* folder. Delete 51013.ipt.

8. Switch to Autodesk Autoloader. Scan the files again.

   All files are opened and resolved successfully. No duplicate files are found.

Task 5 - Complete the Upload

1. Click Next. Log in to the vault.
   - For user name, enter **Administrator**.
   - Leave the password blank.
   - For Vault, select UploadVault.
   - Click OK.
2. On the Map Vault Folders page, note that the project file's search paths are listed on the left and the new vault folders are on the right. Note that three new folders are created below the root folder in the vault.
3. Under Resultant Vault View, right-click the Designs folder. Click Rename. In the Rename Folder dialog box, enter **Products**. Click OK to rename the vault folder.

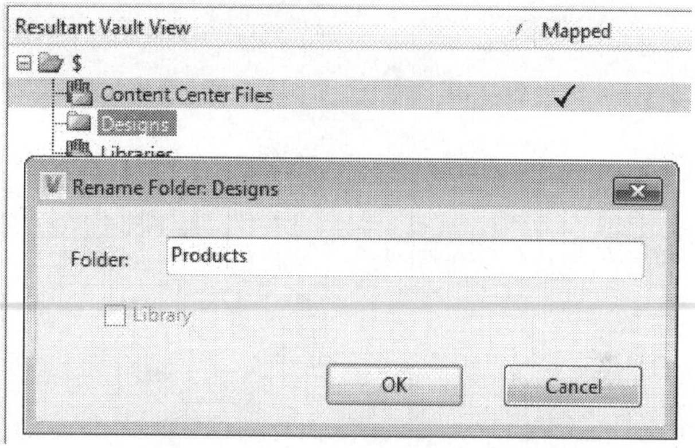

4. Under Folder to Check In, double-click Winch.
5. In the Browse Vault for Folder dialog box, select the Products folder. Ensure that the Direct Mapping check box is not checked.

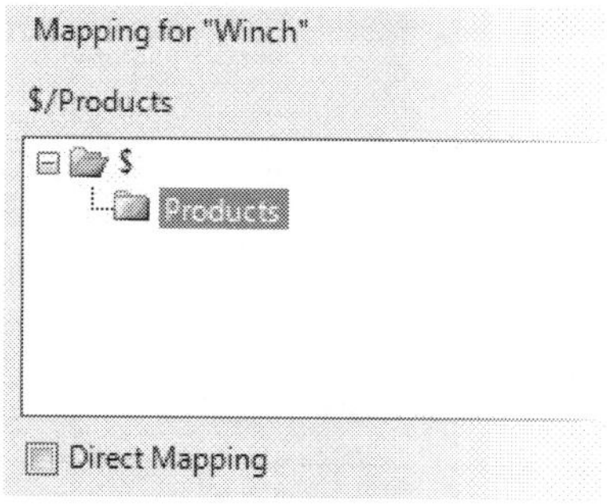

6. Click OK. The workspace folder from the project file is mapped to the new folder in the vault.

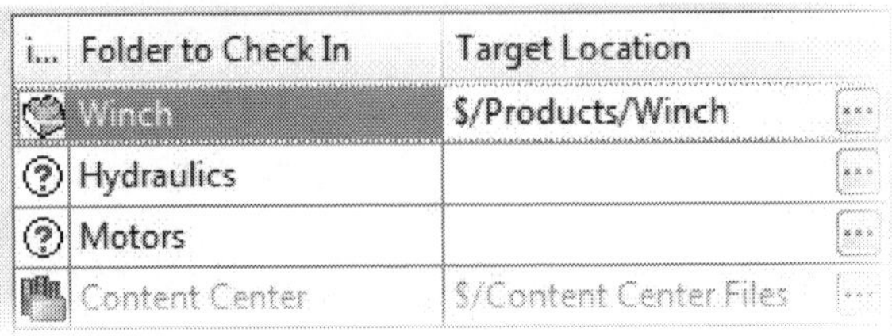

7. Under Folder to Check In, double-click Hydraulics. In the Browse Vault for Folder dialog box, click Products. Click New Folder.

8. In the Create Folder dialog box, enter **Common Components**. Click OK.

9. In the Browse Vault for Folder dialog box, click Common Components. Click OK. A Hydraulics subfolder is created automatically.

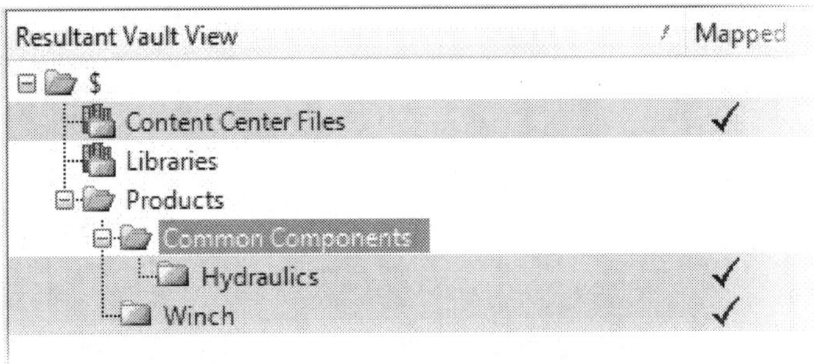

10. Under Folder to Check In, double-click Motors. In the Browse Vault for Folder dialog box, click Common Components. Click OK.

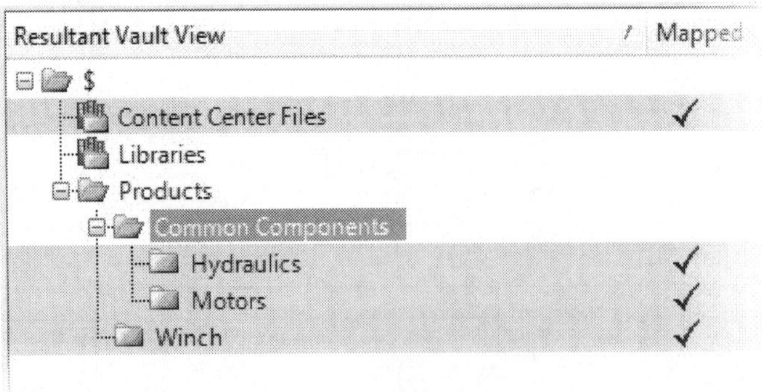

11. Click Next.

12. On the Copy & File Redirection Progress page, wait until the operation is complete. Click Next.

13. On the Specify Data Subsets page, examine the resulting structure of files in the vault.

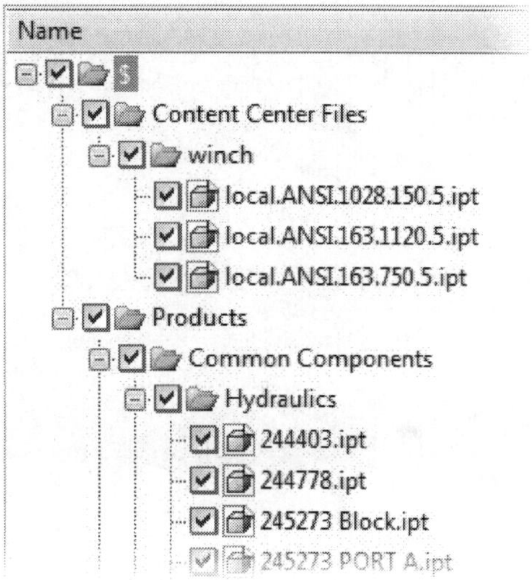

14. Click Upload.

15. On the Autoloader Progress and Report page, make note of the report location and filename.

16. Click Done.

Task 6 - Review the Results

1. Start Autodesk Vault.
   - For user name, enter **Administrator**.
   - Leave the password blank.
   - For Vault, select UploadVault.
   - Click OK.

2. In the root folder of the vault, Vault Explorer ($), note that there is a project file named Designs.ipj.

3. View the contents of the other folders.

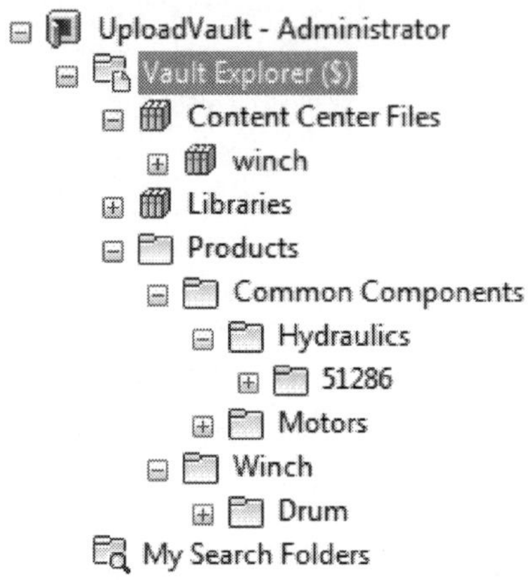

4. Exit Autodesk Vault.

9.3 Chapter Summary

How you organize Inventor files in the vault greatly affects how Inventor and Vault operate together. In this chapter, you learned how Autodesk Inventor files are organized for the best results with Vault. You also learned how to prepare existing projects and upload them to a vault using Autodesk Autoloader.

Having completed this chapter, you can:

- Describe how Inventor project and model files are organized for the best results with Vault.
- Add existing models to a vault using Autodesk Autoload.

Chapter 10

Managing Vault

As a Vault administrator, you are responsible for maintaining vaults and files, including managing user accounts and managing the integrity and performance of the vaults.

Learning Objectives in This Chapter

- Set up vaults.
- Manage users and groups.
- Manage file properties.
- Backup and restore vaults.
- Maintain a vault.

10.1 Setting Up Vault

Overview

In this lesson, you learn about the components of the vault server, typical Vault installation methods, how to create a vault, and how to set up the Vault environment.

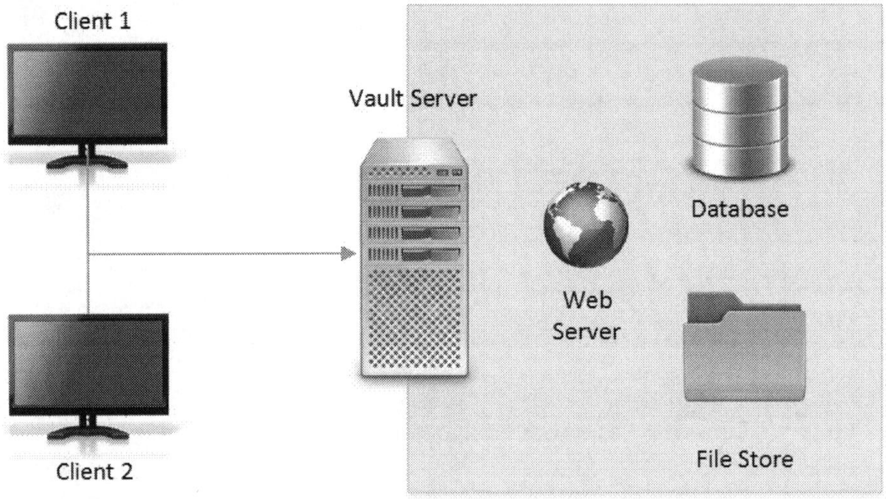

Objectives

After completing this lesson, you will be able to:

- Describe the components of an Autodesk Vault installation.
- Create a new vault.
- Enable unique filenames, set working folders, and enable visualization files.

Components of Autodesk Vault

When you install Autodesk® Vault, several software applications and their associated data files are stored on the vault server. You should understand the purpose of each application and where each component is installed in order to correctly manage Vault.

Autodesk Vault consists of a server and one or more clients that access data on the server. The server manages the vault file store, where the files you add to the vault are stored. The server also manages the vault databases where the property data from the files and the files' relationships are stored.

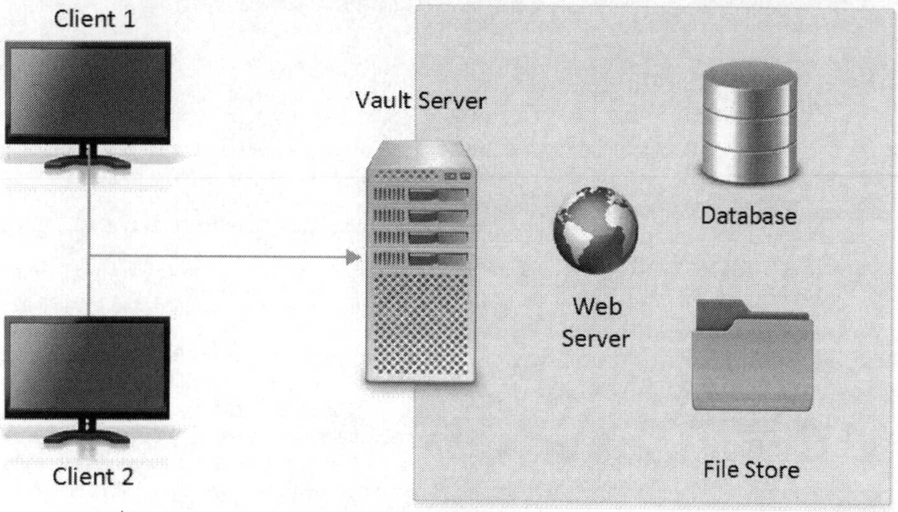

The vault clients are installed on each user's computer and are used to view, extract, and add files and data from the vault. The clients communicate to the vault server through XML-based web services using standard HTTP protocol.

About the Vault Server Software

The Autodesk Vault server consists of the hardware and software that receives transaction requests from clients, processes those transactions, and returns data back to the clients. The software on the Vault server consists of three applications working together to manage the Vault databases and file stores as shown in the following image.

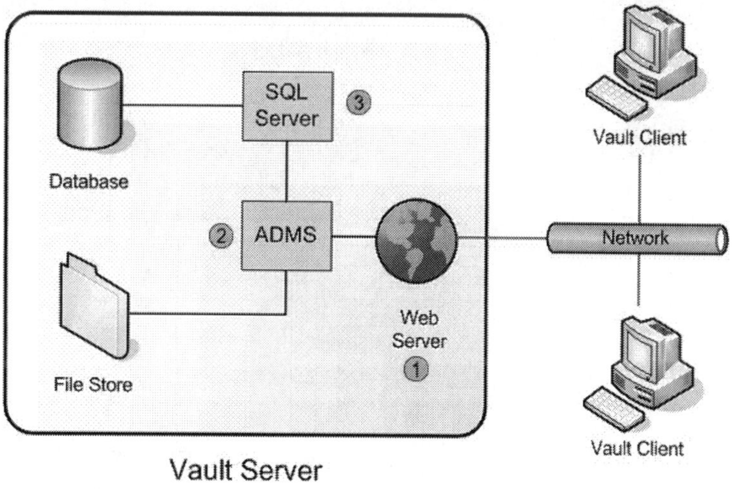

Components of the Vault server:

1. The web server manages web requests and responses between Vault clients and the Vault server. Microsoft Internet Information Services (IIS) is required for the installation of Vault on a stand-alone workstation or on a server that more than one user accesses. You must install IIS before you install Autodesk Data Management Server.

2. Autodesk Data Management Server (ADMS) manages all requests from clients, such as receiving client requests, sending requests to the database server, packaging and returning data back to the clients, and storing and retrieving files from the file store.

3. The database server manages the databases and handles requests for data. By default, Microsoft SQL Server Express, a free, but limited, version of Microsoft SQL Server is installed. Microsoft SQL Server Express has a limit on the size of the databases. The limitations outside the metadata limit are one processor and concurrent users might be limited by the operating system. The full version of SQL Server supports multiple processors as well as many concurrent users, and it has no limit on the database size. If you install Microsoft SQL Server before you install Vault, you can use it instead of Microsoft SQL Server Express. In a true production environment SQL Express is not ideal from a performance perspective.

Setup Scenarios

You must make several decisions before you install Autodesk Vault. The software and hardware you use and how you configure your network are dependent on the number of users, the size of the databases, the size of the file store, and the expected network activity. The typical scenarios outlined below are general guides. Before you install Autodesk Vault, review the Autodesk Vault Implementation Guide.

Single-User Setup

To use Vault in a single-user, single-workstation environment where you do not need to share data with other users, you can install Vault on the same workstation as the CAD application. All components required will be installed during installation of Autodesk Vault. This is typical of a training installation.

Multi-User Setup

When two or more users need to share design data, the Vault must be installed on a computer that is on a network and is accessible to the design team.

For small teams, you can use either one of the design team's workstations, a dedicated workstation, or a dedicated server. Install Vault on either a Windows server operating system or a Windows desktop operating system. You must install Microsoft Internet Information Services before you install Vault because more than one user will be accessing the vault. You can start with Microsoft SQL Server Express and then upgrade to Microsoft SQL Server when your vault databases approach the size limit.

For large teams, consider using a dedicated server running a Windows server operating system. For more than 10 users, you should install Microsoft SQL Server.

Creating Vaults

Most Vault installations use just one vault for their master design data, because data and mappings cannot be shared across vaults. However, you might want to create additional vaults for training so that users can become familiar with Vault procedures without affecting the main vault. You can also use more than one vault to isolate design data. For example, a contractor might want to isolate data from different clients who each have separate libraries and shared content.

After you create a new vault, you need to grant permissions to existing users. If you are creating the vault for training, consider creating different user accounts for training that are granted access to just the training vault so that users don't accidentally add data to the wrong vault.

Process: Creating a Vault

The following process describes how to create a vault.

1. Start Autodesk Data Management Server Console (ADMS Console). Expand the node in the left pane to reveal Vaults. Click Vaults. Click Actions menu>Create.
2. Enter a name for the vault. Accept the default file store location or specify a location.

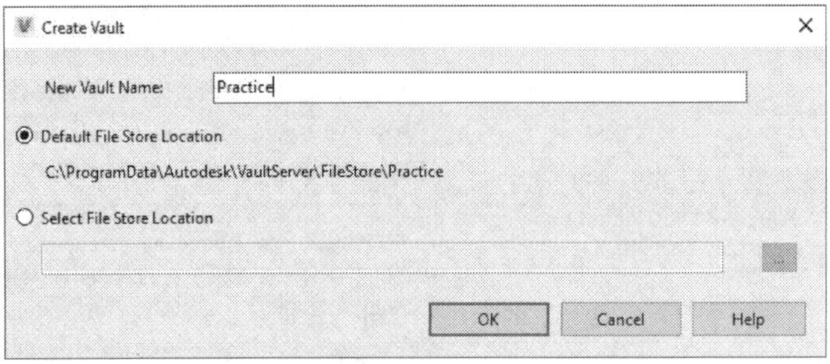

3. Expand Vaults node to reveal the new vault and select it. Review the new vault's properties.

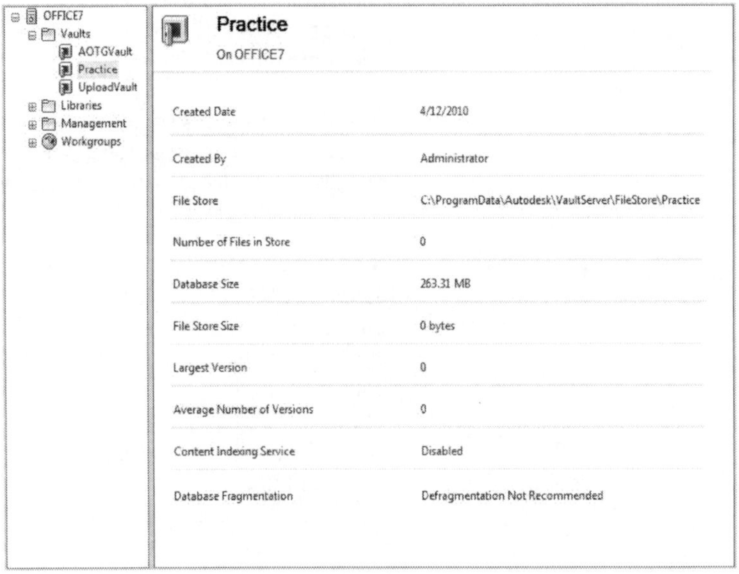

4. Select Tools menu>Administration. Use the Groups and Users workflows to grant users access to the vault.

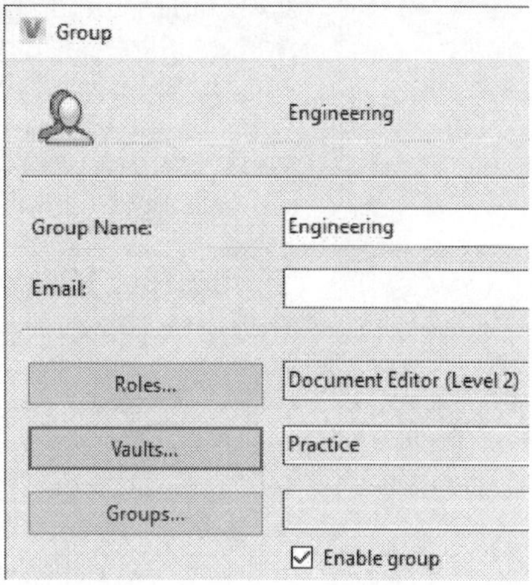

Setting the Environment

When you create a new vault, you must decide whether to enforce unique filenames and to define a working folder for all users or enable users to define their own working folders, and whether or not to enable or disable automatic visualization file attachments.

About Enforcing Unique Filenames

When unique filenames are enforced, files in the vault must each have a unique, identifying name.

This rule is enforced when files are added to the vault, renamed in the vault, or restored to the vault. If unique filenames are going to be enforced, it is recommended that you set this option before any files are added to the vault, although it can be toggled on at any time.

If unique filenames are enforced, and you want to add a project that contains files with names that match files in the vault, you can temporarily disable unique filenames. After you add the project to the vault, locate the duplicate filenames and then rename the duplicate files. When you have finished renaming the files, enforce unique filenames again.

Disabling the Checking In of Design Files in Vault

CAD files should always be added to the vault using the Vault add-in in the CAD application so that file relationships are preserved. By default, users are prevented from adding CAD files using Autodesk Vault. If you want to enable users to add CAD files using Vault, CAD files that have relationships to other files will not maintain those relationships in the vault.

Defining a Working Folder and Autodesk Inventor Project File

A default working folder for all new vaults is predefined as My Documents\Vault, allowing users to immediately begin working with a vault. The default working folder location can be changed by a user to another location. The vault administrator can also enforce a working folder for all users so that users cannot define their own working folder, eliminating the need for users to create a working folder and making a consistent location for vault files on user workstations.

The enforced working folder path can be the following:

- Network path: \\ designco\users\pdollan
- Local path: C:\users\bdunn
- Path containing a system variable for a directory: \\ designco\users\%username%
- Path beginning with My Documents: My Documents\Vault

When the working folder is enforced, any previous working folder settings are replaced with the new path. If an enforced working folder location cannot be applied to a user's settings, the previous user-defined location is used. If there is no previous user-defined location, the default location My Documents\Vault is used.

The default Autodesk Inventor Project file can be set by a user unless the vault administrator enforces a consistent project file for all users. Enforcing a consistent project file for all users can help ensure successful file resolutions when renaming files, for example.

About Visualization Options

Vault uses visualization files (typically DWF™ and DWFx) to display CAD files in the vault. By default, visualization files are automatically created and attached to the corresponding CAD file when you check files in to the vault. Automatic creation can be disabled if you want to reduce the size of the vault or if you do not plan to use visualization files.

Visualization files can also be generated and stored in a folder outside of the vault so that other users who do not have access to the vault can see your designs. As an administrator, you can specify a default folder location for the published files.

If you enable the automatic creation of visualization files, users are not forced to create visualization files each time they check in or add a file. Enabling creation enables the settings in the add-ins so that users can toggle creation on or off. If you disable automatic creation, the settings in the add-in are disabled so that users cannot create visualization files.

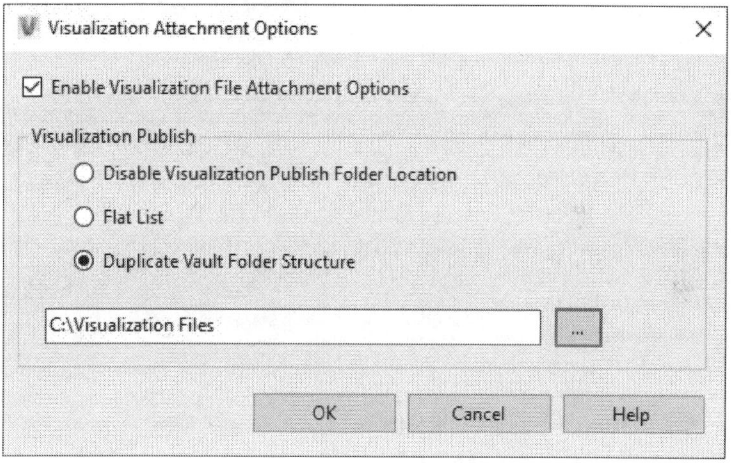

Visualization Publishing Options

A variety of options are available for you to specify what gets published, select the type of visualization file, and fine tune the output of visualization files. The settings are available on an application basis. For example, you can specify different settings for AutoCAD® files, 2D Inventor files, and 3D Inventor files for various releases in the case of Inventor.

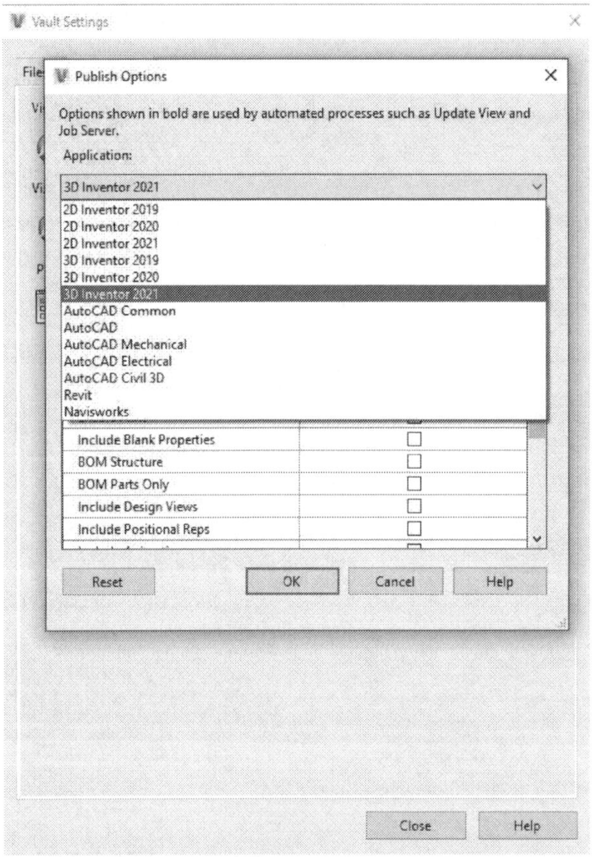

Visualization Commands

The Visualization Commands options enable you to specify which commands break the link between a data file in the vault and its corresponding visualization file. When an operation causes a file to be versioned forward, the link to the visualization file is removed, preventing an out-of-date visualization file from being attached to the data file.

If a command is unchecked, then when that command is performed, the Visualization Compliance property for the data file is set to Not Synchronized to indicate that the visualization file attached to the data file is out of date and might not accurately represent the contents of the data file. When the data file is viewed, you are warned that the visualization file is not synchronized. You can either update the visualization file or manually verify that the visualization file is correct. When a visualization file is verified, the Visualization Compliance property for the data file is set to User Verified.

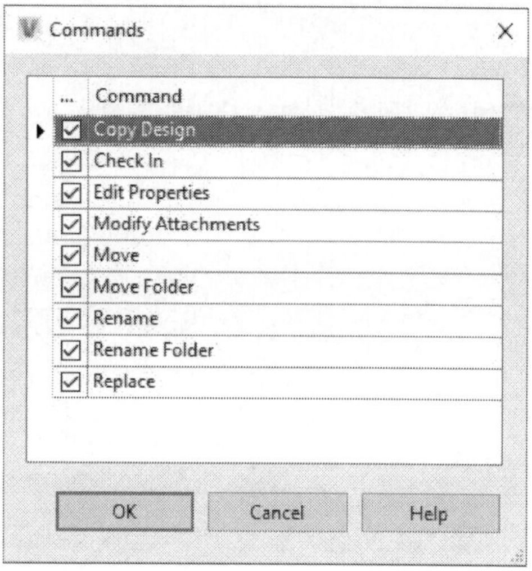

Procedure: Setting the Vault Environment

The following steps describe how to enforce unique filenames, set the working folder, and configure visualization files.

1. Log in to Autodesk Vault as an administrator.
2. Click Tools menu>Administration>Vault Settings.

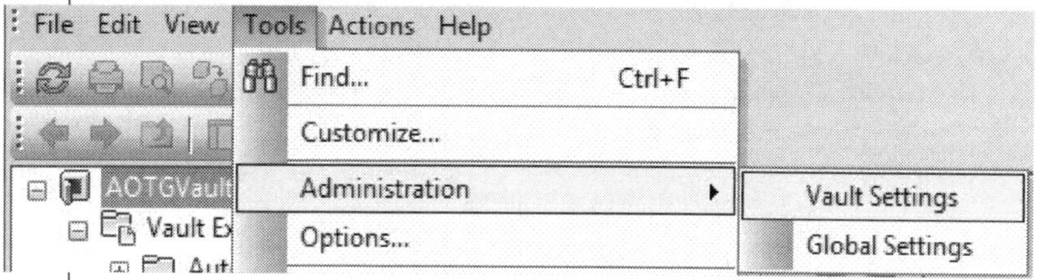

3. The Vault Settings dialog box is displayed.

4. To enforce unique filenames, in the Files tab, under Options, select the Enforce Unique File Names check box.

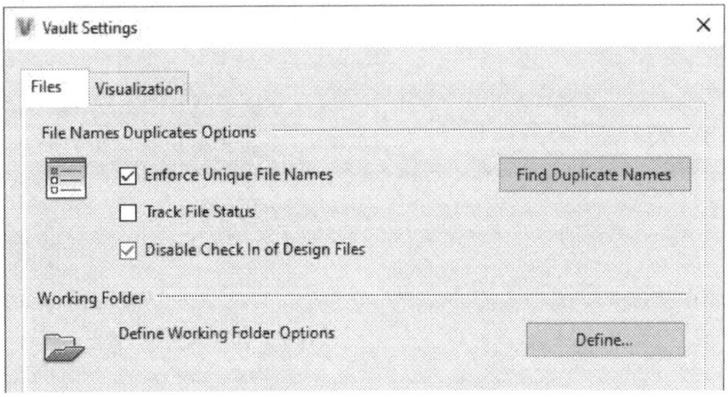

5. To enforce a working folder for all users:
   - Under Working Folder, click Define.
   - In the Working Folder Options dialog box, select the Enforce Consistent Working Folder for All Clients check box.
   - Enter or select a folder name.

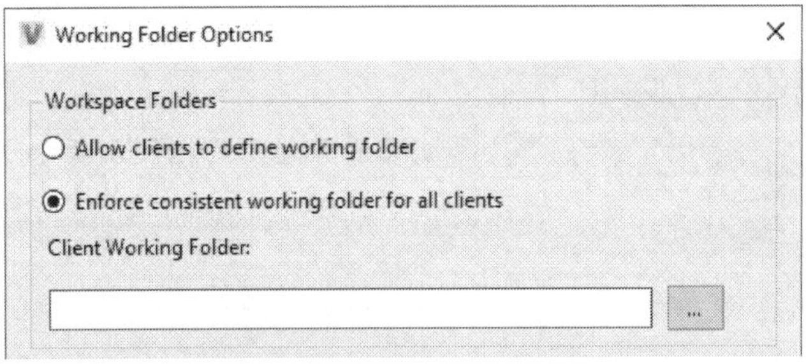

6. To enforce a consistent project file for all users:
   - In the Working Folder Options dialog box, select the Enforce Consistent Project File for All Clients check box.
   - Enter or select a project file.

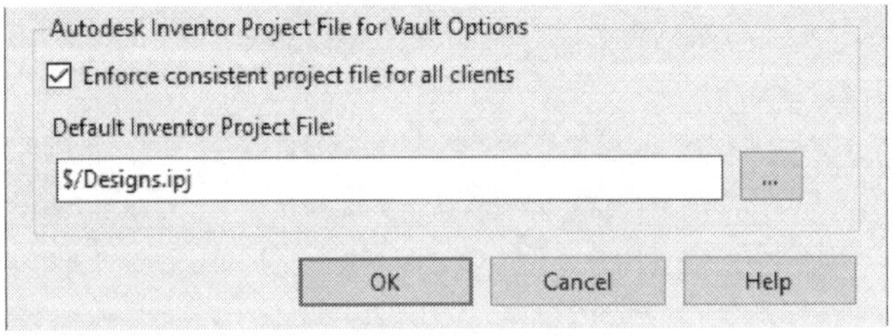

7. To set visualization options, click the Visualization tab.

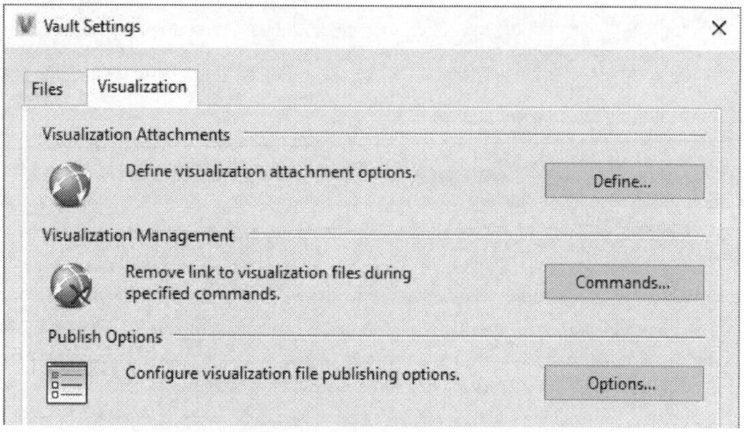

8. To set visualization file attachment options:
   - Under Visualization Attachments, click Define.
   - In the Visualization Attachment Options dialog box, select Enable Visualization File Attachment Options to enable or disable the attachment options in Vault add-ins.
   - To publish visualization files to a location outside of the vault, under Visualization Publish, select an option. Enter a folder name if appropriate.

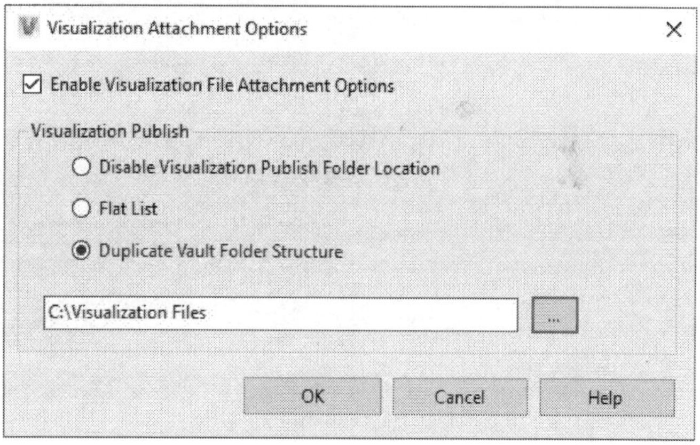

9. To remove the link between a visualization file and its underlying file when a specified command is executed, do the following:
   - On the Visualization tab, under Visualization Management, click Commands.
   - Select which commands should cause the link to be removed.

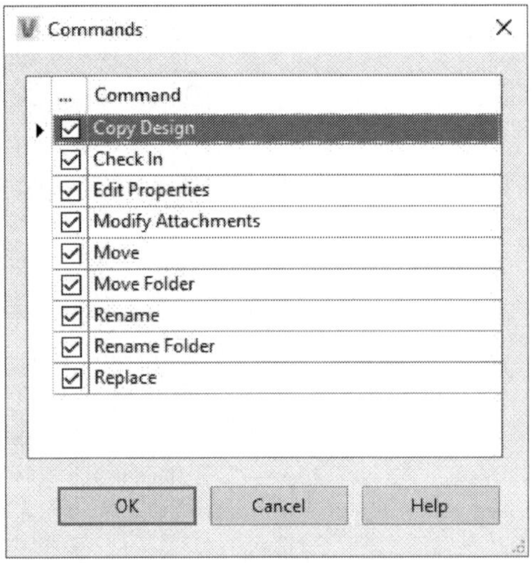

10. To specify the visualization file format, select what's included in visualization files, and tune visualization file settings:
    - On the Visualization tab, under Publish Options, click Options.
    - Select the Application to which the visualization settings will apply.
    - Select the appropriate settings.
    - Repeat for all of the applications you are using.

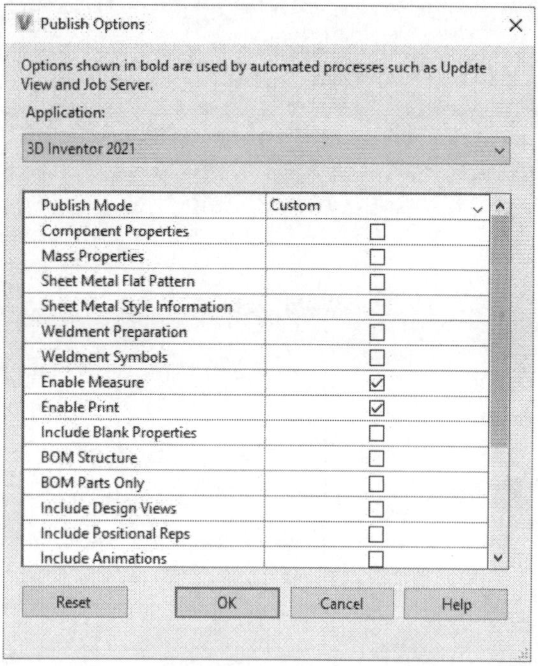

Practice 10a Create and Set Up a Vault

In this practice, you create a vault, review vault settings, and set a common working folder. You then add a file to the vault and examine both the vault databases and vault file store.

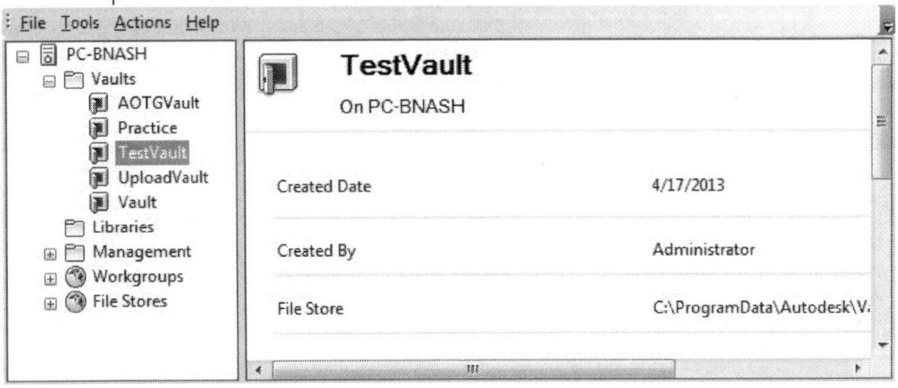

The completed practice

1. Start Autodesk Data Management Server (ADMS) Console. Log in as an administrator. The password is blank.
2. In the list of vaults, expand the Vaults folder. View the existing vaults.
3. Right-click the Vaults folder. Click Create.

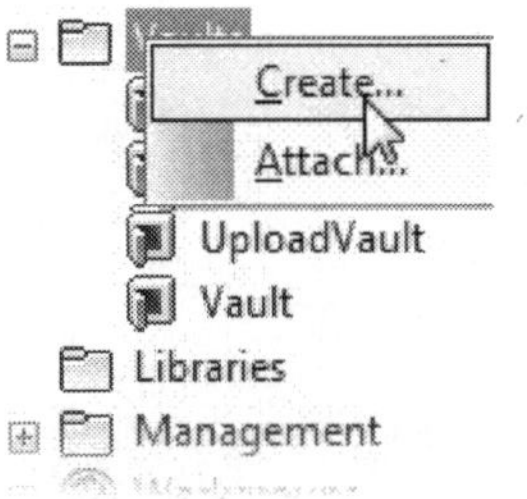

4. Enter **TestVault** for the new vault name. Review the default file store location. Click OK.
5. When the message box is displayed to indicate that the vault was successfully created, click OK to close the message box.

6. In the list of vaults, click TestVault. Review the database size and the file store location.

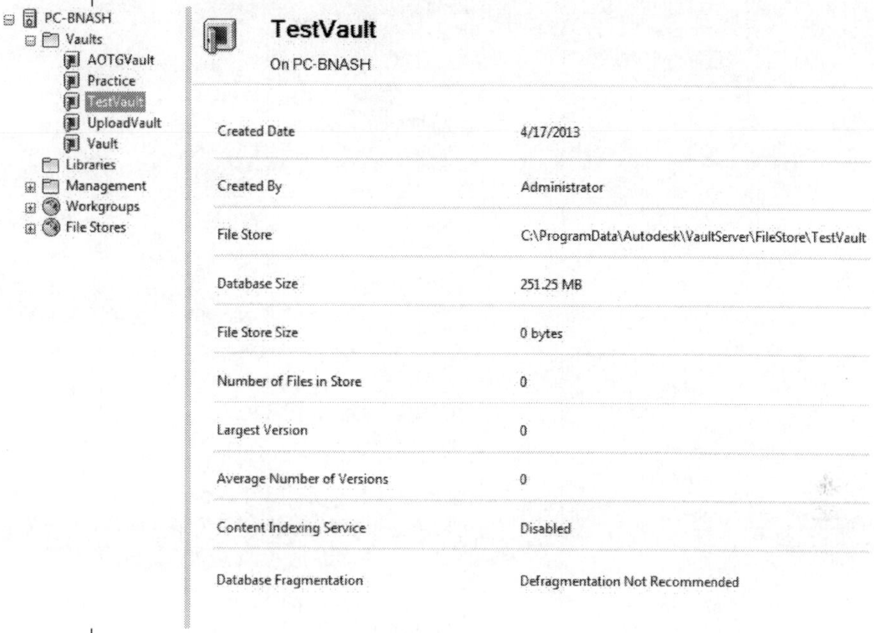

7. Start Autodesk Vault. Log in as an administrator to TestVault. The password is blank. If you were already logged in to Autodesk Vault, log out and then log back in.

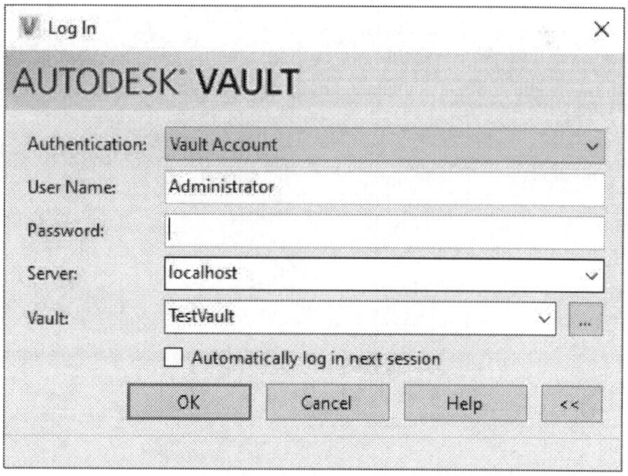

8. Click Tools menu>Administration>Vault Settings.

9. On the Files tab, under Options, select the Enforce Unique File Names check box to toggle it on.

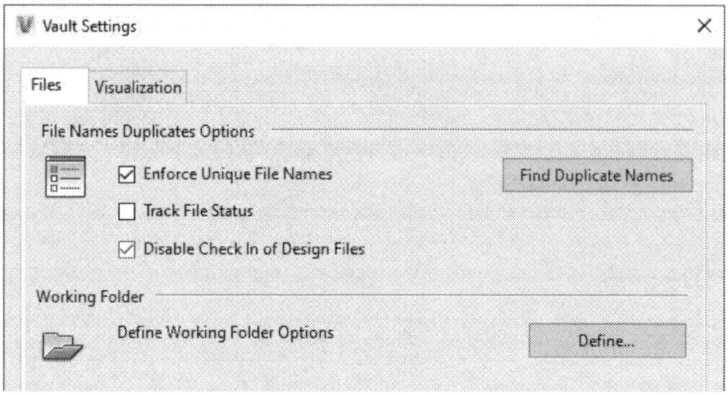

10. Under Working Folder, click Define.

11. In the Working Folder Options dialog box, click Enforce Consistent Working Folder for All Clients. For Client Working Folder, click [...]. Create the folder TestVault under *C:\Users\Public\TestVault.* Click OK.

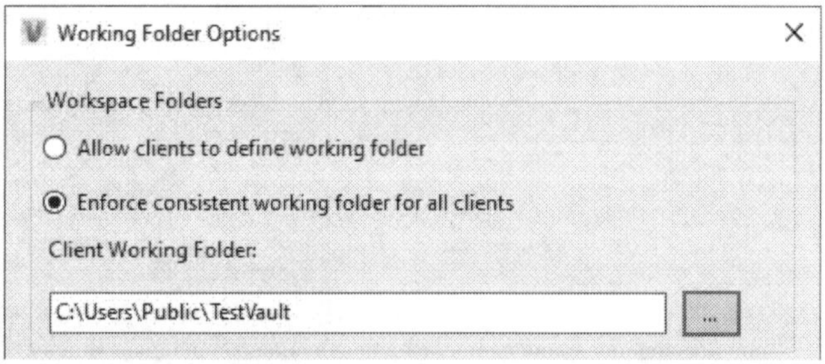

12. Click OK to close the Working Folder Options dialog box.

13. Select the Visualization tab. Under Visualization Attachments, click Define. In the Visualization Attachment Options dialog box, review the settings. Click OK.

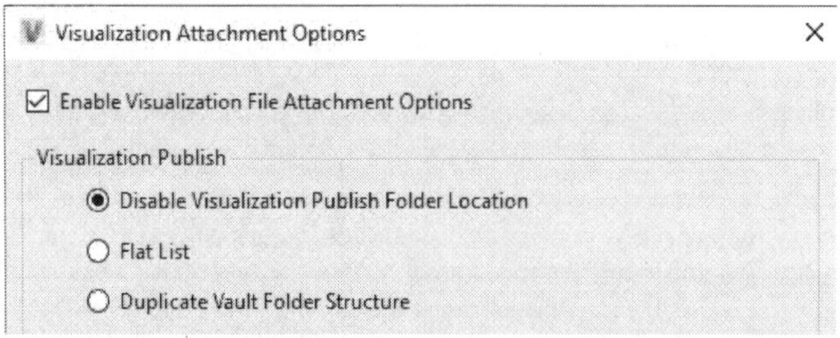

14. Under Visualization Management, click Commands. Confirm that all check boxes are selected. Click OK.

15. Under Publish Options, click Options. In the Publish Options dialog box, under Application, select 3D Inventor 2021. Select the Include Positional Reps check box to include positional reps in DWF files. Click OK.

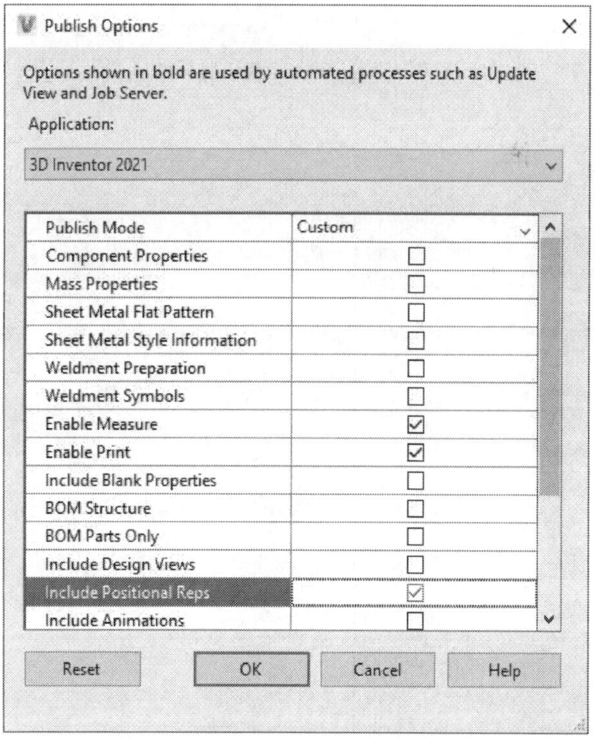

16. Click Close to dismiss the Vault Settings dialog.

17. In the Tools menu, select Administration and then Global Settings, to display the Global Settings dialog.

18. Under Users section, click Users...

19. Note that you can access the same User Management dialog box as you did from the ADMS console.

20. Close the User Management and then the Global Settings dialog boxes.

21. Click Tools menu>Options. Under Options, select the Show Working Folder Location check box. Review the other options. Click OK.

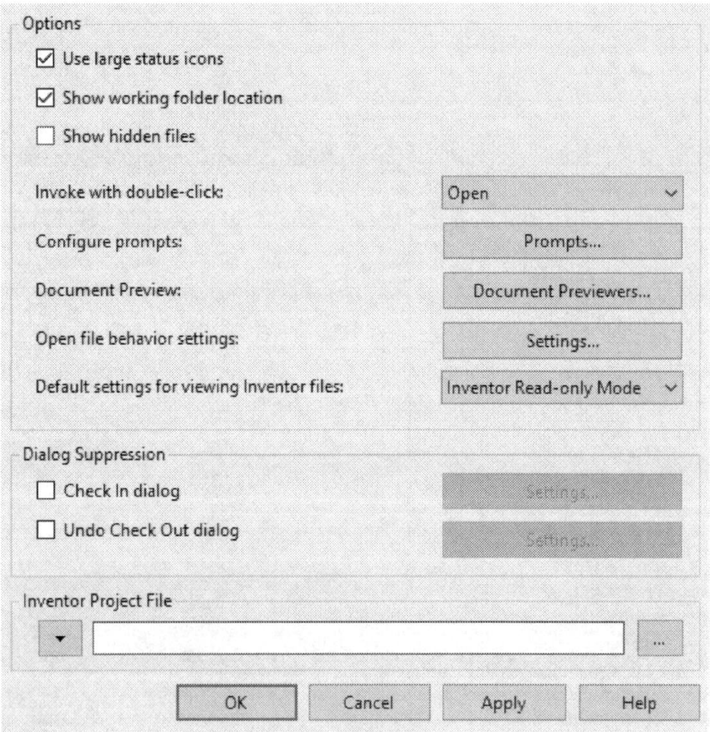

22. Click File menu>Log Out. Log in again as an administrator.

23. Click OK to close the Enforce Working Folder dialog box.

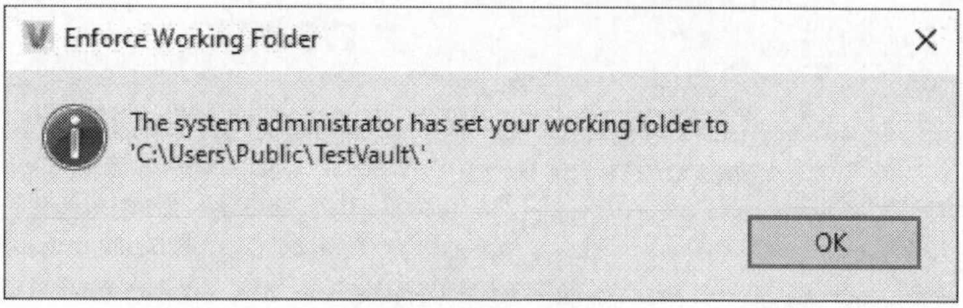

24. Confirm that the working folder is displayed in the title bar.

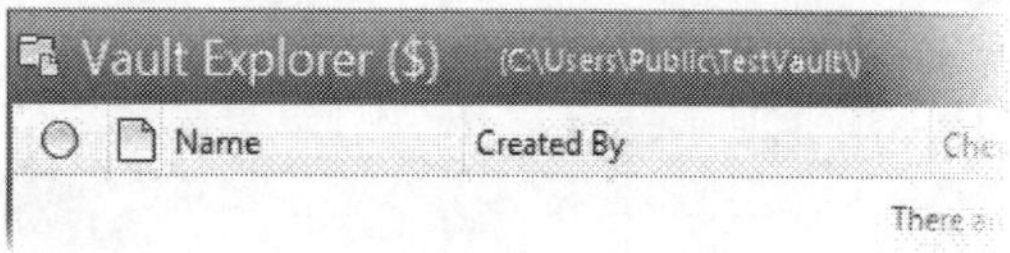

25. Add a non-CAD file to the vault using any of the methods you have learned in previous practices. Use a simple file such as a Microsoft Office document or text document.

    Tip: Drag the file into the vault. Due to vaulting restrictions, you will not be able to drag a CAD file into the vault.

26. In Windows Explorer, navigate to the file store for TestVault and continually expand the folders until you locate the file that you added. Note that the file was renamed but the file is stored in its native format.

    Tip: The location of the file store is displayed on the property page in ADMS Console.

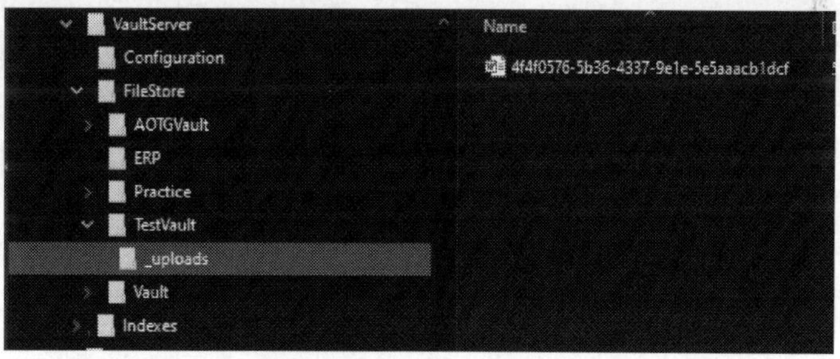

    Note: Do not rename, delete, move, or change files in the file store.

27. Close both Autodesk Vault and ADMS Console.

10.2 Managing Users and Access

Overview

A user must have an account before logging in to a vault. The administrator is responsible for creating new user accounts, creating groups of users, assigning roles to users or groups, and granting access to vaults.

You manage users in the Global Settings dialog box as shown in the following image.

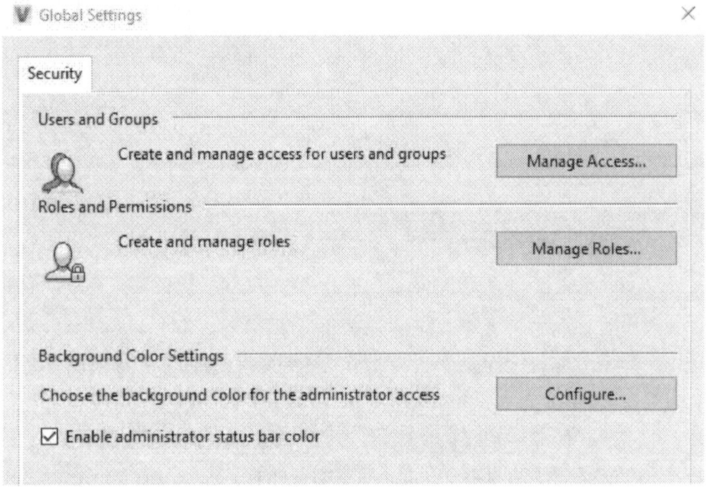

Hint: Windows Authentication

In this lesson, you employ the user authentication that is built in to Autodesk Data Management Server. If you use Vault Professional, you can also use Windows authentication to manage user access. See Help for more information.

Objectives

After completing this lesson, you will be able to:

- Describe how groups and roles are used to control user access.
- Create users and groups, assign roles, and grant access to vaults.

Creating Users and Groups

A user account is required before a user can log in and access vault data. The administrator can specify which vaults a user can access and the user's permissions. User permissions can be controlled for individual users or for groups of users.

The following image displays the Global Settings dialog box where you access tools to administer users.

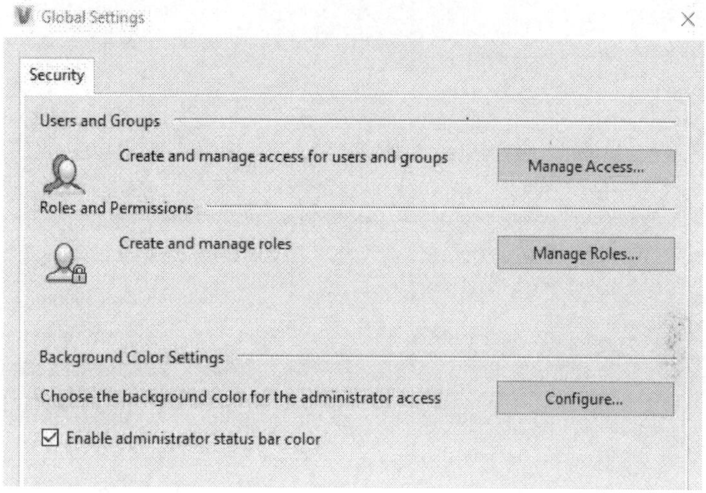

About User Accounts

In Vault, permissions control the access at the vault level. If you assign a user or group to a vault, the permissions apply to all files and folders in the vault.

To access a vault and its associated data, a user must have an account with the appropriate access permissions. As an administrator, you can add users, group users together for easy management, define roles, and assign access permissions. You should create unique user accounts for each user of Vault to ensure that Vault transactions are secure and can be tracked.

About User Roles

You assign access permission to vaults by assigning one or more predefined roles to users or to groups of users. The permissions for that role apply to all files and folders in the vaults to which the user or group is assigned.

You can also create your own custom roles. You can do this by creating a new role, editing a role, or copying an existing role to then edit. For example, you can copy the Document Editor Level 2 role and then remove the Folder Create permission so that users cannot create their own folders within the vault.

You can assign users to several predefined roles. Some roles apply to users of Autodesk Vault and some apply to the Autodesk Inventor Content Center as listed in the following table. Privileges are additive, so a user assigned multiple roles has all the privileges of the assigned roles.

Role	Permissions
Document Consumer	Read folders and files Read labels Set Vault get options Edit the user profile
Document Editor (Level 1)	Includes all the permissions of a Document Consumer plus: Check out, create, and add files Create folders Create labels Override file status Modify visualization attachments
Document Editor (Level 2)	Includes all the permissions of a Document Editor (Level 1) plus: Move, rename, and delete files Rename and delete folders Delete labels
Content Center Editor	Includes all the permissions of a Document Editor (Level 2) plus: Add and delete categories Publish content
Content Center Administrator	All tasks of the Content Center Editor plus: Manage libraries
Administrator	All tasks listed above plus: Manage users, vaults, and libraries Log in to ADMS Console

About Groups

Individual users have roles and permissions assigned to them that define what actions they can take and to which vaults they have access. To manage multiple users efficiently, you can create groups of users and assign roles and permissions to the group. As a member of a group, a user has all the permissions and roles assigned to the group.

Groups can be composed of users or other groups. Groups can be disabled, thereby toggling off all permissions assigned to the group.

Guidelines for Managing Users and Groups

Follow these guidelines to manage groups efficiently:

- Assign most permissions at group level: If you use groups, consider assigning most permissions at the group level and not for each individual user. For example, to assign most users the Document Editor (Level 1) role, create a group, add the users, and assign the group the Document Editor (Level 1) role. If one or two users also need to be Content Center Editors, either create another group for those users or assign the permissions at the user level. You will be able to manage users more easily if you are consistent with the way that you assign permissions.

- Disable permissions at the group level: If a group is no longer required or you want to stop access for all of the users that belong to just that group, you can disable the group, removing permissions assigned to the group.

Procedure: Adding a New User

The following steps describe how to add a new user and assign the user to a group.

1. In Autodesk Vault, select the Tools menu>Administration> Global Settings or in ADMS Console, click Tools menu> Administration. For access through ADMS, click the Security tab if not already displayed (there is only one tab when accessing through Vault).

   Note: You can access the user management tools through either ADMS Console or Autodesk Vault. By administering users through Autodesk Vault, you can manage users from any computer on which Autodesk Vault is installed rather than through ADMS Console, which runs only on the Vault server.

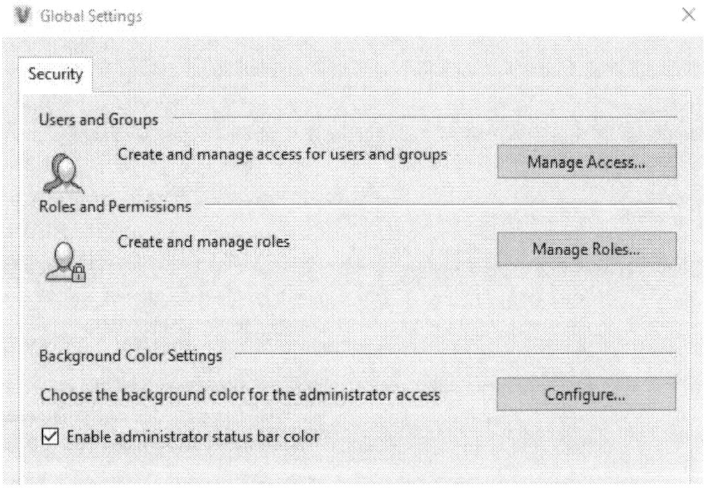

2. Under Users, click Users to display the User Management dialog.

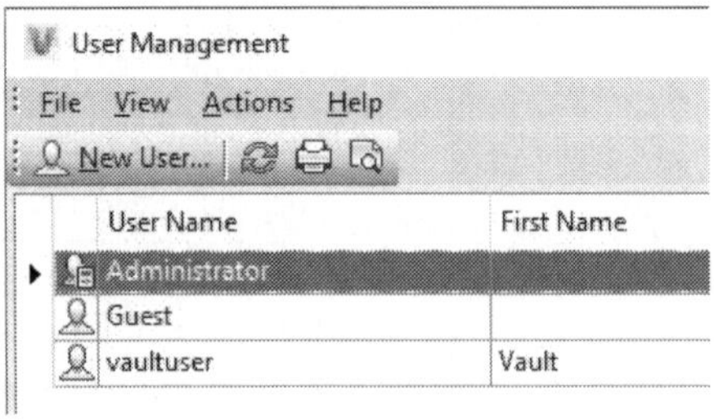

3. Click New User. Enter the user data. Users can change their first and last names, email, and password through Vault Explorer.

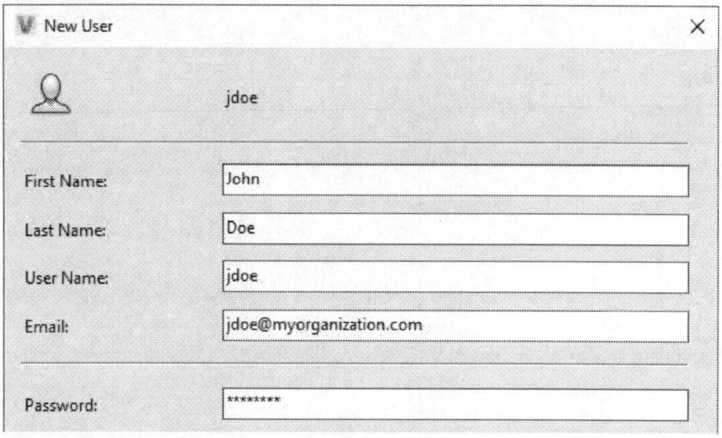

4. If you are controlling permissions using groups, do not enter roles or vaults. If a few users require special permissions, specify the roles and vaults at the user level.

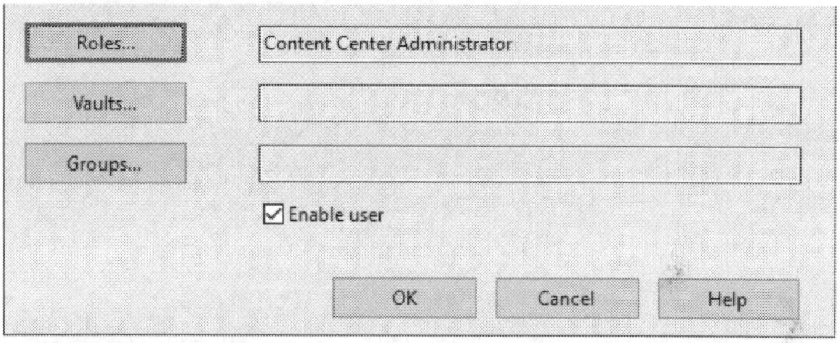

5. To create a new group, on the Security tab, under Groups, click Groups. In the Group Management dialog box, click New Group.

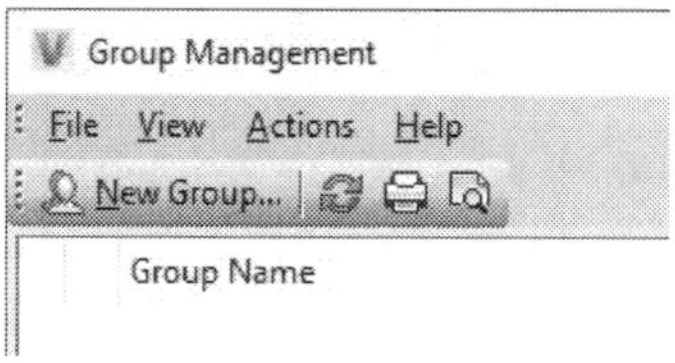

6. In the Group dialog box, enter the name for the group. Select the roles to apply to all members of the group. Select which vaults the group members can access with the selected roles.

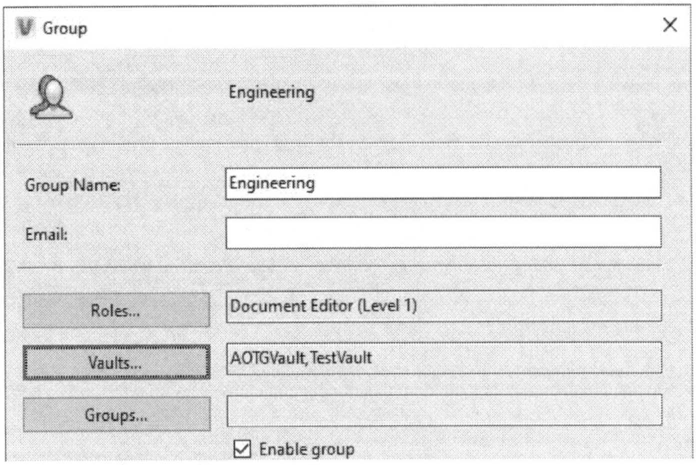

7. Add existing users to the group. Once a group is created, you can also assign users to the group from the User dialog box. A group requires at least one member to be added.

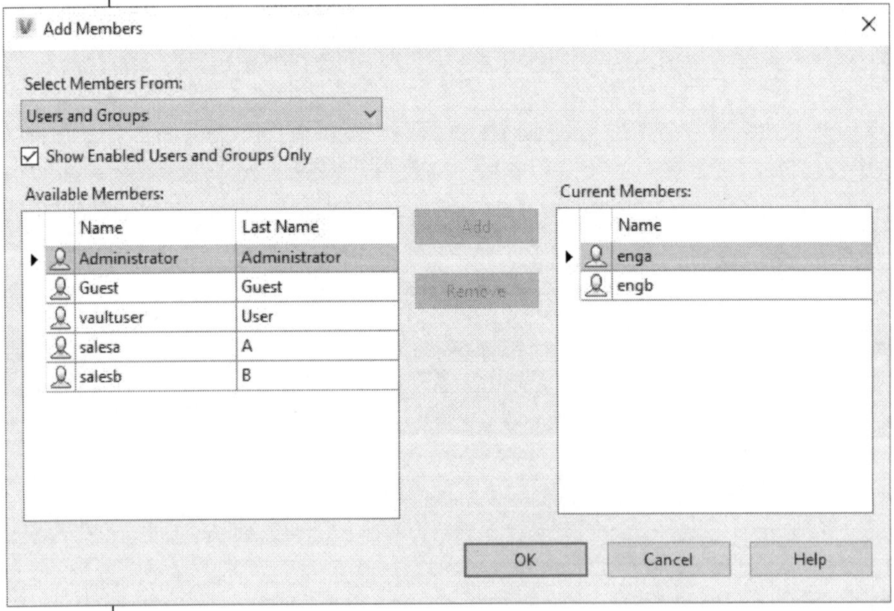

Practice 10b Manage Users and Access

In this practice, you add users and groups to a vault. Users in engineering add models to the vault and require editor permission. One engineering user manages the content center libraries and must be given appropriate permission. All users in sales need read-only access to the vault in order to view models.

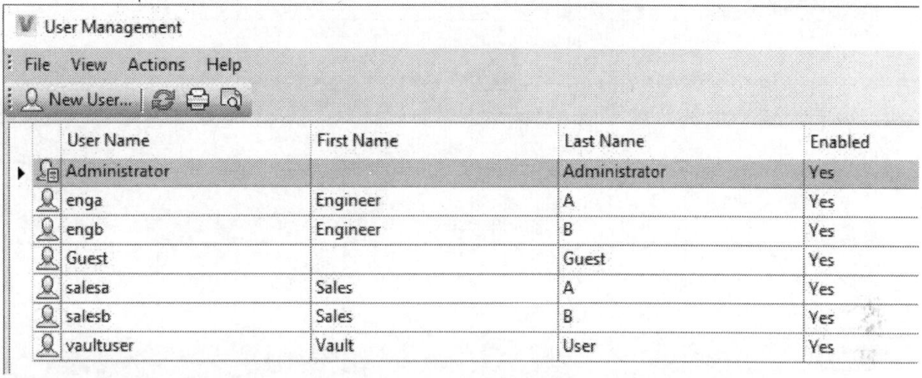

The completed practice

1. Start ADMS Console. Log in as administrator. The password is blank.

   Note: You can also administer users from Autodesk Vault.

2. Click Tools menu>Administration.

3. On the Security tab, under Roles and Permissions, click Manage Roles.

4. In the Roles Management dialog box, review the permissions for the Document Editor (Level 1) and Document Consumer roles. In the Roles Management dialog box, select Document Consumer and click Edit. Review the list in Selected Permissions. Close the Edit Role dialog box. Select the Document Editor (Level 1) and click Edit. Review the Selected Permissions and note the differences compared to the Document Consumer role.

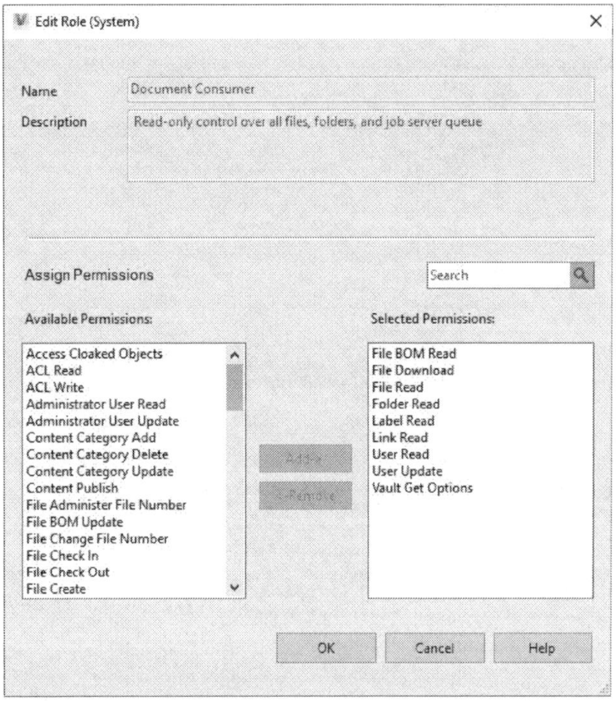

5. Click Manage Users. In the User Management dialog box, click View>By Vault. Review the users for TestVault.

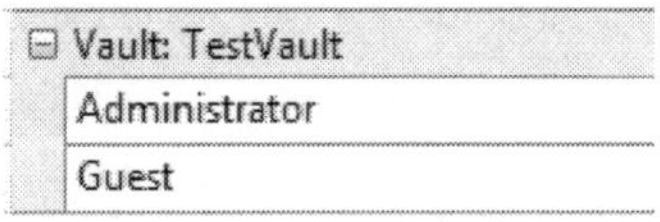

6. Click New User. Create a user with the following data:

- First Name: Engineer.
- Last Name: A.
- User Name: enga.
- Password: vault.
- Roles: leave the box empty.
- Vaults: leave the box empty.

7. Add another user with the following data:

   - First Name: Engineer.
   - Last Name: B.
   - User Name: engb.
   - Password: vault.
   - Roles: Content Center Editor.
   - Vaults: leave the box empty.

8. Add a third user with the following data:

   - First Name: Sales.
   - Last Name: A.
   - User Name: salesa.
   - Password: vault.
   - Roles: leave the box empty.
   - Vaults: leave the box empty.

9. Add a fourth user with the following data:

   - First Name: Sales.
   - Last Name: B.
   - User Name: salesb.
   - Password: vault.
   - Roles: leave the box empty.
   - Vaults: leave the box empty.

10. In the User and Group Management dialog box, note that the users are not assigned to a vault.

User Name	First Name	Last Name
⊟ Vault: (none)		
enga	Engineer	A
engb	Engineer	B
salesa	Sales	A
salesb	Sales	B

11. Close the User and Group Management dialog box.

12. Under Groups, click Manage Groups. In the Group Management dialog box, click New Group.

13. In the Group dialog box, enter the following data:

   - Group Name: **Engineering**
   - Roles: **Document Editor (Level 1)**
   - Vaults: **TestVault**

14. Under Group Members, click Add.

15. In the Available Members list, select enga and engb. Click Add. Click OK twice to close both the Add Members and Group dialog boxes.

16. Add another group named Sales. Grant Document Consumer access to TestVault. Add salesa and salesb as group members.

17. In the Group Management dialog box, review the two groups.

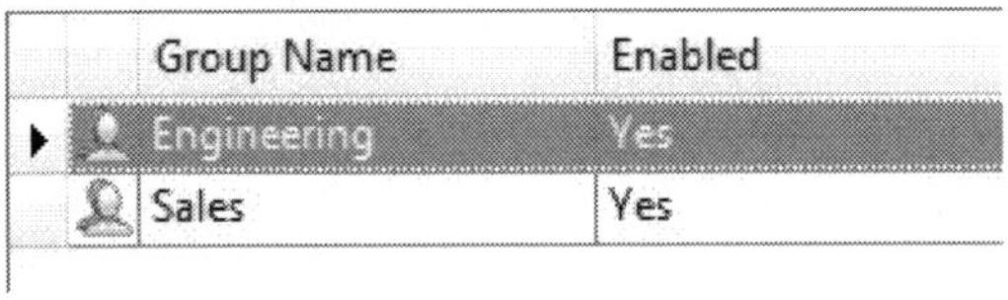

18. Close the Group Management dialog box.

19. Close the Global Settings dialog box.

20. Start Autodesk Vault. Log in using the following information:

- User Name: salesa.
- Password: vault.
- Vault: TestVault.

21. Click File menu>User Profile. Change the password to sales. Click OK.

22. Log out of Autodesk Vault. Log back in to confirm that the password was changed to sales.
23. Try to create a new folder in the vault.
24. Because salesa does not have adequate permissions, the user cannot create a folder.

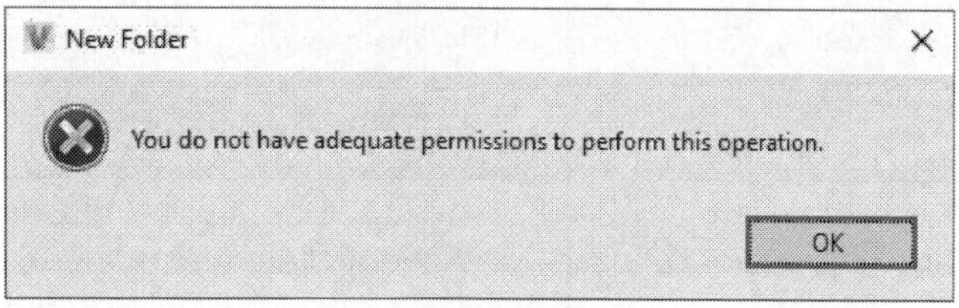

25. Log out and then close Autodesk Vault. Close ADMS Console.

10.3 Managing File Properties

Overview

When you add a file to the vault, the file's properties are stored in the vault database. The group of properties, called metadata, is used for tracking and finding files in the vault. It is important to manage properties so that users can efficiently use properties in their vault workflows.

Two types of properties are in Autodesk Vault. System properties are predefined and are included in every file's database record in the vault. A default set of User Defined properties are shipped with the system and mapped to the most common file properties. The values of these User Defined properties are automatically set when you add a file to the vault. As an Administrator you can add additional User defined properties that are used in your company and map them to the file properties of common applications or change the mapping of the default set. The administrator can also rename file properties, select which file properties should be searched, and perform other property management tasks.

The following image displays the Property Definitions dialog box where you manage properties.

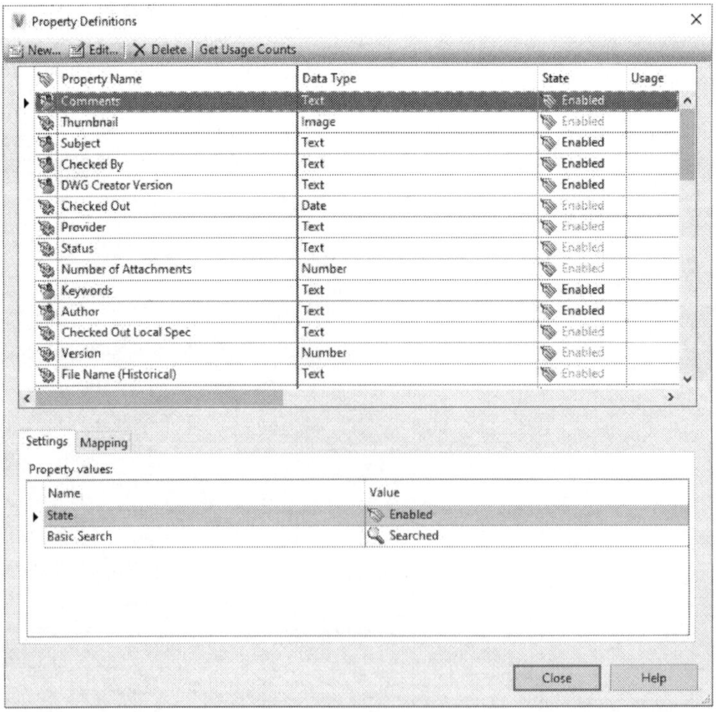

Objectives

After completing this lesson, you will be able to:

- Rename properties.
- Remove properties from a vault.
- Map User Defined Properties to indexed file properties.
- Add AutoCAD block attributes to a vault as properties.
- Add properties for other file formats.
- Re-index vault databases to reflect property changes.

Renaming Properties

File properties are important for locating and organizing files in the vault. When a file is added to the vault, the file's properties are extracted from the file and stored in the vault database. The names of file properties (in the file) are determined by the company's standards. The names of user-defined file properties in the vault are determined by the vault administrator, also generally based on company standards. They can be the same as the actual file properties, or can differ to be more readable in Vault, for example. Vault adds several more properties, called system properties, whose names are predefined.

Each property has two names, the property name and the display name. If the property name for a file or system property is not meaningful to users or does not meet your company's standards, you can change the display name.

Procedure: Renaming Properties

The following steps describe how to rename a property.

1. Log in to Autodesk Vault as an administrator.
2. Click Tools menu>Administration>Vault Settings. On the Files tab, click Properties.

Click a column header to sort by that column.

3. In the Property Definitions dialog box, select the property to rename. Click Edit.

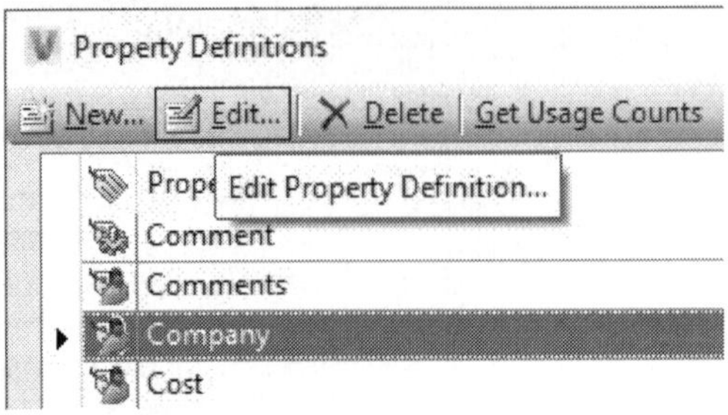

4. For Property Name, enter a new name.

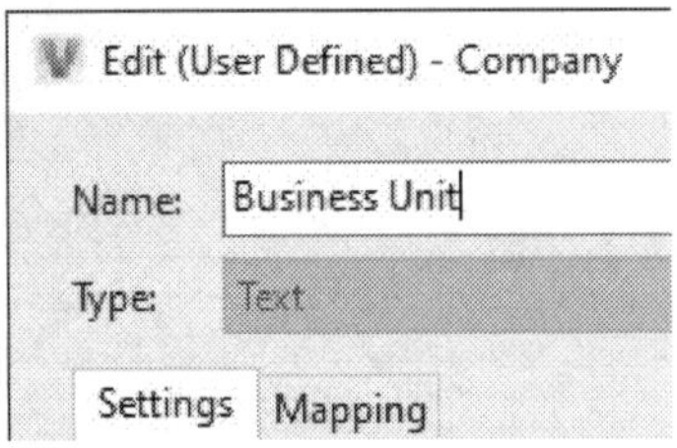

Changing Property States

Vault properties are updated from the file when there is a mapping between the property of a file and that of the vault. Additionally, the Vault only extracts values of properties from files where a mapping exists between the file property and a vault property. All others are ignored. This keeps databases small for improved performance and reduces confusion by limiting the number of properties that users can access.

You can change the state of a file property from "Disabled" to "Enabled" if you plan to use the property for searching or reporting. The state of system properties cannot be changed; they are always in the database.

By default, the values of a property are searched when you perform a basic search from the Find dialog. If there are many properties in a large database this could impact the performance of the Find operation. You can change this default by setting the Basic Search value from "Searched" to "Not Searched." Later, if you find that you need to be able to search these you can re-enable them so they are again searched. Note that you can always search an enabled property from the Advanced tab of the Find dialog.

Procedure: Changing Property States & Basic Search

The following steps describe how to change a property's state and basic search values.

Change the state of more than one property by selecting multiple properties before you click Edit.

1. Log in to Autodesk Vault as an administrator.
2. Click Tools menu>Administration>Vault Settings. On the Files tab, click Properties.
3. In the Property Definitions dialog box, select the property to change. Click Edit.

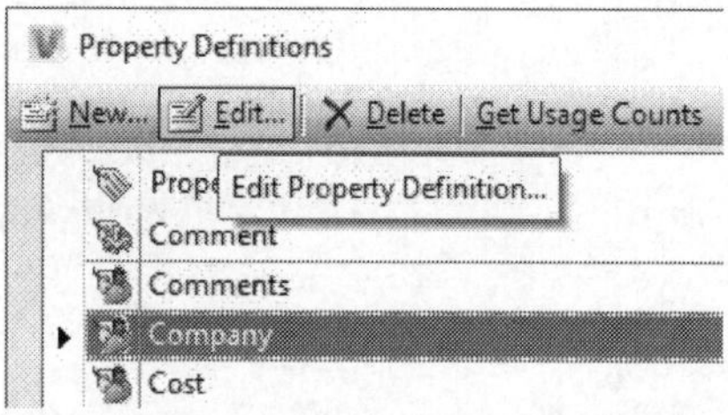

4. Change the state to Enabled or Disabled.

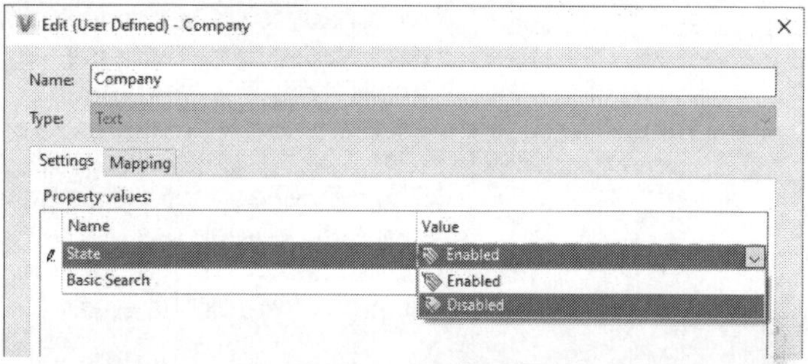

5. You can also make the property available in the Basic Search tool by changing the Basic Search field from Not Searched to Searched.

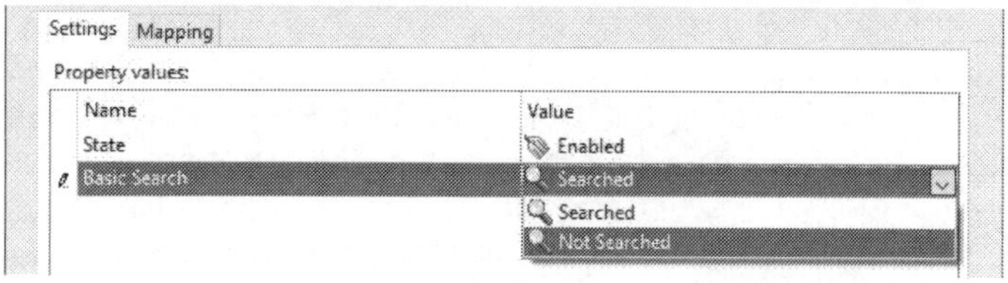

6. Log in to ADMS Console. Re-index the properties for the corresponding vault so that the values of new in-use properties are added to the database and not-in-use properties are removed.

Mapping Properties

Many companies need to manage model files from different applications or with different standards. If a certain property is named differently in different files, you can map the different properties into one user defined property.

About Mapping Properties

Different file formats use different names for similar properties. Also, some files include properties that are similar and it is difficult to determine which property holds the data.

You can manage several file properties as one Vault property by mapping them. When you map two or more file properties, the values of those properties are used to set the value of a single user defined property. Conversely, if you edit a user defined property value using the Edit Property command, mapping enables you to set the value of the mapped file properties from the new value of the user defined property. That way, you can change the value of a mapped user defined property in the Vault and when you check out the file in the authoring application the file property value is correct. You can also control the order in which values are set. This is useful in cases where there is older data whose property name might be different for the same application. The first property value that is not blank is used to set the property value.

The following image displays the results of merging the Engineer and Author properties into one user defined property Engineer. It indicates how it is mapped from Autodesk Inventor and two different Word documents.

The user defined property is mapped to the iProperty Engineer in Inventor. When an Inventor file is checked in, if the Engineer iProperty has a value it will be used to set the value of the user defined property.

Now take the case of a specification document written in word. Some of the Engineering groups have consistently used the standard Word property Author. However, another Engineering group has a template with a custom property Engineer that is used to specify the responsible engineer. In this case Vault will first look to see if the custom property Engineer exists and has a value. If not, it then looks to see if the standard property Author has a value.

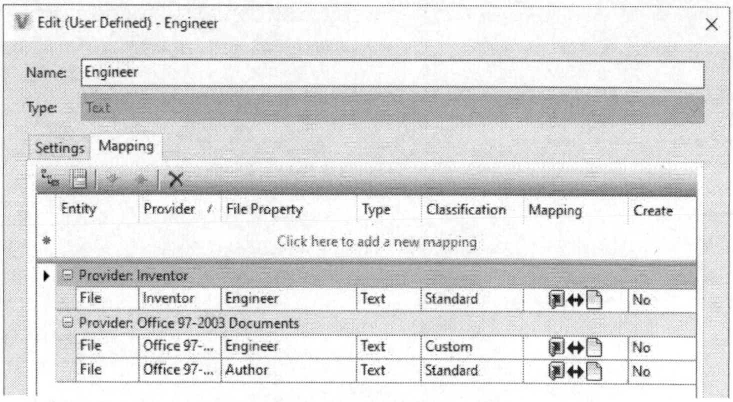

Note that in the case where there is no value, for either the Inventor or the Word document, the user defined property value will not be set.

Mapping Property Rules

The following rules apply when you map properties:

- Generally, only user defined (non-system) properties can be merged. Originator, Original Create Date and Thumbnail are exceptions.
- Properties of different types can be mapped with some exceptions. There are special considerations when mapping properties of different types.
- Put the most important or most commonly used property first. The order of the merged properties is important. When a merged property is assigned a value, the merged properties are checked in the order in which they are defined. The first nonblank property is used for the merged property's value. The remaining properties are not checked.

Procedure: Mapping Properties

The following steps describe how to map property values for a new user defined property.

1. Log in to Autodesk Vault as an administrator.
2. Click Tools menu>Administration>Vault Settings. On the Files tab, under Properties, click Properties.

3. Create the user defined property and ensure that it is enabled.

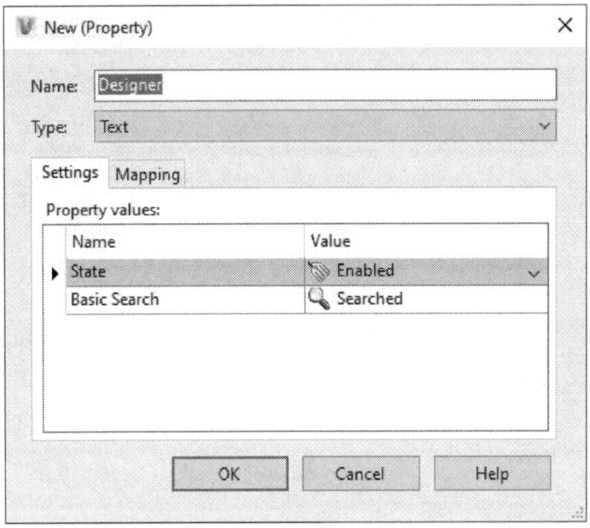

4. Select the Mapping tab and click on the space Click here to add a new mapping.

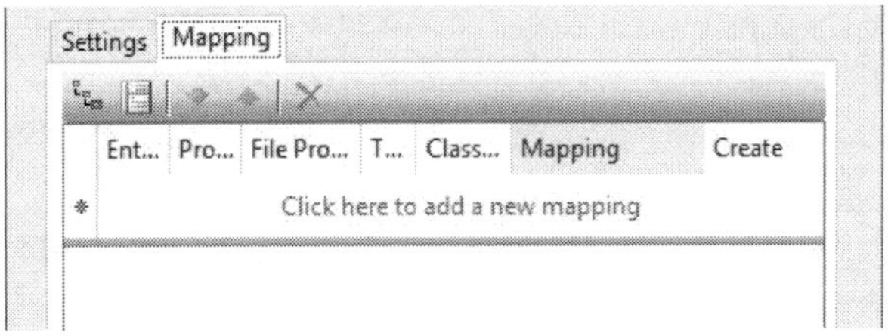

5. In the Provider field, select the application.

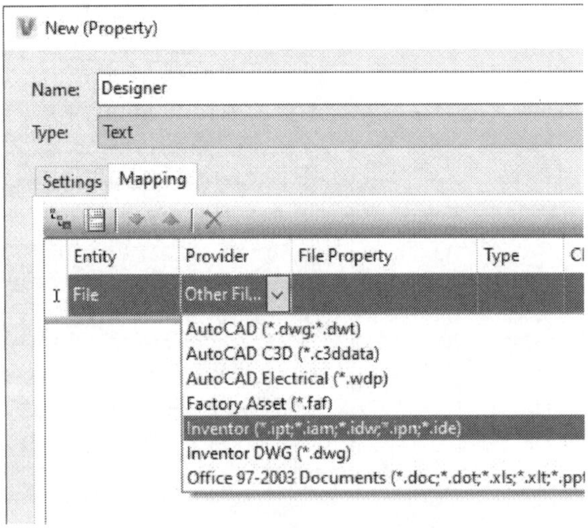

6. In the File Property field, select the property to map to. You will need to Import Properties from a representative file in the vault which contains a file property with a value.

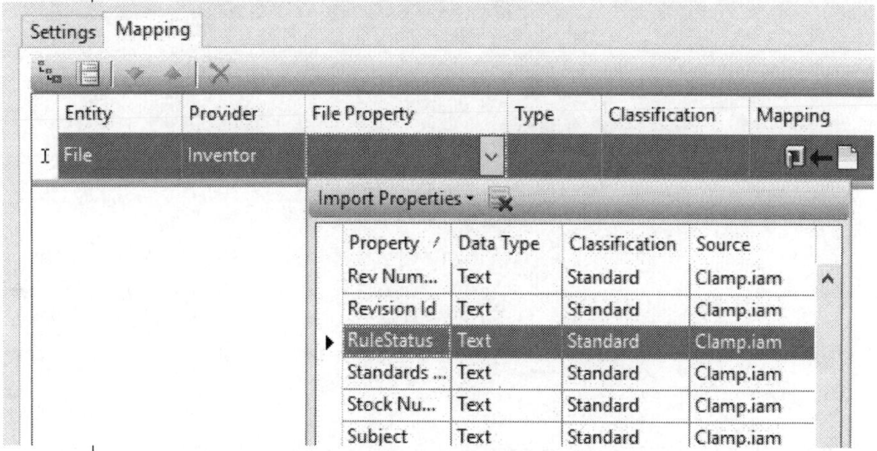

7. Specify the Mapping. Select if you want the file property to write to the user defined property, the user defined property to write to the file property, or both.

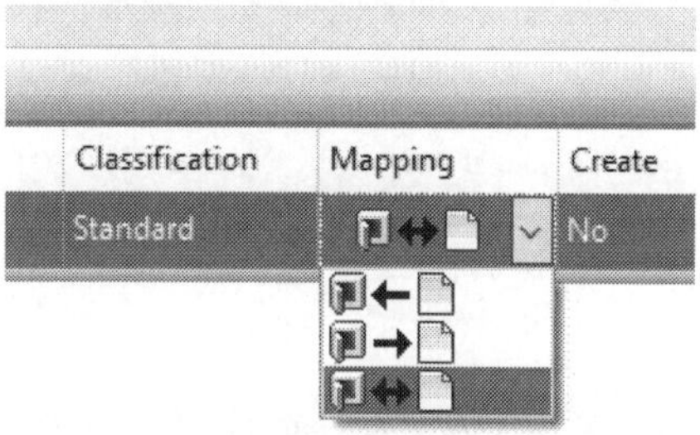

8. Specify the Create option. The Create option applies to write mappings; if the file property does not exist when a value is pushed to the file, the administrator can choose whether the file property is created or not.

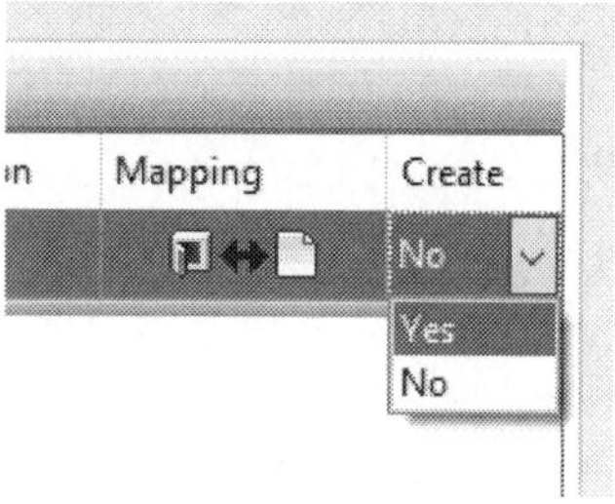

9. Specify the second application, if required.

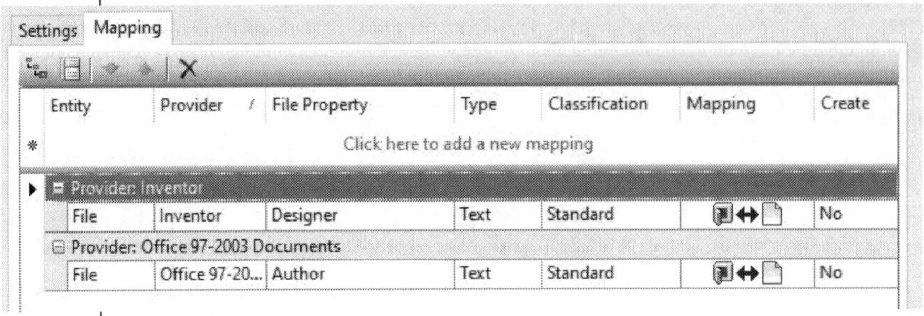

10. If there are files from the same application to be managed that have a file property that might be different than the ones mapped, specify it. Use the Up and Down arrows to specify which value to check first.

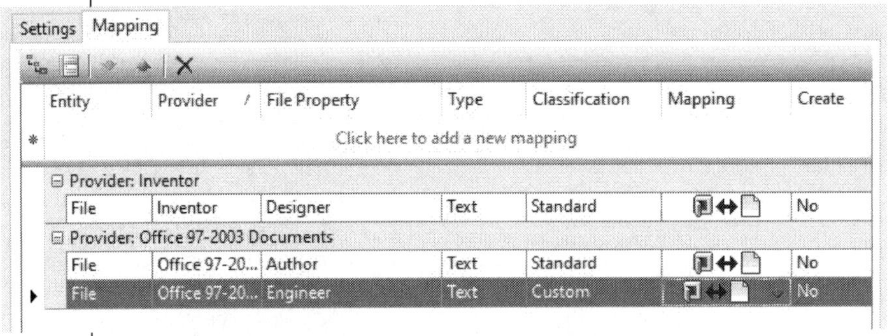

11. Select OK to create the user defined property with the specified property mappings. You will need to re-index the properties in order to set any files with property values already in the vault.

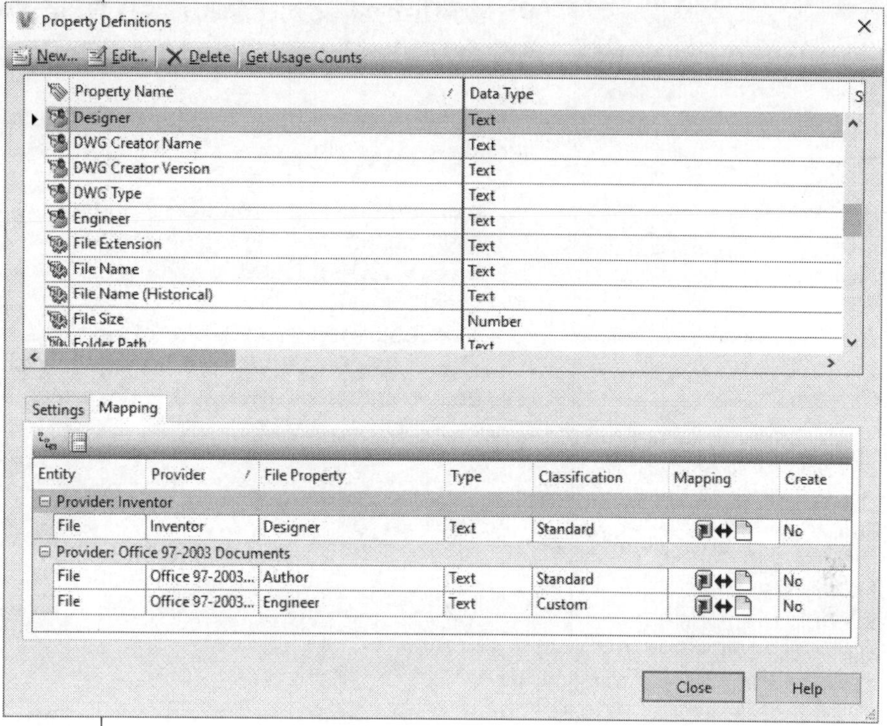

Adding AutoCAD Attributes

Many companies store important information about AutoCAD drawings in attributes. For example, the drawing number, description, designer, and latest revision are often stored in the title block. By default, attribute values are not extracted from AutoCAD files when the files are added to the vault; however, you can set up Vault to add block attribute values as properties.

In Vault, you can define a property, and name it as you see fit. You can then assign a mapping to an attribute in an AutoCAD titleblock. The names do not need to match. Attribute tag names are not always meaningful; therefore, you can also extract the attribute prompt and use the prompt as the property name.

An AutoCAD block can include more attributes than you want to use in Vault. If you do not need some of the properties, you can exclude them from the database indexes. If a property is similar to other properties in the vault, you can merge the new AutoCAD block property with the existing vault properties so that users see just one property for all files rather than having to view or search on different properties when they work on different file formats.

Procedure: Adding AutoCAD Block Attributes Properties

The following steps describe how to add AutoCAD block attributes to the vault.

1. Open the drawing in AutoCAD and record the name of the block. Ensure that the case is correct.
2. Log in to ADMS Console.
3. Select a vault.
4. Click Tools menu>Index Block Attributes.
5. In the Index Block Attributes dialog box, click New. Enter the name of the block. The case must match the name in AutoCAD.

You can use the prompt instead of an attribute tag. To use the prompt when it is available, enable the "Extract attribute prompt when available" check box. If this check box is toggled on and there is no prompt, the attribute tag is used.

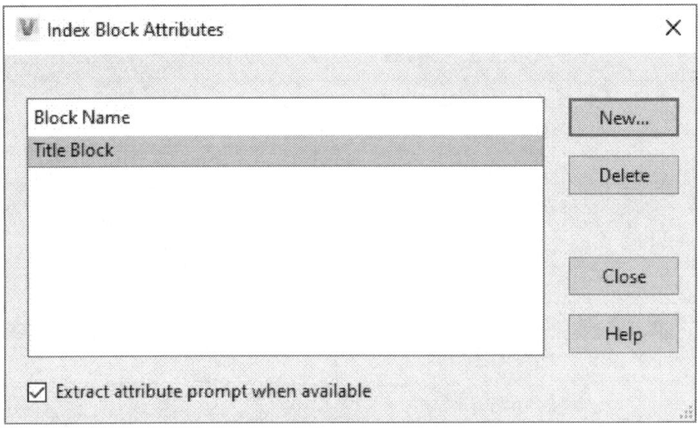

6. Close the Index Block Attributes dialog box.
7. Click Actions menu>Re-Index File Properties to re-index the properties.
8. Re-index the vault.

   You can create mappings to the attributes within the AutoCAD titleblocks in the same way you created mappings to Inventor iProperties and Word document properties.

Adding Other Properties

Autodesk Vault automatically adds properties from any application that has a Vault add-in. If you store other types of files in the vault, you can include their properties in the vault database by installing the appropriate iFilter. For example, if you store Adobe® Portable Document Format (PDF) files in the vault and need to organize and search for the files using properties, you can install the iFilter that supports PDF files. Some iFilters read just file properties while others read both a file's properties and the file's contents.

Procedure: Adding Other Properties

To add properties from other file formats, do the following:

1. Purchase or download an iFilter for the appropriate file format.
2. Install the iFilter on the computer that hosts the vault server.
3. In ADMS Console, re-index the vault database. If the iFilter can read the file contents and you want to search on file contents, enable the content indexing service.

Re-Indexing Vault Databases

Re-indexing scans the selected vault database, extracts and indexes properties from the files in the vault database. The extraction and indexing process uses the latest available iFilters/Content Source Property Providers for the files. Only properties currently set to Enabled and properties that have read-mappings are re-indexed. During re-indexing, existing property (e.g., user-defined property) values are updated.

Reasons for re-indexing:

- New iFilters or Content Source Property Providers have been added that extract more relevant information.
- Property definitions have been set to Enabled.
- Read-mappings have been modified.

Procedure: Re-Indexing the Databases

The following steps describe how to re-index the vault databases.

1. Log in to ADMS Console.
2. In the list of vaults, select a vault to re-index.
3. Click Actions menu>Re-Index File Properties.
4. In the Re-Index File Properties dialog box, select whether to re-index all files or just the latest and released versions only. Clicking Status lists the status of a active re-index procedure, or the results of the last re-index procedure. It does not determine whether re-indexing is required.

5. Vault maintains re-index status for every file. Although certain criteria are selected for a re-index operation, it is not required that all files that fall under the criteria be re-indexed. This is because some files might already be up-to-date. However, the Administrator can choose to force a re-index on all files that meet the selected criteria by selecting the Force Re-Index option. To force a re-index, click Expand (>>) and select the Force Re-Index check box.
6. To determine how many files will be affected, click Calculate.

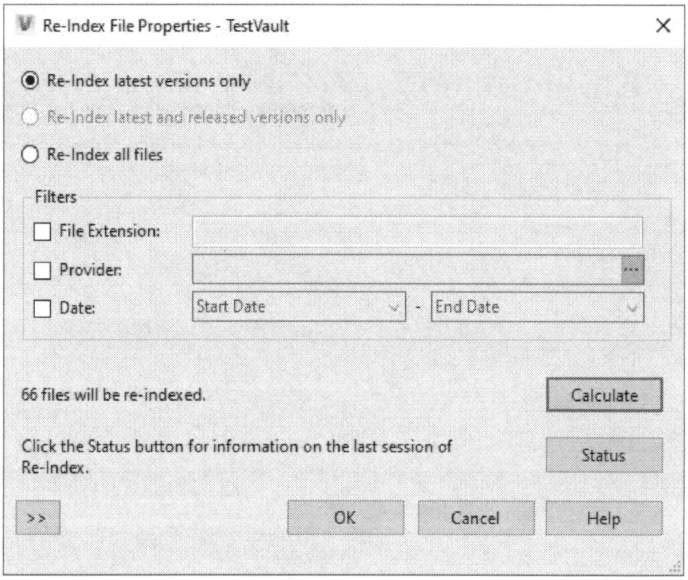

7. Click OK to run the re-indexing service.

   Note: It might take a while to re-index the properties.

8. To check if the re-indexing operation is complete, do one of the following:
   - Select the command again. If the operation is not complete, the Re-Index Properties Status dialog box displays the status of the current re-indexing operation. If the operation is complete, the Re-Index Properties dialog box is displayed.

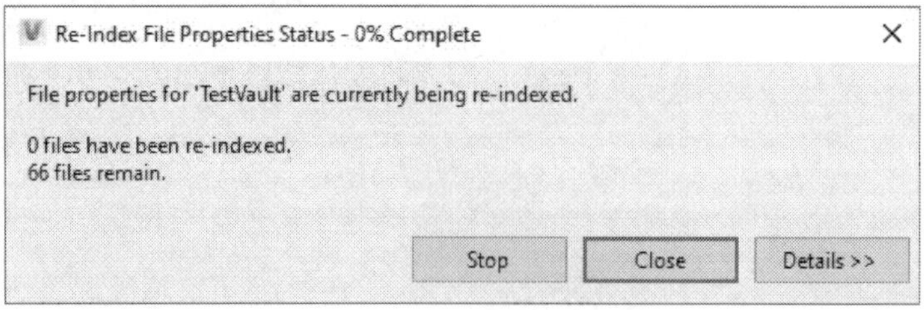

- Check the Server Log to see if the Property Re-index task is complete.

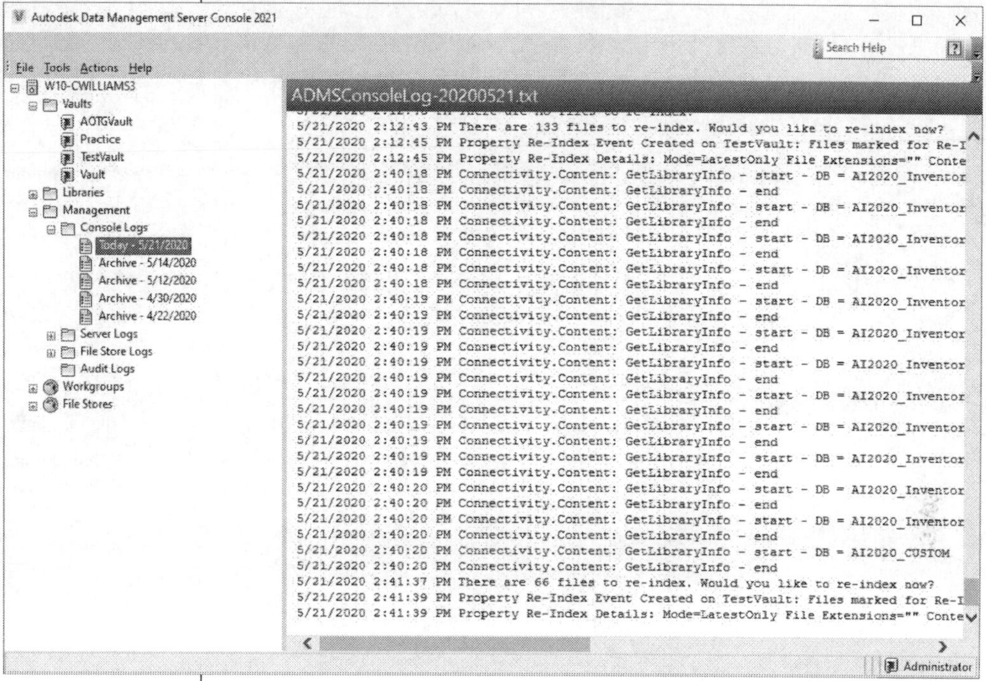

Practice 10c Manage File Properties

In this practice, you add AutoCAD attributes as properties, map properties, disable properties, and re-index the vault databases to update the property indexes.

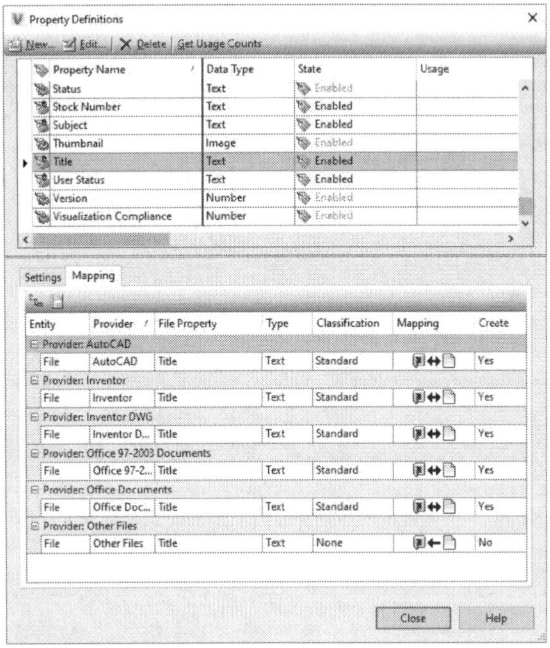

The completed practice

Task 1 - Add AutoCAD attributes as a property.

1. Start Autodesk Vault. Log in to TestVault as an administrator. The password is blank.
2. Click Tools menu>Administration>Vault Settings.
3. In the Vault Settings dialog box, in the Files tab, under Options, clear the Disable Check In of Design Files check box.

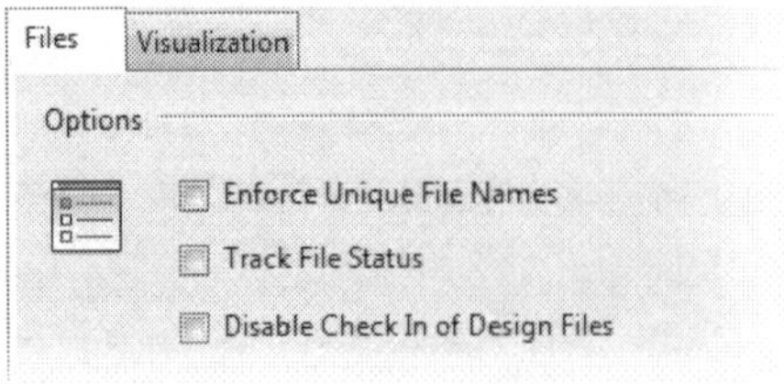

Note: Normally, you should add design files using the vault client in the CAD application. For the purpose of this practice, the design file that you add to the vault is a drawing that is not related to other files so it can be added using Autodesk Vault.

4. Close the Vault Settings dialog box.
5. Add the files AutoCADBlockAttributes.dwg and Document.doc from *C:\AOTGVault\Chapter 10* to the vault using any method. The location does not matter.

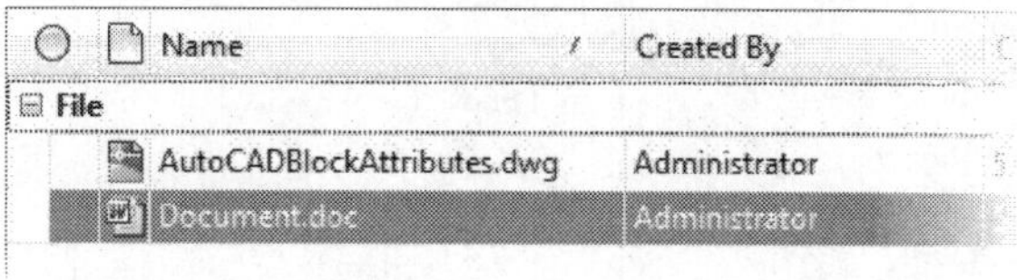

6. Start ADMS Console. Log in as administrator.
7. The password is blank.
8. Expand the list of vaults. Select TestVault.
9. Click Tools menu>Index Block Attributes.
10. In the Index Block Attributes dialog box, click New.
11. For Block Name, enter **Title Block**. Click OK.

    Note: You must enter the block name with the correct case and a single space between the two words.

12. Verify that the Extract Attribute Prompt When Available check box is selected.

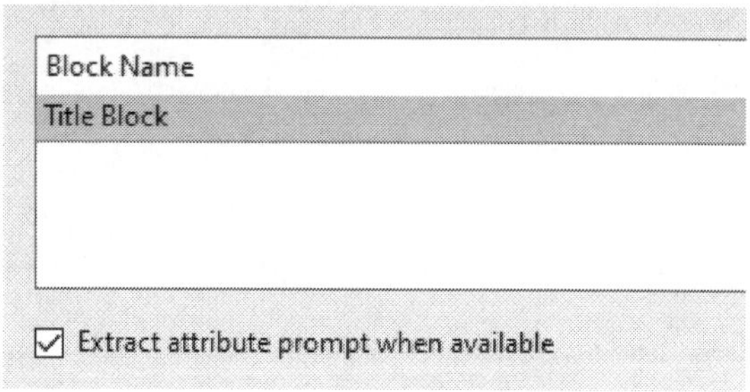

13. Click Close.
14. Click Actions menu>Re-Index File Properties.

15. In the Re-Index Properties dialog box, ensure that Re-Index All Files is selected. Click Expand (>>) and click Force Re-Index. Click OK and click Yes to re-index now.

    Note: It might take a while to re-index the properties. To check if the re-indexing operation is complete, select the command again. If the operation is not complete, the status of the current re-indexing operation is displayed. If the operation is complete, the Re-Index Properties dialog box is displayed.

Task 2 - Map and remove properties.

1. In Autodesk Vault, click Tools menu>Administration>Vault Settings.
2. In the Vault Settings dialog box, on the Files tab, click Properties.
3. Click on the Property Name column header to sort by Property Name.
4. In the Property Definitions dialog box, hover over the Property Type icon to display the Filter icon. Select the Filter icon to filter the list, selecting System.

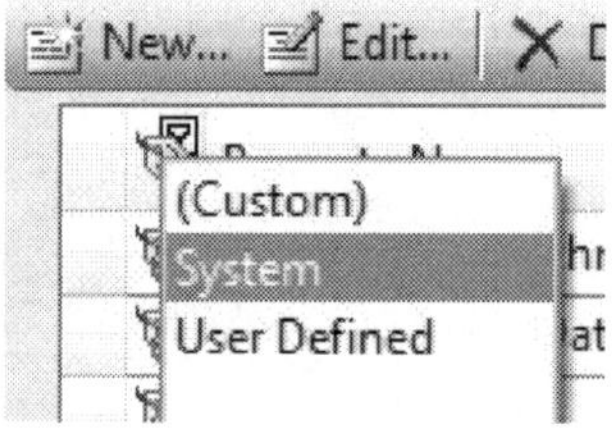

5. The Property Type column and the Filter Settings indicates that all of the displayed properties are system properties.

6. From the Filter Settings, select the red 'X' to remove the filter. All properties are displayed.

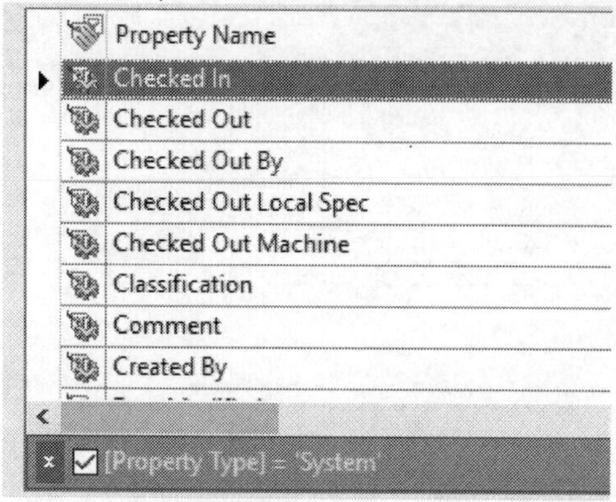

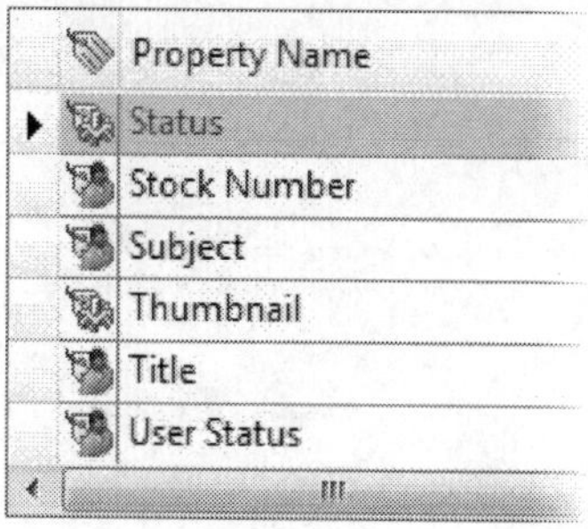

7. Hover over the Data Type column header until the filter icon displays. Select the Filter icon and select Number.

   Only properties with the Number data type are displayed.

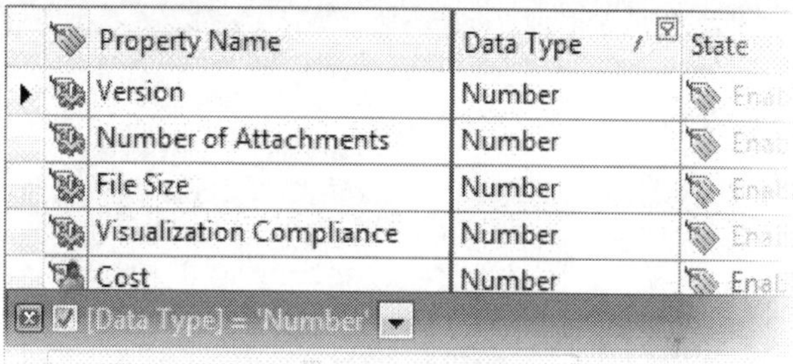

8. Click the red 'X' to remove this filter.

9. All properties are displayed.

10. Select the Title property in the property list and the Mapping tab to reveal its mapping.

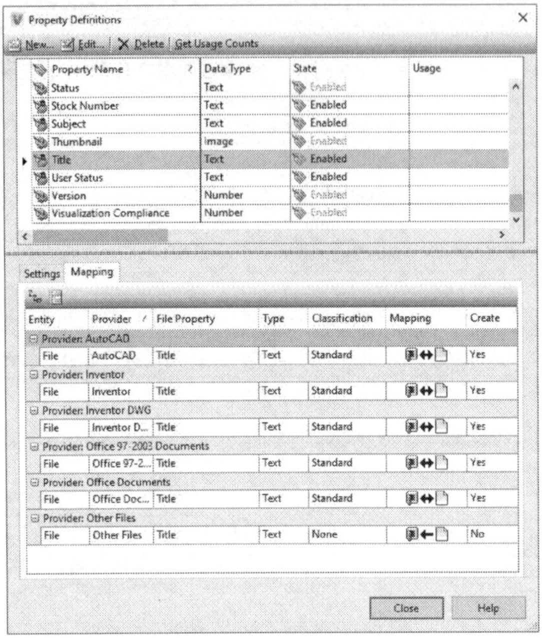

Title is a standard attribute that is associated with many different document types. As such, the Title property is shipped as a default user defined property with vault and is mapped to the standard Title file property for Autodesk and Microsoft Office document types. However, for our example we want to include a mapping to the Block Attribute Drawing Title in the AutoCAD file.

11. In the Property Definitions dialog, select Edit to reveal the Edit dialog for the Title property. Select the Mapping tab to display the default mapping.

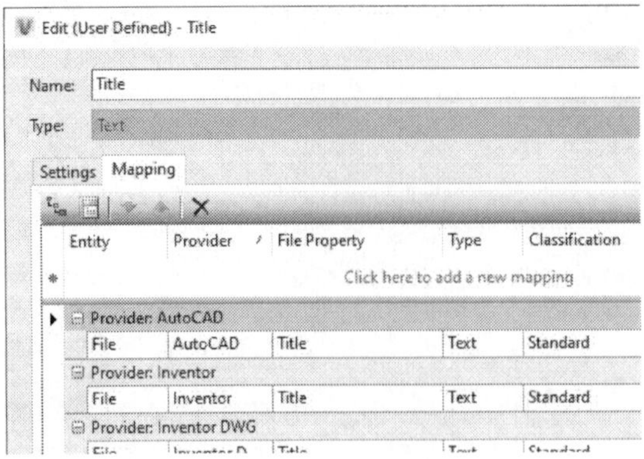

Note again the default mappings. For AutoCAD the property is already mapped to the Title file property. We will add a mapping that first looks in the Title Block attributes. If it does not find a value there it will then look for a value in the standard file property named Title.

12. Click in the Click here to add a new mapping area of the Mapping display. In the Provider drop-down select AutoCAD (*.dwg;*.dwt).

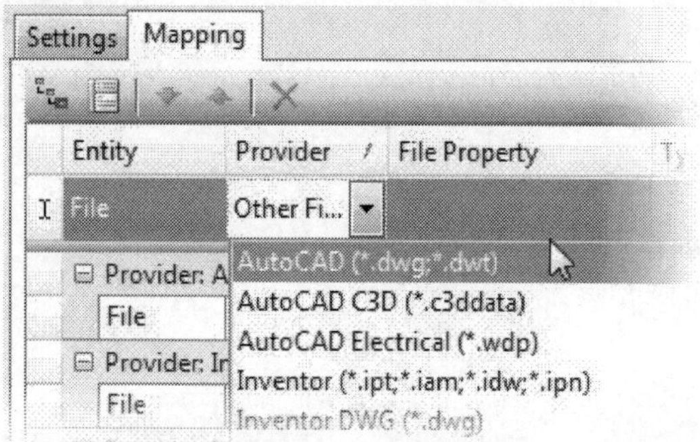

13. In the File Property drop-down, select Import Properties and Import from Vault.

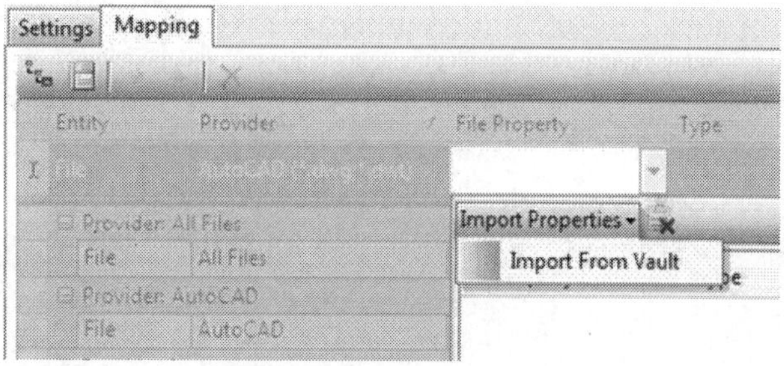

14. Select AutoBlockAttributes.dwg. From the list scroll down until you find Title Block.Drawing title. Select this row and then select OK.

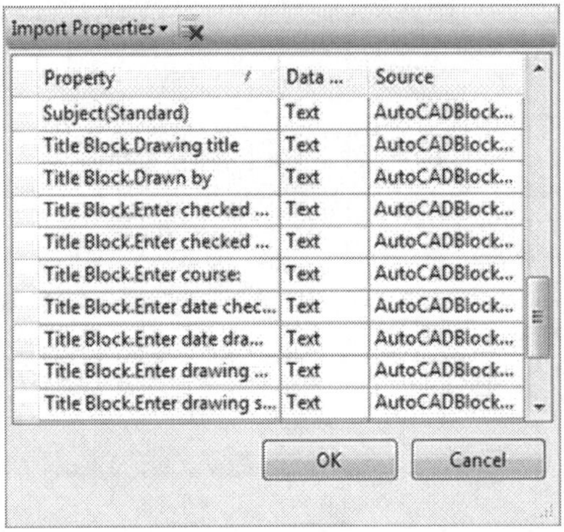

Note: Drawing Title is an attribute in the title block of the AutoCAD drawing that you added to the vault. If Drawing Title is not in the list, you might need to run a repair of the Autodesk Data Management Server in Add/Remove Programs. Adding drawing attributes to the server can be affected if you installed AutoCAD products after installing ADMS.

15. Click on the row Provider: AutoCAD to display the new mapping.

For AutoCAD files the system will first look for the Title file property and then the Title Block. Drawing title Block Attribute.

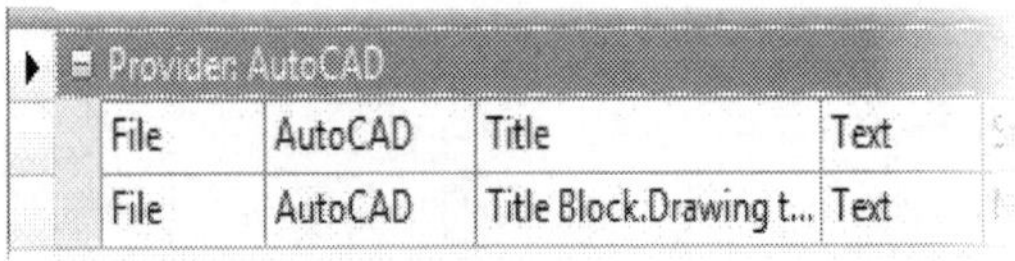

We want to change the order of the mapping so that the system first looks for a Block Attribute for the Drawing title. If it does not find a value there then look for the standard Title file property.

16. Select the second row in the Provider: AutoCAD section. Select the up arrow in the Mapping toolbar to move it before the Title file property.

17. Select OK to dismiss the Edit (User Defined) – Title dialog.

18. In the Property Definition dialog, select New to create a new user defined property.

19. In the New (Property) dialog, enter Project for the Name of the new property.

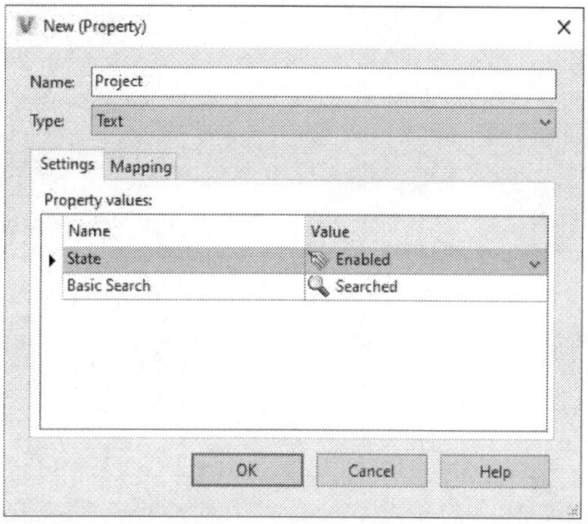

20. Select the Mapping tab and select Click here to add new mapping.

21. In the File Property field, select Import Properties. Browse to the Word document you added to the vault and select Open.

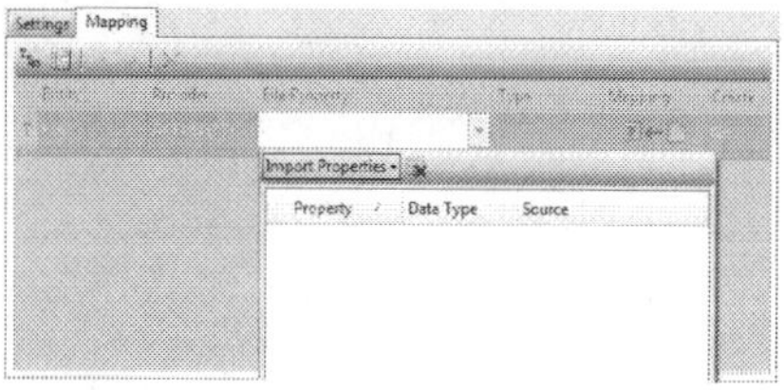

22. In the list of imported properties, scroll down to find the custom property Project. Select it and then dismiss the dialog by selecting OK.

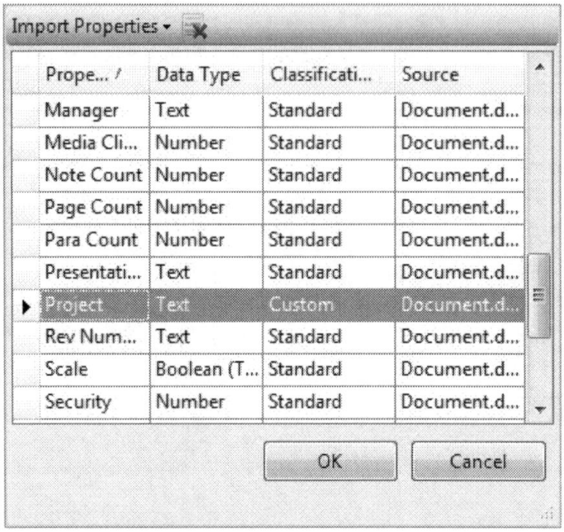

23. Select OK to create the user defined property.

24. In the Property Definitions dialog, select the properties with Property Names Company and Cost Center by pressing Ctrl button. Since these are not relevant to our organization, we will disable them. Click Edit.

25. In the Edit – Multiple Properties dialog, select the Value for State (File Properties Only) and select Disabled.

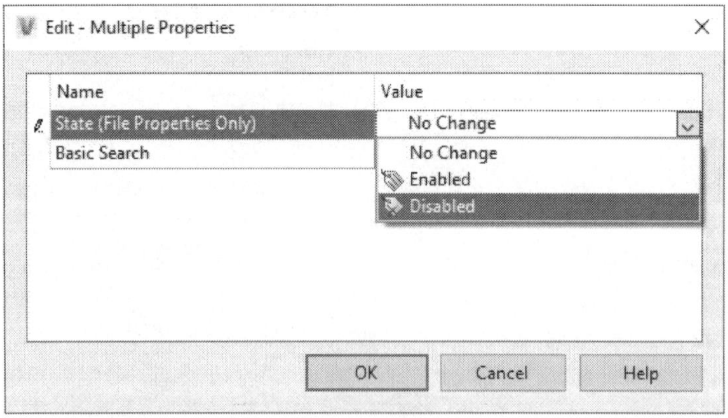

The properties are disabled. In the future, if these properties are used and you want to include them in column customization or find / search workflows, they can be re-enabled.

26. Select OK to dismiss the Edit – Multiple Properties dialog box.

27. Click Close. Click OK to close the Warning message that states that you must re-index the vault. Close the Vault Settings dialog box.

28. Switch to ADMS Console. Ensure that TestVault is selected. Re-index the properties.

29. Below the list of vaults, expand the Management and Server Logs folders. Click Today.

30. Scroll to the bottom of the log file. Confirm that Property Reindex started and completed.

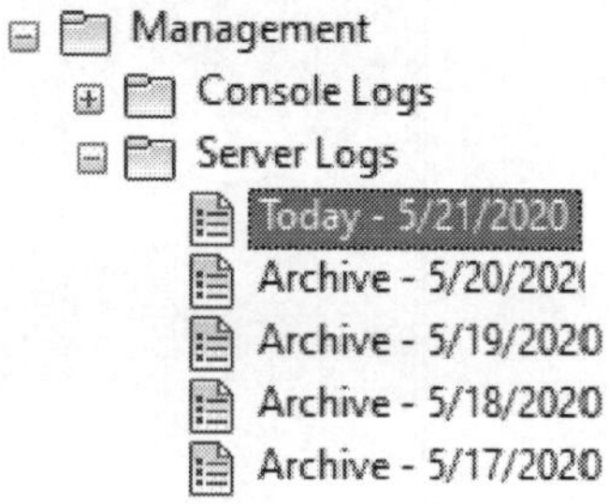

Task 3 - Display Properties in Vault Explorer

1. In Autodesk Vault, navigate to the folder that contains the document and the AutoCAD drawing that you added to the vault earlier in the practice.

2. Click in the file pane. Click View menu>Customize View.

3. In the Customize View dialog box, click Fields.

4. In the Customize Fields dialog box, under Select Available Fields From, select Any. Review the properties. Properties whose states are set to Disabled (Company, Cost Center) are not displayed.

5. Under Available Fields, select Title. Click Add to add it to the list of fields to show. Select Title and Project from the Show these files in this order list and move them up until they are just after the Name field. Click OK.

6. Close the Customize View dialog box.

7. Note the Title for the two files and the Project for the Word document.

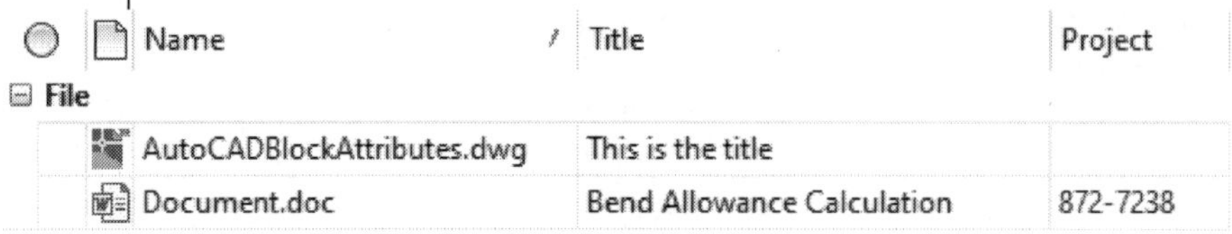

8. Close Autodesk Vault and ADMS Console.

10.4 Backing Up and Restoring Vaults

Overview

You must back up Vault files and databases on a regular basis so that you can restore them if they are accidentally corrupted or deleted. In this lesson, you learn how to back up and restore vaults and their associated files.

In the following image, the vaults are being backed up to a local drive.

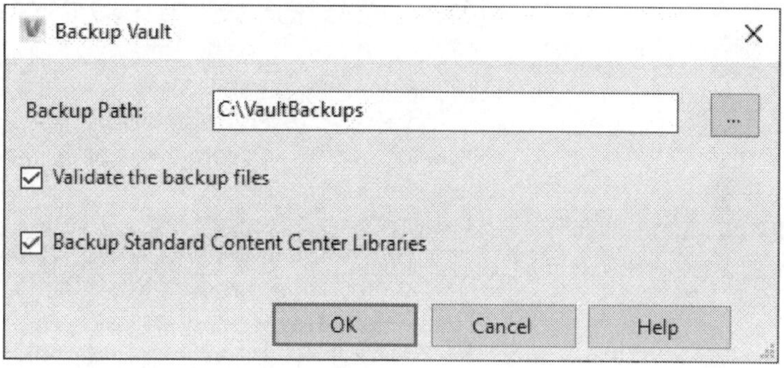

Objectives

After completing this lesson, you will be able to:

- Back up a vault.
- Restore a vault.

Backing Up a Vault

You should back up the Vault file store and databases regularly in case files in the vault are accidentally corrupted or lost. The backup tool backs up all attached vaults and libraries including the master database, vault databases, and vault file stores.

To guarantee that a vault can be restored without problem, the file store and databases must be backed up at the same time while ensuring that no database transactions take place during the backup procedure. The backup tool is preferred over other backup strategies because it automatically stops the Vault service and groups all required files into one folder, guaranteeing that the vault files can be successfully restored.

In the following image, the vaults are being backed up.

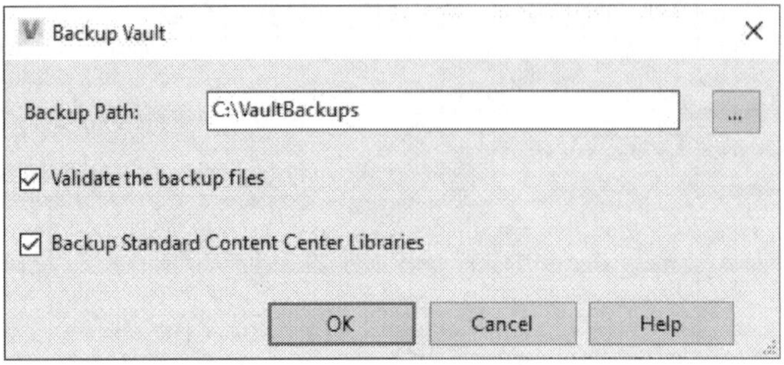

Excluding Vaults or Libraries from a Backup

If you have vaults or libraries that do not contain important data, you can exclude them from a backup to reduce the size of the backup. For example, a practice vault might not need to be backed up.

You can exclude individual vaults and libraries by detaching them before running the backup tool. When the backup tool is finished, you must reattach them. As an option, you can exclude all of the standard content center libraries during the backup procedure.

Procedure: Backing Up a Vault

The following steps describe how to back up vaults.

1. Log in to ADMS Console. If you do not want to include individual vaults or libraries in the backup, detach them. You do not need to detach the standard content libraries because you can exclude them using the backup tool.

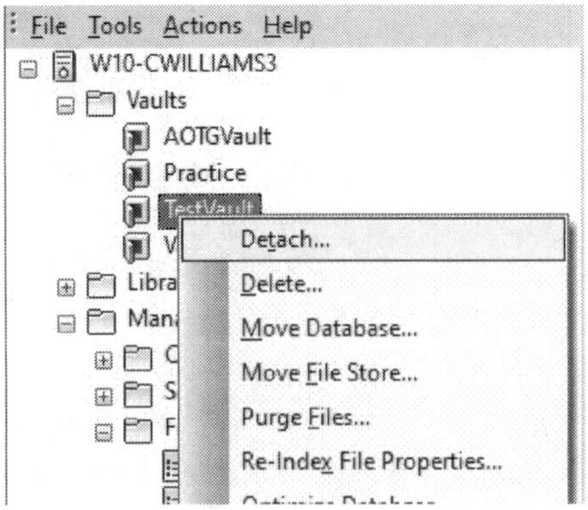

2. Click Tools menu>Backup.

3. In the Backup Vault dialog box:
   - Specify a location for the backup files.
   - Select the Validate check box to validate the backup files.
   - Select the Backup Standard Content Center Libraries check box if you want to include them in the backup. Typically, you can leave standard content center libraries out of the backup because you can restore them from the installation disks if they are lost or corrupted.

4. The Vault databases and file stores are backed up to the location that you specified.

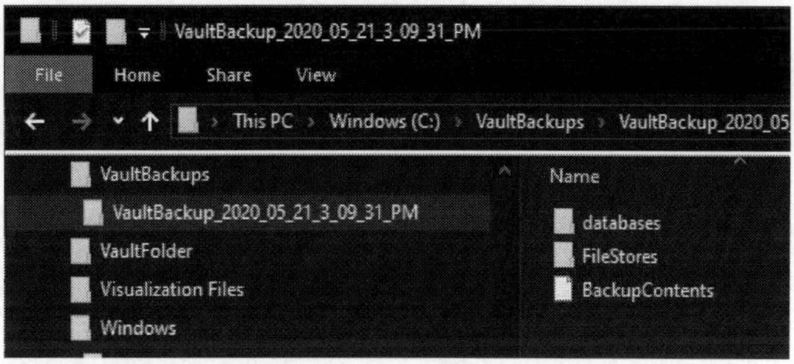

5. Check the Console Log if you want to confirm the status of the backup operation.

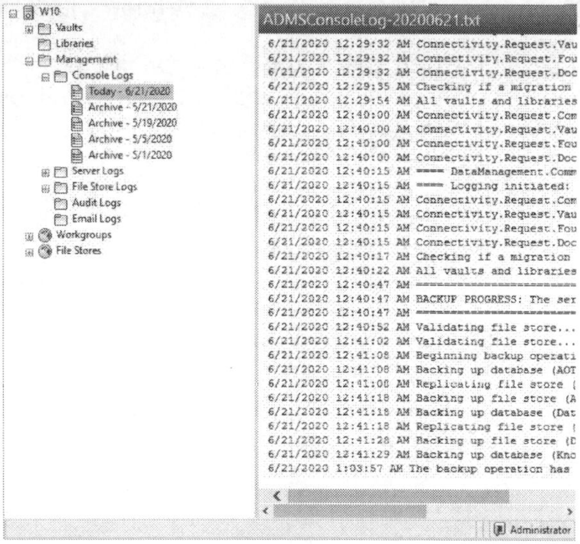

6. If you manually detached any vaults or libraries before you ran the backup tool, reattach them.

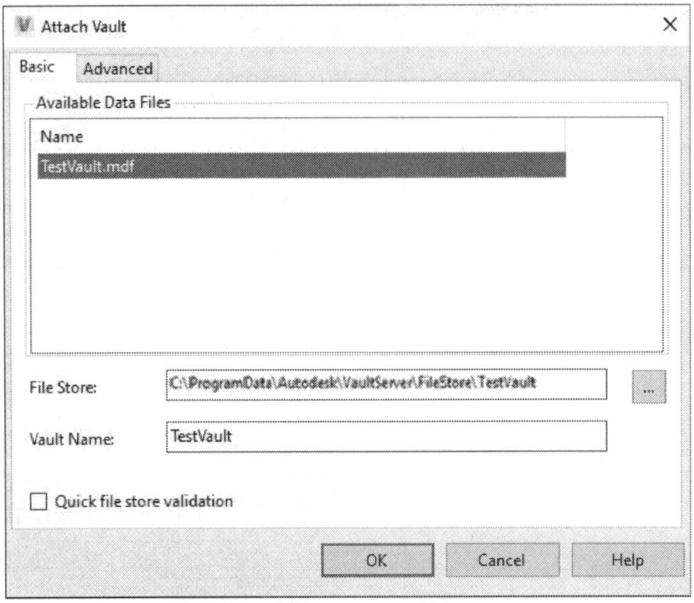

Automating Backup Using Batch Files

To schedule vault backups at regular intervals, you can run the command line version of the ADMS Console from a batch file. You can create a batch file that performs all of the operations required to back up your vaults, and then schedule the batch file to run at regular intervals using a task scheduler, such as Microsoft Windows Task Scheduler.

The command line version of the Vault Manager is named Connectivity.ADMSConsole.exe and is located in the ADMS installation folder.

The following is a sample command line call:

Connectivity.ADMSConsole.exe -Obackup -BC:\Backup -DBSC -VUadministrator -VPadmin -S -VAL -LC:

\Backup\BackupLog.txt

The command line arguments are described in the following table.

Argument	Description
C:\...\Connectivity. ADMSConsole.exe	Specifies the location and name of the executable file.
-O<operation>	Specifies the operation as a backup.
-B<folder>	Specifies the backup directory.
-VU<username>	The Vault administrator account user name (required).
-VP<password>	The Vault administrator account password (required unless password is blank).
-WA	Use Windows Authentication instead of -VU and -VP.
-DBSC	Excludes the standard content center libraries from the backup. The libraries are detached before the backup procedure, the vaults are backed up, and then the libraries are reattached.
-L<backup log name and location>	Specifies the name and location of the log file. If the log file exists, the log data is appended to the file.
-VAL	Validate the backup. Errors are recorded in the log file.
-S	Runs the command in silent mode so that dialog boxes are not displayed.

Restoring a Vault

If a problem arises with your vaults, you might need to restore them from a backup. When you run the restore procedure, all of the attached vaults and libraries are deleted and are replaced by those from the backup. If you excluded vaults or libraries from the backup, you can detach those files before restoring the vault and then reattach them after the restore operation is finished.

If the vault databases in the backup are from a previous version of Vault, the databases are automatically migrated to the current version when you use the restore tool from ADMS Console.

Restore Options

The Restore Vault dialog box and its options are displayed in the following image.

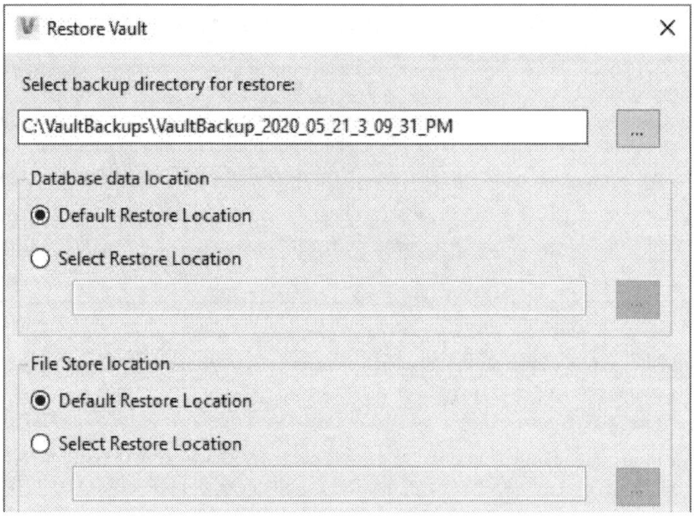

Backup Directory	The directory where you saved the backup.
Database Data Restore Location	By default, when you restore a vault, the Vault databases are restored to their default locations on the server, which might not be the locations from which they were backed up. If you have moved the databases from their default location, you must specify the locations rather than using the default location. When you restore the vaults, the databases are deleted from their current location and the files from the backup are restored to the specified location.
File Store Location	By default, when you restore a vault, the Vault file stores are restored to their default locations on the server, which might not be the locations from which they were backed up. If you have moved the file stores from their default location, you must specify their locations rather than using the default location. When you restore the vaults, the file stores are deleted from their current location and the files from the backup are restored to the specified location.

Practice 10d Back Up and Restore a Vault

In this practice, you back up a vault, examine the vault backup folder, and restore the vault.

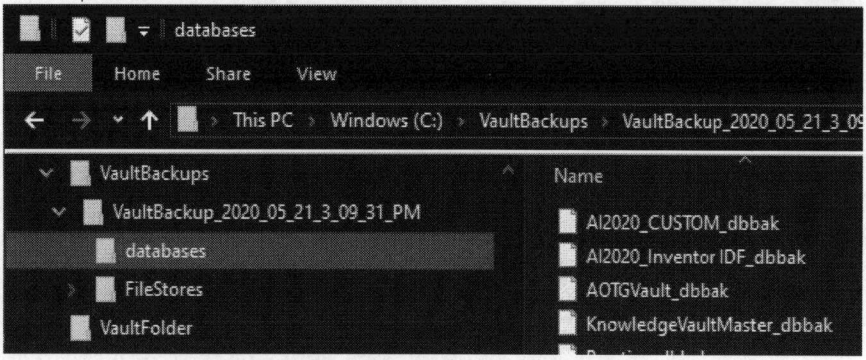

The completed practice

1. Start ADMS Console. Log in as administrator. The password is blank.
2. Review the total size of the vaults, libraries, file stores, and the number of days since the vault was backed up.
3. Click Tools menu>Backup.
4. In the Backup Vault dialog box, for Backup Path, create and select the folder *C:\VaultBackups*. Select the Validate the backup files check box to toggle on validation. Clear the Backup Standard Content Center Libraries check box.
5. Click OK. The Backup Progress dialog box is displayed.
6. When the backup operation is complete, click OK.

7. In Windows Explorer, navigate to the VaultBackups folder. Do the following:

   - Confirm that the folder name contains the current date and time.
   - Open the folder that contains the backup and confirm that the backup includes all of the Vault databases and file stores. The databases for the standard content center libraries should not be included.

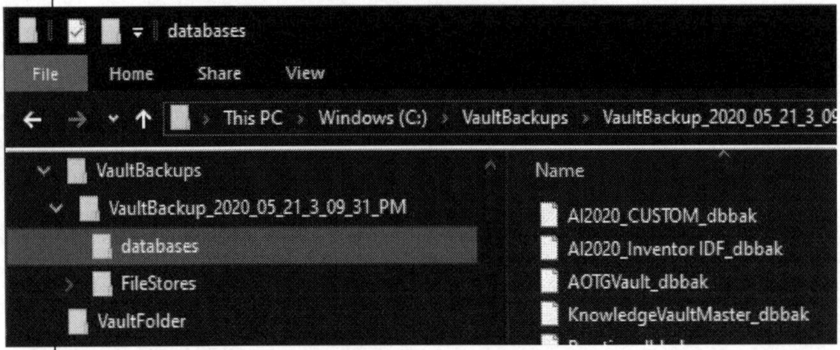

8. In ADMS Console, click Tools menu>Restore.

9. Click Yes to delete the current datasets and file stores.

10. In the Restore Vault dialog box, select the vault backup folder that was created during the backup operation.

11. Click OK.

12. In the Restore Progress dialog box, when the restore operation is complete, click OK.

13. Review the Console Log. Confirm that the restore operation succeeded.

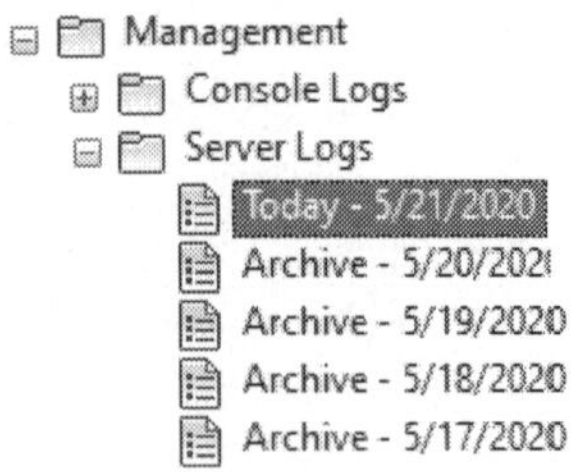

14. In ADMS Console, examine the vaults and file stores.

15. Close ADMS Console.

10.5 Maintaining Vault

Overview

As the Vault administrator, you need to perform routine maintenance on vaults and file stores. In this lesson, you learn how to get statistics about a vault and how to perform various maintenance tasks.

In the following image, the statistics for a vault are displayed.

Objectives

After completing this lesson, you will be able to:

- View information about a vault.
- Purge versions of files from a vault.
- Determine the status of files in a vault.
- Enable or disable full-text search.

Viewing Vault Statistics

The status of vault databases and the size of the databases and file stores must be monitored to determine whether the vault is performing optimally and if maintenance is required.

In the following image, the statistics for an individual vault are displayed.

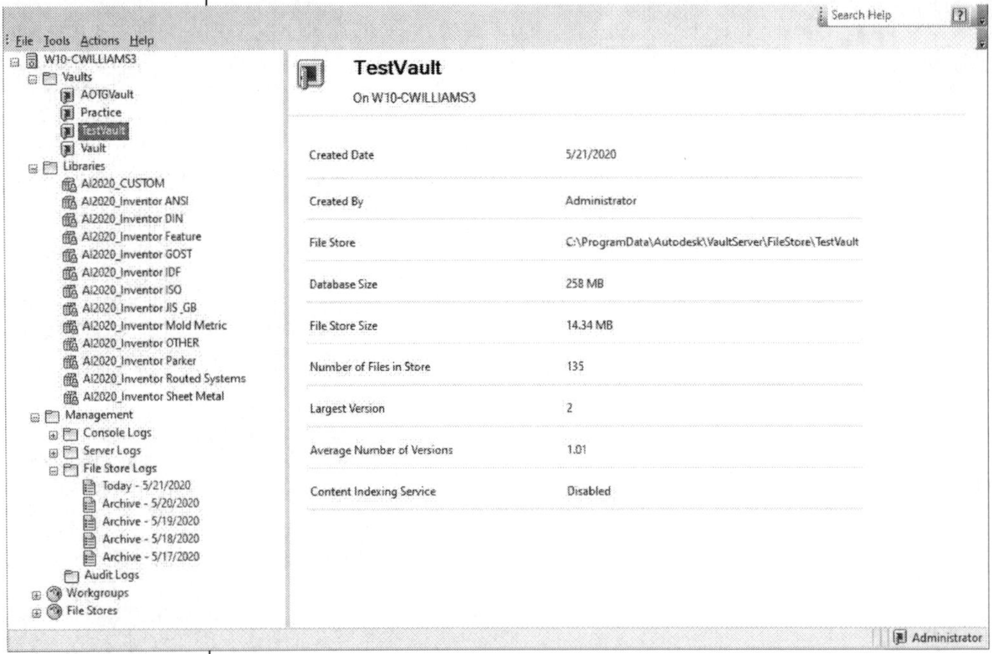

Vault Properties

The following image displays the properties that are displayed for all vaults and libraries.

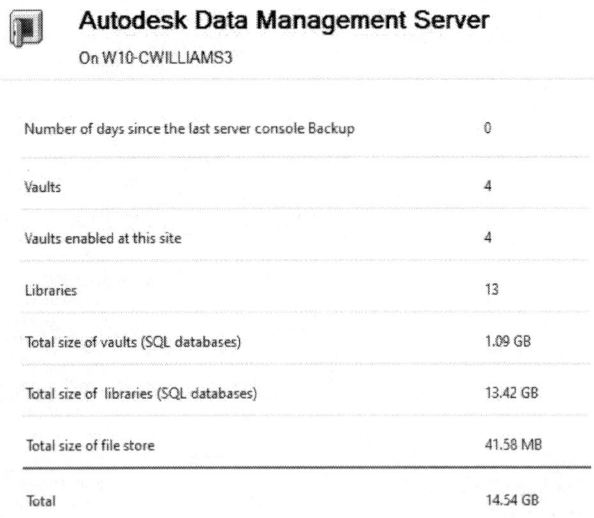

Number of days since the last backup: Helps you to determine whether the vaults should be backed up.

Number of vaults and libraries: Indicates the total number of vaults and libraries.

Total size of vaults: Displays the total size of the vault databases. Use the total vault size to determine whether the total size for all databases is approaching the limit for your database server. Note that this is only true in a one Vault site. The database limit relates to individual vault sizes not to the total vault size, which could be more than one vault. If the size approaches the limit, you can reduce the size of the vault databases by removing unused properties and purging unnecessary versions.

Total size of libraries: Displays the size of the libraries that are managed by the server.

Total size of local file store: Displays the total size on disk for all files in all file stores. You can use this to determine whether you should move the file stores to another partition, drive, or computer, or if you should purge files to reduce the number of files in the file stores.

The following image displays the properties that are displayed for an individual vault.

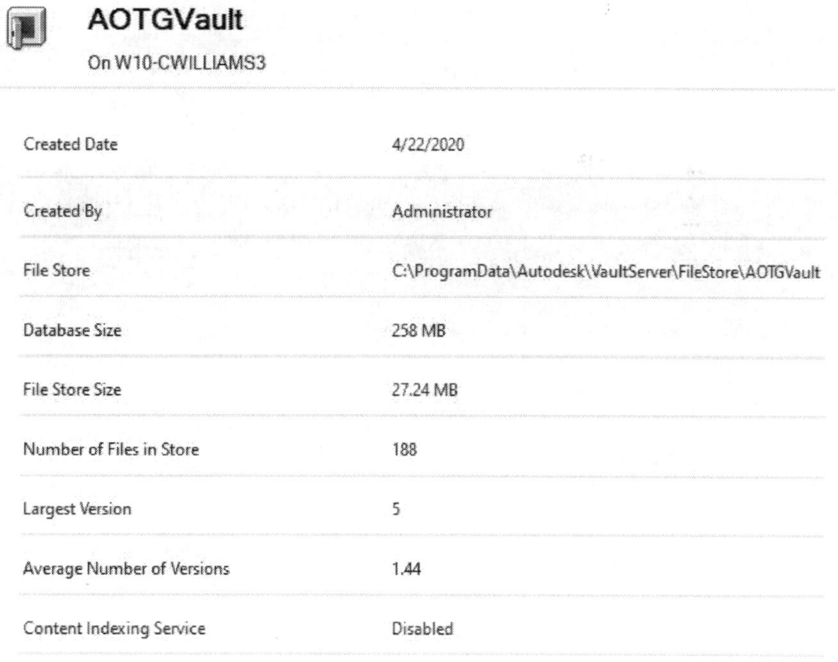

File Store: The location of the file store. Helps you to locate the file store and confirm its location.

Number of Files in Store: The total number of files in the file store including all versions.

Database Size: The total size of the MDF and LDF file for the selected vault. Use this information to help you determine whether you should reduce the database size or update the SQL server.

File Store Size: The total size on disk for all files in the file store. You can use this to determine whether you should move the file store to another partition, drive, or computer, or if you should purge files to reduce the number of files in the file store.

Largest Version and Average Number of Versions: The largest and average version number of the files in the vault.

Content Indexing Service: The search capability. When you enable the content indexing service, users can search for text in files when they use the Advanced Find command in Autodesk Vault.

Database Fragmentation: The databases can become fragmented as files and properties are deleted, resulting in reduced performance. If defragmentation is recommended, run the Defragment tool.

Procedure: Viewing Vault Statistics

The following steps describe how to view information for all vaults and for specific vaults.

1. Log in to ADMS Console as an administrator.
2. Click the top-level folder to view information about all of the vaults and libraries.

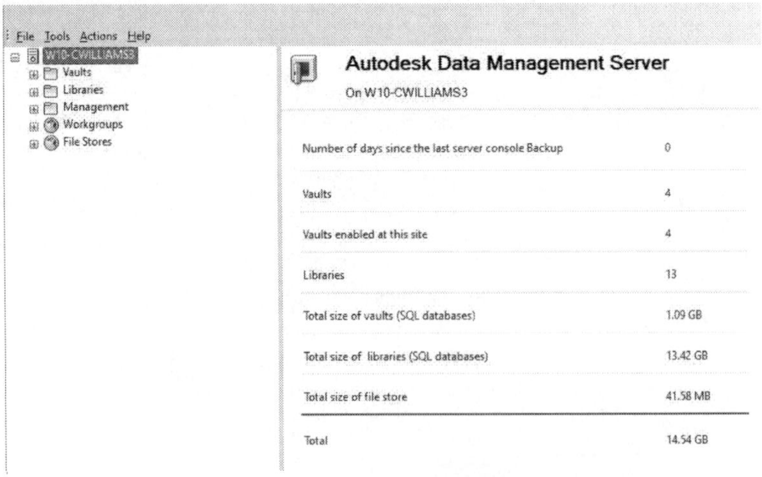

3. Select an individual vault to view information about it.

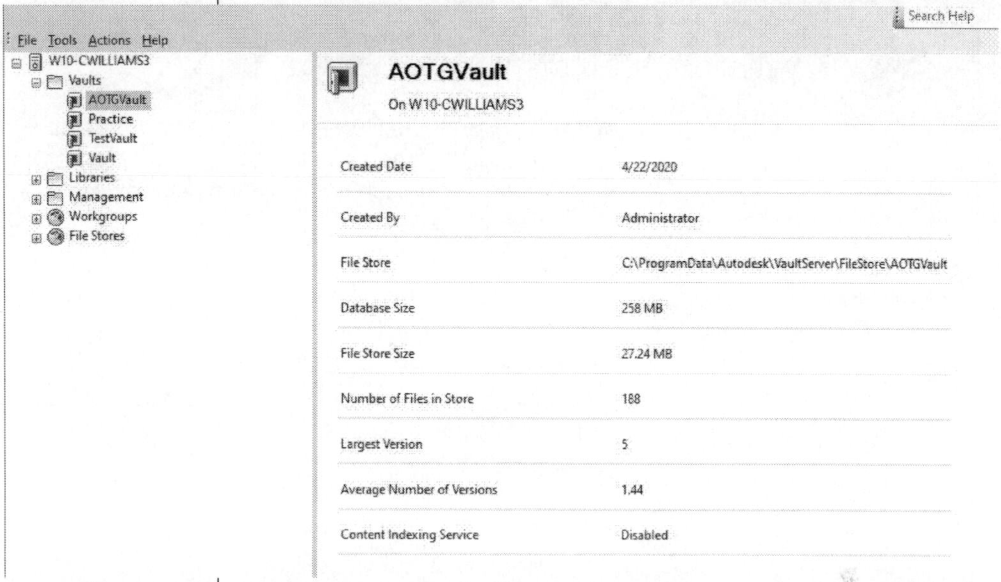

Purging Versions

Each version of a file takes up disk space in the file store and databases. You can remove versions periodically from the vault to reduce disk space and increase performance.

When you purge files, the files are removed from the file store and their properties are removed from the vault database, thereby reducing the size of both the file store and database. Files are purged based on the criteria you specify.

Accessing the Purge Command

You can purge files from both ADMS Console and from Autodesk Vault.

In ADMS Console, the Purge command operates on all files in the selected vault. When you run the Purge command from Autodesk Vault, you can specify which files to purge as shown in the following image.

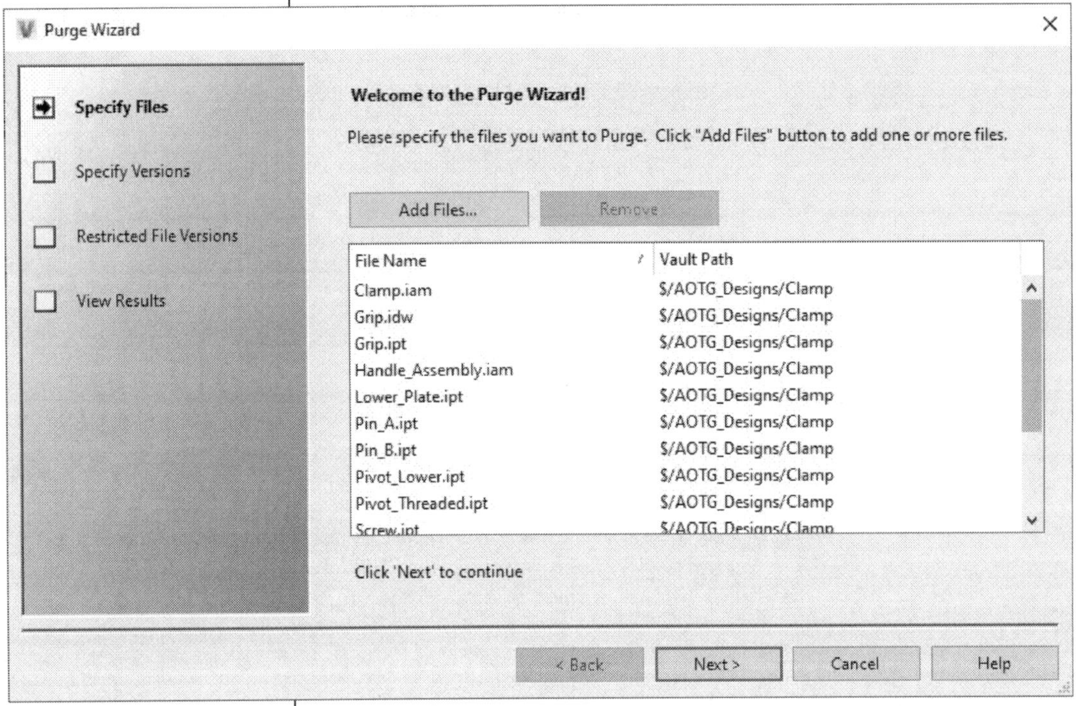

Purge Criteria

The purge criteria are shown in the following image. The criteria are the same whether you run the Purge tool from ADMS Console or from Autodesk Vault.

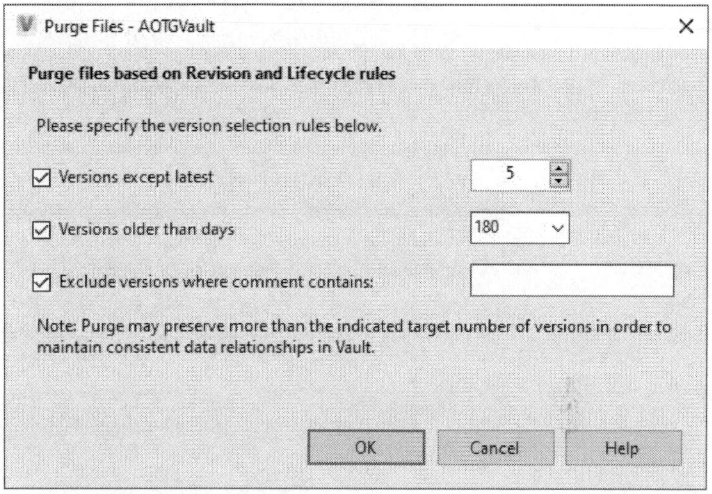

The following are the purge criteria:

Versions Except Latest: Specify how many file versions to leave in the vault.
Versions Older Than Days: Specify how old the files to purge should be.
Exclude Versions Where Comment Contains: Any files with comments that contain this string are excluded from the purge process.

Purge Rules (including Vault Workgroup and Vault Professional)

In addition to the version selection criteria that you specify, the following rules also apply:

- The latest version in a revision cannot be purged (the revision is never removed). To remove a file and all of its versions from a vault, use Delete.
- The leading version of a revision cannot be purged.
- File versions linked to items in Vault Professional cannot be purged. To remove a version linked to an item, the item must first be deleted from the item master.
- File versions that are labeled cannot be purged.

- File versions marked as Controlled by the life cycle definition cannot be purged.
- Only the first, last, or first and last versions in a released state can be purged.
- Older versions of files that are currently checked out can be purged.
- Children with a dependent parent version cannot be purged until the parent version has been purged.
- The Administrator role can override purge restrictions and force the removal of versions, except for versions that are linked to items.
- For Autodesk Vault Workgroup and Vault Professional. Files are purged based on revision and lifecycle rules unless version selection rules are defined during purge set-up.

Procedure: Purging Files

The following steps describe how to purge files from a vault.

1. Log in to ADMS Console as an administrator.

   Note: The Purge command can also be accessed from Autodesk Vault. The command is similar except that in Autodesk Vault you can select individual files to purge.

2. Back up the vault. If you accidentally purge required files, you can restore the vault to recover the files.
3. In the list of vaults, select a vault. Click Actions menu>Purge Files.
4. In the Vault Version Purge dialog box, specify the criteria for purging. The vault must be locked so that users cannot access it during the purge operation. Before the Purge tool runs, you are prompted to lock the vault.

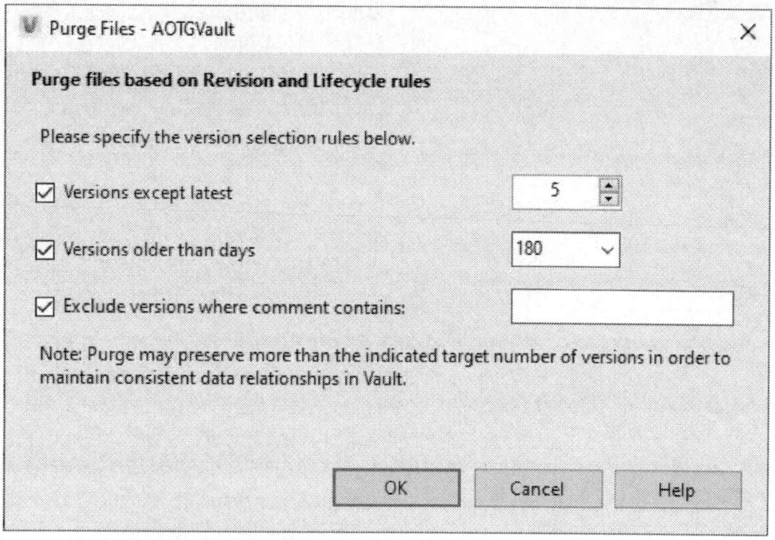

5. To review the results:
    - On the Tools menu, click View Server Tasks.
    - In the Server Tasks dialog box, from the list of Server tasks, select File Purge.
    - Click Details.

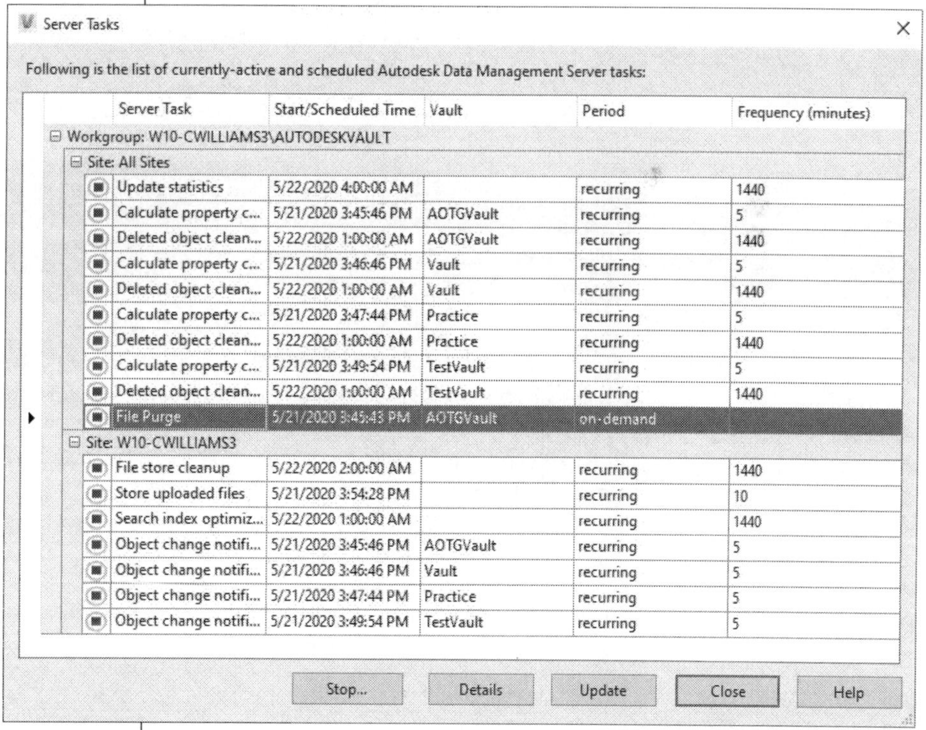

Note: If using Vault Professional, you can also purge items from the ADMS Console or Autodesk Vault client using Actions>Purge Items. Item versions are purged based on their lifecycle control settings. When a lifecycle state is created, the administrator must identify which item and file versions in that state are retained during a purge. For example, a lifecycle state can be defined so that all items in the Review State are purged except for the latest version when the Purge command is invoked.

Tracking File Status

A parent file in a model might not always reference the latest versions of its children. For example, several users might work on parts or subassemblies of a larger assembly. If the main assembly or drawings are never checked out and updated, they will reference previous versions of their children. In Vault, you can track file status to quickly identify parent files that do not reference the latest children.

The Status property indicates if a parent file in the vault references the latest versions of its children. You can display the Status property in Vault as shown in the following image.

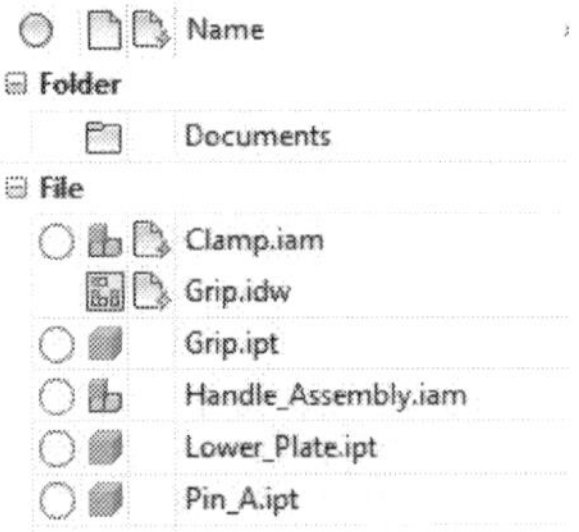

About File Status

You can customize the view in Autodesk Vault to display the Status property. The following table describes the three file statuses.

Icon	Status	Description
	Unknown	The file status needs to be updated. Run the Update File Status command from ADMS Console.
	Needs Updating	The file uses a version of a child that is older than the latest version.
	Up to Date	When no icon is displayed, the file is up to date because it references the latest versions of all children.

Procedure: Tracking File Status

The following steps describe how to track the status of files in the vault.

1. In Autodesk Vault, click Tools menu>Administration>Vault Settings. In the Administration dialog box, click the Files tab. Select Track File Status. Click Close.

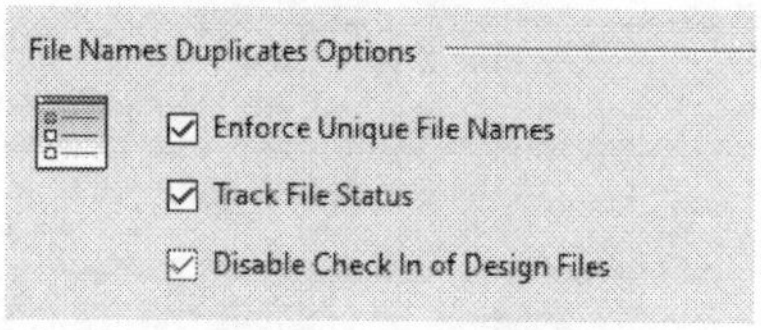

Note: If you do not toggle on Track File Status from Autodesk Vault, you can toggle it on from ADMS Console when you run the Update File Status command.

2. In ADMS Console, select the vault that you want to check. Click Actions menu>Update File Status.

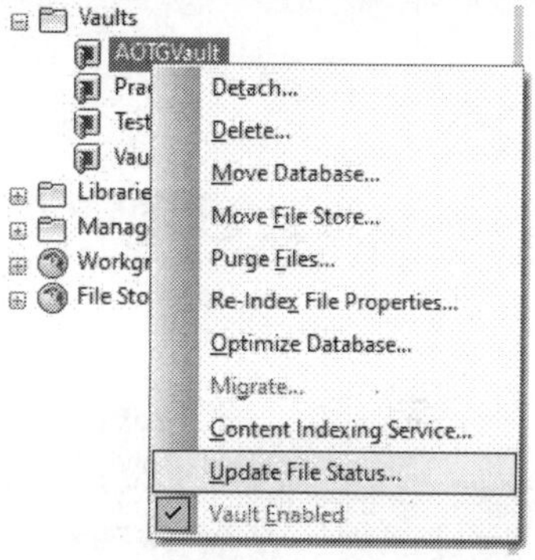

3. In Autodesk Vault, customize the view to display the Status property.
4. Browse the folders of your designs and view the status. Find the Needs Updating icon. To find all files in the vault that need updating, use an Advanced Find with Status is Needs Updating as the search criterion.

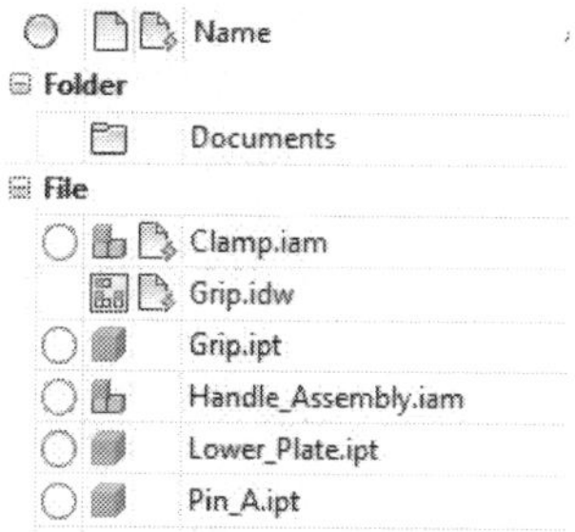

Note: A user with Document Editor (Level 1) or greater permissions can manually override the status property, changing the status to either Needs Updating or Up to Date. When the Update File Status command is run from the ADMS Console, user overrides are removed and the true file status is displayed.

5. If a file needs updating, press CTRL and click the File Status icon.

   The reason for an update is displayed. The child file(s) that are newer than the files referenced are listed.

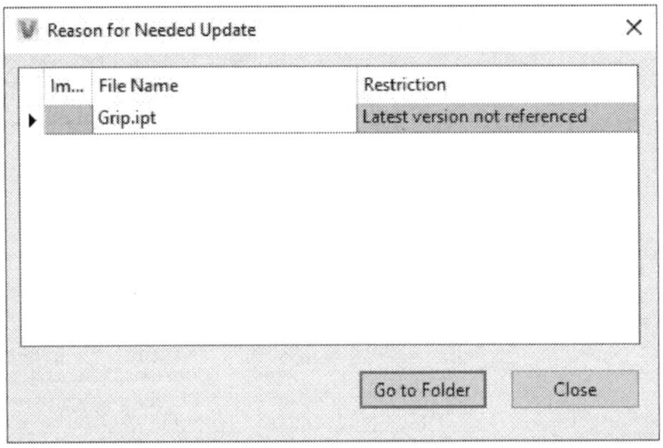

6. Click Go to Folder to open the folder that contains the child file. Use the Where Used tab to determine which versions are referenced.
7. To update the parent file:
   - Get the latest versions of the parent and children.
   - Check out the parent file.
   - Edit the parent file and save it.
   - Check the parent file back in to the vault.

Indexing File Contents

By default, you can search for files in the vault based on file properties. To search for files based on the content of text in files, you must enable content indexing.

When you add a file to the vault, the properties of the file are extracted and added to the vault database. To locate a file in the vault, a user can search for property values. However, important information is often in the contents of documents. If you enable content indexing, users can search for files based on both properties and the contents of files.

The content indexing service requires the appropriate indexing filter (iFilter) to access the properties and contents of a file. By default, iFilters are installed for files whose application has a Vault add-in client. To enable full content searching of other file formats, install additional iFilters on the Vault server. When the indexing service indexes the files, the properties and contents of files supported by the iFilter are added to the index.

Procedure: Indexing File Contents

The following steps describe how to toggle the file content indexing on or off.

1. Log in to ADMS Console as an administrator.
2. Expand the list of vaults. Click a vault. Click Actions menu>Content Indexing Service.

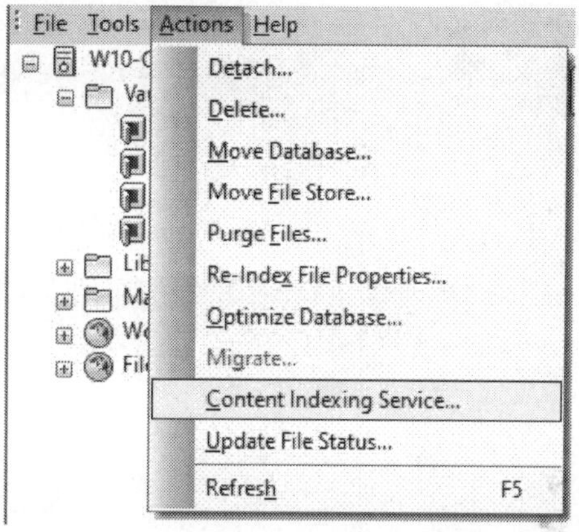

3. In the Content Indexing Service dialog box, toggle it on or off as required.

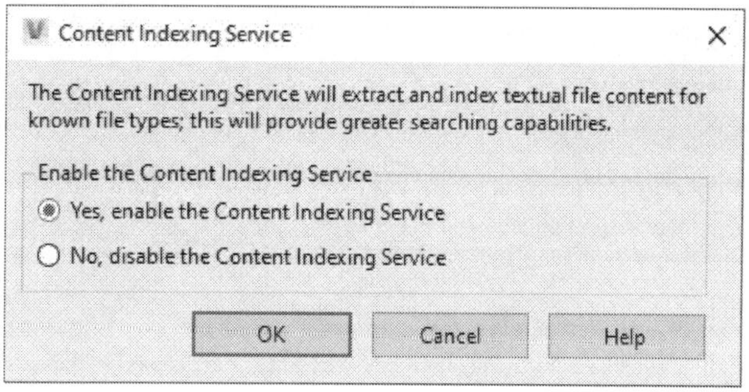

4. Confirm that the content indexing service is enabled.

Largest Version	[illegible]
Average Number of Versions	1.21
Content Indexing Service	Enabled
Database Fragmentation	Defragmentation Recommended

If searching file content is enabled, it will remain so until the user disables it. Searching file content can cause searches to take slightly longer than usual, as it is searching an additional database of information.

5. When you perform a basic search, toggle on Search File Content to search for content in files.

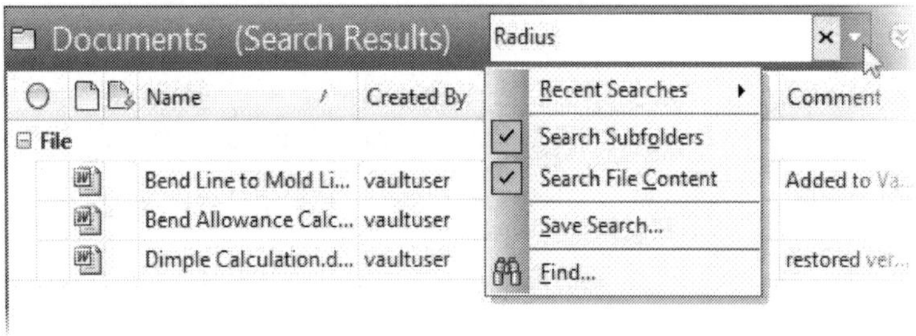

Practice 10e Perform Vault Maintenance

In this practice, you determine the status of vaults, update file status, and index file contents.

Task 1 - Enable content indexing.

1. Log in to ADMS. Expand the Vaults folder. Click each vault and review its statistics.
2. Select TestVault.
3. Click Actions menu>Content Indexing Service. In the Content Indexing Service dialog box, select Yes, Enable Content Indexing Service. Click OK.
4. Click OK in the message box that is displayed. On the statistics page for TestVault, confirm that Content Indexing Service is enabled.

Content Indexing Service	Enabled

5. Start Autodesk Vault. Log in to TestVault as an administrator. In the search box type Radius and select the drop-down to enable Search File Content. Select the search button.
6. The Word Document Document.doc that you added in the previous practice should be shown. Open the file and note the word Radius.

$$(0.0078T + 0.0174R) * D$$

Where:
R = Radius
T = Sheet metal thickness
D = No. of degrees

Task 2 - Track file status.

You upload an Autodesk® Inventor® model to the TestVault vault, enable file status tracking, make a change to a part in Autodesk Inventor, and then review the results.

1. Start Autodesk Vault. Log in to TestVault as an administrator.
2. Click Tools menu>Administration>Vault Settings. In the Vault Settings dialog box, clear the Enforce Unique File Names check box. Click OK.
3. **Note:** You use Autoloader to load a model into the vault. You cannot use Autoloader if unique filenames are enforced.
4. Start Autodesk Autoloader. Select Next.
5. In the Select Data Source window, select the folder *C:\AOTGVault\Chapter3\ AOTG_Designs\ICU Valve*. The Select Project dialog is displayed.
6. Browse for the project file *C:\AOTGVault\ManageVault.ipj*. Click OK to dismiss the Select Project dialog box.
7. Click Next.
8. Scan the files. When the scan is complete, click OK. Click Next.
9. Log in to TestVault as an administrator. Leave the password blank.
10. Map the ICU Valve folder to the Designs folder in the vault. Ensure that the Direct Mapping box is checked.
11. Click Next.
12. When the Copy and Redirection is complete, click Next.
13. Click Upload. When the upload is complete, click Done.
14. Return to Autodesk Vault.
15. In Vault:
    - Refresh the display.
    - Display the contents of the Designs folder.
    - Select ICULBUTN.ipt.
    - Click the Where Used tab.
    - Note all of the files where ICULBUTN.ipt is used.

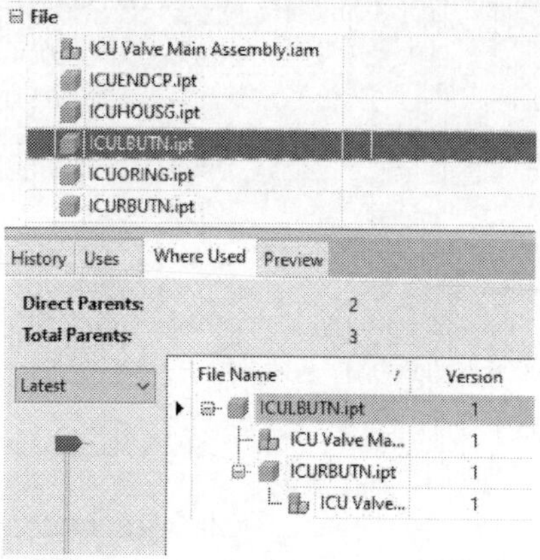

16. Click Tools menu>Administration>Vault Settings. In the Administration dialog box, on the Files tab, select the Track File Status check box to toggle on file status tracking. Click Yes in the Warning dialog box. Click Close.

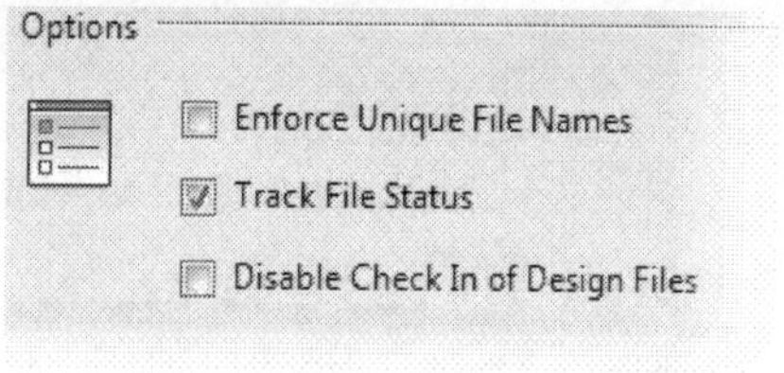

17. Click View menu>Customize View. Select Fields to display the Customize Fields dialog. Select Any from the Select available fields from drop-down. Select Status from the Available fields list and Add -> to add it to the Show there fields in this order list. Use Move Up to move it so it is before Entity Icon. Select OK to dismiss the Customize Fields dialog and Close to dismiss the Customize View dialog.

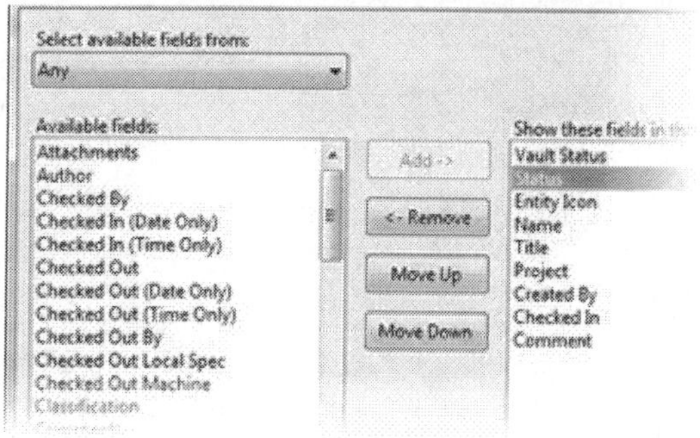

18. Place the cursor over an icon in the File Status column to display the tooltip. The status is unknown because it has not been updated from ADMS Console.

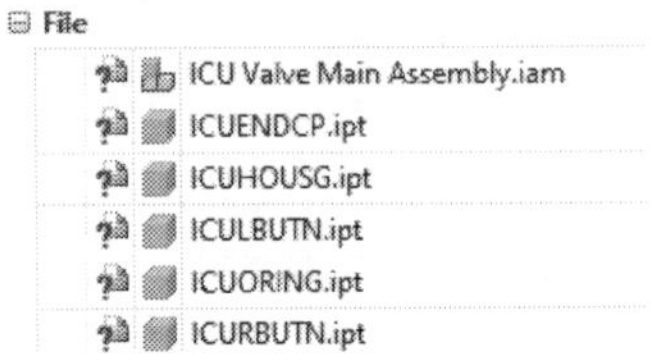

19. Switch to ADMS Console. Select TestVault.

20. Click Actions menu>Update File Status.

21. Click Yes to lock the vault. Click Yes to confirm that you will lose file status overrides. When the status update is complete, click OK.

22. Switch back to Autodesk Vault. Refresh the view. All files are up to date.

23. Select ICULBUTN.ipt.

24. Click Edit menu>Edit Properties.

25. On the Property Edit dialog, select Select Properties and do the following:

    - In the Select available fields from drop-down box select All fields.
    - Find Title from the Available fields list and use Add -> to add it to the Show fields in this order list. Remove any other fields except for Entity Icon and Name.
    - Select OK to dismiss the Customize Fields dialog.

26. In the Property Edit dialog, enter the title **ICU Valve Left Button.**

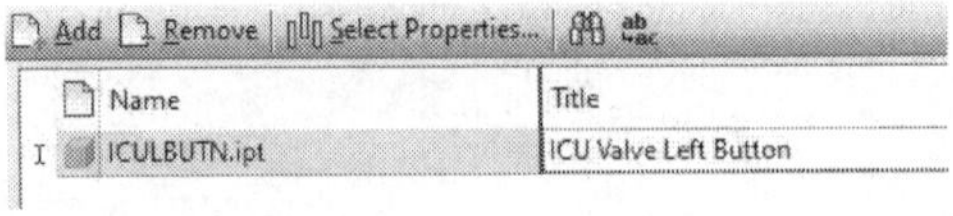

27. Click OK.

28. View the results of the Property Edit and then close the Property Edit Results dialog.

29. Refresh the Vault. Note that the version of ICULBUTN.ipt has incremented because you modified the file.

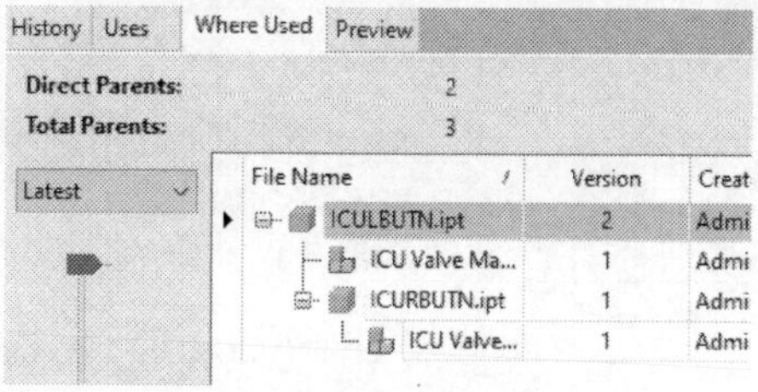

30. Review the icons in the file status column.

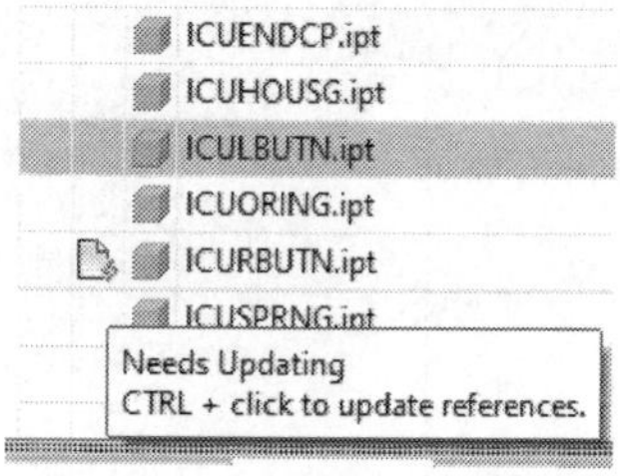

31. Press the CTRL key and click one of the file status icons. Review the reason that the file needs updating.

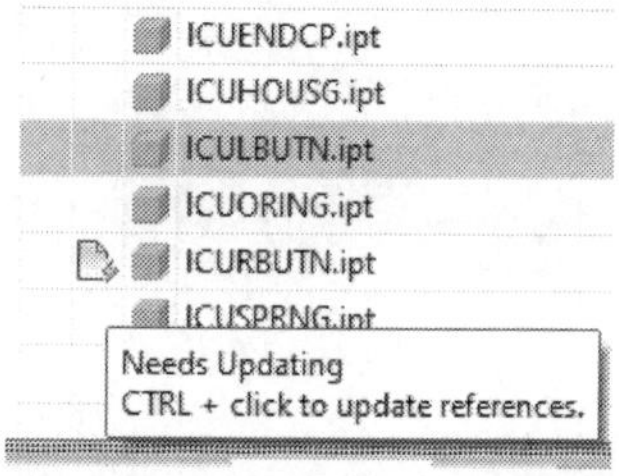

32. Review the reason that the other files need updating.

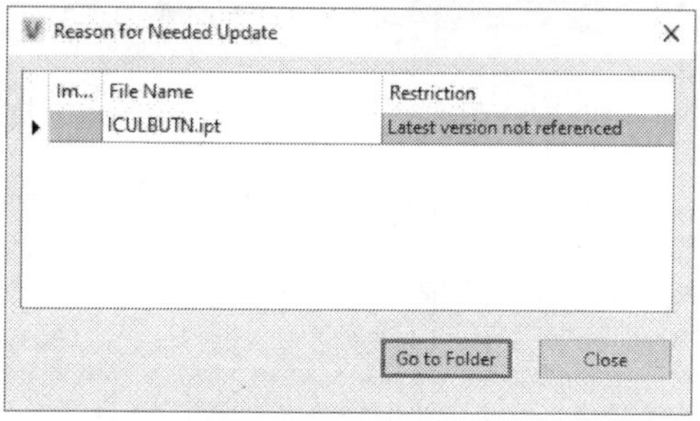

You do not update the parent files in this practice. To update the parent files, get the latest versions of all files, open each parent file in Autodesk Inventor, check it out, save it, and then check it back in to the vault.

33. Close Autodesk Vault and ADMS Console.

10.6 Chapter Summary

As the Vault administrator, you are responsible for maintaining vaults and files, including managing user accounts and managing the integrity and performance of the vaults.

Having completed this chapter, you can:

- Set up vaults.
- Manage users and groups.
- Manage file properties.
- Backup and restore vaults.
- Maintain a vault.

Appendix A

Vault Basic Integrations

Additional Autodesk software supported with Vault Basic that has not been covered in other chapters includes:

- Autodesk® 3ds Max®
- Autodesk Simulation software, such as Autodesk® Simulation Mechanical, Autodesk® Simulation Multiphysics, Autodesk® Simulation Moldflow® Adviser, and Autodesk Simulation Moldflow® Insight WS.
- Autodesk® Navisworks® Manage and Autodesk® Navisworks® Simulate.

Additional Vault Basic Integrations

The typical workflows and commands used when working with Autodesk Vault Basic and the additional Autodesk software add-ins are described below.

Autodesk 3ds Max

1. In the Autodesk 3ds Max software, from the File menu, click Reference>Asset Tracking Toggle. The Asset Tracking manager is the equivalent of the Autodesk Inventor Browser or the AutoCAD External References palette. From the Asset Tracking manager, all Vault interactions, settings, etc., are performed.

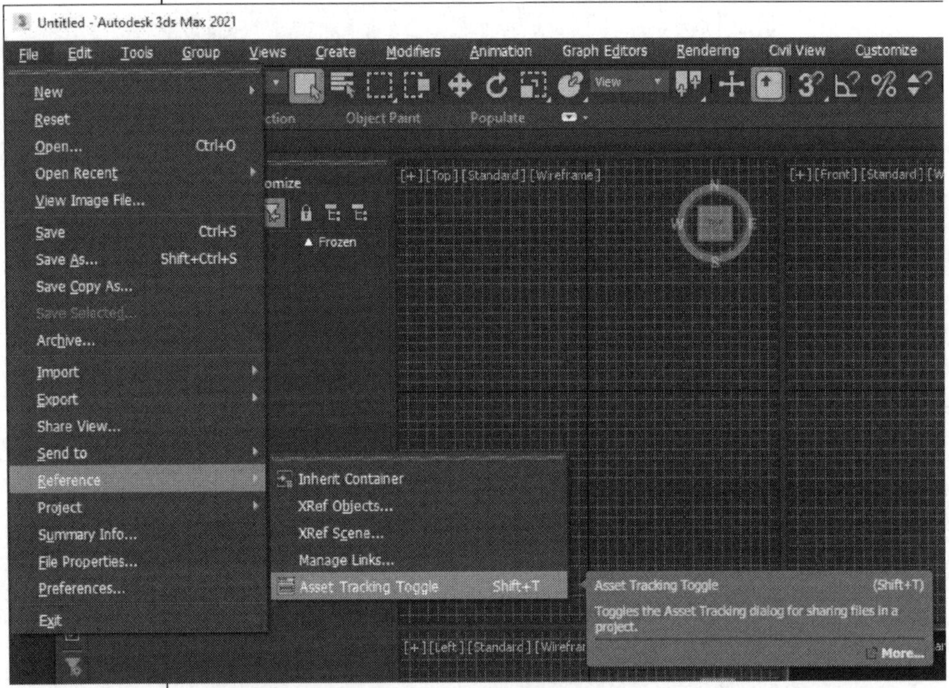

2. Select Log in from the Server pull down menu.

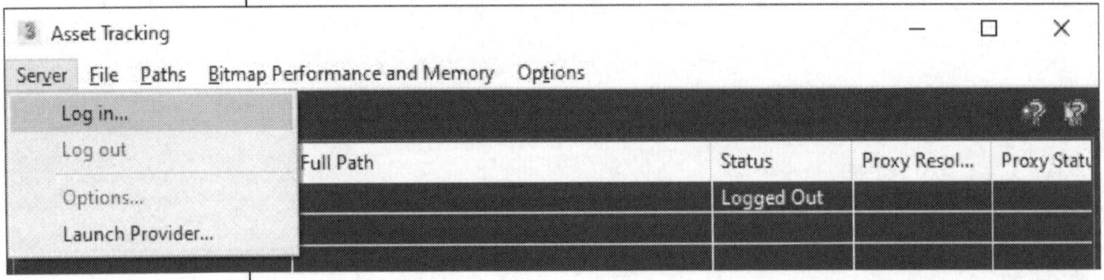

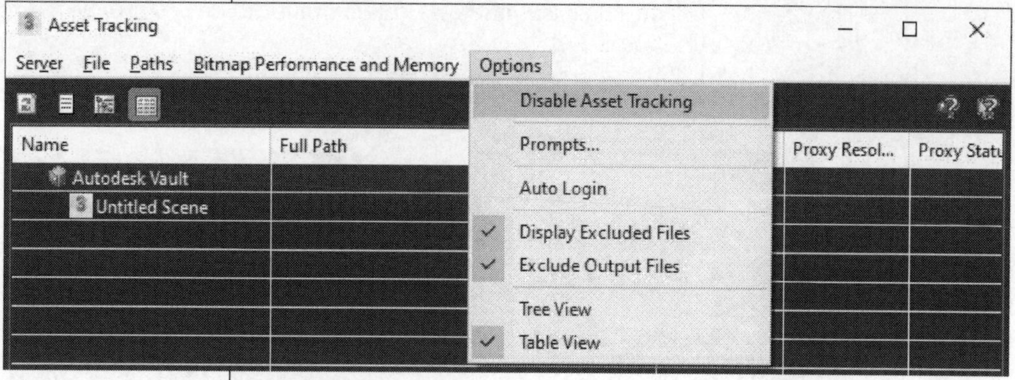

Note: If the Login menu is grayed out, click Options and uncheck Disable Asset Tracking.

3. Enter your User Name, Password, Server, and Vault information and click OK to login.

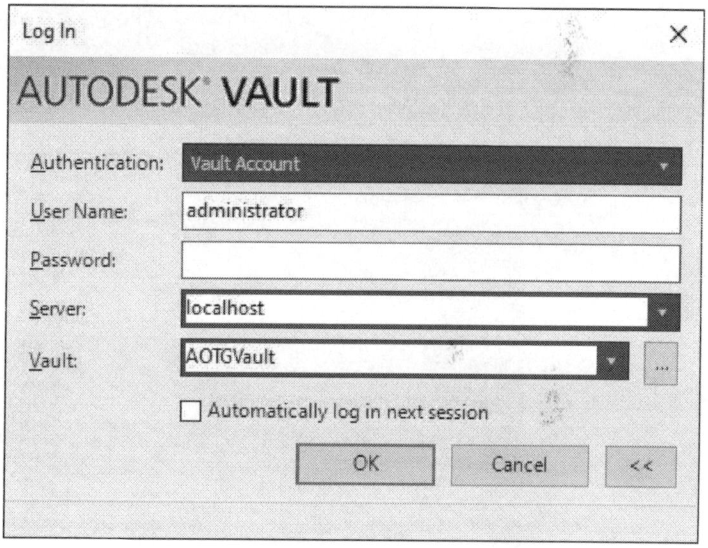

4. Click Paths >Set Project Folder to set your project's root folder.

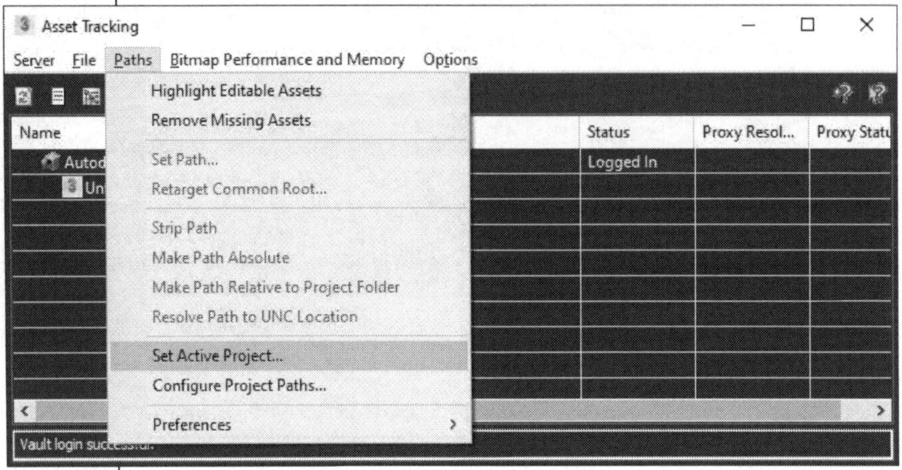

5. Click Paths>Configure Project Paths to set paths for scenes, materials, etc.

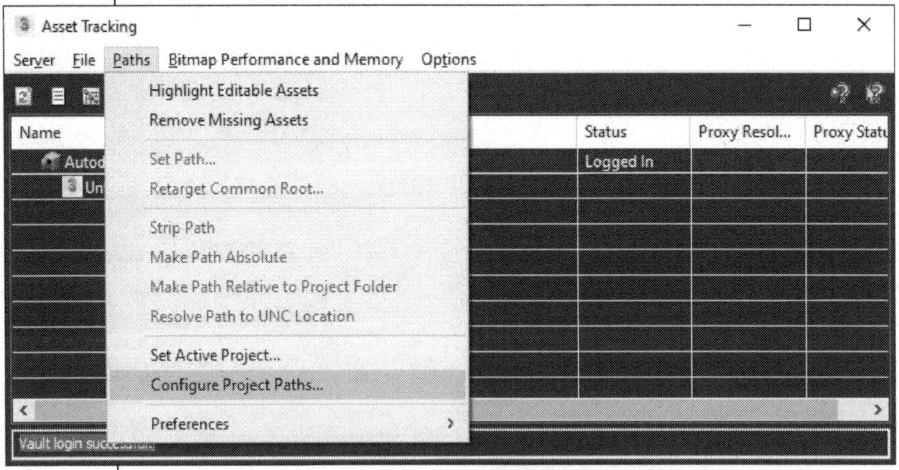

6. To add files to the vault, click File>Add Files. This checks in the scene and all related image files.

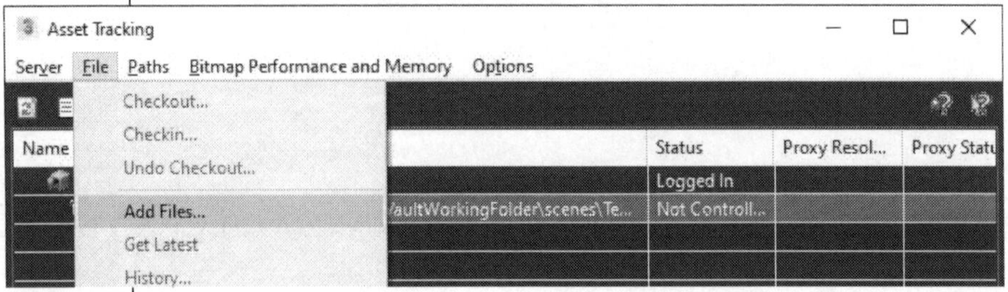

7. Use the commands from the File menu or the context menu (shortcut menu) to work with the Vault Add-in.

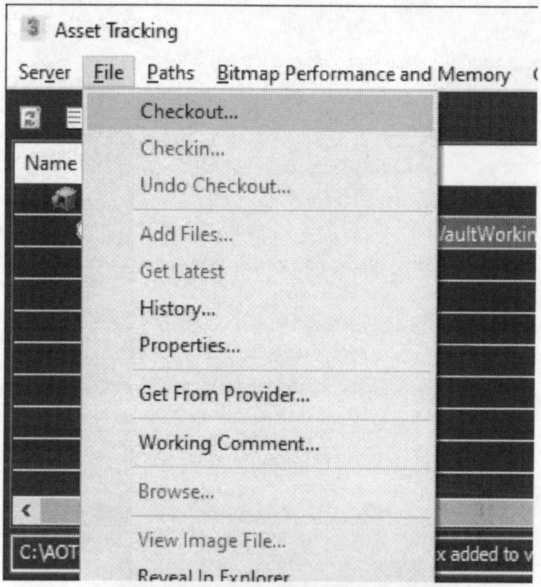

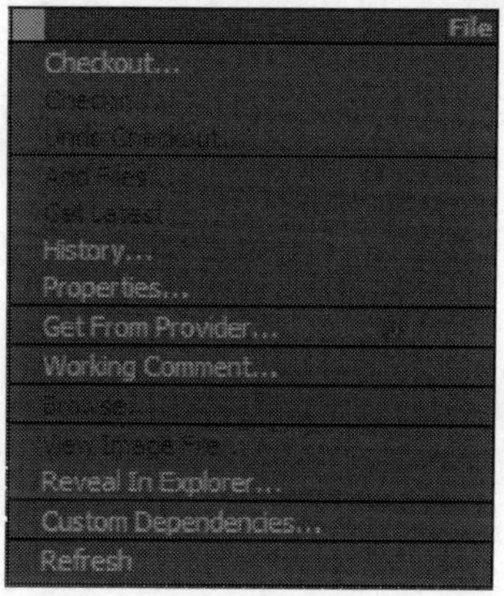

The File commands are described in the following table:

Option	Description
Checkout	Check out highlighted assets.
Checkin	Check in highlighted assets.
Undo Checkout	Undo file checkout.
Add Files	Enables you to add files to the vault database.
Get Latest	Downloads the latest version of the highlighted asset from the database.

History	Opens a read-only dialog box that displays information about the highlighted asset, such as vault and local locations, versions, and check-out status.
Properties	Opens a read-only dialog box that displays information about the highlighted asset, such as vault and local locations, versions, and check-out status.
Get From Provider	Enables you to copy files from the database to the local working folder.
Working Comment	Opens a dialog box containing a common text buffer for the current session. When you check out a file, any comment you enter in the Asset Tracking dialog box is copied to the Working Comment dialog box.
Browse	Enables you to browse the local directories for missing files, such as bitmaps.
View Image File	Opens a window showing the highlighted image file.
Reveal in Explorer	Opens a Windows Explorer dialog box showing the location of the highlighted asset.
Custom Dependencies	Opens a dialog that enables you to specify files to be dependents of the current scene.
Refresh	Reloads the asset listing from the local scene and updates the window contents.

Autodesk Simulation Software

1. In the Autodesk Simulation software, click the Vault tab and click Log In.
2. Use the following commands to work with the Vault add-in:

Option	**Description**
Go to Vault	Launch the Vault Explorer.
Log In	Log in to the Autodesk Data Management Server.
Log Out	Log out of the Autodesk Data Management Server.
Open	Open files from the vault.
Refresh	Refresh files from the vault.
Check in	Check in all files.
Check out	Check out all files.
Undo check out	Undo file checkout.
Options	Set options for working with the vault.

Note: The vault files are referenced to one another so that Check in, Check out, or Undo check out are performed on all related files simultaneously.

Autodesk Navisworks Manage and Autodesk Navisworks Simulate

1. Click the Vault tab and click Log In on the Access panel.

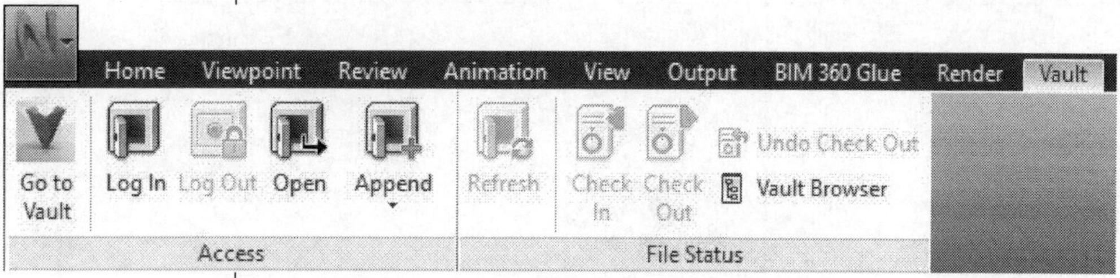

2. Use the following commands to work with the Vault add-in:

Option	Description
Go to Vault	Launch the Vault Explorer.
Log In	Log in to the Autodesk Data Management Server.
Log Out	Log out of the Autodesk Data Management Server.
Open	Open files from the vault.
Append/Merge	Adds the selected files to the currently opened scene. Merges the selected files into the currently opened scene.
Refresh	Refresh files from the vault.
Check In	Check in all files.
Check Out	Check out all files.
Undo Check Out	Undo file checkout.
Vault Browser	Open the Vault Browser.

3. Use the Vault Browser to view the file status and structure of the current file. You can also perform basic vault related operations, such as check in and check out.

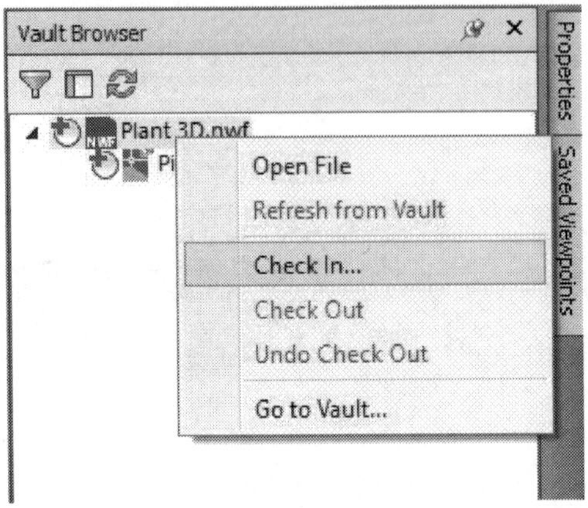

Note: If the Vault tab is not showing, click Options under the application button. In the Options Edit dialog, expand the Tools node, click Vault, and select the Show in User Interface check box.

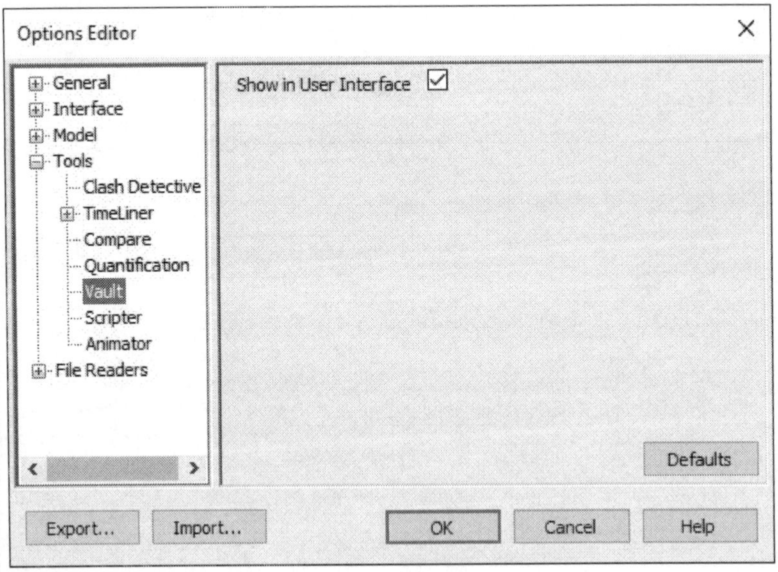

Appendix B

Additional Resources

A variety of resources are available to help you get the most from your Autodesk® software. Whether you prefer instructor-led, self-paced, or online training, Autodesk has you covered. These resources include:

- Learning Tools from Autodesk.
- Autodesk Certification.
- Autodesk Authorized Training Centers (ATC®).
- Autodesk Subscription.
- Autodesk Communities.

Learning Tools from Autodesk

Use your Autodesk software to its full potential. Whether you are a novice or an advanced user, Autodesk offers a robust portfolio of learning tools to help you perform ahead of the curve.

- Get hands-on experience with job-related practices based on industry scenarios from Autodesk learning guides, e-books, self-paced learning, and training videos.
- All materials are developed by Autodesk software subject matter experts.
- Get exactly the training you need with learning tools designed to fit a wide range of skill levels and subject matter—from basic essentials to specialized, in-depth training on the capabilities of the latest Autodesk products.
- Access the most comprehensive set of Autodesk learning tools available anywhere: from your authorized partner, online, or at your local bookstore.
- To find out more, visit http://www.autodesk.com/learning.

Autodesk Certification

Demonstrate your experience with Autodesk software. Autodesk certifications are a reliable validation of your skills and knowledge. Demonstrate your software skills to prospective employers, accelerate your professional development, and enhance your reputation in your field.

Certification Benefits

- Rapid diagnostic feedback to assess your strengths and identify areas for improvement.
- An electronic certificate with a unique serial number.
- The right to use an official Autodesk Certification logo.
- The option to display your certification status in the Autodesk Certified Professionals database.

For more information:

Visit www.autodesk.com/certification to learn more and to take the next steps to get certified.

Autodesk Authorized Training Centers

Enhance your productivity and learn how to realize your ideas faster with Autodesk software. Get trained at an Autodesk Authorized Training Center (ATC) with hands-on, instructor-led classes to help you get the most from your Autodesk products. Autodesk has a global network of Authorized Training Centers that are carefully selected and monitored to ensure you receive high-quality, results- oriented learning. ATCs provide the best way for beginners and experts alike to get up to speed. The training helps you get the greatest return on your investment, faster, by building your knowledge in the areas you need the most. Many organizations provide training on our software, but only the educational institutions and private training providers recognized as ATC sites have met Autodesk's rigorous standards of excellence.

Find an Authorized Training Center

With over 2,000 ATCs in more than 90 countries around the world, there is probably one close to you. Visit the ATC locator at www.autodesk.com/atc

to find an Autodesk Authorized Training Center near you. Look for ATC courses offered at www.autodesk.com/atcevents

Many ATCs also offer end-user Certification testing. Locate a testing center near you at www.autodesk.starttest.com

Autodesk Subscription

Autodesk® Subscription helps you minimize costs, increase productivity, and make the most of your Autodesk software investment. With monthly, quarterly, annual, and multi-year options, you can get the exact software you need for as long as you need it. For a fee based on the term length, you receive upgrades released during your contract term. Subscribers can also get licensed software to use on their home computer.

- For more information, visit www.autodesk.com/subscription.

Autodesk User Communities

Free products are subject to the terms and conditions of the end-user license agreement that accompanies download of the software.

Autodesk customers can take advantage of free Autodesk software, self-paced tutorials, worldwide discussion groups and forums, job postings, and more. Become a member of an Autodesk Community today!

Feedback

Autodesk understands the importance of offering you the best learning experience possible. If you have comments, suggestions, or general inquiries about Autodesk Learning, please contact us at learningtools@autodesk.com

As a result of the feedback we receive from you, we hope to validate and append to our current research on how to create a better learning experience for our customers.

Useful Links

Learning Tools

www.autodesk.com/learning

Certification

www.autodesk.com/certification

Find an Authorized Training Center

www.autodesk.com/atc

Find an Authorized Training Center Course

www.autodesk.com/atcevents

Autodesk Store

store.autodesk.com

Communities

www.autodesk.com/community

Student Community

students.autodesk.com

Blogs

www.autodesk.com/blogs

Made in United States
Orlando, FL
04 November 2026

90205881R00297